D1034220

Management Principles
for
Nonprofit Agencies
and Organizations

Management Principles
for
Nonprofit Agencies
and Organizations

Gerald Zaltman
VOLUME EDITOR

A Division of
AMERICAN MANAGEMENT ASSOCIATIONS

Library of Congress Cataloging in Publication Data

Main entry under title:

Management principles for nonprofit agencies and
    organizations.

    Includes index.
    1. Corporations, Nonprofit—United States—Management—
Addresses, essays, lectures.   I. Zaltman, Gerald.
HD38.M31865   658'.04'8   79–15453
ISBN 0-8144-5518-2

© 1979 AMACOM
A division of American Management Associations, New York.
All rights reserved. Printed in the United States of America.

This publication may not be reproduced, stored in a retrieval system, or
transmitted in whole or in part, in any form or by any means, electronic,
mechanical, photocopying, recording, or otherwise, without the prior
written permission of AMACOM, 135 West 50th Street, New York, N.Y.
10020.

First Printing.

812978

LIBRARY
ALMA COLLEGE
ALMA, MICHIGAN

To H. J. Zoffer

In acknowledgment of his creative
leadership in management education

LIBRARY
ALMA COLLEGE
ALMA, MICHIGAN

Contents

Introduction

THERE HAS BEEN dramatic growth in the number and size of nonprofit organizations in the past decade. Most significant about this growth is not the absolute increase in the number of people and agencies involved but rather the causes. Much of the increase is in response to important, unmet social needs in health, education, and welfare.

The needs and problems addressed by nonprofit organizations are significant, ranging from the provision of mental health services for specific disadvantaged groups to the provision of cultural benefits for a broader segment of society. They also include the provision of educational services and a host of other vital services. Humanitarian and cultural services warrant great care in the management of their associated activities, because such services are too important not to be delivered well. The financial and nonfinancial resources available to nonprofit organizations are often barely adequate and demand great care in their management. These two considerations—the importance of the problems addressed by nonprofit organizations and the frequent paucity of available resources to address them—place a burden of heavy responsibility on those who manage nonprofit organizations to do so effectively and efficiently.

The effectiveness and efficiency with which responsibility is discharged depend on many factors that fall under the rubric of "management"— the process of planning, organizing, and controlling the activities of an organization. *Planning* determines what the goals of the organization are and how they are to be achieved. *Organizing* allocates resources and responsibilities and coordinates them effectively. The monitoring of an organization's various activities falls to *controlling*. None of these processes is simple, because they involve a subtle blend of art and science. How well

1

these functions are conducted may account for one of the most critical factors affecting the success or failure of nonprofit organizations.

A senior official in the U.S. Department of Health, Education, and Welfare recently confided to the editor of this volume that the major costs of inattention to management issues in nonprofit organizations are not financial; they are human. These human costs may be measured in lives lost, prolonged suffering, and unnecessary unhappiness among substantial numbers of people. This same observation has been made many times by leaders of major nonprofit organizations all over the world. The basic point they make is that good management does make a difference, whether for a small senior-citizen center or for a large government agency; the difference is one that can dramatically affect the quality of the lives of those being served.

It is thus vital that managers in nonprofit agencies improve their management skills. This volume is designed to provide materials that will enrich its readers' current management skills. It is intended to introduce the newcomer to the management field to the important concepts and tools he or she should be sensitive to. Both newcomers and more experienced managers will become familiar with current thinking in the field along with discussions of its practical implications. Some ideas will have immediate applicability to problems currently being faced; others will broaden understanding of basic management issues and the nature of the tasks faced by the manager's colleagues.

WHAT DOES GOOD MANAGEMENT INVOLVE?

The basic tasks involved in the management of any organization are the same, although how these tasks are performed varies according to the nature of the organization. Each chapter in this book addresses one or more of these basic tasks and describes how they are best performed in various nonprofit settings.

Organizing

The organizing task (or process) includes several considerations. First, it involves a sensitivity to classic management functions, even though individual managers may not be deeply involved in all of them. Chapter 1 discusses these functions, each of which is later discussed in detail in other chapters. Second, organizing requires the exercise of effective *leadership,* the subject of Chapter 2. Effective managers are especially concerned with the professional development of their colleagues as human resources whose continuing growth assures the achievement of organizational goals. Thus the topic of *human resource development* is the focus of Chapter 3.

The development of employees to help achieve organizational goals should not be the only concern of a manager. Employee mental health is important not only for human dignity but because poor mental health can be deleterious to an organization's mission. Consideration of the psychological and sociological well-being of employees as people is often neglected in order to achieve organizational goals. Sensitivity to *mental health* in organizations is addressed in Chapter 4. Leadership, manpower development, and mental health are especially important to organizations undergoing change to better meet present challenges or to meet new challenges. The task of instituting *organizational change* is addressed in Chapter 5.

Planning

Planning involves determining what the organization is to achieve and how it will be accomplished. An obvious first task is *defining the problems* to be solved and *identifying and understanding the client* who is experiencing the problems. Thus Chapter 6 is concerned with problem definition, and Chapter 7 is concerned with client or consumer analysis. Knowing the nature of the problem and identifying the clients an organization should serve are two important planning tasks. The determination of what program to offer is another important planning activity. The selection of a program or service involves *cost-benefit analyses*, the subject of Chapter 8. Knowing who has what problem to be addressed by a program or service is essential for the next task, *strategic planning*, which is the focus of Chapter 9.

The formulation of an action or *marketing program* to implement strategic planning considerations is another essential planning task and is discussed in Chapter 10. Effective planning, especially with regard to the subject matter of Chapters 6 through 10, requires appropriate information. Having appropriate information at the appropriate time requires a systematic approach to information gathering and processing. Thus Chapter 11 is concerned with designing an effective *management information system*.

Control

Control is the process of monitoring the internal and external activities of the organization. Internal control includes the tasks of *fund accounting* and *accounting for operating decisions*. These are two crucial activities in any organization and are treated in Chapters 12 and 13. Chapter 14 examines in detail the special concept of *zero-based budgeting*. External control involves evaluating internal changes which have been instituted or simply assessing the functions of certain organizational procedures related to employees. Either aspect of control involves *evaluation research,* which is the topic of Chapter 15.

The tasks of organizing, planning, and control (see Figure 1) include many important subtasks. Whether thinking in terms of the larger tasks or the subtasks, the reader should understand that there is no special sequence assigned to their performance. Management is a multifaceted activity in which many tasks are performed simultaneously. How one task is performed affects others. When evaluation research is conducted to assess the impact of a program on clients, organizational changes may be suggested to better serve clients, or it may be found that a problem or client group has been wrongly defined. Implementation of a management information system may require special human resource development activities to use the system effectively. Sensitivity to the mental health of organizations may require an internal evaluation system. The financial accounting procedures used may influence the type of information available for conducting cost-benefit analyses. Figure 1 suggests that the overall tasks of organizing, planning, and control—and their subtasks—are in-

FIGURE 1. *Critical management tasks.*

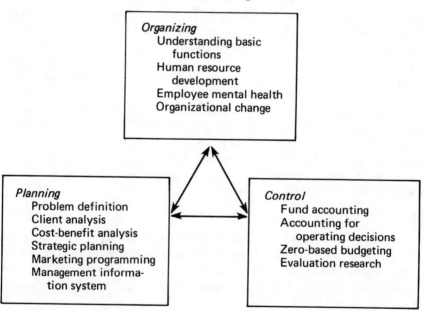

terrelated. This should be kept in mind when considering the issues and techniques of each chapter.

THE NATURE OF NONPROFIT ORGANIZATIONS

A nonprofit organization is one whose major goal is not the maximization of monetary gains. Operationally, whether an organization is classified as nonprofit depends on decisions of the U.S. Internal Revenue Service. The IRS lists 293 classifications for nonprofit organizations, suggesting a large diversity of such enterprises. A large number of criteria for conferring this status on an organization also exist. Table 1 provides a sense of how diverse the list is.

An important issue that recurs in the literature on nonprofit management concerns the distinctiveness of nonprofit organizations as a group in contrast to for-profit organizations. Some authors argue that important differences exist between nonprofit (especially government) organizations and business organizations, and that it is useful to distinguish between them (Levitt, 1973; Etzioni, 1973). Organizations that primarily pursue financial goals may be able to evaluate their performance more readily than organizations whose primary goals are not measured as easily. Consumer influences can be very weak on nonprofit organizations and stronger on for-profit ones.

TABLE 1. *Nonprofit enterprises grouped by services rendered.*

Services Performed	Enterprises	Services Performed	Enterprises
Health	Hospitals Nursing homes Clinics	Cooperatives	Insurance Savings banks Utilities Marketing
Education	Universities Schools Trade institutes	Other private	Religious Scientific research Associations
Social	Welfare Child care Family counseling		Clubs Unions

Arts and Culture	Orchestras
	Libraries
	Museums
		Other government	Uniformed
			  Military
			  Police
			  Fire
			Civilian
			  Regulatory
			  Fiscal
			  Justice

Source: William H. Newman and Harvey W. Wallender III, "Managing Not-for-Profit Enterprises," *Academy of Management Review* (January 1978), p. 25.

Some writers argue that for-profit and nonprofit organizations are not inherently different, that there is an increasing convergence of management processes for the two types of organizations as differences in decision making and goal definition disappear (Murray, 1975; Genck, 1973). For example, a close examination of recruiting procedures for top-level positions in government and industry suggests that formal credentialing systems and informal contacts (who do you know?) play similar roles in both. At one time, it was believed that formal credentialing systems were dominant in industry, with informal contacts being dominant in government. Whether or not this was ever true, it does not appear to distinguish between the two sectors now.

Some commentators maintain that the nonprofit (or not-for-profit) classification is far too broad, because the differences among nonprofit organizations are greater than the differences between nonprofit organizations as a group and for-profit organizations as a group (Newman and Wallender, 1978). It is claimed that nonprofit organizations can vary greatly in terms of the influence on internal decisions exerted by contributors of outside funds. A museum may have a few donors who contribute a majority of its operating capital and thus be influenced greatly by these donors. The funding structure of other organizations makes any one contributor relatively unimportant. Some business firms, such as small suppliers of construction equipment, are often extremely dependent on a few customers who do, indeed, influence such internal decisions as who to buy from. In this regard, a museum may resemble a business firm more closely than it does other nonprofit organizations.

There are also other perspectives (see Pauly and Redisch, 1973; McGill and Wooton, 1975; Roberts, 1975), none of them mutually exclusive. The authors of this book hold the position that there are differences between for-profit and nonprofit organizations even though some of the differences may diminish as managers of both increasingly use the same tools. In other words, not all nonprofit organizations are alike. There are great variations between a federal law-enforcement agency and a museum or between a hospital and a small liberal-arts college. In fact, each chapter in this volume indicates, for its subject matter, what the unique differences are between nonprofit and for-profit organizations. Some of these differences are especially relevant for certain types of nonprofit organizations but not for others.

The authors display a sensitivity to the characteristics of any organization which are especially relevant to the tools and concepts discussed in their respective chapters. For this reason, we shall not discuss here any unique set of factors associated with nonprofit organizations. There are unique factors, but from the reader's standpoint, the ones that are important depend on the management concept or tool under consideration as well as on the nature of the organization the reader is in. Again, each author identifies general facets of nonprofit organizations which are important for the management issues discussed. The reader may choose to give greater or lesser prominence to these factors, depending on the nature of his or her own organization.

THE NATURE OF MANAGEMENT

It is not uncommon to hear or read debates on whether management is an art or a science. The authors of this volume view management as a subtle blend of both. They feel that managing is a process—doing—and thus may appropriately be labeled an art. When thoughtfully exercised, the process is also based on knowledge; thus it can also be called a science. In some areas of management, the knowledge base is well developed and well organized; in other areas it is inexact and disorganized. The author(s) of each chapter indicate both the well-developed and ill-developed aspects of their topics.

Each chapter provides an inventory of the most up-to-date and important knowledge in its topic area—the "knowns." These items of knowledge may not always be well integrated, exact, or advanced, but the reader should not expect it to be otherwise. Management is an exciting, challenging activity precisely because it involves a tremendous number of factors that operate more or less at once. The chemistry between these factors adds to their variability and challenges the creation of order among them.

When the authors were invited to participate in this volume, each was also asked to translate his or her knowledge into action, which is the artistic dimension of management. Like other craftsmen, each contributor has his or her own style and has exercised his or her sense of the art of management somewhat differently. Some authors give listings of specific principles or guidelines throughout the chapter, while others summarize them at the conclusion. Some authors are highly assertive and specific; others are suggestive. But all the authors are prescriptive and provide the reader with expert interpretations of the practical implications of their ideas.

One source drawn on by all the authors is the current research in the scholarly literature, to which they are also important contributors. Another source of their knowledge is found in the principles which appear to underlie the behavior or decisions of successful managers. There are many practicing managers who, through trial and error, have developed a personal theory of management. They have learned that these factors are interrelated, and their knowledge of the interrelated factors enables them to explain and even to predict and control the management process. (A theory, of course, is simply a set of interrelated factors which helps explain, predict, or control a phenomenon.) Many effective managers deny that they possess a theory, even though they freely describe a rich array of interrelated factors which they feel are important to understand and use if one is to be a good manager. They dislike the term "theory" because it suggests something abstract and unusable. The authors of this volume all work closely with managers who possess sophisticated but practical theories. Accordingly, they were asked to present as part of their inventory of knowledge the practical implications of what these managers do and what knowledge appears to underlie this practice. Thus the common practices shared by effective managers are supplied along with their underlying knowledge bases.

This volume is unique in two ways: (1) Each chapter examines the aspects of nonprofit organizations that are most important to the critical management activities discussed. In the authors' view, all nonprofit organizations are not alike, nor are they always different from for-profit organizations in the same ways. (2) Each chapter presents a set of important management concepts and tools derived from both traditional research and the behavior of unusually effective managers. The practical implications of these concepts and tools are given in detail.

REFERENCES

Etzioni, Amitai. "The Third Sector and Domestic Missions," *Public Administration Quarterly,* July–August 1973, pp. 314–327.

Genck, Frederick H. "Public Management in America," *AACSB Bulletin,* April 1973, pp. 1–13.

Levitt, Theodore. *The Third Sector: New Tactics for a Responsive Society* (New York: AMACOM, 1973).

McGill, Michael E., and Leland M. Wooton. "Management in the Third Sector," *Public Administration Quarterly,* September–October 1975, pp. 444–455.

Murray, Michael A. "Comparing Public and Private Management: An Exploratory Essay," *Public Administration Quarterly,* July–August 1975, pp. 364–371.

Newman, William H., and Harvey W. Wallender III. "Managing Not-for-Profit Enterprises," *Academy of Management Review,* January 1978, pp. 24–31.

Pauly, Mark, and Michael Redisch. "The Not-for-Profit Hospital as a Physicians' Cooperative," *The American Economic Review,* March 1973, pp. 87–99.

Roberts, Marc J. "An Evolutionary and Institutional View of the Behavior of Public and Private Companies," *The American Economic Review,* May 1975, pp. 415–427.

PART I
Organizing

CHAPTER 1

Management Functions: What to Do and When

Dennis P. Slevin

Editor's Note   *A manager's task is a complicated and difficult one. The success of any nonprofit organization often relies directly on the effectiveness of the individual managers and how they accomplish their respective jobs. This chapter looks analytically at what a manager does and attempts to provide the reader with better insight concerning his or her management performance.*

The modern descriptive view of how managers spend their time is presented. The impact of modern technology and changing environment is shown to have caused dramatic differences in the way that present-day managers spend their time. A time span model is presented to demonstrate the importance of getting control over the day-to-day interruptions so that time can be spent on the important managerial functions.

The traditional views of managerial functions are summarized by the acronym POSDCORB: Planning, Organizing, Staffing, Directing, COordinating, Reporting, and Budgeting. Because of the frenetic nature of a manager's day, the successful manager must know not only the intellectual content of these functions but also how to schedule and do each of them.

Planning involves outlining the things to be done and the methods to be adopted to accomplish an organization's objectives. Most managers express a desire to spend more time in planning. Good managers are good planners. The author presents

11

management by objectives (MBO) as a sound planning device and stresses the importance of effective scheduling and self-discipline.

Organization is the establishment of a formal structure of authority through which work subdivisions are arranged and coordinated. The structure of an organization is critical to its effectiveness and should change with the environment. Organizations need differentiation (specialization) as well as integration (the linking of specialized subgroups into a meaningful whole) to function effectively.

Staffing is the personnel function of hiring, training, maintaining, and motivating employees. Staffing well includes the development of job descriptions, the evaluation of applications, interviewing, the evaluation of interviews, the checking of references, formation of a global evaluation for each candidate, and hiring.

Directing is the ongoing task of making decisions, embodying them in specific or general orders, and leading subordinates. To improve their directing capabilities, managers should take sufficient time to gather the necessary information and delegate as much work as possible.

Coordinating is the important duty of interrelating the various parts of a manager's responsibilities. A consensus test can help with coordination.

Reporting and budgeting are closely related. Reporting is keeping those to whom one is responsible (superiors and subordinates) informed as to what is going on. To do reporting well, managers should both get and give all the information needed from and to all the parties concerned. Budgeting is a control mechanism that should be used for feedback.

The emphasis of this chapter is both conceptual and pragmatic. On a conceptual level the basic management functions are defined and explained. On the pragmatic level the reader is told not just what to do but also how to do it and when to schedule it. A number of flowcharts, checklists, and examples are included for this purpose.

Finally, the author advises the manager to make a personal diagnosis to see if the POSDCORB functions are being accomplished and to form plans for positive changes in weak areas.

What does it mean to be a manager? The purpose of this chapter is to answer this question for you and to provide you with pragmatic tools for increased managerial effectiveness. A number of specific action principles are provided.

For over half a century scholars have attempted to define the functions that a manager performs. Their thinking in this area is best represented by the acronym POSDCORB. You may have heard of it; it was developed by Gulick and Urwick over 40 years ago. The initials stand for *P*lanning, *O*rganizing, *S*taffing, *D*irecting, *CO*ordinating, *R*eporting, and *B*udgeting. We will go into some depth defining and explaining each of these functions later in the chapter. But first, let's put the POSDCORB approach in some perspective.

THE IMPERIAL VIEW

One of my students recently called this the "imperial view" of management. And that's probably a fitting label. It represents the stereotype of the manager who in princely fashion sits in his large office, behind a wooden desk, smokes his pipe and thinks calmly and collectedly about his management problems. He receives his subordinates as they come in with problems, carefully considers the alternatives, makes decisions, and dispatches them to implement his solutions. He is a thinker, a planner, and a schemer (in the positive sense of that word). He is interested in the long-term success of the organization and makes all decisions with those considerations in mind. He operates much the way a prince would run his castle—always in control and with very few interruptions or changes in his schedule.

This view may have been correct (although I doubt it) at the turn of the century, but it is certainly not accurate today. Modern technology and a rapidly changing environment have become allies in making the manager's job more difficult. At the turn of the century a manager was not deluged by paperwork emanating from a phalanx of memory typewriters, electronic digital computers, and high-speed duplicating machines. He could not pick up the telephone and direct-dial London, hoping he had the five-hour time differential calculated correctly. And if things weren't going right in another city, he could not climb on a jet in the morning and return that evening after having attended several business meetings. These are all modern advantages that we obviously would not want to do without. However, they have combined to make the professional manager's job one characterized by interruptions and overload. Some recent empirical work has shed important light on the way that a manager really operates. The classical or "imperial" stereotype is no longer appropriate; its replacement, the descriptive view, brings with it some major surprises.

THE DESCRIPTIVE VIEW

In the mid 1960s a behavioral scientist at McGill University named Henry Mintzberg became interested in what managers do. He first attempted to talk to them or ask them what functions they performed and how they did them. This didn't work very well, so he tried a new tack: he followed practicing managers around and recorded precisely what they did—formal meetings, informal meetings, telephone calls, dealing with subordinates, and so forth. His results were quite surprising and destroyed many of the myths concerning what practicing managers did. For example, in the study of five chief executives (five days of observation each) of smaller firms, he found:

- 78 percent of their time was spent in verbal (oral) communication.
- 50 percent of their activities lasted less than nine minutes, and only 10 percent exceeded one hour.
- 40 percent of their contact time was spent in activities devoted exclusively to the transmission of information.
- 93 percent of the verbal contacts were arranged on an ad hoc basis.
- The five chief executives initiated on their own—that is, not in response to something else—a grand total of 25 pieces of mail during the 25 days they were observed (5 days each).
- The chief executives met a steady stream of callers and mail from the moment they arrived in the morning until they left in the evening (Mintzberg, 1973, 1975).

In short, Mintzberg found that the management job was not characterized by reflection and planning, but rather by interruptions and fragmentation. The typical manager's job could be described by the acronym ROFFS. It contained *role overload*—many people made demands of his time, and although none of these demands was unreasonable in itself the total accumulated to a 16-hour day. In an attempt to cope with overload and interruptions, the manager engaged in *frenetic activity*—trying to get things done as quickly as possible. He became *fragmented*—working on two or more tasks simultaneously. And this finally led to *superficiality*—making decisions quickly with inadequate information and reflection.

This research is not presented as a criticism of practicing management today; rather, it is a description of how the process actually occurs. This description is accurate from the executive suite down to the shop floor and it holds great significance for you as a practicing manager. It means that if you want to get the planning, organizing, staffing, and other tasks done—as you must to be a successful manager—you must not only know *what* to do but also *how to schedule it*. The remainder of this chapter looks at the classical functions of management (they're still as appropriate today as they were) and offers some pragmatic tips that you might follow in order to get them done effectively.

PLANNING (FREQUENCY, CONSTANT; PROPORTION OF TIME, 16%)*

Planning is working out in broad outline the things that need to be done and the methods for doing them to accomplish the purpose set for the enterprise (Gulick and Urwick, 1937).

Let's start out with a little quiz. Are the following statements true or false?

1. Managers do a lot of planning.
2. Planning should occur in the planning group—it is not the individual manager's primary responsibility.
3. The more planning a manager does, the more he is paid.

Statement 1 is false. Most practicing managers I have talked to spend a very small percentage of their time in planning. It is rare to talk to anyone who spends more than 20 percent of his time in the planning function. Also, most managers seem to express a desire to spend more time in planning than they actually do. In short, planning plays too small a role in most management jobs. Statement 2 is false. Planning is an integral and central function of every manager's task. If you don't plan, you become a crisis manager, responding to rather than driving the environment of your job.

Statement 3 is probably true. Management is a forward-looking job, and the more forward-looking, probably the more responsible. Chairmen of the board and presidents are constantly dealing with five- and ten-year time horizons, while blue collar workers on the production floor may be dealing with time horizons of only a few minutes. The longer the time frame, the more responsible the job, and the higher the pay.

Elliott Jaques, a well-known English behavioral scientist, has found consistently high correlations between felt fair pay (what people think individuals *should* make) and the time span of jobs in a variety of organizations (Jaques, 1970, 1977). Every manager has jobs or projects in his in-basket that have varying times to completion. The *time span* of a manager is defined by Jaques as the time required to complete the longest task. Jaques maintains, and I believe I have to agree, that:

An individual is not a manager unless his time span is at least three months.

---

*Description in parenthesis indicates frequency with which function should be performed. Percentage indicates proportion of time spent by one sample of line managers (managers having subordinates and budget and decision-making authority), as opposed to staff specialists with few or no subordinates and primarily advisory authority.

A Short Study of Management Time Allocation

A group of 38 managers in the 1978 executive MBA program at the Graduate School of Business, University of Pittsburgh, were polled concerning the nature of their jobs and time they spent in the various management functions. A total of 26 usable responses were obtained: 17 were from line managers, 9 were from staff. The responses were analyzed, and the percentage of time that line managers indicated spending in each of the POSDCORB functions is shown in parentheses in the major headings of this chapter. Complete results are summarized below.

	Line Managers	Staff Managers
Age	35	38
Number of immediate subordinates	4	3
Total supervised	36	6
Number of years of work experience	12	14
Hours per week on job	48	51
Number of incidents per day	59	32
Duration of each incident (minutes)	13	17
Number of interruptions per day	23	15

	Percentage of Time Allocated	
Function	*Line Managers*	*Staff Managers*
Planning	16.0	16.1
Organizing	12.2	12.2
Staffing	8.8	3.2
Directing	17.6	10.8
Coordinating	22.4	16.1
Reporting	9.0	10.1
Budgeting	4.5	5.2
Other	10.5	24.8
	100.0	98.5

Using Jaques' model, we can construct Table 1–1.

So you see, planning is central for both organizational and individual success. The best individual managers of my acquaintance have always been excellent at planning. Whether it involves formulating a long-range plan or deciding how to spend their vacation at the beach, they just seem to have a well-developed skill in this area. Poor managers have trouble planning, especially as they move up through the organization. As Jaques says:

Ineffective managers borrow against their longest tasks.

It's easy to do, isn't it? It's easy to be constantly worrying about alligators and to keep putting aside swamp drainage. Have you ever taken over

TABLE 1–1. *Organizational level and time span (time required to complete the longest task in your in-basket).*

Level	Time Span	Responsibility	Felt Fair Pay
6	10 years	Chief executive officer and president	Highest
5	5 years	Vice president/general manager	↑
4	2 years	Upper middle management	
3	1 year	Middle management	
2	3 months	Lower middle management	↓
1	Less than 3 months	Nonmanagement	Lowest

from a manager who constantly borrowed against his longer tasks? It's a terribly frustrating situation, because you must invest tremendous time to get the longer tasks under control—and usually they don't show any immediate payout. Some managers have made careers out of moving into positions, doing an excellent job on the short-term tasks and moving out before the longer-time-span tasks catch up with them. They accumulate what looks like an impressive track record, leaving shambles behind them.

The level ⟶ time span causal arrow may work in both directions. Not only do people at higher levels have longer time spans, but people with longer innate time spans tend to move to higher levels. In our civilization, people with longer time spans generally command greater respect. Socrates, Aristotle, Churchill, Da Vinci, Washington, Lincoln all had a "sense of history"—a view of the long-term consequences of current activities. Management is a futuristic task, and people with this orientation are more likely to succeed. I would even go so far as to say:

If you have a long time span, you are much more likely to rise to the organizational level appropriate to it.

And as you rise, you must continue to increase your time span. As one of my students suggested, perhaps the "level of incompetence" hypothesized by Laurence Peter is in part due to a person rising to a job for which he has too short a time span (Peter and Hull, 1969).

How to Do Planning

The message is clear on an individual level. Planning takes self-discipline. Planning involves the longest-time-span activity in the manager's in-basket and, therefore, is quite often the most neglected function. It consists of looking at the future, setting objectives, and developing action plans for accomplishing them. On the individual level, I would suggest that you consider the MBO (management by objectives) process as a planning device. Entire books have been written on this subject, but as a useful personal tool it works as shown in Figure 1–1.

Objectives are set in the following categories:

1. Routine—recurring tasks you have to do.
2. Problem solving—fighting brushfires or potential trouble spots.
3. Innovation—new and creative processes, procedures, solutions.
4. Personal—goals *you* want to accomplish.

Progress is reviewed quarterly to:

1. See where you are.
2. Modify or add objectives—be flexible.

An accomplishment report replaces the traditional performance appraisal. In the accomplishment interview, the employee does a self-analysis of his accomplishments (with his boss) and uses his progress to set the basis for the objectives for the next year. (Bonoma and Slevin, 1978, p. 75).

Use the model in Figure 1–1 with yourself and your subordinates. You will find it helps both planning and goal attainment. At a minimum, use a checklist to specify objectives and action plans (Figure 1–2). For each objective, list the specific action plans you will use to accomplish it. This will provide you with a compact, personal framework for being successful as a planner.

FIGURE 1-1. *Management by objectives.*

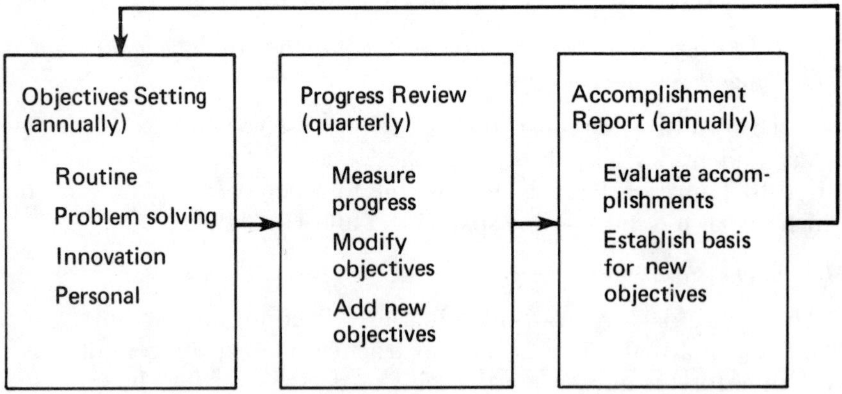

Source: Thomas V. Bonoma and Dennis P. Slevin, *Executive Survival Manual* (Belmont, Cal.: Wadsworth, 1978). Adapted from Dennis P. Slevin and William Wolz.

FIGURE 1–2. *Checklist of objectives and action plans.*

	Objectives	Date
1.	_____	_____
2.	_____	_____
3.	_____	_____
4.	_____	_____
5.	_____	_____

	Action Plans	
1.1	_____	
1.2	_____	
1.3	_____	
1.4	_____	
2.1	_____	
2.2	_____	
2.3	_____	
2.4	_____	
3.1	_____	
3.2	_____	
3.3	_____	
3.4	_____	
4.1	_____	
4.2	_____	
4.3	_____	
4.4	_____	
5.1	_____	
5.2	_____	
5.3	_____	
5.4	_____	

How to Schedule Planning

Given a frenetic day filled with interruptions, the only way a manager will accomplish futuristic activities is with good scheduling and self-discipline. Try the following pointers:

1. Schedule some uninterrupted time—a minimum of one hour per week—for your personal planning. Put it on your calendar.
2. Engage in regular meetings (at least monthly) with your subordinates in which planning is the primary topic.
3. Insist on meetings with your superiors during which you address future plans. They will be amazed at your maturity and you may be rewarded by moving to a level in which an even greater time span is appropriate!

ORGANIZING (FREQUENCY, MONTHLY; PROPORTION OF TIME, 12%)

Organizing is the establishment of the formal structure of authority through which work subdivisions are arranged, defined, and coordinated for the defined objective (Gulick and Urwick, 1937).

A recent annual report of International Harvester Company described a "complete reorganization of the company into five basic business groups with worldwide scope and further delegated authority and responsibility." It also discussed the rapid rate of change faced by the company in the business and social environment. Why would a company be so concerned about organization as to mention it in an annual report? For two reasons:

1. Organization structure (who does what and who reports to whom) is crucial to organizational effectiveness.
2. A rapidly changing environment dictates certain specific changes in organization structure.

This section provides a straightforward, pragmatic model for organization design. It presents the relationship between environment and organization structure and is designed to help you fulfill the organizational aspects of your management job. Listed below are a few of the positions necessary for a hospital to function (Arnold, Blankenship, and Hess, 1971).

Admitting officer
Business manager
Controller
Credit manager
Director of office services
Director of volunteer services

Employment interviewer
Employment manager
Executive housekeeper
Food and drug inspector
Food service supervisor
Hospital administrator
Hospital engineer
Hospital librarian
Local executive
Local health officer
Medical engineer
Personnel director
Public relations director
Purchasing agent

The size of this list implies two things for the practicing manager: (1) there are many different specialized people in any large organization, and (2) the manager must bring together the activities of these specialized individuals to form a meaningful whole. In the words of the organization designers, it means that the design of any social organization must include two key variables: differentiation and integration (Lawrence and Lorsch, 1967).

Differentiation and Integration

Differentiation means different people doing different things. It is a function of the number and diversity of specialized positions in the organization. It is a measure of the degree of specialization that occurs in the organization. *Integration* is the coordination that takes place, linking the activities of the specialized subgroups into a coordinated whole.

If you use these two concepts, you will find that many of your organizational design problems become more straightforward and understandable. There are some key principles that you should keep in mind as you attempt to use these concepts.

Differentiation and integration are antagonistic. The more differentiation you have, the harder it is to achieve the required integration. If you needlessly differentiate your organization, you are going to have to spend a lot of money in integration activities.

Complex environments require more differentiation. The more dynamic the environment faced by the organization, the more differentiation required. As the external environment becomes more changing and more complex, additional differentiation is required. In other words, the differentiated specialists are matched to the various elements in the environment.

Integration leads to higher levels of performance. Research has indicated that business firms with higher levels of integration experience higher profits. Every manager knows that coordination is important, and integration is key in determining whether the organization operates effectively. Even at the individual level, if you think about successful managers that you have known, you will probably conclude that they had a high level of intrapersonal (within themselves) integration. They "had their act together" in terms of coordinating their own activities.

Integration costs; it should be viewed as overhead. Although integration leads to higher levels of performance, it is expensive. Integrators don't really do the operating tasks of the organization—the differentiated specialists do them. Therefore, although integration is essential and key to successful performance, it also is expensive and not productive in and of itself. The message is clear; in order to design your organization, you must do the following (see Figure 1–3):

1. Set the differentiation required by the environment.
2. Set the integration necessary to coordinate the differentiated activities.

Figure 1–4 shows an organization chart of a statewide department of public health with the following properties:

• It is highly differentiated. Vital statistics, management analysis, data processing, statistical consultation services, administrative services, public health contract services, and regional coordination are separate bureaus.

• The level of integration is very low. The food and drug laboratory is a part of the division of laboratories, while food and drug inspection is a bureau in the division of environmental sanitation. Similarly, the bureaus of vital statistics and management analysis are under the division of administration, while the bureaus of data processing and statistical consultation services are under the research division.

• The span of control in the administration, laboratories, and preventive medical services divisions are very close to the upper limits normally recommended. On the other hand, the span of control for the division of dental health is zero; for the division of alcoholic rehabilitation it is only two.

The reorganized chart in Figure 1–5:

• Pools the various bureaus under three major functions—community health services, preventive medical services, and environmental sanitation.

• Makes each of the divisions self-sufficient in terms of the laboratory facilities and administrative services required.

• Pools the original bureaus within each division to form functionally viable departments. The bureau of food and drug inspections and the food and drug laboratory have been put under the department of food and drugs.

FIGURE 1-3. *The design process.*

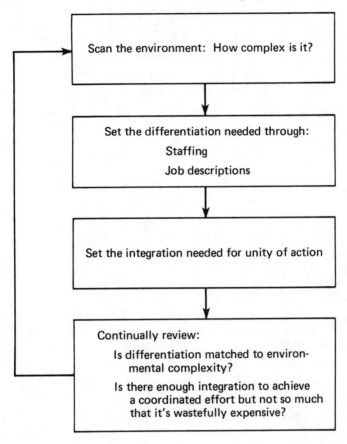

The reorganization achieves better integration as well as a more evenly distributed span of control. Also, in some places, the degree of differentiation has been reduced.

STAFFING (FREQUENCY, AS NEEDED; PROPORTION OF TIME, 9%)

Staffing is the whole personnel function of bringing in and training the staff and maintaining favorable conditions of work (Gulick and Urwick, 1937).

The most intermittent and yet probably the most important job of the manager is that of staffing. If you hire good people, you really don't have to "manage" them—they do it themselves. If you hire bad people, no amount of "management" techniques and time is going to solve your problem. And yet we often staff under crisis circumstances, hiring because

FIGURE 1-4. *Organization chart: a state department of health.*

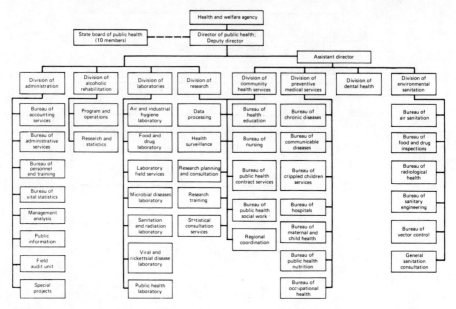

Source: Copyright © 1971 by Aldine-Atherton, Inc. Adapted, with permission, from Mary F. Arnold, L. Vaughn Blankenship, and John M. Hess, *Administering Health Systems* (New York, Aldine Publishing Company).

we need people in a hurry, and then regretting it at our leisure. I've known terribly bright managers who just couldn't staff well. They would surround themselves with incompetents and then spend a tremendous amount of time undoing the crises that arose. *Remember, one good staffing decision is worth several good decisions in the other POSDCORB areas.*

How, then, does one staff well? The answer to that question lies in following the sequence of activities listed below:

1. Job description—form ideal stereotype of candidate.
2. Identify key dimensions.
3. Score application/résumé.
4. Interview—collect data only.
5. Score interview.
6. Check references.
7. Administer and score in-basket.
8. Form global evaluation of each candidate.
9. Make hire decision and pray.

FIGURE 1-5. *Reorganized organization chart: a state department of health.*

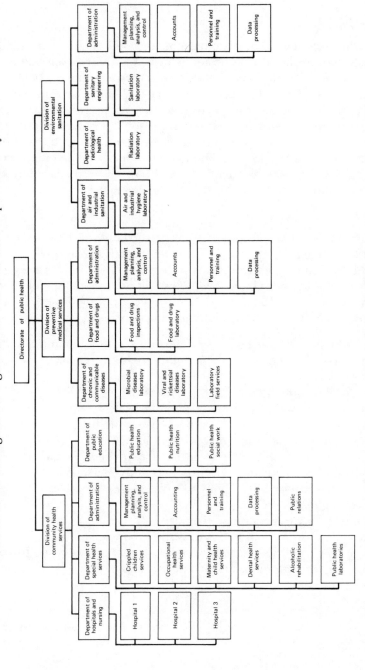

Source: Copyright © 1971 by Aldine-Atherton, Inc. Adapted, with permission. from Mary F. Arnold, L. Vaughn Blankenship, and John M. Hess, *Administering Health Systems* (New York, Aldine Publishing Company).

Let's look at each of the above items in sequence to see how they are done.

Job Description

This sounds rather straightforward, but you'd be amazed at the number of people that are hired into positions in which the responsibilities are unclear. The job description does two things for you. First, it enables you to form a stereotype of the perfect candidate. You can then match each of your applicants against this perfect stereotype. Second, it gives applicants the opportunity to self-select out of the job if it is inappropriate for them. I am never upset if someone turns me down for a job that I have offered. The candidate himself knows better than anyone else whether he fits into the position, and I wonder if I haven't been spared making serious mistakes in some cases by the candidates themselves.

Identify Dimensions

The assessment center technique has emerged in the 1970s as the most powerful management appraisal device we have available. I will not describe the assessment center process here, but will say that it uses a set of behavioral dimensions on which the candidate is scored quantitatively on each. Look at the following list and select from it those ten or so dimensions that are key to your job selection problem.*

Impact. Ability to create a good first impression, to command attention and respect, to show an air of confidence, and to achieve personal recognition.

Energy. Ability to maintain a high activity level.

Oral presentation skill. Effectiveness of expression when presenting ideas or tasks to an individual or a group given time for preparation (includes gestures and nonverbal communication).

Oral communication skills. Effectiveness of expression in individual or group situations (includes gestures and nonverbal communication.)

Written communication skill. Ability to express ideas clearly in writing in good grammatical form.

Creativity. Ability to generate, recognize, and/or accept imaginative solutions and innovations in business situations.

Range of interests. Breadth and diversity of interests, concern for personal and organizational environment, and a desire to participate actively in events.

---

*Development Dimensions 1977–1978 Catalog (Pittsburgh: Development Dimensions, 1977), pp. 38–39. Used with permission.

Stress tolerance. Stability of performance under pressure and opposition.

Motivation for work. Importance of work in personal satisfaction, and the desire to achieve at work.

Work standards. Desire to do a good job for the job's own sake.

Career ambition. Desire to advance to higher job levels; active efforts toward self-development.

Leadership. Effectiveness in getting ideas accepted and in guiding a group or an individual toward task accomplishment.

Sales ability and persuasiveness. Ability to organize and present material in a convincing manner to gain agreement or acceptance.

Sensitivity. Skill in perceiving and reacting to the needs of others. Objectivity in perceiving impact of self on others.

Listening skill. Ability to extract important information in oral communications.

Flexibility. Ability to modify behavioral style and management approach to reach a goal.

Tenacity. Tendency to stay with a problem or line of thought until the matter is settled; perseverence.

Risk taking. Ability to weigh alternatives and make decisions in which a calculated risk is taken to achieve maximum benefits from the decision.

Initiative. Actively influencing events rather than passively accepting; self-starting. Taking action beyond what is necessarily called for. Originating actions rather than just responding to events.

Independence. Taking action based on one's own convictions rather than through a desire to please others.

Planning and organization. Ability to efficiently establish an appropriate course of action for self and/or others to accomplish a specific goal, make proper assignments of personnel, and appropriately use resources.

Management control. Skill in establishing procedures to monitor (or regulate) processes, tasks, or the activities of subordinates. Ability to evaluate the results of delegated assignments and projects.

Delegation. Ability to use subordinates effectively and to understand where a decision can best be made.

Problem analysis. Skill in identifying problems, securing relevant information, and identifying possible causes of problems.

Judgment. Ability to develop alternative solutions to problems, evaluate courses of action, and reach logical decisions.

Decisiveness. Readiness to make decisions, render judgments, take action, or commit oneself.

Ability to learn. Ability to assimilate and apply new information.

Resilience. Ability to handle disappointments and rejection while maintaining effectiveness.

Integrity. Maintenance of societal, ethical, and organizational norms in business practices.

Development of subordinates. Efforts to maximize human potential of subordinates through training and development activities related to current and future jobs.

Financial analytical ability. Ability to understand and analyze financial data.

Adaptability. Ability to maintain effectiveness in different situations, handle changing responsibilities, live and work in different areas under different circumstances.

Technical translation. Ability to translate a technical document or technical information to understandable form for laymen.

Organizational sensitivity. Skill in perceiving the impact and implications of decisions on other components of the organization.

Political sensitivity. Awareness of changing societal and government pressures from outside the organization.

Score Application and Résumé

Using the ten or so dimensions that you've selected from the above list, assign a quantitative score to each based on information that you've obtained from the paper documents you have in front of you. Use whatever scale you are comfortable with. I personally prefer a 10-point scale, but 5- or 7-point scales should work equally well. If it's impossible to assess a dimension from the paperwork alone, merely leave it blank. You might feel that this process is unnecessary, since you plan to talk to the applicant. On the contrary: research has shown that application blanks and résumés are more predictive of job success than the selection interview. Sounds surprising, doesn't it?

The Interview

The personal interview is the single worst selection device available to the management. Yes, that's not a typographical error. I said, "worst." Yet everybody uses it. Over 95 percent of all social organizations use the selection interview in staffing decisions. Research has indicated that if two individuals interview the same candidate, they are not likely to agree on their evaluations. This has been demonstrated consistently in numerous research studies. And yet it is a surprise to all of us, because we all use the interview and hope we use it well. If the interview doesn't work, then why do we use it? It can work. Studies have shown that if the data are collected in the interview and the evaluation is performed afterward, the interview tends to be much more effective. The problem with the selection interview is that we tend to make very quick decisions, often based on inappropriate cues such as dress, personal attractiveness, and verbal fluency, and then spend the rest of the interview searching out confirmation for our hastily drawn conclusions. When you are interviewing:

Keep evaluation out of the interview.

Use the interview for data collection only. Write copious notes concerning facts about the candidate. Do not attempt to score or evaluate any of this information until at least one day after you have collected it. Separating evaluation from data collection will greatly increase the accuracy of your interview ability.

Score Interview

Scoring is a relatively straightforward step. Review the notes that you have taken under each of the dimensions selected. Place a quantitative score for the interview for each applicant under the appropriate dimension. You might even have a sheet of the dimensions typed with several spaces between each and use it to record your descriptive information on each dimension during the interview. Then merely use your best judgment for the evaluation.

Reference Checks

You'd be amazed at how many people are hired without their references being checked. References can provide you with valuable insight into the candidate. For any key job, I would strongly suggest that you check references. Ask specifically about each dimension that you have selected. Then consider the following questions:

1. What are the candidate's strengths?
2. What are the candidate's weaknesses?
3. Would you hire him back?

I am always suspicious of job candidates who list the president or vice president of their previous organization as a reference, and yet hesitate when you ask them if you can contact their previous boss. It's always good to talk to the person who was the individual's immediate supervisor. It is always amazing how much valuable and new information can be obtained from an insightful reference.

In-Basket Exercise

One of the assessment center devices that is particularly effective in job selection is the in-basket exercise. It places the candidate in a hypothetical situation where he has just replaced someone in a job and must handle 30 or so items in that individual's in-basket. The items may range from urgent notes from the president to anonymous hate letters from the production floor. The candidate is asked to respond in writing concerning what he would do about each. I have used this technique a number of times and find it to be quite powerful. It is especially good in helping you to get a handle on the dimensions of planning, organization, and control. Some people don't interview well; yet they do fantastic jobs when hired. With others the reverse is the case. The in-basket technique will help you avoid these types of errors. Although you should be trained in the use of the technique in advance, I believe that any first-rate manager should be able to gain a lot of insight from evaluating in-basket results. I would strongly suggest that you use this technique for hiring decisions. In-baskets are available from a variety of sources. Probably the most comprehensive range of in-baskets can be acquired from Development Dimensions, Inc. (Suite 303, 250 Mt. Lebanon Blvd., Pittsburgh, PA 15234).

Use the flowchart in Figure 1–6 to make sure that you follow a deliberate plan in the staffing process. Take your time and do it well. Your reward will be effective and motivated subordinates.

DIRECTING (FREQUENCY, CONSTANT; PROPORTION OF TIME, 18%)

> Directing is the continuous task of making decisions, embodying them in specific as well as general orders, and serving as the leader of their enterprise (Gulick and Urwick, 1937).

Ambrose is a "tight-fisted" manager. He spends a lot of time monitoring his employees, "looking over their shoulder," and he constantly knows how they are doing in their jobs. Bascombe, on the other hand, doesn't much care. He assigns tasks to his subordinates, and then never follows up to see when or how they're done.

Now try a short quiz. Are the following statements true or false?

1. Ambrose is the better manager because he has better "control," and he knows what's happening with his subordinates.
2. Ambrose is the worse manager of the two because his nitpicking and overseeing demotivate his employees.
3. Bascombe is the better manager because he is "participatory" and gets a higher level of motivation from his subordinates.
4. Bascombe is the worse manager of the two because his subordinates sense he really doesn't care about their work.

The truth of the matter is that there are true and false elements to each of the above statements. Neither individual is a good manager, for the following reasons:

FIGURE 1-6. *Staffing flowchart.*

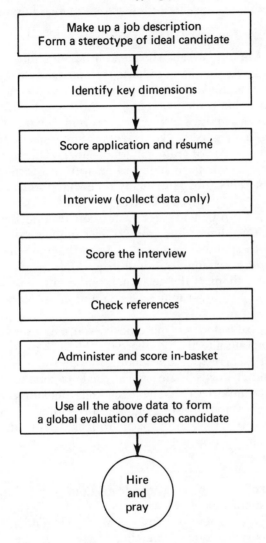

Ambrose manages by suffocation.
Bascombe manages by abdication.

Management is a job of, among other things, directing. This means making decisions, delegating work to others, and in general leading subordinates. Your performance as a manager in the directing function can be improved if you (1) take sufficient time to get the information you need before making decisions, and (2) delegate effectively as much work as possible. Let's look at each of these two principles in more detail.

Set Aside Enough Time for Decisions

My dentist, some time ago when I went to him with a rather vague tooth pain, said: "Action taken in haste is worse than no action at all." In this particular case, he was right. No intervention was needed with the tooth, not even a filling, and in a relatively short time the discomfort went away. And this principle is also true concerning many of the decisions that we make as managers. We know from recent research that the typical management day is one of fragmentation, superficiality, and frenetic activity. Decisions are made in haste, often with insufficient information and insufficient reflection. How many times have you made a decision quickly only to regret it at your leisure?

Analyzed on a fundamental level, decision making is nothing more than (1) generating alternatives, and (2) selecting from those alternatives (Maier, 1977). In spite of the hurry and the flurry of the management day, you must resist making decisions too quickly, or without setting aside adequate time for them. If the decision is important, you can and should make time to do it right. It may save you tenfold in trying to undo bad decisions in the future.

When you make a decision too quickly, you may do two things. You may fail to generate alternatives that you should have considered, and you may select incorrectly from among the alternatives that you have generated. In other words, haste can get you both coming and going, and it is particularly important that you set aside decision-making time in order to do a good job of directing. The principles set forward in the discussion on planning are appropriate to making sure that you do this part of "directing" appropriately.

Delegation

Another part of directing concerns delegation—the distribution of your work to your subordinates. Most managers I have evaluated delegate insufficiently for a variety of reasons. Managers tend to be obsessive/compulsive personality types. They like activity and like to be involved in the "action." They find it difficult to release to others tasks that they have done before. They tend to leap on a task and "get it done" rather than to take the time to delegate it by instructing someone else.

The only way that you will rise to the top of your organization is to delegate effectively. Think about it. The president of your organization delegates to everyone in the organization, either directly or indirectly. He can't possibly perform all the tasks that have to be done, and that is the reason for social organization. When you delegate, follow the following guidelines:

1. Explain to your subordinates the general objectives and guidelines that you would like them to follow in fulfilling the task. It is important that they understand almost as well as you the nature of the objectives of the task if they are going to do an effective and motivated job.

2. Explain to your subordinates the level of initiative that goes with the delegated task. Three basic levels of initiative (authority) might be considered:

- Act; notify routinely.
- Act; notify at once.
- Recommend; but take no action without prior approval.

In general, if you have confidence in your subordinates, the higher the level of initiative, the better. This releases you for time spent on other activities.

3. Establish a control system for every delegated task. This simply means that you set a time when your subordinate will report to you concerning progress that has been made to date. When you specify objectives for the task, you should also include the time frame in which you hope it is completed, and the times at which progress reports are expected.

If you delegate effectively, both you and your subordinates will do a better job. You will have more time. They will be developed in their management capabilities, and their motivation will increase. Any healthy organization will have a substantial amount of effective delegation occurring at all levels.

COORDINATING (FREQUENCY, CONSTANT; PROPORTION OF TIME, 22%)

Coordinating is the all-important duty of interrelating the various parts of the work (Gulick and Urwick, 1937).

Recently one of the major highways leading to the University of Pittsburgh was resurfaced. It wasn't an ordinary repaving job, but the entire street was torn up and the old pavement was removed down to the base. It took some time and many faculty members, students, and businesspeople in the area suffered through single-lane traffic for an extended number of months. Shortly after the job was completed, we were informed that the local gas company had not installed a new pipe down the center of the street while the pavement was torn up and would have to dig up the new pavement for its extensive work in the area.

This story demonstrates a lack of coordination. When a manager does not coordinate, he ends up spending a lot of wasted motion, a lot of his own and others' time and energy on tasks that had they been coordinated would take considerably less time. Much of the material in this section has already been covered when we talked about the organizing function. Integration in an organizational design is nothing more than coordination. But a few points should probably be emphasized here.

Good coordinators (integrators) rise to the top of their organizations. Good managers are good integrators. Good integrators tend to be placed in highly visible positions where they have the ability to get things done through others—the essence of the management task. As a consequence, if you have high aspirations for organizational advancement, you should attempt to seize upon opportunities to perform coordination (integration) functions.

Make sure that you have the information necessary for coordination. This item is treated more fully in the description of the Bonoma-Slevin leadership model in Chapter 2. However, it is redundant to say that no coordination can take place without information exchange. Make sure that you are getting the information that you need to perform your coordinative functions. This information need not be in the form of fancy reports and lengthy documents. It could be simply handwritten performance figures submitted on a regular basis.

Make sure that you have agreement on important decisions between yourself and the individuals that you are coordinating with. I have often seen management group and committee meetings move on from one topic to another with what seems to be implied agreement. However, if what the behavioral scientists call a "consensus test" is used—asking each individual how he feels about the decision—quite often lack of consensus is revealed. Don't be afraid to "consensus test" when you are coordinating with other people. Don't assume that mere head nods and smiles indicate agreement with decisions that are being made. Instead specifically test by asking them direct questions about their opinion of the decisions that are about to be made.

REPORTING (FREQUENCY, WEEKLY OR MONTHLY; PROPORTION OF TIME, 9%)

BUDGETING (FREQUENCY, MONTHLY OR YEARLY; PROPORTION OF TIME, 5%)

Both these topics will be discussed under the same heading, since they are so closely related.

Reporting involves keeping those to whom the executive is responsible informed as to what is going on. This includes keeping himself and subordinates informed through records, research and inspection.

Budgeting includes fiscal planning, accounting, and control (Gulick and Urwick, 1937).

Quite recently a notorious embezzler was arrested by the FBI while on a trip to Las Vegas with his friends. He was a civil servant, and had bilked the federal government out of close to $1 million. He wasn't very remorseful, saying that "he hadn't really cheated anybody individually, just the federal government." But the interesting point of the story was how he got started. Mr. Embezzler went to his boss and slipped in a voucher along with others that the boss was signing to generate a check to Mr. Embezzler in excess of $50,000. He did this many times, generating checks in his own name in varying amounts that totaled nearly $1 million. Merely a cursory review of the vouchers would have told his boss that something was wrong; nonetheless, the boss signed his name mechanically without even reading the name of the payee. I'd say this boss had a reporting/budgeting problem, wouldn't you?

Necessary Evils

This area is probably the least interesting in management, because it entails a number of time-consuming tasks that nonetheless must be accomplished. But I can give you a few important pointers about the reporting/budgeting process:

Get the information you need, even if you must have special reports (weekly or monthly) generated. Many managers make decisions without sufficient information. Often a rather informal report generated by the appropriate subordinate can provide an excellent data base for future decisions.

Provide information to others who need it. Part of your responsibility in management is not only to get all the information that you need, but also to give information to others who need it for decision making. If you do provide them with information that is needed, you will be appreciated.

Don't be afraid to modify routine reports. Some time ago a friend of mine assumed a new management position. He soon discovered that a substantial amount of his subordinates' time was spent preparing reports that were then circulated throughout the organization. One week when the reports were prepared, he merely placed them in his desk drawer rather than circulate them. He subsequently received special requests for only 10 percent of the information that was being routinely transmitted. The net result was a substantial savings not only in his subordinates' time but also that of the individuals who were receiving unnecessary reports.

Although budgeting is an unpleasant process for many managers, it does provide a valuable scorecard for measuring performance throughout the year. This is especially true in nonprofit organizations. The absence of a "bottom line" or profit statement makes it even more essential that budgets be used as a feedback device. Although books have been written about this topic, it is not the intention here to get into the mechanics of the budget process. From the management and behavioral standpoint, I can provide you with two suggestions:

Remember that budgeting is a negotiation process. Use principles of good negotiation such as planning, setting high targets, and anticipating your opponent. Maximize the budget that you need to perform your responsibility effectively.

Use your budget as a feedback device. Every good manager should keep at least monthly updates on his budget to indicate the extent to which expenditures are on schedule. Most nonprofit organizations have reasonable internal computer systems that provide this information. If you budget effectively, you will generate the resources that you need to accomplish your objectives, and at the same time have a better idea of the progress that you are making toward those objectives.

FIGURE 1–7. *Management functions checklist.*

Function	Percentage of Time		Action Plan
	Spent Currently	Should Spend Ideally	
Planning			
Organizing			
Staffing			
Staffing			
Directing			
Coordinating			
Reporting			
Budgeting			

The time span of my job is _____ months.

Am I doing a good job on the long time span tasks? ☐ Yes ☐ No

Am I borrowing against my long time span tasks? ☐ Yes ☐ No

CONCLUSION

So you're a manager, are you? Or are you aspiring to be one? After reading this chapter I hope you'll have a better idea of what management is. Now that you understand it, do some personal diagnosis. Are you getting the POSDCORB functions accomplished? Are you strong on some and weak on others? Are you getting your long-time-span tasks accomplished? Do you have the authority and the information to do a first-class job? Use the checklist in Figure 1–7 to diagnose your current situation and to form an action plan for positive future change. Being a good manager is somewhat analogous to being an athlete. You have to practice and get feedback in order to improve.

REFERENCES

Arnold, Mary F., L. Vaughn Blankenship, and John M. Hess, eds. *Administering Health Systems* (Chicago: Aldine, 1971).

Bonoma, Thomas V., and Dennis P. Slevin. *Executive Survival Manual* (Belmont, Cal.: Wadsworth, 1978). (Adapted from Dennis P. Slevin and William Wolz.)

Development Dimensions. *1977–1978 Catalog* (Pittsburgh: Development Dimensions, 1977), pp. 38–39.

Gulick and Urwick, 1937. As adapted in Thomas V. Bonoma and Dennis P. Slevin, *Executive Survival Manual* (Belmont, Cal.: Wadsworth, 1978).

Health Career Guidebook (Washington, D.C.: U.S. Department of Labor, 1972).

Jaques, Elliott. *Equitable Payment* (Carbondale and Edwardsville: Southern Illinois University Press, 1970).

Jaques, Elliott. "Conversation: An Interview with Elliott Jaques," *Organizational Dynamics,* Spring 1977.

Lawrence, Paul R., and J. Lorsch. *Organization and Environment* (Boston: Division of Research, Graduate School of Business Administration, Harvard University, 1967).

Maier, Norman R. F. Interview by Marshal Sashkin in *Group and Organization Studies,* December 1977, pp. 399–418.

Mintzberg, Henry. *The Nature of Managerial Work* (New York: Harper & Row, 1973).

Mintzberg, Henry. "The Manager's Job: Folklore and Fact," *Harvard Business Review,* July–August 1975.

Peter, Laurence J., and Raymond Hull. *The Peter Principle* (New York: Morrow, 1969).

CHAPTER 2

Leaders and Followers

Wesley J. Johnston
Thomas V. Bonoma

Editor's Note *Effective management requires the formalizing of leadership roles within the organization. It is important for every manager to understand the principles of leadership, to be able to evaluate himself or herself as a leader, and to make appropriate improvements. This chapter is about leadership and reviews various behavioral studies in leadership, deriving a set of useful principles from them.*

The authors review three traditional theories of leadership: trait theory, behavioral/functional theory, and contingency theory. The trait approach focuses on enduring personality characteristics that make one person a leader and another a follower. The authors suggest that the research to date shows no consistent set of traits that are conducive to leadership superiority in all situations. The behavioral approach focuses on behavior patterns and identifies the three styles as being autocratic, democratic, and liberal, no one of which characterizes all leaders in all situations. The contingency approach combines the other two approaches and proposes that the best leader is one who is adaptive and changes style as the situation demands, who has certain personal values, and who participates in identifiable group values. Pressure tends to push organizational leaders toward different styles; the authors urge leaders to be aware of this and to modify leadership approaches as necessary.

The effects of leadership styles on the behavior of followers are also explored. Generally, people-oriented styles are associated with group satisfaction, whereas task-oriented styles are associated with higher group productivity. But no simplistic theory of leader behavior and group response can be effective.

The concepts of authority, conformity, risky decisions, and groupthink are also

discussed. Authority represents the control given to a leader through the institu-
tionalization of his or her role. A good leader should be able to encourage conformity
or diversity, as the situation demands, while remaining aware that groups tend to
make riskier decisions than do individuals working alone. Groupthink develops
when people are deeply involved in a cohesive in-group and a striving for unanimity
overrides the motivation to appraise alternative courses of action realistically. The
chapter stresses the importance of being aware of the problems and opportunities
associated with these phenomena.

Three problem areas specifically about leadership in nonprofit organizations are
also identified: the lack of tight management control, fuzzy organizational goals,
and the prominence of organizational conflicts. The authors believe these problems
call for higher quality of leadership and drive than may be necessary in for-profit
organizations.

As long as men and women jockey for social dominance, the phenomenon of leadership will be prominent in their lives. Wherever there is organization or a need for concerted action, there is the concomitant need for someone to be a director. Equally important is the need for those who will be directed—the people who make the role of leadership possible by being followers.

This chapter is about leadership in general, and about the special problems of leadership in not-for-profit organizations in particular. It is intended to both inform and persuade—that is, both to present a review of the various leader behavior studies and to provide, where appropriate, a set of managerially actionable principles.

We begin the examination with a consideration of the meaning of leadership itself. We then look at some of the major theories offered by behavioral researchers to account for the leadership phenomenon. And, since it is impossible to discuss leadership without discussing "follower-ship," we include a consideration of the effects of various leadership styles on follower behavior. Finally, we present our best sense of how the leader's task in a not-for-profit organization is made more difficult by some of the environmental factors found in this type of setting. At the end of each major section we present a set of principles or guidelines concerning leadership. These principles are marked with a bullet (•) for easy identification. They contain the most important conclusions that can be drawn from this chapter.

THE PROBLEM

Because of their central importance to social organization, leaders and leadership have been commented on almost since the beginning of recorded history. Plato discoursed at length on three types of proposed leaders for society. He placed a philosopher-statesman at the top (to rule the public) and managers at the bottom in order to satisfy the citizens' lower appetites. The English word "leader" can be traced in common usage to the year 1300. Stogdill's *Handbook of Leadership* (1974) attempted to accumulate all the published evidence on leadership, reviewing over 5,000 abstracts of books and articles. When we speak about leadership, we are therefore dealing with a social phenomenon that has long been of interest to philosophers and scientists, with massive amounts of opinion, theory, and research for consideration attached to it. We can do no more than select and review some of the best of it for you here.

With all the time and effort put into the study of leadership, you might think that, by now, we know a lot about the subject. Unfortunately, this is not quite the case. The only unqualified statement that can be made about leadership is that there is currently no generally accepted theory of how it functions. There is also no one set of principles that can be offered to managers for taking effective action in all situations. In fact, a large number of differing accounts exist about what a leader is.

DEFINITIONS

The major problem in defining what a leader is, or what constitutes leadership behavior, is that the definition depends on what aspects of an organization are chosen for analysis. Carter (1953) identified five different ways of defining leaders and leadership, including both the *sociometric* approach, where the group is asked to name its best-liked or most leaderlike member, and the *group goals* approach, where the person who is most capable of helping a group reach its performance goals is called the leader.

However, the definition gaining widest acceptance in the social sciences nowadays for the terms "leader" and "leadership" is attached to the concept of social influence, in which a leader is the person who exercises the most influences on a group's performance. This leader directs, coordinates, and supervises others while group members perform different tasks with a common purpose. Leadership becomes the quality or qualities that allow a person to exercise a strong influence over others.

Several qualifications are in order, though. First, the kind of influence over a group we are talking about must be positive (Shaw, 1976). That is, leaders are those individuals who exercise the kinds of influence they *intend* to exercise over a group. Many people have strong deleterious effects on group behavior, but this kind of influence is not what we would label "leadership."

Even though leadership involves planning, coordination, control, and supervision, the idea that leadership is synonymous with management is not precisely correct. More correctly, management is the formalizing of the leadership role in an organization. It is important to remember that leaders also exist in informal groups, where they are not always accorded the formal role of manager. Also, not everyone assigned the formal role of leader leads effectively. Consequently, the proposition that all leaders are also managers is not valid; nor is the one which asserts that all managers are leaders.

Though we have defined leader and leadership in terms of social influence, this is just the first step. What is needed in addition to this broad definition is *how* influence is exercised. Are certain types of individuals more adept than others at being leaders? Most leadership strategies vary, depending on the group's situation. What behaviors are most closely associated with having a high influence over a group's actions? These are the causes and correlates of positive influence, to which we now turn.

Guidelines

• The terms "leader" and "leadership" are best defined in relationship to having "positive social influence."

• The idea that leadership is synonymous with management or that management is identical to leadership is incorrect.

APPROACHES TO LEADERSHIP

Three traditional ways of looking at leadership have been identified. They are the trait approach, the behavioral/functional approach, and the contingency approach. Each is only partly correct in accounting for what makes leaders effective influences.

The Trait Approach

The questions asked by the earliest leadership research were: "What qualities can make one person a successful leader while permitting another person to fail in the same situation?" Or, in different form, "Are there 'great men' who are born leaders?" Thus early investigations of leadership focused on isolating those enduring personality characteristics, called traits, that make one person a leader and another a follower.

Hundreds of studies were conducted during the 1920s and 1930s in an attempt to identify the personal characteristics (or traits) of leaders. Both leaders and nonleaders were compared on all types of personality and intelligence scales to determine the differences among them. Reviews of this research, reach the same basic conclusion (see Stogdill, 1974): *There is no consistent pattern of traits that characterizes leaders in all situations.*

But the following conclusions were supported by positive evidence from 15 or more of the 5,000 studies surveyed by Stogdill (1974):

1. The average leader exceeds the average group member in:
   Intelligence (brighter).
   Scholarship (performs better at academic tasks).
   Dependability in exercising responsibilities.
   Activity and social participation.
   Socioeconomic status (upper middle or upper class).
2. The qualities, characteristics, and skills required of people in leadership positions are largely determined by the demands of the situation.

Intelligence remains the one personal characteristic most consistently related to leadership, with two qualifications: (1) many exceptions exist, and (2) if the gap is too wide between the intelligence of the leaders and that of followers, the resulting interaction can defeat leadership attempts.

While there is validity in the notion that who you are determines how good a leader you will be, the evidence is largely disappointing. The trait approach overemphasizes the personality and other characteristics of the leader. That the situation, the type and abilities of followers, and prevailing group interactions can also determine a leader's behavior were ignored by the trait theorists. The trait view still holds considerable sway in many corporations and organizations, even though research findings show it is not a complete way to explain who influences group behavior.

Guidelines

• There is no consistent pattern of traits that characterizes leaders in all situations.

• Intelligence is the one characteristic most consistently related to leadership.

• The trait approach to leadership is incomplete, because it concentrates solely on the leader and ignores other important aspects of the leader-follower equation.

• It is unwise for an organization to select its leaders only on the basis of personality or other individual characteristics.

The Behavioral/Functional Approach

While the trait approach to leadership emphasizes the personal qualities and virtues of the leader, the behavioral approach focuses on a leader's behavioral patterns, referred to as "leadership style."

Early research on leadership styles attempted to determine the effect of three types of style on group behavior: (1) the autocratic leader, who leads by command; (2) the democratic leader, who acts in direct contrast to the autocratic leader; and (3) the laissez-faire leader, who allows a high amount of group freedom (see Lewin and Lippitt, 1938).

The notion of behavioral styles was advanced to replace personality traits and caused a movement to "rethink" what leadership is. Important studies of the functions of leaders, carried out during the 1940s and 1950s, emphasized leadership styles and attempted to identify leaders by the functions they perform, leading to various analyses of group and leader tasks. This research concentrated on the typical activities engaged in by leaders (Halpin and Winer, 1952; Hemphill, 1950; Likert, 1961, 1967).

For example, a large research program was organized after World War II by Rensis Likert and others at the University of Michigan's Institute for Social Research. The purpose of most of these studies was to discover the principles and methods of effective leadership, because Likert felt that leadership is a relative process in which leaders must consider the expectations, values, and interpersonal skills of their followers. The leader should behave in a manner perceived by group members as being supportive of their efforts and cognizant of their personal worth. Followers should be permitted to participate in making decisions affecting their welfare and work. The leader's influence should be used to further task performance and the personal welfare of followers. Group cohesiveness and motivation for productivity should be built up by providing freedom for responsible decision making and the exercise of initiative.

Two distinct styles of leadership were identified in all of Likert's functional studies of leadership:

1. *The job-centered leader* practices close supervision, ensuring that specified procedures are used by subordinates performing their tasks. The influence of the job-centered leader is based upon coercion, reward, and legitimate types of power.
2. *The employee-centered leader* feels that a subordinate's personal advancement, growth, and achievement are important. Techniques such as the delegation of authority and individual need satisfaction are used to build a supportive work environment.

The research findings of those pursuing this theory seem to indicate that the employee-centered leader is more effective in influencing group behavior.

A second popular behavioral way of thinking about leadership uses the "managerial grid" (Blake and Mouton, 1964, 1965). As shown in Figure 2–1, this framework assumes there are two dimensions upon which a

FIGURE 2-1. *Managerial grid.*

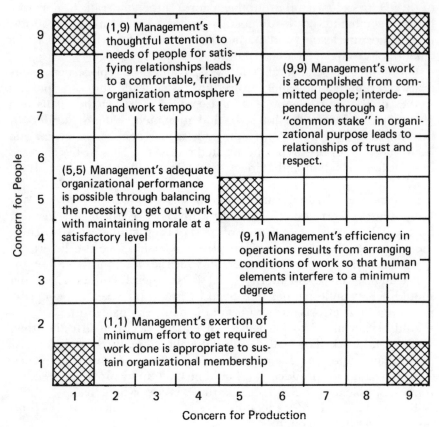

Source: Robert R. Blake and Jane S. Mouton, *The Managerial Grid*
(Houston: Gulf Publishing, 1964), p. 10.

manager's attitudes can be measured. Concern for people represents the vertical axis, while concern for production represents the horizontal one. Leaders may score either high or low on both concerns or they may be high on one and low on the other. Concern for people and production may be complementary rather than mutually exclusive. The leader who scores high on both is effective in achieving performance results and developing followers who are committed to the accomplishment of work and whose sense of interdependence leads to trust and respect.

The assumptions made by the Blake-Mouton model about leadership are that (1) individuals exhibit varying styles of leadership behavior—they are 1,9 *or* 5,5 *or* 9,9; (2) the 9,9 style of leadership is the ideal approach to many leadership situations; and (3) by undertaking a training program, leaders may be able to learn to move from their current style to the preferred 9,9 style.

While each behavioral/functional theory differs from the others, they share several common properties:

1. Each theory defines "leadership style" in terms of broad dimensions of leadership behavior.
2. All the theories are predicated on the belief that the style of the leader is the important variable in the process of leadership.
3. Taken collectively, the theories suggest that the primary functions of leaders are organizing, directing, and supporting subordinates.

Although these theories provide an improvement over the trait approach, they fail to capture the full complexity of the leadership process and offer lists of styles instead of lists of traits. They ignore the situational constraints on leadership, as well as the human nature of lower-level group members, providing no more of a complete account for how a leader effectively influences a group than does the trait approach.

Guidelines

• There is no one style of leadership that characterizes all leaders in all situations.

• The behavioral/functional approach is less than totally successful because it searches for the "best" style of leader behavior for all situations and ignores many situational or group factors.

• It is unwise for an organization to select or dictate a single leadership style for all members to follow.

The Contingency Approach

The contingency approach to leadership combines the trait approach and the behavioral/functional approach by proposing that "the best leader is the one who is adaptive, who can change his style depending on the situation, the group, and his personal values" (Bonoma and Slevin, 1978). The contingency approach predicts that a leader's contribution to group effectiveness depends on both the characteristics of the leader and the favorableness of the situation for leadership. In situations that are either very favorable or very unfavorable, directive leadership is more effective. When the situation is only moderately favorable, nondirective leadership is often more effective.

One typical contingency approach (Fiedler, 1967) starts with the style of the leader as a basic in understanding effective leadership. Two leadership styles were identified by Fiedler:

1. Relations-oriented leaders, who stress the importance of good personal relations between followers and themselves.
2. Task-oriented leaders, who concentrate on structuring the relationships and activities of subordinates toward more effective task accomplishment.

Fiedler also posits three situational variables that affect the outcome of organizational performance:

1. The leader's legitimate power—the degree to which the position provides formal authority and support to aid the leader in obtaining compliance from other group members.
2. The structure of the task—the degree to which the specific task is straightforward and clearly defined with step-by-step procedures for accomplishment.
3. The personal relationships between leader and members—the degree to which the leader is trusted and liked by other group members.

With groups ranging from basketball teams to open-hearth furnace shops, Fiedler's contingency approach was generally able to predict which styles of leadership work most effectively in different situations. For example, a task-oriented leader performs best in situations where either the task is highly structured (such as budgeting) and good leader-member relations exist or where the task is totally unstructured (long-range strategic planning) and poor leader-member relations exist. A relations-oriented leader also works best in a mixed-task structure situation (marketing strategy), where the leader can have only a moderate influence over the group.

The contingency approach argues that there is no universally successful style of leadership. The leader who desires to be successful must adopt different styles that accord with the types of situations encountered. A change in the leader's environment can also aid in more effective group performance. For instance, by changing the task structure, changing the leader's legitimate power, or changing the personal relationships between the leader and group members, a situation more or less favorable to the appointed leader can be created.

The Management-Targeted Approach

While Fiedler's model is helpful in illustrating relationships between leader styles and leadership situations, there is another, more recently developed contingency model that was designed specifically to aid managers in implementing effective leadership styles.

In their *Executive Survival Manual* (1978), Bonoma and Slevin note that "despite the development of a variety of normative models and completion of uncountable empirical studies, it is still extremely difficult for the practicing manager to implement the recommendations of leadership research. . . ." To solve this problem, they developed a two-variable model of leadership that simplifies management decision-making problems and helps managers make leadership control decisions just as they make other decisions.

To make effective leadership style decisions, the manager needs the answers to only two basic questions: "Where (from whom) do I get the information I need?" and "Where should I place the decision-making authority for this problem—on myself or my group?" These questions capture the leadership style dimensions of information input and decision-making authority. The two dimensions are then plotted on a graph, as shown in Figure 2–2. The Bonoma-Slevin grid uses information input and decision-making authority in an active way to help the manager make leadership decisions.

Bonoma and Slevin depict several ideal points on the grid in Figure 2–2 for their stereotypical or practical importance:

• Autocrat (10,0) represents stereotypical managers who solicit little or no information input from the group and who also make managerial decisions solely by themselves.

• Consultative autocrats (10,10) are the stereotypical managers who elicit intensive information input from group members but retain all substantive decision-making authority for themselves.

• Consensus managers (0,10) are characterized by throwing open a problem to the group for discussion (information input) while simultaneously allowing or encouraging the entire group to make relevant decisions.

• Shareholder managers (0,0) are poor managers who permit little information input and exchange to take place within the group while giving the group all authority to make final decisions.

Table 2–1 outlines how Bonoma and Slevin elaborate on their basic grid to indicate how movement on it can be brought about by problem attribute pressures, leader personality pressures, and organizational group pressures. This model argues that an effective leader or manager cannot inflexibly occupy only one square of the grid in Figure 2–2 but must be able to move in any direction on the grid, as problems or the organization require. Since the styles of organizational problems vary,

FIGURE 2-2. *The Bonoma-Slevin leadership model.*

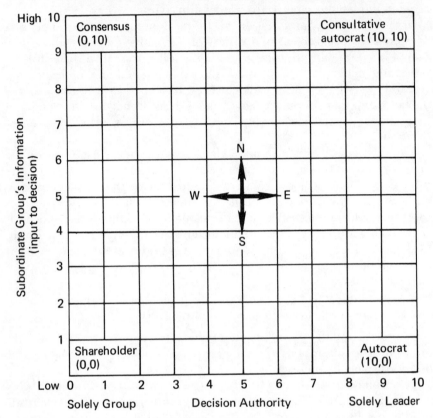

Source: Adapted from T.V. Bonoma and D.P. Slevin, *Executive Survival Manual*
(Cambridge, Mass.: Cahners Books, 1978).

Bonoma and Slevin argue that the best leader in management is the one
who is the most flexible in shaping a leadership style to meet specific
problem requirements. The totally inflexible manager is also totally ineffective in many group dealings. In this view, there is no best style of
leadership.

The contingency approach is a good start toward the integration of
leadership styles and situational factors as determinants of group effectiveness. Models like this are important, not only because they propose
that leadership is situation specific but also because they attempt to specify
the leadership styles that may be most effective in differing situations.

TABLE 2–1. *Leadership style pressures.*

Type of Pressure	Direction of Pressure
Problem attribute pressures	
The problem is ambiguous.	North: Pressure toward the need of increasing information input, regardless of authority.
There is not enough time to make decisions adequately.	East: Pressure toward placing increasing decisional authority solely in leader; possibly also South to the extent information inputs and exchange require time.
The decision is important or critical to the organization.	North: Information search is maximized; also possibly East, maximizing decisional control.
The decision is personally important to the leader.	East: Possibly Northeast; Maximize personal control and information.
The problem is structured on routine.	East: Spend as little time as possible on decision making.
The decision's implementation by subordinates is not critical to its success.	East, South: Input and sharing not required.
Leader personality pressures	
The leader has a lot of power over subordinates or is in great need of power (task oriented).	East: Maximize personal control.
The leader is high in need for affiliation (people oriented).	North: Maximize information input; possibly West.
The leader is intelligent.	East: Maximize abilities to demonstrate personal competence.
The leader has a high need for achievement.	East: Maximize personal control.
Organizational group pressures	
Conflict is likely to result from the decision.	North, West: Maximize the participative aspects of decision making.
Good leader-group relations exist.	North, West: Maximize the participative aspects of decision making.
Formalization of the organization is high.	North: Maximize information input and exchange.

Source: Adapted from T. V. Bonoma and D. P. Slevin, *Executive Survival Manual* (Cambridge, Mass. Cahners Books, 1978).

Guidelines

• Successful leaders must be capable of adopting different leadership styles, depending on the factors in the leader-follower situation.

• Various pressures tend to push the style of organizational leaders in different directions; leaders in organizations should therefore be aware of such pressures and modify their leadership approaches accordingly.

THE EFFECTS OF LEADERSHIP STYLES

One of the primary reasons for the large amount of research on and interest in leadership is the belief that the style of leadership within a group has an important effect on the group's functioning. Effective leadership makes for an effectively functioning group. If organizational leaders are to adapt successfully to various leadership situations by varying their leadership styles, they must be aware of the potential effects of their style on the groups they lead.

The main research effort up to now has been to identify the relationships that exist between a leadership style or behavior and group performance. If leader-follower links are understood, the outcomes of group functioning can be shaped by changing the leadership variables of style (or traits), training, and environment (situation). If happy and satisfied group members are the goal, one type of leadership can be selected. If high productivity is the goal, the best type of leadership can be chosen for that purpose. But perhaps there is a leadership style that can serve both purposes. Use of the guidelines for organizational leaders given below must always be tempered by consideration of the organizational milieu and the situation at hand. For instance, while research has found that hostility is thirty times as great in autocratic as in democratic groups, no one would really prefer a democratic pilot on a malfunctioning jet airliner.

Authoritarian, Democratic, and Laissez-Faire Styles

Table 2–2 outlines the three types of leadership examined by early studies of leadership styles. The findings of one study (White and Lippitt, 1968) can be summarized as follows:

- A laissez-faire style is not the same as a democratic one.
- Democracy can be an efficient management style.
- Autocracy can create much hostility and aggression, including aggression against group scapegoats.
- Autocracy can create discontent that does not appear on the surface.
- There is more follower dependence and less individuality with autocratic styles than with the two others.
- There is more group-mindedness and more friendliness in democracy.

The important findings of an earlier study (Lewin and Lippitt, 1938) included:

- Hostility is thirty times as great in the autocratic as in the democratic groups.

TABLE 2–2. *Leader behavior styles.*

Authoritarian	Democratic	Laissez-faire
Determination of all policy is done by the leader.	All policies are a matter of group discussion and decision, encouraged and assisted by the leader.	Complete freedom for group or individual decisions exists, with a minimum of leader participation.
Technique and activity steps are dictated by the authority, one at a time, so that future steps are always uncertain to a large degree.	The activity perspective is gained during a discussion period. General steps toward group goals are sketched; when technical advice is needed, the leader suggests two or more alternative procedures from which a choice can be made.	Various materials are supplied by the leader, who makes it clear information will be supplied when asked for. Leader takes no other part in work discussions.
The leader usually dictates the particular work task and work companion of each member.	The members are free to work with whomever they chose. The division of tasks is left up to the group.	Complete nonparticipation by the leader.
The dominator tends to be personal in praising and criticizing the work of each member; remains aloof from active group participation, except when demonstrating.	The leader is objective or fact-minded when giving praise and criticism and tries to be a regular group member in spirit without doing too much of the work.	Infrequent spontaneous comments on member activities by the leader, unless questioned, and no attempt made to appraise or regulate the course of events.

Source: Adapted from Ralph White and Ronald Lippitt, "Leader Behavior and Member Reaction in Three 'Social Climates,'" in D. Cartwright and A. Zander, eds., *Group Dynamics*, 3rd ed. (New York: Harper, 1968), pp. 318–335.

- Aggression is eight times as great in the autocratic as in the democratic groups.
- Scapegoating is far more prevalent in the autocratic than in the democratic or laissez-faire groups.
- The democratic leader is better liked by more group members than the autocratic leader.
- The laissez-faire leader is better liked by more group members than the autocratic leader.
- The quantity of work is greater in the autocratic groups, but not reliably so.

- The quality of work in the democratic groups is judged to be superior.
- There is less work done under laissez-faire leadership than under either democratic or autocratic leadership.
- The quality of work done is poorer under laissez-faire leadership than under either democratic or autocratic leadership.

In addition to these findings, some interesting effects were noted after changes of leadership style were made within the groups: (1) When the leadership style was initially autocratic and then followed by the laissez-faire style, aggressive actions by group members rose dramatically. (2) When laissez-faire leadership was followed by autocratic and democratic leadership styles in turn, aggressive acts remained relatively stable, gradually declining across the three periods of leadership.

According to Foa (1957), even workers' expectations about what kind of leadership style will prevail in a group setting can affect their satisfaction. Groups with either authoritarian or permissive expectations about a leader are relatively satisfied if the leader turns out to be permissive. But when the leader turns out to be authoritarian, workers who have authoritarian expectations generally become more satisfied than workers who had held expectations of a permissive leader.

When considering whether to lead in a permissive or restrictive manner, it is important to consider the outcome of each style. Group productivity and cohesiveness are *not* consistently higher under either type of leadership. Follower satisfaction appears more often to be associated with permissiveness than with restrictiveness.

Relations-Oriented and Task-Oriented Styles

Relations-oriented leadership can be referred to as a "group-oriented," or "employee-centered," a "human relations" approach. No matter what the title, it implies effort by leaders to maintain friendly, supportive relations with their individual followers. It does not necessarily imply a high degree of permissiveness. In fact, these leaders can and do maintain high performance standards. The findings of studies concerned with these styles of leadership conclude that:

- Both member satisfaction and group performance are higher under a relations-oriented style.
- Effective supervisors regard others as individuals with motives, feelings, and goals of their own.
- Workers under employee-centered supervisors have more group pride than those under work-centered supervisors.

- High levels of group performance in one company were associated with satisfaction with supervisors' supportiveness, open communication, mutual understanding, and worker autonomy on the job.
- A supportive attitude toward workers and belief in the group method of supervision, combined with high group loyalty and attitude toward management, is associated with increased productivity and the desire for responsibility.

However, the evidence is not all positive. A number of studies have found that no relationship exists between leader style and productivity or even satisfaction in the relations-oriented style. Some negative results showed that (1) managers of scientific teams highly skilled in human relations were rated low in leader effectiveness, and (2) in simulated business groups, productivity was positively related to close rather than general supervision.

In summary, it appears that job satisfaction is higher, in most cases, under a relations-centered leader, but whether productivity is increased or decreased by a relations orientation is unclear.

Participative and Directive Styles

Participative leadership implies that leaders permit or encourage group members to participate actively in discussion, problem solving, and decision making. In directive leadership, leaders play active roles in problem solving and decision making and expect group members to be guided by their decisions.

In changing group opinion, participative leadership is more effective than directive leadership. Research has shown that:

- Participatory leaders and followers changed their attitudes about the task more than supervisory leaders and followers.
- Participatory group members were more satisfied with the group's final product.
- Participatory group members felt that the task was more interesting and meaningful than did supervisory-led members.

Permissive leadership resulted in the highest productivity when employees were involved in the planning and execution of tasks. The members also felt a greater commitment to goals of productivity. The effectiveness of directive leadership also depends on (1) ready acceptance by groups whose membership is closely restricted, with a stratified status structure and low dependence of group members, and (2) group cohesiveness and satisfaction in business and government increasing with more directive leadership and decreasing with leadership sharing. The overall findings support the conclusions that:

- Satisfaction of group members is higher with a participative style of leadership.
- Group cohesiveness is higher with a participative style of leadership.
- Productivity of the group appears to depend on factors other than participative or directive styles of leadership (the findings have been highly inconsistent).
- Opinion change occurs more readily under participative leadership.

Research on the effects of leadership style on follower behavior does not confirm simplistic or polarized explanations of leader behavior and group response. The pattern of behavior effective in one situation is not necessarily effective elsewhere. Generally, a person-oriented leader promotes the satisfaction of group members. Those with more task-oriented styles are often rewarded with more group productivity.

Guidelines

- Democratic, relations-oriented, and participative styles of leadership can be efficient styles of management.
- Autocratic, task-oriented, directive styles of leadership can create discontent that often results in hostility, aggression, scapegoating, and lowered morale.
- It is not clear whether task- or relations-oriented styles produce more heightened group productivity.
- Because the types of leadership, changes in leadership styles, and expectations about a new leader can affect group attitudes, organizations must be especially careful when replacing one leader with another.
- Group satisfaction and morale tend to be higher in a democratic, relations-oriented, participative atmosphere, though output or productivity is not as clearly affected in such situations.

OTHER LEADERSHIP FACTORS

Just defining leadership, specifying the interaction of leadership styles and leadership situations, and noting the effects on followers is not the end of the puzzle. Leaders exist within hierarchies, whether established by their followers or by the organization to which they belong. They need to deal with the problems and effects of their legitimate authority apart from the effects of their leadership styles. When human beings get into groups, they are often unpredictable. In addition to the problems posed by authority, there are three other unusual group phenomena: conformity, the risky shift, and groupthink.

Authority

The terms "authority," "power," and "influence" are often used inter-changeably. But authority has a narrower meaning than do influence or power. It stands for only that control given the leader through the institutionalization of the leader's role, the formal power of the leader vested in the role he or she holds within the organization (Tedeschi, Schlenker, and Bonoma, 1973).

Who legitimizes the leader's power to give it the status of authority? How are the areas in which a leader may legitimately exercise authority determined? Can the leader's authority be delegated or shared with others in the organization's hierarchy? Two different theories attempt to answer these questions: the theory of formal authority and the acceptance theory of authority.

The theory of formal authority views the leader's institutionalized power as being derived from higher levels in the organization. Authority is said to be legitimate when a leader's superiors are consistently supportive of a particular type of influence assertion. If the leader has support from above, he or she is felt to possess authority under the theory of formal authority.

The acceptance theory of authority requires legitimization from below—that is, acceptance of the leader's power by the followers or subordinates within the groups. Because this theory emphasizes legitimization from below, real authority is lacking when the upward acceptance fails to materialize, regardless of how much formal authority has been given the leader.

Neither theory is entirely true by itself; if taken together, however, both are true. Research has consistently shown that, to be maximally effective, a leader needs support both from above and from below. Lacking support from above, a leader's effectiveness is limited to the small group or department directly controlled. Lacking support from below, even the most legitimate demands or requests either go unsatisfied or are met by hostility, subversion, and aggression.

When individuals join a formal organization, they contractually agree (often only implicitly) to accept authority in return for a share in the rewards and membership in the organization. This agreement is not a blanket acceptance of all directives; a "zone of indifference" exists within which employees permit authority to be exercised. Attempts to exercise authority outside this zone are generally rejected by the organization's members, with actual behavior not conforming to formally defined patterns.

While an organization may establish rules concerning employee behavior both on and off the job, employees may legitimize only those prescriptions they feel fall within the zone of indifference. Whether formal or informal, there are limits to authority. Employees questioned about what management might legitimately require of them and the things over which management should have no authority gave the answers listed in Table 2–3. It appears that employees feel strongly that it is legitimate, or within the zone of indifference, for management to influence the work environment or direct job performance, but that personal affairs and family matters clearly fall outside the zone of indifference.

Another way to evaluate the strength of authority as compared with other personal or organizational factors is to measure its power to affect decision making. The reasons one individual seeks a decision from another on work-related matters are given in the order of frequency mentioned by managers (Filley and Grimes, 1968):

- Responsibility and function—the person with authority is responsible for that particular matter.
- Formal authority—the person with authority is generally in a position to make decisions.
- Control of resources—the person with authority controls money, information, and so on.

TABLE 2–3. *Managerial authority items with high and low legitimacy.*

Item	Mean Score
High legitimacy	
The amount of time spent talking to a spouse and children on the telephone while at work	78
The tidiness of the manager's office	77
Working hours	77
The kind of temperament exhibited on the job	76
How much importance is attached to getting along with other people	69
The amount of time spent doing job-related reading while at work	67
How the working day is divided among various duties	66
Low legitimacy	
The church attended	−95
Where charge accounts are maintained for personal shopping	−94
Where vacations are spent	−94
Schools children attend	−93
Political party affiliation	−93
The kind of person spouse is	−90
The kind of car driven	−90
Whether house is owned or not	−88
Whether spouse works or not	−88
The kind of house or apartment lived in	−85
How much entertaining is done	−83

- Collegial—a group of peers has the right to be consulted.
- Manipulation—the person with authority can get the decision made in the desired manner.
- Default or avoidance—the person with authority is available and will deal with the problem.
- Bureaucratic rules—the rules specify the person to consult.
- Traditional rules—custom, tradition, or seniority specify the person to consult.
- Equity—the person with authority is a fair decision maker.
- Friendship—the person with authority is liked personally.
- Expertise—the person with authority has a superior knowledge of the subject.

The list contains nonauthority reasons, formal authority views, and some items that accord with acceptance theory. The thing to note is that the majority of reasons given for consulting someone else before making decisions relate to the ascription authority.

Guidelines

- Authority stands for the control given a leader through role institutionalization.
- To be truly effective, a leader needs support from both above and below in the organizational hierarchy; he or she must be backed by superiors and supported by subordinates.
- Subordinates make an agreement to accept authority for a share in the rewards of their organization.
- Authority is not without its limits. The area in which authority is given a leader by subordinates may extend only to job-related matters, known as the "zone of indifference."
- The need for an authoritative answer is often why one individual seeks advice from another in formal organizations.
- An effective leader understands the basis of his or her authority as well as its extent.

Conformity

Confusion often arises when the terms "conformity," "compliance," and "conventionality" are used. Each word has a separate meaning. The following discussion attempts to clarify the differences and explain some of the important and complex relations involved in social influence situations that are likely to affect leader-follower relations.

Conformity is generally taken to mean (1) going along with the group, behaving in a way consistent with that of the majority; (2) a change in attitudes or beliefs as a result of group pressure; or (3) a basic personality trait. These definitions refer to the behavioral uniformity that society expects of individuals in groups.

The opposite of conformity is independence. If conformity is yielding to group pressures, independence is not yielding to those pressures. However, it is also more than that. For group members to be truly independent, they must choose their own positions regardless of whether they agree with the position taken by the group. The individual must then be either totally unaffected by group norms and positions or totally unaware of them. Simply reacting negatively or in opposition to a group position is anticonformity and is not true independence. The main ingredient for an independent follower's response is the holding of a private opinion that contradicts a majority opinion.

The manager's problem is to learn how to manage conformity, to be able to encourage it when it is appropriate or in the best interests of the organization and to be able to encourage diversity or independence when that is appropriate. Let us first identify the personal or social attributes of managers that promote group conformity: (1) *expertise,* the manager's competence for the task at hand; (2) *attraction,* the positive relationship between manager and workers; (3) *status,* the manager's formal role in the organization; and (4) *esteem,* the manager's reputation for being competent. The more a manager possesses these attributes, the more successful he or she will be in getting others to conform to group norms and methods.

Conformity is also promoted through *idiosyncracy credits*—the positive impressions of leaders held by their followers (Hollander, 1963). Idiosyncracy credits represent status and are spent by individuals by deviating from norms, innovating, and influencing. Credits are accumulated through perceived conformity to group norms and competence in accomplishing group goals. This explains why the newer members of a group, who have fewer credits, are constrained to conform more, while members of long standing, with considerable idiosyncracy credit balances, are free to deviate without being chastized. Credits can be spent on either nonconformity or influence. Eventually, however, the bank account of goodwill is used up.

Individuals of higher status generally have greater freedom to deviate. This fact is useful in understanding the potential for innovation associated with leadership. In pursuing the achievement of goals, high-status leaders are permitted to deviate from group norms to a greater extent than low-status leaders because of their store of idiosyncracy credits. The longer someone has been successfully interacting within a group, the greater the number of idiosyncracy credits he or she has built up and the less likely it is that deviation will be punished.

Judgments should not be made about the inherent goodness or badness of conformity, since it has complex sources and effects. Neither conformity nor diversity should be valued for its own sake. The yes-person and the anticonformist both have places in an organization. Independent thinking can be a valuable asset when applied appropriately.

Guidelines

• One problem faced by leaders is how to manage conformity. Being able to encourage conformity, diversity, or independent thinking as the situation demands is an important leadership skill.

• The qualities of expertise, positive relations, status, and esteem enable a leader to obtain conformity more easily from others.

• Even though innovation requires deviation from established procedures, leaders and other group members of long standing are freer to be innovative than newer group members.

• Nonconformity can cost an individual group goodwill.

• Conformity is inherently neither good nor bad. Every organization can use some independent thinking, but total conformity can undermine the overall purpose of the organization.

The Risky Shift

In group decision making, the "risky shift" phenomenon tends to result in groups making riskier decisions than individuals working alone would. Thus, in the story about Dr. H (see box), the groups assigned to reach a consensus on whether he should buy a Lear jet would be more likely to give answers with lower odds than would an equal number of solitary individuals.

It is not clear why the risky shift phenomenon occurs in groups, though it has been speculated that it is due to the fact that responsibility for the risk is shared. All things being equal, groups tend to make suboptimal decisions—that is, they do not require a high return from a risky alternative before they recommend its adoption.

Another danger related to group decision making is group inaction. Groups usually have so many things to tend to that they wind up making no decision at all. Or if a decision is made, it is often not implemented, because no action ensues or no one person is held to blame if the decision is not carried out. The diffusion of responsibility in groups, where no one individual is responsible for a decision and its consequences, may be suspected as responsible for both inaction and the risky shift problem.

Dr. H is a physician who specializes in heart transplants. He does a lot of consulting work in all parts of the United States and Canada, which necessitates a lot of traveling. Dr. H is considering two alternative means of travel: he can purchase a Lear jet and hire a pilot or he can continue to use public transportation. Public transportation has become somewhat undesirable to him because it means he must conform to the scheduled flights and seat availability on public airlines. This makes it more difficult to be involved in emergency operations in distant places. It also means spending a lot of time waiting for planes or sitting in planes. Dr. H considers this wasted time, since he finds it difficult to concentrate on reading scientific reports in this environment.

But even during bad weather conditions public transportation is fairly readily available to most locations. That is, because of their sophisticated equipment, airlines often operate when private planes remain grounded. In addition, using public transportation has the advantage of not involving any long-term commitments of Dr. H's time or resources.

Purchasing a Lear jet and hiring a pilot would offer more convenience and flexibility of scheduling as well as a certain amount of prestige and status. Since Dr. H has a very high income, he could afford the initial cost of the plane as well as the other upkeep expenses involved. However, owning the jet might involve other disadvantages. There is the remote possibility that Dr. H would be offered a position at a large research hospital. If this happened, he would stop traveling and would devote most of his time to research. In this event, he would be stuck with the plane. The market for used Lear jets is not good, since most people or firms who are interested in purchasing such an item are willing to spend the additional amount to get a new plane. Thus Dr. H would probably have to spend a lot of his valuable time searching for a buyer for the jet and would probably have to take a loss on the plane.

Gain-Loss Summary

Alternative 1: Using Public Transportation

Attractiveness. The availability of public transportation during bad weather and the absence of any long-term commitment is worth + 35 S.U.s (satisfaction units) to Dr. H; while the inconvenience associated with conforming to airline schedules and crowds is worth − 30 S.U.s to Dr. H. The total attractiveness of this alternative for Dr. H is + 5 S.U.s.

Odds. The chances that Dr. H will receive these S.U.s if he chooses public transportation are 10 in 10.

Alternative 2: Purchasing a Lear Jet

Attractiveness. The occupational and personal satisfaction of having a Lear jet available for business trips is worth + 75 S.U.s to Dr. H. The financial and personal costs associated with owning a Lear jet if his practice changes are worth − 65 S.U.s to Dr. H.

Odds. Suppose that you are Dr. H. You are considering the probability or odds (from 0 in 10 to 10 in 10) that your private practice will remain the same. What is the *lowest* probability that you would consider acceptable to make it worthwhile for you, as Dr. H, to purchase the Lear jet?

Guidelines

• The final decision of a group should be carefully scrutinized to determine that it is an acceptable, responsible, and not an overly risky solution to the problem. Remember, it is said that the camel was a horse designed by a committee.

• A good leader keeps in mind the possibility of a risky group decision and guards against it.

• A good leader does not let a meeting terminate without outlining actions to be taken by individual group members.

Groupthink

The concept of "groupthink" occurred to Irving L. Janis (1972) while he was reading about the United States' involvement in the Bay of Pigs. The Central Intelligence Agency's plan for the invasion of Cuba and eventual overthrow of Fidel Castro was ill conceived, contained many flaws, and ended in great embarrassment to the U.S. government. Janis at first found it difficult to understand how "bright, shrewd men like John F. Kennedy and his advisers [could] be taken in by the CIA's stupid, patchwork plan" (Janis, 1972, p. 111).

Janis began to wonder whether a psychological contagion similar to social conformity had interfered with the alertness of the decision makers. By making a further analysis of this incident, Janis noticed that the behavior of the decision makers fit a specific pattern of concurrence seeking. He had noticed this behavior in other kinds of face-to-face encounters, especially when there was a strong "we feeling" or solidarity present. From these observations, he came to believe that group processes had prevented Kennedy and his advisers from debating the real issues inherent in the CIA's plan and carefully appraising its risks.

In reviewing other miscalculations in U.S. policymaking (failure to be prepared for the attack on Pearl Harbor; the invasion of North Korea; escalation of the Vietnam War) that emanated from meetings of small groups of government officials, Janis concluded that the phenomenon of the Bay of Pigs was not an isolated incident.

The term "groupthink" was developed to refer to the mode of thinking that arises when people "are deeply involved in a cohesive in-group, when the members' strivings for unanimity override their motivation to realistically appraise alternative courses of action" (Janis, 1972, p. 197). Janis identified eight main symptoms as belonging to groupthink (pp. 197–198):

1. An illusion of invulnerability, shared by most or all group members that creates excessive optimism and encourages taking extreme risks.

2. Collective efforts to rationalize in order to discount warnings that might lead group members to reconsider their assumptions before they recommit themselves to their past policy decisions.

3. An unquestioned belief in the group's inherent morality, inclining the members to ignore the ethical or moral consequences of group decisions.

4. Stereotypical views that interpret enemy leaders as being too evil to participate in genuine negotiations or too weak and stupid to counter the risks that might defeat their purposes.

5. Direct pressure brought on any group member who expresses strong arguments against any of the group's stereotypes, illusions, or commitments, making it clear that this type of dissent is contrary to what is expected of all loyal members.

6. Self-censorship of deviations from the apparent group consensus that reflect each member's inclination to minimize the importance of personal doubts and counterarguments.

7. An illusion of shared unanimity concerning judgments that conform to the majority view, resulting partly from self-censorship of deviations, augmented by the false assumption that silence means consent.

8. The emergence of self-appointed mind guards—members who protect the group from adverse information that might shatter their shared complacency about the effectiveness and morality of their decisions.

Although the major condition promoting groupthink is cohesiveness, not all cohesive groups are doomed to be victims of self-defeating patterns of concurrence seeking. Janis offered nine prescriptions to defeat the occurrence of groupthink in policy- and decision-making groups:

1. Encourage group members to air objections and doubts; discourage them from soft-pedaling their disagreements. Criticism is valuable; be open to it.

2. Limit policy-planning briefings to unbiased statements about the scope of the problem and the limitations of available resources. Be impartial; do not advocate specific proposals.

3. Set up several independent policy-planning and evaluation groups to work on the same problem.

4. When alternative approaches are being surveyed, divide the group into two or more subgroups: have them meet separately from time to time and then come together to work out differences.

5. Have group members discuss deliberations periodically with trusted associates in their own departments and report back to the group on the reactions received.

6. Invite outside experts to each meeting on a staggered basis to challenge group views.
7. Assign at least one group member the role of devil's advocate at each meeting devoted to evaluating alternatives.
8. Spend time considering warning signals and alternative scenarios for rivals' behavior. Be prepared for counterreactions.
9. After reaching a preliminary consensus about the best alternative, wait a while and then hold a second-chance meeting. Encourage group members to express residual doubts and rethink the entire issue before approving the final decision.

The leader must be aware of the problems of conformity, risky decisions of groups, and groupthink in order to prevent developments stemming from them. The major way to do this is not to get rid of these phenomena, because it cannot be done. Rather, it is to manage and control them consciously.

SPECIAL PROBLEMS OF THE NOT-FOR-PROFIT MANAGER

Up to this point, the assumption has been that for-profit (private) and not-for-profit (public) organizations require the same management and leadership styles. While there is no good research evidence to cite, our strong sense is that the two sectors impose quite different constraints on their leaders. Consequently, we would like to offer our set of speculations, and they are only speculations, on the special constraints and problems of the public sector manager which might impede him from being an effective leader. We have identified three major areas in which the public sector seems to differ radically from the private one. These differences, which bear on leadership behavior, are (1) lack of tight managerial control, (2) fuzzy organizational goals, and (3) the prominence of organizational conflicts.

Lack of Managerial Control

One of the primary problems facing would-be leaders in the public sector is born of the dual requirements of public accountability and multiple management hierarchies. Because of these requirements, nonprofit managers often lack the same types of managerial controls that are available to leaders in the private sector. To explain what we mean by this lack of control, we'll speculate on three major areas impinging on public sector managers which might affect their leadership latitude. They are (1) the tenure phenomenon, (2) the budgeting process, and (3) the supervision and incentive dilemma.

Tenure. Though a functional kind of tenure may be encountered in the private sector, especially at the upper levels, nowhere is tenure so well entrenched as in the public sector. We are not referring here only to universities, where faculty members become almost unremovable after a few years, unless a severe moral fault is uncovered. The phenomenon we are talking about also occurs at the local, state, and federal levels, where civil-service employees and others, after a short probation period, literally cannot be removed from their jobs except for the most gross sorts of negligence and absenteeism.

The effects of functional or legitimate tenure are simply to remove many of the normal control mechanisms and incentives from the bag of the manager who organizes and controls the behavior of subordinates. In most instances, no meaningful punishment for employee infractions exists, since worker continuance is assured by virtue of employment guarantees. While advancement and other significant incentives may be withheld because of only adequate or mediocre performance, there often is no real incentive for tenured workers to perform at more than mediocre levels. Obviously, in this kind of situation, the manager's job becomes all the more difficult.

Budgeting. Public sector managers also often face two budgeting problems that their private sector counterparts can avoid in part. First, when budgets are set up, the specification of line items is a firmer process in public agencies than in private corporations. This is because public agency budgets are frequently drawn from tax dollars and are therefore often scrutinized and cast in concrete well in advance of expenditure. There are just more people to be consulted in advance in the public sector. The second problem is that the average public sector manager has less budgetary control than does his private sector counterpart. While the latter may be able to switch money from one line item to another, eliminate items, or add new items as needed, most public sector managers are severely limited by their previous decisions in coping with changing reality.

Incentive. When employee incentives are considered along with the budgetary constraints imposed on the public sector manager, it becomes clear why it is hard to run a rewards-for-performance shop in the public sector. Raise sizes are often either legislated or fixed in across-the-board amounts applicable to all workers. The manager often has little or no latitude in redistributing incentive income to those who most deserve it, while disincentives for poor performance are either lacking or difficult to implement within budgetary constraints. If every employee at a university gets merit raises ranging from 4 to 7 percent, the difference between being the poorest performer and the best is marginal and largely of only social significance. Thus public sector agencies cannot and do not usually reward or punish their workers with any clear relationship being evident between performance and pay.

Fuzzy Organizational Goals

By "fuzzy" organizational goals we do not mean that public sector goals are any less clear than those in the private sector. But most public sector organizations or service agencies specialize in dispensing services and satisfying consumers. These variables are notoriously hard to evaluate on a cost-benefit basis, thus making it extremely hard for managers or leaders to discriminate between good and bad performance.

Many public sector organizations are in the business of deferral, such as keeping the mentally ill from becoming patients or keeping the sick from dying. It is always harder to measure the accomplishment of negative goals than positive ones. Unitary commodities like money often do not exist for measuring public sector organizational goals. And since these agencies often deal in the subjective quantities of service delivery and human satisfaction, managers in a public sector agency have a much more difficult time than do their private sector counterparts. The latter can often rely on straightforward return-on-investment indices or other conventional performance indicators.

Organizational Conflicts

We do not mean to suggest that organizational conflicts are more prevalent in public sector agencies, at least not the kind where different individuals come into conflict. But it has been speculated that public sector workers are generally less satisfied with pay and other incentives than workers in private sector jobs, because these jobs allow a greater degree of freedom than do equivalent jobs in the private sector. Thus the public sector manager is often in the position of leading a group of individuals whose utility is only partially consistent with organizational goals and who may have significant other things going "on the side" in which they are deeply invested.* Needless to say, it is difficult to lead followers who are only partially committed.

This is not to say that public sector employees are generally less vigorous, motivated, or able than their private sector counterparts. Because of working conditions, pay levels, and lack of clear incentive-performance relationships, plus a host of other factors, public sector employees often find it convenient to establish other areas in which they can measure their

---

*The Pittsburgh policeman who ran an off-hours security business for pornography warehouses is a dramatic example.

personal worth. Job tenure and the often greater freedom in working hours afforded public sector employees only further encourage this trend.

The Public Sector Leader's Dilemma

When all these factors are taken into account, it is clear that the job of the public sector leader is a difficult one at best in most organizations. He or she must work in a difficult organizational environment, where situational factors like budget inflexibility and the lack of differential incentives often overcome personal style variables. He or she must attempt to deliver service and provide human satisfaction, knowing that they are long-term propositions as well as extremely hard to measure effectively. And he or she must deal with a workforce and even colleagues who are only marginally satisfied in their positions and have made substantial commitments to other endeavors.

All this is to say that the quality of leadership in public sector organizations on the whole must be higher than it is in the private sector if it is to achieve the same effect. The public sector manager must do more with less. He or she must be so competent and display such a strong facilitative style that the work not only gets done, but gets done superbly—in the face of strong organizational constraints. In effect, the good public sector manager is composed of equal thirds of leader, politician, and magician.

U.S. AIR FORCE LEADERSHIP CHECKLIST

The following checklist* can give you a more concrete understanding of the principles of leadership discussed in this chapter. It also allows you to evaluate yourself as a leader and to identify areas for possible improvement. Eleven principles of leadership are listed. Used wisely, they can increase your leadership abilities. The questions under each principle are designed to help you understand its application. If you can think of other principles to be used in your organization, add them to the list.

1. *Know your job. Do you:*
    - Understand your goal and how it contributes to the goal of the next higher unit?
    - Frequently review the requirements of your goal to be sure that each requirement is being fulfilled by a designated individual or group?
    - Know the general provisions of directives governing your job and review them frequently for currency?
    - Keep informed on the new developments in your specialty?

*Adapted from *Leadership in the Air Force*, a Squadron Officer School textbook (SOS-2), 1978.

2. *Know yourself and seek self-improvement. Have you:*
   _ Determined your career objectives?
   _ Identified the qualifications you need to meet your objectives?
   _ Considered the areas for improvement?
   _ Reviewed your performance appraisal report to find out the areas it suggests can be improved?
   _ Discussed with your personnel manager or immediate superior the policies governing career progression in your specialty?
   _ Determined what continuing education courses are available to you?
   _ Kept abreast of current events and analyzed their implications?
   _ Established a self-improvement program?
   _ Started on the first step of that program?

3. *Know your people and look out for their welfare. Do you:*
   _ Have an understanding of basic human psychology?
   _ Show sincere interest in your subordinates and encourage them to discuss their problems with you?
   _ Know the name, home town, family status, educational level, capabilities, and limitations of your immediate subordinates?
   _ Systematically check the progress of your people, especially those who have been recently assigned to your work unit?
   _ Give public recognition to subordinates for superior performance?
   _ Avoid showing favoritism?
   _ Get the facts on gripes?
   _ Handle grievances promptly, but take time in handling emotionally charged issues?
   _ Understand the union contract rules that apply to your people?
   _ Permit subordinates to explain their mistakes?
   _ See that advancement goes to the most deserving?

4. *Keep your subordinates informed. Do you:*
   _ See that your people understand the organization's objectives, situation, and immediate goals?
   _ Explain policy and procedure changes to your people giving reasons for them?
   _ Keep your people in the know on future plans?
   _ Judiciously use formal letters, memoranda, conferences, talks, informational and educational materials, and bulletins to inform your people?
   _ Insure that the personnel affected know the schedules?
   _ Keep alert for false rumors and stop them by giving the facts to your people?
   _ Make sure that your key subordinates inform their workers?

5. *Set the example. Do you:*
   _ Conduct your life each day as you would like to see your subordinates conduct theirs?

— Keep yourself physically fit, mentally alert, well groomed, and correctly dressed?

— Maintain self-control?

— Cooperate willingly with other sections and units?

— Support the decisions and policies of your superiors?

— Refrain from criticizing one person to another?

— Suppress loose talk and gossip?

— Share danger and hardship with your subordinates?

— Live by your moral principles?

6. *Be sure that the task is understood, supervised, and accomplished. Do you:*

— Give clear, complete instructions, taking time to explain and answer questions when necessary?

— Give orders only when needed and avoid overdirecting?

— Check to see that the work is progressing on schedule?

— Frequently visit your people on the job?

— Refuse to be satisfied with lower quality work than your people are capable of producing?

— Insist on an honest day's work from your subordinates?

— Frequently review procedures, looking for more efficient methods?

7. *Train your people as a team. Do you:*

— Develop teamwork, showing how each person's job contributes to the total effort?

— Identify and begin training replacements for key personnel who will be leaving your unit?

— Have a productive on-the-job training program?

— Train your people in several different jobs?

— Give your key subordinates authority to do their job and insist that they make decisions within their area of responsibility?

— Standardize procedures for routine jobs?

— Encourage and carefully consider subordinates' suggestions?

— Occasionally test your unit's capability by demanding maximum performance for a short time?

8. *Make sound and timely decisions. Do you:*

— Carefully and objectively consider the facts available before making a decision?

— Use the scientific problem-solving method to arrive at the most logical decision?

— Use technical advisers and organizational staff when their assistance is indicated?

— Analyze your decisions to determine why some were good and others bad?

— Give your subordinates a decision as soon as possible so that they will have time to plan?

— Seek and consider the advice of superiors, contemporaries, and subordinates?

9. *Seek responsibility and develop a sense of responsibility among subordinates. Do you:*
   — Look for ways to do the job efficiently instead of looking for reasons why you should not do it?
   — Try to understand decisions from up the line and support them fully, or do you present them as "this is what the boss wants"?
   — Know the duties and responsibilities of your immediate superior?
   — Assign responsibility and delegate authority, supervise, and intervene only when necessary?
   — Provide opportunities for subordinates with the potential to move into more responsible jobs?
   — Correct errors in judgment so that the initiative of subordinates is encouraged?
   — Accept responsibility for your subordinates' mistakes?
   — Report to your superior or take appropriate action yourself on all cases that justify disciplinary action?
   — Insure satisfactory housekeeping of the work areas you supervise?

10. *Employ your authority according to its capabilities. Do you:*
    — Analyze any task you assign in relation to the capabilities of your unit?
    — Try to assign your people to jobs that fit their specific talents?
    — Review past performance when determining assignments?
    — Protect your work unit against arbitrary, unnecessarily heavy workloads?
    — Initiate action for additional people if the workload is greater than your authorized manpower can do reasonably?

11. *Take responsibility for your actions. Follow up. Do you:*
    — Admit mistakes, analyze the cause, and make corrections gracefully?
    — Carry out your superiors' policies and directives as though they were your own?
    — Make promises you can keep and keep the promises you make?
    — Follow the authority hierarchy and insist that your subordinates also follow it?
    — Make sure that a subordinate does not fail as a result of your actions or failure to act?
    — Adhere to what you know to be right; have the courage of your convictions?
    — Have the nerve to change when the situation warrants it?

REFERENCES

Blake, R. R., and J. S. Mouton. *The Managerial Grid* (Houston: Gulf, 1964).

Blake R. R., and J. S. Mouton. "A 9,9 Approach for Increasing Organizational Productivity," in E. H. Schein and W. G. Bennis, eds., *Personal and Organizational Change Through Group Methods* (New York: Wiley, 1965).

Bonoma, T. V., and D. Slevin. *Executive Survival Manual: A Program for Managerial Effectiveness* (Boston, Mass.: CBI Publishing Co., 1978).

Carter, L. F. "Leadership and Small Group Behavior," in M. Sherif and M. O. Wilson, eds., *Group Relations at the Crossroads* (New York: Harper, 1953).

Davis, K. "Attitudes Toward the Legitimacy of Management Efforts to Influence Employees," *Academy of Management Journal,* Vol. 11 (1968), pp. 153–161.

Fiedler, F. E. *A Theory of Leadership Effectiveness* (New York: McGraw-Hill, 1967).

Filley, A. C., and A. J. Grimes. "The bases of Power in Decision Processes," *Proceedings of the Academy of Management,* 1967.

Foa, U. G. "Relation of Worker's Expectation to Satisfaction with Supervisor," *Personnel Psychology,* Vol. 10 (1957), pp. 161–168.

Freedman, J. L., J. M. Carlsmith, and D. O. Sears. *Social Psychology* (Englewood Cliffs, N.J.: Prentice-Hall, 1970).

Halpin, A. W. *Theory and Research in Administration* (New York: Macmillan, 1966).

Halpin, A. W. and B. J. Winer. *The Leadership Behavior of the Airplane Commander* (Columbus: Ohio State University Research Foundation, 1952), mimeographed.

Hemphill, J. K. *Leader Behavior Description* (Columbus: Ohio State University Personnel Research Board, 1950).

Hollander, E. P. *Leaders, Groups, and Influence* (New York: Oxford University Press, 1963).

Janis, I. *Victims of Groupthink* (Boston: Houghton-Mifflin, 1972).

Lewin, K., and R. Lippitt. "An Experimental Approach to the Study of Autocracy and Democracy: A Preliminary Note," *Sociometry,* Vol. 1 (1938), pp. 292–300.

Likert, R. *New Patterns of Management* (New York: McGraw-Hill, 1961).

Likert, R. *The Human Organization* (New York: McGraw-Hill, 1967).

Shaw, M. E. *Group Dynamics,* 2nd ed. (New York: McGraw-Hill, 1976).

Stogdill, R. M. "Leadership, Membership, and Organization," *Psychological Bulletin,* Vol. 47 (1950), pp. 1–14.

Stogdill, R. M. *The Handbook of Leadership: A Survey of Theory and Research* (New York: Free Press, 1974).

Tedeschi, J. T., B. R. Schlenker, and T. V. Bonoma. *Conflict, Power and Games* (Chicago: Aldine, 1973).

White, R. K., and R. Lippitt. "Leader Behavior and Member Reaction in Three 'Social Climates,'" in D. Cartwright and A. Zander, eds., *Group Dynamics: Research and Theory* (New York: Harper, 1968).

CHAPTER 3

Managing Human Resources

James A. Craft

Editor's Note *Employees represent a major but often underutilized resource in a nonprofit organization. In an era of shrinking resources and increasing performance demands, a manager who is able to manage and utilize human resources has a better chance of achieving organizational goals. This chapter presents some of the basic concepts of human resources management and practical guidelines of specific importance to not-for-profit managers.*

First, the evolving set of assumptions about people underlying management theory is discussed. The administrative model is traced, starting from the scientific management movement and Hawthorne studies to the work of McGregor and Herzberg. The newly evolved concept of Man indicates that, in addition to monetary and social factors, people are often interested in and motivated by such things as recognition, achievement, and opportunities for personal development and challenge.

Using the new concept of Man, the author develops a human resource planning approach with four broad steps. The first step is to review the operating and strategic plans and objectives of the organization over a relevant planning horizon. The next step is forecasting human resource needs and the potential supply of talent. The next phase is programming—that is, determining how an organization's quantity and quality manpower requirements will be available at the appropriate time. The final step is the continuous monitoring of previous forecasts and ongoing programs to facilitate changes for improvement.

The next issue dealt with is how to motivate employees to higher performance levels and fuller use of their capabilities. Using the concept of needs developed by Maslow and others, guidelines are developed for motivational programs for subordinates, with techniques to enhance motivation.

The questions of measuring, appraising, and evaluating employee performance are also addressed. Four basic approaches to performance appraisal are described and evaluated: trait assessment, employee comparison, behavior assessment, and goal achievement. The author recommends a combination of the behavior assessment and goal achievement approaches. Further guidelines are suggested for establishing and maintaining an appraisal system, improving the rating process, and appraisal feedback.

Finally, the subject of human resource development (HRD) is discussed. HRD is an approach for enhancing the development and growth of employee skills, judgment, and maturity so that both organizational and individual goals can be better and more certainly met. HRD represents a planned change, an individual approach, and is a continuous, broad-based process which is a key element of a larger organization human resource system. A model of HRD is presented that highlights the key areas of career planning and development, and training and development. Guidelines are included to help managers formulate and implement programs.

Managers in all types of organizations are reaching the conclusion that their employees are a major organizational resource. Management rarely views today's employees as mere hands to get the work done or as factors of production substitutable one for another. The emerging view is that employees are unique individuals, each representing a significant pool of talent, skills, and abilities. Tight budgets and pressures for increased productivity and job security have made it clear that management must develop appropriate procedures to effectively utilize and maintain these human resources if the organization is to achieve its goals. This chapter introduces some of the concepts of human resources management and presents guidelines for managing employees.

CHANGING CONCEPTS AND EXPECTATIONS

Among the many forces that have led to the development of the human resources management concept, probably none has been more significant or had more impact than the evolving administrative model of Man. This model, which provides the conceptual basis for management theory, is basically a set of assumptions about people and their behavior in organizations. Such assumptions guide managers in their interaction with employees. They will be reflected in the management policies, personnel programs, operating procedures, and leadership styles used to manage the organizational work force.

In the early part of this century, when the so-called scientific management movement was in full flower, the prevailing assumptions underlying management thought were hardly flattering to the average employee. In fact, the common assumptions were that people had little real interest in work, that they were rather lazy, and that they were motivated on the job primarily by monetary incentives. Generally, management seems to have held rather low expectations about employee initiative and performance. Emphasis was placed on the need for strong management control and close direction of each employee.

By the early 1940s, a new set of assumptions about Man in the workplace was gaining prominence in management thought. Research findings by Harvard psychologists in the monumental Hawthorne studies focused attention on the social and emotional aspects of the job. Common assumptions regarding employees were that they were strongly interested in social affiliation and acceptance on the job. This was a powerful motivator—perhaps more important than money incentives. Also, workers bring emotional and personal problems to the job, and this affects their behavior. It was assumed that they were often not capable of dealing with these problems on the job and needed support assistance from management.

The major response by management, the emergent human relations movement, emphasized the development of personnel programs and practices to make workers feel they were being cared for, that they belonged and were appreciated. The basic unit of administrative activity moved from the individual to the group. Attention turned to issues such as developing and utilizing effective groups, improving morale, developing sympathetic leadership styles, and providing counseling assistance to employees.

By the mid-1960s, new research and changes in the labor force led to significant modifications in the administrative model of Man. The work of Douglas McGregor (1960), Rensis Likert (1967), Frederick Herzberg (1966), and numerous others (combined with the practical manager's disenchantment with the be-nice-and-do-good approach of the human relations movement) led to the development of this new model of Man. It recognized that money and social relations are powerful influences on worker behavior, but each had been overemphasized in the past, to the exclusion of other factors.

The new concept of Man pointed out that, in addition to monetary and social factors, people are often interested in and motivated by such things as recognition, achievement, and opportunities for personal development and challenge. People are also capable of higher levels of performance and self-control than had been assumed in the past. This evolving concept seemed to be consistent with the increase in educational level and the growing number of people employed in professional, technical, managerial, and service jobs. Some of the specific assumptions of this evolving concept of Man were:

1. People do not dislike work *per se;* in fact, they enjoy opportunities that use their skills in productive ways, that make them feel they are making a contribution.
2. People are willing to accept responsibility and can exercise self-control and direct their own activity without tight management control.
3. Employees often want an opportunity to grow and develop within the organization; such opportunities can be powerful factors in motivating behavior.
4. Most employees desire recognition for their accomplishments and wish to enhance their feelings of self-esteem.
5. Employees seek what they believe is an equitable return on their personal investment in the job.

These assumptions view people as being capable, interested, and intelligent contributors to the achievement of organizational objectives. With the recognition that individuals vary in experience, attitudes, interests, and abilities, these assumptions form the basis for much of contemporary management thought and technique. As such, they are an important influence on the development of an effective human resources management program.

Accompanying the emergence of a new concept of Man are changes in employee attitudes and expectations about work. Not long ago, when people accepted their jobs, they did as the boss ordered, without question or suggestion. Employees expected to perform their jobs as they were defined by the engineer or boss, regardless of whether the work was satisfying. They expected fair pay for the work and hoped for equitable treatment by the boss. Hard work, even at a demeaning task, was a virtue.

While today's employees continue to expect fair pay and reasonable treatment on the job, and work still retains much of its traditional moral significance, new expectations and attitudes have arisen. Workers now seem less willing to accept jobs they consider menial or degrading. They increasingly express dissatisfaction with repetitive, low-level, deadend positions. There is a growing expression of interest in working—in a "good" job. There is greater concern that a job have dignity, earn respect from peers, and provide an opportunity for growth. There is the expectation that a job allow one to get ahead.

There also seems to be a redefinition among workers of the meaning of success. Success has often been identified with income, job status, and material possessions. While these are still important, nowadays people seem to be more concerned with what they trade off for them. There is often more interest in developing a satisfactory lifestyle than in maximizing income. People seem more intent on holding jobs that offer opportunities to make contributions and allow personal expression. They want to use their skills and to grow in the organization. Thus there is generally more interest in the quality of work life when defining job success (Yankelovich, 1974).

Along with the points mentioned above, there seems to be a lessening of concern with economic security. In an increasingly affluent society, money is often a less powerful incentive than it was in the decades before World War II. Economic security is not the dominant theme expressed by the current generation of employees.

Here is a summary of what seem to be the current trends in employee expectations from the job:

- Employees feel that career opportunities should be available; there should be a chance for growth and advancement on the job.
- Employees expect that personal skills and abilities will be utilized on the job and that the job should be challenging.
- Employees increasingly expect that wages and salaries not only should be fair but should be part of a larger remunerative package that includes health care, paid holidays, insurance, pensions, and other benefits.
- Employees feel that work should be personally fulfilling; the job should be satisfying and make a meaningful contribution.
- Employees expect that every worker must be treated with dignity and respect as a human being and as a contributor to organizational objectives.

While these expectations are not shared completely or with the same intensity by all workers, they do reflect current trends and indicate the shape of things for the future. Such expectations and attitudes must be kept in mind as administrators develop policies and programs for managing human resources.

HUMAN RESOURCE PLANNING

If managers are to achieve an organization's goals at minimal cost, while simultaneously providing opportunities for the development and growth of employees, human resource programs must be formulated and implemented in a planning framework. Drawing on ideas developed by Eric Vetter (1967) and others, human resources planning can be viewed as the process by which the managers responsible for an organizational system determine how the system will develop from its current position (in terms of the number of people and types of skills available) to a desired one in

order to achieve organizational objectives and provide improved opportunities for the employees.

Planning and Programming

There are four broad steps in developing a planning approach to meet
organizational human resource needs, as outlined in Figure 3–1. The
first step in developing a human resource planning system is to review
the operating and strategic plans and objectives of the organization for
a specific planning period. The plans and objectives may be defined formally, assessed from the obvious direction in which the organization is
proceeding, or discerned from discussions with top management and
those in policymaking positions. Relevant planning horizons will vary by
type of organization, market stability, the budgeting process, and other
variables.

By reviewing organizational goals, plans, and objectives, planners seek
information that will give them insights into the organization's personnel
needs of the future. The following types of information might be needed:
proposed changes in the extent or type of activities of the organization;
the introduction of new products or services over the next few months
or years; the possible introduction of new technologies to carry out organizational operations; and the establishment of new locations for delivery of organizational output.

The next step is forecasting human resource needs and the potential
supply of talent to meet those needs. This involves taking the information
gathered from reviewing organizational plans and goals and translating
it into estimates of the numbers and types of people needed to achieve
the defined objectives. For example, if the expected rise in a school district's enrollment is 50 percent over the next two years (given mandated
class sizes, types of courses to be taught, new teaching technologies available, and so on), a reasonable estimate can be made of the number and
types of teachers needed.

After an estimate of the demand for manpower has been made, a
forecast of the available supply of people to meet these needs must also
be made. The following kinds of questions might be asked when attempting to forecast supply: How many people currently employed can now
handle the tasks projected for the future? What is the expected attrition
of employees over the planning period (from retirement, transfer, promotion, turnover)? What is the expected availability of people with the
necessary skills in the external labor market?

When both the supply and demand for human resources have been
estimated for the specified time horizons, the human resource planner
must determine foreseeable organizational shortfalls or surpluses in the

FIGURE 3-1. *The human resource planning process in nonprofit organizations.*

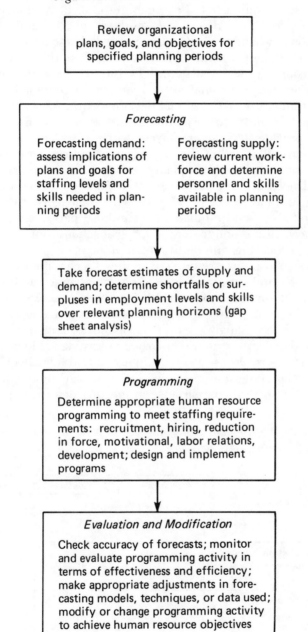

Review organizational plans, goals, and objectives for specified planning periods

Forecasting

Forecasting demand: assess implications of plans and goals for staffing levels and skills needed in planning periods

Forecasting supply: review current workforce and determine personnel and skills available in planning periods

Take forecast estimates of supply and demand; determine shortfalls or surpluses in employment levels and skills over relevant planning horizons (gap sheet analysis)

Programming

Determine appropriate human resource programming to meet staffing requirements: recruitment, hiring, reduction in force, motivational, labor relations, development; design and implement programs

Evaluation and Modification

Check accuracy of forecasts; monitor and evaluate programming activity in terms of effectiveness and efficiency; make appropriate adjustments in forecasting models, techniques, or data used; modify or change programming activity to achieve human resource objectives necessary manpower. He will want to make his estimates explicit—perhaps using a "gap sheet" format, as illustrated in Figure 3–2.

The third step requires that the human resource planner take the data developed previously and determine how the required quantity and quality of manpower will be available when needed. These needs can be met either by developing personnel currently available in the organization or by hiring from outside the system. The internal development of employees to meet organizational needs requires programmatic thrusts in training; incentive and motivational development; assessment and evaluation of performance; career planning; and labor relations. These programs can provide current employees with career advancement and growth opportunities within the organization and can be important in motivating and retaining high-quality employees. If it appears that organizational needs cannot be met solely from within, recruitment and hiring programs have to be developed. When managers have made an effort to look ahead and estimate organizational personnel needs, they are in an excellent position to determine what actions should be taken to minimize future staffing and motivational problems.

The final step in human resource planning is a continuous monitoring of the forecasts and programs to assess their accuracy and determine what changes, if any, need to be made. The forecasts must be monitored in light of changes in plans and objectives or unexpected external events (such as new laws, changing economic pressures, and war). Forecasts should be updated and revised regularly. Forecasting methods should be modified and improved as new techniques and additional information become available. Programs also need to be revised continually and assessed with regard to their relevance in meeting defined objectives. (Is

FIGURE 3–2. *Gap sheet for human resource planning in nonprofit organizations.*

	Planning Horizons		
	6 months	*12 months*	*24 months*
Estimated need for human resource (demand) (1)			
Estimated availability of internal human resources (supply) (2)			
Estimated gap between needed and available human resources (1 – 2)			

the training program effective in providing new skills? Is the performance evaluation system providing needed information for administrative and developmental decisions?)

MOTIVATING EMPLOYEES

If employees are recognized as major organizational resources that must be effectively managed, the question arises as to how the manager can stimulate use of their skills and abilities to achieve organizational objectives. The issue is clearly how to motivate employees to high performance levels.

What Is Motivation?

Motivated behavior is goal-oriented and has objectives. People behave in ways that make sense to them and help them achieve an objective that satisfies personal needs. In an organization, employees do not behave in a particular way unless they feel their performance will attain goals that satisfy their needs. A brief example can help illustrate the point:

The office manager of a local government agency wants Joe, a bright young employee, to increase the number of reports he processes each day. The manager feels that Joe is more intelligent and has more potential to become a manager than most of his other subordinates. The group of employees of which Joe is a part has never been a highly productive unit, but it has always done satisfactorily. Several members of the group have been employed in the agency for many years, and all the members tend to produce about the same amounts. One day the manager approached Joe and advised him that, if his productivity increased to a certain level, he would be nominated for a step wage increase at his next evaluation. Also, with good performance, Joe might be considered for a management position in the future.

The manager's approach is direct and seems to make good sense outwardly, since people do work for money and promotion (or success). If Joe is given a chance to make more money with a hint of a possible promotion later, then his behavior should be directed to help him achieve these goals. The manager has, in effect, assumed certain needs for Joe and consequently has designed a motivational program to affect Joe's behavior.

From Joe's point of view, however, things look somewhat different. He is not unhappy with his present salary, although he could use the raise. However, if he could get anything he wanted on the job, he would really like to be accepted by the other people in the office who do the same kind of work he does. He greatly admires the two men in the group who seem to be the leaders. He often feels left out of things that are going on in the group, and he would like to get to know the other members better personally. He has a strong need for social acceptance and approval and little current need for a slightly higher income or uncertain growth indications for the future. He knows that if he starts picking up the pace in processing the reports, he runs the risk of making the others look bad, and they may dislike him for it. Given the motivational program designed by the manager, it seems unlikely that Joe will increase his output. In effect, the manager has not structured the situation so that Joe can satisfy his needs by producing more.

Needs in Motivation

A need is a drive or a desire that stimulates activity to satisfy it. Some needs are innate or inherent, while others are learned and may be limited in terms of the number of individuals who experience them. Innate needs include such things as the need for food, water, and oxygen. Learned needs are acquired from interaction with other people and other experiences in the world. They include such things as the need to achieve, the need for power, and the need to enjoy a certain standard of living. Learned needs are as important and powerful in motivating behavior as are innate needs.

One useful way of looking at human needs is to group them into major types and to place them in a hierarchy. Using ideas developed by Abraham Maslow (1954) and others, we can say there are three essential classes of needs: basic, social, and higher-order.

Basic needs are those innate needs referred to above. These are basic survival needs such as those for food and sleep. They also include the need for security and personal safety. Such needs are universal and require immediate satisfaction if a person is to survive. Most people gratify them in much the same way. When satisfaction of these basic needs is threatened, they then become the most important motivators.

Social needs motivate a person to seek affiliation with others. Most people want to be accepted and appreciated by others, to be loved and esteemed by those they respect. Such acceptance provides support for feelings of personal worth. These needs usually emerge *after* basic needs have been reasonably satisfied. They generally do not require immediate gratification, but are important in the long run for the health and development of an individual's personality.

It is not difficult to see how social needs influence behavior in the workplace. Employees want to be part of the gang and enjoy the jokes, the concerns, and the fellowship of their colleagues. When such needs are strong, the work group can have tremendous influence over the behavior of someone who values membership in the group and wishes to retain the friendship and respect of peers. The group establishes rules of behavior for its members. Some of these rules may, in fact, be contrary to the achievement of organizational objectives. People with a strong need for social acceptance by fellow workers may be motivated to perform in ways that are not consistent with the achievement of organizational goals. In fact, they may perform in ways that appear to be irrational in light of the motivational systems established by management.

While recognition of the social needs of the individual on the job is important in understanding and motivating employees, the human relations movement overemphasized social needs at the expense of considering other types of individual needs that might be equally or more important.

Higher-order needs involve people's views of themselves and feelings of personal value and achievement. This includes the need for a positive self-concept—to believe that one is valuable as an individual. People have a need to use their skills and talents, to express themselves through things they can do best. They want to learn about themselves and develop their unique capabilities. In our affluent society, such needs seem to be increasingly important. There is increasing interest in such things as a satisfactory lifestyle at work, "doing your own thing," opportunities for personal growth, and individual development on the job. These interests reflect more concern by workers for satisfying higher-order needs in the work environment. In fact, these higher-order needs (along with social needs) may be the most important ones today for managers to consider when they design programs to motivate and better utilize available human resources.

Often these differing types of needs are viewed as a hierarchy in which a higher-level need emerges as the major motivating force when lower-level needs are met at least minimally. An employee who is having difficulty meeting personal financial obligations may be more immediately interested in the opportunity to earn overtime income on the current job than in the opportunity to learn a new job that may be more interesting but offers no immediate pay increase. On the other hand, an employee who feels he has an adequate or reasonably good income, and who is accepted by peers and administrative superiors as a significant member of the work organization, might have a strong interest in learning new skills, gaining performance recognition, and having a chance at personal and professional growth in the organization. In each of these cases, different types and levels of needs exist within the employee, and he is motivated to behave in ways to satisfy these needs.

Motivating Human Resources

Employees will behave in a particular way only if they are capable of doing so and if they believe that such behavior will lead to outcomes (goals) that will satisfy their important needs. Managers can motivate subordinates to behave in ways consistent with organizational objectives if they can structure the situation and manipulate conditions so that the employees can meet their needs through effective performance. Managers must take action to *integrate* the need satisfaction of employees with the achievement of organizational goals.

1. *Be sensitive to the needs of subordinates.* If managers are to motivate employees effectively, they must have an awareness and understanding of their employees' needs and what workers seek from the job. Ideally, a manager should develop a sensitivity to the particular needs of groups as well as of individual employees, tailoring work assignments and rewards to provide opportunities that satisfy those needs. Assessing needs is more than finding out what employees want; it is getting a feeling for why employees want something.

In attempting to assess employee needs, managers should be careful not to assume they already know them. Just because the administrator of a family counseling agency was once a caseworker does not necessarily mean he knows the current personnel and professional problems and needs of the counseling staff. Managers' assumptions about what employees want from their jobs and why are often incorrect. In many established motivational systems, management has defined what the employees "need" and then established the incentive structure based on these assumptions. Such systems frequently have a minimal effect on employee behavior in terms of desired management objectives. Reality is what employees see it to be, not what management thinks it is or what management would like it to be. Management should make an effort to assess employee needs before establishing a motivational program.

The following approaches and tools can be used to better understand employee desires and needs:

Surveys. Special surveys can be used to determine employee desires and needs on an overall basis as well as to assess the differences between groups. Morale surveys can provide information on employee feelings about the job and possible problems. Attitude surveys regarding organizational policies, programs, and procedures can provide indications of employee needs and feelings.

Observation of behavior. Management can take an honest, hard look at how employees behave on the job and observe their responses to stimuli such as different styles of leadership, opportunities for training and development, and wage incentives. For example, in a family counseling agency, how do the caseworkers (who consider themselves professionals and must exercise discretion and good judgment with clients) respond to the agency requirement that they be at their desk by 8:00 A.M., whether or not they have a counseling appointment?

Employee counseling and interviews. When the supervisor or human resources manager counsels and interviews employees in performance reviews or development sessions, information can be gathered on individual employee aspirations, problems facing employees, expressed needs from the job, and individual interests and hopes. This can be a rich source of information about employee needs, goals, and potential incentives.

Personal knowledge of employees. Managers can get to know their subordinates beyond the point of simply considering them as one of the staff or an employment number. For example, the head nurse of a hospital unit who develops personal knowledge and a respectful, friendly relationship with staff nurses can make them feel much easier in discussing their needs, problems, and hopes on the job, and it is likely that this supervising nurse will structure jobs and recommend policies that reflect the needs of the employees.

2. *Tie outcomes desired by employees to behavior that is consistent with organizational objectives.* The more people value an outcome that satisfies a need and believe that the outcome depends on their own actions, the more they are motivated to behave in a way to attain the outcome. Take the situation of a job placement counselor in a vocational rehabilitation agency who strongly desires a merit increase because of personal financial needs. If it is well established that merit increases are awarded in the agency on the basis of the quantity of client placements, and placements result directly from efforts at job development in the community, it can be expected that the counselor will put a great deal of effort into job development. Utilization of this basic guideline requires that the following conditions be met:

The employee must believe that a certain pattern of behavior or level of performance will lead to a need-satisfying outcome. It must be made clear that there is a relationship between behavior and reward, and the relationship must be a consistent one.

The employee must believe that his behavior or effort will be assessed accurately and fairly. If, for example, the employee does not trust the performance appraisal system or feels that it does not accurately represent performance, he may not work to achieve the valued outcome. He may feel that efforts to perform will not be assessed accurately and that it is unlikely that goals can be attained, regardless of what is done. It is important, then, if management is trying to develop certain employee behaviors, that the method used to appraise performance be accepted as valid and meaningful by employees.

The employee must feel able to work in a manner or at a level that leads to high performance. It is necessary, therefore, that management establish realistic performance goals for each person, given his past experience and physical and intellectual capabilities. Someone who does not believe he is able to perform (or is incapable of performing) in a certain way is unlikely to make the effort to obtain higher performance even though the outcome of such performance is desirable.

3. *Create a climate of mutual respect and personal security.* It must be remembered that employees are dependent on their bosses for rewards and opportunities to satisfy their needs on the job. The boss is obviously in a powerful position to affect the climate of work relations and the attitudes employees have about their jobs, and job performance. When a boss demonstrates respect for subordinates and recognizes the value of their contributions, employees become less hesitant to suggest ideas for procedural improvements and perform better. They know where the boss stands with regard to performance. They know that they are respected as individuals and that the boss is willing to consider personal situations as they affect job performance. In such a climate, managers are much better able to learn of the needs and goals of their employees.

4. *Maintain high but realistic expectations for employee performance.* Research indicates that when a manager demonstrates confidence in the abilities of his subordinates, they respond positively to the high performance expectations. For example, if a fire chief has expressed pride in the record of the employees in the fire prevention unit and has set high but obtainable goals for inspectors in order to further reduce the incidence of fire hazards in the community, it is likely that those inspectors will want to live up to their reputations and will work to justify the confidence placed in them.

Expectations must not be too difficult to achieve, but they must be set at a level that stretches the employee's current abilities. They must be realistic and achievable, given the experience and capabilities of the subordinate, but they must offer a challenge to go beyond the current performance level. As employees achieve the goals set for them, the manager's belief that they are capable of high-level performance is reinforced. Such achievement is also likely to raise the employees' level of aspiration for future performance.

In addition to achieving the goals of both the organization and the employee, this process contains significant motivational elements through the development of competency in performing tasks. Employees may receive satisfaction from doing their jobs well, being successful, and meeting recognized high expectations, and are motivated to demonstrate that they have the talent necessary for outstanding performance. As they master the tasks or meet performance expectations, new goals that are challenging but realistic can be established. Over time, a self-reinforcing cycle of success can emerge to motivate effective behavior.

Illustrative Approaches to Motivation

A variety of strategies, programs, and techniques have been established to enhance employee motivation on the job. These approaches generally represent attempts to motivate employees by providing some opportunity to satisfy needs through performance.

Building a positive self-concept. Each person holds a self-image that reflects feelings of personal worth and adequacy. The self-concept is developed through past experiences and integrates the values and beliefs held by an individual. Work plays an important role in shaping the self-image because it offers a tangible indication of one's value, and it provides a personal identity. The need for a positive self-concept is universal. Most people behave in ways that are consistent with their ideal image and that reinforce a favorable self-perception. At work, employees are motivated to perform at levels and in ways that are consistent with their self-images. They receive feedback from bosses and other employees on the job which they use to assess how well they are measuring up to their desired self-concepts. Such feedback and experience can also help modify the self-image over time.

Clearly, a person's self-image can affect behavior and motivation to perform on the job. If management consistently criticizes and denigrates an employee, he may find the job dissatisfying and, over time, develop low self-esteem. This can lead to low expectations and poor performance on the job. If the threat to the self-concept becomes too great, the employee may leave the organization. On the other hand, if management works to build a positive self-concept for each worker, is supportive of accomplishments and improvements, encourages the development of the self-perception of being important and valuable to the organization, employees are likely to perform in ways that maintain and enhance their positive self-images. In short, management can take actions that can make people feel they are winners or losers. People with high self-esteem and the feeling that they are important and can succeed will have high aspirations, perform more effectively on the job, and be more likely to rise to meet the challenge of high performance expectations.

Participation in goal setting and decision making. Another approach used to enhance subordinate motivation is participation. It has been advocated as a useful practice because it can improve decision making and have a motivational impact on those involved. Decisions may be improved in uncertain situations, since subordinates may bring unique and useful information to the decision process which would never have been considered by the manager acting alone. For example, the supervisor of a municipal road construction gang may seek input from the crew to help estimate the time necessary to complete the renovation and resurfacing of a city street. Crew members may have an experience-based knowledge of drainage problems, an understanding of the condition of equipment available for current use, and knowledge of problems with materials that are now used—all of which can aid greatly in making a more accurate assessment of the time requirements for the job. This kind of input can also prompt the crew's interest in getting the job done in the time estimated.

In these situations, motivation to implement a plan or to achieve certain levels of performance may be enhanced, since the individual employee involved in achieving the goal has a role in developing it and assumes some personal responsibility for it. The subordinate is aware of how and why the plan or goal was established, and this can provide a rationale for his effort.

However, research findings on the usefulness of participative management for employee motivation are mixed. It seems that the participative approach is most useful with employees who are predisposed toward involvement in decision making, either by personality characteristics or from training (as in the case of certain professionals). It is also likely to be most useful in uncertain and ambiguous task situations where no clear-cut options for action are apparent. Clearly it will have few commitment or ego involvement effects if the participation is on an issue that is not meaningful to those involved. It seems likely that participation can be most useful in motivating workers who are seeking satisfaction of higher-order needs (such as recognition and esteem), who are mature in behavior and outlook, and who would like to have a larger role in dealing with the events that affect them.

Job enrichment. In recent years, a major emphasis has been placed on redesigning jobs to increase worker motivation. When jobs are restructured to incorporate more planning and control activities and a wider variety of tasks, the work becomes more challenging and offers more opportunities for achievement and development, thus becoming intrinsically more motivating. The emphasis on job enrichment has resulted from findings that (1) certain workers are dissatisfied with repetitive and unchallenging jobs and (2) other workers are motivated by jobs with high opportunities for achievement, development, recognition, and responsibility. Clearly, this strategy for motivation of employees focuses on their assumed need to satisfy higher-order needs on the job. It is also consistent with current administrative assumptions about employees.

It appears that the usefulness of job enrichment as a motivational strategy is mixed. Some people seem to be happy with repetitive work and do not respond positively to an enrichment program. Job enrichment as a motivational approach seems to work best with employees who are seeking higher-order need satisfaction on the job, who want variety and autonomy in their work, and who do not exhibit feelings of alienation (powerlessness or meaningless). Work may be a central life interest for these people, who tend to respond positively to opportunities for need satisfaction through job enrichment.

Paying for performance. A widely advocated approach to motivating employees is the strategy of paying for performance. The underlying concept is that compensation of employees on the basis of the relative merit of performance stimulates and reinforces desired employee behavior. This approach has broad appeal, since it is consistent with both the assumptions underlying the old scientific management concept of Man and the current human resources model. Because pay can satisfy basic needs as well as some higher-order ones (such as esteem and self-worth), it has found wide acceptance as a motivator.

If a pay incentive program is to be implemented, management has to make it clear that pay is, in fact, directly related to desired performance levels. Management has to demonstrate this relationship visibly to employees, not just state that it exists. If the link is not clearly established, there is a substantial risk that a program can lose its motivating potential. As noted earlier, employees must believe that performance evaluation results do reflect their individual performance. Managers must be willing to assess subordinates' performance carefully and award differential pay increases directly on the basis of evaluated performance.

Management must also be aware of employees' perceptions of equity in pay levels and increases. For example, hospital employees often compare their pay with that of people in similar jobs or in other area hospitals. Major discrepancies can lead to pay dissatisfaction. Also, employees compare the effort they expend to achieve pay increases with what they believe to be the effort of others in relatively similar circumstances. If a hard-working and high-performing subordinate discovers that he is being rewarded only marginally above someone with lower performance whom he feels exerted much less effort on the job, the motivational impact of the "pay for performance" system will be inhibited.

Pay as a motivator can satisfy a wide range of needs, but it calls for careful administration and recognition of the fact that its many meanings open the door to complex problems.

Anxiety. Management may attempt to motivate employees by increasing their anxiety level. Research indicates that to a certain point increased anxiety can motivate a person to higher levels of performance. Excessive anxiety, however, can lead to dysfunction and declining performance. Anxiety is usually created by management's threats to take away something of value or to punish for failure to perform. Such an approach to motivation was characteristic of management thinking around the turn of this century, and it persists as the carrot-and-stick approach.

Anxiety seems to be most effective as a short-term behavior motivator. Used over the long term, it can encourage employees to seek employment elsewhere and lead to self-protective and defensive actions by employees. It can probably be used effectively to stimulate performance on routine and simple jobs but would be less effective in motivating those performing creative, complex, and higher-level jobs. It might also be effective with those who are working basically for extrinsic rewards on the job, such as money. But it must be kept in mind that excessive reliance on anxiety as a motivator can lead to employee dissatisfaction, fear, and dislike of management.

APPRAISING PERFORMANCE

The review and assessment of employee performance on the job is a major aspect of human resources management. Performance appraisal can be both formal and informal. The informal system includes personal observations that are not used specifically as justification for salary increases or other such administrative decisions but rather are used for decisions regarding interpersonal and work relationships. Personal assessments can affect allocation of job assignments, internal communication flows, and social interaction patterns of the job. Formal evaluation systems usually consist of a procedure established by management to systematically collect data about individual effectiveness on the job. Most often, an instrument or specific process is used in assessing job performance as it relates to organizational goals. Formal appraisal systems generally have two basic objectives: (1) employee motivation development and (2) administrative decision making.

As far as the motivation/development objective is concerned, the performance appraisal (PA) system provides employees with feedback on how they are doing, indicates how they might improve performance, and provides opportunities for them to discuss personal growth and development on the job and in the organization. With regard to the objective of administrative decision making, the PA system provides information that assists managers in planning the use of human resources, making informed decisions with regard to training and development needs, al-

locating financial rewards, making salary adjustments, and other person-
nel-related decisions.

Factors Affecting Performance Appraisal

While PA is an important and necessary part of the human resources
management system, its utility and effectiveness can be undermined. For
example, management may attempt to use one set of appraisal data for
justifying administrative decisions about an employee (for example, layoff
or salary adjustment) and also for counseling and developing the employee. In some cases, the data collected are simply not suitable for both
purposes, and the PA program can only lose credibility in the eyes of the
manager and the employee. Also, if one set of PA data is used for both
purposes, the employee may find that while he wants honest and complete
feedback on performance, he does not want negative information known
that will undesirably affect decisions about rewards (such as salary increases and promotions). He may therefore not fully disclose information
to the organization which would detract from his evaluation. If negative
information is presented in the appraisal interview to justify a salary
decision, the employee may become defensive; and such criticism, even
when offered in good faith, may not lead to a change in behavior or
performance.

For a PA system to work effectively, supervisors and managers must
understand its objectives, and they must show that they are willing to
implement it conscientiously. In many cases, raters are not fully aware
of how the results are to be used, what the items on the evaluation form
actually mean, or what behavior top management considers important.
They also have little input on the format or structure of the evaluation
system.

It is understandable that many managers are reluctant to spend much
time on the PA process when they are uncertain of its usefulness to them.
Some supervisors feel PA takes too much time away from "important"
job activities to carefully evaluate each employee. Other supervisors are
reluctant to be critical of employees, finding it difficult to face subordinates and tell them they are not doing well. Finally, some supervisors feel
they are not qualified to evaluate employees or feel inadequate conducting
interviews and providing feedback.

The PA data collected should be valid and represent accurate reflections of employee performance. A number of factors can negatively influence the reliability and validity of employee evaluations. Some supervisors are very lenient in their ratings, rating no one lower than average.
Other raters are overly stringent and rate only a few people above average.
Some never use the extreme ends of a rating scale, tending to bunch

everyone at the center. Such diversity makes the interpretation and comparison of ratings difficult. Another pitfall for evaluators is the "halo effect," whereby a high opinion of an employee in one important area influences ratings of him on all other characteristics. For example, if a teacher is known to have good interpersonal relations with students, this perception may positively bias the principal's assessment of that teacher's knowledge of the subject matter.

Finally, managers may not maintain adequate records of performance and behavior for employees over a period of time, in which case they may forget earlier actions and rate someone only on very recent behavior or performance. Other factors such as personal bias and lack of understanding of items for evaluation can also lead to problems in the PA system.

MEASURING PERFORMANCE

There are four basic approaches to performance appraisal: trait assessment, employee comparison, behavior assessment, and goal achievement.

Trait Assessment

The trait assessment approach emphasizes evaluation of employee characteristics. Management defines the personal characteristics or traits it feels are important for effective performance, depending on the group being rated and the objectives of the evaluation. Obviously, the traits used for appraising hourly workers will differ from those used for clerical or managerial employees. Illustrations of personal qualities that have been used include initiative, cooperation, leadership, maturity, and learning ability.

The graphic rating scale. Trait appraisals are usually made on a graphic rating scale. A set of traits or characteristics is given to a supervisor, who is then requested to evaluate each employee on an accompanying scale for every trait listed. Figure 3–3 is an illustration of a segment of a graphic rating scale. The traits may be presented as shown, with little supporting information, or they may be defined with lengthy descriptions. The scale usually ranges from five to nine points. A scale with too few points does not allow for adequate differentiation, while a scale with too many points can confuse raters by calling for distinctions that are too fine and unrealistic.

The general advantage of trait assessment is that the instruments are reasonably easy to construct and use. The evaluation data can be used to provide information for administrative decision making. Unfortunately, the approach suffers from most of the potential PA errors noted earlier

FIGURE 3–3. *Graphic rating scale.*

Instructions: Circle the point on the scale that best represents your judgment of the health officer being rated.					
Dependability	1 low	2	3 average	4	5 high
Loyalty	1 low	2	3 average	4	5 high
Leadership ability	1 low	2	3 average	4	5 high

(leniency, stringency, halo effect, and bias). It is quite subjective, and it does not supply the kind of detailed information on specific behavior that employees find useful as feedback for personal development.

In an attempt to get some global rating for an employee, the numerical ratings for all traits may be summed. This can lead to the false impression that trait assessment is an objective and precise measurement technique. In addition, such global scores can be misleading with regard to relative abilities. For example, two employees who have quite different capabilities and potential may receive an identical overall score, because equal weight is given to each trait. If equal weights are not used for each trait, the problem arises of defining the appropriate relative weight for each of the traits. Because of the subjectivity and interpretational problems of the trait assessment approach, some organizations are abandoning it and seem to be relying more on newer types of rating systems.

Employee Comparisons

The employee comparison approach requires that the rater compare each employee individually with all the others being rated. Interpersonal comparisons can be made with one or more items, or employees may be compared globally.

Ranking. Using this technique, the rater ranks his subordinates from the best to the poorest on a series of defined job dimensions or on an overall basis. Many supervisors tend to rank employees informally anyway; this technique may simply formalize the process. When a large number of employees must be ranked, the process can be tedious and difficult. One approach that makes ranking somewhat easier is "peeling," in which the extreme ends of the scale are ranked first. For example, in the first round, a school principal might choose the teacher who seems to prepare lesson plans best and the teacher who does it most poorly and place them in their respective end positions on the ranking list. The process is then repeated until all teachers are ranked.

Paired comparisons. Here, the rater compares each individual to be evaluated with every other employee, making comparisons in pairs. For each pair of names, the preferred employee is rated for either a trait or overall performance. An employee's score or standing is based on how many times he is chosen over others. All employees are thereby placed in ranked position vis-à-vis their peers. This technique can be rather cumbersome when large numbers of people have to be rated; for example, if 25 employees have to be evaluated, the supervisor has to make 300 comparisons.

Forced distribution. This technique requires the rater to distribute a specific percentage of employees to each of several groupings. It is based on the concept that there is a natural distribution among people, with most falling around the average and fewer on either end of the distribution. For example, a supervisor might specify the highest 10 percent of those being evaluated, then the next 20 percent, followed by the middle 40 percent, the 20 percent who are just below average, and finally the lowest 10 percent.

A major advantage of employee comparison techniques is that they eliminate the kinds of leniency and stringency that place everyone at either the top or the bottom of the evaluation scale. These techniques are useful in providing information for such administrative decisions as salary increases and promotions, since top performers are readily identified.

A severe disadvantage of employee comparisons is that they place people in a position relative to one another and do not tell *how much* better or poorer one employee is from another. Is the gap great or infinitesimally small between the person rated number one and the person rated number two? This information can be important for both administrative and developmental decisions. Comparison techniques also require that some people be placed into the lowest categories, regardless of the acceptability of their performance. This may not be realistic in situations where all employees are of top quality. For example, in a community legal assistance organization with a group of highly dedicated and competent attorneys as staff members, it might be very difficult, if not impossible, to rank or distribute them by performance. Such a process could have undesirable motivational effects on people who find themselves in the bottom of the group and who, for all practical purposes, have performed satisfactorily. Information useful for counseling and developmental purposes is not provided. Finally, employee comparison techniques are rather laborious and time-consuming for the evaluator, who may be unwilling to go through the tedium of the process.

Behavior Assessment

The behavior assessment approach is designed to improve evaluator accuracy by using actual observations of an employee's job behavior rather than a rating of personal traits or peer comparisons. The supervisor observes the employee's behavior when performing job tasks and uses the data obtained as the basis for an appraisal. Two major techniques of behavioral assessment are behaviorally anchored rating scales and the critical-incident method.

Behaviorally anchored rating scales (BARS). This technique uses a set of scales—at least one for each major job dimension—on which the rater evaluates the employee's performance. Each scale has specific statements of behavior which anchor the various points along the scale. A rater evaluating employee performance indicates the point on the scale where the description best illustrates the employee's actual behavior on the job. Figure 3–4 illustrates a BARS scale. The scales are generally developed by the supervisors who use them (and in some cases by the employees). The supervisors generate the items of behavior, assign them to particular areas of performance (knowledge, judgment, teaching skill, and so on), and determine at which point the items belong on the scale to represent a certain level of performance. The establishment of a BARS rating system is a participative process that engages those who will use it, thus enhancing the probability of the scale's being used with accuracy.

The critical-incident method. This technique requires that a supervisor identify, classify, and record the employee job behaviors that lead to success or failure. Department heads carrying out normal functions observe and record the specific actions and behaviors of subordinates that tend to be critical to effective performance. These observations are grouped under the major areas basic to the job to provide a record of specific employee behavior that can then be used when evaluating and providing feedback to the employee.

The behavioral assessment approach has much to recommend it because it focuses on specific observations of behavior, with employee evaluation based on actual job behavior. As an objective technique, it is likely to gain the acceptance of the rater as well as the employee. In addition, from the appraisals, employees can easily see what types of behavior are necessary for improved performance ratings. Managers can better determine the type of developmental activities that can help employees meet

FIGURE 3–4. *A behaviorally anchored rating scale (BARS): Interpersonal rela-*
tions with students—the professor's rapport with and sensitivity to
students.

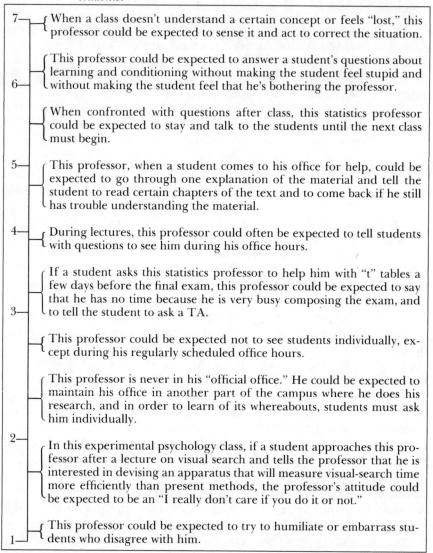

7— When a class doesn't understand a certain concept or feels "lost," this
professor could be expected to sense it and act to correct the situation.

6— This professor could be expected to answer a student's questions about
learning and conditioning without making the student feel stupid and
without making the student feel that he's bothering the professor.

When confronted with questions after class, this statistics professor
could be expected to stay and talk to the students until the next class
must begin.

5— This professor, when a student comes to his office for help, could be
expected to go through one explanation of the material and tell the
student to read certain chapters of the text and to come back if he still
has trouble understanding the material.

4— During lectures, this professor could often be expected to tell students
with questions to see him during his office hours.

If a student asks this statistics professor to help him with "t" tables a
few days before the final exam, this professor could be expected to say
that he has no time because he is very busy composing the exam, and
3— to tell the student to ask a TA.

This professor could be expected not to see students individually, except during his regularly scheduled office hours.

This professor is never in his "official office." He could be expected to
maintain his office in another part of the campus where he does his
research, and in order to learn of its whereabouts, students must ask
him individually.

2— In this experimental psychology class, if a student approaches this professor after a lecture on visual search and tells the professor that he is
interested in devising an apparatus that will measure visual-search time
more efficiently than present methods, the professor's attitude could
be expected to be an "I really don't care if you do it or not."

This professor could be expected to try to humiliate or embarrass stu-
1— dents who disagree with him.

Source: Oren Harai and Sheldon Zedick, "Development of Behaviorally Anchored Scales for the Evaluation of Faculty Teaching," *Journal of Applied Psychology*, October, 1973, pp. 261–265. Copyright © 1973
by the American Psychological Association. Reprinted by permission.

behavior expectations. It also reduces the problems of leniency, halo, and stringency that are characteristic of trait rating.

It should be noted, though, that the behavioral assessment approach has limitations and disadvantages. For one, the BARS technique is costly to develop. It takes time for supervisors to develop appropriate behavior items and scale them. Also, separate forms may have to be developed for each job or job family in which performance is to be evaluated. The critical-incident technique may not be implemented by supervisors conscientiously because it requires a willingness to record critical incidents as they occur or soon afterward. This can be tedious and may give the impression that the supervisor is watching employees closely for mistakes.

In addition, supervisors may not give timely feedback to employees. If, for example, the manager of a consumer cooperative foodstore discusses incidents he has observed that led to a checkout clerk's failure to deal satisfactorily with customers too long after the occurrence of that behavior, it may not be particularly useful to effect behavior modification.

Even with these limitations, the behavioral assessment approach, particularly the BARS method, seems to be growing in interest and popularity as a method for PA. Part of the interest is due to the need for more specific and objective data to facilitate development and make administrative decisions in light of government requirements for equal-employment opportunities.

Goal Achievement

The goal achievement approach was developed in response to the inadequacies and subjectivity of trait assessment and employee comparisons. It focuses on the establishment of specific goals to be achieved within a specific time period. The goals are objective and clear-cut; a person's progress and accomplishment can be measured in terms of achievement. Perhaps the most widely known technique of the goal achievement approach is management by objectives.

Management by objectives (MBO). It is common for the supervisor and the subordinate to jointly establish performance goals for the subordinate that are to be achieved in a specified time period. The supervisor contributes the needs of the organization, and the subordinate inputs with regard to personal capabilities and the constraints faced. The objective is to establish specific and realistic goals. After establishing these goals, an implementation plan is developed, representing a statement of the various things that must be done to achieve the goals in the designated time. With the passage of time, the subordinate's progress is reviewed, with the performance goal then modified as changes in the environment or unexpected problems warrant. When the target date is reached, both subordinate and boss review employee performance in terms of goal achievement, and the cycle begins again.

The goal achievement approach has gained substantial support in recent years as a PA tool. It focuses on objective outcomes and performance rather than subjective assessments and can be used for administrative decision making while allowing subordinates to set challenging goals to enhance their own development. It emphasizes the need for unique and individual goals for each person, and provides a high participation framework in which employees can influence their evaluation.

On the negative side there is the possibility that subordinates will establish PA goals that are too low. There is also the difficulty of comparing two subordinates who achieve their respective goals. Also, an important limitation is that this technique does not provide specific information on the particular behaviors employed to achieve goals.

Overall, the goal achievement approach has been favorably received by a number of organizations. It is clearly one of the more widely discussed of the PA methods currently available.

A Combined Approach

In light of current knowledge about employee expectations, attitudes, and motivation to high levels of performance, as well as the need for objective measures to demonstrate equal-opportunity compliance, managers should consider employing a combination of behavioral assessment and goal achievement approaches. When used together creatively, these systems can provide an environment that sets realistic employee challenges and yet provides specific behavioral feedback to the employee during the year and at performance review time. Such periodic feedback can help employees learn the new patterns of behavior that assist in achievement of objectives and development of capabilities to meet future organizational challenges. The establishment of a joint system can enhance the developmental and motivational potential of an organization's appraisal system while accumulating adequate data for administrative decision making.

Establishing an Appraisal System

Assuming there is managerial interest in establishing an appraisal system or in reviewing an existing one to enhance its effectiveness, research and experience suggest the following guidelines for consideration.

Define why a performance appraisal system is needed. What are the objectives of a system to measure and assess employee performance? Those interested in the performance appraisal system should list all the operational objectives they have in mind for the system (for salary increases, for promotions, to define training needs, for criteria in selection validation, to provide personal employee counseling, and so on). These objectives should be listed in their order of importance to assist in defining what information the PA system is expected to provide and to focus on the issue(s) of greatest importance.

Use job analysis to define the performance dimensions for each type of job. A thorough job analysis should be made of each job that will be included in the performance evaluation system. The job analysis defines the performance domain of the job as well as the job's important activity dimensions. These data provide the basis for the factors to be developed and used on the performance evaluation form. Job analysis insures that the performance appraisal tool is job-related, clear, and meaningful.

Determine the performance appraisal approach and technique to be used. After reviewing the alternative approaches and techniques available for a PA system, select those that best meet the most important objectives specified and that can best measure the performance dimensions defined by job analysis. Consider who will be using the system—that is, who will do the rating and who will use the outcomes. Consider the technique or approach that will be most meaningful and useful given their capabilities and needs. Finally, consider the organizational climate. What approach would be best under prevailing leadership practices, the current assumptions about people, and the operating programs in the organization? It might be foolish to implement a very participative technique in a not-for-profit agency characterized by tight administrative control and authoritarian leadership.

Obtain the support of top management. Top management must be committed to the need for a performance appraisal system; it must be willing to support the implementation of an appropriate method for gathering relevant performance data. This support enhances the perceived importance of the appraisal system and provides an incentive for managers at all levels to use the PA system.

Obtain the acceptance of those who will be using the system. It is critical that the people who will be using the PA system accept its necessity and believe its appraisal technique is valid and useful for measuring performance. If the managers and supervisors who will be using the system don't believe in it, they will undermine its effectiveness by either implementing it inappropriately or not at all. It is usually best to involve line managers early in developing an appraisal technique that addresses the organization's needs and climate. When they have helped to specify the needs and have assisted in designing the system, line managers are more likely to implement it as intended.

Train those who will use the appraisal system. Even the best-devised appraisal system may be ineffective if the people who are to use it have differing perceptions of its meaning, do not understand its use, or unwittingly allow personal bias to enter into the evaluation process. In hospitals, social agencies, municipal governments, and virtually all other types of not-for-profit organizations, supervisors are continually asked to evaluate employees when the only knowledge they have of rating procedures comes from the briefest of instructions included on the rating form or perhaps a few words from an administrative superior.

Substantial improvement in individual abilities to rate people with an appraisal tool can result from training the managers and supervisors who are to use it. They should develop an understanding of the types of errors that can unknowingly enter into an evaluation. They should be aware of the intended use of the evaluations and the meaning of the terms and concepts employed on the evaluation form or in its process. They should have opportunities to practice using the technique and should be given feedback on how they perform. They should be given written material, perhaps in the form of a manual, to which they can refer and which will provide a standard for future reference on appraisal questions.

Develop appropriate procedures for giving employees feedback. If appraisals are to be useful in modifying or reinforcing employee behavior, their results must be communicated back to the employees. Management should carefully consider the approaches best suited to giving employees the kind of accurate information that can lead to a better understanding of their contributions to the organization and that will motivate better performances.

Three methods for conducting a performance appraisal interview were suggested by industrial psychologist N. R. F. Maier (1958): "tell and sell," "tell and listen," and "problem solving." In the tell-and-sell approach, the interviewer acts as a judge, communicating the evaluation to the employee and then attempting to persuade (sell) him or her to improve. The tell-and-listen approach also places the interviewer in the role of judge, this time to communicate the evaluation and allow the employee to express his or her feelings. The expectation is that by allowing employees to express defensive feelings, they become more willing to accept proposed changes. In the problem-solving approach, the interviewer is a helper, discussing job problems with the employee, listening to feelings and ideas, and helping the employee define how to perform the job better. These models are alternative strategies for providing feedback and working for change; each may be useful under the right circumstances. Other, more detailed, guidelines to consider in establishing an appropriate appraisal interview format will be discussed later.

Periodically assess the performance appraisal system. As with any program, the PA system needs to be evaluated occasionally to make sure it is meeting its objectives. In universities, for example, faculty performance appraisal systems have to be assessed to determine if they provide the necessary information on research capability and teaching effectiveness. Are the performance evaluation data relevant to and useful in making decisions regarding salary increases, promotions, and so forth? More broadly, does the system really provide useful information for stimulating and rein-forcing behavior consistent with organizational objectives? Is the system being used by all managers? What type of errors or bias seem to influence the system? Much information can be obtained by reviewing the actual ratings, observing the rating process, and discussing the system with the managers and employees who are implementing it or being appraised under it. Modifications necessary to meet defined objectives should be made in ways that retain the acceptance of all parties involved.

PERFORMANCE APPRAISAL IMPROVEMENT

While we previously suggested guidelines for establishing and main-taining a performance appraisal system in a nonprofit organization, this section provides guidelines for improvement of the appraisal process.

Guidelines for Rating

The following guidelines are a synthesis of research findings and or-ganizational practice; they should prove useful in defining ways to im-prove the assessment of employee behavior.

Appraisal should be done by those with the best knowledge of employee perfor-mance. Performance appraisal is frequently done best by the immediate supervisors of those being evaluated. They usually have the most complete information for making valid ratings. They know subordinates' jobs and most likely have made more numerous relevant observations regarding performance than have other coordinate supervisors or higher-level man-agers. There is evidence that, while higher-level managers may have knowledge of a wider range of employees, they are unable to make useful discriminations among individual employees on particular areas of performance.

There may be circumstances, however, when it is more appropriate to have ratings made by subordinates, groups of supervisors, peers, or even by the employees themselves. For example, in the research unit of a public health agency, those scientists who do esoteric research might best be evaluated by peers who can understand what they are doing; self-appraisal might even be appropriate here.

The raters should use specific job behavior or objective measures. By using examples of specific behavior or measurements of goal achievement, raters can focus on relevant and tangible activities that affect job performance and not on subjective (personal) traits. This helps both parties better understand the basis for the evaluation and reduces the chances of personal bias entering into appraisals. For example, if one aspect of a social worker's performance appraisal is concerned with the problem of consistent tardiness in arriving at scheduled meetings with clients, this issue can be dealt with much more clearly and objectively if the behavior itself is noted rather than being reflected indirectly (and combined with other things) as a rating on a scale termed "interest in clients." The raters should be encouraged to maintain records of incidents and behaviors related to job effectiveness that can be used when it is necessary to conduct performance evaluations.

The raters should have a thorough knowledge of what is being rated. Raters must have an understanding of which activities, behaviors, goals, or traits are being considered in an evaluation. They then know what to look for and can make more relevant observations. When raters have been trained in the objectives of the appraisal system and understand the elements of the appraisal instrument, they can be more efficient and accurate in gathering relevant on-the-job data.

Raters should be aware of their personal biases. Raters should be sensitive to the fact that personal feelings and biases can adversely influence appraisal systems. When they are aware of their own predispositions and prejudices, personal feelings can be dealt with and will be less likely to be major influences. Also, all raters should be made aware, through training, that such errors as leniency, halo, and stringency may creep into the rating process so they can guard against them.

Raters should make appraisals regularly. Rating is often done only annually, while evaluations might better be made at other intervals. Certain jobs have work cycles that lend themselves to assessment on weekly, monthly, or bimonthly bases. Evaluations conducted at those times (or at least making concrete observations to be used later) would seem appropriate. However, it is probably inappropriate to conduct an appraisal just before significant administrative action is to be taken regarding the employee, because the pressures felt by the rater can lead to an assessment that might be less accurate than if the evaluation had been done at a time when its impact was not as immediate on the employee.

Appraisal Feedback Guidelines

The communication of performance appraisal results to an employee is important and sensitive. Each person wants to know where he or she stands. Management can use the occasion to reinforce good behavior, motivate the employee to better performance, and discourage dysfunctional behavior. The situation is sensitive because it provides information relating to an employee's contribution and behavior in the organization. The positive or negative feedback can affect the employee's self-concept and feelings about the job, the boss, and the organization. The following guidelines offer principles to be considered when developing a system to provide employees with feedback.

Use separate appraisal interviews for administrative and motivational-developmental purposes. It appears that combining salary reviews with motivational and developmental appraisal interviews can lead to problems. The combining of them often turns into a prolonged discussion about the justification for the salary action. In some cases, the employee may become defensive, the result being little opportunity for constructive interaction regarding personal needs and development in the organizational system. It would seem better to separate feedback sessions that have different objectives.

Communicate feedback at relevant intervals. The type and timing of feedback should respond to the circumstances and meet employee and organizational needs. For motivational and developmental purposes, appraisal feedback is probably best provided on a regular basis, as the employee performs a job and outcomes are available. Constructive behavioral feedback consistent with the job cycle can be effective for learning and modification of performance. Depending on employee experience, competence, and need for feedback, appraisal information can be given on a day-to-day coaching basis or at longer intervals. For example, the supervisor in a municipal agency that has just hired a disadvantaged person for a subsidized public-service job might want to provide assistance and performance appraisal information in an empathetic way more often than for a long-term employee in the same agency. The important point is that, for development and motivation, giving regular feedback that is adapted to the characteristics of the job or to individual needs is better than simply using an administrative cycle for giving appraisals.

For the purposes of administrative decision making, there may be little choice but to provide interview information at mandated times to accord with budgeting, specified promotion review periods, and so forth. In other cases, where the supervisor has control over rewards and the timing of reviews, the choice might be made to review at the completion of a job, and tie rewards to the accomplishment of the individual. In such cases, when employees are interviewed, if they have had continuous feedback, they should not be surprised about the rewards, since they already have reasonably good understandings of how they have been doing.

Develop employee participation in the review. At performance appraisal reviews, employees should have the opportunity and feel free to express their feelings about the job, their performance, needs, and behavior. This can include opportunities for employees to assist in establishing performance goals and objectives and to work cooperatively with their bosses in reviewing and assessing goal achievement. Such involvement and participation can lead to improved relations between manager and employees, with a more favorable attitude by both toward the appraisal system. The employee feels the manager is helpful and job problems can be more readily cleared up. The manager benefits by learning about expectations, feelings, and aspirations of the job. This can be helpful in developing motivational and developmental programs to meet both employee and organizational needs.

Focus on goal achievement or specific behavior. The most constructive results seem to come from focusing on objective and specific aspects of job performance rather than on personal and subjective things, such as traits. Discussions of goal achievement and actual behavior are more likely to be accepted by both the manager and the employee as valid and are more likely to lead to positive suggestions for change and development.

Avoid being excessively critical. There is evidence that, in general, criticism does not have a positive effect on goal achievement. This is particularly true when interviewers make large numbers of critical comments during evaluations. There seems to be a point at which additional criticism is no longer heard by employees. People become defensive and try to justify their actions when they face severe criticism. They are so busy thinking up reasons to defend themselves that they do not hear what follows. While criticism can be useful, managers should be aware of the problems of presenting excessive criticism.

Use praise when it is deserved. Experience seems to be mixed regarding the use of praise in performance evaluations. Praise may not be useful for motivational purposes if it is used as candycoating for subsequent criticism. When used indiscriminately, its value may be reduced when applied to important accomplishments. However, if it is used with discretion and is given as deserved on a day-to-day basis, it can reinforce good performance, enhance employee self-esteem, and be a useful reward and motivational tool.

Maintain an attitude of helpfulness. Performance appraisal interviewers should work with employees in a helpful manner and demonstrate interest in them. Interviewers need to learn to let the other person talk, to really listen and learn from employees. They should reflect the ideas and feelings of the people talking to them and help them see their strengths and weaknesses. They should not make statements about employees or their behavior without prior consideration and review of their potential consequences. Managers can increase their understanding of employees and can increase mutual respect and rapport if they approach appraisal interviews with a helpful attitude.

Communicate in language that has meaning to the employee. When discussing job performance, interviewers are more effective when they use terms, concepts, and ideas that are job-related and that the employee understands. In general, reference to nonoperational or tentative organizational goals, esoteric research, and concepts or materials with which the employee is not familiar do little to create trust or communicate helpful ideas that can improve performance.

HUMAN RESOURCE DEVELOPMENT

With acceptance of employees as a basic organizational resource, there is growing interest in developing the reservoir of talent and ability this resource represents. Human resource development (HRD) is a planned approach to enhance the development and growth of employee skills, abilities, judgment, and maturity to better meet overall organizational and individual employee goals. HRD programs are implemented to develop employee capabilities to carry out current job functions more effectively and to meet projected staffing needs. Organizations require trained, competent people to integrate and use new technology and need qualified people both to replace those lost through attrition (turnover and retirement) and to meet the expanded requirements of growth. In addition, by developing the capabilities of certain minority groups, organizations can meet their social responsibilities as well as their operating goals. Finally, organizations must maintain a high-quality labor force and minimize the costs and problems of personnel obsolescence.

Employees have a major interest in organizational HRD. It is through this development system that they can achieve their personal objectives in the organization and become better able to visualize their opportunities and determine if their aspirations can be realized within a particular organizational context. They can plan for their professional growth, define their developmental needs, and have a chance to satisfy higher-order needs through skill development, promotion, work achievement, and recognition.

Characteristics of HRD

HRD represents planned change in employee behavior, growth, and development. It is not a random training process, with no basis other than what may seem like a good idea at the moment. An HRD program is established to meet defined personal and organizational needs. It is integrated with the human resource planning system so that projected manpower requirements are considered as careers are being planned and training strategies are being established. For example, administrators can define the skills needed in the organization for the next several years on the basis of estimated demand and mix of services, thus determining the types of training necessary to develop current employees to the point where they will have the necessary skills, certifications, and experience to meet those expected requirements.

HRD emphasizes an individualized approach to employee growth. In some cases, the orientation is global, since certain skills, knowledge, abilities, and attitudes may be generally required for success in the organization. However, the HRD approach recognizes differences among individual employees and attempts to focus on developing each individual's potential within the context of organizational needs.

HRD is continuous and ongoing. Employees learn behavior and develop skills continually as they participate in the organization. HRD emphasizes the need for a complementary and reinforcing relationship between formal planning and training and informal everyday activities. For example, the training of police officers does not end with formal training sessions; the learned behavior must be reinforced in the department by the chief and supervisors, as well as by patrolmen peers.

HRD deals with long-term human resource needs. HRD is not limited to training for the improvement of current job performance; it also focuses on preparation for long-range personal development and organizational requirements. It goes beyond the immediate technical requirements of the job. There is a concern with the dynamic problems of staffing needs for the future and the evolution of individual career plans.

HRD is a key element in a larger set of human resource activities. HRD is integrated with and depends on the human resource requirements for the future. It interrelates strongly with issues of human resource utilization and motivation. It provides the basis for individuals to develop necessary skills for employment on jobs that can lead to social and higher-order need satisfaction. HRD activities can bring the most useful employee skills to full development, with maximum use of all talents being made. Performance evaluation also plays a critical role in the assessment of development needs and the evaluation of development outcomes.

HRD is an investment in organizational employees. By assisting with career planning and in implementing training and development programs, organizations are allocating monetary resources to people rather than to capital or other investments. Investments in human resources are expected to have long-range payoffs in terms of low turnover, improved productivity, loyalty to the organization, job satisfaction, heightened levels of motivation, and low cost in recruiting needed skills from outside the organization.

The HRD Concept

The diagram of the HRD process presented in Figure 3–5 suggests the flow of activity in an organizational HRD system. This model demonstrates that HRD draws heavily on the human resource planning system of an organization. Once personnel and skill needs are forecasted for the near and long-term future, career opportunities and plans can be formulated consistent with the organization's projected needs.

Career planning occurs at both the organizational and individual levels. At the organizational level, management uses its understanding of organizational needs to specify and group-related jobs to form career paths in the organization. It establishes an organizational internal labor market in which job information flows freely and employees are made aware of opportunities throughout the organization. Management establishes a performance appraisal system that provides realistic feedback to help employees assess their qualifications and needs. Counseling programs may be established by the organization to assist employees to define their aspirations more clearly and develop a better understanding of their own abilities. It is management's responsibility to define the job structure in order to meet organizational needs while providing opportunities for employee advancement and growth. It must create a climate that encourages employees to seek growth opportunities and development in the system.

Individual employees have the responsibility of seeking information about opportunities for careers in the organization and evaluating them in light of their own needs, aspirations, and life goals. The employees must try to assess their interests and objectives in the work environment realistically. In conjunction with management, they should try to determine how these objectives can best be met in the organizational career

FIGURE 3-5. *Personal growth in a human resource development planning framework.*

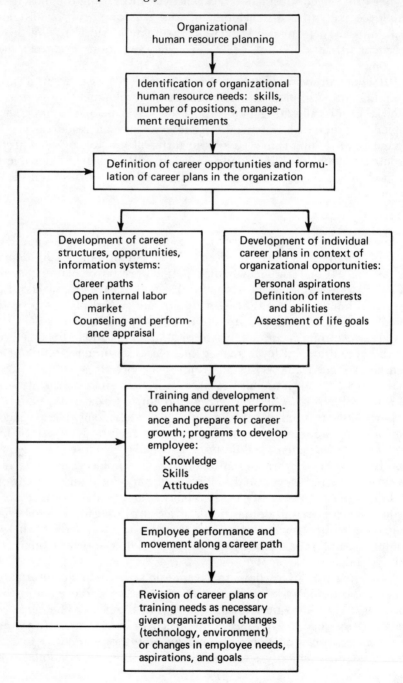

system. For example, a scientist in a nonprofit research organization should define his or her preferences and determine if the type of opportunities desired are available in that organization. The scientist may then choose to stay at the bench and progress through the various research positions or may choose to go into administration and take responsibility for directing research activity. In either case, he or she needs accurate feedback and information from management with regard to performance and opportunities that will be available in the organization in order to plan on obtaining the necessary skills and abilities to meet career goals.

Once career opportunities and plans have been developed, the next step is to define the specific types of training and development necessary to prepare employees to obtain their career objectives while meeting organizational needs. There is a need to define the types of programs that will be most useful to develop the necessary knowledge, skills, abilities, and attitudes for movement along the career path. These training programs must then be made available and their effectiveness and utility evaluated.

Modifications in certain aspects of career planning and training may be necessary due to significant changes in the organization's technology, legal requirements, or other unanticipatable environmental changes. Alterations may also be made necessary because of changes in individual employee personal needs, job aspirations, and life goals, requiring reformulation of career opportunities and plans or redirection of training and development activities.

Career Planning and Development

The growing expectation by workers that they should have opportunities for growth, development, and achievement on the job has led to an increasing interest by organizations in planning for employees' careers. Increasing pressures on organizations for the retention and more effective use of human resources has also encouraged an emphasis on career planning and development.

Career planning and development in an organization requires that the organization identify and communicate career opportunities within the system to its employees. It must also provide an environment conducive to individual self-assessment and realistic career path planning. For individual employees, it involves defining overall career objectives and specifying interim job and work goals. Employees define the sequence of jobs or positions they hope to hold in the organization to achieve career objectives. Such planning requires interaction and cooperation between individual employees and management if it is to be done realistically and options are to be correctly understood.

Career planning and development is important for several reasons. (1) It provides employees with the knowledge and understanding of the opportunities that are available in the organization. (2) It provides a framework that encourages each employee to better define his or her employment objectives and career goals. (3) It helps the organization gain a better idea of which employees are interested in growth opportunities, and provides an indication of future hiring needs. (4) It assists in defining a framework for determining appropriate training and development activity. As career paths are defined in light of organizational needs, training can be focused on providing the skills, knowledge, and attitudes which will enhance the opportunities for career success and meet organizational manpower requirements.

Employees should conduct self-assessments. Such self-assessments are useful in defining work goals and aspirations and in determining how they fit into overall life objectives. Many people never bother to consider how their jobs fit into their life plans or what they hope to achieve from the world of work. Without such planning, they find themselves in jobs that do not develop along with their life expectations, leading to dissatisfaction with the job, poor morale, lower productivity, and turnover. Self-assessment and definition of career objectives help employees to make better matches between life and work goals and to turn career goals into actual plans for development and movement along career paths.

Employees differ in their interest in and capability for self-assessment and career planning, with some needing more help than others. An organization may want to encourage its supervisors to work with subordinates in thinking about such problems. Some organizations have special counselors who work with employees to help them develop more realistic understandings of their abilities and the opportunities for careers within the organization. Other organizations run career workshops, set up employee group sessions for the sharing of thoughts on career development, and provide self-assessment and career planning manuals to assist employees in defining their needs and aspirations. Career development is self-development. But management must provide the environment and opportunities for such self-development to occur.

Performance feedback should be given to employees regularly. If employees are to realistically assess their prospects for careers in not-for-profit organizations, they need an understanding of how they are doing on the job now and how they are shaping up for future opportunities. Performance appraisal plays an important role in providing feedback. Performance- and behavior-related feedback can indicate areas where development is needed. In addition to regular performance appraisal information, organizations need feedback systems for employees who were rejected for promotion or transfer. When given accurately, honestly, and in a constructive manner, such feedback can help overcome disappointment and can assist employees to better prepare for future openings that are more consistent with proposed career paths and abilities. For example, if a bookkeeper puts in a bid for a job opening as an accountant and is turned down, he or she deserves an honest explanation for not being selected for the job and some counseling on what must be done to be competitive the next time such a position opens. Too often, employees do not receive adequate or useful feedback, which inhibits personal planning and growth.

Job families and career path opportunities should be identified and communicated to employees. Management should make realistic appraisals of career opportunities and expected job openings on an organizationwide as well as a departmental and other subunit basis. It should identify clusters of jobs with related but differential skill requirements and specify possible lines of progression and movement in the organization. These potential job paths should not represent only traditional promotion or transfer patterns but can also incorporate expectations with regard to future change and growth. Job paths and job families may be vertical progressions, such as promotions, but they may also represent horizontal movement in the form of transfers that build new skills and experience. Management must be certain it understands and communicates the requirements and qualifications for job path movement. While the organization may formulate general career paths and define relevant job families, individuals can use such information to work with management in defining realistic individually tailored career plans.

Identify high-potential employees and monitor career progress. In addition to a performance appraisal system, an organization should have other mechanisms that insure it makes the best possible use of its available human resources and provides maximum opportunities for them. An organization might maintain a comprehensive human resource information system that includes information on employee interests, education, skills, work experience, hobbies, evaluations, and career aspirations. This information can be used to help identify people who have the abilities and interests for an open position, and it should be updated as employee interests and characteristics change. Other approaches, such as assessment centers, can be used for identifying employee talent and potential. The assessment center can help employees better understand their strengths and weaknesses in important skill areas and can give the organization a good indication of employee potential.

Establish an open internal system so employees can freely seek opportunities. If an organization is to be successful in promoting the development of its human resources, it must be willing to provide information on available opportunities and create a climate in which employees feel free to seek new positions within the system. HRD is difficult, if not impossible, in organizations where managers are able to hoard high-quality personnel. In these organizations, managers may not recommend their subordinates for promotion or may hesitate to give them opportunities to develop new skills because they do not want to lose capable people. Some organizations restrict employee opportunities by allowing promotions to be made on the basis of friendship or acquaintance. In such cases, high-quality personnel may never know of the availability of certain jobs. This may work to the detriment of both the individual and the organization.

To provide maximum opportunity for personnel career development and the best use of human resources, an organization should be certain that jobs are openly advertised, perhaps through job posting. Many government agencies, for example, regularly post a list of available jobs and invite applications from all qualified employees. If people are aware of job opportunities and understand the qualifications required to fill them, these people are better able to direct their efforts toward meeting job requirements and to move along their career paths.

An organization can also use a rotational system for certain professional and supervisory employees to familiarize them with a variety of managers, departments, and jobs. They are not bound to any one manager or department, and they will have more information about possible openings within the organization. In addition to employees enjoying more information under this system, the organization has a broader perspective on the adaptability and potential of a wide range of possible candidates for immediate job openings and for long-range manpower planning.

Training and development activities for personal development should be made available. If certain behaviors, skills, knowledge, or attitudes are necessary for meeting requirements for job advancement and movement along a career path, employees must be given the opportunity to develop them. The organization must provide adequate training programs to prepare employees to meet expected challenges and to prepare them for better current and future performance. Such programs and training activities may be internal (organizational training departments that offer courses) or external (sending employees to special seminars, degree programs, or institutes). Supervisors can often play a major role in personal and career development through their leadership style and performance expectations. Supervisory trust of subordinates, willingness to delegate increasing responsibilities, willingness and ability to reward and reinforce behavior for high-quality job performance, and a high level of expectation for employees all influence employee development on the job. Employees must seek out particular training and development in areas of recognized personal weakness. They must seek to define life and career goals, taking the final responsibility for utilizing the developmental opportunities provided.

Training and Development

As a key element in the HRD process, training represents the implementation of a strategy to change the behavior of employees to better meet organizational objectives and enhance individual movement along defined career paths. Training also provides for employee participation in organizational development processes. For example, employees become involved with planned change by acting as trainers and helping develop skills in others. This is quite common in on-the-job training activity, which occurs in virtually all nonprofit organizations. Employees also become involved through participation as learners in training programs and activities. Such participation contributes to the development of personal self-esteem, and the competence developed in training can lead to higher motivation. Personal growth and organizational development depend greatly on the design and effectiveness of an organization's training activity.

1. *Formulate training programs on the basis of assessed needs.* Before designing and implementing training programs, management should assess organizational and individual needs so the training is relevant and effective. With regard to organizational needs, the first step is to determine the type and nature of training needed to improve the efficiency and effectiveness of *current* organizational operations. One or more of the following techniques may be used to make an assessment.

Observe organizational processes. Management should remain sensitive to problems in the daily operation and processes of the organization. For example, by simply observing the daily operations of the agency, department, or organization, managers may see obvious problems that can be corrected through training. Problems such as poor human relations skills, inability to use time effectively, and inadequate report-writing abilities may be clear to someone who stops to look.

Interview supervisors. Management can learn a great deal from the first-line supervisors who can identify individuals with the potential for development and can specify problem areas where training is necessary to improve organizational production or service delivery.

Seek information from employees. A basic source of information about training needs is the employees themselves. Suggestion systems or direct interviews can provide an indication of what the employees feel is necessary to better perform their jobs. They can suggest the special skills needed and can point to bottlenecks or inefficiencies that could be eliminated by adequate training.

Analyze operating reports. Indicators of potential training needs are organizational operating reports that reflect such things as turnover, cost effectiveness, and grievance rates. They can be helpful in identifying employees, supervisors, and departments where training can help improve organizational effectiveness.

Review performance appraisals. Information from performance appraisals of employees can assist in identifying people who might benefit from training to improve current performance. Performance appraisal information may be particularly useful if the behavior assessment approach is used. In a child-care organization, for example, the employee who is overly aggressive with the children can be identified. Needed skills and behaviors can be clearly specified, and training can be designed to meet current inadequacies. The review of performance evaluations can help in determining which supervisors need training in implementation of the performance appraisal system. If a supervisor continually makes errors of leniency in his employee evaluations, he may be in need of training on how to use the evaluation procedure.

In addition to the assessment of needs to improve current employee effectiveness, management must consider *projected* needs for skills and knowledge. Management must forecast organizational personnel needs in the intermediate and long range, and determine the appropriate paths to meet those needs through training. This will call for an analysis of the most useful *sequence* in training activity over the defined time horizon. Training must be viewed as part of a sequential, developmental process rather than as a one-time effort for short-term benefits.

Finally, the definition of training requirements must consider employee needs. Employees may not require training to improve current performance; but they may need training to move in projected promotion patterns or to prepare for bidding on jobs to which they aspire. Training programs should be devised so employees recognize that the organization is concerned with providing the background necessary for them to compete for opportunities in the system, as well as for assisting in movement along a career path. Such training programs are most appropriately developed when projected organizational needs and employee career planning and development are considered simultaneously.

2. *Utilize training methods that address defined needs.* After organizational and individual needs for training have been specified and training objectives established, appropriate training methods and techniques must be selected.

On-the-job (OJT) training. This approach focuses on learning while the person is on the job. Usually, instruction comes from supervisors or fellow employees. The major advantage of OJT is that it is conducted in the actual job situation where the trainee will be required to work; this leads to an excellent transfer of learning. Being on the job offers a strong incentive to quickly learn how to meet expectations and to handle an appropriate share of the work. It offers the opportunity to practice the new behavior in a realistic setting.

The major disadvantages of OJT are that the pressure of the job can create anxiety that inhibits performance and retards learning. It is also possible that supervisors may lack interest in training, may not have adequate time to spend with the trainee, or may have poor training skills themselves, all of which can result in ineffective training. The specific methods of OJT include job rotation, coaching by supervisors, special assignments to learn new tasks, apprentice training with a professional or skilled craftsman, and internships as assistants to managers or supervisors.

Off-the-job training. Some training may be conducted away from the job, usually when OJT might cause such operational problems as delays, breakage, or distractions to others. In some cases, learning is enhanced when trainees are away from the pressures of the job and work environment, where they can then focus total attention on the training activity. The major advantages of off-the-job training are that trainees can (1) make mistakes while learning that are less costly; (2) experiment with new ideas and behavior; and (3) draw on readily available trainers and resource personnel to maximize the value of the learning experience.

The major disadvantage of off-the-job training is that it may lack transferability to the work environment where the new behaviors or ideas are to be implemented. Off-the-job training methods include lectures, conferences, and seminars away from the job; case-study sessions; roleplaying simulations; programmed instruction; vestibule training; and T-group or laboratory training.

In selecting appropriate training methods and techniques, it is critical to consider the objective of the training. The objective of most training is to modify behavior through skill development, knowledge acquisition, and attitude development or change. When the objective of the training is to develop particular skills (for example, psychomotor skills to run a machine or the social skills of interviewing), training will be most effective if it uses methods which *involve* the trainee and allow him or her to practice developing the skills. The following training methods are useful in developing skills: apprentice training, vestibule training, role playing, OJT with coaching, and case studies.

On the other hand, if the training objective is to transmit information and help trainees acquire knowledge, effective learning can be somewhat more passive, and practice may be less important. For knowledge acquisition, such training methods as lectures, films, television, and programmed instruction are among those that are most effective. Finally, if attitudinal change is the goal of training, active trainee involvement and heavy participation are generally necessary. Training methods to change or modify attitudes include conferences, case studies, role playing, training groups, buzz groups, and other incentive and participative techniques.

   3. *Employ concepts and knowledge of human learning in designing and implementing training programs.* For training to be effective in creating a learning experience, the basic principles of learning have to be considered in the design and implementation of the training program and strategy.

   Motivation. Learners must want to learn. A motivated trainee learns more quickly and retains what has been learned better than one who is not motivated. Trainees must see how the training can help them meet their needs and achieve desired goals. For example, a social worker's desire to learn a new counseling technique can be increased if he or she sees how the training will help with better job performance, lead to a promotion or a raise, or achieve some other goal that is important in meeting the employee's needs.

   Knowledge of results. When people are learning, they need feedback on how they are doing. Coupled with explanations of why certain results occur, feedback provides a basis for adjustment and learning more appropriate behavior. Specific feedback should be given to trainees as soon as possible after responses are made. Feedback can be motivational and enhance the learning process as trainees begin to feel that they are making progress.

   Reinforcement. Reinforcement refers to an action taken that increases the probability of certain behavior being repeated. For example, if nursing aide trainees are rewarded when they successfully assist a patient, that kind of behavior is likely to be repeated. It has been found that positive reinforcement of desired behavior tends to increase the chance that the desired behavior will be repeated. However, punishment for undesirable behavior does not always lead to a decrease in that behavior. Emphasis, then, should be placed on reward for desired behavior.

   Practice. People usually learn by doing. Learning is best achieved when trainees are actively involved in what is being taught. Practice is most effective when it is spaced over a period of time rather than compressed in a short time span. Continuous, active practice may lead to "overlearning" of skills and behavior so that trainees no longer need to think before responding in the ways desired. In effect, they have internalized the behavior pattern into their response sets.

Whole or part learning. Research provides no definitive answer on whether trainees should learn tasks in segments or whether they should try to learn a whole task at one time. It seems to depend to some extent on who is being trained and the nature of the behavior, knowledge, or skill being learned. Some evidence indicates that the whole method is more useful with more intelligent trainees or when the material to be learned is best presented and developed as an integrated unit. When the material or set of tasks to be learned is diverse and one is dealing with, say, disadvantaged workers, the part method may be most effective. By learning each part of the task, trainees can obtain a reasonably quick feeling of accomplishment and be motivated to continue. If the whole method were used, they might become discouraged at the early lack of success.

4. *Evaluate training for effectiveness.* Many organizations accept the value of training without assessing its utility. If an organization uses training as part of HRD, it must formally evaluate this activity. Only through evaluation can an organization determine the effectiveness of a particular program or the relative usefulness of different techniques and methods and obtain a rational base for the justification and design of future programs. Evaluation should be undertaken as each training program is being developed. It is an integral part of the training strategy and should be built into the program from its inception. Some aspects of evaluation that must be considered include the following.

Training criteria. This refers to the problem of what is to be measured when determining training effectiveness. To a great extent it depends on a training program's objectives. If, for example, the training is intended to familiarize supervisors with the contents of a collective-bargaining agreement covering employees in their departments, the criterion might be their knowledge of the agreement. On the other hand, a different measure of training effectiveness might be needed for supervisors who had gone through an experiential training program to enhance their human relations skills. Evaluation criteria can be qualitative (such as asking trainees how they felt about the learning experience) or quantitative (production records, test scores, and so on).

Evaluation time frames. The appropriate time frame for conducting the evaluation must be determined. In certain training situations, results may be apparent shortly after the training (for example, training on how to complete forms dealing with employee benefits). A quantitative assessment of training effectiveness can be made in a reasonably short time after the training takes place. In other situations, it may be months or possibly years before the results of the training can be determined (for example, general management development and leadership skill training). In such a case, it might be desirable to develop criteria for immediate and intermediate assessment in addition to long-run criteria. One might collect participant perceptions immediately after the training, supervisor assessments in the intermediate period, and relevant performance criteria in the longer run.

Evaluation design. Many organizations, if they conduct any formal evaluation at all, may simply try to look at employee performance before and after training to determine effectiveness. The problem with this approach is that, if there is a change, it is not clear whether it is due to training or to other factors. There are a variety of experimental and quasiexperimental designs that can be used, but the most effective plan uses before-and-after measures for both an experimental group and a control group. Such a design gives a rational basis for assessing training effectiveness. Two groups of employees are formed by random assignment that assures their being relatively similar. The performance of each group's members is measured before training, and then training is given to the experimental group. After training, the performance of the members of both groups is again measured. The impact of the training on performance can be estimated.

5. *Reinforce behavior acquired through training.* If an organization is to fully realize the benefits of its training, it must maintain an environment that supports and reinforces what has been learned in the training process. If the organizational climate and reward system are not supportive of newly acquired behaviors or attitudes, the results are likely to be wasted training expenditures by the organization, low interest in training activity by employees, and frustration on the part of those who have completed the training programs. In such a climate, behavior learned in training remains restricted to the training environment and is not carried back to the job.

Top management support for training makes it clear that management is involved in and expects the training to be a major factor in the maintenance of a high-quality workforce. Management must reward subordinates on the basis of how well they use and encourage the application of newly learned behaviors on the job. Management should have a clearly spelled out policy indicating the importance of HRD and training.

Supervisors play a key role in supporting and reinforcing training, since they will be developing assignments, designing jobs, and setting goals for employees. The leadership style, method of performance appraisal, and coaching procedures they use can either reinforce newly learned behavior or work against it.

The work (or collegial) group also plays a significant role in the transfer and use of behavior acquired in training. If, for example, the work group feels that the learned behavior is consistent with peer group welfare (in supporting production norms or consolidating the group), it is likely to support its application on the job.

Finally, the organization's incentive system must support the behaviors learned in training. If valued outcomes such as praise, recognition, raises, promotions, and time off are tied to the use of such behavior, then one can expect motivated learners in the training system and significant use of newly learned behavior on the job.

CONCLUDING COMMENTS

This chapter has emphasized that employees represent a major but often underutilized resource of nonprofit organizations. If managers are to successfully meet expectations of increased productivity and effectiveness while financial and physical resources are becoming increasingly scarce, they have to make efforts to better manage and utilize the vast potential of their organizations' human resources.

A number of major concepts and practical guidelines have been presented that should assist the not-for-profit manager to:

1. Better plan for organizational human resource needs in the near and long-term future by forecasting and establishing a framework for human resource program development.

2. Better utilize the skills and capabilities existing in the organization through assessment of employee needs and the design and implementation of policies, programs, and behaviors that enhance employee motivation.

3. Better assess and record the contributions of employees to the organization that can aid in making more accurate and acceptable administrative decisions based on employee performance.

4. Better provide constructive feedback to employees on their strengths and weaknesses relating to organizational performance, thus aiding them in personal and career development decisions and aiding the organization by directing employee behavior in ways that meet organizational needs.

5. Establish more effective training and career programs to develop organizational human resources and meet expected needs over a forecasted time horizon.

The concepts and guidelines presented offer a solid basis for establishing or modifying an organization's human resources management system. Naturally, managers will need to review this chapter's guidelines in light of the specific characteristics and idiosyncrasies of their own organizations.

SELECTED BIBLIOGRAPHY

General and Background Reading

Beatty, Richard W., and Craig Eric Schneier. *Personnel Administration: An Experiential Skill-Building Approach* (Reading, Mass.: Addison-Wesley, 1977).

Craft, James A., and Jacob G. Birnberg. "Human Resource Accounting: Perspectives and Prospects," *Industrial Relations*, February 1976, pp. 2–12.

Hamner, W. Clay, and Frank L. Schmidt. *Contemporary Problems in Personnel*, rev. ed. (Chicago: St. Clair Press, 1977).

Heneman, Herbert G., III, and Donald P. Schwab, eds. *Perspectives on Personnel/Human Resource Management* (Homewood, Ill.: Irwin, 1978).

Pigors, P., et al., eds. *Management of Human Resources*, 3rd ed. (New York: McGraw-Hill, 1973).

Sayles, Leonard R., and George Strauss. *Managing Human Resources* (Englewood Cliffs, N.J.: Prentice-Hall, 1977).

Human Resource Planning

Burack, Elmer H., and James W. Walker, eds. *Manpower Planning and Programming* (Boston: Allyn and Bacon, 1972).

Cassel, Frank H. "Manpower Planning: State of the Art at the Micro Level," *MSU Business Topics*, August 1973, pp. 107–117.

Coleman, Bruce. "An Integrated System for Manpower Planning," *Business Horizons*, October 1970, pp. 89–95.

Drandell, Milton. "A Composite Forecasting Methodology for Manpower Planning Utilizing Objective and Subjective Criteria," *Academy of Management Journal*, September 1975, pp. 510–519.

Heneman, Herbert G., III, and M. G. Sandver. "Markov Analysis in Human Resource Administration: Applications and Limitations," *Academy of Management Review*, October 1977, pp. 535–542.

Milkovich, George T., et al. "The Use of the Delphi Procedures in Manpower Forecasting," *Management Science*, December 1972, pp. 381–388.

U. S. Civil Service Commission. *Planning Your Staffing Needs: A Handbook for Personnel Workers* (Washington, D.C.: Government Printing Office, 1977).

Vetter, Eric. *Manpower Planning for High Talent Personnel* (Ann Arbor, Mich.: Bureau of Industrial Relations, University of Michigan, 1967).

Walker, James. "Human Resource Planning: An Odyssey to 2001 and Beyond," *Pittsburgh Business Review*, March 1978, pp. 2–8.

Walker, James. "Manpower Planning: An Integrative Approach," *Management of Personnel Quarterly*, Spring 1970, pp. 38–42.

Motivation

Carroll, Stephen J., and Henry L. Tosi. *Organizational Behavior* (Chicago: St. Clair Press, 1977).

Herzberg, Frederick. *Work and the Nature of Man* (Cleveland: World, 1966).

Lawler, E. E., III. *Motivation in Work Organizations* (Monterey, Cal.: Brooks/Cole, 1973).

Leidecker, Joel, and James Hall. "Motivation: Good Theory—Poor Application," *Training and Development Journal*, June 1974, pp. 3–7.

Likert, Rensis. *The Human Organization: Its Management and Value* (New York: McGraw-Hill, 1967).

McGregor, Douglas. *The Human Side of Enterprise* (New York: McGraw-Hill, 1960).

Maslow, Abraham H. *Motivation and Personality* (New York: Harper & Bros., 1954).

Steers, R. M., and Lyman W. Porter. *Motivation and Work Behavior* (New York: McGraw-Hill, 1975).

Vroom, Victor H. *Work and Motivation* (New York: Wiley, 1964).

Yankelovich, Daniel. "The Meaning of Work," in J. M. Rosow, ed. *The Worker and the Job* (Englewood Cliffs, N.J.: Prentice-Hall, 1974).

Yoder, Dale, and Herbert G. Heneman, Jr., eds. *Motivation and Commitment.* Volume II of *ASPA Handbook of Personnel and Industrial Relations* (Washington, D.C.: Bureau of National Affairs, 1975).

Performance Appraisal

Burke, R. J., and D. S. Wilcox. "Characteristics of Effective Employee Performance Review and Development Interviews," *Personnel Psychology,* Autumn 1969, pp. 291–305.

Cummings, L. L. "A Field Experiment Study of the Effects of Two Performance Appraisal Systems," *Personnel Psychology,* Winter 1973, pp. 489–503.

Cummings, L. L., and Donald P. Schwab. *Performance in Organizations: Determinants and Appraisal* (Glenview, Ill.: Scott, Foresman, 1973).

Levinson, H. "Appraisal of What Performance?", *Harvard Business Review,* July–August 1976, pp. 30–36, 40–46, 160.

Maier, Norman R. F. *The Appraisal Interview: Objectives, Methods, and Skills* (New York: Wiley, 1958).

Meyer, H. H., et al., "Split Roles in Performance Appraisal," *Harvard Business Review,* January–February 1965, pp. 123–129.

Oberg, Winston. "Make Performance Appraisal Relevant," *Harvard Business Review,* January–February 1972, pp. 61–67.

Schwab, Donald P., et al. "Behaviorally Anchored Rating Scales: A Review of the Literature," *Personnel Psychology,* Winter 1975, pp. 549–562.

Careers and Training

Alfred, Theodore. "Checkers or Choice in Manpower Management," *Harvard Business Review,* January–February 1967, pp. 157–169.

Bowen, Donald D., and Douglas T. Hall. "Career Planning for Employee Development: A Primer for Managers," *California Management Review,* Winter 1977, pp. 23–35.

Campbell, John P., et al. *Managerial Behavior, Performance, and Effectiveness* (New York: McGraw-Hill, 1970).

Carroll, Stephen J., et al. "The Relative Effectiveness of Training Methods—Expert Opinion and Research," *Personnel Psychology,* Autumn 1972, pp. 495–510.

Goldstein, Irwin L. *Training: Program Development and Evaluation* (Monterey, Cal.: Brooks/Cole, 1974).

Gutteridge, Thomas G. "Organizational Career Development and Planning," *Pittsburgh Business Review,* March 1978, pp. 3–14.

Hinrichs, John R. "Personnel Training," in Marvin D. Dunnette, ed., *Handbook of Industrial and Organizational Psychology* (Chicago: Rand McNally, 1976).

Kellogg, Marion. *Career Management* (New York: AMACOM, 1972).

This, Leslie, and Gordon Lippitt. "Learning Theories and Training," *Training and Development Journal,* April 1966, pp. 2–11.

CHAPTER 4

Management of Mental Health in Nonprofit Organizations

James A. Wilson

Editor's Note *All organizations should strive to enhance the mental and emotional lives of their employees. Many organizations do not do it, although maintaining the quality of life of organizational members is an ethical issue every manager should be concerned with. This chapter explores this issue.*

The author maintains that the situation in nonprofit organizations is ripe for conflict between lower-level staff and professionals. The potential for conflict arises partly out of the fact that these people tend to be polarized by their tasks, with support people feeling they have lesser status and prestige, even if they do see themselves as having equal importance. The result is increased anxiety, withdrawal, and aggressive behavior.

The various positive and negative factors that contribute to and detract from good mental health are discussed here, with suggestions of what might be done by managers to improve the employee work environment. The essence of managing mental health involves enhancing positive experiences and lessening negative ones. Self-esteem is a significant indicator of health. People with high self-esteem tend to be less punitive, moralistic, and judgmental in their appraisal of themselves; they experience less anxiety, loneliness, depression, and alienation. The organization should deliver positive reinforcement in the form of praise, recognition, and minor material rewards to build employee self-esteem. But negative situations do exist, and are sometimes unavoidable.

Any organization can provide a number of essentials that contribute to good mental health: a place to be, fulfilling roles, status, people to relate to and enjoy, stimulation, challenge, education, and reduced concern over economic survival. On the negative side, there are the competing demands between job and family. Threats to mental health lie in the impersonal bureaucratic structure of many organizations where power is imperfectly distributed, with more at the top and less at the bottom. Real or felt lack of power can contribute to the feeling of being manipulated and exploited.

The author suggests that, if an organization truly values the mental health of its members, it protects them, even if it must do so seemingly at the expense of productivity. However, there is little evidence that productivity goes down when an organization is concerned with the mental health of its employees.

This chapter focuses on management's attitude toward mental health in organizations in general and nonprofit organizations in particular.* Many excellent volumes concerned with mental health in organizations exist and should be consulted by those who wish to extend their understanding of these issues (see especially Jennings, 1965; Schoonmaker, 1969; and Levinson, 1970).

Some early discussion and definition of these central concepts may be helpful toward setting the stage for the materials that follow. It is assumed that nonprofit organizations differ from organizations that seek profit (in the traditional sense). If this is so, the management of nonprofit organizations obviously differs from the usual business or corporate model. However, even if organizations and the style, methods, and goals of their management differ, many aspects of this issue will be similar in both.

The writer's knowledge is derived from theory and from observation and actual work experiences in profit and nonprofit organizations such as corporations, consulting firms, the military, hospitals, universities, and research establishments. Considerable data are derived from working with executives in psychotherapeutic settings.

---

*I am indebted to Professor Donald Bowen (University of Tulsa, Oklahoma), Dr. Arthur Erbe (of Oakmont, Pennsylvania), Professor Ian Mitroff (University of Pittsburgh), Dr. Raghu Nath (University of Pittsburgh), and Dr. Thomas Kellaghan (Educational Research Centre, Dublin, Ireland) for substantive and helpful comments on early drafts of this chapter. They saved me from a number of errors; of course, they are not responsible for any that remain. I am also indebted to Mrs. Maureen Jenkins, whose typing and clerical assistance was invaluable.

THE PSYCHOLOGY OF NOT-FOR-PROFIT
ORGANIZATIONS

What kinds of psychological and sociological factors differentiate non-profit from profit organizations and how do these differences affect the dynamics and management of such organizations? It would be difficult to specify the common factors that unify the diverse range of nonprofit organizations (military, hospital, religious, research, government, educational, political, and social). Therefore, I will confine myself to statements that appear to be true about service organizations, in which monetary profit is not the primary operating purpose. Nonprofit or service organizations often distinguish more clearly than profit organizations between the services they provide—the content of their mission—and the management or administrative activity that supports this mission.

In the nonprofit organization, there is a clear and distinct feeling that the service provided—such as education, hospital care, or social work—is more important than the management or support functions that keep the organization running to deliver the essential service. Management or support people (hospital administrators, accountants, clerical workers, and custodians) often feel that they are second-class citizens in relation to professional workers, especially if they are not as well paid. Their social status as people, as well as the status of their jobs, is reflected by the reduced status assigned to them in the organization structure; it is even recognized by clients. By contrast, in profit-making industrial organizations, the distinction between mission and management is much less clear, because these two functions have become blended and blurred. In general, the manufacturing function and the management of the firm are considered parts of one process. Management as a process, profession, and function was born in the commercial sector. Only in the last few decades has its study been included in the education of personnel for government, the military, hospitals, schools, and social agencies.

Thus managers of service organizations often have to contend with two feelings of inferiority. First, although they work in a hospital, for example, they are not physicians, nurses, or medical technicians. Second, their status as managers is considered to be lower than that of industrial managers, because it is felt by many that administrators of service organizations are less competent than their industrial counterparts. Industrial managers manage everything that takes place in the firm. Nonprofit managers, however, contend with teachers, social workers, nurses, physicians, scientists, and others who are content- or mission-oriented professionals and may not have a high regard for management skills. In addition, the managers of service organizations frequently operate under moral, legal, and professional constraints, because they are not qualified or even licensed to provide the services offered by the organization and are thus unable to direct the organization's professional function.

While it is true that many physicians, nurses, and teachers, work as managers, if their primary role is administration and management, they are no longer functioning as the professionals they were trained to be. The fact that managers of service organizations are not in contact with their clients or customers, or are in contact with them only infrequently, can also contribute to their lesser status.

In a service organization, administrators are likely to feel heavily controlled and influenced by people who do not share their concerns and problems or perhaps do not even understand what management is about. Because of this feeling, these administrators may be less organized, seemingly less rational, or less efficient than they would be in profit-making firms. Frequently, they feel that they are patronized by the line personnel, with resultant feelings of being threatened, vague martyrdom, and even mild paranoia.

When working extensively with nonprofit organizations, it is not long before one is told by administrators: "We had this fine idea about how to cut costs and deliver better service, but the physicians, nurses, teachers, and social workers would not accept it." Such a situation can give rise to feelings of frustration and of being manipulated that, in turn, can lead to alienation and withdrawal. These feelings and emotions are not dissimilar to those reported by staff personnel in relation to line personnel in industrial organizations; and they exist for similar reasons. Thus second-class feelings do not exist only in service organizations. However, they tend to be more pronounced and widespread in organizations where a schism exists between mission (line) and administrative (staff or support) workers. These generic statements will be more or less true of various organizations, depending on such factors as size, degree of bureaucratization, amount of teamwork, and whether the organization is owned privately or by the government.

By contrast, feelings of inferiority are often found cheek by jowl with feelings of superiority, grandiosity, and arrogance because of the altruistic, service, or charitable nature of the organization. ("We who work and exist for service are better and more worthy than those who merely make widgets for profit".) And such feelings can be shared by everyone in a service organization, not merely the managers and administrators. Superior feelings can conflict with the "mendicant mentality," a concomitant of the beggar's role that makes people in nonprofit organizations feel they are constantly begging—for budgets and salaries from government, foundations, and wealthy philanthropists whom they may see as donors, constrainers, enemies, or friends.

Service organizations often achieve a high degree of commitment by their personnel to the organization's mission. This frequently surpasses the commitment expressed and felt by personnel in profit organizations, who know that they provide a needed service with what they make but seldom cloak this function in high-sounding rhetoric about public, social, and moral responsibility. Workers in service organizations are more likely to feel an ownership of the organization and an identity with its mission and the services it provides for philosophic, ethical, religious, or other deeply personal reasons (such as the cancer researcher whose parents died of cancer). Service workers often have a profession whose goals, values, and ethics transcend those of the organization they work for. They express these goals, values, and ethics within and through the organization, imbuing the organization with them and producing the aura of humanitarianism and high purpose that marks social agencies, hospitals, and research centers.

A consequence of noble professional feelings is that personnel in nonprofit organizations often express boredom with taking inventory, checking cash accounts, purchasing towels, and keeping sidewalks clean, discounting these functions as mechanical housekeeping—busywork. This does not help those who work at these activities, without which even the best organization can flounder.

The situation in service organizations is ripe for conflict between staff (support services) workers and the professional or mission workers. Different people are drawn to various kinds of work, and this can set the stage for personality differences. Both the work they do and its training differ. The work differs in status and prestige, with the professionals tending to feel they are what the institution is all about and support people having lesser occupational or social status and prestige, even when they see themselves as having equal importance. Aside from such substantive causes of conflict as the resource allocations that occur in any organization, the negative feelings described can cause the kinds of conflict that tend to increase anxiety, withdrawal, and aggressive behavior.

We have not begun our discussion of mental health *per se* in nonprofit organizations, and yet, in merely indicating the nature of these organizations and the kinds of people drawn to them, we have identified a potential for mental health problems and the need for management of such problems.

SOME ASSUMPTIONS ABOUT MENTAL HEALTH

More difficulties arise from the human condition itself than from work situations. In understanding mental health in business or in the professions, it is essential to know that neurosis, anxiety, defenses, and coping mechanisms are not distinct or separate from life itself. Mental health and ordinary emotional problems are related to childhood, family, work, love relationships, relationships with self (sometimes referred to as identity), and how we relate to and cope with the process of being alive. The ability to transcend the organic and animal levels of existence is deeply entwined in mental health and is not separate from philosophy, religion, and cosmology. Man, nature, and our collective destiny deeply affect everyone's psychology. Mental health is not separate or distinct from concerns about sex or race.

Women cannot ignore the status of women in general or their own status in particular, or fail to see the relationship between their femaleness and the way they experience life. Likewise, men who are insensitive to the benefits and problems of being male are naive or deluded. Race is important in that blacks, Amerindians, Chicanos, or Asian-Americans who ignore or fail to see that minority status and experience affect mental health are at a double disadvantage (see Grier and Cobbs, 1969). Mental health cannot be separated from culture and the sociological marks of our identity: age, ethnic heritage, regional origin, and social class.

Mental and emotional problems can also differ over time. For example, during the Victorian period, "neurasthenia" was a common diagnosis for minor depression and was quite fashionable among genteel people. Today, cases of mild depression can be treated with chemotherapy or short-term psychotherapy. Alienation—the feeling of powerlessness over one's life, of not having access to one's own emotions and identity—is also a preoccupation of some mental health authorities. Neither depression nor alienation can be separated from economics, business, politics, occupation, standard of living, or profession. The employing organization has an impact on mental health, and it is especially true of bureaucratic and authoritarian organizations in both the profit and nonprofit sectors.

Individual mental health is related to environmental and societal health. It is next to impossible to be a healthy fish in badly polluted waters. The ability to be happy, content, and oblivious in the midst of severe environmental and social disorganization suggests an unhealthy denial of reality. Likewise, someone so crippled, depressed, or angry at this same bad state of affairs as to be unable to function in a healthy and sometimes even happy fashion would not be mentally healthy. A healthy posture—feeling stable and functioning fully—involves having an awareness of the disorganization around one and doing what can reasonably be expected to ameliorate it, as well as whatever is required for oneself.

Much pop psychology and even some formal "adjustment" psychology seems to suggest that we can ignore our environment, ignore fellow humans, "mind our own business," get on with our personal goals—both internal and external—and to hell with the rest. This is an impractical view, because the world will not allow us to be completely indifferent to it. For example, we cannot escape the slums, poverty, crime, and filth of the large city by fleeing to the suburbs, since the city pursues us in the form of business usage taxes, shared transit costs, disturbing newscasts of the city left behind, and an inability to "use" the city at night.

Normalcy

The concept of "normality" or "normalcy" does exist. It can be looked at and analyzed. But it is almost impossible to define. It is easier to note how the concept is applied. If normality exists, is it possible for anyone to be entirely normal? How much abnormality can a person or personality sustain and still be called normal? Can abnormal people be normal in some aspects of their lives and behavior? If so, is only a part of them ill—and what part?

One of the assumptions our society makes is that normality exists, has distinguishing characteristics, and is good. Though most people are normal, each might admit to being a little bit neurotic. Acceptance of these statements depends on which criterion of normality one uses. It is generally agreed that what most people do most of the time constitutes normality. In one sense, such a criterion is statistical, a kind of gross majority rule. But it is also cultural, in that people do not spontaneously come to similar forms of behavior. Rather, they conform to what they have been taught and transmit it as correct, best, and proper.

Every culture provides continuous and demanding lessons in normality that can be confused with what is right and good, even with what is true and beautiful. In general, the members of a culture agree that the way the majority behaves most of the time is normal. Such popular concepts of normality attest to the suggestion of anthropologists that culture is possible only because so many of us are alike in so many ways. Statistical definitions of normalcy, then, are really cultural definitions. Using these definitions, what we feel to be normal depends on the culture of which we are members and the extent to which we conform to that culture; and it colors how we evaluate the behavior of others. A culture defines health, pathology, and normalcy in ways that create or support its beliefs, with a system of meanings that explains the nature of existence.

Another common definition of normality is the medical one, which defines mental health as it does physical health, in terms of the presence or absence of pathological symptoms. In the case of mental and emotional disorders, pathology includes the presence of undue stress or anxiety, depression, delusions, hallucinations, or such systems of neurotic behavior as compulsion, inappropriate repression, and hysteria. But culture intervenes in medical definitions also, since physicians in different cultures do not define illness similarly. Even professionals in the same culture do not always agree, depending on what school of psychology or psychiatry they follow. The definitions of mental and emotional disorder discussed here are not pure. Each of them is influenced by other definitions. Physicians and psychiatrists are influenced by the culture they work in, with their work and definitions in turn influencing the public's popular definitions of mental health and disorder.

Freud is reported to have responded to a question about what normal people are able to do well by answering: "To love and to work" (Gorney, 1972). Building on Freud, Gorney (1972, p. 317) and Riesman (1953, pp. 174–205) discuss the benefits and meaning of love, work, and play. These functions not only signify health but are themselves health-producing experiences. Thomas Szasz (1969), a controversial American psychiatrist, suggests that physicians in particular are too quick to apply traditional models of symptoms and methods for their treatment to mental disorder. He suggests that all of us have difficulties and problems in living. If these problems sometimes weigh us down with anxiety and depression, it is normal. When the problem is poverty or the lack of money, he suggests that money, not a pill, will remove the symptoms.

William C. Menninger (1966), an influential American psychiatrist, suggested several criteria for "emotional maturity." These include:

- Having the ability to deal constructively with reality.
- Having the capacity to adapt to change.
- Having a relative freedom from symptoms produced by tensions and anxieties.
- Having the capacity to find more satisfaction in giving than receiving.
- Having the capacity to relate to other people in a consistent manner, with mutual satisfaction and helpfulness.
- Having the capacity to sublimate, to direct instinctive hostile energy into creative and constructive outlets.
- Having the capacity to love.

Humanist and existentialist thinkers appear to be more philosophic when defining normalcy. They suggest that, in order to be fully human, one must accept and be at peace with one's own body and nature and the human species in general. Perhaps this is one of the most difficult definitions of normality to accept, since few of us believe we have achieved all of these qualities to the fullest extent. Indeed, many of us are deeply alienated and do not have access to or are not in touch with nature, our bodies, or other humans.

Other thought systems such as Calvinism, individualism, and the success (or work) ethic also contribute to folk concepts of normalcy. Some of them suggest that normal life is a problem to be solved, a task to be done, or a race to be won. Unfortunately, aside from those for whom mere survival is a problem, most of us are caught up in this very definition of normalcy. It defines our world as being composed of solving problems, doing tasks, and winning races. We are doomed to being unhappy and feeling inadequate or unworthy when we are not doing these things, and we feel satisfied and worthy when we are. This tends to be more true of people over the age of 30 who have drunk more deeply of Calvinism and the so-called Protestant (work) ethic because there was more of it about when they were growing up. However, the current tone of many young people, especially university-trained people, is one of seriousness and concern for their careers as contrasted with the self-conscious hedonism of the 1960s.

It then follows that whether or not one is normal depends on which definition of the term is accepted or used. We tend to define and evaluate ourselves in terms of perceptions of normality, with obvious consequences for our self-esteem (this mental health concept will be discussed later). For the self, the acceptance and application of a concept of normality is more important than a decision as to which of the various definitions is true and which is not. When making such a decision, we construct ourselves—that is, we form an identity and become the kind of person we believe we are. This process of making oneself and forming an identity is continuous, emergent, and cumulative. We grow, change, and form ourselves all the time in both large and minute ways by taking a multitude of actions. Furthermore, we change ourselves by accretion and deletion, dropping off behavior as well as adding it.

It follows from the many definitions of normalcy that others can dispute our normality. This is equally true over time, and from place to place; a person's behavior can be normal in one place but not in another, at one time but not at another. To some extent, normality is a function of the person who asks the question rather than of the subject or the behavior in question.

For those of us interested in the management of mental health in nonprofit and other organizations, when normality is equated with good mental health ("normal is best"), it becomes our management goal. It is not necessary to accept one definition of normality to the exclusion of others, since they all intimate what can be expected from effective management of mental health. It is more important that we merely have a sound idea of what constitutes good or normal mental health, because, as we will see later, the demands of mental health can and often do conflict with the demands of the organization.

Organizations usually maximize their own interests and attempt to shape the behavior of their employees around those interests. Organizational interests supersede the interests of the employees, but some organizations try to integrate their interests with those of their employees. Should any adjustment be required, it is invariably the employees' interests that are sacrificed to those of the organization. Almost no organization moves by plan against the good mental health of its employees. Yet, in the day-to-day activities of an organization, there is frequently a significant lack of agreement between what is good for the organization and what is good for the mental health of its employees.

THE GOALS OF MENTAL HEALTH MANAGEMENT

One of the truisms of medicine and therapy is that if something positive cannot be done for a patient, one should do nothing to make him or her worse. It should also be one of the minimum goals of mental health management to resist tampering with the mental health that exists in employees when they join the organization. It is less obvious that an organization should enhance or increase the mental health of employees.

A case can be made on utilitarian as well as humanitarian grounds that healthy workers are likely to produce more, with lower rates of absenteeism, turnover, and tardiness, and, perhaps, fewer grievances. Some economic benefits should result. Critics of this concept usually counter with questions concerning the costs of such undertakings. For example, should an organization be asked to make contributions to the mental health of employees to its own financial detriment? Should an organization refrain from using techniques that contribute to its income but that operate against the mental health of employees?

Most for-profit organizations view such questions as economic and argue that, if an organization makes too many decisions in the interests of its employees and against its own interests, it will not survive—and neither will the jobs of its employees. Obviously, economics, costs, and survival must be brought into the equation, but the issue is also a "value" question insofar as the organization expresses its values in the nature and quality of its decisions and techniques. There is no doubt that the issues are complex. If anything, they are more complex for the nonprofit organization, whose existence relates to the services provided its clientele. If taken to the extreme, an organization can maximize the conditions for internal mental health at the cost of fewer services provided outside. A balance must be maintained by management that reflects the values of the organization.

The Theory of Self-Esteem

Another essential criterion of mental health is the need for a person's positive relationship with the self, which is usually called self-esteem. It is perhaps the most important part of human identity. The concept is discussed under a number of names that overlap, such as "self-acceptance," "love of self," "liking yourself," and "self-confidence." They all mean the desire to think well of the self, to have the self support the self in whatever is undertaken and to feel no crippling anxieties about the worth or value of the self.

The person with low self-esteem questions his or her personal worth or value, puts himself or herself down, predicts failure rather than success for the efforts of the self, and sometimes refuses to try to succeed. Such a person is anxiety ridden, lacks confidence, feels inferior, and behaves in a number of defensive ways (shifting, for example, from withdrawal and dependency to expressions of hostility). The meaning of the behavior is usually the same: the self is convinced that it is "not OK" (Berne, 1973, pp. 84–89).

This appraisal or evaluation of the self by the self suggests a benchmark or criterion against which self-worth is judged. This criterion is referred to psychoanalytically as the "ego ideal"—what we actually wish for the self in reality and in fantasy. It is our hopes, dreams, aspirations, and all the statements we make that begin with "If only . . . ." This criterion is future-oriented. It deals with those things, goals, and happenings we want to possess for ourselves—achievement, success in all its aspects, and the esteem and admiration of others.

It is the desire for self-esteem and the esteem of others that provides the motivation for attempting to achieve the things that deliver admiration and esteem. This is one of the strongest motivators known. In accomplishing something that makes us feel good about ourselves, we also kill off or escape having the doubt and anxiety about ourselves that can be so painful and crippling. With every success, our self-esteem tends to heighten; with every failure, it decreases. Anxiety heightens with failure and lessens with success.

The process of building self-esteem is a powerful one, lying as it does at the center of our being. We want to think well of ourselves and escape the anxiety that attends our vulnerability. There is a part of a person that takes up arms against itself, a part that sees itself as the problem, attempts to expunge the things that cause feelings of anxiety about self-worth. This is not surprising, given the reflective nature of human beings. People can reflect on and objectify their own existence and behavior, making objects of themselves in their own thoughts, and then object to their own behavior on moral or other grounds.

There is a basic punitive aspect to the process of building self-esteem in which people attempt to make real the dreams and aspirations they have for themselves. The positing of an aspiration may involve a negative evaluation of self, an indictment for lacking something, a feeling of in-adequacy, or a feeling of being something less than ideal because of a lack of some quality. To an extent, then, each person creates his or her own courtroom in which he or she is indicted, tried, convicted or vindi-cated, awarded damages or benefits, and in which he or she plays all the roles.

It may be that we are task, success, and productivity oriented because we have been placed in more social, psychological, and historical jeopardy in terms of our own self-evaluations than are people in other societies. Some people, when placed in jeopardy, quit, withdraw, take drugs, or commit suicide, while others attempt to do good in order to enjoy the adulation and achieve the rewards that can make them feel better about themselves.

The jeopardy in which Americans find themselves has to do with such factors as the high expectations transmitted to many American males about "getting further than their fathers did." It is as if they are running a competitive race with their fathers. These expectations are translated into upward mobility as sons climb the class structure on their trek to "success" and, possibly, higher self-esteem. It is unfortunate for the so-cially mobile that the process of transcending the economic and social state of the father has much ambivalence attached to it for both fathers and sons. Fathers, although they may wish the success of their sons, are also conditioned to competition and to winning, even against competing sons. Further, the connotations of "failure" can plague a father, who, while he may have done much better than *his* own father, is passed by a still more successful son. On the other hand, sons often experience guilt and remorse, as well as pleasure, as they pull ahead of their fathers. Insecure fathers, with low self-esteem, will be especially vulnerable to such negative feelings. Indeed, "success" constitutes a unique hazard for which many people in our society are not prepared.

While the need for self-esteem may be virtually universal, the norms and criteria for achieving it differ from person to person. But the end sought is the same: the self-esteem that provides affirmation of one's existence in the world and the worth and value of that existence. Existence should not be treated casually. There are many people whose very existence is in jeopardy. There are people who experience themselves as being without faces, voices, names, or identity, and who have suffered loss of being, selfhood, and self-esteem. (See Ralph Ellison's *The Invisible Man* and James Baldwin's *Nobody Knows My Name* as examples.)

Such feelings are the result of social interactions. How we are treated by significant others and how they feel about us affect how we feel about ourselves. This is "internalization"; it involves the incorporation of another's feeling and evaluation into the self. It is part of the socialization process because we are speaking of how others contribute to the shaping of our opinions of the world and of ourselves, which, in turn, will be reflected in our behavior and in our feelings about ourselves and about others.

Self-esteem can also be spoken of as a liking or loving of the self. It is also closely related to the concept of "self-validation." Gorney (1972, p. 318) suggests that self-validation is "confirmation of the existence and worth of the self." Humans apparently are not born with a definite sense of their own existence or of the worth and value of that existence. Such a sense or feeling is built up over time, as the result of experiences with and in the world. Self-validating experiences result in higher self-esteem, which confirms one's existence and place in the world.

Internalization is not necessarily a one-to-one process, whereby the actual feelings of one person are replicated in another. It is more complex than that. What we internalize of another's feelings about us is related to the feelings we already hold for that person and for ourselves. For example, if we love our parents, we tend to duplicate their behavior and feelings. But if we dislike, reject, or fear our parents, we may either accept those feelings or suppress them and internalize contradicting ones—a concept that sheds light on the observation that drunken parents can produce both alcoholics and teetotalers. Parents also differ in the way they treat each child, with differences in the children's internalizations giving rise to siblings with different characteristics.

Though people differ in *what* they internalize, internalization does occur and has to do with how we feel about ourselves. The more self-esteem we have, the less vulnerable we are to the negative evaluations and feelings of others. The less self-esteem we have, the more vulnerable we are to the negative evaluations of others, especially if those others are more powerful and more successful than we are and already possess what we aspire to.

Thus the amount of self-esteem we have is controlled largely by sources in the environment and in the self-validating experiences the environment provides or fails to provide us with. Parents, peers, reference groups, superiors on the job, and other authority figures (teachers, spouses, lovers, and professional clients) are all sources of self-confirming or nonaffirming experiences (see Coopersmith, 1967).

Self-Esteem and Positive Experiences

To attempt to list all the positive and negative effects on self-esteem that flow from human experience is a monumental task. We can point out only the most general kinds here. Positive experiences (often termed "success experiences") result in higher self-esteem, given the friendly conditions discussed earlier, with the resultant feeling that the self is "OK" (Berne, 1972). People with more life-affirming experiences and the resultant higher self-esteem exhibit greater self-confidence, satisfaction with the self, and acceptance of others; more toleration of the faults and foibles of others; less need to blame or to scapegoat others (including a lessened tendency toward anti-Semitism and racism in all its forms); less anxiety and frustration; increased feelings of potency (strength in all its forms) and autonomy (having the freedom, power, and will to control, direct, and enjoy one's life); increased capacity for love (the giving and receiving of it); and even higher performance on the job.

People with high self-esteem tend to be less punitive, moralistic, and judgmental in their appraisals of others, although they may hold extremely high standards of performance and behavior for themselves. They also tend to experience less anxiety, loneliness, depression, and feelings of alienation, which is the social scientist's term for those who feel themselves to be powerless in their own lives and in the lives of others—who do not have the ability ("access") to express the emotions they feel at a conscious level and who are politically powerless in all senses of that word. As Coopersmith (1967, p. 261) indicates:

> Children with high self-esteem appear to learn quite early that they must respond to the challenges and troublesome conditions they encounter.... Our study provides clear indications that the individual with high self-esteem feels capable of coping with adversity and competent enough to achieve success, and that the individual with low self-esteem feels helpless, vulnerable, and inadequate.

Because of their high evaluations of themselves, people with high self-esteem need to defend themselves against the criticism of others less strongly and are much less affected when they are criticized. They balance their own views with those of others and objectively sift the evidence presented. Those whose self-esteem is low or in jeopardy feel the need to defend themselves against the criticism of others in order to contain the anxiety that the critical evaluations of others arouse. This added anxiety is more than the safety or equilibrium of a person can sometimes bear. Such feelings can affect a person's performance on the job and will be discussed later on.

Low Self-Esteem

Low or lowered self-esteem can be severe and destructive. As Coopersmith (1967), who has carried out considerable research among adolescents, suggests:

> Children with low self-esteem are likely to be obedient, conforming, helpful, accommodating, and relatively passive . . . more inclined to be overtly submissive and accepting. . . . [They] have higher levels of anxiety, more frequent psychosomatic symptoms, are rated less effective, and are likely to be more destructive than persons who regard themselves with considerable worth.

This kind of anxiety is one of the major results of lowered self-esteem. At its extreme, anxiety becomes the nervous breakdowns that send people to the hospital, the extreme form of stress that can no longer be coped with, contained, or controlled. In a lesser degree, it can take the form of stomach-knotting worry that prevents people from eating or sleeping properly; it can also drive people to drink. Anxiety can be the nameless panic we are consciously aware of, or it can be a response to a real situation that is beyond our control.

Guilt can also cause anxiety; but not all anxiety is due to guilt. Guilt is concern about worthiness—as a person, as a son or daughter, or as a member of a religious group. Or it can be the feeling of having let God down. People who feel they are sinners, and suffer because of it, have moral and theological problems as well as an anxiety problem. Anxiety can resemble fear, except that there is nothing there to be afraid of. But the feeling is much the same.

Feeling is the central word here. Anxiety is an emotion—hugely subjective and arising out of a myriad of situations and the feelings they engender. Some people feel considerable anxiety because they love their parents too much and are afraid of losing them, while others feel anxiety and guilt because they do not love their parents enough. Anxiety can be an irrational and unreasonable taskmaster. It shapes our actions by pushing us toward behaviors that lessen pain and discomfort and away from behaviors that heighten negative feelings. Anxiety can stem from specific stimuli, or it can be generalized, arising from we know not what and discoloring all our thoughts and feelings. Some forms of anxiety are inescapable, such as the existential ones that surround those facets of existence that cannot be changed—aging or the reality of death.

Anxiety can be felt as something we are conscious of, or it can be largely unfelt and repressed. Even in this latter form, it continues to influence our behavior, feelings, and likes and dislikes as we attempt to lessen it or defend ourselves against it. The problem is that there is no word to adequately represent the unfelt feelings that operate as pressures, tendencies, or energy to influence our behavior without our knowing why. This is the meaning of "unconscious."

People respond to anxiety very differently. Some become quiet and withdrawn; others yell and scream. Some begin drinking; others stop eating. Some people become highly agitated and are always doing something, while others become immobilized.

Lowered self-esteem also tends to produce the alienation, withdrawal, and low expectations that can influence people not to want to compete or to involve themselves with others—resulting in self-recrimination or feelings of wanting to escape. People who are alienated because of low self-esteem find it difficult to make emotional and social contact with others, to achieve the satisfactions derived from being involved in the lives of others. They have a decreased ability to express the emotions they feel or even to feel appropriate emotions. They tend to be defensive and inhibited sexually, or they express their sexuality passively and inappropriately, such as in voyeurism or exhibitionism. Contradictorily, some also become highly aggressive and hostile.

Those who lack the self-validating experiences that result in higher self-esteem tend to be prone to psychosomatic difficulties. Increased internal tension due to anxiety has been shown to be behind many disorders, such as ulcers, asthma, colitis, and hemorrhoids. Alcoholism is frequently the result of low self-esteem, manifested either as an incipient condition alleviated by the intake of alcohol or as the guilt and self-recrimination that result from alcohol abuse.

SELF-ESTEEM AND THE ORGANIZATION

An organization should do nothing to detract from or lessen the self-esteem of its employees. More positively speaking, it should do all it can to provide an environment in which employees can increase the self-esteem they feel. It is difficult to operate on self-esteem directly. Still, many managers feel that if enough positive reinforcement is offered in the form of praise, recognition, encouragement, and minor material rewards, self-esteem will increase, resulting in higher levels of performance and production. Small improvements over brief periods may be attained in this way, but attitudes toward the self are deep, perennial, and not that malleable.

If changes are to be made in people's self-esteem, something has to be set in operation in them that is as strong as the basic experiences that laid down the negative self-attitude in the first place. A serious and enthralling love affair can have an enhancing effect on the ego and on self-esteem, because it is positive and deeply involving. (A love affair tends to force the internalization of positive feelings about the self, because the source of those positive feelings cannot be ignored or passed over.) But deep-seated feelings of inadequacy can make it possible to reject more superficial kinds of positive feedback. The defenses against changing a low self-estimate operate in the interests of stability by encouraging disappointment and maintenance of a vision of the real world that protects the poor self-image.

Few organizations can or do deliver only positive feedback to employees. Even excellent workers occasionally experience failure or decreased performance, some of which is not within their control. Negative situations exist in any environment and are sometimes inescapable. The result can be temporary minor depression or self-pity. Self-esteem is also related to such terms as "inferiority," "self-hatred," "self-pity," and not being "OK" (Harris, 1969). All these feelings appear on a continuum of low self-esteem that ranges from deep self-hatred to cloying but not overly destructive self-pity (expressed by "Everything happens to me").

People with high self-esteem tend to reach out and grasp new experiences, seek challenges, and achieve satisfaction in making contact with the new and the novel. Those with low self-esteem withdraw, become passive and repetitive in their experiencing of the world, and are more dependent on others in their lives than on themselves. Not only can the world influence the attitudes the self holds of itself and the world, but how the world is seen, experienced, and dealt with depends on those same attitudes toward the self. The world we live in is the world we use and need to corroborate our attitudes toward the self at the same time as we are responding to the appraisals the world delivers to us.

Managers and Self-Esteem

Self-esteem is a significant index to the health of a person. Just as high or low performance on the job has an impact on self-esteem and mental health, so self-esteem affects the performance delivered to the organization. Though people with low self-esteem tend to withdraw and be passive, they may also be overbearing and unduly domineering. They may seek power; but once it is gained, they are unable to be sustained by it. This affects their managerial style and performance. A clear one-to-one relationship between low self-esteem and low performance does not exist, but there are a number of reasons for suspecting there is some relationship between them. For example, someone who is low in self-esteem has a sense of being in conscious or unconscious jeopardy most of the time.

These heightened defenses may act as a brake on more positive behaviors, such as providing support to others; or they may act as filters on reality, either to deny the original source of anxiety or to fantasize anxiety-producing elements in the environment.

People with high self-esteem are supportive of others, initiate activity more frequently, are assertive, and are socially skilled. They usually do not distort information; they communicate effectively. These traits contribute significantly to good job performance. Mental health and good performance on the job thus contribute to each other. One need never choose between them, because they are parallel qualities. What is good for mental health is generally good for performance, and what is bad for performance is generally against mental health. An organization in which virtually everyone is failing but claims to have good mental health is a contradiction. So is an organization where everyone's performance is extremely successful but where mental health is thought to be less than good. An inverse relationship between performance and mental health might exist for brief periods of time, but in the long run they tend to catch up with each other.

Employee Self-Esteem

It is surprising how little time most organizations spend in plotting a strategy for the better mental health of employees. The concept of corporate social responsibility will probably be brought to bear on this need eventually. But unless an organization possesses a medical department that includes a lead-taking psychiatric function, managers are likely to give very little time to maximizing employee mental health and minimizing the factors that detract from it.

One might expect that such health-oriented organizations as hospitals, community health centers, and nursing schools would do better in this regard, but there is virtually no evidence that these organizations are more concerned about employee mental health than others. In fact, because of pressure, overwork, and poor management or organization, they are often thought to do less about employee mental health than other kinds of organizations.

Organizations can provide a number of essentials to mental health in the form of a place to be, roles to fulfill, status to be enjoyed, people to relate to and enjoy, jobs that are satisfying, services to take pride in, and successes—all of which can be internalized to raise self-esteem. How frequently we hear people say "I don't know what I would do without my work." Work and the organization can provide a point of stability as well as opportunities and stimuli for creativity, self-expression, and growth. Affiliations with fellow workers can also contribute to fulfilling social needs that drive back feelings of alienation or of being a nobody. On the job, and in feelings about work, each worker can be a somebody who is needed and depended upon by others.

For many people, self-esteem needs are fulfilled only on the job. If these needs were not met, many of them would be even more open to depression, anxiety, and facelessness. We are a nation of people whose identities tend to be reduced to the nature and features of our work and jobs; our identities have been institutionalized to make us mere extensions of our work. However, this should not lead us to reject the healthful benefits of work and job. But it should be borne in mind that jobs and work *alone* cannot make and keep people mentally and emotionally well, just as jobs and work *alone* cannot make them sick.

Human beings are a living tapestry, woven of many strands: psychic and family lives, social and love lives, and religion—as well as work. A corner of this fabric can become unraveled, but if the whole cloth is basically tough, the person can survive, even if the psyche becomes a bit frayed. Battles are less important than surviving the fray. Some people are deeply threatened by their own successes, often because of a poor fit between their low self-estimates and the positive feedback they get from the world. There is no doubt that when one's job or personal relationships are not going well, there are serious consequences for mental health.

The work performed in organizations can provide stimulation, challenge, and excitement. It is difficult to list all the joys of managing and administering, but many managers so enjoy their work physically and mentally that it makes essential contributions to their sense of self, well-being, and happiness. They enjoy the competitiveness, the intellectual opportunities, the problem solving, the political machinations, and the human relations. Underlying a good deal of this pleasure is the fact that much organizational work is creative. Raw materials and thoughts are fashioned into something productive. This is the kind of pleasure that can be felt at all levels of an organization.

While for-profit businesses probably make much more of self-serving profit motives than they should at the expense of noting opportunities for service to others, the issue of altruism is close to the surface in service organizations. It is unfortunate that our culture has so overemphasized competitiveness, individualism, and being a winner that it has made altruism almost subversive, to the point of creating guilt in those who feel it or act on it. Modesty is one thing, but some people deny their own altruism or desire to do good in the face of their own behavior because do-gooders have given doing good a bad name.

Other contributions to mental health are the formal and informal educational benefits gained in organizations. They assist in providing the feelings of confidence and of understanding the world better that accrue to personal growth. Many people who move upward in an organization learn how to contribute more and are then more heavily rewarded with greater status, higher income, and more sophisticated levels of culture and leisure, all of which increase their self-estimates as well as the estimations of others. There are obvious problems of value judgment here; it is not meant to suggest that such people are better per se or that more money is always better than less money. Rather, we are pointing to the experiences and feelings of people who feel and think that life is richer and more satisfying as they progress in their occupations or professions.

Organizations and working effectively in them can reduce anxiety about economic survival, the ability to support dependents, self-worth, and the ability to make a contribution—because they provide a stage on which to strut our stuff. They provide mutual support systems of friends and colleagues who can assist us and see us through in the face of whatever difficulties beset us. Many mental health difficulties can be avoided when organizations are fairminded and conscious of equity issues, when they are effective in matching people to jobs and jobs to people, when they are able to match personal and organizational goals, and when they balance authority with responsibility, delegate properly, and knit the informal, organic side of the organization with its formal one. *A major contribution to mental health is the avoidance of unnecessary threats to it. Perhaps what we are saying is that bureaucracies can be more benign than many which exist today, but much will depend upon how aware the organization is of its own impact on mental health.*

Many critics of organizations make much of organizational impersonality, ruthlessness, and upward-striving competitiveness as factors that alienate one person from another, create anxiety, and foster depression as well as low self-esteem. There is no doubt that this is true in many organizations. But many organizations are also experienced as providing challenge, satisfaction, growth, social and intellectual benefits, material rewards, high status, and even freedom, not to mention escape and diversion. In such organizations, people's lives and beings have not been dehumanized; they have been made whole.

NEGATIVE CONTRIBUTIONS TO MENTAL HEALTH

Organizations are not the sole authors of mental well-being or mental and emotional ill health. But employers can make positive contributions to mental health, and they can make negative ones. In terms of their impact on people, much depends on what is going on in the rest of their lives. A negative impact from the work sector, although felt deeply, can be minor in its effect. But if all is not well in other aspects of someone's life, a negative experience at work can have considerable destructive effect, as anxiety-producing factors pile up and tear down defenses and coping mechanisms. Such factors have different impacts on various character types. For example, people with a tendency toward *hysteria* underreact or overreact, while obsessive-compulsive personalities engage in rituals or involve themselves in ever-deepening spirals of repetitive and conforming behavior in order to barricade themselves against the threatening outside world.

One of the most deeply felt conflicts that produces anxiety is the feeling of being torn between the worlds of job and family in terms of one's time, energy, and commitment. Most people want to give their best to their families, but they also want to excel and make contributions to their jobs or professions. These competing demands frequently give rise to conflict. Energy and time must be carefully allocated if commitments and needs are to be met in both worlds.

In addition to the elementary conflicts of time and energy and commitments, a movement toward either pole at the expense of the other can give rise to considerable guilt about letting the family or job down. Only recently have we come to realize the complexity of balancing and fulfilling the needs of home, marriage, children, and job or profession. As women move deeper into the work world, they inevitably experience the same conflicts and anxieties men always have, as they too attempt to do their best in both worlds. For this reason, the graduate business schools at Harvard and Pittsburgh have included courses on the executive family and mental health in their curricula.

The two-world conflict reflects the feeling of a divided self, the split between organization and personal life. The handling of a life divided between two worlds demands its own repertoire of skills and behavior. The primary technique of defense is roleplaying: one thinks, feels, and behaves one way on the job and another way off the job. This appears to decrease the conflict between the two, but it can also create as many difficulties as it solves. An obvious difficulty is that one is clearly not living an integrated life. Fragmentation of one's life can lead to fragmentation of the self and a decrease in the amount of satisfaction achieved, because neither part of life is allowed to enrich and inform the other. A life lived this way can lead to alienation, as well as to a tendency to keep the commitment to either part shallower than it otherwise might be.

Organizational life, in general, and the business world, in particular, call for and reward behavior that is rational, logical, impersonal, and bureaucratic. Executive behavior is ego-oriented, exhibiting patterns that are reasonable, planned, and rather unemotional, lacking either the warmth or hostility that characterize behavior on the personal level. On the other hand, in one's personal life behavior is usually self-expressive, warm, understanding, supportive, and frequently other-oriented rather than self-oriented. Families and friends tend to emphasize feeling, affection, love, and mutual support.

- How is one to handle the obviously different demands and needs of the two worlds?
- How much of one world can be carried over to the other?
- Does one tell the work self to switch off the cold bureaucrat and turn on the warm, supportive person?
- Does one tend to take some of the warmth of the home to the office and some of the coolness of the office home?
- Does each self flatten out into a composite of the two, forming a neutral self, neither warm nor cold?

All of these strategies are used to minimize the conflict between the two worlds and reduce the anxiety and fragmentation that can result from it. Each strategy can be effective on the conscious level, but just as often the conflict and anxiety are not conscious. Thus, they may always be present and unresolved, in turn debilitating and lessening effectiveness in both worlds.

Differing and competing role demands result in the desire not to contaminate the personal world with the problems and values of the work world as well as the wish to maintain a life for the self aside from work. Most people tend to keep the two worlds separate and function with two behavior repertoires. This can be done consciously by switching off, or it can be done unconsciously, in which case the dichotomy is often denied by the person. If the demands of both worlds become so great that anxiety and conflict build to intolerable levels, usually the personal life is sacrificed to the job, appropriate rationalizations being made. Younger executives, however, appear to be placing more value on their families and their family roles. They work hard and are ambitious, but they have placed conscious limits on the amount of sacrifice they are willing to accept for the job, as well as on the amounts of conflict, guilt, and loneliness they will tolerate from it. When these limits are reached, they are willing to accept less success or even seek jobs that do not demand as much.

Although mobility is less extensive in not-for-profit organizations, the mobility of executives and their families can make them vulnerable to loss of cultural and family roots and support systems, and give them a life that becomes increasingly less satisfying. This gives rise to the growing perception that, if executives and their families can be moved about at the will of an organization, the executives' wishes and their families' needs do not count for much. Such feelings can reduce feelings of autonomy and self-esteem and increase alienation. Though many families do thrive on the novelty and challenge offered by new areas to explore and master, others, like some good wines, do not travel easily.

Organizations can respond to such situations in a number of ways. They can place employees' families higher on their value scales, thus making the families clients of the organization. They can also consciously opt to decrease or end some of the anxiety executives and their families experience by placing transfers, extended work assignments away from home, and educational programs demanding absence from home on a voluntary basis. Organizations should be aware that, in attempting to maximize their efficiency, productivity, and services to their clients, they may be doing it at great cost to the lives and families of their employees. If these hidden costs were included in their accounting systems, many successful organizations might drop dangerously close to the failure line.

Families differ among themselves, and some members cope adequately with problems and threats that destroy others. But some executives and their families clearly ought not to be attached to organizations that demand more allegiance than they can provide. Just as clearly, however, some organizations ought not to demand what some families find burdensome or impossible. Many organizations operate in a manner which suggests that they value themselves over the lives and families of their executives. A case can be made that the family is as valuable as the organization. Some people feel that the person and the family should be valued more highly than the existence and contributions of the organization. Ideally, however, neither should be held hostage for the success of the other

Some people seem to assume that if family life is valued too highly, less energy will be spent on the job and less productivity will result. As far as I know, no such situation has been tested empirically, but I would like to hypothesize that it is just as likely that productivity would increase as anxiety about the family's welfare is reduced. In the latter situation, employees would be motivated to work better and smarter, realizing that they were working for a humane organization rather than for an uncaring bureaucratic one.

ORGANIZATIONAL TRAPS

Many threats to mental health stem from the impersonal and bureaucratic structure of organizations. The size of the organization can be a mental health factor. As organizations grow, function after function becomes bureaucratized and institutionalized, until relationships move from being fluid, informal, and cohesive to being awkward, wooden, and mechanized. Humans seem to benefit most from warm, close, supportive relationships with others. One of the threats of the bureaucratic organization is the impersonalizing of human relationships. Managers and others are often told to disengage themselves from friends as they move up the line, to withhold themselves from relationships and keep cool, lest they be forced to evaluate or criticize a friend. They are told to mistrust attempts by others to establish warm, human relationships or interactions because of the possibility of their being motivated by political reasons.

We need not belabor this point, for the impersonality of many organizations is well known. The reason for this, however, is perhaps less well known, unless one accepts what appears to be the circular rationalization involved in counseling a person toward *coolness* because the organization is single-minded in its thrust toward task achievement and success, and cares less for humans and human relationships. In effect, because an organization is bureaucratic and impersonal, a member of it must be cool, suspicious, and detached in human relationships. And, of course, because an organization is made up of cool, suspicious, and detached people, it is cold, bureaucratic, and mechanized in its interpersonal human behavior. In essence, employees are constantly being told that the organization itself and the goals of the organization are everything—are, in fact, ends— and that the human beings in the organization are means to those ends. When organizations exist to achieve goals that are mere abstractions, such as a given set of numbers on a balance sheet, or "services rendered," or so many "clients served," and not to serve the people inside and outside the organization, bureaucracy is inevitable.

One of the myths about Americans is that we are a warm, friendly, open, "folksy" people who do not stand on ceremony, are indifferent to social class, and dislike formal ritual. Although there are people (and perhaps some regions of the country) about which this is still true, by and large we are a deeply individualistic and competitive people, still vaguely Calvinistic and moralistic, repressed and fearful of intimacy in most of its forms, and very interested in upward social climbing and in exhibiting our material possessions as our forefathers exhibited trophies of the hunt (Slater, 1976).

When put in large, pyramidal organizations where power is exercised hierarchically, people are going to behave competitively, politically, and rationally, emphasizing the acquisition of material goods and aware that power and rewards will go to the strongest competitors. It means that in our organizations and in our lives, we will be tight and repressed emotionally, rather obsessive, slightly hysterical (like the Felix Unger character in Neil Simon's *The Odd Couple*), cool and suspicious of others, competitive and defensive, calculating, assertive and aggressive in human relations, and overly preoccupied with ourselves.

However, because we like to think of ourselves as jolly, fun-loving, gregarious folk, we maintain the myth as we go about affecting these qualities in our human relationships—thus the ambiguity about many North Americans that European visitors often sense. Many Americans will warmly invite someone they have just met at a party to "drop by any time," but they will be quite amazed if the European actually does show up, as a Britisher would on Sunday afternoon, unannounced and uninvited.

Given the hierarchical and pyramidal structure discussed earlier, how do we behave in an open and spontaneous way with bosses who can and do fire people on short notice, with peers who compete with us for the same promotion, and with subordinates who need strong support and guidance and who interpret any expressed weakness or emotionality as incompetence? Obviously, in such organizations, trust among fellow employees will be low and relationships will often be paranoid or adversary. Dependent emotions as such will be repressed (because they render the expresser of the emotion vulnerable to negative interpretation), communication will flow downward but not upward, and decisions will tend to be defensive and uncreative and will involve little risk.

The design of organizations must reflect what we know of human beings and of their capacities and needs for mental health. We cannot counsel people to open up in contemporary organizations when doing so can render them vulnerable to personal, political, and professional attack. Becoming open in a closed organization is a prelude to resignation or termination. In the interests of mental health, an organization must make provision for spontaneity and close, warm, intimate relationships. Support must be given to emotional expression in order to decrease alienation, anxiety, and depression and move in the direction of heightening employee self-esteem. The structure and climate of the organization have to be consonant with such changes, and the organization's values must reflect this commitment to mental health and life-giving (Maccoby, 1972).

It is paradoxical that, as the interfaces between people open up and people become more trustful, self-expression increases. More risks are taken and conflict appears to increase, but adversary relationships tend to decrease simply because the dimensions of conflict are now open and known. The character of such conflict tends to alter quickly, and people soon master the skill of confronting and challenging one another in nondestructive ways within the organizational arena. This approach seems more positive than the one in which conflict exists *sub rosa*, where either side is vicious.

Many managers and mental health authorities are loath to say that organizations make people sick. Organizations, like families, are seldom all good or all bad. It is difficult to measure in a viable and scientific way the positive and negative contributions of organizations, because it is extremely difficult to isolate and control for organizational impact as opposed to the many other factors that affect the lives of people and society. Further, some effects are obvious and conscious, while others are less obvious and operate unconsciously.

Many mental health problems appear to grow out of the dependency inherent in the pyramidal and hierarchical character of organizations. Many forms of dependency are beneficial and even delightful, such as friendship and love. But in some situations, dependency can be destructive, painful, and prevent mature growth. When people are placed in a dependent state in relation to a superior, where they expect support, encouragement, and protection, they can be debilitated by being reminded of feelings they had as children about their parents. Regression to an earlier, childlike state can give rise to hostility, because such a situation is frustrating to an adult. Sometimes the very words used for superiors and mentors (godfather, champion, sponsor, and father) suggest that an employee cannot make his or her way through the maze of organizational politics without the supporting hand of a parental figure.

Transference and displacement also occur, as feelings for our parents and other authority figures are transferred to the powerful authority figures in the workplace. This can make perennial organizational children of employees and can lead to the acting out of feelings of frustration, hostility, and anxiety on the job—much as rebellious children do.

A portion of this process extends to experiencing the self in the organization as a spare part in someone else's machine. When one is a nobody, merely carrying out the desires, wishes, and goals of another, there are feelings of powerlessness and the self is experienced as a sham, an empty façade, a meaningless role lacking definition and selfhood. Simply put, this appears to be a loss of the sense of one's own being, existence, and worth, along with an obvious negative impact on self-esteem. People who begin their organizational lives with a threatened or diminished sense of self are especially vulnerable to this process, and they are damaged more deeply by it than those who have a well-developed sense of self and of self-worth.

Power and Mental Health

As defined here, power is the ability to guide events in the direction of one's own values, interests, and goals. The problem with power in organizations is that it is imperfectly distributed, with more at the top than at the bottom, less for workers than for management, more for males than for females, less for minorities than for others, and more in the hands of the old than the young. But power does not require the holding

of line authority; one can have personal or informal power in organizations, as well as the power of consultative or participative influence.
The option of initiating and sending communications up the organizational ladder and being heard can be a source of considerable power,
though such two-way communication is relatively rare.

Lack of power, on the other hand, produces the there-is-nothing-
I-can-do-about-it syndrome, where powerlessness is felt as being forced
to act in another's interests. Feelings of helplessness, guilt, regression,
withdrawal, and suspension of the self in one's own behavior (detachment
or disengagement) are usual responses to severe expressions of this destructive process. This feeling of helplessness, personified in the statement
"There is nothing I can do about it," is one of the most destructive and
debilitating emotions that one can feel, because it speaks of nothingness,
nonbeing, and counting for nothing in the lives of others.

The corollary to "There is nothing I can do about it" is "They don't
care," one example of which is the organization that fails to take reasonable precautions concerning worker safety. In other organizations, some
employees continue to feel—unnecessarily—that their jobs are in jeopardy, right up to the day of their retirement, and after perhaps some 40
years of service. A lack of employment security occurs when an organization fails to make a firm commitment about the worth of its employees,
probably because of the mistaken fear that employees, hearing of such
a commitment, will let down on the job. *This is a naive view, because pride
of workmanship and commitment to organizations and their goals cannot develop
in situations in which workers fear the loss of the ability to work and to commit
themselves.* The feelings that result from a real or imagined lack of power
can also contribute to feelings of being manipulated and exploited, of
being used. These feelings can also be due to a lack of feedback about
performance or from being obliged to overwork to the detriment of
physical health.

Morality and Mental Health

A seldom-discussed feature of the destructive nature of organizations
is the dilemma created when employees are asked to do what they feel
is unethical or immoral, with the only alternative being to refuse and be
thought of as disloyal. The employee cannot win in such a situation. The
requests usually begin with mundane issues, such as lying about products
or services, pricing or fee procedures, or delivery dates. They then move
on to more serious issues, such as carrying out racist, sexist, ageist, or
unsound ecological policies when the employees' values contradict such
policies.

Many executives and employees have serious and responsible commitments to moral, philosophic, and religious values that make it impossible or existentially painful for them to carry out requests they find objectionable. Some employees are asked to operate institutionalized systems of rebates, bribes, or kickbacks that they find repugnant (Jacoby, Nehimkiss, and Eels, 1978). Engineers are sometimes asked to design inferior products they know are deficient or even dangerous. This is a moral failure, because the organization is doing something that should not be done (or may even be illegal), and there is the fact of moral pain and guilt caused to those whose values are contrary to organizational policy.

This is another instance of the inability of the person to express his or her personhood, a move against human autonomy and in the direction of alienation and powerlessness. Some organizations not only take action against their moral and ethical employees for disloyalty; they also fail to reinforce the humanitarian or highly moral employee who moves to assist human beings at the expense of short-term, organizational goals. An organization that views the moral, ethical, and humanitarian values and commitments of its employees as threats to the firm is itself a threat to employees, their mental health, and society.

The destructive process often extends to making it impossible for employees to express themselves about what has happened either inside or outside the workplace. The talk is almost always seen and experienced as political and threatening, giving rise to paranoia, suspicion, and self-repression. When "I can't talk about it" becomes "Nobody wants to listen or hear," "They don't care" and "I don't care" usually follow. At that point, the system and the person have made the self into an object that feels but cannot express; that hurts and cannot cry out or defend itself against the attacker; that thinks but cannot contribute; that seeks to be moral but cannot act morally.

Institutionalization of the Person

A person placed in an institutionalized situation can feel considerable frustration, anxiety, and anger. Some have these feelings more than others. All of us, however, seem to have a baseline of free-floating anxiety derived from early childhood experiences, to which is added the anxiety we feel as a result of the conditions and experiences of daily life. When baseline anxiety is already high and more anxiety is added by the job situation, the increased level of anxiety can produce symptoms of nausea, stomach upset, diarrhea, loss of appetite, inability to sleep, backaches, headaches, irrational fears, nervous fidgeting, loss of sexual interest, impotence, feelings of being trapped, and excessive blaming of the self, in addition to painful feelings of fear, dread, panic, or loathing that freeze us in our tracks. The latter type of severe anxiety reactions can extend to fainting or amnesia, and are particularly damaging, resulting in hospitalization if experienced for any length of time. The symptom picture resembles the battle fatigue experienced by combat personnel. It is, in fact, the so-called (and badly named) "nervous breakdown," in which we but not our nerves break down—emotionally and physically.

Depression is another response to the debilitating attacks on the person we have been discussing. Together with anxiety, depression constitutes more than 50 percent of all mental difficulty reported. Anxiety, coupled with long periods of work under pressure, appears to be the source of much physical stress, including the oversecretion of hormones that ready us for flight or fight. However, we usually neither flee nor fight, except politically or verbally, so the body is buffeted by the chemical residue of a fight or a retreat that does not take place. These hormones heighten blood rate, increase blood pressure, shut down the digestive processes, and send increased amounts of blood cells, sugar, and oxygen to the muscles of arms and legs.

Chronic stress reactions can contribute to a long list of organic and psychosomatic difficulties, such as migraine headaches, peptic ulcers, hypertension, ulcerative colitis, emphysema, neurodermatitis, asthma, heart attacks, and cancer. Stress, anxiety, and depression, with their attendant debilitating physical symptoms and responses, are killers, whether the final blow is to the self in suicide or the all-too-frequent heart attack. The negative and destructive elements in a person's psychological and external life should be reduced wherever possible in order to reduce pathological reactions.

A major difficulty in contemporary organizations is that many people feel they are incapable of reducing or controlling the amount of stress, anxiety, or depression they experience. Whether this is true or not, these feelings are thought to be in the control of managerial others, who impose demands, evaluate, motivate, hire, and fire. (This is another of the expressions of power discussed earlier.) However, many employees of organizations transcend this experience, internalize their superiors' demands, and take over their own motivation, evaluation, and demand levels. That is, they become institutionalized in another sense, developing into self-starters who probably need to be held back from work, because they are overcommitted to the job to their own detriment as well as that of the organization.

Such people allow themselves to be overpowered by their desire for approval, status, or success to the point of allowing overwork, fatigue, too little sleep, and more pressure and anxiety than is good for them to shorten their lives and, thus, their years of contribution to their organization and society. Their drives can stem from deep-seated feelings of inadequacy that date back to childhood, or from feelings of guilt resulting from a need to make up for past inequities, or from the fact that their lives are unrewarding and unsatisfying. Some people have an intense need for the feelings of legitimacy that success on the job provides. Success of any kind can seldom put such strong feelings to rest; it is very much like the lust for money and material objects; that is, there is never "enough."

Sometimes feelings of lack of power can be traced to poor or inadequate job definition and classification when people are in the dark about what they should be doing. Indefinite assignments, ambiguous orders and directives, little or no feedback as to performance, receiving only negative feedback when performance has also been good, receiving no recognition for contribution to an organization or being unable to feel secure about the future within an organization can contribute to low self-esteem, high anxiety, and frustration.

These feelings can arise before a job is even undertaken, with guilt and lowered self-esteem resulting from the secrecy, subterfuge, and telling of falsehoods that occur during hiring when attempting to shape oneself into the product that appears to be desired. It can be said that no one needs to lie to get a job, but that is contradicted by the feelings of many people. There can be a lack of honesty and candor on both sides of the interview table.

Depersonalization

A lack of power and influence, coupled with institutionalization, frequently results in a combining of the job and person to the point where many people say "I am my job; my job is me." It is very similar to psychological repression. When repression is complete, it is usually not as damaging as less than complete repression. For the person who has been subsumed by the job, guilt and anxiety over a loss of identity would be meaningless. But people who behave as if they have been subsumed by the job or are truly on the verge of it often experience doubt, guilt, anxiety, and frustration. Both of these situations are widespread, especially in middle-management ranks, where competition for escape is rife, the ability to affect policy is slight, and only the power to implement exists.

These negative factors affecting mental health are often exacerbated by the debilitation of physical health. The stronger one's commitment and loyalty to an organization, the more severely one's skills tend to become limited and relegated to one service area, one industry, or even only one or two organizations. One is now occupationally vested and deskilled for other undertakings and may feel obliged to move against the best interests of physical health. Inordinate travel demands coupled with long hours, too little exercise, eating junk food due to lack of time, and overexposure to rich foods and alcohol as part of the ambience of any organization can itself be a contributing factor to the destruction of some personalities. Tiring executives to the extent that they have insufficient energy for family or other personal and social interests can also contribute to poor physical and mental health.

Physical and mental health are reciprocal; each affects the other. For this reason, some businesses and nonprofit organizations support physical-fitness programs and provide annual physical examinations and counseling sessions for high-stress employees, alcoholism programs, and other mental and physical health programs.

WHAT THE ORGANIZATION CAN DO

Mental health is a legitimate concern and should be a constant preoccupation of any organization that values the lives and contributions of its employees. It follows that, if people are to have autonomy and feelings of freedom, they need to be able to affect the policies and regulations that bear on their work and personal lives. This can be done, minimally, by merely listening to them, taking their counsel, and accepting as many of their suggestions as is possible under the circumstances.

It is important that the ethical and moral positions and values of employees be viewed as significant resources. While each employee cannot be satisfied as to what should be done in every situation, none should be asked to do that which is morally or ethically repugnant. Such a position implies that a commitment to the value of human life needs to be made within the organization.

Mental health and what furthers it are not matters of opinion. The assumption that they are is a rationalization that serves those who fear what they may find or who do not want to change procedures that produce negative emotional and psychological effects. Anxiety, frustration, hostility, fear, insecurity, depression, and alienation have well-known effects on physical and mental health. It is true that health professionals do not always agree about what to do about these problems, but they do agree that the problems exist. Much that goes on in organizations damages psyches, lives, and families; of equal importance, it can prevent the happiness and satisfaction that would obtain if changes were made.

There are a number of things organizations should do because they are the correct thing to do. Many organizations do what is right only because it is mandated by law or because of public scrutiny. Some organizations do not do even that. However, movement toward greater humanism and more concern for emotional and mental health is already under way in many organizations, as evidenced by the inclusion of the topic of mental health in this volume.

One can fantasize philosophic issues being raised about invasion of personal privacy by the organization and the larger question of whether an organization ought to concern itself with issues that are over and above its mission. The organization that is concerned about the personal lives of its employees and their legal rights as citizens is probably not the organization that will knowingly overstep the bounds of privacy. Authoritarian organizations, in which people are afraid to speak out, will tend not to be very concerned about the privacy of employees.

CONCLUSION

No conclusive empirical evidence exists about the positive relationship between productivity and good mental health practices in organizations. We do not know that productivity improves when organizations introduce practices that further mental health and expunge those that do not. We also know how to decrease absenteeism, tardiness, and turnover. Most authorities believe that loyalty to the organization is enhanced, that cohesion in groups is improved, and that time spent by management settling conflicts and dealing with complaints is lessened. But an organization that attempts to improve the conditions for mental health *solely* for productivity reasons probably doesn't value or care enough about its employees to carry out such an effort with credibility. Efforts in this area cannot be simulated; they are easily seen through by the employees they affect. Managers or administrators who feel they project concern by compulsively asking "How's the family?" are insincere and proclaim their indifference to others, who perceive it and react directly opposite to the way they are expected to.

Organizations that attempt positive change for the wrong reasons do well to stay in the authoritarian and directive mode they were in originally and remain honest and direct about it. Organizations, managers, and administrators should not attempt to humanize their organizations toward better employee mental health if they are not genuinely interested in the outcome and value of this goal for itself. When organizations truly value the lives and mental health of their members, they can act at the expense of productivity by writing it off as "optimizing."

There is little evidence that productivity goes down when organizations become concerned with the mental health of their employees. However, that family life improves, that more personal satisfaction is gained, that one enjoys one's work, and that society benefits if mental and emotional life is enhanced are all virtually taken for granted by most authorities. At a superficial level, it is the symptoms of mental anguish and suffering that are destructive of relationships—such symptoms as nervousness, displaced hostility, withdrawn depression, agitated depression, violence, and scapegoating (including racism, sexism, anti-Semitism, and ageism). Not only do people go to hospitals in extreme cases, but they *legitimately* miss much work due to their illness and its symptoms; they may cause conflict in committee work, disrupt interpersonal interfaces, and take up much administrative time in their need to be counseled.

The victims of their symptoms too may need to be calmed and "treated," in the personnel sense. Some of this is entirely unnecessary because it can be prevented by the intelligent, well-tempered organization that cares enough to prevent what it can and correct what it should. Such an organization will also move to enhance the mental and emotional lives of employees whenever and however it can. However, organizations that do not face up to the issue will not entertain the possibility that such destructive forces exist within their own boundaries. They will deny the right and responsibility of the organization "to look into the lives of its employees."

It is paradoxical that well-tempered and well-intentioned organizations have probably already done whatever can be done to realize the life-fulfilling and self-validating undertakings described here. The organization that is indifferent to mental and emotional well-being probably will not make such efforts, no matter what information comes its way.

Ask yourself which of these models best represents your own organization.

REFERENCES

Baldwin, James. *Nobody Knows My Name* (New York: Dell, 1961).

Berne, Eric. *What Do You Say After You Say Hello?* (New York: Bantam, 1972), pp. 84–89.

Coopersmith, Stanley. *The Antecedents of Self-Esteem* (San Francisco: W. H. Freeman, 1967).

Ellison, Ralph. *The Invisible Man* (New York: Vintage, 1972).

Gorney, Roderic. *The Human Agenda* (New York: Simon and Schuster, 1972).

Grier, William H., and Price M. Cobbs. *Black Rage* (New York: Bantam, 1969).

Harris, Thomas A. *I'm OK, You're OK* (New York: Avon, 1969).

Jacoby, Neil H., Peter Nehemkis, and Richard Eels. *Bribery and Extortion in World Business* (New York: Macmillan, 1978).

Jennings, Eugene Emerson. *The Executive in Crisis* (East Lansing, Mich.: MSU Business Studies, 1965).

Levinson, Harry. *Executive Stress* (New York: Harper and Row, 1970).

Maccoby, Michael. "Emotional Attitudes and Political Choices," *Politics and Society*, Winter 1972.

Menninger, William C. *Personal Communication (Business Card)*, (Topeka, Kan.: The Menninger Foundation, 1966).

Riesman, David. *Individualism Reconsidered* (New York: Doubleday/Anchor, 1954).

Scarf, Maggie. "Normality Is a Square Circle or a Four-Sided Triangle," *The New York Times Magazine,* October 3, 1971, p. 16.

Schoonmaker, Alan N. *Anxiety and the Executive* (New York: American Management Association, 1969).

Slater, Philip. *The Pursuit of Loneliness,* rev. ed. (Boston: Beacon, 1976).

Szasz, Thomas S. *The Myth of Mental Illness* (New York: Dell, 1969).

Wilson, James A. "Morality and the Contemporary Business System," *Journal of Contemporary Business,* Summer 1975, pp. 31–58.

CHAPTER 5

Managing Change in Organizations

Robert A. Cooke

Editor's Note *Change is often a more complicated process in not-for-profit organizations than in for-profit ones. Change management is applicable to all managerial levels, and all managers must be familiar with it. This chapter focuses on the problem of change and includes some strategies to facilitate change in nonprofit organizations.*

Change in an organization involves alterations or modifications to any of its facets, including its tasks, technology, structures, or components. Forces inside or outside the organization can generate change and also complicate its management.

The author reviews organizational environments, tasks, technology, members, and structures. The external environment is comprised of cultural, political, ecological, economic, and technological forces. Organizations have to adapt to significant changes in any of these sectors and must import energy from the environment to carry out their tasks. Among the tasks performed by nonprofit organizations are transaction, transmission, maintenance, transformation, and creation. These tasks are carried out by members, who are the basic components of organizations. Members accomplish organizational tasks by means of various technologies or techniques. The structures of an organization typically are designed to support the tasks being performed and the technology being used. However, they are not always useful for introducing change in organizations and may have to be supplemented by special change-supporting structures.

The author outlines a strategy for facilitating systemwide change and establishing change-supporting structures. Most of the changes or innovations introduced in organizations are due either to authority or to collective decision making. The availability of structures that support both processes allows an organization to alternate between the two. Collective innovation decision processes can be facilitated by establishing new role and communication structures to support them and by

154

providing members with the skills necessary to use these structures. A program designed to do this for schools is described; managers can use its framework to create programs suited to their organizational needs.

The author also describes innovation processes among individual members of an organization. He discusses innovation attributes and individual characteristics that may inhibit change and suggests various tactics to overcome these obstacles. A basic model of innovation at the individual level suggests a cyclical process, consisting of the states of knowledge, attitudes, and behavior linked by learning, attitude formation, and decision-making subprocesses. Managers can use tactics directed toward each of these subprocesses to increase the likelihood that members will implement innovations. For example, managers can make continuing education an integral part of members' work roles when lack of education and poor conceptual skills inhibit change.

Professionals and specialists are the ones most likely to acquire knowledge about innovations. Managers can increase specialization to promote change in their organizations. If possible, complex innovations should be broken down into less complicated components, since complex innovations may be difficult to understand. Defensiveness and selective perception by members can interfere with the adoption of innovations. This can be counteracted by demonstrating how innovations work and providing more task feedback. Organizational members are likely to have low expectations about innovations that are costly in terms of time and money and that require substantial physical and mental effort. Innovations can be highly risky, uncertain, or low in compatibility with members' qualifications and objectives. The author identifies tactics that managers can use to reduce these problems.

Innovations cease to be attractive after a specific time. Therefore, managers should be sensitive to such terminal points and prepared to facilitate the timely introduction of change. Employee feelings of role overload, lack of autonomy, and responsibility inhibit change. Creating organizations conducive to change can overcome some of these problems.

This chapter focuses on the problem of change and on some strategies that can be used by managers to facilitate change in nonprofit organizations. The problem of change is a recurring one. It is therefore likely to be highly important to managers and administrators of hospitals, schools, social service agencies, and other nonprofit organizations. Change may be required on an almost routine basis—for example, as the clients and community being served place new demands on the organization, as innovative ways of accomplishing the work of the organization are developed, and as the needs and expectations of members change over a period of time. Members, clients, and the community may all feel a certain sense of ownership over the organization and expect it to be responsive to their changing needs.

Pressures for change can be strong and may require great adaptability on the part of the organization. At the same time, however, various factors can make it difficult to successfully initiate and implement change. Because so many different groups have a stake in nonprofit organizations, it can be impossible to get all the relevant parties to agree that a particular change should be made. Change efforts can be complicated further due to the fact that the services provided by these organizations tend to be complex and difficult to evaluate. Managers may not be able to convince members that the organization's performance needs to be improved and that a change has to be made; members may resist change on the grounds that it is risky and unnecessary. While nonprofit organizations experience strong pressures for change, they also experience strong pressures for stability.

In some organizations, forces for stability prevail. These organizations may be managed and structured in ways that render them incapable of responding to pressures for change. Their managers may go to great lengths to define unambiguous roles for members and make clear the lines of vertical communication and authority. These and other structures can provide an important base on which members can rely to carry out their work in an orderly and efficient way, but they may do little to support, and may even impede, efforts to introduce change and innovation. Highly stable and predictable organizations can thus become extremely efficient in carrying out a task no longer relevant to the community or highly proficient in using an outdated technology.

In other organizations, however, the forces for change as well as those for stability are accommodated. The structures of these organizations provide a base not only for the efficient performance of the organization's work but also for change and innovation. This chapter focuses on the nature of these change-supporting structures as well as on some of the strategies and tactics used by the managers of these organizations to promote change on an ongoing basis.

Basic concepts are presented here that are likely to prove useful to managers in understanding and dealing with the problem of change in their organizations. Organizational environments, tasks and technologies, and members and structures are reviewed in terms of how they give rise to the need for change and, at the same time, complicate the management of change. A model of change processes at the organizational level is presented, and a strategy for facilitating these systemwide processes and for establishing change-supporting structures is outlined. Innovative processes at the level of individual organizational members are then described. The attributes of innovations and the individual characteristics that present obstacles to change are identified, and some tactics for overcoming these obstacles are suggested.

ORGANIZATIONS AND CHANGE

Change in an organization involves an alteration or modification in the tasks, technology, structures, or components of the system. Change implies innovation when the alteration or modification involves something that is perceived to be new by an organization's members. Regardless of whether innovation is involved, a change in an organization is likely to reverberate throughout the system. For example, changes in the basic tasks performed by an organization are almost inevitably accompanied by changes in technology. Changes in tasks and technology usually require alterations to the structures of the organization, including changes in the patterns of authority and communication as well as in the roles of members. These technological and structural changes can, in turn, necessitate change on the part of members—the basic components of the organization. Members may have to acquire additional knowledge and develop new skills to perform their modified roles and work with the new technology (Leavitt, 1965).

Changes in organizational tasks, technologies, structures, and components are often introduced in response to changes outside the system. Every nonprofit organization exists as part of a larger suprasystem; changes elsewhere in the suprasystem (that is, in the environment) can generate external pressure for change and innovation. Organizations obtain input from the larger system that includes members, information, funds, and materials. If they fail to adapt to changes in the environment, this input may no longer be forthcoming. Thus schools, hospitals, social service agencies, and other nonprofit organizations must respond to changes in community norms, the legal system, and the state of technology if they are to survive as viable social systems.

Forces within the organization can generate internal pressures for change. For example, the members of an organization may be dissatisfied with a particular program because it is difficult to work with and does not seem to be responsive to the needs of the clients being served. Unless change is introduced, these members may reduce the amount of energy they put into their work or may leave the organization altogether. Thus organizations must respond to internal as well as external pressures if they are to maintain their resources and operate efficiently. Unfortunately, the same factors that generate the need for change also can render change more difficult to initiate and implement. When there is uncertainty regarding the effectiveness of a program, the effectiveness of alternative programs also may be uncertain. Managers may therefore have trouble identifying a viable alternative and gaining members' acceptance of a new program.

Three major principles of relevance to managers are emphasized throughout this chapter:

1. Change is likely to involve all facets of the organization.
2. Forces both within and outside the organization can generate pressures for change.
3. The same forces that give rise to the need for change can also complicate the management of change in the organization.

The External Environment

Virtually everything within an organization is directly or indirectly affected by forces beyond its boundaries. These external forces can be viewed by managers as comprising the cultural, political, ecological, economic, and technological sectors of their organization's environment (Katz and Kahn, 1978). Certain nonprofit organizations are in a relatively powerful position vis-à-vis these environmental sectors; they may be able to effect changes in some sectors and resist changes in others. Nevertheless, even the most powerful organizations have to adapt to significant changes in these sectors.

The *cultural sector* represents the value patterns of the larger society and communities within which the organization operates. While value patterns change only gradually and the adaptation of organizations to such changes may be slow, the potential impact of values on organizations is significant. Even churches, which strive to define and promote value patterns, respond to cultural changes and alter their stances on issues such as the role of women in the church hierarchy. Educational organizations also respond to changes in values by adding new programs and courses and defining new roles for students.

Changes in the *political sector* reflect changes in the cultural and other sectors and can promote innovation in organizations in a variety of ways. Recent legislation or court rulings permit organizations to undertake new activities or get things done in new ways, as exemplified by changes in statutes that allow teacher associations and other public employee unions to negotiate with employers. New laws can promote change even when they are only indirectly related to particular innovations. Legislation permitting long-term contracts between municipalities and private firms, for example, facilitates the adoption of new technologies such as resource recovery systems.

Changes in the political sector also can *require* change in organizations. Equal-opportunity laws lead to changes in hiring practices; environmental laws require technological changes; and legislation regarding the rights of consumers brings about a variety of changes in organizations. Changes in the tasks, technology, and structures of public nonprofit agencies can be required in even more direct ways by new legislation. The services offered by the local offices of the Social Security Administration change significantly each time new legislation is enacted to expand the responsibilities of the system.

Changes in the *ecological environment* can also lead to important changes in organizations (Katz and Kahn, 1978). Extreme changes in the weather can turn a drought-control agency into a flood-control agency. As suggested by this example, ecological factors are most likely to affect nonprofit organizations via the political sector. Many of the changes introduced by transit authorities, drain commissions, parks departments, and natural resource agencies are directly attributable to legislation based on ecological considerations.

Advances in the *technological or information sector* can promote changes in organizations. New developments in computer software represent changes in the technological environment of research institutions, government agencies, and other nonprofit organizations. Programmed instruction in education, telemetry in emergency medicine, and pyrolysis in solid-waste management are examples of changes in the technological environments of schools, hospitals, and municipalities, respectively. Advances in the technological environment provide organizations with the opportunity to innovate, perform their tasks more efficiently, and provide clients with higher-quality services. But adoption of technological innovation is not always voluntary; sometimes organizations must adapt to the technological environment in order to compete successfully or to comply with legal constraints.

Organizations also operate within an *economic (input-output) environment*. All organizations—including nonprofit ones—face competitive markets and competition for their members' energy, raw materials, and information. Although hospitals typically are not profit-making institutions, a community hospital may find itself competing with a church-operated hospital for patients. Research institutions openly compete with one another for government contracts and grants; colleges and universities compete for students and faculty members; and the post office competes with private carriers for parcels to be delivered. Public elementary and secondary schools, though fairly well protected from the forces of competition, compete with other public agencies for local tax dollars. Even voluntary associations, social clubs, and churches compete for members and for monetary contributions. The economic environment of nonprofit organizations, while not necessarily the same as that of for-profit institutions, can create the need for organizational change and innovation. Competitive pressures can make it necessary for an organization to alter its tasks, adopt new technologies, or change its structures to keep its clientele and maintain its funding base.

Task and Technology

Much of the energy received by organizations from their environments is used to carry out a particular task or set of tasks. Organizational tasks can be viewed in terms of the services being offered or the product being produced. The tasks of nonprofit organizations involve such productive activities as educating students, curing patients, rehabilitating prisoners, conducting aeronautical research, or performing dramatic plays. In carrying out these tasks, organizations employ a technology that is usually designed to accomplish the task rationally and efficiently. Both task and technology are likely to be the focus of change and innovation in non-profit organizations.

Organizational tasks. The tasks performed by nonprofit organizations are diverse and difficult to classify concisely and comprehensively. At least some of these tasks can be placed in one or more of the cells shown in Table 5–1. This table distinguishes between the general nature of the task and its focus. The predominate nature of an organization's task can be:

1. *Transaction,* or negotiation or mediation between two or more individuals, groups, or other systems (credit unions, for example, mediate between people who want to save money and people who want to borrow money).
2. *Transmission,* including communication, dissemination, and transportation (public broadcasting networks transmit educational programs to local television stations).
3. *Maintenance,* or preservation, storage, or custodial functions (police departments maintain law and order).
4. *Transformation,* involving some change or alteration of another system (Lamaze associations work with parents-to-be to better prepare them for childbirth).
5. *Creation,* or the development of something new (the executive branch of government creates new commissions, agencies, and departments).

These tasks can focus on at least three different kinds of systems:

1. *Nonliving systems* include machinery, raw materials, certain elements of the ecological system, and money. The postal service transmits mail; museums maintain works of art; the municipal drain commission transforms sewage; and artists work with clay, paint, or other materials.

2. *Living systems* include individuals, groups, organizations, and communities. Employment agencies carry out transactions between individuals and organizations as they place people in jobs; transit authorities move people; nursing homes maintain the well-being of senior citizens; schools educate and change students; and political organizers create new committees to support candidates.

3. *Abstract systems* include scientific knowledge, abstract forms of art, legal systems, and other types of information. Zoning boards interpret local ordinances in mediating between developers and local residents; extension services disseminate new information to potential users; and R&D labs develop basic research findings into practical or applied knowledge.

Many of the changes introduced in nonprofit organizations are subtle and involve only minor alterations in the tasks performed by the system. Sometimes, however, they are dramatic and, in terms of Table 5–1, move the organization from one cell to another. For example, at one time, prisons were responsible primarily for maintaining offenders in custody and segregating them from society. Today, many of these institutions are

TABLE 5–1. *Some tasks performed by nonprofit organizations.*

Nature of the Task	Focus of the Task		
	Nonliving Systems	*Living Systems*	*Abstract Systems*
Transaction	Social Security	State employment placement agencies	Arbitrators; zoning boards
Transmission	The postal service	Local transportation authorities	Agriculture extension services
Maintenance	Public libraries; museums	Prisons; nursing homes	Data banks
Transformation	Sewage and drain commissions	Schools; hospitals; mental health clinics	Research and development laboratories
Creation	Artists	DNA research laboratories; executive branches; political organizations	Basic research organizations; performance groups; composers; writers.

heavily involved in rehabilitating the inmates and preparing them to reenter society. This is a major change—from a maintenance to a transformation task. An equally radical change in task has been experienced by many state unemployment agencies and commissions. Initially involved only in dispersing monetary benefits to the unemployed (transaction), these agencies have become active in placing clients in jobs and in developing the skills and abilities of these clients (transformation). Changes of this kind typically are made in response to changes in the environment.

Changes in the political and cultural sectors, or competition for resources and clients, may make it necessary or desirable for an organization to redefine its task or to do more for its clients. Redefined and expanded services generally lead to a higher degree of complexity in the organization's task, and therefore require concomitant changes in the organization's technology.

Organizational technology. Changes in technology involve modifications in the basic techniques and equipment used to accomplish the tasks of an organization. Technological change can involve changes in members' jobs, in the way work flows through the organization, and in the interdependence of members' work efforts.

Technological change may be introduced as the result of a decision to alter the task of the organization. Many prisons, for example, have adopted new techniques (behavioral modification and educational technologies) to carry out the task of rehabilitation. Technological change may also be introduced directly in response to changes in the competitive or technological sectors of the environment. Teachers in a secondary school may implement a contract or independent learning system for advanced math students. Agents in a law enforcement department may use new electronic equipment to communicate with other agencies. Or counselors in a free clinic may try out the latest therapy techniques in their group sessions. While technological changes do not always imply a modification of the task being carried out, they usually lead to changes with respect to the efficiency, quality, or potential magnitude of task accomplishment.

A technological change that is introduced to accomplish a more complex task can greatly increase the amount of uncertainty members must deal with in carrying out their work. The example of a state unemployment agency illustrates how such a change can increase uncertainty. If the agency is engaged exclusively in paying out benefits to the unemployed, its members can carry out this relatively straightforward task through the use of standardized procedures. Most of the required transactions are routine, and guidelines can be developed to handle nonroutine cases. Individual clients can then be handled by individual members independently, and the activities of these members can be coordinated with rules and regulations. However, if the agency takes on the additional tasks of placing clients in new jobs and training them for these jobs, the technology and the flow of work through the system become more complex. New techniques are needed to assess the work interests and capabilities of the clients, training programs have to be introduced, and mechanisms for matching clients with prospective employers must be put into place. These new techniques can create some uncertainty, with their effectiveness remaining ambiguous and their appropriateness varying for different types of clients. Furthermore, the efforts of the various members carrying out testing, training, and placement are likely to become highly interdependent and difficult to coordinate solely through the use of rules and regulations. The members responsible for training would have to adjust to the activities of those responsible for testing and placement, and those responsible for placement would have to adjust to the activities of those doing the training. These complex interdependencies generate additional uncertainty that must be dealt with by members. Members must be prepared to change their behavior and organizational structures must be modified if this uncertainty is to be absorbed. The kinds of task and technological changes in the above example almost inevitably require changes in the organization's structure and components.

Structure and Components

Organizations are composed of components—that is, members with particular qualifications—who are coupled or interconnected by means of various structures (see Georgopoulos, 1972). Communication, role, authority, and other structures can be established by managers, or they can evolve naturally and gradually from interactions among members which recur over time. In either case, the characteristics of the structures that emerge are determined in part by an organization's task and technology.

Organizational structures. Organizations that perform transaction or transmission tasks and deal mainly with nonliving systems are often traditionally structured. For example, agencies directly involved in collecting taxes can function most efficiently and fairly when they are structured bureaucratically. Clear-cut rules and regulations, though they are sometimes complex and unwieldy to administer, enable the agency to deal with taxpayers in a somewhat consistent and defendable manner. The roles of members can be clearly specified, and their activities can be coordinated by means of a centralized authority structure and a vertical, predominately downward communication structure.

As the tasks and technologies of organizations become more complex and uncertain, traditional structures become less appropriate. These structures may not be adequate for organizations involved in transformation or creation activities or organizations whose tasks focus directly on living or abstract systems. The tasks of schools, hospitals, research organizations, and mental health clinics tend to be too complex to carry out and coordinate solely on the basis of rules and regulations. Individual members must use discretion to solve a variety of unusual problems. Members must also adjust their activities to other members and to the reactions of individual clients to the techniques being used. Roles cannot be completely specified, vertical communication structures may be inadequate for communication, and a centralized authority structure may limit the discretion of those members closest to the work problems. Flexible roles, decentralized authority structures, and horizontal communication structures may be needed if these organizations are to perform their tasks effectively.

The kinds of structures most appropriate for an organization depend on the nature of the tasks being performed and the technology being used. The above-mentioned state agency for the unemployed would have to establish new structures (such as decentralized authority structures) in order to cope with the uncertainty of its new technology and properly carry out its expanded tasks. Similarly, managers of a local transportation authority would have to make structural changes when introducing minibuses. Minibuses are designed to pick up and drop off passengers at the time and location of their choice; the routes followed by the drivers must be constantly rescheduled to accord with passenger needs. Planning rather than standardization must be used to coordinate the activities of drivers, two-way communication between drivers and dispatchers must be maintained, and drivers' activities must remain flexible and readily subject to change.

Other factors besides task and technological changes can promote alterations in an organization's structure. Cultural changes in the environment may require that the organization become more decentralized and participative, or changes in the needs and attitudes of members and clients can necessitate modifications. Structural changes to promote participation have been made in such diverse organizations as unions, political parties, schools, and voluntary associations to satisfy the needs of members and to better reflect the democratic norms of the society.

Organizational components. Members are the basic components of all organizations. They provide a critical source of energy for performing the work of the organization, for solving systemwide problems, and for implementing changes and innovations. Members bring knowledge and skills to the organization and are recruited on the basis of these qualifications. The nature and focus of the tasks being performed, as well as the organization's structure and technology, define the qualifications required for membership. People with sophisticated skills and specialized knowledge generally are needed when organizational tasks involve transformation or creation and when these tasks focus on living or abstract systems. These people are also needed in organizations characterized by sophisticated technologies, regardless of the task performed.

Even when the qualifications of members are high, a modification of task or technology can require additional skills and knowledge. Unless new people with the necessary qualifications are hired, managers have to find ways to provide members with the skills and knowledge required by a new program or procedure. A school changing from traditional to open classrooms has to provide its teachers with the new skills needed for the different learning activities. Assuming that members are able to absorb new knowledge, they are then in a position to modify their behavior in ways consistent with the new task or technology. However, additional knowledge is not always sufficient to change behavior.

The probability that members will change their behavior is largely determined by their attitudes toward the new task, technology, or structure. As members gain knowledge about a proposed change, they form attitudes toward it that can lead them to accept or reject the change. Unfavorable attitudes toward an innovation may develop if members believe they are not capable of implementing it successfully, or negative attitudes may emerge if they feel that the innovation will reduce the quality of services provided to clients or will lead to some other undesirable outcome. In either case, members would not be motivated to modify their behavior in ways consistent with the proposed change. Organizational change, therefore, depends not only on behavioral change on the part of members but also on basic changes in their beliefs, attitudes, and values.

The Management of Change

Significant changes in organizations tend to involve many facets of the system. The tendency for change to be pervasive can make its management difficult. Change management is further complicated by the fact that many characteristics of nonprofit organizations and their environments create not only pressures for change but also pressures for stability. In view of these problems, it is unlikely that managers can rely on any single strategy to facilitate change. Changes necessitated by external factors present their own kinds of complications and should be managed differently from change necessitated by internal factors.

External factors and change management. The environment can determine the extent to and frequency with which changes are needed in an organization. An organization operating in a highly dynamic environment has to change constantly to adapt to its instability. Rapid and continuing changes in, for example, the demand for an organization's services or product can make it necessary to modify the tasks performed by the organization on an ongoing basis. An organization that operates in a highly complex environment has to introduce changes more frequently than does an organization operating within a relatively simple one. Complexity implies high interdependence with many sectors of the environment and with many systems (including groups, organizations, and individuals) within each of these sectors. The multiple interdependencies increase the probability that external changes will affect the organization.

Although environmental complexity and instability require organizational change and adaptation, they are likely to complicate the management of change. An innovation introduced in response to competitive forces or to advances in the technological environment may not be consistent with the demands placed on the organization by other sectors. Educational innovations might not be adopted because they are at variance with community values (cultural sector); resource recovery systems may be rejected by municipalities because of legal constraints (political sector); and a new piece of medical equipment may be resisted by administrators because it is already owned by too many other hospitals in the community (input-output sector). The implementation of such changes by managers requires changing the environment as well as the organization.

Many other environmental characteristics, besides instability and complexity, have implications for organizational change. The conservatism of a community can make it difficult to introduce curriculum changes in a school. Similarly, the low salience of competition for inputs may make it difficult for educational administrators to justify innovations, even if the proposed changes might improve their school's effectiveness. The environment can contain complex and sometimes contradictory implications for an organization—change may be mandated by one sector and prohibited by another. Managers not only have to monitor the environment and identify the need for change; they must also identify innovations that are consistent with the requirements of all sectors.

In large organizations, externally generated change can be handled more effectively by teams than by individual managers. A change team can be composed of representatives from the research and development department, the legal staff, the finance and public relations groups, and other departments directly involved in dealing with the various sectors of the external environment. The team approach can be useful also in small organizations, including those where specialists in boundary-spanning positions are not available. A group of people can bring more energy to a change effort than can an individual manager; this additional energy can then be directed more effectively toward the relevant sectors of the environment.

While the team approach appears to be appropriate for organizations of all sizes, it is likely to be most useful in organizations that have complex and dynamic external environments. This approach alone, however, is not sufficient to facilitate change in all types of organizations; complementary strategies are needed, particularly in those organizations where internal factors generate pressure for change.

Internal factors and change management. The tasks and technologies of nonprofit organizations can be substantially more complex and uncertain than those of for-profit organizations. Many organizations that operate on a not-for-profit basis carry out tasks that center directly on people; the clientele of these human-service delivery systems often are heterogeneous and change constantly. The tasks frequently involve transformation, and the technologies used may be somewhat ambiguous with respect to their reliability and appropriateness for different clients. Children in schools differ significantly from one another in terms of their needs and capabilities and thus respond differently to educational technologies. Some of the patients served by a mental health clinic may respond less positively than others to particular therapeutic approaches. Given the instability and complexity of the clientele of such organizations, pressures for change are likely to arise from within the organization. Similar internal pressures for change may arise in organizations where tasks focus on abstract systems. This does not necessarily mean that these organizations face more pressure than do organizations whose tasks focus on concrete systems, but it does suggest that they may face more internally generated pressure for change and innovation.

Internal pressures can be quite strong due to the characteristics and backgrounds of the people who carry out the work of nonprofit organizations. Hospitals, social service agencies, and schools generally have well-educated professional staffs who are able to identify problems that require innovative solutions, offer information about relevant changes, and disseminate the information to others in the organization.

The characteristics of nonprofit organizations and their members that create pressures can also make change and innovation difficult to accomplish. There is evidence that professionalized personnel are reluctant to accept certain types of changes (Newman and Wallender, 1978). The complex tasks performed by nonprofit organizations and the tendency of these tasks to focus directly on people can also complicate change processes. Changes must be accepted not only by the people who carry out the work of the organization but also by the clients or consumers of the organization's product or service. To the extent that the clients themselves are transacted, transmitted, or transformed, their acceptance of changes becomes more critical and problematical. A new curriculum introduced by a community college cannot be successful unless it is accepted by the students as well as by the faculty.

Change and innovation may also be made difficult by the uncertainty that characterizes the technologies of nonprofit organizations. A new rehabilitation program may not be accepted in a prison because it cannot be demonstrated that it works; a new treatment approach may be rejected by a drug clinic because its long-term impact on abusers is difficult to discern; and a new medication may be rejected by the staff of a hospital because of erratic side effects.

Managing change is complicated further by the complex internal interdependencies of nonprofit organizations. When the activities of members are highly interdependent, a change implemented by one member is likely to have repercussions throughout the system. Even an innovation that initially seems to affect only a few members can affect many others; its successful implementation may depend on its acceptance by all members of the organization.

The structures of nonprofit organizations also can complicate and inhibit change. The initiation of change can be particularly difficult in organizations with highly specified roles and centralized authority and communication structures. While these structures may provide a base for efficiently carrying out some tasks, they are not adequate for change and adaptation. Members may view the organization as being highly inflexible and may believe that the probabilities of successfully changing the system are slim. They therefore may not bother to identify problems or suggest relevant changes. Even when they are motivated to initiate a change, they may find that they have neither the contacts nor the influence to get other members interested in the idea.

It is easier to initiate change in organizations that have loosely defined roles, horizontal communication structures, and relatively decentralized authority structures. But members here may have trouble seeing changes through. The implementation of a change involves a great amount of uncertainty. When this uncertainty cannot be reduced with well-defined roles and clear lines of authority, members may become frustrated and abandon the change effort.

Regardless of the nature of an organization's work structures, they are usually not entirely appropriate for supporting change and innovation and have to be supplemented by other structures that provide a base for adaptation. One set of structures is the management change team mentioned earlier as an approach to responding to external pressures for change. The team approach, however, may not be adequate for responding to internal pressures for change and overcoming internal obstacles.

When the need for change arises from within the system, those members closest to the work of the organization may be in the best position to identify the need and suggest appropriate changes. But these members are invariably excluded from the early stages of the change process in organizations where change can be introduced only at the top. Managers can rectify this problem in at least three ways. First, they can try to increase members' participation in administrative change decisions. For example, representatives of the members who carry out the work of the organization might be asked to serve on the change team. Second, managers can use various strategies to promote change initiation by individual members of the organization. (Some of these strategies are reviewed in the final section of this chapter.) Third, managers can establish change-supporting structures to provide a base for collaborative problem solving and change initiation by members. These change-supporting structures are particularly appropriate for nonprofit organizations, where highly qualified members carry out complex tasks by means of uncertain technologies. Examples of the kinds of structures that can support collaborative change processes are discussed in the following section.

ORGANIZATIONAL CHANGE

Most of the changes and innovations introduced in organizations, aside from those implemented by individual members on an optional basis, are the result of either authority or collective decision processes. *Authority innovation decision processes* start at the top of the organizational hierarchy, where a decision is made to implement a change, and proceed down to those members who are responsible for carrying out the change (Hage and Aiken, 1970). *Collective innovation decision processes* are those in which the members expected to carry out a change are the ones who decide whether or not it should be implemented (Rogers and Shoemaker, 1971). Both authority and collective processes can be used to introduce change in nonprofit organizations.

Authority processes are used in most organizations to solve such problems as allocating resources; with only minor modifications, the same structures that support these problem-solving processes can also be used to support authority innovation decision making. While it may be relatively easy in many organizations to create a management change team for introducing innovations through authority processes, collective innovation decision processes may be less consistent with the existing structures of the organization. These processes are based on horizontal communication and shared influence and place responsibility for organizational decisions in the roles of all members. Similar structures appear to be available in organizations such as hospitals for carrying out and coordinating work activities, but these work structures may not be entirely appropriate for collective innovation decision making and tend not to be used for it. Managers of many nonprofit organizations, therefore, may have to establish new structures or at least modify existing structures to provide a base for collective innovation decision processes.

A normative or ideal model of the collective decision process is illustrated in Figure 5–1. The process begins with the identification and diagnosis of problems by organizational members on a collaborative basis. The collective nature of these *evaluation* activities requires organizational members responsible for implementing decisions to be either directly or indirectly involved in identifying problems and situations requiring change. The evaluation stage involves defining the appropriateness of organizational objectives and tasks in light of environmental factors. It can also involve assessing the appropriateness of the technology being used, the adequacy of organizational structures and processes, and the fit between structure, task, and technology.

Solution generation involves the identification of possible changes and potential solutions to organizational problems. Innovative as well as more traditional alternatives can be proposed and considered at this stage. After a preferred solution is identified, the proposed changes are *internally diffused* to other organizational members who are interested in the problem or who might be affected by the change. Solutions can be communicated to relevant people outside the system as well as to those organizational members who were not directly involved in evaluation or solution generation activities. This stage promotes the participation of all inter-

FIGURE 5–1. *The collective decision process.*

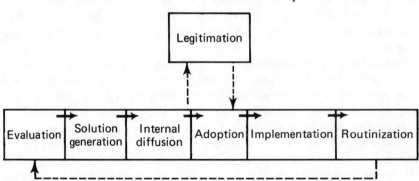

ested parties in decision making, provides those most directly involved in it with feedback from others with different perspectives, and generates ideas for modifying and improving the solution in terms of its quality and acceptability.

At the *legitimation* stage, the proposed solution is communicated to and, when necessary, submitted for the approval of administrators, policymakers, and others with the formal or legal authority to sanction a change decision. The acceptance of the solution in its final form (after possible modification by administrators) reflects the *adoption* of the change. At this point, plans are made for implementing the change and preparing the system for the introduction of the new tasks, technology, structure, or program.

The change is put into practice at the *implementation* stage, during which organizational members make the transition from the old way of doing things to the new way. *Routinization* is the process of identifying and solving problems arising from the change as well as the merging of the new program with existing programs and procedures. At this point, the change is evaluated and the collective decision process begins again.

The Need for Collective Processes

The need for collective innovation decision processes is likely to be more pressing in some types of nonprofit organizations than others. Nevertheless, a minimal amount of collective decision making may be required in all organizations because of the inherent limitations of authority processes. The managers responsible for initiating authority decisions are poorly positioned within the organization for identifying technical problems and suggesting relevant innovations. Managers frequently do not come into direct contact with these problems and, because upward communication in hierarchical organizations is often less than adequate, they may not have complete information about them. Subordinates have been known to distort and repress information that might affect them adversely and filter out information that is potentially objectionable to superordinates. In organizations that perform complex and uncertain tasks, the resulting information gap can seriously restrict the ability of managers to identify the need for change and propose relevant alternatives. The members performing the basic work of the organization, however, may have the required information and may as a group be better able to communicate upward information regarding problems and possible solutions.

Managers of nonprofit organizations may not be in the best political position to initiate certain types of changes. Because their organizations are responsive to the pressures of many other organizations and groups, the administrative function of these managers tends to become one of "maintaining a working equilibrium of at best antagonistically cooperative forces" (Spindler, 1963, p. 42). Managers may therefore find it difficult to take a consistent stand or promote certain changes. Teachers, nurses, social workers, and other people who are not responsible for maintaining equilibrium may be in better positions to initiate changes and innovations. While change initiation through collective processes generates another set of pressures with which managers must contend, such pressures can replace internal forces for stability and help managers make their organizations more proactive.

Authority processes are limited also in failing to tap the problem-solving and change initiation capabilities of organizational members at all levels. This shortcoming can be particularly costly in the nonprofit organizations whose members have direct access to information about innovations, are committed to the goals of the system, and are favorably disposed toward change. By centralizing change decisions, authority processes do not take advantage of all the information about innovations that may be available in the organization. These processes also fail to capture the energy of members who are highly committed to the objectives and tasks of the organization. This energy, which could be used to identify and solve system problems, may be particularly abundant in organizations comprised of volunteers, dedicated professionals, and persons committed to public service. Untapped energy might also be used to attain a change mass—the impetus needed to implement change. In organizations where members are favorably disposed toward innovation, a change mass can be obtained most effectively through collective processes.

Another problem concerns members' satisfaction with and acceptance of authority decisions. Numerous studies have shown that the acceptance of decisions is positively associated with participation in the decision-making process. When decisions to change are made through authority processes, members may not fully understand the reasons for the change, may not be highly motivated to carry out the change, and may discontinue using the new program or procedure even if they initially implement it.

Dissatisfaction with changes introduced by managerial directives can be especially strong when professionals hold dominant roles in an organization. Professional methods and standards can impose rigidity when adjusting to environmental changes (see Newman and Wallender, 1978), and innovations introduced through authority channels are frequently likely to be dismissed by those expected to carry them out. Collective processes offer members a mechanism for modifying new programs and procedures in ways that are consistent with their standards. While such modifications can decrease an innovation's responsiveness to a particular problem or need, they can increase the likelihood that members will implement it.

Change can be facilitated if collective as well as authority decision processes are used in an organization. The availability of both collective and authority processes implies a degree of flexibility missing in organizations that use one process to the exclusion of the other. The availability of structures which support both processes allows the organization to alternate between collective and authority decision making as needed. For example, authority processes are needed when there is little time available to decide on a change, because collective decision making requires meetings and other time-consuming activities. When some time is available, however, collective processes can be more appropriate, particularly if there is uncertainty regarding how the problem is to be solved and the type of change to be made.

The appropriateness of collective versus authority processes also depends on the innovation or change required. Collective processes can be particularly useful when a problem requires a pervasive solution that involves changes throughout the organization. The active involvement and input of all members may be needed to successfully implement this kind of solution. Changes that are relevant to the work of members and require a high level of commitment on their part should be initiated collectively. By affording members an opportunity to influence change, collective processes increase the probability that members will feel satisfied and be willing to implement it. Changes that are not likely to be pervasive or relevant to members' work can be made more efficiently through authority processes.

The availability of structures that provide a base for both authority and collective processes provides managers with flexibility in other ways. They can alternate between the two structures *within* the process of carrying out a particular change. Collective processes can be used at the early stages, when the participation of members is needed to solve a problem and identify an appropriate innovation. Authority processes can be used at the later stages to reduce the ambiguities that arise when changes are being implemented. Collective processes are important for nonprofit organizations not only because they offer a better way of managing certain types of change but also because they can complement authority processes and provide an organization with alternative mechanisms for change initiation and implementation.

Facilitating Collective Innovation

Managers can facilitate collective decision processes by establishing structures to support these change processes and providing members with the skills necessary to use these structures. These structures and skills can be developed by using planned organizational change or organization development programs designed to improve interpersonal relations, communication, and problem solving. Though some of these programs are too expensive or otherwise inappropriate for nonprofit organizations, others have been designed explicitly for organizations like schools and hospitals. One program focuses on the development of organizational structures to support collective decision processes in educational systems. This task-oriented, problem-solving program has been shown to promote change and improve the satisfaction of members in certain schools (Duncan et al., 1977). This program is not likely to be relevant to all types of nonprofit organizations, but many of its components can be modified by managers to create their own programs.

The major components of the school program include *survey feedback* for the definition of problems and the need for change, *task-oriented problem solving* for the identification of innovations and solutions to problems, and *collective decision structures and roles* for the communication, legitimation, and implementation of changes. The program relies on: (1) the *training* of organizational members to lead and monitor problem-solving activities and (2) an *overlapping group* structural configuration to sustain change in the organization. Before any groups are established, members should be provided with information about the purpose of the program, its components, and its implications for members. This information is more likely to be understood and accepted if the members are involved in tailoring the program to the needs of their organization.

Managers can initiate the program by providing members with time to serve on one or more groups: the problem-solving group, the review committee, or the policy committee (see Figure 5–2). These overlapping groups act in concert and are designed to superimpose a collective decision-making configuration over the existing authority structure of the organization. As shown in Table 5–2, an elementary school problem-solving group could be composed of all the faculty members and run by a faculty program leader and a program monitor who are elected by the teachers. Problem-solving group functions include interpreting the results of a task-oriented survey administered to members, identifying faculty problems, determining what action can be taken to alleviate problems, communicating problems and recommendations upward to the review committee, and implementing changes.

The review committee operates at the school level and includes the principal, program leader, program monitor, and another member designated by the principal. Its functions include sanctioning problem-solving group recommendations, suggesting ways in which solutions proposed

FIGURE 5-2. *Overlapping group structure for an elementary school.*

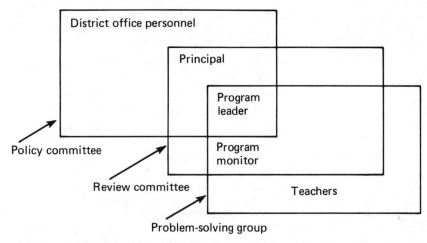

Source: R. B. Duncan et al., "An Assessment of a Structural Task Approach to Organizational
Development in a School System," final report to the National Institute of Education
(Ann Arbor, Mich.: Institute for Social Research, 1977).

by the group might be improved, explaining why certain solutions cannot be implemented, and communicating information upward to the policy committee and downward to the problem-solving group. The policy committee operates at the district level and includes the superintendent, principal(s), and program leader(s). Its functions include: responding to questions and recommendations coming from the problem-solving group via the review committee, approving changes, and explaining why particular changes cannot be implemented.

(The overlapping structure described here is designed for elementary schools and probably would not be entirely appropriate for other types of organizations. The structure would be different even for secondary schools, where multiple problem-solving groups would be needed along with a coordinating committee for program leaders. Generally, problem-solving groups should be created with a reasonably small number of members whose jobs are similar or whose work efforts are interdependent.)

Elected faculty leaders serve as key members on all three committees. The collective decision program for schools includes skill development training to prepare leaders for their linking roles. The training focuses on change processes, conflict resolution, survey feedback, communication skills, group behavior and problem solving, and leadership. Group monitors also have a central role in the program and receive training on how

TABLE 5–2. *Elementary school committee memberships and activities.*

Group	Functions
Problem-solving group Program leader, monitor, and faculty of the school	To interpret survey results for their own group. To identify the group's key work problems and needs. To diagnose the basic reasons and causes underlying work problems. To determine what action can be taken at the school level in solving problems and meeting needs. To discuss problems and possible solutions with other members of the system who might be affected by the problem or proposed changes. To communicate to the review and/or policy committee the group's thinking and recommendations regarding alternative proposals for solving problems and meeting needs. To obtain from the review and/or policy committee reasons and explanations for existing top-level policies, programs, procedures, and action. To plan for the implementation of solutions.
Review committee Principal, program leader, and monitor	To plan and schedule survey administration, feedback, and problem-solving meetings. To approve proposed changes and innovations proposed by the problem-solving group. To explain why proposals for change cannot be approved and to suggest modifications of proposals for further consideration. To facilitate upward and downward communication between the policy committee and problem-solving group.
Policy committee Superintendent or district representative, principal, and program leader from the school(s) interested in the particular problem	To respond to questions, suggestions, and recommendations of problem-solving groups. To sanction and suggest changes in innovations emerging from problem-solving groups.

to record and evaluate the activities of the problem-solving group. Their training parallels that for the program leader and places special emphasis on group dynamics, problem diagnosis, and feedback. Administrators are also central to the success of collective decision making and receive training to sharpen their skills in communication and group problem-solving processes.

Skill training, an integral part of organization development programs, is critical to the success of any change effort. When initiating their own program, managers should spend time identifying the kinds of training needed by members of their organization. Planning can be done in collaboration with in-house specialists or external consultants. Consultants can also be instrumental in carrying out the training program. When consultation is unavailable or beyond the means of the organization, other arrangements should be made to provide members with a training experience.

In the absence of members who possess the skills needed to use the structure, an overlapping group structure can become time-wasting and ineffectual. Managers and elected program personnel might do well to enroll in courses on group processes, organization development, or communication that are likely to be relevant to various phases of the collective decision process. Another possibility is for managers and elected program leaders to carry out their own training programs. Experiential training manuals designed for the college classroom (see Morris and Sashkin, 1976) can be used to identify relevant literature and exercises. The skills developed through this training experience can be supplemented by using the guidelines presented below for the various stages of the collective process.

Evaluation. The evaluation stage of the collective decision process can be initiated by using survey feedback procedures. Survey feedback involves administering questionnaires to group members and systematically returning the data to the group. The questionnaires should include items that pertain to the work being performed and the technology in use, which are issues of general interest to members. A problem-solving group can select an existing survey, develop its own questionnaire, or supplement a standardized instrument with questions particularly relevant to its own organization.

The use of standardized surveys can minimize the participation of system members at this stage of the process; however, they offer important advantages, especially when used simultaneously by multiple groups or organizations and average scores for a number of groups are computed and fed back to provide a benchmark against which each group can evaluate its own scores. Survey feedback can be supplemented by other data, such as accounting information, absenteeism and turnover records, and data from questionnaires administered to clients (see Nadler, 1976).

The focal unit for data feedback and problem identification is the problem-solving group. Feedback at the group rather than the individual level is preferred because groups provide a greater potential for: wide, experience-based contributions to problem solving; the general recognition by all members of shared problems; the pooling and sharing of information that facilitates solution generation; and the development of mutual expectations to implement decisions agreed upon by members (Mann and Likert, 1952).

Discussions centering around feedback data can be particularly productive if the group is comprised of members whose status within the organization is roughly equivalent. Communication tends to be more open and problem solving more creative in peer groups than in groups whose members differ significantly in status and power. While managers should make themselves available to attend meetings and provide information, they should also encourage groups to hold survey feedback and problem-solving meetings on their own.

Survey data can be fed back to a group by its program leader. To do it properly, the leader must fully understand the data and be prepared with a good feedback strategy. There is evidence that the best feedback strategies involve both written and oral presentations of the data. Figure 5–3 illustrates a type of feedback chart that can be used by program leaders to supplement oral presentations of data. (The data presented in the figure are simulated for illustrative purposes.) The chart includes scores for sets of questionnaire items (not individual items) and is designed to help members identify general problem areas. Problem identification is facilitated by profiling the group's own scores alongside those of similar groups. The profiles of contrasting scores enable group members to quickly identify discrepancies between their group and others. Negative discrepancies can motivate members to clarify their objectives, generate solutions to problems, and implement those solutions (Nadler, 1976).

Preliminary discussions should focus on defining the importance of the problem areas identified by the survey data. Only problems relevant to the group should be discussed in further detail. Interest and motivation of members to solve problems can be maintained only if less pertinent problems are filtered out and handled through authority processes. Detailed feedback charts presenting data on each questionnaire item can be used to guide in-depth analyses of relevant problems. The program leader should move the group toward specifying problems precisely, defining underlying reasons and causes, and defining specific change goals.

Discussion should focus on various facets of the organizational system, with, for example, a task problem being directed to include consideration of technology, structure, components, and external environment. Here are some guidelines from the school program that can be used to facilitate discussion:

1. *Diagnose problems first; suggest solutions later.* Initial stress is placed on problem definition and specification; the generation of solutions is de-

FIGURE 5-3. *Elementary school survey—general profile.*

Group profiled: School Z	Legend: ○ School
No. in group: 23	△ District overall

Percent Favorable Response

Category	0 10 20 30 40 50 60 70 80 90 100
1. Administrative practices	△○ (≈30)
2. Professional workload	△ (≈35) ○ (≈55)
3. Nonprofessional workload	○ (≈45) △ (≈50)
4. Materials and equipment	△ (≈30) ○ (≈45)
5. Buildings and facilities	○ (≈25) △ (≈35)
6. Educational effectiveness	△○ (≈45)
7. Evaluation of students	△ (≈30) ○ (≈45)
8. Special services	△○ (≈30)
9. School-community relations	○ (≈25) △ (≈45)
10. Supervisory relations	○ (≈50) △ (≈55)
11. Colleague relations	○ (≈55) △ (≈60)
12. Voice in educational program	○△ (≈30)
13. Performance and development	△ (≈45) ○ (≈50)
14. Students	○ (≈25) △ (≈30)
15. Reactions to survey	△○ (≈55)

Source: Adapted from R.J. Coughlan, *School Survey Program Feedback Guide* (Chicago: University of Chicago Press, 1967).

ferred. Suggestions and opinions are solicited regarding whether the survey results reveal problems and, if so, what they are.

2. *Subproblem identification.* The objective is to identify and delineate problems and break them down into key components. The leader is responsible for moving the group from the symptom to the problem to the subproblem definition.

3. *Basic reasons and causes.* In an effort to identify underlying organizational dynamics, each subproblem is analyzed for specific reasons and causes.

4. *Members' suggestions.* An attempt is made to have the total group contribute to the discussion.

5. *Titles, not names.* To keep the discussions objective and factual, emphasize organizational roles and relationships rather than personal and interpersonal problems. Group members are encouraged to use job titles or organizational functions rather than names.

6. *Group feelings.* Group members are encouraged to say, "Perhaps the group feels this way because . . ." rather than "I feel so because . . ." to keep discussions on a less personal level. (This rule was designed to help members express their thoughts as group members rather than as individuals.)

7. *No leader evaluation.* The program leader is encouraged not to evaluate member contributions. The objective is to have all members contribute ideas and opinions without the feeling that their statements will be judged by the leader as good or bad.

8. *Understandable specification of problems.* Problems must be stated precisely and be understandable to people in other parts of the system.

Solution generation. If group members do not feel competent to solve a particular problem, relevant information should be communicated to the review committee for problem solving and decision making through authority processes. If the problem under consideration falls within the members' sphere of expertise, the group should move on to solution generation. As during the evaluation stage, the program leader's role is to facilitate task-oriented communication without emphasizing such subjective elements of group interaction as those focused on in sensitivity training.

Problem-solving group members should be encouraged to be objective and factual and approach problems in terms of situations and roles rather than personalities, outlining difficulties to be overcome and goals to be achieved. The assumption is that members of many organizations are more willing to discuss interrole relations than interpersonal problems. Also, leaders with only limited training may find it easier to facilitate meetings that focus on tasks rather than personalities.

Program leaders can set up groundrules for guiding problem-solving group meetings. The guidelines below are designed to effect creative problem solving, promote a task orientation, and standardize group decision-making processes:

1. *Disagreement as a source of ideas.* The leader and members should perceive member disagreement as a source of ideas rather than as an obstacle to problem solving.

2. *Multiple alternatives.* The group is encouraged to identify many possible solutions for each problem rather than settle for just one or two.

3. *Decisions later.* As ideas for improvement are generated, it is understood that solutions will not be evaluated immediately. Final evaluation of alternatives and selection of the best solution is postponed until alternatives have been carefully examined.

4. *Avoidance of financial remedies.* The group is discouraged from generating only solutions that require more money. Attention is directed toward proposals that involve more efficient uses of existing resources. As part of the process, the group is encouraged to engage in cost-benefit analyses of proposed remedies.

5. *Action to take.* After alternative solutions have been evaluated, the group selects what it perceives to be the best course of action. This includes steps to be taken at the school level within the purview of teacher authority as well as those recommendations to be referred to the review and policy committees.

6. *Schedule.* A timetable is kept of the action program initiated for each problem analyzed. This includes starting dates, interim progress reports, and completion dates.

7. *Positive statements.* Group members are asked to word problems and offer suggestions in the form of positive statements, such as "Communication between X and Y can be improved by . . .," rather than stating vague complaints.

8. *Written communications.* Decisions requiring legitimation at the review and policy committee levels should be forwarded in written form. The problem and proposed solution should be clearly stated, with responsibilities delineated.

9. *Request response.* Matters forwarded to the review committee can be accompanied by a request for action by a certain time. This can be done inoffensively by saying something like, "We would like the response of the review committee three days before our next problem-solving group meeting on . . . ."

10. *Follow-up on results.* Each problem area is periodically reviewed by the program leader or the group to determine what has been done, how well solutions have been implemented, and what the overall results are.

Attempts should be made to have all group members contribute to the discussion, to avoid conformity effects, and to defer solution generation until various interpretations of the problem have been explored (see Coughlan, 1967). The problem-solving group should be encouraged to identify a number of possible solutions for each problem and to withhold final selection until a number of alternatives have been discussed and carefully reviewed (Maier, 1970).

Alternatives should be assessed and evaluated along a number of dimensions. For example, a solution involving a change in technology should be analyzed to identify concomitant changes in structures and components that might be required. The probability that the solution can be successfully implemented should be considered, and estimates should be made as to the likelihood of the solution really solving the problem. The group should also attempt to identify other effects of the solution and the extent to which these outcomes might be acceptable to organizational members. Each alternative should be evaluated in terms of its quality and acceptability.

After the alternatives have been properly evaluated, the group can select the best solution and define a course of action. When the proposed change is minor and has no effect on persons outside the group, members can plan for implementation. In most cases, proposed changes will have implications for other members, so the immediate course of action should be to discuss the proposal with these individuals.

A timetable should be developed for each action program to maintain the momentum of the group. The timetable can be developed by the group monitor, who is also responsible for recording the ideas expressed during the meetings. The names of the group members proposing the ideas should be excluded from these minutes, with members reviewing the minutes and other documents prepared by the monitor to ensure that they accurately reflect the group's thinking. In general, the purpose of these procedures is to formalize the group and provide a basis for ongoing collective decision activities. These procedures and guidelines are made impersonal and task-oriented to reduce their threat and anxiety content and minimize the social and psychological costs of suggesting new alternatives.

Internal diffusion. As discussed earlier in this chapter, the activities of members of many nonprofit organizations are highly interdependent. These interdependencies tend to become more visible when a change is introduced. An innovation initiated by one group in the organization almost invariably has a direct or indirect effect on other groups. Two important problems arise when decision making is not responsive to these interdependencies and when a new idea is not promptly disseminated throughout the organization: First, certain members may be unaware of the proposed change and may not understand it well enough to cooperate in its implementation. Second, the change may be initiated by members with a particular perspective and thus may be unresponsive to the needs of other members. This implies that the change will not be fully accepted throughout the organization or may actively be resisted by members who were not involved in proposing it.

Problem-solving groups composed of individuals whose activities are interdependent promote the internal diffusion of new ideas to these participants. However, many proposed changes affect people either in or outside the organization who are not members of the problem-solving group. Since effective completion of the diffusion stage involves discussing problems and solutions with all relevant personnel, special efforts must be made to gain the participation of people outside the group who might be interested in the change. They can be contacted by group representatives who have interacted with them on previous occasions and who are likely to understand their perspective. Selected personnel from other parts of the organization can also be invited to a meeting of the problem-solving group. These expanded meetings can be used to advise the guests of problem situations and possible solutions as well as to gain their points of view and insights regarding alternative proposals. The objective is to improve the changes being proposed as well as to gain acceptance of them. Prior to conducting an expanded meeting, program leaders should familiarize themselves with the factors that promote resistance to change and tactics that can be used to reduce resistance. (Some of the tactics outlined in the final section of this chapter can be helpful here.)

The internal diffusion process becomes more difficult to carry out if the solutions being considered by a problem-solving group can impact on the entire organization or if two or more groups are simultaneously dealing with the same problem. Under such circumstances, the active involvement of managers can be critical, because they can call for an ad hoc meeting of a coordinating group composed of the relevant program leaders and representatives from other parts of the organization. During this meeting, the program leaders can exchange information regarding the problem and preferred solutions. The leaders can then provide their own problem-solving groups with feedback concerning the attitudes, perceived problems, and ideas of other groups. Following these meetings, the leaders can reconvene to modify proposed solutions to better fit the needs of the entire organization.

The different subenvironments of the units or departments within an organization can make it difficult to identify changes that are acceptable throughout the system. Managers and program leaders may have to rely on conflict resolution skills and strategies when developing mutually agreeable solutions (Morris and Sashkin, 1976). They first should determine whether differences are real or are merely the result of miscommunication and misunderstandings. When the differences are real, the ad hoc group may be able to remove the basis for the conflict. It is sometimes possible to rearrange the work of the organization so that two different changes can be implemented simultaneously in different subunits. Alternatively, the group may be able to identify superordinate solutions that override and encompass the basic elements of two or more seemingly inconsistent solutions. If superordinate solutions cannot be found, the conflict might have to be resolved through bargaining or authority decision making.

Legitimation. The legal structure of many nonprofit organizations places substantial decision-making authority in legislative bodies, boards of directors, and their administrative representatives. Some of the decisions that members are competent to make in problem-solving groups may have to be approved by administrators, unless operational authority over these decisions is formally delegated to the group.

Legitimation activities may be desirable even in the absence of legal constraints. High-quality change decisions in organizations are made in consideration of both internal and external factors. Through collective processes, members may focus on internal problems and constraints and may inadvertently neglect or selectively filter out certain external factors. The opposite may be true for administrators operating within the authority structure. Consequently, the proper integration of these decision-making structures may be necessary if change decisions are to be responsive to forces both within and outside the organization.

The collective decision program designed for schools relies on an overlapping group configuration (Figure 5–2) to achieve integration and legitimation. A similar group structure might be used in other organizations to provide a mechanism for the legitimation of problem-solving group proposals, as well as for the collective legitimation of managers' proposals. This legitimation process is initiated at review committee meetings attended by the manager, program leader, program monitor, and another member designated by the manager. The meetings provide a forum for discussing the problems and solutions identified by the problem-solving group.

Figure 5–4 illustrates a communication form around which review committee discussions might center. This form can be prepared by the program monitor and should be distributed to review committee members prior to the meeting. A written communication can be helpful in accu-

FIGURE 5–4. *Survey feedback and problem-solving communication form.*

Date:_____	
The Problem and Its Key Aspects	*Basic Causes*
Goal of Changes	*Solution*

rately conveying the ideas of the problem-solving group and in providing review committee members with the information necessary to prepare for their meeting. Written communications can also help to formalize collective decision processes and reduce the likelihood that ideas for change will be forgotten after the early stages of the process.

Recommendations can be approved, rejected, or modified by the review committee. In some cases, recommendations approved by this committee might have to be sanctioned at a higher level. Further approval may be needed if the solution has policy implications and if the manager on the review committee does not hold a position at the top of the organization's hierarchy. For example, a faculty proposal to adopt a new set of math texts would require central office approval; a proposal by social workers in a public agency to offer a new counseling service would have to be approved by the top administrator; and a recommendation from police officers to modify the procedures for dealing with domestic quarrels would need to be reviewed by the chief.

A meeting of a policy committee (see Figure 5–2) might be called to initiate the review and approval of changes with policy implications. The committee meeting could be attended by members of the change team, if one has been formed, so that the proposal can be considered in light of the relevant sectors of the external environment. The communication forms should be distributed to committee members prior to the meetings to provide a focus for the group's discussion. They can also be used after the meeting to communicate information to other relevant groups, such as the board of directors or other governing body.

Though certain change proposals in all organizations have to be approved at the policy committee level, the collective decision process is more straightforward when final authority to accept or reject a proposal is vested in the review committee. When a change is rejected at this level, the committee should define why the proposal is unacceptable and how it might be modified to increase its feasibility. The committee can formalize its reactions by preparing a memorandum that specifies (1) the aspects of the proposal that are acceptable; (2) suggestions for modifications; (3) the aspects of the proposal that are not acceptable, with an explanation; and (4) a schedule for further action. The problem-solving group can then reformulate its proposal on the basis of this new information.

The overlapping group approach facilitates the legitimation subprocess by providing a base for more effective vertical communication. First, the committee structure enhances members' ability to interact constructively with managers by promoting communication between groups rather than individuals. This group orientation should counteract many of the natural barriers to effective upward communication. Second, the structure replaces the communication of poorly developed and inconsistent statements of problems by individual members with documented statements of carefully analyzed problems and possible solutions. Third, problems are stated in impersonal and task-oriented terms; organizational titles are used rather than names; and unconstructive criticism and negatively worded statements are avoided. These factors can minimize defensive reactions and increase the likelihood that the information will be accepted and acted on. Finally, communications from managers to members should increase in relevancy and efficiency as feedback from the review committee focuses on those policies and external pressures directly related to solutions proposed by the problem-solving group.

Adoption. There should be relatively high acceptance by members of solutions and innovations generated through the collective process. Acceptance is expected to be high as a result of the amount of member involvement and group interaction involved in the early stages of the process. High involvement on the part of members in decision-making activities can promote their understanding of the problem, influence over the decision, and awareness and understanding of selected alternatives. A high level of group interaction can broaden the organizational perspective of members and speed up the diffusion of new ideas within the organization. These factors, along with members' perceptions of group commitment and consensus, should heighten the acceptance of and the innovativeness of the change proposals (Zaltman, Duncan, and Holbek, 1973).

Adoption is concerned with acceptance of the solution in its final form—after legitimation and possible modification. The final solution is likely to be accepted if vertical communication channels have been used effectively to promote members' understanding of the problem area and related organizational constraints. Solutions should also be accepted by administrators if their viewpoints have been considered in the decision-making process. The assumption is that undistorted and objective vertical communication can bring about consistency across organizational levels regarding members' and managers' attitudes toward problems and preferences for alternative solutions.

When members of a problem-solving group support a collectively initiated change, it is likely that they will be willing to invest time in planning its implementation. As a result of studying, for example, the logistics of alternative solutions, a certain amount of preliminary planning will have already taken place. Final planning can then be done for facilitating the implementation of change. This final planning can be handled by a subcommittee of the problem-solving group, whose members should assume responsibility for identifying the resources needed to properly implement the change or innovation, as well as any modifications in the components and structures of the organization that would facilitate implementation.

Some members might have to be provided with more information about the practical aspects of the change, and other members might need training in order to carry out the new task or work with the new technology. Modification may also have to be made in the roles of members, the flow of information, or the distribution of decision-making authority. The subcommittee also should prepare a timetable that specifies who is to do what by when. If the change is complex, this timetable can specify the sequence in which the innovation's components should be implemented. This type of detailed timetable is particularly appropriate when implementation of some components depends on the prior implementation of others.

Implementation and routinization. When carried out properly, the collective decision process can counteract the tendency that change and innovations have to evaporate in organizations. The process should facilitate the implementation of new programs and procedures by promoting intragroup cooperation and personal and group commitment. The implementation of change should be facilitated both by formalizing each group decision as an action to be taken and scheduling change activities. The good intentions of the group are translated into the realities of everyday behavior to the extent that the group monitor carefully records each decision outcome and the specific action for which each member is responsible. Scheduling and setting deadlines should increase members' willingness to engage in the nonroutine change activities.

An important objective at this stage is to reduce the uncertainty associated with the implementation of change. This objective can be met by planning, scheduling, and assigning responsibility for specific change activities to individual members of the group.

Uncertainty can also be reduced by switching to the authority structure at this stage. Implementation through authority processes taps both the managerial expertise and the advantageous organizational location of administrators for supervising change efforts. Managers can coordinate the efforts of the various members involved in carrying out the change, serve as a clearinghouse for collecting and disseminating information pertinent to the change, and assist individual members in solving the problems which inevitably occur when changes are being introduced. In addition, managers can help gather the resources needed at this stage and activate the change team to provide organizational members with assistance they might need to facilitate implementation. Whether implemented through collective or authority processes, change is routinized successfully only when managers and members are sufficiently committed to working through the unanticipated problems that arise during implementation.

At the routinization stage, it is important for the problem-solving group to follow up on changes initiated by members. The program leader or a specially commissioned subcommittee of the problem-solving group can assume responsibility for periodically evaluating the extent to which recommendations have been implemented and the degree to which new programs or procedures have alleviated problems. Each change should be assessed in terms of (1) the specific subproblems at the evaluation stage that gave rise to the need for change; (2) the various criteria at the solution generation stage that were used to select the alternative; and (3) the needs and perspectives of the various groups who, at the internal diffusion stage, expressed interest in the problem and solution. Any unanticipated and dysfunctional consequences of the change should also be documented. If a change has had negative effects or has failed to solve a particular problem, it must be singled out for further intensive analysis. This analysis involves renewed evaluation and problem identification activities and therefore implies a recycling of the collective decision process.

Follow-up activities implicitly include evaluation by problem-solving group members of the adequacy of collective decision processes. Their evaluation is likely to be favorable to the extent that the collective decision process and group recommendations are being successfully implemented. However, collective decision making can be difficult to carry out successfully, and the process can break down at various stages.

Group monitors can be instrumental in evaluating the effectiveness of the process and in identifying ways that it needs to be improved. For example, monitors can periodically interview members of the problem-solving group to see how they feel about collective decision activities. The form illustrated in Figure 5–5 guides interviews in elementary schools and can be modified for use by other organizations. The data collected through these interviews are used to identify specific problems in group processes; they can signal the need for better communication, additional training for the leader, or more support from managers.

For many organizations, collective decision making is an innovation in itself. It implies a basic modification in the structures and components of the organization and is likely to be viewed as something new by members. A collective decision program, therefore, is subject to the same problems inherent in most innovations. The program may be highly appropriate for some organizations and inappropriate for others. Any decision to implement this kind of program should consider the needs of the organization and the relative merits of other organizational change programs (see Katz and Kahn, 1978).

Collective decision making is a complex process that is not likely to work very well the first time around. Managers and members must be willing to work through the problems of implementing the program and modifying it to meet the particular needs of their organization. Like all innovations, a collective decision program has to be initiated carefully. Members throughout the organization should participate in the decision to implement the change. They should understand the purpose of the program as well as their roles in the collective decision process. Members should also understand that the program is not necessarily going to be successful and cannot serve as a mechanism for solving all the problems of the organization.

Collective processes should be used initially to tackle minor problems and introduce small-scale changes. This approach gives members the opportunity to go through the process a few times and sharpen their problem-solving skills. Cycling through the process in this way can also

FIGURE 5–5. *Periodic faculty feedback monitoring form and tally sheet.*

School _____   Date _____   Number Responding _____

Number of meetings since last Faculty Feedback Form _____

INSTRUCTIONS: For each respondent, make a mark in the response category space that he or she checked on each item. To arrive at an item mean:

1. Multiply the total number of responses in each response category times the score of that category.
   Notice that in some cases the favorable response (7) is on the left and in others it is on the right.
2. Total the scores for all categories within the item.
3. Divide the total by the number of respondents.

The scores will range from 1 to 7, with a high number indicating a more favorable response by the faculty.

Example: In the following example, 8 teachers filled out the item. Three individuals responded with a 1, two individuals with a 2, two individuals with a 4, and 1 individual with a 6.

$3 \times 1 = 3$ $2 \times 2 = 4$ $4 \times 2 = 8$ $6 \times 1 = 6$ Total $= 3 + 4 + 8 + 6 = 21$ Score $= 2.6$

Mean score $= 21/8 = 2.6$

| 1 | 2 | 3 | 4 | 5 | 6 | 7 |

1. Value of time in meetings   Total =
| 1 | 2 | 3 | 4 | 5 | 6 | 7 | Mean =

2. Organization   Total =
| 7 | 6 | 5 | 4 | 3 | 2 | 1 | Mean =

3. Individual or faction domination   Total =
| 6 | 7 | 5 | 4 | 3 | 2 | 1 | Mean =

10. Fair consideration to recommendations   Total =
| 1 | 2 | 3 | 4 | 5 | 6 | 7 | Mean =

11. Review committee—all communications   Total =
| 1 | 2 | 3 | 4 | 5 | 6 | 7 | Mean =

11a. Constructive   Total =
| 1 | 2 | 3 | 4 | 5 | 6 | 7 | Mean =

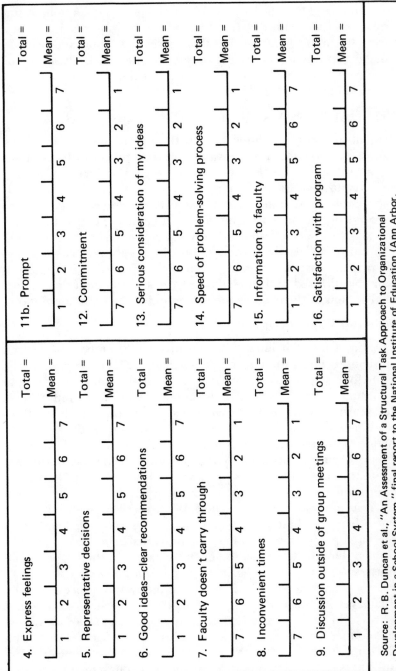

4. Express feelings   Total =

    1   2   3   4   5   6   7   Mean =

5. Representative decisions   Total =

    1   2   3   4   5   6   7   Mean =

6. Good ideas—clear recommendations   Total =

    1   2   3   4   5   6   7   Mean =

7. Faculty doesn't carry through   Total =

    7   6   5   4   3   2   1   Mean =

8. Inconvenient times   Total =

    7   6   5   4   3   2   1   Mean =

9. Discussion outside of group meetings   Total =

    1   2   3   4   5   6   7   Mean =

11b. Prompt   Total =

    1   2   3   4   5   6   7   Mean =

12. Commitment   Total =

    7   6   5   4   3   2   1   Mean =

13. Serious consideration of my ideas   Total =

    7   6   5   4   3   2   1   Mean =

14. Speed of problem-solving process   Total =

    7   6   5   4   3   2   1   Mean =

15. Information to faculty   Total =

    1   2   3   4   5   6   7   Mean =

16. Satisfaction with program   Total =

    1   2   3   4   5   6   7   Mean =

Source: R. B. Duncan et al., "An Assessment of a Structural Task Approach to Organizational Development in a School System," final report to the National Institute of Education (Ann Arbor, Mich.: Institute for Social Research, 1977).

help to gradually establish the new role, influence, and communication structures associated with collective innovation decision making. These structures can complement the ones that currently support authority decision making in the organization and can provide a wider base for collaborative problem solving and the subsequent initiation of even more significant changes.

INDIVIDUAL INNOVATION

Individual innovation is important to the organization in two ways. First, authority and collective innovation decision processes focus on organizational change; but both involve change by the individuals who comprise the organization. It is the individual members who must ultimately adopt and implement an innovation if any systemwide change is to take place. Second, organizational change and adaptation depend on the ability of individual members to independently initiate change outside the context of authority or collective processes. Individual or optional innovations not only may increase the adopting member's effectiveness but also may eventually be diffused and implemented throughout the organization. This final section of the chapter focuses on individuals and innovations.

Individual Innovation Processes

Innovation at the individual level is a process of temporally ordered stages or subprocesses. Rogers and Shoemaker (1971) conceptualize the process in four stages: (1) gaining *knowledge* of the innovation and an understanding of how it works; (2) forming a favorable or unfavorable attitude toward the innovation (*persuasion*); (3) engaging in activities leading to the *decision* to adopt or reject the innovation; and (4) seeking information to support the decision (*confirmation*) or reversing the decision on the basis of new information. Other models of the process are consistent with this one. The process proposed by Robertson (1971) involves a series of similar stages: problem perception, awareness, attitude, legitimation, trial, adoption, and dissonance. While there are some important differences between these and other formulations, most of them center on three basic properties or "states" of individuals: *knowledge, attitudes,* and *behavior*. The models are also generally based on three underlying subprocesses: *learning, attitude formation,* and *decision making*.

An individual-level model. A basic model of innovation processes at the individual level is presented in Figure 5–6. The model suggests a cyclical process, revolving around knowledge, attitudes, and behavior as distinct states linked together by learning, attitude formation, and decision making. This simplified model of the innovation process subsumes the detailed substages included in other formulations. Though the process sug-

FIGURE 5-6. *An innovation-expectancy model.*

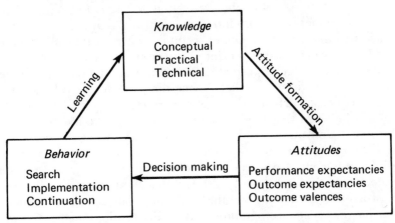

gested by this model does not begin with a specific subprocess or state, it seems reasonable to assume that it usually starts with learning and knowledge. Knowledge provides a base on which attitudes are formed and decisions are made; thus, learning may be a prerequisite to changes in attitudes and behaviors.

Learning can take place during the course of day-to-day activities or as a result of a purposeful search for new information. In either case, it can lead to at least three different types of knowledge. First, learning can increase an individual's *conceptual knowledge* or awareness and understanding of abstract concepts, including new ideas and innovative approaches to getting tasks accomplished. Second, it can increase *practical knowledge* or the how-to knowledge required to use an innovation. Third, learning can improve an individual's *technical knowledge* or understanding of cause–effect relations. Through experience or exposure to new information, one can learn about the extent to which the present way of doing things achieves the intended results. Knowledge can also be gained about the effectiveness of new approaches toward achieving these results.

On the basis of knowledge, individuals develop beliefs and attitudes about traditional and innovative ways of doing things. The attitude formation process may be best understood in terms of expectancy-value theories of motivation, which posit that an individual's motivation to perform at a certain level or to behave in a certain way depends on his or her attitude toward that behavior. These attitudes are defined by the individual's performance expectancies, outcome expectancies, and outcome valences (Cooke, Uhlaner, and Quinn, 1975; Lawler, 1973).

After learning of an innovation, people are likely to develop effort →

performance expectancies or beliefs regarding the probability that an effort on their part to implement the innovation will lead to successful performance. Members of an organization might feel that they cannot work effectively with a new and complex technology even if they make a great effort. Low performance expectancies can result from a lack of the skills and how-to knowledge required to use the innovation. Potential adopters are also likely to develop beliefs concerning the successful use of the innovation. These performance → *outcome expectancies* reflect the extent to which it is believed that the innovation will lead to the intended results and to other outcomes. On the basis of past experience or recently acquired knowledge, organizational members may believe that an innovation—if implemented properly—is highly instrumental in achieving its intended results. Members may also feel that the innovation will have a high probability of leading to other outcomes. Some outcomes, such as higher pay or greater recognition, may be the result of changes in work performance associated with use of the innovation.

Different outcomes vary in attractiveness to different individuals, and these *outcome valences* help to define the utility of innovative and traditional ways of doing things. Organizational members may attach positive value to some outcomes of an innovation and a negative value to others. These valences may gradually change as new knowledge is acquired and are important in understanding why people eventually adopt or reject innovations. In combination with their performance and outcome expectancies, members' preferences for outcomes define their attitudes toward an innovation and their motivation to use it. Organizational members can be motivated to implement a new program if they feel they can successfully work with it *and* if they believe that the program will lead to valued outcomes. This motivation—or psychological state of adoption—can be particularly strong if the new program is expected to lead to more highly valued outcomes than present programs. Motivation will be low if the new program seems difficult to use or if it is expected to lead to negatively valued outcomes. Rejection may be particularly strong if present programs are seen as easier to use or are associated with fewer negative results.

Expectancies and valences provide the basis for decision making which affects behavior relevant to new programs and procedures. An individual who is unhappy with traditional procedures (because they do not lead to desired outcomes) may be motivated to reject the tradition and decide to *search* for alternatives. Other organizational members who are already aware of alternatives may be motivated to adopt a particular innovation. They are likely to decide to *implement* the new program or procedure, unless they perceive constraints (such as a lack of funds to pay for a costly innovation) which would render the implementation decision difficult to carry out. Members who are already using an innovation are likely to gain new knowledge from this experience, form new attitudes about it, and decide to *continue* or discontinue its use. The three behavioral states of search, implementation, and continuation can lead to learning and renewed knowledge.

Managers can use this individual-level model to analyze and understand the innovative or noninnovative behavior of members of nonprofit organizations. Consider the example of a nurse in an outpatient clinic who is responsible for educating patients about their medical conditions and teaching them how to take care of themselves at home. As a result of ongoing contacts with patients, the nurse learns that many patients are not following their medical regimens. This experiential learning points to a change in the nurse's technical knowledge. Present patient education programs are obviously not leading to the type of self-care they were intended to promote. Such technical knowledge can lead to changes in the nurse's attitudes toward present programs.

Though the nurse knows how to work effectively with the existing programs, she does not believe these programs have a high instrumentality for patient self-care. Since self-care is undoubtedly highly valued by the nurse, her attitudes toward the traditional techniques will become less favorable. An ideal state of affairs would be a higher rate of compliance on the part of patients. The discrepancy between the actual and the ideal may lead the nurse to change her behavior.

The nurse may be motivated to actively search for alternatives by reviewing recent journals for relevant articles or attending professional meetings to discuss the problem with other nurses. Assuming the decision to search is not constrained by organizational obstacles or other factors, the resulting search can promote learning and increase the nurse's conceptual and practical knowledge. The nurse may then become aware of a new strategy, such as the social support approach,* and acquire some of the how-to knowledge needed to use the strategy properly. Beliefs and attitudes about the new approach will be formed on the basis of this knowledge. The nurse might believe that she has both the practical knowledge and the skills required to provide patients with socioemotional support. If so, the performance expectancy associated with the innovation will be high. Furthermore, this approach may be viewed as having a high probability of leading to a highly valued outcome, such as patient compliance, and the nurse may be motivated to use it.

---

*The social support approach involves providing patients with information about their condition and treatment; socioemotional support through face-to-face interaction with the nurse; and additional encouragement from a "partner" at home.

This motivation will be translated into behavior after some decision making. The nurse may decide to try the social support approach if its relative advantage over the present program is great enough to offset the usual cost involved in changing routines. Various factors, however, could lead to a decision against using this approach. The rules governing the nurse's activities may be so rigid that it would be difficult if not impossible to try something new. Or the workload may be so great that the nurse cannot take the time needed to introduce the social support system. Thus the nurse's decision to try the innovation depends not only on motivation but on situational factors that can constrain behavior.

Implementation of the social support approach to patient education, even on a trial basis, can promote experiential learning. More specifically, the nurse may gain both technical and practical knowledge about this approach. The functional and dysfunctional effects of the social support approach become more apparent at this point. This new knowledge can reinforce or change the nurse's attitudes toward the innovation. If the approach seems to be too difficult to use effectively or does not seem to lead to patient compliance, motivation to continue using it will be low. Alternatively, the new procedures might be considered highly workable and effective in achieving patient compliance, in which case the nurse would be motivated to continue using the innovation on a sustained and ongoing basis.

This example illustrates only one of many ways in which an individual can go through the innovation process. The process in this case began with learning (gaining technical knowledge about traditional programs) that led to a search for new alternatives. The process can also begin with knowledge about an innovation that leads a person to compare current programs with the innovation, to assess the relative advantages of the innovation, and to decide whether to implement it. Or the process can begin with attitude formation or decision making when the adopter has little knowledge about the innovation. Organizational members are sometimes directed to use a new program by higher-level personnel. When this happens, however, members may have too little knowledge to implement the program properly, and they may fake acceptance. Even if they do try working with the innovation, they may develop unfavorable attitudes toward it and revert to the traditional way of doing things.

Facilitating Individual Innovation Decision Processes

Innovation decision making by individual members is probably most successful, at least in terms of leading to the continued use of innovations, when the process begins with knowledge. Furthermore, these processes are probably most successful when carried out by certain types of individuals and with respect to particular kinds of innovations. A substantial amount of research suggests that various *individual characteristics* and *innovation attributes* are associated with the adoption and implementation of change. Table 5–3 specifies some of these characteristics and attributes and the subprocesses and states they are most likely to affect. The ways these factors complicate learning, lead to low motivation, and negatively influence a decision regarding the implementation of an innovation are discussed below, along with tactics that can be used by managers to counteract these negative effects.

Learning: conceptual and practical knowledge. A variety of research has identified numerous characteristics of individuals that are related to their innovativeness (see Rogers and Shoemaker, 1971). Many of them are associated with innovativeness because they are related to the ease with which individuals learn about innovations. Socioeconomic background, personality, and interpersonal behavior can limit the likelihood that knowledge about new ideas will be brought into an organization and used by its members. Some managers may recognize that the members of their organizations are not the type to learn about innovations; they may also feel that it is impossible to change their members in ways that can promote innovation. Nevertheless, certain strategies can be used to promote learning even by those members who otherwise might be unlikely to acquire any knowledge about innovations.

People with relatively little education and poor conceptual skills adopt innovations later than do others. Though managers may not be able to sharpen the conceptual skills of members, they can do a good deal to improve education and training. Managers can make continuing educa-

TABLE 5–3. *Some innovation attributes and individual characteristics affecting the change process.* *

	Innovation Attributes	Individual Characteristics
Learning		
Conceptual knowledge	Radicalness	(Professionalization)
Practical knowledge	Operational complexity	(Training)
Technical knowledge	(Visibility of consequences)	Selective perception
Attitude formation		
Performance expectancies	(Clarity, reliability)	(Security, status)
Outcome expectancies	(Compatibility)	(Integration)
Decision making		
Implementation	(Reversibility)	Intolerance of ambiguity

*Parentheses indicate that the change process is impeded when individuals or innovations are *low* in terms of the characteristic or attribute.

tion an integral part of members' work roles. Educational expenses can be subsidized, rewards can be offered for additional training, and in-service or on-the-job training experiences can be arranged. This strategy is exemplified by managers of emergency medical service systems who are working to upgrade the educational level of ambulance drivers and attendants. These employees are frequently asked to attend symposia and community college courses designed for emergency medical technicians and paramedics. This educational experience promotes knowledge of the latest medical protocols and equipment and provides a conceptual base for understanding and learning how to use future innovations.

Another reason some members of nonprofit organizations do not quickly learn about innovations has to do with their interpersonal behavior. More specifically, certain people may do little to seek out information about new ideas and may have minimal contact with other organizational members who could provide them with such information. These people are unlikely to acquire knowledge about innovations, particularly if they work within organizations where members work independently and where formal structures for horizontal communication are weak. Teachers in self-contained classrooms and social workers out in the field may not learn about the new techniques their colleagues are using other than through informal channels.

Managers can supplement informal channels (which may exclude certain members) with formal structures for horizontal communication. Problem-solving meetings or other kinds of group meetings and in-house newsletters can effectively get information about new programs and techniques even to those members who are otherwise isolated. In addition, managers can encourage members to work together or observe one another. This tactic is particularly useful in promoting the dissemination of ideas that are difficult to communicate verbally and makes it easier for those with poor conceptual skills to understand those ideas. It also permits members to observe the effects of the innovative approach and facilitates technical learning.

Members who identify with a profession, have expertise in a specialized area, and are cosmopolite (that is, have reference groups outside their organizations) are more likely than others to acquire knowledge about innovations. When organizational members are neither highly specialized nor professionalized, managers can use information linkage tactics to connect organizational members with sources of information that can guide and motivate change (Zaltman, Florio, and Sikorski, 1977). Consultants or field agents can be brought into the system to provide information about new ideas; sales representatives can be asked to interact directly with members regarding new products; and outside researchers can be invited to evaluate new programs, procedures, and techniques within the organization. Articles, books, and other professional literature can be made available to members; demonstrations can be conducted; and workshops or in-service meetings can be arranged. Managers can also establish and maintain communication channels between their members and other organizations that provide information about innovations on an ongoing basis.

These tactics can be used in conjunction with others that increase the professionalization or specialization of members. In some organizations, managers can create specialized roles and hire new people to fill them. Reading specialists can be hired by schools as can be ombudspersons by public agencies and pediatric nurses by outpatient clinics. These people are likely to identify with professional groups and provide information about new ideas in the field.

In some organizations, the roles held by present members can be made more specialized. For example, the members of a family counseling agency might begin specializing in specific problems (marital problems, alcoholism, financial problems, and so on). A move toward specialization must be supported by resources that can be used by members to acquire additional training and participate in meetings and other professional developmental activities. If carried out properly, efforts to increase specialization and professionalization can put members in a position that enables them to recognize a need for change and have better access to information about relevant innovations.

The probability that organizational members will learn about a particular innovation also depends on the attributes of the innovation under consideration. Members are likely to become aware of and gain an understanding of an innovation high in communicability. The probability that this conceptual knowledge will be achieved is low, however, if the innovation is complex or radical. Though it may be difficult (and counterproductive) to decrease the radicalness or complexity of an innovation, steps can be taken to increase the likelihood that members will learn about it.

Radical innovations are high in novelty and creativity and differ significantly from other alternatives (Zaltman, Duncan, and Holbek, 1973). Innovations may be radical because they are based on premises or assumptions that differ from those currently in use.

Years ago, the human relations approach to management was viewed as a radical innovation by many administrators because it is based on assumptions that were at variance with those that underlay then current managerial styles. The assumption that people are inherently lazy was consistent with the prevailing scientific approach to management and inconsistent with the new school of thought based on the assumption that people work hard when properly motivated (McGregor, 1964). The educational strategies used to promote managers' understanding of the human relations approach often emphasized these underlying assumptions. Generally, organizational members may be able to gain a better understanding of a radical innovation if they are provided with information about the assumptions on which the innovation is based.

Highly complex innovations that involve multiple and sophisticated ideas can also be difficult to understand. If a complex innovation is divisable, managers can break it down into less complicated components to facilitate learning by members. If a complex innovation is low in communicability, other tactics can be used. Complex innovations often are not communicable because they have been developed within highly specialized fields that use their own languages. Thus, a police officer may have trouble understanding a new approach to improving community relations couched in psychological and sociological terms. Managers and external change agents can promote conceptual learning by translating technical terms into everyday language. In addition, managers can demonstrate the innovation or arrange to have members observe persons in other organizations who are using the new technique or idea. Demonstration can be particularly helpful if the innovation is highly abstract and difficult to quantify.

Managers can employ similar strategies to help members acquire practical knowledge about an innovation. These strategies are especially useful if the innovation is high in operational complexity and low in consistency. *Consistency* implies that the skills and how-to knowledge required to use an innovation are similar to those required to use the present program, procedure, or equipment. In some cases, managers may be able to modify an innovation to increase its consistency. In other cases, they may be able to select a particular version of an innovation consistent with members' knowledge. A manager interested in having employees use a new miniaturized computer can make a model available to them that is similar to the calculators currently being used. This strategy can minimize the amount of time needed for the employees to familiarize themselves with the basic computer operations and allow more time for the learning of complex functions.

The operational complexity of an innovation can also affect acquisition of knowledge. Potential adopters are likely to have trouble learning how to use an innovation that requires a variety of sophisticated skills. The problems caused by complexity can be reduced if the innovation is operationally divisible. Divisibility permits members to initially use the parts of the innovation that are consistent with their present skills and then gradually learn how to use the other parts. When division is impracticable or undesirable, the innovation might be modified to make it easier to acquire the requisite practical knowledge. For example, the continuing development of statistical computer software packages has made it increasingly easy for members of research institutions to gain the skills required to use computer hardware. This technique is particularly effective when users become involved and when their skills and practical knowledge are kept in mind as the innovation is developed.

Learning: technical knowledge. Two things that can interfere with the learning subprocess are defensiveness and selective perception. Some people may purposefully or unknowingly avoid information that is inconsistent with present behavior. This can minimize their conceptual and practical knowledge and, possibly more important, their technical knowledge about innovative programs and the programs they currently are using. Managers may be able to counteract this tendency by having innovations demonstrated to members and providing members with the results of action-research and experimental studies on the innovation. These tactics, however, may increase members' defensiveness and their resistance to new information. An alternative approach is to increase members' technical knowledge about present programs and procedures. Jobs can be modified to give members more task feedback or information about their performance gained in the course of working. When this tactic is not practical, members can be provided with external feedback on the quality of their work.

Teachers can be given information about the progress of their former students; doctors can be provided with medical audit data; and priests and rabbis can collect information about the satisfaction, contributions, and attendance of the members of their congregations. When such feedback data are presented in a confidential and nonthreatening manner, they can help identify performance gaps and promote a search for alternative programs and techniques. The feedback tactic can also make members responsible for evaluating their own performance and give them experience in assessing cause–effect relations. This experience can be valuable in the acquisition of information and interpretation of technical data for new programs.

Even when organizational members are not highly defensive or selectively perceptive, the attributes of innovation can make it difficult for them to acquire relevant technical knowledge. They may not be able to get adequate information about an innovation if the cause–effect time span is long. The impact of some educational innovations is difficult to discern because the effects are not evident for many years. Technical knowledge can be elusive when visibility of consequences is low. A social worker or psychologist may have trouble learning about the effectiveness of a new counseling technique because the intended effects are subtle changes in self-esteem or assertiveness.

Technical knowledge can be a problem when the effects of an innovation are variable or conditional. To the extent that heterogeneous clients are served by an organization, the appropriateness of technological innovations is likely to vary from one client to another. For example, a new training program for the unemployed may be highly effective for certain clients but totally inapplicable to others.

When the effects of an innovation are long term, low in visibility, and variable, it is important for managers to make available to members information on its impact or that of similar programs. When such information does not exist, managers may be able to arrange to have the innovation evaluated by an outside group or get an expert opinion on its effectiveness. When this is too costly, managers can encourage members to experiment with the innovation and gain technical knowledge through experience.

The differential effects of an innovation for different clients or under different circumstances can be estimated by randomly assigning groups of clients to the new program and following their progress systematically. Intermediate criteria for evaluation can be identified if the intended effects of the innovation are long term, and corollary criteria can be identified for low-visibility effects. This way, a teacher might acquire technical knowledge about an alternative learning program for potential dropouts by using it on a small scale. Assuming it is ethical and practical to randomly select students for the experimental program, it is possible to compare their progress with that of students who have not been selected for the program. The program could be assessed in terms of intermediate criteria (student satisfaction, absenteeism, dropout rate) associated with basic long-term objectives that are more difficult to measure. While the experimental approach is time-consuming and involves risks, it may be the most practical way to increase members' technical knowledge about an innovation.

Attitude formation: performance expectancies. Attitudes toward innovations are based partly on expectations about being able to work effectively with new programs or procedures. Attitudes toward a particular innovation may be less than favorable if members expect their efforts will not ensure the effective use of the innovation. Attributes of innovations can lead to low performance expectancies in three ways. First, the level of effort required to use an innovation may be significantly higher than the level on which members' performance expectancies are based. Second, the innovation may be objectively unreliable, and any effort to use the innovation, regardless of the level of that effort, would not necessarily result in effective performance. Third, the innovation may be ambiguous; because people are unclear about what the innovation really is, there is uncertainty about being able to use it effectively.

Organization members are likely to attach low expectations to innovations that are costly in terms of time and money and that require a high level of physical or mental effort. Members may feel that they will not be able to work with these innovations, given the amount of energy they currently allocate to the activities toward which the innovation is directed. Managers may be able to counteract this problem by having innovations developed in ways that are consistent with the resources of the organization and its members. Development efforts carried out with the involvement of members can be particularly effective in achieving this consistency and reducing the effort required to use an innovation. Assuming that costs and energy requirements are reduced through development, members may readjust their thinking and raise their performance expectancies.

When the amount of time, effort, and money required to use the innovation cannot be reduced, managers can use a manipulative strategy to raise members' expectancies. One tactic involves providing members with released time from other activities if they agree to implement a time-consuming innovation. For example, a principal could reduce a teacher's classroom workload so that he or she can assume responsibility for leading a new problem-solving group. Another tactic is subsidizing the innovation by providing members with additional resources that support its use. Either tactic can lead members to base their performance expectancies on a higher level of effort; this adjusted level of effort may be great enough to increase the expected probability that the innovation can be used effectively.

Expectancies can also be low if the innovation is unreliable. Some ideas are so new and untested that they do not always work, regardless of the effort expended. In a research organization, for example, members may attach low performance expectancies to a new computer program that has not yet been debugged. These expectancies may be realistic and managers may have a difficult time raising them. More viable tactics might be to lower members' aspiration levels about the reliability of new programs or make it acceptable for members to spend time and money on programs that may not work. Furthermore, managers can encourage members to consider the future reliability of the program. This approach seems legitimate, since reliability should increase if the program is tried out and properly debugged.

Another reason why members may hold low performance expectancies concerns ambiguity of the innovation. Certain innovations are so unclear or abstract that potential adopters cannot define what proper role performance means. This problem can be illustrated by the attempts of teachers to implement a new role model designed to help them work with a special group of children. The model was unclear, and teachers were not certain about the role performance required by the innovation. While this problem made it difficult to use the innovation, it also probably depressed the teachers' performance expectancies. Efforts are not likely to be seen as leading to effective performance when performance expectations are unclear. This problem can be dealt with by clearly specifying the innovation, having it demonstrated to members, and letting them try it out under simulated conditions.

The limitations of members can also be responsible for low performance expectancies. Members may not have the qualifications necessary to successfully implement an innovation. Awareness by members of their own limitations can be useful if it leads them to reject innovations that are beyond their capabilities. However, this awareness can be dysfunctional if it leads them to reject important innovations which are within their capacity to carry out. In this case, managers can suggest that members evaluate their performance on a learning curve and consider their future capabilities. Members' capabilities then can be enhanced by using some of the tactics outlined above for acquiring practical knowledge.

Other tactics can be used when members do not have the necessary qualifications or when there is no time to develop those qualifications. Managers can allow two or more members with complementary qualifications to cooperate in implementing a change or give them access to technical specialists and assistants. Either approach can increase performance expectancies.

People who have the necessary qualifications but who feel insecure or low in status may shy away from an innovation, because such feelings can lead them to underestimate their chances of success at doing something new. Even if they do not underestimate their capabilities, they may emphasize the probability of failure rather than that of success. Managers can try to overcome these problems by providing members with additional resources and training. When this approach does not work, they can try to reduce the costs associated with failure.

Member's costs can be reduced if they are rewarded for effort rather than performance. This tactic is particularly useful when environmental pressures for change are great but when members are uncertain about their capabilities. Costs to the organization can be reduced if the failure experience is viewed as a learning opportunity. Knowledge gained from a small-scale failure can be helpful in selecting more appropriate changes and in avoiding more costly mistakes in the future.

Attitude formation: outcome expectancies and valences. Attitudes can be un-favorable even toward an innovation that is considered workable. This is the case when people do not believe that an innovation is likely to lead to desired outcomes. Innovations can be uncertain or risky in that they may have an unknown or low probability of resulting in outcomes that are positively valued. They can also be low in compatibility when the expected outcomes are not highly valued or are negatively valued by members.

Managers may be able to reduce uncertainty by using some of the tactics already described. Experimentation and evaluation can help to define the conditions under which a new program or procedure is likely to lead to desired outcomes. Managers can encourage working toward uncertain or risky innovations by not holding potential adopters responsible for out-comes, emphasizing instead definition of the uncertainties and identifi-cation of ways of reducing the uncertainties.

The problem of increasing the compatibility of an innovation is com-plex, because outcomes can be inconsistent with members' values in mul-tiple and subtle ways. First, an innovation may be technically incompatible when its effects are not valued by organizational members. Employees in a social services agency who value personalized service may dislike a proposed assembly-line approach to handling clients even though it might enable them to serve more people. Second, the activities and processes implicit in an innovation may be inconsistent with those valued by po-tential adopters. The personnel in the social services agency may value working with a client from beginning to end and dislike the prospect of performing only one activity numerous times for many different clients. Third, innovations can lead to undesirable secondary outcomes. Members might believe that, by implementing a certain innovation, they will lose status in the organization or become easier to replace.

When an innovation favored by management is perceived to be tech-nically incompatible by members, it may indicate that members are not properly integrated into the organization. Members may not accept some of the basic goals and objectives of the system. Technical incompatibility can also indicate that organizational objectives are improper or misguided. In either case, technical incompatibility means that conflict exists within the organization, and managers may want to deal with it with conflict resolution tactics.

The conflict resolution approach can lead to basic changes in an in-novation or in the way it is implemented. For example, the extent to which an assembly-line method is implemented in a social service agency might be limited as the result of a conflict resolution meeting. Managers and members may agree that the new system can be used for routine cases if the old system is retained for clients with nonroutine problems.

While this solution may reduce the number of clients that might otherwise be handled, it maintains an element of personalized service for those who need the most attention and is more likely to be acceptable to members. By developing this kind of solution, managers can become more sensitive to members' objectives and members can become more aware of organizational goals.

Managers can also modify an innovation that involves activities negatively valued by members. In the social service agency example, members might have been more willing to use the assembly-line system if it did not make their jobs so simple and monotonous. The monotony could be reduced by compromising. Each member could be made responsible for two or three activities rather than one. Or a job rotation plan could be instituted along with the new system, to provide the members with variety.

While compromise solutions cannot always be identified, they can be helpful in motivating members to implement a change and implement it properly. When power strategies are used and members are forced to implement a change that makes their jobs less interesting, they are likely to become dissatisfied and less motivated to perform their jobs well (Lawler, 1973).

Two other tactics can be used when an innovation has indirect or secondary outcomes that are negatively valued by members. One is to reduce the likelihood that the innovation will lead to the unattractive outcome either by modifying the innovation or by making a change in the organization. If members believe that an innovation will make them easy to replace, the manager may be able to guarantee their job security. A second tactic involves tying positively valued outcomes to the innovation to counterbalance the unattractive ones. For example, members can be offered a pay raise if they agree to implement an innovation that might otherwise reduce their status in the organization. The objective here is to improve members' outcome expectancies in ways that increase the perceived relative advantage of the innovation.

Decision making: implementation. Managers may sometimes find that a change or innovation is not implemented even though a member's attitudes toward it are favorable. A number of factors with little bearing on an individual's attitudes toward a particular change may explain this failure. Factors leading to a decision against implementation can involve the innovation itself as well as the characteristics and organizational position of the adopter.

The "terminalism" of an innovation can lead members to decide against implementing it. A terminal is a specific point in time beyond which implementation of an innovation becomes impossible or less rewarding (Zaltman, Florio, and Sikorski, 1973). Members may be unlikely or unable to implement certain changes if a terminal is missed. Managers should therefore be sensitive to terminals and facilitate the timely introduction of a change. A principal, for example, may be able to help a teacher implement a curriculum innovation in time for the next school year by cutting through the bureaucratic red tape. A similar tactic would be appropriate when a member is reluctant to implement an innovation because of the large number of gatekeepers who must sanction the change. A staff psychologist in a large rehabilitation center might decide against introducing an attractive new counseling technique simply because it has to be approved by everyone from the chief psychologist to the state department of corrections. Managers can counteract gatekeeper problems by personally assuming responsibility for getting the change approved or by bringing together in a single meeting the various individuals whose approval is required.

Another reason why members may decide against an innovation concerns the irreversibility of certain implementation decisions. Even if an innovative program is believed to be associated with more positive outcomes than a traditional one, its perceived marginal utility may not be great enough to offset the fact that the decision cannot be reversed. Thus, an evaluation researcher in a government agency may decide not to use a promising new experimental design because the program being evaluated would be irrevocably committed to that design. The problem here is that even a small chance of failure cannot be tolerated, since it is not possible to start over again. Managers can help members with irreversible decisions by getting additional people involved who can analyze the proposal from different perspectives. An in-depth analysis of an irreversible innovation may indicate that the risks associated with the proposed changes are acceptable from the organization's perspective.

The time and costs involved in dismantling an old program and implementing a new one can lead a potential adopter to decide not to implement an innovation. Changes imply certain start-up or transitional costs that, in some cases, may be great from the perspective of the individual but relatively inconsequential from the perspective of the organization. For example, a lighting director in a theater group may feel very positive about a new computerized lighting system but may be concerned about the amount of time and effort required to install it. This level of effort, however, may be acceptable from the vantage point of the group, since over the long run the system would be economical and would add to the quality of the group's performance. Under these and similar circumstances, managers can promote a decision in favor of implementation by providing members with the time and resources required to install the change.

The characteristics of the potential adopters also can explain why positively valued changes are sometimes rejected. A person with a low tolerance of ambiguity may reject a change simply because its implementation would increase uncertainty temporarily. Other people may reject changes because of the strategies or rules they use to make decisions. Though an innovation might be implemented by the people whose decisions are based on the rule of maximizing the probability of positive outcomes, the same innovation might be rejected by those people whose decisions are based on minimizing the probability of negative outcomes.

Certain organizational members may decide not to implement changes because of the way they perceive their roles. Some members of nonprofit organizations feel they are overworked. Role overload can lead them to avoid changes that will be time-consuming to implement. Others may perceive a lack of autonomy and feel their roles are too highly structured to allow for change and innovation. Yet other members may believe it is not their responsibility to introduce change and thus may never get around to making an implementation decision.

Managers can respond to such problems by creating an organizational climate that is supportive of change, innovation, and experimentation. This climate can be promoted by rewarding members for success rather than penalizing them for failures, by providing members with the autonomy they need to try out new ideas, and by compensating members for the time and effort they might expend to introduce changes. Managers can formally expand members' roles to include problem-solving and change-initiation responsibilities.

A final strategy for creating a supportive climate is to establish structures that support systemwide change. An organization that actively responds to pressures for change can prompt its members to introduce innovations on their own more readily than an organization that is stagnant and inflexible. Change-supporting structures may be useful not only for generating change at the organizational level but also for creating an organizational climate that encourages change initiation on the part of individual members.

REFERENCES

Cooke, R. A., L. M. Uhlaner, and R. P. Quinn. "The Decision to Recycle: Applying Motivation and Innovation Models to Environment Research," final report to the Institute for Environmental Quality (Ann Arbor, Mich.: Institute for Social Research, 1975).

Coughlan, R. J. School Survey Program Feedback Guide (Chicago: University of Chicago Press, 1967).

Duncan, R. B., Susan A. Mohrman, Allan M. Mohrman, Robert A. Cooke, and Gerald Zaltman. "An Assessment of a Structural Task Approach to Organizational Development in a School System," final report to the National Institute of Education (Ann Arbor, Mich.: Institute for Social Research, 1977).

Georgopoulos, B. S., ed. *Organization Research on Health Institutions* (Ann Arbor, Mich.: Institute for Social Research, 1972).

Hage, G., and M. Aiken. *Social Change in Complex Organizations* (New York: Random House, 1970).

Katz, D., and R. L. Kahn. *The Social Psychology of Organizations,* 2nd ed. (New York: Wiley, 1978).

Lawler, E. E. *Motivation in Work Organizations* (Monterey, Cal.: Brooks/Cole, 1973).

Leavitt, H. J. "Applied Organizational Change in Industry: Structural, Technological, and Humanistic Approaches," in J. G. March, ed., *Handbook of Organizations* (Chicago: Rand-McNally, 1965).

Maier, N. R. F. *Problem Solving and Creativity in Individuals and Groups* (Belmont: Cal.: Brooks/Cole, 1970).

Mann, F., and R. Likert. "The Need for Research on the Communication of Research Results," *Human Organization,* Vol. 11, No. 4 (1952), pp. 15–19.

McGregor, D. M. "The Human Side of Enterprise," in H. J. Leavitt and L. R. Pondy, eds., *Readings in Managerial Psychology* (Chicago: University of Chicago Press, 1964).

Morris, W. C., and M. Sashkin. *Organization Behavior in Action: Skill Building Experiences* (New York: West, 1976).

Nadler, D. A. *Feedback and Organization Development: Using Data-Based Methods* (Reading, Mass.: Addison-Wesley, 1977).

Newman, W. H., and H. W. Wallender. "Managing Not-for-profit Enterprises," *Academy of Management Review,* Vol. 3 (1978), pp. 24–31.

Robertson, T. S. *Innovative Behavior and Communication* (New York: Holt, Rinehart and Winston, 1971).

Rogers, E. M., and F. F. Shoemaker. *Communication of Innovation: A Cross-Cultural Approach* (New York: Free Press, 1971).

Spindler, G., ed. *Education and Culture: Anthropological Approaches* (New York: Holt, Rinehart and Winston, 1963).

Zaltman, G., and R. B. Duncan. *Strategies for Planned Change* (New York: Wiley, 1977).

Zaltman, G., R. B. Duncan, and J. Holbek. *Innovations and Organizations* (New York: Wiley, 1973).

Zaltman, G., D. Florio, and L. Sikorski. *Dynamic Educational Change: Models, Strategies, Tactics, and Management* (New York: Free Press, 1977).

PART II
Planning

CHAPTER 6

Problem Management: A Behavioral Science Approach

Ralph H. Kilmann

Editor's Note   *Problems that are simple in for-profit organizations are usually ill defined when they occur in nonprofit organizations. With increasingly dynamic and changing environments surrounding organizations, problem management has become one of the most difficult tasks faced by managers in nonprofit organizations. It is very important, therefore, that the reader understand techniques for managing problems.*

This chapter defines the five generic steps of problem management, highlighting what constitutes effective problem solving and the types of errors to be avoided. These five steps are (1) sensing the problem, (2) defining the problem, (3) deriving solutions, (4) implementing particular solutions, and (5) evaluating outcomes of implemented solutions.

The processes and structures involved in problem management are distinguished from one another. A distinction is also made between problems of individuals and interpersonal problems. Each of these action areas is studied separately and all are integrated with the five generic steps of problem management.

Process denotes events, sequences, or episodes that take place over time within organizational members or between them. Structure denotes the conditions, forces, or constraints that influence behavior in organizations, and may refer either to the stable attributes or personality characteristics of people or to stable external conditions such as interpersonal interaction and organizational designs, goals, or reward system. These two basic distinctions in combination create four possible areas of focus in problem management: external–process, external–structure, internal–process, and internal–structure.

Internal–structure refers to the various attitudes, characteristics, and abilities of individuals that can affect the performance of various participants in problem management. Internal–process refers to the thought processes individuals use in addressing a problem. External–structure is the arrangement of individuals into groups (or intergroup combinations) to best utilize problem management resources in the organization. Five different group design structures may be adopted, depending upon the conditions: ad hoc, personality, vested interest, task and people preference, and random assignment design. External–process concerns interactions that take place among individuals once they are placed in various group and intergroup arrangements.

The Problem Management Wheel, illustrated in the chapter, shows how these elements are interrelated and dependent on each other.

Managers are continually beset with problems. Some of these are very well structured, concrete, easily definable, and solvable. For example, which of three photocopiers is most economical to purchase or lease given the projected duplicating needs of the high school? Which of two candidates would best fit the job of assistant to the hospital administrator? Which of three methods of inventory control would minimize out-of-stock inconveniences with regard to the welfare agency's reporting forms? Other problems are very ill structured, vague, and difficult to define, and it is not often known if lasting solutions can be found, since the nature of the problem keeps changing. For example, should the university's goals be altered? How should civil service employees be effectively motivated? What new charitable programs should the organization formulate and implement? Which new medical science technologies can and should be developed?

One might even define the essence of management as problem defining and problem solving, whether the problems are well structured, ill structured, technical, human, or even environmental. Managers of organizations would then be viewed as *problem managers,* regardless of the types of products and services they help their organizations provide. It should be noted that managers have often been considered as generic decision makers rather than as problem solvers or problem managers. Perhaps decision making is more akin to solving well-structured problems where the nature of the problem is so obvious that one can already begin the process of deciding among clear-cut alternatives. However, decisions cannot be made effectively if the problem is not yet defined and if it is not at all clear what the alternatives are, can, or should be. (For a more comprehensive discussion, see Kilmann and Mitroff, in press.)

THE NEED FOR PROBLEM MANAGEMENT

It has become apparent to most management scholars and practitioners that contemporary organizations are facing increasingly dynamic and changing environments. This poses more complex and ill-defined problems than organizations have previously had to address. (Alvin Toffler's *Future Shock* presents an excellent discussion on the pervasiveness of such changes and how this fosters complex problems.) Further, complex problems often involve the entire organization, not just one or two departments or one or two individuals. These problems can never be completely resolved, since they are always present (for example, relevance of organizational goals to changing societal needs). This suggests that the shift of the manager from decision maker to problem definer and solver (that is, problem manager) is quite appropriate.

Organizations, however, are designed for performing specific, day-to-day activities and for providing well-defined products and services—not for addressing complex and changing problems. In particular, organizations have operational subunits (medical specializations as in hospitals, teaching programs as in schools and universities, social programs as in government agencies) to pursue fairly well-defined goals and tasks. But how can the organization engage in effective problem management if it is primarily designed for day-to-day concerns and if complex and changing problems do not fit well into the design categories or boxes on the organization's chart? Also, what if people in the organization are trained and expected to spend most or all of their time managing daily matters in their specific departments and not ill-defined and fuzzy matters that cut across department lines? What if routine matters and goals of "productivity" drive out planning and creativity? Perhaps effective problem management is becoming a much needed function for organizations. Perhaps available knowledge about individual and organizational behavior should be applied to suggest how effective problem management can be designed and conducted (see Kilmann, 1977).

While the above arguments are as relevant to profit as well as nonprofit organizations, the latter seem to require more explicit problem management. Briefly, profit-based organizations have available a number of yardsticks for decision making and problem solving which nonprofit organizations do not. And even though profit-based, economic decision models are often far removed from the real-world conditions of uncertainty and incomplete information, they nevertheless provide some guides for decisions and actions (see Downs, 1966). Some simple problems for profit organizations (decision making) become more ill defined when these same types of problems are considered for nonprofit organizations. For example, a rather straightforward cost-benefit analysis for developing a new product in a particular market for a profit organization becomes broadened to include political, geographical, and legal "fuzzy" issues when a nonprofit organization considers expanding its services.

This chapter seeks to provide a comprehensive discussion on problem management especially suited for nonprofit organizations. Questions to be explored include: Who should be selected to engage in problem management? What should the criteria of selection be? What type of special logic or thought process is especially suited to defining problems? How should individuals be composed into groups in order to partake in problem management effectively? How does one assess effectiveness in problem management? How should individuals interact with one another so that problems are defined and solved properly? How should individuals resolve their differences if they disagree on the nature of the problem? Are there certain basic steps to go through to assure that problems will be managed effectively? What errors can take place at each step?

Because all these questions demonstrate just how complicated problem management is, a special effort is made to organize the discussions into frameworks and diagrams which will help in sorting the material into meaningful, related subparts. This chapter first presents a definition and discussion of the five generic steps of problem management. Included is a discussion of what constitutes effective problem management and the types of errors which need to be either avoided or minimized at each step. The *processes* are then distinguished from the *structures* involved in problem management and attention is directed to whether these processes and structures take place and exist within individuals or between individuals (as in group interactions). These distinctions form four very different but equally important action areas of problem management—that is, areas for acting upon and addressing the types of questions noted above. The four action areas are explored separately, with suggested principles and guidelines for ensuring that each is identified and conducted appropriately. Finally, the chapter presents the Problem Management Wheel, an integrated diagram portraying not only the four separate action areas and the five generic steps of problem management, but also how these need to be linked together in order to foster overall effectiveness.

THE GENERIC STEPS OF PROBLEM MANAGEMENT

Most people in organizations experience and act upon problems, either implicitly or explicitly. Sometimes managers (for example, school administrators) bring in outside consultants (curriculum specialists) to help them solve organizational problems. While managers or consultants may differ in how they approach problems, one can define certain ideal or typical steps that should or can be conducted whenever the issues emerge as to what is wrong and what can be done about it. In fact, it can be argued that styles of problem management differ according to how the ideal or typical steps are conducted as well as whether certain steps are emphasized and others ignored.

Figure 6–1 shows the five general steps of problem-defining and problem-solving processes: sensing the problem, defining the problem, deriving solutions to the problem, implementing particular solutions, and eval-

FIGURE 6-1. *The five generic steps of problem management.*

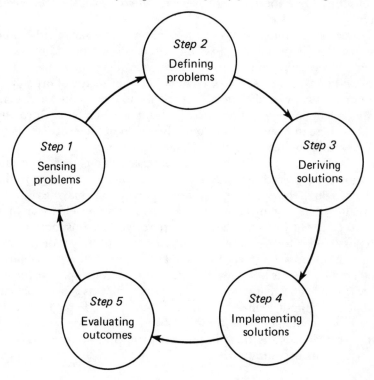

uating the outcomes of the implemented solutions. The cycle then repeats by noting whether a problem is still sensed. Certainly, one could list other decisions or action steps in this process (for example, choosing various strategies for implementing solutions or choosing approaches for evaluating outcomes), but these could be incorporated into the key five steps.

Step 1: Sensing the Problem

One would logically expect the process to start at a point where one or more individuals in the organization sense that something is wrong or that some problem exists. A problem is here defined as a discrepancy between what is (current performance) and what could or should be (expected performance or organizational goals). Once the gap between what is and what should be goes beyond some threshold, a problem is perceived. For example, the turnover rate in a museum may be 15 percent per year, which may be expected given the nature of the labor force and the general mobility expected. However, if the turnover rate became as high as 40 percent, individuals may well perceive some problems, since this rate significantly exceeds their expectations or threshold levels. This type of sensing or experiencing has been referred to as the "felt need for change."

Any number of indicators, both formal and informal, can be used to assess whether a problem exists: increased cost of providing services, smaller appropriation of resources, decrease in clientele, competing agencies providing the same services, change in public image of organization, low morale, turnover, absenteeism, increase in complaints, and general anxiety or frustration on the part of civil service members. Once any or several of these indicators break some threshold of tolerance, individuals in the organization usually perceive that problems exist.

An exception to this might be when goals, aspirations, and expectations are so low that everything seems fine even though the organization is slowly decaying. Here the organization's perceptions may be out of line with reality. The organization may be denying its problems or may be afraid to confront problems because it perceives itself as ineffective. All these possibilities for denying the existence of a problem (or not recognizing a problem) are referred to as a Type 0 error: the probability that a problem exists but is not sensed. For example, any complex government agency which claims that it does not have *any* problems is probably stating its problems without realizing it and is commiting a Type 0 error. Likewise, a large school system without problems simply does not exist. The question is: What is the most important problem to address, given the resources of the organization?

Step 2: Defining the Problem

Once it is sensed that a problem exists, step 2 is to define just what the problem is. For example, is the museum's high turnover the result of interpersonal conflict, low job satisfaction, few promotion opportunities, competitive job offers from other organizations, a change in the nature of the job market, a basic problem in job description, or outdated organizational tasks? Any or several of these possible problem definitions could be the reason behind the high turnover rate. Specifically, the problem is viewed as the *cause* for an indicator breaking the threshold. The object of this step, therefore, is to work backward from the perceived difficulty to try to determine or suggest what really caused it.

Problem definition is probably the least understood step in the whole process, because it is the most ill structured. How does one know when a problem is defined properly? What are the alternative definitions to a problem situation (as distinguished from solutions), and how can these alternative definitions be generated? How should alternative problem definitions be evaluated and a single or integrated (synthesized) definition be chosen?

Because problem definition is so ill structured and often subjective, it is not surprising that problem managers as well as consultants often bypass this part of the process. They simply assume that they know what the problem is. In particular, it appears that each external consultant or internal manager applies his approach to the problems of the organization without carefully considering whether that approach is indeed suited for the organization's particular problem. Of course, most individuals assert that it would be inappropriate and even unethical to use approaches, including their own, if these were not germane to the organization (that is, if they would not solve the organization's problems). But one must consider whether the problem manager can really be objective in such a decision. This is especially the case if, like most professionals, he is trained in one or at most two specialties and therefore cannot assess whether other approaches would really be better suited to the problem at hand.

It is natural, for example, to expect that a human resource manager or consultant trained in interpersonal relationships and group dynamics would perceive that the inefficiencies in the organization are caused by less than adequate interpersonal relationships and group processes; that a manager specializing in marketing would view the same situation as being caused by ineffective advertising campaigns; and that an industrial engineer would see the identical situation as stemming from man-machine interface problems or the inefficient flow of work materials. The same "selective perception" and biases could also be expected from managers specializing in operations management, accounting and finance, management information systems, and so on.

While the major error of problem sensing is denying the existence of a problem and assuming that everything is fine (Type 0 error), the major error of problem definition is formally referred to as the Type III error: the probability of solving the wrong problem instead of the right problem (Mitroff and Featheringham, 1974) or solving the trivial problem rather than the most important problem given the resources and needs of the organization. But how do managers of the organization define what the basic problem is that is causing the various perceptions? More often than not, as has been suggested, individuals assume that their view of the world (their specialty) defines the essence of the problem. Alternatively, some top manager or person "close to the problem" defines what it is and all attention, including the time and energy of other managers and consultants, is devoted to solving that definition of the problem. And when one asks, "Why are you implementing that particular solution or approach?" the response is, "Because such and such is the problem." "And why is that the problem?" The response follows, "Because the director says it is so."

One might wonder if such implicit problem definitions do not typically result in significant Type III errors—solving the wrong problem. Experience has shown that a particular definition of the problem is addressed because that is the way it was always done, even if the existence or sensing of the problem never disappears or gets resolved. An example is the hospital administrator who defines the problem of needing better doctors when the real problem is that the existing doctors (or even new doctors) cannot communicate across their medical specialties to address complex patient ills.

Step 3: Deriving and Selecting Solutions

Step 3 in the process concerns the derivation of solutions to the already defined problem and the selection of a single solution. Most discussions on decision theory, management decision making, and even statistical decision analysis concentrate on this aspect of the process. One can usually construct a "decision tree" indicating the alternatives that are available in the situation (as branches of the tree), with associated costs and probabilities of leading to the desired outcome (generally with respect to optimality). Sometimes, alternate action steps follow beyond each main alternative resulting in branches leading off from other branches. Then, a cost-benefit analysis or a calculation of the expected net value for each alternative enables the decision maker (problem manager) to choose a single solution to the previously defined problem. (Because this part of the process is well documented in other literatures, further details are not presented here. (see, for example, Schlaifer, 1959.)

Two related errors have been discussed extensively with respect to choosing between two well-defined alternatives in statistics which can be generalized to choosing among several alternative solutions to a problem. Type I and Type II errors are the probability of not rejecting alternative A when B is in fact "true" or the best, and the probability of accepting alternative B when A is in fact "true" or best, respectively. These two errors, of course, assume the relevance, importance, and rightness of the problem definition for which the alternative solutions are desired. But if a Type III error has been committed (defining the problem incorrectly), consideration of Type I and Type II errors is meaningless and irrelevant. Type I and Type II errors concern the appropriate choice among the branches of a given decision tree, while Type III errors concern whether the right decision tree was chosen when compared with alternative *whole* decision trees.

Perhaps an anecdote (modified from Ackoff, 1960) would help to distinguish these important errors relative to problem definition and alternative solutions. This story takes place in a large university building where the administrator began receiving more and more complaints from students concerning the long time spent waiting for elevators. Sensing there was a problem (from the many complaints), he consulted his engineering staff for a solution. Naturally, the staff defined the problem implicitly as a technical one. In fact, it seemed as though the problem definition was not even an issue; it was simply assumed. The engineers suggested two alternatives for a decision tree: speed up the existing elevators or install new elevators. Both alternatives incurred a very high cost.

As the administrator was weighing these alternatives, he shared the problem with another person on his staff who had a background in psychology. This person suggested that the problem was a human one—that the perception of time is subjective and perhaps the students complain because they cannot do anything else while time passes waiting for the elevators. Defining the problem in these terms suggested two alternatives: place mirrors in the hallways at the elevator entrance on each floor, or place display cases there containing interesting and informative materials or news items. These alternative solutions were much cheaper than the first two, and actually solved the problem when implemented (there were fewer complaints).

This anecdote illustrates how a different problem definition (human versus technical) not only addresses the problem situation quite differently but does so with entirely different solution alternatives. Choosing the psychological type of definition versus the engineering type of definition is an example of a Type III error (in choosing a whole decision tree). Once a given definition is chosen, the choice of alternative solutions is an example of Type I and Type II errors (in choosing a branch of the given decision tree). While the rightness or wrongness of the problem definition in this anecdote may come down primarily to money considerations, in other problem solutions the issues might include morale, public image, ease of implementation, and other intangible yet real consequences of alternative problem definitions.

Step 4: Implementing Solutions

Step 4 in the process concerns the implementation of the chosen solution. It is one thing to derive what appears to be the optimal or best solution and quite another to implement it effectively in the organization. One can usually cite many examples of excellent solutions which were implemented poorly, not at all, at the wrong time, by the wrong people, or simply in the wrong way. Implementation should not be taken for granted—one should not assume that a good solution will automatically be accepted and find its way into the mainstream of organizational activity. There is resistance to change in any organization—members may perceive costs and psychological losses as outweighing the benefits of the proposed change. In addition to the technical and purely economic aspects of implementing solutions, therefore, there are psychological and social aspects. The latter are often a more powerful deterrent to successful implementation than the former.

The literature on organizational innovation has provided a view of the innovation process which is quite analogous to an organization adopting or implementing something new or some newly derived solution to a problem. A number of factors have been specified as affecting the likelihood that a given innovation or solution will be accepted and utilized by the members of the organization. Specifically, the model includes the following factors as perceived by organizational members: (1) the new or target level of performance of the organization (or subset of the organization considering the chosen solution), (2) the organization's current level of performance, (3) the costs associated with adopting the solution, (4) the rewards associated with adopting the solution, (5) the probability that adoption of the solution will lead to achievement of the target level of performance, and (6) the probability that the target level can be achieved without the adoption of the solution (Slevin, 1973; Schultz and Slevin, 1975). The target level or level of performance can be generalized to any indicator wherein the organization first sensed a problem, defined it, and then chose a particular solution. This solution is intended to bring the current level of the indicator up to the desired target level.

Various combinations or comparisons of the above factors can highlight different types of constraining forces acting on implementation. Comparing the target level of performance with the current level indicates the aspirations of organizational members for improving the organization. The perceived costs relative to the perceived rewards of implementing the solution are an important indicator of the incentives operating in the situation (for example, incentives that motivate or demotivate member acceptance). Also, differences in the probabilities of achieving the target level of performance with or without the adoption of the solution suggest members' expectations concerning the possible impact of the implemented solution.

These concerns and issues suggest the many ways in which the implementation step can fail to achieve expected results. Basically, the members of the organization, for many reasons, may not accept the implemented solution, resist it, modify it, or even sabotage it. Not planning for implementation and not anticipating obstacles, resistances, and forces operating to keep things the same results in the Type IV error: the probability of not implementing a solution properly (Slevin, 1973; Schultz and Slevin, 1975). No matter how well the other steps in the process have been conducted and to what extent the other errors have been minimized (Type I, II, and III errors), committing a significant Type IV error can nullify the total effort at effective problem management.

To use the example of the elevator problem discussed earlier, a Type IV error would occur if the administrator had selected the solution of installing mirrors at each floor, but the mirrors that were installed were asthetically unappealing to waiting students, or if the mirrors were too small or were not located in convenient places near the elevators, or if the halls were too dark to make appropriate use of the mirrors. Certainly the assumption behind installing the mirrors and managing the Type III error was that the mirrors would be used while students waited for the elevators. Ignoring the logistics and psychological factors which affect the *use* of the solution results in a Type IV error. Alternatively, even if the solution of installing more elevators were chosen, the new elevators would have to be regarded as safe, pleasant, and efficient. Otherwise, the students might prefer to wait for the old elevators—which demonstrates a Type IV error on top of a Type III error.

Step 5: Evaluating Outcomes

The final step in the process shown in Figure 6–1 is evaluating the outcomes resulting from the implemented solution. Step 5 thus asks if the implemented solution actually solved the initially sensed problem. If the indicators focused on previously are no longer beyond the threshold levels, the organization may assume that the problem has been managed properly—if it is sure that it is not committing a Type 0 error. It is possible, however, for the problem to "go away" by itself, without any effort from the organization. In either case, the organization does not need to be concerned about the problem further (at least at this time). But solving the initial problem may lead to the creation or perception of other problems, and these newly identified problems may motivate the organization to continue the cycle.

If the initial problem is still sensed after the organization has gone through all five steps, it is likely that one of the steps was done incorrectly or that one or a combination of Type I, II, III, or IV errors was committed. The evaluation step is critical in attempting to pinpoint which error or errors were made prior to going through the process again in order to manage the initial problem effectively. This assumes, of course, that the evaluation step is conducted correctly in the sense of accurately measuring the "performance" and outcome of each preceding step. Perhaps a Type V error can be defined as the probability of evaluating the problem management process incorrectly. Recent research on program evaluation is seeking to minimize this error (Weiss, 1972), but for now we will assume that the organization can conduct this step appropriately.

If the initial problem is still sensed, was the problem defined correctly? Because the Type III error is the most pervasive of all the errors, this question should be asked first. Subsequent discussions in this chapter will consider the ways in which the Type III error can be minimized. This can be done by the explicit use of multiple problem definitions developed by diverse representation throughout the organization. Also helpful is the use of various individual, group, and intergroup processes in order to first debate and then synthesize these multiple perspectives. Type I and II errors, although important, are not as critical as Type III. However, the cost-benefit analysis can be rechecked to see if the wrong solution was chosen. Perhaps efforts should also be directed to discovering or creating solutions that were not considered in the first analysis but that may turn out to be much better solutions after all.

Finally, the Type IV error has to be questioned. The organization must assess whether various unanticipated resistances, obstacles, or unintended consequences overcame the benefits which could be potentially derived from the chosen solution. If a Type IV error is detected, steps have to be taken to implement the solution in a different way, taking the new awareness of implementation obstacles into account.

When a full assessment has been made, the first part of step 5 is complete. The second part of step 5 involves a strategy for re-engaging in steps 2, 3, and 4, depending on where the errors were made. That is, a strategy is developed for performing one or more steps differently from before in order to manage the initial problem more effectively. The cycle of steps is then repeated, arriving back at step 5, where the question of whether the initial problem has been resolved is again addressed. Going through the cycle of problem management once or just a few times should resolve the initial problem or at least help to continually manage very complex recurring problems.

Figure 6–1 suggests that the effectiveness of a problem management effort is a multiplicative function of all five steps. That is, if a major error is made in any step, the overall effectiveness is zero (anything multiplied by zero is zero). Failing to implement the right solution (Type IV error) and implementing a solution to the wrong problem (Type III error) are probably the most obvious examples. Selecting a weak solution rather than a better solution (Type I and Type II errors), failing to sense the existence of a significant problem (Type 0 error), and incorrectly evaluating the impact of a solution on a problem situation (Type V error) are more subtle examples of the multiplicative relationship among the five steps.

BEHAVIORAL ACTION STEPS FOR PROBLEM MANAGEMENT

The foregoing discussion has outlined the generic problem-defining and problem-solving process and has defined the effectiveness of problem management in terms of the five basic steps. It is necessary, now, to relate this process to an organizational setting and to consider the specific *behavioral* actions by which steps 1 through 5 can best be executed. In other words, the initial view of problem management has to be expanded to include such questions as these: Who should be involved in the process? From what parts of the organization should they come? What abilities or attributes should these members have in order to engage in the process effectively? Do we need different people for different steps? How should these members be designed into organized groups so that the process can be conducted efficiently as well as effectively? How should these members interact with one another in designed groupings so that the most can be made of their expertise in addressing the problems of the organization?

Thus, although Figure 6–1 helps to describe and define the steps involved in problem management in some *abstract* sense, practicing managers and consultants need concrete principles and guidelines on how to carry out this process for problems in their specific organization. Basically, what is needed is a translation from theory to practice in order to answer the above questions. A framework (adapted from Kilmann and Thomas, 1978) will now be presented which sorts the above questions into four areas of action steps that managers can utilize in any problem situation so that the potential for effective problem management can be realized.

Figure 6–2 shows the framework for organizing the important action areas for problem management. The four areas are defined by two basic distinctions: process versus structure and internal versus external. The process-structure distinction refers to the types of variables or action options available to the problem manager. Process denotes events, sequences, or episodes which take place over time among organizational members (the people who will be engaging in the generic process shown in Figure 6–1). Structure denotes the conditions, forces, or constraints which influence or guide behavior in organizations and may refer either to the stable attributes within people or the stable conditions existing outside people, in the *environment* of behavior. Consequently, while the process perspective places people in a sequence of events, the structure

FIGURE 6-2. *Four action areas for problem management.*

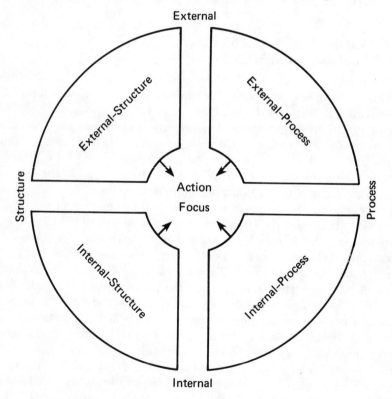

model places people in a web of forces as an explanation of people's behavior or as a strategy to change or influence behavior.

The internal-external distinction, as implied above, refers to whether the focus for action or choice is within people, as in mental activity (process) or personality characteristics (structure), or outside people, as in interpersonal interactions (process) or organizational designs, goals, or reward systems (structures). Combining the two basic distinctions results in four possible areas of action in problem management in an organization: external–process, external–structure, internal–process, and internal–structure. The four action areas shown in Figure 6–2 are meant to provide a basis for translating the abstract process into problem management activity in the organization.

Internal–structure represents the various attitudes, characteristics, abilities, dispositions, and beliefs of individuals that may bear upon the effectiveness of organizational members in the steps of problem management. Certain individuals, because of their personality characteristics, may be better at sensing problems or defining problems, while other personality types may be better at problem solving and implementation. Bearing in mind the relationship between personality style and the steps of problem management will help managers select individuals from the organization to engage in problem management activities, or at least will help them appreciate how different styles are likely to address the same problem situation.

Internal–process represents the mental activities, thought processes, or logic with which individuals "work through" a problem. Here the concern is whether individuals are applying the type of logic suited to the nature of the problem. One action area for problem managers is to help individuals think about problems in new ways and to make their analysis or thought process explicit when inquiring into alternate definitions of the problem or different solutions. For example, making one's assumptions explicit is an important mental activity which bears strongly on the effectiveness of how different problem definitions are illuminated and analyzed.

External–structure is concerned with the design of problem management groups—that is, the arrangement of individuals into groups as well as intergroup combinations in order to best utilize the problem management resources in the organization. Groups can be more powerful and effective than separate individuals in problem management as well as in other organizational activities. Setting up useful group structures is therefore an essential part of moving members of the organization through the five steps of problem management effectively.

Finally, external–process concerns the interactions (processes) which take place among individuals once they are designed into various group and intergroup arrangements. Which type of interaction is most conducive to creativity, the articulation of differences, and the resolution of differences? Are different modes of interaction appropriate to each different aspect of problem management? Specifically, external–process focuses on ways in which conflicts or differences are addressed and managed, since the five generic steps have much to do with the development and management of conflict. And how conflict is handled has much to do with the quality of the problem definition as well as the acceptance of the implemented solution by organizational members.

Each of the four action areas will now be explored in more depth in order to develop specific guidelines or principles for conducting problem management effectively. The chapter will then conclude with a comprehensive, integrated model, the Problem Management Wheel, which summarizes all the important aspects of problem management.

Internal–Structure

The personality typology of C. G. Jung (1923) has been shown to be quite useful in explaining the effect of individual differences in organizational settings. Specifically, the Jungian framework considers individuals as having developed characteristic ways of taking in information and then making decisions on the basis of this information. Much of organizational activity in general, and problem management in particular, includes sensing or collecting information and making decisions (choosing a problem definition, selecting an alternate solution, deciding on an implementation strategy, and so on). It is therefore apparent why this framework has received so much attention. In addition, the Jungian personality characteristics to be described below, are expected to be fairly stable attributes of people. People prefer a certain style of taking in information and making decisions. This style remains fairly constant over time and thus fits well into the action area of internal–structure.

There are two basic ways in which people take in information: sensation and intuition. Sensation refers to the preference for taking in information directly by the five senses. It focuses on the details, facts, and specifics of any situation, the here and now, the immediately tangible data, the itemized parts, and so on. In contrast, intuition is a preference for the whole rather than the parts, for the possibilities, hunches, or future implications of any situation, the extrapolations, interpolations, and any unique interrelationships among pieces of information. Thus with intuition the focus is beyond the parts; with sensation the focus is on the parts themselves. According to Jung, people develop a preference for one type of information-taking mode; and although individuals can do both if required, they cannot do both equally well, nor do they like to do both equally well—they simply *prefer* one over the other. In fact, the information-taking mode which is not preferred is often referred to as an individual's blind side or his weaker function.

There are two basic ways in which individuals arrive at decisions: thinking and feeling. Thinking refers to a very impersonal, logical, analytical, reasoned preference for making a decision. If such and such is true, then this and that follow, based on logical analysis. Feeling, on the other hand, is a very personal, value-laden, unique mode for making a decision. Does the person "like" that alternative? Does it fit with his values and the image he has of himself? While the development of such a conclusion is not logical, it is not illogical either. Rather, feeling is alogical, or simply based on a different style of reaching decisions. Just as they do with sensation and intuition, individuals develop a preference for either thinking or feeling. Although individuals can apply either when required, they may be uncomfortable and simply not sure of themselves and their decision when they utilize their weaker function.

The two personality characteristics associated with information and decision making, when combined, result in four personality types: sensation–thinking (ST), intuition–thinking (NT), sensation–feeling (SF), and intuition–feeling (NF). Each type represents a particular combination of an information-taking and decision-making preference which is manifested when individuals engage in any aspect of problem management. Consider the following:

ST (sensation–thinking) individuals prefer the well-structured aspects of problem management. They prefer clear-cut alternatives, supported by detailed information on every consequence of a decision, and they choose a particular alternative on the basis of a logical, impersonal analysis (such as a cost-benefit calculation). STs seek single answers to all questions and prefer the answers to be clearly right or wrong, as determined by some analytical assessment. It is not surprising, then, that STs are most comfortable with step 3 of problem management, where specific solutions are derived and, better yet, each alternative is carefully analyzed in order to pick the best solution to implement. STs are uncomfortable with uncertainty, imprecision, subjective criteria, and personal interactions, but these qualities are not heavily germane to step 3.

NT (intuition–thinking) individuals prefer the development of many possible ways of looking at a complex situation, where each way is a broad, abstract perspective. NTs have a high tolerance for ambiguity, perhaps because they prefer not to get down to details; therefore, at a very general level, differences can be managed easily. In addition, however, NTs recognize that there are always alternative views, especially in complex situations. They get bored, in fact, with well-structured, routine types of problems. NTs therefore are generally most comfortable with step 2 of problem management, where alternative problem definitions are considered and then synthesized. Such a synthesis is facilitated by the NT's analytical ability, if only at an abstract, theoretical level. But because of their preference for thinking, NTs require some initial structured input—perhaps an indication that some problem already exists.

NF (intuition–feeling) individuals enjoy the most ill-defined, ambiguous situations. In fact, it might be said that NFs thrive on uncertainty and ambiguity. They thus function best when there is a minimum of structure or order, or when problems have not even been defined or sensed. NFs are most comfortable in noting when something is wrong or sensing that some problem exists. Because of their preferences, however, they become uncomfortable with moving past step 1. This would take them into the more structured realm of problem management which is their blind side or weaker function.

SF (sensation–feeling) individuals enjoy interpersonal interactions with specific people. This satisfies their preference for concrete details as well as their personal, value-laden preference for being with people (where subjective, qualitative, and "liking" criteria are paramount). SFs enjoy the people part of problem management. They are concerned with the unique needs of particular people in the organization—rather than with analytical aspects of problem management (ST or NT) or the broad aspects of problem sensing (NF). SFs therefore are most natural for step 4: implementing solutions. Their orientation enables them to best consider the impact of the solution on the members of the organization—the kinds of needs, resistances, fears, and other unique reactions which are likely to be manifested. Such sensitivity enables SFs to guide implementation effectively.

It should be emphasized that the above description of personality types applied to problem management portrays the extremes (see Kilmann and Mitroff, in press). One should not conclude that only NFs can sense problems, NTs define problems, STs derive and choose solutions, and SFs guide implementation. Rather, these *preferences* as personality characteristics (internal–structure) enable certain aspects of problem management to be performed better than others. It is not that an ST cannot sense problems or guide implementation, but that an NF and SF, respectively, will be more natural at it and might do it a little better as a result. But because NF is the exact opposite of ST, the latter will have greatest difficulty in problem sensing while the former will have greatest difficulty in calculating solutions. Similarly, an SF will have the most difficult time defining complex problems, while an NT will really have to push himself in guiding the implementation of a solution.

It is not surprising to suggest, therefore, that one person or persons of only one type will have difficulty performing the entire problem management cycle. This is especially evident in step 5 (evaluation), where, if the initial problem is still sensed, each prior step has to be examined to see how well it was performed and whether any errors were made. Different steps in the cycle, therefore, require different personality preferences. Consequently, a problem manager selecting members to engage in the cycle should be guided by the following:

- Include people with diverse personality types in problem management so that resources are available to do each step in the cycle well.
- When possible, have NFs focus on problem sensing, NTs on problem defining, STs on problem solving, and SFs on implementation.
- Be aware of these different personality types and know how each contributes to overall effectiveness.
- Develop your own personality preference so that you can begin to perform (and not just appreciate) each step in the cycle.

Managing by the above guidelines is expected to facilitate a valid evaluation of the problem-solving process, since each separate step can be properly evaluated only if its unique features are appreciated and learned.

In addition to capitalizing on personality differences in members, it is important to keep in mind other criteria for selecting people to engage in the five-step process of problem management. Certain areas of expertise—for example, in accounting, marketing, and the service that the organization is providing—need to be represented in the people involved in problem management, depending on the extent and complexity of the problems in question. In other words, it is necessary to have knowledgeable people as well as certain personality types in order for problem management to be effective.

Furthermore, commitment and member involvement are fundamental in considering whether the implementation of a solution to the problem will be *accepted* by organizational members. The varieties of resistance to change and of forces to keep things the same were discussed in the section on step 4—implementing the chosen solution. In general, the more that individuals are involved in making decisions (or affecting decisions) which concern them, the more likely they will be to accept and be committed to the decisions (Leavitt, 1965). Involvement fosters ownership and a feeling of oneness with the organization. Lack of involvement on matters directly relevant to the individual fosters alienation, resistance, and even rejection. Consequently, in addition to personality and expertise considerations, participants in problem management should be chosen because they will be potentially affected by whatever solutions are implemented. For complex problems, this often includes representation from most segments of the organization and even representation from outside sectors (such as clients, consumers, and lobbying groups).

The following additional guidelines are therefore offered for selecting members according to the internal–structure aspects of problem management:

- Select people who are experiencing the problems.
- Select people who have the expertise to define and solve problems in various specialties.
- Select people whose commitment to the problem definition and resulting solutions will be necessary in order for the solution to be implemented successfully, and who are expected to be affected by the outcomes of any effort to solve or manage the felt problem.

These guidelines presuppose that the problem managers can anticipate the eventual definition of the problem, its solution, and the manner in which the solution will be implemented. Naturally, if this could be done exactly, there would be little need to involve many people in the process of problem management except for fostering commitment and acceptance. However, the Type III error is especially likely when only a few people are involved in a complex problem. Therefore, *as many people as possible,* drawn from general areas of expertise and related to expected issues of acceptance and commitment, should be involved in managing the problem, if only in an intuitive manner—the same type of psychological function which may have sensed the problem to begin with. Perhaps what is more important is that as the process of problem management proceeds through the five basic steps, the selection of people can be altered as more becomes known about the problem in question. Therefore, flexibility in the selection of people with certain stable attributes (internal–structure) is the key, rather than being constrained to initial, highly tentative selection decisions.

Internal–Process

Besides the relatively stable personality characteristics of people, managers must also consider what particular mental processes are relevant to problem management and how to make these processes as effective as possible. In other words, besides the fundamentally different preferences of thinking versus feeling, for example, and their relevance to particular steps of problem management, there are certain mental processes which need to take place in all steps—but primarily in problem definition and implementation. It is in these stages that Type III and Type IV errors are undoubtedly the most critical (compared with Types I, II, and V). Internal–process thus explores the aspects of mental activity which need to be fostered regardless of whether individuals are ST, NT, SF, or NF.

Assumptions in the definition of problems and the derivation and implementation of solutions are critical mental processes that are generally implicit, unconscious, or (by definition) taken for granted. Yet assumptions have a major impact on what individuals expect will happen, can happen, or should happen. Assumptions are the driving force behind the support for various problem definitions or plans for implementation. Associated with assumptions are *stakeholders*—individuals, groups, or any collection of individuals who have a stake in the organization in question (such as employees, stockholders, consumers, and competitors). Individuals in an organization implicitly make assumptions about what the various stakeholders want, believe, expect, value, and learn, about how they make decisions or engage in activities themselves, and about the outcomes from stakeholder decisions and activities. Assumptions may be defined as the premises or contingencies from which certain conclusions (decisions or viewpoints) can be derived. For example, if certain assumptions are true or what is being assumed does materialize, then a particular conclusion is correct. But if certain assumptions are actually incorrect or what is being assumed does not materialize, then some other conclusion is warranted. Most often, however, individuals assume that things in the past will automatically be the same in the future, that everyone is basically the same and wants the same things, that people make decisions in a totally rational manner, that the organization is primarily interested in being maximally effective, that the clients of the organization need the particular service that the organization offers, that the clients can easily discern the value of the organization's service, that organizational growth is always desirable, and so on. In other words, people accept very basic and sometimes simplistic assumptions, only because these assumptions have never been questioned or exposed for questioning. Yet so much of what individuals may argue for (for example, continuing to provide the same exact service to clients, designing certain advertising compaigns, proposing budget increases to offer more services) may be based on inaccurate assumptions or simply outdated assumptions. In fact, one could reverse each of the "typical" assumptions just stated (forming counter-assumptions) and realize that these "atypical" assumptions are also plausible but lead to very different conclusions!

Alternative problem definitions can usually be generated quite easily by altering assumptions. Actually, being locked into a given set of assumptions can limit the likelihood of alternative definitions of the problem being entertained and seriously considered. For every different set of assumptions, a different problem definition can be derived. Furthermore, when various strategies are being considered for implementing solutions, different assumptions will again suggest different strategies. For example, assumptions regarding how those affected by the solution will react are obviously critical to how the solution is presented to the organization.

Internal–process is concerned with making assumptions explicit, questioning these assumption, formulating new and/or counterassumptions, questioning these new assumptions, and then deriving the problem definitions and implementation strategies that follow from these assumptions. Questioning an assumption involves an assessment of its validity—now that the assumption is stated explicitly, is it true? Since truth and falsity often depend on probabilistic events or simply future happenings, part of the questioning may also involve stating the relative certainty or uncertainty of the assumption. If the assumption is very uncertain, perhaps further information should be collected or forecasting should be done to reduce the uncertainty. Finally, questioning entails an assessment of importance: How important is this assumption to the conclusion being offered (the problem definition)? Will the conclusion change drastically if this particular assumption is altered? It is clearly more critical to question the validity and certainty of assumptions which are most important to the issue at hand (Saaty and Rogers, 1976).

A sequence (primarily a mental process) which gets at the substance and questioning of assumptions might be as follows. State your definition of the problem (or strategy for implementation). Then list all the relevant stakeholders that might have some bearing on the problem as defined— either in the cause of the problem or in its solution. Formulate one or more assumptions which must be true for each stakeholder so that the definition of the problem is maximally supported and can be derived explicitly. In other words, what aspects, decisions, activities, outcomes, or beliefs of each stakeholder would have to exist to argue most strongly for your definition of the problem? (This assessment ensures that no major assumption is missed by ignoring one or more key individuals or groups that bear on the problem.)

Next, assess the importance and relative certainty of each assumption in order to highlight the few assumptions that are most important and also most uncertain. Develop counter-assumptions for the most important and most uncertain assumptions. (Because of their uncertainty, the assumptions can be changed easily, and they will still be plausible. Their importance suggests how changing the assumptions can significantly alter the desired conclusion.) Then develop alternative problem definitions on the basis of the counterassumptions (or variations thereof) that have now been formulated. Finally, examine each set of assumptions and its corresponding problem definition and select one set or a synthesized set in order to minimize the Type III error (defining the problem incorrectly on the basis of wrong or inaccurate assumptions) or the Type IV error, if implementation strategy is being considered. Each of the foregoing steps should be conducted in such a manner that conclusions are directly derived from assumptions—that is, what ordinarily remains hidden and therefore not subject to debate and questioning is made explicit and *is* examined.

This sequence of steps can be performed by one person, several people, one group, or several groups. However, internal–process by itself cannot present the whole range of action steps necessary for effective problem management in an organization. The other action areas are needed as well.

External–Structure

Most efforts at problem management make very little use of the problem-defining resources of the organization in diagnosing a problem situation and developing an implementation strategy to best address the defined problem. More often than not, one or a few managers with or without the aid of a consultant perform the steps of problem management. Recent research and practice in the field of organization design, however, demonstrate some alternative means to more systematically and efficiently involve members in the problem definition process by means of *designing* problem-defining groups. It is expected, in fact, that such structural designs (that is, external–structure) will result in a better problem definition (because a broader base of expertise is brought to bear in the process). Further, an implementation strategy to address the defined problem will receive greater commitment and involvement from organizational members, precisely because of their greater participation in the process.

More specifically, for complex, ill-structured problems there are a number of alternative definitions. These not only are feasible but are likely to be proposed and considered as the problem facing the organization by different individuals (because of specialization, selective perception, vested interests, or personality differences). However, different people proposing different problem definitions are viewed as a set of resources which can be *designed* into action—that is, combinations of problem definers with expressed views of problem definitions can be formed into groups to discuss, debate, synthesize, and better formulate their views. Such designed groups, moreover, are considered more powerful than separate individuals conducting isolated diagnoses of the organization.

("Powerful" means more influential owing to the greater mobilization of expertise, motivation, cohesion, and commitment that results from the proper use of groups.) Furthermore, designing more than one group and making these groups as different as possible will maximize the likelihood that different problem definitions will be entertained and fully considered. That is, each group will develop a distinct definition of the problem. These definitions can then be debated and synthesized.

Table 6–1 shows five structural designs for problem management groups. Each group design has these aspects in common: (1) designing individuals into various groups; (2) having each group formulate and present its views on what is causing various problems in the organization; (3) debating different views, assumptions, and beliefs across the several groups; and (4) developing a synthesized statement of the problem situation. What varies across the different designs and is the major concern here, however, is that each type of group structure has its corresponding advantages and disadvantages.

Following is a brief summary of each design alternative. The assumption is that a variety of individuals throughout the organization (or subsystems) in question have been brought together to participate in problem management. Also, even though the external–structure action areas can be formulated for each of the five generic steps in problem management, the discussion concentrates on designs for problem definition, since this is viewed as one of the most critical contributions of external–structure (that is, managing the Type III error).

The ad hoc design. A collection of individuals is asked to generate, either separately or in small groups, a list of problems that they are experiencing in the organization. The total list that is generated is then categorized into major themes, by type of problem or by functional area in the organization affected by the problem (or by some other categorization which may appear to be useful in highlighting *different* ways of conceptualizing the organization's problems). This categorization then becomes the basis for forming problem-solving groups—groups that are to spend time in further defining the problems listed under the various categories, debating their views with other groups, and so on. Individuals are designed into these groups by task preference. That is, each individual chooses to work in a particular group on the basis of his or her preferences for the categories of problems. The group size is regulated by asking individuals in the larger groups with marginal or multiple interests to switch to the smaller groups.

The ad hoc design is fairly easy to utilize since it requires no formal assessments of interest. Rather, as problem types emerge, individuals self-select into groups. Balanced against its ease of use, however, is the

TABLE 6–1. *Structural designs for problem management.*

Alternative Designs	Consequences	
	Advantages	*Disadvantages*
Ad hoc	Quick; no assessment required; no data analysis; free and immediate choices	Basis for grouping unknown; does not assure different groups; people may not feel free to make open choices
Personality type	Defines basis for group differences; assures different problem perspectives; intuitively pleasing and plausible; tends to generate involvement	Assumes valid assessment of personality; requires taking of personality scales; personality differences may not be important criteria for different problem perspectives
Vested interest	Tends to produce strong differences between groups; easy to form groups along functional or interest lines	May produce rigid group outcomes without possibilities for synthesis; may stifle creative perspectives; may override other differences
Task and people preference	More systematic and takes account of more variables in forming groups; based on research findings and rigorous design techniques	Requires extensive assessments and complicated analysis for designing groups, even with MAPS; requires much more time to create designs
Random assignment	Impersonal; quick; no vested interests; differentiation of groups based on chance	Impersonal; not rooted in any theory of group formation; unknown lines of differentiation; design quality left to chance factors

uncertainty of who determines (and how) the problem categorization that is the basis for group formation and differentiation. It may be the consultant, the top manager, or a few vocal individuals who propose the categories, but the process is likely to be less than systematic and all-encompassing.

In essence, the important task of forming ad hoc groups is first based on an unsystematic method of categorization coupled with individual preferences to be in a particular group (working on a prespecified category of problems). While the latter is likely to foster commitment (because of choice), one cannot be sure that the individuals in each group will work well together—since it is only task preference, not people preference that determines group composition. The importance of this design issue will be evident later as the other designs for external–structure are discussed.

The personality type design. Instead of allowing individuals to self-select into groups or to let some unsystematic categorization of problem items determine the task focus for each group, individuals can be distinguished on some personality dimension which is considered salient to organizational diagnosis. Different types of personalities might be expected to define and view problems quite differently, and such a distinction could well contribute to designing different problem-solving groups. Naturally, the choice of both the personality scheme to use and the measuring instrument which is applied to assess individual personality types, is critical. The instrument must be reasonably valid and reliable, and the personality dimension must distinguish important problem perspectives.

Most research on organizational behavior has shown that individual differences do not play a major role in what takes place in organizations. Nevertheless, the psychological typology developed by C. G. Jung, as measured by the Myers-Briggs Type Indicator (Myers and Briggs, 1962), has proved to be a useful framework for problem definition purposes. Specifically, in 10 to 15 minutes individuals can be assessed and sorted into the four personality groups discussed above. These four groups usually present four very different views of a complex problem situation, and since the psychological typology is quite broad and encompassing, the four designed groups tend to consider most of the important issues in the situation.

An advantage to using the personality type design is that since the basis of group differences is known, the results of the group can be predicted to a certain extent. Moreover, the participants tend to get involved in the problem-solving process because of the intuitively pleasing basis for categorization and its uniqueness to most organizational members.

A disadvantage of the personality-based design is that some individuals do not like taking "personality tests," consider them an invasion of privacy, and view the assessment as invalid ("You can't sort me into a group on the basis of that test!"). Since personality scales and measurements are not 100 percent valid, there is some truth to these opinions. It is also possible that the personality framework selected to distinguish groups is not appropriate to highlight important aspects or different views of the problem situation. In some situations no personality framework may be appropriate, and in that case some other basis for designing groups might be much more powerful in bringing out differences in viewing the problem situation. But whether or not the personality type design is chosen (external–structure), members may be selected partly on the basis of personality attributes (internal–structure) so that each generic step of problem management can be done well.

The vested interest design. Different definitions of what constitutes the organization's major problems are often rooted in identifiable, already existing groups. For example, functional areas in the organization, service departments, professional or disciplinary associations, and simply memberships in any ongoing group may greatly determine the way individuals will perceive the organization's problems. The vested interest design attempts to make the most of these natural or ongoing differences. Thus, groups are designed by explicitly maintaining existing group memberships (for example, nurses versus doctors versus administrators) in order to generate the correct problem definition. What has to be decided, however, is which set of vested interests should be the basis for a particular design. Should it be functional area, disciplinary training, management versus worker, or something else?

Consequently, one disadvantage of the vested interest design is that it assumes that the critical vested interests are apparent in any situation. However, this is often not the case. And just as the personality-based design can err on the side of choosing an inappropriate dimension of personality to distinguish groups, so the vested interest design can choose the wrong vested interest groups. Another disadvantage of this design is that very strong vested interest positions may result, with little or no probability of developing integrated or synthesized viewpoints. The separate groups may rigidly stick to their initial positions. The same rigidity may also stifle creative or new perspectives, since the groups may become locked into stereotyped attitudes. In other words, some other design of groups could possibly foster new ideas instead of the status quo.

But if the differences between the vested interest groups do not become overwhelming, the organization can depend on the strong expression of different viewpoints with this design alternative. Also, if groups already exist along clear interest lines, it certainly is easier to form these groups than to utilize personality tests or rely on unsystematic methods of problem categorization (as in the case of the ad hoc design). Finally, individuals are generally quite comfortable in their natural interest groups in contrast to some other, less familiar form of group composition. Membership in an interest group, at a minimum, does provide a strong support base for individuals.

The task and people preference design. This design is probably the most complex in terms of the number and variety of variables taken into account. In essence, individuals indicate those fellow organizational members they can best interact with in a problem-defining group as well as their problem and task preferences. Individuals with similar preferences are placed in the same group.

The dimensions of tasks and people are chosen because of the support in the literature for these two general types of variables in determining effective group behavior (Blake and Mouton, 1964). Briefly, a group can be expected to have difficulty in completing its assignment if members do not have some similarity or compatibility of viewpoints to suggest what tasks are important. On the other hand, if the individuals within a group can agree on what issues are critical to defining the organization's problems but cannot get along with one another and therefore cannot form into a cohesive group, it is unlikely that the group will make the most of its expertise and other member resources. Consequently, the effective group must be designed from certain task *and* people similarities. Further, to maximize the motivation and commitment of each group under this design, the members themselves are expected to choose the relevant task and people characteristics on the basis of their preferences and beliefs, rather than having some outside consultant or other person assign people to a group without their participation in the design decision.

The task and people preference design thus goes beyond the ad hoc design in that it is determined by both task and people considerations. However, rather than having one or a few people perform the group design in a qualitative, ad hoc manner, the task and people design can be conducted by the MAPS Design Technology—a computerized procedure for systematically using individual responses to task and people questionnaire items in order to efficiently cluster individuals into groups. The computer process is designed to draw out similarities in task and people preferences from the inputs of all individuals participating in the problem management design (Kilmann, 1977).

The major advantages of the task and people preference design include the systematic integration of task or problem issues and the formal consideration of task and people dimensions in designing groups. Utilizing the MAPS procedure with the aid of a computer facilitates the analysis of many variables which separate individuals cannot calculate, let alone comprehend. Also, because of the impersonal nature of the computer, the resultant design stems not from a few individuals' perceptions, but from the inputs of all individuals.

The primary disadvantage of this design is its complexity. It takes much more time to form the groups, and individuals typically need some preliminary understanding of how the process works (particularly if MAPS is used) before they can become committed to the design. Furthermore, while the impersonality of the computer is an advantage to some (because it may appear to be more objective and certainly more systematic), others meet it with disdain ("I am not going to let some computer program determine what group I get assigned to, whom I work with, and what I work on!").

The random assignment design. Individuals may also be assigned to groups strictly on a chance or random basis (as in a control group for research purposes). The advantages of random assignment are that it is impersonal, is easy to administer, takes little time, and by chance can be expected to form groups composed of diverse people so that strong functional vested interests are not localized in a single group.

One can expect, however, a number of disadvantages or negative consequences to this design method. First, its very randomness does not allow one to define how each group is differentialy designed. Therefore, it is not at all certain whether groups will in fact develop different perspectives. It is conceivable that all differences, in the extreme, are randomly distributed across the groups. Thus the important differences regarding the definition of organizational problems become suppressed in the process of each group developing a consensual position to debate with the other groups (that is, the groups may turn out to be quite similar). Second, while the random process may seem impersonal and not tied to vested interests, it is also seen as devoid of substance. That is, groups are not designed according to some substantive theme, whether derived by ad hoc categorization of issues, personality types, vested interests, or a computer analysis of problem issues via questionnaire responses. Some individuals see the random design process as a "copout" in attempting to structure problem management.

A comparison of designs. The foregoing discussion has summarized five alternative designs for problem management. While other structural designs are certainly plausible (designs based on age, sex, hierarchical level, values, and so on), the five designs discussed demonstrate the variety of ways in which the organization could increase the likelihood of obtaining a correct problem definition and commitment to implementing solutions to the identified problems.

When presenting even five alternatives, however, one must consider a metatheory: a set of principles for selecting each design under particular circumstances. This assumes, of course, that the five designs are not all equal but have advantages and disadvantages for the organization. It seems appropriate, therefore, to briefly consider some guidelines for selecting the different designs.

Table 6–2 compares the five designs according to three criteria: (1) the *cost* or energy involved in implementing the design (including assessments

TABLE 6–2. *Net benefits derived from selecting a given structural design.*

Alternative Designs	Net Benefits*		
	Quality	Acceptance	Cost
Ad hoc	M	M	L
Personality type	M	M	M
Vested interest	L	H	L
Task and people preference	H	H	H
Random assignment	L	L	L

*H = high; M = medium; L = low.

and analysis of assessments, relatively speaking), (2) the expected *quality* of the problem definition based on the likelihood of different viewpoints and a well-balanced synthesis of these viewpoints, and (3) the expected commitment and *acceptance* generated by organizational members as a result of the type of individual participation anticipated by the design, compared to an average level of commitment fostered by participation in any group design.

Criteria 2 and 3 follow from a very basic model of group effectiveness— that is, *effectiveness = quality of decision × acceptance of decision* (related to Type III and Type IV errors, respectively). The multiplicative relationship emphasizes again that if either component is low or zero, so will be total effectiveness (anything multiplied by zero is zero). Criterion 1 recognizes that there is a cost (energy usage) associated with the implementation of each structural design in terms of individual assessments, data analysis, time for explaining results of personality variables, addressing questions concerning the use of more complex designs, and so on.

Assuming that appropriate scales could be developed for the three criteria, one might propose a general equation as follows, where criteria 2 and 3 represent potential benefits to a given design and criterion 1 represents its costs:

Net benefits derived from a given design = (quality × acceptance) − costs

In each cell of Table 6–2 a qualitative assessment has been made of high, medium, or low to reflect the advantages and disadvantages of each structural design. For example, the random assignment design scores low in terms of costs of implementing, but is also low in quality and acceptance. In contrast, the task and people preference design is the most costly to implement but it is also expected to have high quality and acceptance because of its systematic and involving nature. The vested interest design is high in acceptance, since the design follows preexisting groups; but it is expected to be low in quality, since a creative synthesis across strong vested interest is not expected. However, the vested interest design is relatively easy to implement. The ad hoc design is expected to have many of the same benefits as the personality-based design, but the latter is a bit higher in costs of implementation.

Although it would be tempting to compare the five designs and to select one over the other for all situations, it must be emphasized again that the scaling in Table 6–2 is very rough, qualitative, and based only on gross expectations. In addition, different organizational situations or climates would weigh each of the three criteria differently. Thus, in one situation quality rather than acceptance might be the most important criterion, especially if organizational members are willing to utilize any of the five designs. In a different organizational setting, however, the cost factor might be critical. For example, members may be skeptical or resistant to any design other than the ad hoc because they do not "believe" in personality theory, computer analysis, or any other type of systematic method of group composition. In this case a substantial cost would be evidenced which would offset the benefits to be derived from using the personality type or the task and people preference design.

A number of guidelines will now be summarized to aid the action steps in the external–structure area:

• Developing the correct problem definition, the best implementation strategy, and other decisions in problem management can be aided greatly by the use of group structures rather than simply individual efforts, particularly for complex problems.

• Groups can be composed along a number of dimensions (for example, personality type, vested interest, ad hoc), but the choice in a particular situation should be based on what composition will make the separate groups most different with regard to the issue at hand (for example, problem definition), while also being open to a creative synthesis. The chosen design should also not be too costly given the climate and resources of the organization.

• Once the separate groups are formed (a manageable number is three to six groups, each containing four to seven members), each group is expected to develop a position statement, a preliminary problem definition, or an implementation plan in a reasonable period of time. Then a debate among the groups is encouraged in order to set the stage for a synthesis—helping members to understand the reasons for the group differences and the advantages and disadvantages of each position. Finally, representatives from each group meet to form a synthesis group (or several synthesis groups). The objective is to develop a creative synthesis by maximizing the advantages or strengths of each position while minimizing the disadvantages or weaknesses.

Utilizing group designs as suggested above is expected to make the most of the problem management resources of the organization, not only to derive a higher-quality definition and solution to the problem, but to provide for a successful implementation program.

External–Process

The fourth and final action area, external–process, concerns the interactions (processes) which take place between individuals (external) once they have been designed into various group and intergroup structures. Of the several possible conceptual frameworks for understanding the nature of interactions and interpersonal processes, conflict and conflict management (Thomas, 1976) would seem to be most relevant to the present discussion. In essence, at each step of the generic process of problem management there is the likelihood that conflict will be experienced—different people will propose different definitions of the problem, different solutions, and different strategies for implementation. The action areas presented previously emphasized the need to generate and highlight differences. Differences in group problem definitions (external–structure), differences in assumptions (internal–process), and differences in personality types (internal–structure) were all viewed as valuable resources to effective problem management, *if these differences could be utilized constructively.* Conflict is the experience of these differences, and conflict management is the manner of addressing or managing these differences constructively.

The focus of this section, therefore, is on the alternative ways in which people can approach situations (interact) when they find moderate or even extreme differences in viewpoints (including objectives, beliefs, assumptions, perspectives, values, and attitudes). The concern is to specify which of these alternative ways of approaching conflict is best for each of the five generic steps of problem management, or at least to suggest which alternative ways of interacting are more likely to result in the constructive use of conflict.

A framework has been developed whereby five conflict-handling modes can be defined by two basic dimensions: assertiveness and cooperativeness (Thomas, 1976). Assertiveness is the behavioral effort to get one's own views accepted by the other people in the situation. Cooperativeness is the behavioral effort to get others' views accepted. By combining various levels of assertiveness and cooperativeness, we can define five basic behavioral efforts with regard to addressing differences: competing (assertive but uncooperative), collaborating (both assertive and cooperative), avoiding (both unassertive and uncooperative), accommodating (unassertive but cooperative), and compromising (intermediate in both assertiveness and cooperativeness). Figure 6–3 plots the five conflict-handling modes of interacting on the two dimensions.

Competing is thus behaving in a manner to win one's own position with little concern for the other's point of view. Collaborating, on the other hand, is an attempt to reconcile both viewpoints, to get at some synthesis whereby each person feels that his views are a substantial part of the final position. Avoiding is not being concerned with either one's own or the

FIGURE 6-3. *Dimensions of conflict-handling behavior.*

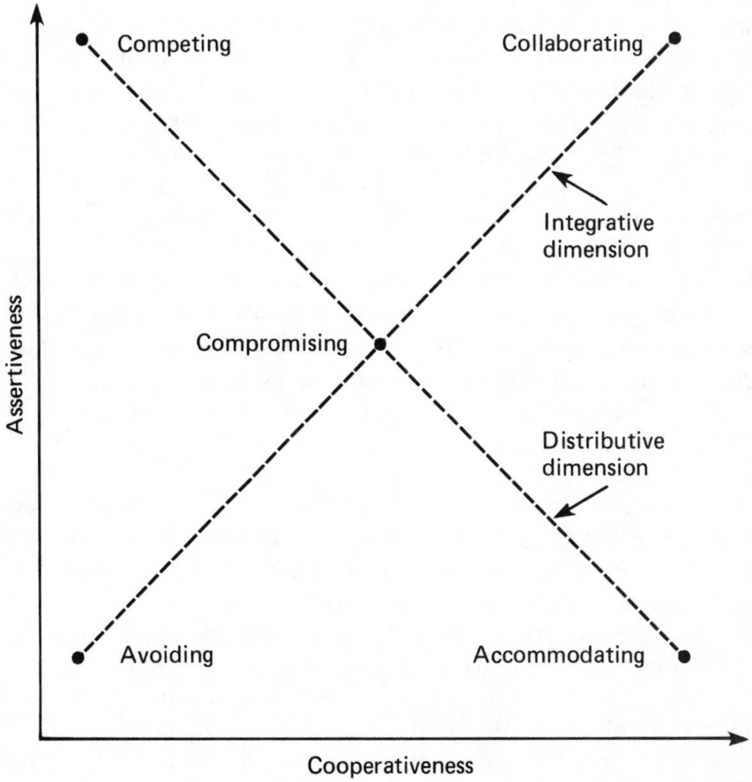

Source: Adapted from Figure 1 of R. H. Kilmann and K. W. Thomas, "Interpersonal Conflict-Handling Behavior as Reflections of Jungian Personality Dimensions," *Psychology Reports,* Vol. 37 (1975).

other's viewpoint and behaving accordingly (for example, by leaving the problem situation). Accommodating is being primarily concerned with the other's point of view and minimally or not at all concerned with having the "final" position reflective of one's own views. Finally, compromising is splitting the differences, or attempting to arrive at a position where each person gets some portion of his own views incorporated; but unlike collaborating, no effort is made to achieve a creative synthesis so that all people fully accept and feel ownership of the final position.

Every person is able to use each of these five modes of resolving differences. The prime issue is knowing when each mode is most effective or likely to result in the best solution for all involved in the conflict situation. For example, collaborating is best when creative solutions are possible, whereas competing is best when either/or decisions have to be made. In any event, an important part of problem management is to encourage the use of those modes that will resolve differences constructively at each step of the generic process of problem management. In fact, the problem manager who initially institutes the process, guides the process, and moderates the various group discussions at each step serves as a model to the other participants. By demonstrating how one type of conflict handling results in better resolutions (problem definitions, solutions, or implementation plans) than other types, the problem manager can foster effective use of the external–process action area.

The five conflict-handling modes can also be defined according to two additional dimensions: distributive and integrative. (see Figure 6–3). The distributive dimension describes a give-and-take effort at resolving differences, with competing (taking) and accommodating (giving) at the extremes and compromising intermediate. There the effort is focused on just how much each person gets, assuming a fixed amount of what is being distributed. The more one person gets, the less the others get—a process that has been referred to as a zero-sum game. Stated differently, the size of the pie is fixed, and the issue is dividing it up into pieces of certain sizes and distributing them to the people in question. This is analogous to the final position in a problem situation having separate parts that come directly from the different people—as a form of compromise. Naturally, the more people or views in the situation, the less the final resolution or position will reflect any one person or view. Rather, the identified pieces of the total solution get smaller and smaller, and perhaps so does the acceptance of, and satisfaction with, the final position.

The integrative dimension, however, is quite different—collaborating and avoiding are at the extremes and compromising is intermediate. The "size of the pie" is not fixed but can be enlarged, in line with the creative ability of the people involved, to formulate a synthesis of their differences.

This synthesis can actually provide each person with most or even all of his viewpoints even though initially there seemed to be some overriding differences. Sometimes, however, what appears to be initially a zero-sum situation can be broadened to include a larger package of issues as a result of synergistic, integrative interpersonal interactions—where the final resolution goes beyond what any one person first anticipated or desired. Here the final resolution is more than the summed viewpoints of separate people. Integrative solutions should never be accepted below the distribution dimension, since people would get less than they could have gotten in total from even a distributive solution. In fact, anything below the distributive line represents spite behavior, reflecting the attitude of taking less for oneself "to make sure the other people don't get what they want."

Integrative solutions, whether they refer to problem definitions or implementation strategies, would appear to be the ideal. What has to be recognized, however, is that only under certain special conditions is it feasible to expect integrative as opposed to distributive solutions. This is especially the case when a solution is desired that moves well beyond the integrative-distributive intersection, all the way to a complete collaborative solution. The primary conditions necessary for integrative solutions are (1) multidimensional or nonzero-sum issues, (2) a balance of power among people in conflict, and (3) an atmosphere of trust in the problem situation.

The first condition indicates that an integrative solution is not possible if the issue is strictly zero-sum or is perceived to be. Developing synthesized problem definitions or solutions cannot be done on an either/or issue or an issue that varies along a single dimension. The latter forces the resolution along the give-and-take distributive line in Figure 6–3. Only if an issue can be seen as multidimensional—as having several alternative but not exclusive aspects—can individuals prepare a synthesis that combines these aspects into totally new packages of proposed resolutions. Broadening the scope or definition of a problem, for example, to include different aspects of the organization can often synthesize what initially seemed to be two totally exclusive, narrow, and different definitions of the problem.

The second condition states that a balance of power is necessary for developing integrative solutions. "Balance of power" means that each individual or group has an equal input into the process of deriving a final resolution. Otherwise, if one person or group has greater influence in the process (because of organizational position and authority, for example), from the perspective of the more influential person there is no need to develop an integrated solution. The person can influence the resolution toward his viewpoint (as in competing), supported by power or other resources. Only when each person must rely on his own expertise, persuasiveness, or line of argument might there be motivation to achieve an integrated solution. (The strengthening of labor unions to counter the traditional power of management over the worker is an example of developing a balance of power—to foster integrative as well as more equal, distributive solutions.)

The third condition emphasizes the importance of trust in developing integrative solutions. If people do not trust each other in the problem situation, they may not openly share all their viewpoints, beliefs, and values, but may offer only those that are conspicuous and safe. The fear is that the other person or group may, at some later date, use this information against the person who expressed the controversial or risky viewpoint. Sometimes, for example, top managers seem unwilling to hear the many problems of the organization, especially those problems that might stem from possible mistakes of top managers; therefore, the middle and lower-level managers are careful to develop problem definitions in some other domain, in a narrow manner. This restriction of information, however, prevents the "problem" from being seen in a much broader or different light, which, as was suggested earlier, may limit the multidimensional aspects of the issues and thus limit the possibilities for integrative solutions. Further, the lack of trust tends to limit the zany, the provocative, and even the ridiculous from being seriously considered as part of a solution package. But even the seemingly ridiculous or zany viewpoints might provide a creative basis for an integrative solution—as long as people feel free to suggest all possibilities without fear or intimidation.

To the extent that the three conditions exist together—that an atmosphere of trust exists so that all possible viewpoints can be openly revealed, that a balance of power is evident so that individuals will be motivated to develop jointly satisfying solutions, and that the issues surrounding the conflict can be portrayed as multidimensional and multifaceted—there will be a greater likelihood that an integrative resolution can be developed. Although integrative solutions are clearly desirable, since everyone involved would have his viewpoints supported by the resolution (which also fosters acceptance of the resolution), it might not be realistic to always expect the three conditions to be evidenced, and hence to expect integrative solutions. Even if there is trust and a balance of power, issues may well be unidimensional (or at least consisting of a few rather than many aspects), suggesting that only distributive solutions can be expected. In fact, an organization may have more control over developing trust and ensuring a balance of power during problem management than over the complexity of issues. Whether issues are unidimensional or multidimensional is primarily a function of the nature of the problem situation even when all effort has been expended on viewing issues in the broadest possible way.

Looking back at the five generic steps of problem management shown in Figure 6–1, one might expect that an atmosphere of trust and a balance of power could be developed throughout the five steps. These two conditions arise from the climate of the organization engaged in the process and the manner in which all steps of problem management are conducted (that is, whether "democratic" or "autocratic"). However, it becomes quite evident that the conditions of unidimensionality and multidimensionality vary as one moves from one step of problem management to another. As discussed earlier, some steps are better defined and structured than others. Specifically, defining the problem (step 2) and implementing solutions (step 4) seem to have more facets—more critical alternatives—than deriving and selecting solutions (step 3). Step 3 seems closer to being unidimensional. Furthermore, even though sensing a problem (step 1) is an ambiguous task, the *resolution* of this step is usually an either/or decision—either a problem is said to exist or not—which suggests that it is unidimensional. Finally, evaluating the outcomes (step 5) is necessarily unidimensional even though it involves an assessment of each preceding step. The assessment or resolution to be made is a question of validity. That is, was each step performed correctly and were the errors minimized? This is quite different from resolving the objective of each step in the first place.

In summary, then, differences about whether a problem exists are expected to be resolved largely by the distributive modes (competing, accommodating); differences about what constitutes the definition of the problem are expected to be resolved by the integrative modes (various forms of collaborating); differences about what constitutes the best solution to the already defined problem are expected to be resolved with the distributive modes; differences about what implementation strategy would be best, given all the possible obstacles and resistances to change, are expected to be resolved by the integrative modes; and differences about whether each preceding step was performed effectively are expected to be resolved by the distributive modes.

These expectations reflect the best or highest that can be achieved under the assumption that an atmosphere of trust and a balance of power exist at each step of the problem management process. A next or lower solution to an integrative one is the distributive, and the next lower solution to a distributive one is a spiteful solution, as discussed earlier. These lower solutions will be developed for the above differences if the other conditions for integration are not met or are even seriously reversed.

It should be evident, however, that the conditions for integrative so-lutions presuppose that the group structures have been designed effec-tively and that members have the necessary abilities and expertise to engage in problem solving effectively (internal–structure and internal–process). Thus, the action area of external–process depends strongly on the other three action areas. This suggests that for the overall process of problem management to be effective, each action area must be conducted in a particular way and each area must be supportive of the others. The following guidelines are offered to facilitate understanding of the exter-nal–process action area. Even though other process issues are certainly relevant and important, the resolution of differences seems to be the key, given the focus of the other action areas.

- Be aware of and appreciate the different modes of resolving differences.
- Attempt to state issues in the broadest terms feasible in order to foster multidimensional as opposed to unidimensional issues and hence to enhance the possibilities for integrative resolutions.
- Attempt to establish a climate of trust and a true balance of power in order to foster motivation and the open exchange of information and hence to enhance the possibilities for integrative solutions.
- Encourage (through modeling and instruction) the use of integrative modes (such as collaborating) especially for problem defining and implementation planning, when conditions of trust and a balance of power can be established.
- Encourage the use of distributive modes (such as competition and accommodation), especially for resolving differences in sensing the problem, deriving solutions, and evaluating outcomes, if the integra-tive modes are not feasible because of unidimensional differences.

TOWARD AN INTEGRATION: THE PROBLEM MANAGEMENT WHEEL

The first part of this chapter described the five generic steps of problem management and the critical types of errors that must be minimized. These steps were necessarily abstract and conceptual in order to define the basic, idealized processes. The second part of this chapter presented many of the key actions that a problem manager must consider and decide upon if the abstract process is to be operationalized in real organizational settings. Important action areas examined were (1) the selection of or-ganizational members according to various psychological and substantive criteria; (2) the types of mental activities, especially assumption testing, required of problem-defining and problem-solving efforts; (3) the design of group structures according to various group composition criteria to make the most of an organization's problem management resources; and (4) the behavioral modes of members attempting to resolve their differences at each step of the process.

The Problem Management Wheel (Figure 6–4) shows how all these elements of effective problem management are interrelated and dependent on one another. In the center of the wheel are the generic five steps—the core or hub of problem management. Surrounding this core are the action areas that guide, condition, and enable each step to be performed effectively. The reader is encouraged to look back at the specific guidelines provided in earlier sections for a brief summary of each action area.

FIGURE 6-4. *The Problem Management Wheel*

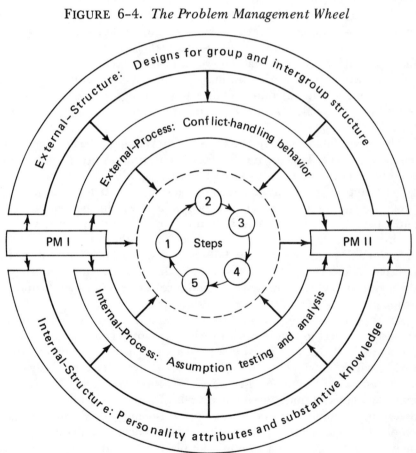

In order to understand how the various action areas are interrelated, it is necessary to define two integrating links. The first link specifies that processes occur within structures, more than vice versa. In other words, structures shape the conduct of processes, providing the constraints as well as the freedom to take part in certain sequences of activity. For example, the structure of groups is expected to guide the interacting modes within the groups to a greater extent than interacting modes affect the design of group structures. Similarly, the stable attributes of individuals (psychological types) are expected to guide various mental processes (such as assumption testing) and enable these to take place in a certain manner over time to a greater extent than mental activities affect the development of stable personality attributes.

The second integrating link proposes that *external* structures act more strongly on *external* processes than on any other action areas (that is, internal–structure and internal–process). Likewise, *internal* structures act more strongly on *internal* processes than on any other action areas (that is, external–structure and external–process). In other words, it seems more reasonable to argue that the two external areas (outside individuals) and the two internal areas (inside individuals) are each linked together more strongly than any other combination—recognizing that in both external and internal linkages the structural area dominates the process area.

These two linkages were the basis for developing the Problem Management Wheel. That is, the structural action areas are shown on the outermost edge of the wheel, as the major guiding force for the five generic steps of problem management and as further influenced by the processes that take place between people and within their minds. The latter processes are shown to be guided by the more basic structures. Furthermore, the top half of the wheel shows the two external action areas linked together, while the bottom half shows the linkage of the two internal action areas. The arrows between the various action areas suggest the major direction of influence or guidance of one action area to another action area and then to the five generic steps.

An important implication of these linkages is that the problem manager should *first* select individuals with various personality attributes and substantive knowledge and provide a particular structural design of groups for these individuals. Thus, the internal–structure and external–structure action areas represent the first level of action taking by the problem manager. For example, these individuals may be formed into groups to determine if some important problems are being sensed in the organization. The *second* level of action would be to encourage the appropriate modes of interaction that should take place within and between groups by the individuals involved, and to foster the types of assumption analyses on the part of the selected individuals that are conducive to the generic step of problem management in question. Thus, as the wheel shows, the external–process and internal–process action areas follow after both structural decisions have been made. While these two levels of action are not meant to be totally fixed and binding, they do suggest a natural priority and action sequence to help manage the complexities of all four action areas.

The two parts of the wheel not yet explained are those labeled PMI and PMII. PMI stands for Problem Management I and suggests where the initiator to the whole problem management effort enters the "system," so to speak. Thus, a problem manager begins the five-step sequence as an implicit or explicit decision, while the four action areas are called into play—that is, members are selected, designed into various groupings, then asked to interact in certain modes and to engage in a particular mental process—at each of the five generic steps. The arrows leading from PMI illustrate this initiation and action-taking effort.

PMII, which stands for Problem Management II, represents the completion of one cycle (turn of the wheel) of problem management and assesses the whole problem management effort—not just how well each of the five steps was conducted but how well each action area was managed. In other words, step 5 of the basic process questions whether the initial problem was resolved and, if not, which of the preceding four steps was done incorrectly regarding that particular problem. PMII questions how well the problem management effort was conducted in general. The hope is that what is learned (or can be learned) after each cycle can be transferred to the next cycle—whether the same problem or a totally different problem is being addressed. Step 5 is thus a micro or very specific evaluation, and PMII is a macro or much broader evaluation of the entire set of decisions and actions that PMI initiated. This is shown by the arrows leading from all sources into PMII, which then is expected to filter back to PMI for the next problem management cycle.

CONCLUSIONS

It may appear from reading this chapter that the management of organizational problems is a complex and difficult undertaking, involving actions on many interrelated variables. It would have been misleading, however, to suggest that important, complex, and ill-defined problems could be addressed effectively with very simple and straightforward routines. The latter could be suggested only for very well-structured problems, but even then "cookbook" formulas are relevant to fewer and fewer organizational problems. Consequently, one has to expect a certain amount of complexity in describing (let alone acting upon) real, complex problems.

A major intention of this chapter was to present a number of frameworks, diagrams, and integrating links to help organize this complex endeavor into an understandable package. The generic five steps of problem management and the four action areas are representative of this effort. The Problem Management Wheel suggests how the major parts can be linked in some meaningful manner. Although one could easily suggest even more variables and issues to consider in making problem management effective, the space limitations required the selection of what was viewed as the most important aspects of the topic.

Problem management is an ongoing effort that is likely to grow in importance as organizations face more dynamic and changing environments. Problem managers are therefore encouraged to modify or add other variables to the Problem Management Wheel that they feel will help them to manage problems effectively, including the development of a larger set of guidelines for action than those given in this chapter. Such an effort at learning would help to operationalize the PMII part of the wheel, where each effort at problem management teaches further principles and guidelines for improving each aspect of the whole endeavor.

REFERENCES

Ackoff, R. L. "Systems, Organizations, and Interdisciplinary Research," *General Systems Year-book*, Vol. 5 (1960) pp. 1–8.

Blake, R. R., and J. S. Mouton. *The Managerial Grid* (Houston: Gulf, 1964).

Downs, A. *Inside Bureaucracy* (Santa Monica, Cal.: Rand, 1966).

Galbraith, J. R. *Organization Design* (Reading, Mass.: Addison-Wesley, 1977).

Hoffman, L. R., and N. R. F. Maier. "Quality and Acceptance of Problem Solutions by Members of Homogeneous and Heterogeneous Groups," *Journal of Abnormal and Social Psychology*, Vol. 3 (1967) pp. 3–21.

Jung, C. G. *Psychological Types* (London: Rutledge, 1923).

Khandwalla, P. N. *The Design of Organizations* (New York: Harcourt Brace Jovanovich, 1977).

Kilmann, R. H. *Social Systems Design: Normative Theory and the MAPS Design Technology* (New York: Elsevier, 1977).

Kilmann, R. H., and I. I. Mitroff, *Strategic Problem Forming and Policy Making* (New York: Free Press, in press).

Kilmann, R. H., L. R. Pondy, and D. P. Slevin. *The Management of Organization Design: Volumes I and II* (New York: Elsevier, 1976).

Kilmann, R. H., and K. W. Thomas. "Four Perspectives on Conflict Management: An Attributional Framework for Organizing Descriptive and Normative Theory," *Academy of Management Review*, Vol. 3 (1978), pp. 59–68.

Leavitt, H. J. "Applied Organizational Change in Industry: Structural, Technological and Humanistic Approaches," in J. G. March, ed., *Handbook of Organizations* (Chicago: Rand McNally, 1965), pp. 1144–1170.

Mitroff, I. I., and T. R. Featheringham. "On Systematic Problem Solving and the Error of the Third Kind," *Behavioral Science,* Vol. 19 (1974), pp. 383–393.

Myers, I. B., and K. C. Briggs. *Myers-Briggs Type Indicator* (Princeton, N.J.: Educational Testing Service, 1962).

Saaty, T. L., and P. C. Rogers. "Higher Education in the United States (1985–2000): Scenario Construction Using a Hierarchical Framework with Eigenvector Weighting," *Socioeconomic Planning,* Vol. 10 (1976), pp. 251–263.

Schlaifer, R. *Probability and Statistics for Business Decisions* (New York: McGraw-Hill, 1959).

Schultz, R. L., and D. P. Slevin. "Implementation and Organizational Validity: An Empirical Investigation," in R. L. Schultz and D. P. Slevin, eds., *Implementing Operations Research/Management Science* (New York: Elsevier, 1975), pp. 153–182.

Slevin, D. P. "The Innovation Boundary: A Specific Model and Some Empirical Results," *Administrative Science Quarterly,* Vol. 18 (1973), pp. 71–75.

Thomas, K. W. "Conflict and Conflict Management," in M. D. Dunnette, ed., *The Handbook of Industrial and Organizational Psychology* (Chicago: Rand McNally, 1976).

Weiss, C. *Evaluation Research* (Englewood Cliffs, N.J.: Prentice-Hall, 1972).

CHAPTER 7

Understanding the Client as a Consumer

Melanie Wallendorf

Editor's Note   *A manager of a nonprofit organization must often interact with a wide range of clients having different needs, attitudes, and relationships to the organization. An organization's success is largely dependent on its ability to provide client satisfaction, both in the long and the short run. A manager who understands his or her client's consumer behavior can be more effective in satisfying those clients, and thus more effective in achieving the objectives of the organization. Thus, an essential task for the manager is to develop an understanding of the client as a consumer. This chapter represents an overview of the consumer behavior process and its implications for nonprofit organizations. Consumers are clients with whom the organization enters into an exchange relationship.*

According to the concept of market segmentation, consumers are divided into groups whose members have similar consumer behaviors. Eight bases of market segmentation which are relevant to the nonprofit organization are age, geographic location, income, lifestyle, volume of usage, benefits sought, use potential, and nature of the exchange. A segments × goals matrix is described which helps a manager formulate strategies for meeting the goals of each segment.

Next, role relationships are examined as a basis for analyzing the manager's interactions with different segments. This analysis helps managers understand consumer attitudes and expectations associated with each of these relationships. A particular model is used to conduct the analysis. Using this model and taking the time to determine relevant attributes, managers can develop better management strategies to change consumer attitudes.

Adoption and resistance of innovations is also considered. Innovations are products, services, or ideas perceived as new by the consumer. Consumers are divided into different adopter categories depending upon the speed with which they accept new ideas or services. In deciding whether or not to adopt the innovation, the consumer passes through various stages. These stages are perception, motivation, attitude, legitimation, trial, evaluation, adoption/rejection, and resolution. The manager must consider how the perceived attributes of an innovation affect the consumer during these stages.

With an understanding of market segmentation, role relationships, consumer attitudes, and the adoption of innovations, the manager is in a position to design communication programs for the chosen market segment. Several ideas for planning communication programs are suggested by the author.

Consumer satisfaction is one of the key variables in measuring the effectiveness of an organization's efforts. Satisfaction results when consumers' expectations about a purchased product or service are met or exceeded; dissatisfaction results when the actual experience does not meet expectations. Many of the commonly used indicators of consumer satisfaction are discussed.

This chapter also discusses consumer research. Research is very popular with managers but often not utilized properly. Some helpful tips are provided to help managers conduct more appropriate and useful research.

Managers of nonprofit organizations must constantly concern themselves with their organizations' clients. For instance, hospital administrators must deal with patients, as well as with physicians, patients' families, and citizens who make contributions of money or time to the hospital. In this chapter we will discuss managers' relationships with these different client groups by drawing from the marketing literature on consumer behavior.

These groups of clients are considered to be the organization's consumers. The nonprofit organization is, in a sense, a seller which enters into an exchange relationship with several different types of consumers. By viewing the relationship between the organization and its clients as one between a seller and a buyer, we highlight the exchange aspect of the relationship (see Chapter 2) and use the exchange paradigm to add to the manager's understanding of the relationship with various client groups.

Who may be termed a client? The definition used in this chapter is broader than everyday usage of the term. We will consider a client as *any person or organization with whom the nonprofit organization enters into an exchange relationship*. In a hospital, for instance, we can determine that patients and their families, physicians and nurses and other medical personnel, suppliers of pharmaceutical products, and citizens who donate money or time to the hospital are all clients. The hospital exchanges its services for dollars from patients and their families, its dollars for services from the medical staff, the use of its medical facility for patient business from physicians, its dollars for supplies from pharmaceutical companies, and plaques on its walls, gratitude, and humanitarian feelings for donated dollars from citizens. These exchange flows are shown in Figure 7–1.

In discussing clients as consumers, we will *focus on those exchange relationships in which the nonprofit organization supplies a client with services or in which it receives dollars or contributed time*. In the hospital example, patients, physicians, and donors will be discussed as consumers. Physicians in this case are categorized as consumers because they receive services from the hospital and are involved in at least a three-way exchange in which the nonprofit organization receives payment. The hospital provides the physician with the use of the medical facility. In turn, the physician provides the hospital with patient business which provides monetary payment to both the physician and the hospital. This exchange network can be further

FIGURE 7–1. *Exchange flows between a hospital and its client groups.*

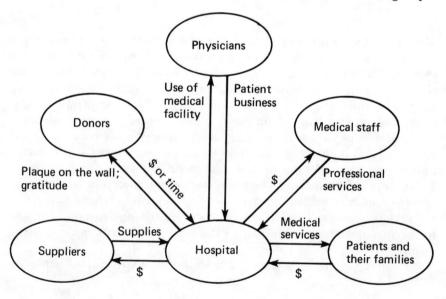

refined by including the patient's insurance company. This is shown in Figure 7–2. In this example the hospital has three clients (the patient, the physician, and the insurance company), the physician has three, and the insurance company has three.

Similarly, a handicapped person is a consumer of a social worker's services even though the payment for the services may come from a government agency rather than from the handicapped person. This example highlights one important aspect of exchanges between nonprofit organizations and their clients: Often the client is a consumer of the provided service, but the fees for the provision of the service are paid by another client group. Thus in for-profit organizations a person or or-

FIGURE 7-2. *Exchange relationships between hospital, physician, patient, and insurance company.*

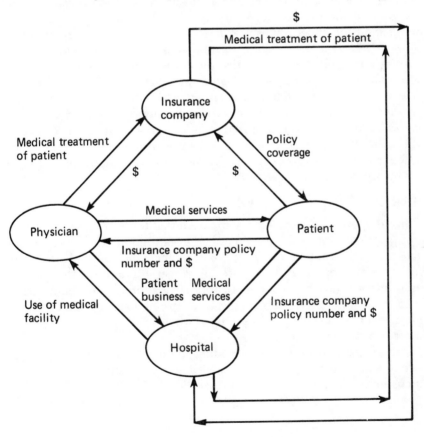

ganization who receives products or services *and* pays for them is called a consumer, but in the case of nonprofit organizations, any person or organization who receives the services of the organization *or* who donates dollars or time to the organization (either as payment for services received by someone else or as a contribution to the organization) is a consumer. Those who perform services for the organization in return for a fee (such as nurses in a hospital) are clients involved in an exchange relationship but are not consumers. Thus of the original set of clients, some are consumers and some are not.

This chapter will cover the ways in which a manager in a nonprofit organization should go about trying to understand clients who are consumers. First to be discussed is *market segmentation,* the process of dividing consumers into groups or segments each of which can be dealt with in a similar way; this concept will help the manager define the groups of consumers with which he or she must interact. Second, *role relationships* will be explained and used as a basis for analyzing the manager's interactions with the defined segments; this analysis will help the manager understand the expectations associated with each of these relationships. Third, *consumer attitudes* will be examined as a way of determining and possibly changing clients' cognitive responses to the nonprofit organization. Fourth, the *adoption of innovations* and consumer responses to new products or services will be discussed. Fifth, the process of *communicating with clients* will be discussed, followed by an analysis of *consumer satisfaction and dissatisfaction* with the nonprofit organization. Finally, *consumer research* will be briefly discussed as a means of measuring how the organization is doing with regard to its clients. The action implications for managers will be presented in each section.

MARKET SEGMENTATION

From Figures 7–1 and 7–2 it is apparent that there are several relevant groups of consumers for the nonprofit organization. For example, in a state university context the groups of consumers include students, sporting event spectators, agencies offering research grants, contributors to endowment funds, and state legislators. This intuitive grouping derives from the fact that as consumers these groups interact with the university in different ways. This is the essence of what is called *market segmentation* in for-profit organizations.

Market segmentation means dividing the market into smaller groups each of which includes people who are similar as consumers. (For a fuller discussion of market segmentation, see Frank, Massy, and Wind, 1972.

This concept is also discussed from a different perspective in Chapter 2.) Since they are similar as consumers, they can be reached by one marketing program. For example, all women beginning to get facial wrinkles may be a market segment for face lift operations because as consumers they are similar in their desire to eliminate the wrinkles that are beginning to appear. However, this group would not be a market segment for ballet tickets, because with regard to this product they are not similar as consumers. Thus market segmentation must be done with respect to a particular product context.

The importance of market segmentation lies in its relation to the marketing concept, which is a consumer-based managerial philosophy. It involves organizing the operation of the organization in such a way that all efforts derive from an attempt to satisfy consumer desires. Instead of producing a product and then trying to find buyers (which is called a selling orientation), the organization must first find out what consumers want and then produce a product or service which is consistent with these desires. Modifications in the marketing mix must then be made as consumers desire change. Managers segment markets when consumers differ in their desires. By grouping people together who have similar desires, managers form market segments. The organization can then decide which of these segments it will service and what the marketing plan should be for each chosen segment. The organization's products or services will then be based on consumer desires.

Segmentation can be done on many bases. Eight segmentation bases which are particularly relevant for nonprofit organizations are (1) age, (2) geographic location, (3) income, (4) lifestyle, (5) volume of usage, (6) benefits sought, (7) use potential, and (8) nature of exchange. Each of these will be discussed briefly.

Age

People in different age groups often differ as consumers. In fact, if there is any one variable which is consistently most important in influencing consumer behavior, it is age. For example, medical services are in greater demand among older persons than among younger persons. Younger persons, however, use more educational services. Consumers' abilities to read and mentally process new information also vary by major age category.

Age must be used cautiously as a basis for segmentation despite its importance. For some things, age in and of itself is important. Specific changes in consumption patterns are uniquely associated with age. The initial entry into public school is one example. Age qualifications for programs such as Medicare form another. For other things, such as medical services, age is simply a surrogate measure of biological changes or social situation changes. Thus, one of the reasons age is so important as a basis for segmentation is that it serves as a convenient, although imperfect measure of other phenomena which cannot be measured easily themselves.

Geographic Location

Many consumer phenomena are the result of where people live. For the most part children attend public schools which are near where they live, although busing has somewhat changed this. People's involvement with the post office is strongly related to where they live. And voters must go to the polls in the precinct where they live.

Over the past few years, several trends in residence location have taken place. Many years ago, the major pattern of movement was from rural areas to the urban areas (cities). People left their farms and went to work in the factories in the cities. Then, about 15 years ago, the suburbs began to grow rapidly. Presently, more people live in suburbia (more than 38 percent) than in either central cities (30 percent) or in rural areas (32 percent) (Masotti, 1975, p. vii). Because of this sudden growth, the suburbs are becoming urbanized and self-contained. Therefore, present movement seems to be in two directions. First, some people whose entire lives have been spent in suburbs, rather than partly in central cities, are moving to suburbs which try to divorce themselves from central cities. Thus, the movement is from suburb to suburb. The second developing pattern of movement is from suburb to exurb or to rural areas (Fava, 1975).

These patterns are very important for nonprofit organizations. As population shifts occur, so must there be shifts in the availability of services in various areas. For example, consumers moving from cities to suburbs to exurbs will still want many of the services they experienced in their previous locations. But will they travel into the city to visit art galleries and museums? If not, the museum should consider setting up temporary exhibits in suburban school auditoriums and charging fees which will cover the costs of transporting and setting up the exhibits. This concept of going to where the people are rather than trying to get them to come to the organization has been used successfully by library bookmobiles and blood bank drives for quite a while. Knowing where to go, however, depends on a thorough analysis of the trends in the geographic location of consumers.

Income

Income is a significant factor in the consumption of the services of some nonprofit organizations. For example, income is used as a basis for determining whether or not persons are eligible for services such as the use of a court-appointed attorney, a college scholarship, food stamps, and government-sponsored job training. In addition, some medical services are rendered on a sliding scale for fees so people with less income are charged less. Income is also a significant factor in determining whether or not an individual may donate money to a ballet company, a political campaign, or a hospital, or whether the person will frequently attend the symphony.

Lifestyle

A person's lifestyle will affect which nonprofit organization services a person is likely to use. People who are somewhat cosmopolitan and who enjoy being involved in the community will be more likely to purchase season tickets to the ballet, attend college sports events, and vote in elections. Lifestyle affects not only whether or not a person will use a particular nonprofit organization's services, but also how or when he or she will use them. For instance, students, homemakers, and retired people will be more likely to go to art galleries during the day, take daytime informal courses (for example, organic gardening, calligraphy), and volunteer their time as hospital aides or Scout leaders. Employed people are more likely to use libraries and visit museums in the evening or on weekends. If these timing differences exist, then the organization should design separate programs for the different market segments.

Volume of Usage

There is a standard marketing rule of thumb which is called the 80–20 rule. This rule states that 20 percent of the consumers will consume 80 percent of the product or service which is used, and the remaining 80 percent of the consumers will consume only 20 percent of the product or service. Translated into a library context, this would mean that about 80 percent of the visits made to the library in a year would be made by only 20 percent of the patrons (who perhaps come every week), whereas the remaining 80 percent of the patrons would account for only 20 percent of the visits. The library may wish to provide special services to either of these segments depending on its goals. If the library is trying to stimulate demand for its services, it may develop a campaign to get the light users into the library more often. If the library is suffering from overuse, however, it may try to restrict the visits of the heavy users by placing limits on the number of books which can be checked out in a specified time period. This example demonstrates how a knowledge of consumer behavior and marketing strategies can be used either to stimulate or restrict demand.

Benefits Sought

Sometimes a group of people are consumers of a particular product or service but should be considered as belonging to different market segments because they are consumers for very different reasons. That is, they are each seeking quite different benefits. For example, two women may both attend a lecture on a nonmechanical, nonchemical method of family planning (such as one based on basal body temperature), but for different reasons. One may wish to use the method in order to avoid conception while the other may wish to use the method in order to determine when is the best time for her to conceive. Two people may sit beside each other at a library, but one could be a student working on a long term paper while the other could be a person looking for a good novel to read. In each case a knowledge of how many people are seeking each type of benefit will help the manager plan how to offer the service. The librarian will need this information in order to plan whether future purchases should be of fiction best sellers or reference books and journals.

Use Potential

The population can be divided into three groups: present consumers, potential consumers, and nonusers. Using this segmentation base, the organization can target its efforts at the right groups. For instance if an organization wants to decrease the number of people using its services, it should develop strategies to change present consumers into nonusers as well as strategies to change potential consumers into nonusers. An organization wishing to increase the volume of services used can either try to persuade present consumers to increase their level of consumption (for example, by getting part-time college students to take a full course load) or try to persuade potential consumers to become present consumers (for example, by getting eligible nonregistered voters to register).

Nature of Exchange

A nonprofit organization deals with several groups of consumer clients, and these groups are different from each other because of the different nature of their exchanges with the organization. For example, in the case of a hospital, patients exchange dollars for medical services, and donors exchange dollars or time for plaques on the wall and humanitarian feelings. These segments are therefore different in the nature of their exchanges with the hospital. The hospital should plan strategies for dealing with consumers involved in each type of exchange.

Using the Segmentation Bases

Any or all of these segmentation bases might be used by a particular nonprofit organization. The purpose is to segment the market in whatever way will be most useful in helping the organization meet its goals. This requires a realistic, clear, operational statement of goals before the process of market segmentation begins. After the segmentation is completed, the organization must decide which segments it will concentrate on in trying to achieve which goals. The goal may or may not be to direct efforts to those people who are currently consumers of the organization's services. Strategies can then be developed for reaching the chosen goals in the relevant segments. A useful way of performing this task is to create a Segments × Goals matrix with the selected strategies filling the cells. A simple Segments × Goals matrix is shown in Table 7–1.

Segmentation Action Implications

• The market for an organization's products or services should be divided into groups of consumers or potential consumers.

• The basis for dividing consumers into segments should reflect differences between people with respect to their use of or preferences concerning the product.

• The manager should choose which segments the organization will try to service.

• The organization's managers should set goals and determine which strategies can be used on each chosen segment for meeting each goal.

ROLE RELATIONSHIPS

The interaction of a nonprofit organization with each of its consumer segments involves a role relationship. A *role* is a set of behaviors which are expected of individuals occupying certain positions as they interact with other people. The performance of a role is a reciprocal process involving a relationship between two or more people. For example, a person is a buyer by virtue of there being a seller.

The role concept has common-sense, everyday use in that people classify each other by the roles they occupy (for example, physician, parent, governor, purchasing agent, student). The concept is also used by sociologists and anthropologists for analytical rather than classificatory purposes. It is in this analytical sense that roles will be discussed here.

Table 7–2 lists 25 role relationships which involve nonprofit organizations and their consumer clients. The relationships have been grouped

TABLE 7–1. *Segments* × *goals matrix for school of nursing at a state university.*

Segment	Goal	
	Higher Ratio of Graduate to Undergraduate Students	*Increased Financial Resources*
Undergraduate students	Increase tuition Raise entrance requirements	Increase tuition
Graduate students	Send brochure on school to major undergraduate schools of nursing	No action
Faculty	Ask for their recommendations of undergraduate students to recruit for graduate program	Minimal pay raises
State legislators	In annual report describe and document current trend of state universities becoming more heavily involved in graduate programs and encouraging attendance at community colleges for undergraduate training	Prepare well-documented budget requesting increase
Alumni	No action	Conduct major drive to raise contributions

by type of organization. By looking at a more complete definition of roles, we can understand the ways in which these are role relationships.

Roles Defined

Nadel (1957) discusses four essential features of roles. First, roles refer to *behaviors*, not merely to characteristics or properties possessed by individuals. Second, roles refer to *relationships* between at least two individuals. For example, one is only a teacher by virtue of (actual, potential, or previous) interaction with other individuals as students. This highlights the important point that role partners (for example, physicians and patients) interact with each other, rather than one (the physician) acting on the other (the patient), as sometimes seems the case in management books. The primary reason for studying consumer behavior (and therefore clients as consumers) is to understand this interaction before planning the manager's future actions. Third, roles are *rule-based*. That is, roles

TABLE 7–2. *Role relationships between nonprofit organizations and their consumer clients.*

Organization	Relationships	Organization	Relationships
Arts	Ballet company manager—patron Gallery owner—art lover Sumphony business manager—symphony patron	Labor	Union official—union member
		Medical	Hospital staff physician—patient Family planning clinic paraprofessional—woman
Civic	Girl Scout leader—Girl Scout Professional Girl Scout worker—Girl Scout volunteer		Community blood bank volunteer—blood donor Hospital executive director—person attending hospital ice cream social
Education	Teacher—student President of state university—state legislator College athletic coach—spectator		Health education seminar lecturer—person in audience
		Politics	Ward leader—voter
Government	Social worker—welfare recipient Police chief—citizen Guard—prisoner Court-appointed attorney—defendant Postal worker—citizen Social Security Administration employee—elderly person	Religion	Minister—church member Pope—priest

derive from normative expectations about incumbents of particular positions. The manager who is trying to understand his or her relationship with clients as consumers must explicate the normative expectations implied by the role relationship. For example, what are the normative expectations of a person occupying the police officer role? Once this set of expected behaviors is described, a study can be done to determine if clients believe that the organization members are fulfilling these expectations. This type of information gathering will be discussed in the following section on attitudes.

The final feature of roles is that they indicate a *bundle of attributes or behaviors* that the role occupant is expected to fulfill. That is, a role is not merely a specification of one behavior. For example, Nadel cites the example of the priest role, which includes performing religious ceremonies, leading a decorous life, remaining celibate, and faithfully following religious beliefs.

To summarize, roles refer to bundles of behaviors which are expected of persons occupying certain positions as they interact with individuals occupying other positions. We turn now to a discussion of the way in which consumption or exchange fits into these role relationships.

Exchange as a Part of Role Behavior

Exchange-related activities are one component of the bundle of behaviors associated with the roles shown in Table 7–2. People do not think of themselves as consumers, but rather as parents insuring that their child will recover from an illness by consulting a physician, or as students purchasing textbooks. Thus people are engaged in day-to-day role relationships a part of which involve exchange.

Nadel indicates that each of the attributes or behaviors which as a set comprise a role can be one of three types:(1) *peripheral,* in which case the variation or absence of the attribute does not affect one's effectiveness in performing the role, (2) *relevant,* in which case the variation or absence of the attribute does affect one's effectiveness in performing the role, and the performance is therefore incomplete or imperfect without the attribute, which may lead to the invocation of negative sanctions, or (3) *basic or pivotal,* in which case the variation or absence of the attribute changes the identity of the role.

Exchange as an attribute of the roles involving nonprofit organizations and their clients can be any of the three types. Exchange activities can be peripheral as in the case of the police officer trying to sell tickets to the Police Officers' Benefit Ball. If the police officer fails to sell any tickets, he or she will continue to be a police officer. Therefore to this role this exchange is peripheral. Consumption may be a relevant attribute of a role enactment such as in the case of the role of a university student. It is expected that students will purchase class texts. However, one can still be a student without carrying out these consumption activities, although it is likely that others (students and professors) will try to encourage role expectation conformity. Finally exchange may be a basic or pivotal attribute of the role performance as in the case of the blood donor role and the ballet patron role.

After segmenting consumers into groups, the manager of the nonprofit organization must determine what the role expectations are for each of these segments of consumers as well as for organization staff members as they interact with each type of consumer. Then the manager must determine whether each role expectation is peripheral, relevant, or basic to the role performance. This information will then be used as a starting point for determining consumers' attitudes toward the organization.

Role Acquisition

Before moving into a discussion of how role expectations affect consumer attitudes, we must further refine the concept of roles. Up to this point we have discussed roles as if a person either does or does not occupy a particular role. However, role acquisition, or the taking on of a role is a temporal process characterized by several different stages (Thornton and Nardi, 1975). First there is the *anticipatory stage,* in which people are exposed to what behavior is expected of a person involved in the role relationship. This occurs prior to the actual occupancy of the role. At the *formal stage* the individual assumes the role and begins to view it as an incumbent rather than as an outsider. During these two stages the stereotypical role behaviors will be strongly expected and enacted by the new role occupant. That is, during these two stages role expectations will be felt most strongly. During the *informal stage* the individual encounters informal and unofficial role expectations. The fourth and final stage is the *personal* stage in which the individual attempts to impose on others his or her own prefences for behavior in the role.

In determining what role expectations exist for interactions with various consumer segments, the manager of the nonprofit organization must determine the role acquisition stages of the consumers. For example, a social worker may have to explain to the new welfare recipient what is expected of him or her as well as what the social worker can and cannot do.

Once the manager has identified the relevant consumer segments and has determined each segment's role expectations as well as each segment's stage of role acquisition, he or she can begin to explore what consumers' attitudes toward the organization and its services are.

Role Relationship Action Implications

• For each segment of consumers, the normative expectations concerning the behavior of the consumer and the provider of services should be explicated (this will often require research to determine how consumers perceive the situation).

• The manager must determine if in fact the normative expectations are being met. If so, then strategies for seeing that the situation continues should be developed. If not, then strategies for rectifying the discrepancy between the expectations and the actual behavior should be developed and implemented.

• If a significant portion of the organization's consumers are in the anticipatory and formal stages of role acquisition, special strategies must be developed for them so they will understand how to fulfill their role as a consumer of the organization's services.

CONSUMER ATTITUDES

Once the manager of a nonprofit organization understands the role expectations associated with relationships between organization people and consumers in the various identified segments, he or she can then begin an analysis of consumer attitudes. This analysis may be done separately for each consumer segment.

The simplest way to define attitudes is to say they reflect a person's general orientation toward something or someone (henceforth called the attitude object). Thus an attitude is the individual's evaluation of the object with respect to some criterion, which is often the object's ability to satisfy the individual in some way. For example, if someone were to say, "I have a favorable attitude toward chocolate fudge," we could infer that the person has evaluated chocolate fudge as being able to satisfy the person's taste buds. However, this positive attitude may not necessarily mean that the person would often or even ever eat chocolate fudge. The person may be on a diet, may be allergic to chocolate, may be a diabetic, may be in a culture where chocolate fudge is not available. Thus there is not always a perfect correlation between attitudes and behavior (as we can also see by thinking of seat belts, periodic vision exams, and actual voter turnout).

In this section we will present a model of attitude structure and then use it as a basis for discussing how information on consumer attitudes can help the manager.

A Model of Attitude Structure

Several models of attitude structure have been developed (see Rosenberg, 1956; Fishbein and Ajzen, 1975, Talarzyk and Moinpour, 1970; Cohen and Ahtola, 1971). Rather than review them here, we will center the discussion on the Fishbein model which has been used in many consumer contexts. The following formula is used to represent the model:

$$A_o = \sum_{i=1}^{n} B_i a_i$$

where A_o = attitude toward the object
B_i = strength of the belief (represented as a probability) that the object has attribute i

a_i = evaluation of attribute i

n = number of relevant attributes

Stating this verbally, we can see that attitude is the product of beliefs times evaluations (also called values). A product or service may have many features or attributes. The consumer will have an attitude toward each of these attributes (where each of these separate attitudes toward an attribute is comprised of a belief times a value). The *sum* of all these attitudes towards attributes, whether favorable or unfavorable, will represent the consumer's overall attitude toward the product or service. This overall attitude represents the consumer's assessment or evaluation of the satisfaction a product is likely to provide.

For example, let us consider the attitudes of a high school student toward two universities which he or she is considering attending. The relevant attributes for this student are cost, distance from home, and number of high school friends who are likely to go to that university. First, we would determine exactly how important each of these attributes is (this is the a_i component of the model).

High cost is

X						
-3	-2	-1	0	$+1$	$+2$	$+3$
very bad						*very good*

Long distance from home is

		X				
-3	-2	-1	0	$+1$	$+2$	$+3$
very bad						*very good*

Many high school friends attending the same university is

					X	
-3	-2	-1	0	$+1$	$+2$	$+3$
very bad						*very good*

Next we would see how the student would rate the probability that each of the two universities would have each of these attributes (this is the B_i component of the model).

Home State College is high in cost

$$\frac{}{-3} \quad \frac{}{-2} \quad \frac{}{-1} \quad \frac{}{0} \quad \frac{}{+1} \quad \overset{X}{\frac{}{+2}} \quad \frac{}{+3}$$

highly   *highly*
improbable   *probable*

Ivy League College is high in cost

$$\frac{}{-3} \quad \frac{}{-2} \quad \frac{}{-1} \quad \frac{}{0} \quad \frac{}{+1} \quad \frac{}{+2} \quad \overset{X}{\frac{}{+3}}$$

highly   *highly*
improbable   *probable*

Home State College is a long distance from home

$$\overset{X}{\frac{}{-3}} \quad \frac{}{-2} \quad \frac{}{-1} \quad \frac{}{0} \quad \frac{}{+1} \quad \frac{}{+2} \quad \frac{}{+3}$$

highly   *highly*
probable   *probable*

Ivy League College is a long distance from home

$$\frac{}{-3} \quad \frac{}{-2} \quad \overset{X}{\frac{}{-1}} \quad \frac{}{0} \quad \frac{}{+1} \quad \frac{}{+2} \quad \frac{}{+3}$$

highly   *highly*
improbable   *probable*

Home State College will be attended by many high school friends

$$\frac{}{-3} \quad \frac{}{-2} \quad \frac{}{-1} \quad \frac{}{0} \quad \frac{}{+1} \quad \frac{}{+2} \quad \overset{X}{\frac{}{+3}}$$

highly   *highly*
improbable   *probable*

Ivy League College will be attended by many high school friends

$$\frac{}{-3} \quad \frac{}{-2} \quad \frac{}{-1} \quad \frac{}{0} \quad \overset{X}{\frac{}{+1}} \quad \frac{}{+2} \quad \frac{}{+3}$$

highly   *highly*
improbable   *probable*

Computing scores for the attitudes we then obtain:

Attitude toward attending Home State College $= (-3)(+1) + (-1)(-3) + (+2)(+3) = 6$

Attitude toward attending Ivy League College $= (-3)(+3) + (-1)(-1) + (+2)(+1) = -6$

Obviously this student has a much more favorable attitude toward Home State College than toward Ivy League College. However, it is interesting to calculate the effects if the student were offered a full tuition scholarship to Ivy League College, thereby making it highly improbable (-3) that Ivy League College is high in cost.

Importance of the Attitude Model to the Manager

The attitude model can be used by the manager of a nonprofit organization in several different ways. First, by examining consumers' role expectations about their interactions with the nonprofit organization, the manager can get a preliminary understanding of the value components for some of the attributes. For example, a hospital administrator who knows that patients expect emergency room staff to offer speedy service will recognize that this will probably be one of the attributes used in forming an attitude toward the hospital.

By using the model and taking the time to determine what the relevant attributes are, the manager will have additional information on which to base management strategies. Merely knowing whether consumers' overall attitudes are positive or negative does not provide this information. For example, if the college president of Ivy League College knew that many high school students, like the one in the previous example, had negative attitudes toward attending the college, he or she would be concerned but would not know what to do. It would be even more damaging to the college if the president *thought* he or she knew why the negative attitudes existed and therefore, for example, spent a considerable sum of money developing a better football team. This would be a waste of money since quality of the football team is not an attribute which is important in determining what the students' attitudes will be. However, if the college president sees the scores which combine to form the overall attitude score, he or she would realize that the college must make efforts to reduce tuition either by cutting costs or (more realistically) offering financial aid to those students whom the college would like to have as students but who have a negative attitude because of their perceptions of the high cost of tuition. The point is that almost any attitude is comprised of mixed evaluations on the various attributes. An understanding of *which* attributes the organization is not doing so well on can help the manager plan strategies.

Information on attitudes can help the manager understand how the nonprofit organization is doing in comparison with its competitors. For example, a hospital could use information on physicians' attitudes to understand why the physicians often recommend other hospitals to their patients. Attitude information could also be obtained from high school seniors to determine how attitudes toward joining the Army compare with attitudes toward taking other kinds of jobs.

Finally, consumers can be segmented on the basis of values they give to each of the attributes. Essentially this is segmentation based on benefits sought (see the section on Market Segmentation in this chapter). For example, a family-planning clinic may find that some women clients evaluate the possibility of including men in the clinic's education sessions as a very positive attribute, while others evaluate this possibility as a very negative attribute. If this is the case, the clinic may wish to designate some education sessions for couples only and others for women only. In this way the clinic can match the benefits sought by each segment.

Basically, information on consumer attitudes can be used to compare the way consumers actually perceive the organization with the way they would ideally prefer the organization to be. This information is invaluable in helping the manager plan strategies for improving the organization's effectiveness in meeting its clients' needs and preferences as the marketing concept states it should.

Consumer Attitudes Action Implications

• The manager should determine what clients' attitudes are toward the nonprofit organization. This should be done separately for each relevant segment.

• The manager should closely examine the scores which combine to form the overall attitude score for a segment and define how the overall attitude can be improved by implementing strategies to modify the key components.

• Information on clients' attitudes toward the nonprofit organization should be compared with information on clients' attitudes toward the organization's competitors in order to determine the organization's relative strengths and weaknesses.

THE ADOPTION OF AND RESISTANCE TO INNOVATIONS

Up to this point the discussion has centered on contexts in which the product or service exchanged with consumers is one which is familiar to all parties involved. Consumers have already formed attitudes toward the service. In this section we will briefly consider the situation in which the product or service is an innovation. An *innovation* is a product, service, or idea which is perceived as new by the consumer. To be called an innovation the product, service, or idea does not need to be new on the market; it only must be new to the individual. However, in most cases the product, service, or idea will be new to individuals when it has also recently been introduced in the market.

It is necessary to consider innovations separately from other products and services for three reasons. First, since role expectations and attitudes toward the innovation have not yet been formed, traditional kinds of analysis of the situation cannot be relied upon. Instead, new ways of gauging consumers reactions to the product or service must be used. Second, goals for the innovation are usually different from the goals for other products or services. An agency sponsoring a new nutrition program may first want to bring the existence of the program to the attention of potential consumers. Thus, at first the agency will undertake an awareness-generating campaign rather than actually striving for a large number of actual consumers. This difference in goals is therefore reflected in different strategies. Finally, the manager of a nonprofit organization should pay particularly close attention to innovations because of the high failure rate for new products. By far, more new products are market failures than are market successes. This fact combined with the fact that introducing a new product or service can be quite costly means that the manager must carefully monitor and plan the introduction of innovations into the market.

In this section we will discuss the diffusion of innovations or the way in which an innovation spreads through the population, the adoption and nonadoption (called *resistance*) of an innovation by individuals, and the attributes of an innovation which affect the probability that the innovation will be adopted.

The Diffusion of Innovations

Diffusion is the process by which adoption or individual commitment to an innovation spreads through the population. One way of thinking of this is that knowledge or use of new products spreads through a group of people just as does a contagious disease or news of an important event.

People differ as to how soon they adopt an innovation after it is introduced. Based on these differences, people can be clustered into groups of consumers who adopt at roughly the same time. This segmentation approach has been empirically verified in a number of contexts (Rogers and Shoemaker, 1971). Figure 7–3 shows this classification. Diffusion follows a normal distribution over time, with few adopters very early in the diffusion process and few adopters very late in the process. Most people fall somewhere in the middle.

An examination of the diffusion process must take into account interpersonal communications which are very significant in decisions to adopt or not adopt an innovation. In particular, it is the early adopters who are likely to tell others about their experience with the new product or service (Baumgarten, 1975; Katz and Lazarsfeld, 1955; Summers, 1971). In addition, early adopters are also likely to be heavy users of the product or service category (Taylor, 1977). Thus, during the initial stages of the introduction of an innovation, managers will want to target their efforts toward those who are likely to be early users and who will influence the decisions of others (see Kotler and Zaltman, 1976).

The Adoption of Innovations

People who have never heard of an innovation have not yet developed role expectations and attitudes toward it. In studying the adoption process we will focus on the stages a person goes through in forming these role expectations and attitudes. It may be helpful to keep in mind a few innovations which have been introduced in the past few years by nonprofit organizations.

• A new Girl Scout program based on recent changes in cultural beliefs about women as well as changes in children's interests. The program

FIGURE 7-3. *Adopter categories based on innovativeness.*

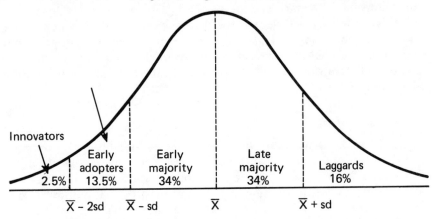

The innovativeness dimension, as measured by the time at which an individual adopts an innovation or innovations, is continuous. However, this variable may be partitioned into five adopter categories by laying off standard deviations (sd) from the average time of adoption.

Source: E.M. Rogers and F.F. Shoemaker, *Communication of Innovations: A Cross Cultural Approach* (New York: Free Press, 1971), p. 23.

includes several new features, including a summer session on women in government, and many badges and programs dealing with pollution, energy problems, career planning, and women's health issues. The main problem with this innovation was spreading awareness of these changes throughout the population in order to change people's images of scouting.

• The introduction of health maintenance organizations (HMOs). These are organizations offering prepaid health plans whereby a person (or the government in the case of welfare recipients) pays a fee and then is entitled to receive health care from the organization's staff. This is different from the traditional fee-for-service plan which characterizes the health care arrangement which most individuals have with private physicians. The main problem with this innovation was convincing physicians to join HMOs rather than remain in their private practices.

• The Equal Rights Amendment, which would provide a mechanism for eliminating all laws which discriminate on the basis of sex. The ERA is different from other attempts to end sex discrimination because it is a generalized measure rather than a statute-by-statute approach. The main problem with this innovation is the amount of misinformation that people have about what its effects will be.

• The proposal that passive restraint systems (for example, air bags) be mandatory equipment on all new automobiles. The main problem with this innovation was reconciling the estimates of different groups (automobile manufacturers, consumer groups, and insurance groups) regarding the costs of passive restraint systems.

Keeping these innovations in mind, we can consider the stages that an individual goes through in the process of deciding whether or not to adopt an innovation. People or groups are considered to have adopted an innovation when they have a commitment to repeating or continuing their usage of the innovation. The stages are shown in Figure 7–4. In the figure the basic adoption process stages are in boxes and run from left to right (perception to adoption). Above each box is the source of resistance to change usually associated with that stage. Only the basic adoption stages will be discussed.

Perception. The internal process of adoption begins with perception. Both the existence of the innovation and the need for it must be perceived by the individual for eventual adoption to occur. Many promotional campaigns to introduce new products or services are aimed solely at increasing the number of people who have reached the perception stage.

Motivation. A necessary step in overcoming resistance to change is motivation. Behaviors which are familiar, such as not using seat belts, are normally resistant to change. Consumer perceptions of an existing need and of the innovation itself must be very positive in order to provide the motivation for further action.

Attitude. The next stage of the adoption process is attitude formation. (The structure of attitudes was explained earlier in this chapter.) As consumers move through the attitude stage, they develop beliefs about the innovation based on information from other people and by reading promotional material and news items.

Legitimation. In the legitimation stage, consumers seek reinforcement for the decision they are contemplating. Of prime importance is the appropriateness of adopting the innovation, which may be determined by observing whether other important people have made similar decisions (if this is possible) or by seeking approval from peers or relatives.

Trial. During the trial stage, the consumer puts the innovation to a personal test prior to complete acceptance. Occasionally, the nature of the innovation or the situation may make personal testing impossible, so the individual may try the product by psychologically sharing the experience of someone else who is actually using the product.

FIGURE 7-4. *A resistance/adoption model.*

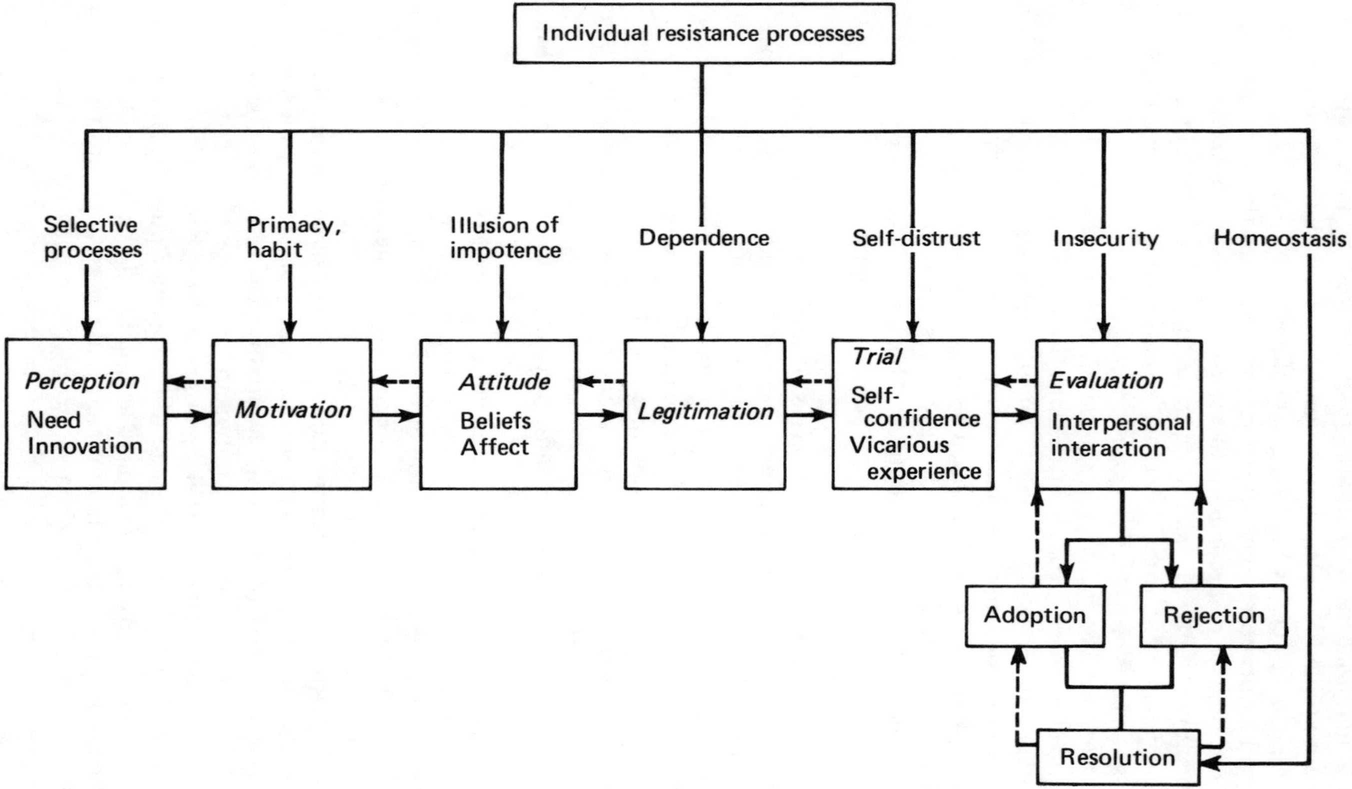

Source: Gerald Zaltman and Robert Duncan, *Strategies for Planned Change* (New York: Wiley-Interscience, 1977).

Evaluation. Following trial, the consumer will review the pros and cons of continued or increased use of the innovation. Informal or very brief evaluation probably follows each stage in the adoption process, but a major evaluation is necessary before a formal commitment is made.

Adoption/rejection. The adoption stage represents the consumer's final commitment to repeated or continued usage of the innovation. The alternative to adoption at this point is rejection. Unsatisfactory outcomes in the process prior to this stage may result in negative feelings or beliefs causing the person to reject the innovation.

Resolution. The final stage is resolution (Campbell, 1966), which includes all the adjustments (some positive and some negative) made as a result of the decision to adopt or not adopt the innovation.

Uses of the adoption process model. The adoption process model can be used by the manager in at least three ways. Goals can be set in terms of the number of people to move from one stage to the next. For instance, in the example of the new Girl Scout program mentioned above, the national directors may decide that they want to develop 100 percent awareness of the changes among present leaders and scouts and 30 percent awareness in the remainder of the population.

A second way that the model can be used is as a gauge of the organization's success in the diffusion of the innovation. If, on the whole, movement through the stages is occurring rather rapidly, it would appear that the innovation might be a success.

Finally, the model can be used as a way of analyzing where consumer resistance might occur. By examining the attributes of the innovation, the manager can get a better idea of the stages at which there might be consumer resistance. With this knowledge, he or she can plan strategies for overcoming the resistance.

Perceived Attributes of Innovations

It is extremely important to understand how consumers will perceive the innovation. Innovations can be characterized by a scheme of attributes. The following are important attributes to consider when evaluating the possible market success of a particular innovation:

Relative advantages—what the new product does that alternatives do not do or do not do as well.

Complexity—(1) how difficult it is to use the new product; and (2) how difficult it is to understand how the product works.

Compatibility—(1) how well the new product fits in with the customer's thinking; (2) how well the new product fits in with the customer's social situation; and (3) how well the new product fits in with other related or connected products.

Trialability—how easily the new product may be tried without full commitment.

Divisibility—how easily the new product can be tried in a mini form.

Reversibility—how easily the new product can be discontinued without adverse effect.

Communicability—how easy it is to receive and send information about the new product.

Adaptability—how easy it is to modify the new product to the unique circumstances of the user.

Cost—the magnitude of the financial and nonfinancial resources required.

Realization—how soon the benefits of having a new product are experienced.

Risk—the magnitude of the dysfunctional consequences of the new product and the likelihood of their being experienced.

To the extent that an innovation has the ratings on these attributes shown below, consumers will find it easier to adopt:

High desirability	*Low desirability*
Relative advantages	Complexity
Compatibility	Cost
Trialability	Risk
Divisibility	
Reversibility	
Communicability	
Adaptability	
Realization (soon)	

The manager should also know the relative importance of the various attributes at different stages in the adoption process. An attribute may be particularly important at more than one stage, as can be seen in Table 7–3.

If the manager knows what attributes of the innovation are not conducive to adoption and when these attributes are most likely to block adoption, he or she can either change the nature of the innovation or develop strategies to lessen the impact of these attributes. For example, libraries minimize the cost to clients of traveling to a central city location (financial costs of travel as well as time) by opening smaller branch libraries and by setting up convenient bookmobile schedules.

Innovation Action Implications

• During the initial stages of the introduction of an innovation, the

TABLE 7–3. *Importance of attributes of innovations in stages in the adoption process.*

Stage	Attribute
Perception and motivation	Relative advantage Complexity
Attitude	Compatibility Communicability Risk
Legitimation	Compatibility
Trial	Trialability Divisibility Reversibility
Evaluation	Cost Realization Adaptability
Adoption/rejection	All attributes
Resolution	Adaptability

manager should target strategies at those individuals who have been iden-tified as being most likely to be early users of the innovation.

• The manager should state goals for the introduction of an innovation in terms of the movement of consumers through particular stages of the adoption process.

• In planning the introduction of an innovation, the manager must design strategies for overcoming resistance to change at each of the adop-tion stages.

• The manager must analyze the innovation's attributes and, where possible, modify them so that they more closely match the desirable char-acteristics of innovations.

COMMUNICATING WITH CONSUMERS

Literally hundreds of books and articles have been written on the pro-cess of communicating with consumers, particularly on designing persua-sive communications in the form of advertising. Therefore, in this section we will not attempt to review or even highlight these writings. The in-terested reader is referred to several excellent works on the subject (DeLozier, 1976; Rogers and Agarwala-Rogers, 1976). In this section, the discussion will focus on how communications with consumers derive from the manager's understanding of consumer segmentation, role expecta-tions, consumer attitudes, and, if applicable, the processes underlying the adoption of innovations.

Persuading consumers to expect, believe, or do something different from what they presently expect, believe, or do is an exceptionally difficult task. Most people vastly overestimate the power of such tools as advertising. If we consider the message of an advertisement to be in many ways an innovation, we can recall the stages in the adoption process and understand all the barriers or resistance factors which may prevent the innovation (the message) from being adopted or implemented. For instance, public service advertisements urging people not to drink and drive have been used on television for many years, yet the number of automobile collisions in which at least one of the drivers has been drinking remains alarmingly high.

A few guidelines will be presented here concerning how to use information about clients as consumers to help increase the probability that a mass communication program will be effective. Market segmentation is an essential first step in planning any communication program. Communications should be designed to appeal to and reach particular segments of the population rather than the population as a whole. In addition, the channel through which the message is carried (radio, television, newspaper, magazine, billboard, leaflet) should be consistent with that segment's lifestyle and media usage patterns. Usage of almost all media is available by demographic segments (broken down by such factors as age, income, geographic location, and home ownership).

An example of a communications program which was designed following market segmentation is one campaign to encourage the use of seat belts (Robertson, 1974). Six messages were designed for television viewing by six different groups: (1) A father thinks about his paralyzed son as they travel to a football game (shown during National Football League games); (2) an injured teenaged girl thinks about her life after a car collision (shown during soap operas); (3) a scarred woman and her husband discuss how the woman feels about going to a party (shown during soap operas); (4) a family who almost has a collision and almost has to deal with an injured daughter is cautioned by a policeman to use seat belts; (5) physicians and nurses discuss car crash cases they have had to treat; and (6) a witch appears to some children and says she makes parents not wear seat belts, and then a good fairy appears and encourages the children to tell their parents to wear their seat belts (shown during children's programs). These messages and the media in which they appeared were designed to reach fathers interested in football, homemakers, families, and children. Each message was written to appeal to one of these groups.

If the advertised product, service, or idea is an innovation, then the goals of the promotional campaign should be defined in terms of the stages in the adoption process. Probably the initial efforts should be targeted toward increasing the number of people who are aware of the innovation. Thus, the effectiveness of such a campaign should be measured by levels of awareness rather than by number of adopters. However, one of the most common mistakes in measuring advertising effectiveness is to examine the increase in the number of customers or in the quantity of the product or service which was used in a certain time period. Instead, measurement of effectiveness should be based on the original goals of the campaign.

Finally, since it is so difficult to persuade people to change their expectations, attitudes, and behavior, special efforts should be made to present the persuasive argument in a way which makes it easy for people to accept it and integrate it into their lives. Not only must the message reach the person and enter his or her thought processes, but it must also make clear to the person exactly how to carry out the desired action. For example, rather than saying, "Help your community," a public service advertisement should say, "Donate blood tomorrow between noon and five at the First National Bank building lower lounge, or call this number and pledge $5 to the American Red Cross."

The key point of this section is that communication strategies should derive from a thorough analysis of clients as consumers. Since advertising is the most visible aspect of marketing, many managers try to plan advertising campaigns as a first step. However, such campaigns will likely be expensive and unproductive unless they are based on a well-researched analysis of consumer segments, and their expectations and attitudes.

Communication Action Implications

• Communication messages and channels should be selected to be congruent with the target market segment.

• The manager must base measurement of advertising effectiveness on the original goals of the campaign.

• Communication messages must be specific about the behavior that they are trying to persuade people to adopt.

CONSUMER SATISFACTION AND DISSATISFACTION

According to the marketing concept the organization should plan its operations to satisfy consumer needs. If consumer satisfaction is to be one of the primary goals of the organization, it is important for the manager of the organization to understand what consumer satisfaction and dissatisfaction are, to be familiar with the processes which may produce them, and to determine whether or not they exist. These topics will be addressed in this section.

What Is Consumer Satisfaction?

The term "consumer satisfaction" may make one think that the process referred to involves an emotion, but it does not. Instead, consumer satisfaction involves an evaluation of previous exchange transactions (Hunt, 1977). Most researchers in this area agree that consumer satisfaction results when a consumer's expectations about a purchased product or service are either met or exceeded. Dissatisfaction results when the actual experience does not meet expectations (see, for example, Aiello et al., 1977; Granbois et al., 1977; Oliver, 1977; Suprenant, 1977; Swan, 1977). Thus, the determinants of consumer satisfaction and dissatisfaction are the consumer's perception of the actual experience as well as expectations and desires as represented in the a_i component of the attitude model. This makes it clear why consumer attitudes are important. The a_i component of attitudes will be compared with actual experience with the product or service to produce consumer satisfaction or dissatisfaction.

How to Determine Levels of Consumer Satisfaction

Given that consumer satisfaction is the organization's goal under the marketing concept, the organization must find a way to measure the extent to which its consumer clients are satisfied in order to evaluate how the organization is doing.

There are several commonly used indicators of the level of consumer satisfaction with the organization which are *not* appropriate for determining how the organization is doing. The organization cannot use the amount of sales or number of clients served as an indicator of the level of consumer satisfaction for three reasons. First, this is a faulty indicator because it does not take into account the number of clients served (present consumers) relative to the number of total clients who could be served (present consumers *plus* potential consumers). For example a blood bank may receive blood donations from 3,000 clients in each of two years, but if the population of the city in which the blood bank is located is growing at a rate of 5 percent per year, then in actual terms the blood bank is losing out. Second, the number of clients served is a faulty indicator because it does not take into account who the clients are. If the blood bank has 3,000 donors in each of two years, but 80 percent of the donors in the first year did not donate in the second year because they found the organization workers to be unfriendly and the facility to be somewhat unsanitary, then there is very high consumer dissatisfaction. In time these unsatisfied donors will tell others about their experience, and the blood bank will find it difficult to find new donors each year. Finally, this is a faulty indicator because some people may be consumers even though they are dissatisfied. For instance, an elderly person may be dissatisfied with the bureaucratic procedures which are necessary for receving Medicare benefits, but he or she may have no other health care assistance alternatives. Therefore, clients may continue to use the services of the organization even though they are dissatisfied because they have no other alternatives.

Examining the number of complaints made to the organization about its services is another faulty measure of the level of consumer satisfaction or dissatisfaction. Many consumers who are dissatisfied do not make a complaint to anyone in the organization. Several studies have reported that the percentage of dissatisfied consumers who do not make a complaint to anyone in the organization is higher than 50 percent (Pickle and Bruce, 1972; Valle and Wallendorf, 1977). Other studies found that approximately one-third of the dissatisfied consumers took no action at all, including making a complaint to anyone in the organization (Day and Landon, 1976; Warland et al., 1975). Furthermore, a change in the number of complaints may not indicate a change in the level of consumer satisfaction. For example an organization may receive more complaints if it makes it easier for dissatisfied consumers to make a complaint to the organization. One strategy which might have this effect would be the installation of a well-publicized toll-free telephone line which consumers could use in making a complaint (Diener, 1977).

Therefore, the only measure of consumer satisfaction on which the organization can rely must be a direct one. The organization must find out from consumers how satisfied or dissatisfied they are with the organization as a whole as well as with its performance on various dimensions. This will mean routinely contacting consumers and asking them to respond to questions about their level of satisfaction.

Researchers have tried to determine what types of questions are best for measuring consumer satisfaction. Considerable controversy surrounds this issue. The interested reader is referred to a collection of papers on consumer satisfaction for details regarding the alternatives and their advantages and disadvantages (Day, 1977). Deciding what questions to ask consumers in order to find out about their level of satisfaction is an important decision which should take into account the specific situation and how it can be best served using existing measures.

Consumer Satisfaction Action Implications

• The manager must measure consumer satisfaction directly rather than indirectly through sales or complaints.

• If the level of consumer satisfaction is lower than is desired, the manager must investigate the problem further so that he or she can design and implement strategies to increase consumer's satisfaction to the desired level.

CONSUMER RESEARCH

Throughout this chapter we have discussed how to better understand one's clients. Often the implication has been that the organization may wish to engage in some research to find out about consumers' needs, expectations, attitudes, or level of satisfaction. Since many textbooks have been written on the subject of marketing research (Tull and Hawkins, 1976; Zaltman and Burger, 1975), this section will include only a few cautions to the prospective market researcher.

Before beginning a survey of consumers, the manager must first determine what information is needed and then find the easiest, least expensive source of this information. After defining exactly what information is needed, the researcher should spend some time in a library to see what relevant information has already been gathered. For instance, a welfare agency may want to know what ages of people in which areas are most in need of financial assistance from the agency. U.S. census data can be used to answer this question. Very complete information on income, age, occupation, family situation, and ownership of certain items (such as refrigerators and television sets) is collected. This information is available for small geographical areas called "census tracts." The important point is that if good or even adequate information is available through secondary sources, then that information should be collected before a consumer survey is even considered.

If it is decided that a consumer survey is needed, then other considerations must be taken into account. Sampling will be a concern. Obviously it is too expensive to ask questions of all consumers, therefore a subgroup or sample will be taken. The sample cannot be limited to current users because they are a self-selected group. For instance, if a hospital is interested in finding out how satisfied physicians are with its services, then the hospital must gather information from physicians who currently use the hospital facility (present consumers) as well as some physicians who either use the facility very infrequently or who previously used it but presently use another hospital (potential consumers). If the sample is biased and therefore does not include the right categories of people, then the information obtained from the sample will be biased and will not provide a sound basis for management decisions.

The researcher must also give serious consideration to which questions to include in the survey instrument. The determination of which questions to include must be predicated upon a clear understanding of what information is needed and how it will be used by the manager. Those questions which merely seem interesting but will not provide information which will be used by the manager should be omitted. Both the researcher and the manager should ask themselves concerning each question, "If we find that responses to this question are _____, how will this be used to make management decisions?" Thus, the major criterion for determining which questions to include is the relevance of the answers for management decisions.

Once the decision has been made concerning which questions to include in the survey instrument, a pretest must be conducted. In a pretest the chosen questions are asked of people similar to those who will be in the final sample. Asking friends, family, or business associates to respond to the questions is not a formal pretest. A pretest should be conducted in order to determine if any of the questionnaire items are difficult for respondents to answer or if they do not elicit the desired information.

Finally, it is extremely important that the researcher as well as the manager give some attention to the ethical issues involved in doing marketing research (see Tybout and Zaltman, 1974). Briefly these issues include not using the conduct of a research project as a guise for selling or promoting something, observing respondents' and nonrespondents' rights to privacy, using qualified researchers during all phases of the research, and preserving the anonymity of respondents and nonrespondents (Tull and Hawkins, 1976). Considering these issues is important not only because of their relationship to respondents' and nonrespondents' rights, but also because of their impact on the quality of the information which is obtained.

Research Action Implications

• In any research project, the manager must begin by determining exactly what information is *needed.*

• The manager must insure that the sample for a survey is appropriate and will provide the needed information.

• The manager must see that a pretest is conducted prior to any survey research investigation.

• The manager must insure that any research investigation does not violate any of the ethical issues involved in doing research.

CONCLUSIONS

Strategies and suggestions for the manager of a nonprofit organization emerge when he or she analyzes the relationship between the organization and its clients as one between a seller and a buyer. In this chapter we have considered any person or organization with whom the nonprofit organization enters into an exchange relationship to be a client. Consumers are clients with whom the nonprofit organization enters into an exchange relationship in which the organization supplies the client with services *or* in which it receives dollars or contributed time.

Consumers can be further subdivided into groups of similar people through a process called market segmentation. Eight bases of market segmentation and their relevance for the nonprofit organization were discussed. The eight bases are (1) age, (2) geographic location, (3) income, (4) lifestyle, (5) volume of usage, (6) benefits sought, (7) use potential, and (8) nature of exchange. Strategies for meeting the organization's goals in each segment can be explored by constructing a segments × goals matrix.

After segmenting the market, the manager must seek to understand the role relationship between the organization and the consumers in each segment. This can be done by examining the way in which exchange is an attribute of roles and the stage of role acquisition of consumers. Then the manager can begin determining what consumers' attitudes are in each segment. This analysis is conducted by using the attitude model presented in the chapter. Strategies can then be developed to change various components of consumers' attitudes (for example, beliefs or evaluations).

The special case of innovations was then considered. Innovations are products, services, or ideas which are perceived as new by the consumer. Consumers can be divided into categories on the basis of when they adopt the innovation. In deciding whether or not to adopt an innovation, a consumer may go through several stages, depending on how far he or she gets in considering the innovation. These stages are perception, motivation, attitude, legitimation, trial, evaluation, adoption/rejection, and resolution. The manager must consider how the perceived attributes of the innovation affect the consumer during these stages.

With this understanding of market segments, role relationships, consumer attitudes, and the adoption of innovations, the manager is in a position to design persuasive communications to direct toward the chosen market segments. Several suggestions were made for planning these communication programs.

In measuring the effectiveness of the organization's efforts, consumer satisfaction will be a key variable to examine. A few suggestions and warnings about measures of consumer satisfaction were discussed.

In order to understand clients as consumers, the manager will in all likelihood conduct some consumer research. This process was discussed briefly and some common pitfalls were examined in the hope that they could be avoided by the manager of the nonprofit organization.

Consumer behavior is an immensely complicated phenomenon, and therefore this chapter has only highlighted some of the key ways in which it operates. By beginning with a sound basic understanding of the consumer behavior of the organization's clients, the manager will be able to design programs and strategies that will be effective in the short run as well as contributing to long-run consumer satisfaction and the optimization of the organization's goals.

REFERENCES

Aiello, Albert, Jr., John A. Czepiel, and Larry J. Rosenberg. "Scaling the Heights of Consumer Satisfaction: An Evaluation of Alternative Measures," in Ralph L. Day, ed., *Consumer Satisfaction, Dissatisfaction, and Complaining Behavior* (Division of Business Research, Indiana University, 1977), pp. 43–50.

Baumgarten, Steven A. "The Innovative Communicator in the Diffusion Process," *Journal of Marketing Research,* Vol. 12 (1975), pp. 12–18.

Campbell, Rex R. "A Suggested Paradigm of the Individual Adoption Process," *Rural Sociology,* Vol. 31 (1966), pp. 458–466.

Cohen, Joel B., and Olli T. Ahtola. "An Expectancy × Value Analysis of the Relationship between Consumer Attitudes and Behavior," *Proceedings of the Association for Consumer Research,* 1971, pp. 344–364.

Day, Ralph L., and E. Laird Landon, Jr. "Collecting Comprehensive Consumer Complaint Data by Survey Research," *Advances in Consumer Research,* Vol. 3 (1976), pp. 263–268.

Delozier, Wayne M. *The Marketing Communication Process* (New York: McGraw-Hill, 1976).

Diener, Betty J. "Consumer Communications—Should They Be Encouraged?" in Ralph L. Day, ed., *Consumer Satisfaction, Dissatisfaction, and Complaining Behavior* (Division of Business Research, Indiana University, 1977), pp. 173–175.

Fava, Sylvia. "Beyond Suburbia," *The Annals of the American Academy of Political and Social Science,* Vol. 422 (1975), pp. 10–24.

Fishbein, Martin, and Icek Ajzen. *Belief, Attitude, Intention, and Behavior* (Reading, Mass.: Addison-Wesley, 1975).

Frank, Ronald E., William F. Massy, and Yoram Wind. *Market Segmentation* (Englewood Cliffs, N.J.: Prentice-Hall, 1972).

Granbois, Donald, John O. Summers, and Gary L. Frazier. "Correlates of Consumer Expectation and Complaining Behavior," in Ralph L. Day, ed., *Consumer Satisfaction, Dissatisfaction, and Complaining Behavior* (Division of Business Research, Indiana University, 1977), pp. 18–25.

Hunt, H. Keith. "CS/D: Bits and Pieces," in Ralph L. Day, ed., *Consumer Satisfaction, Dissatisfaction, and Complaining Behavior* (Division of Business Research, Indiana University, 1977), pp. 18–25.

Katz, Elihu, and Paul F. Lazarsfeld. *Personal Influence* (New York: Free Press, 1955).

Kotler, Philip, and Gerald Zaltman. "Targeting Prospects for New Products," *Journal of Advertising Research,* Vol. 16 (1976), pp. 7–20.

Masotti, Louis H. Preface to special issue entitled "The Suburban Seventies," *The Annals of the American Academy of Political and Social Science,* Vol. 422 (1975), p. vii.

Nadel, S. F. *The Theory of Social Structure* (London: Cohen and West, Ltd., 1957).

Oliver, Richard L. "A Theoretical Reinterpretation of Expectation and Disconfirmation Effects of Posterior Product Evaluation: Experiences in the Field," in Ralph L. Day, ed., *Consumer Satisfaction, Dissatisfaction, and Complaining Behavior* (Division of Business Research, Indiana University, 1977), pp. 2–9.

Pickle, Hal B., and Roy Bruce. "Consumerism, Product-Satisfaction-Dissatisfaction: An Empirical Investigation," *Southern Journal of Business,* Vol. 7 (1972), pp. 87–100.

Rogers, Everett M., and Rekha Agarwala-Rogers. *Communication in Organizations* (New York: Free Press, 1971).

Rogers, Everett M., and Floyd Shoemaker. *The Communication of Innovations* (New York: Free Press, 1971).

Rosenberg, M. J. "Cognitive Structure and Attitudinal Affect," *Journal of Abnormal and Social Psychology*, Vol. 53 (1956), pp. 367–372.

Sternthan, Brian, and C. Samuel Craig. "Fear Appeals: Revisited and Revised," *Journal of Consumer Research*, Vol. 1 (1974), pp. 22–34.

Summers, John O. "Generalized Change Agents and Innovativeness," *Journal of Marketing Research*, Vol. 8 (1971), pp. 313–316.

Suprenant, Carol. "Product Satisfaction as a Function of Expectations and Performance," in Ralph L. Day, ed., *Consumer Satisfaction, Dissatisfaction, and Complaining Behavior* (Division of Business Research, Indiana University, 1977), pp. 36–37.

Swan, John E. "Consumer Satisfaction with a Retail Store Related to the Fulfillment of Expectations on an Initial Shopping Trip," in Ralph L. Day, ed., *Consumer Satisfaction, Dissatisfaction, and Complaining Behavior* (Division of Business Research, Indiana University, 1977), pp. 10–17.

Talarzyk, W. W., and R. Moinpour. "Comparison of an Attitude Model and Coombsian Unfolding Analysis for the Prediction of Individual Brand Preference," paper presented at the Workshop on Attitude Research and Consumer Behavior, University of Illinois, December 1970.

Taylor, James W. "A Striking Characteristic of Innovators," *Journal of Marketing Research*, Vol. 14 (1977), pp. 104–107.

Thornton, Russell, and Peter M. Nardi. "The Dynamics of Role Acquisition," *American Journal of Sociology*, Vol. 80 (1975), pp. 870–885.

Tull, Donald S., and Del I. Hawkins. *Marketing Research* (New York: Macmillan, 1976).

Tybout, Alice M., and Gerald Zaltman. "Ethics in Marketing Research: Their Practical Relevance," *Journal of Marketing Research*, Vol. 11 (1974), pp. 357–368.

Valle, Valerie, and Melanie Wallendorf. "Consumer Attributions of the Cause of Their Product Satisfaction and Dissatisfaction," in Ralph L. Day, ed., *Consumer Satisfaction, Dissatisfaction, and Complaining Behavior* (Division of Business Research, Indiana University, 1977), pp. 26–30.

Warland, Rex, H., Robert O. Hermann, and Jane Willits. "Dissatisfied Consumers: Who Gets Upset and Who Takes Action," *Journal of Consumer Affairs*, Winter 1975, pp. 148–163.

Zaltman, Gerald, and Philip Burger. *Marketing Research* (Hinsdale, Ill.: Dryden Press, 1975).

CHAPTER 8

Cost-Benefit Approach to Capital Expenditure

Prem Prakash

Editor's Note   *In the nonprofit sector, investment projects and policy making have substantial economic, social, and political ramifications. In addition, the absence of the profit motive on the one hand and of competition in the marketplace on the other deprives managers of the usual economic indicators for judging the economic efficiency of their resource utilization decisions. Cost-benefit analysis provides a framework for considering in a systematic way the various economic and social welfare trade-offs that a manager faces in such a situation. In the absence of cost-benefit analysis, the evaluation of alternative courses of action may be excessively subjective. It is important, therefore, for readers to understand some of the concepts involved in cost-benefit analysis as a way of sharpening their own thought processes in allocating resources.*

Cost-benefit analysis is traditionally concerned with the economic efficiency of resource utilization in the aggregate social sense. Questions of social equity, political viability, and ethical values are outside its scope. These questions must be considered by the manager in conjunction with the question of economic efficiency. Cost-benefit analysis views the consequences of a proposed policy or project in terms of the aggregate amount that individual members of society would be willing to pay for the desirable consequences (benefits) and the aggregate amount they would want as a compensation for the undesirable consequences (costs). Thus cost-benefit analysis views all consequences in terms of what society demands or would be willing to pay for, not in terms of what society needs or what is good for it.

In this chapter, the author discusses the ethical, social, and political issues surrounding cost-benefit analysis and introduces the basic economic concepts on which the practice of cost-benefit analysis is founded. Among the economic concepts introduced for the reader are compensating variation, surplus variation, demand schedule, consumer's surplus, and shadow prices.

The issue of accounting for benefit and cost flows is also discussed, using simple examples. The author notes that social benefits and costs are of two types: direct and indirect (or spillover). For each of these, it is important to take into account the relevant cost savings and forgone benefits. The author points out that the valuation of unpriced benefits and costs is the most vulnerable side of cost-benefit analysis. Various means that have been proposed to resolve the valuation problem are reviewed in the chapter. In accounting for future flows of benefits and costs, the analyst has to deal with uncertainty as well. Several methods of handling uncertainty are also discussed in the chapter.

A decision maker needs criteria for evaluating projects, ranking them according to economic efficiency, and allocating limited funds among available projects to maximally enhance social welfare. The problem is made complex by the fact that costs are usually incurred "now" with a view to receiving (uncertain) benefits in the future. This chapter deals with the issues of risk and return and social trade-off of current costs for future benefits.

Nonprofit organizations make public policy and undertake capital expenditures with the intention of increasing the well-being of society. The resources they need often have to be bought in competition with everyone else in the marketplace; but the goods or services they produce do not go through market valuation in competition with other products. In this respect, nonprofit organizations are sharply different from private business enterprises.

In the case of a private business enterprise, the benefit provided by its product is reflected in the price the market is willing to pay for it, and profit is the reward for producing efficiently what society demands. The profit system serves three important functions. First, it provides the motivation for business enterprises to seek new products and services. Second, it provides a criterion for evaluating the worthiness of new projects and the success of old ones. Third, it works to bring about an efficient rationing of society's scarce resources among different productive uses— provided that there are no barriers to trade, that businesses may enter or leave an industry as they wish, pricing and selling their product without collusion or restriction, and that consumers may allocate their funds freely among the goods and services of their choice.

Such a perfectly competitive economy does not exist in practice. But the more an economy is allowed a free and competitive play, the closer it moves to the ideal of efficient resource utilization. The underlying price system then provides a fair schedule of compensation for all private goods and services and for all private costs and sacrifices that trade through the marketplace.

When the profit motive is missing, there is no automatic mechanism to ensure the efficiency of resource utilization. The onus is then on the decision maker to evaluate the worthiness of an alternative from the social viewpoint. This involves ascertaining the economic efficiency of the alternative: Do the benefits of the alternative exceed the costs and sacrifices associated with it? But this is not all. Often, those who receive the benefits from an alternative are not the ones who also bear the associated costs and sacrifices; nor do all resulting costs and benefits trade through a competitive market mechanism. For this reason, evaluating the worthiness of an alternative from the social viewpoint involves making a moral judgment as well: Is the resulting distribution of benefits and costs among the citizens acceptable within the society's norm of equity and fairness?

To illustrate, suppose a project is expected to generate a total benefit worth $1,000 and involves a total cost of $800. The beneficiaries are ten rich families. The losers are twenty poor families. Then the comparison of the total benefits of $1,000 against the total cost of $800 is a consideration of the efficiency of resource utilization. On the other hand, comparison of beneficiaries (ten rich families) versus losers (twenty poor families) is a consideration of distribution and equity. The project might be acceptable on the first count and not on the second.

An excess of benefits over costs indicates economic efficiency no matter who the beneficiaries are and who the losers. To see the underlying rationale, consider again the above illustration. If the beneficiaries were to compensate the losers fully for all costs ($800), then the former would be left with a net benefit of $200 and would be that much better off, while there would be no losers. Thus, all else being equal, society should surely prefer the project to the status quo—provided, of course, a suitable compensating mechanism were devised. One such mechanism, for instance, is competitive market together with price system.

In the presence of a suitable compensating mechanism, the ethical question relating to distribution and equity becomes much less severe, although it might not disappear entirely. For instance, if the norm of society is to reduce the disparity of wealth among its citizens, then, even with suitable transfer of compensation to the losers for their costs, the aforementioned project will not be acceptable to society. This, however, is not a reflection on the project's efficiency of resource utilization, for it allows society the alternative of taxing away $200 from the rich, leaving them no worse off, and transferring the sum to the poor, thereby reducing the disparity of wealth as desired.

COST-BENEFIT ANALYSIS

Cost-benefit analysis is traditionally concerned with the question of economic efficiency of resource utilization; the distribution and equity issue, which is one of moral judgment, is outside its scope. Cost-benefit analysis may be used for appraising both a policy, such as one for water pollution control, and a project requiring capital expenditure, such as construction of a bridge. The approach, which has some formal similarities to the usual profit and loss calculations of a private business enterprise, is outlined below.

1. Each alternative is viewed as a change from the status quo. Careful accounting is made for the following four possible consequences of the change: (a) incremental or additional benefits; (b) cost savings; (c) incremental or additional costs; (d) benefits forgone elsewhere in moving the resources from their existing use to the projected activity—such forgone benefits are called "opportunity costs."

2. The usual financial accounting views all transactions from the standpoint of the business entity. In contrast, cost-benefit accounting views all consequences from the standpoint of the community or society as a whole. No distinction is drawn between benefits that accrue to the consumers and benefits that are appropriated by a producer. Such a distinction is a distributional issue. Care is taken not to delineate the community or "society" too narrowly. For example, in evaluating alternatives for sewage treatment, an incorrect appraisal may result if the communities situated down the river are not included as essential parts of the social whole.

3. What constitutes social well-being is taken to be as revealed by the choices of the people. If, for example, the construction of a highway strip leads some people to move to the suburbs, then such movement reveals the preferences of those who moved. To be sure, they are giving up some of the benefits of living in the city; but that is their business. They must be seeing a net benefit in the move. Or why else would they leave the city? Accordingly, the appraisal of the proposed highway may be made in terms of net benefits, allowing the individuals to net out their own trade-offs. There is no need to account for the trade-offs explicitly by estimating gross benefits that derive from the move and subtracting the benefits given up.

4. The appraisal of benefits and losses may depend upon the law of the land. For example, if the law is silent on the rights of nonsmokers, then a person may enjoy a smoke at will; this, however, is a cost to the nonsmoker, who may be willing to pay the smoker for desisting. On the other hand, if the law protects the rights of the nonsmoker, then not being able to smoke is a cost to the smoker, who may be willing to pay the nonsmoker for allowing, say, one smoke.

5. Often, costs or benefits of a proposed alternative will extend over a substantial period of time—for example, the costs and benefits of a subway system. In some situations, costs or benefits will be contingent on some future event—for example, the benefits from a flood-control reservoir. The appraisal explicitly takes into account such special features of the situation at hand and uses standard methods (explained later) to summarize the evaluation in a single numerical indicator.

6. Not all relevant effects of a proposed alternative can always be meaningfully appraised in their entirety in terms of dollars and cents. For example, no monetary evaluation can fully capture the benefits of saving a life or limb, or the costs of losing one. Furthermore, the distributional effects of a proposed alternative also do not enter into the cost-benefit computation. This is not to say, however, that these relevant effects are ignored in the overall appraisal of the alternatives. Rather, the effects not already counted in the cost-benefit equation are explicitly noted so that the decision maker may weigh them against the net dollars-and-cents benefits in arriving at the final decision.

In the main, cost-benefit analysis is the craft of weighing what is to count and what is not to count in the evaluation of proposed alternatives. Its basic ideas relate to measuring benefits and costs, distinguishing benefits from transfers among economic units, and constructing artificial (or shadow) prices for proper accounting. Although cost-benefit accounting is done with painstaking care, there is no pretension that it yields precise measurements. Its primary usefulness resides in its providing a framework for systematically taking into consideration the various trade-offs. Nonprofit organizations have to make the choices anyway. By quantifying as many trade-offs as possible, even if somewhat crudely, the decision maker is able to get a grasp of the magnitudes involved. In the absence of cost-benefit calculations, the evaluation remains at the qualitative level and decision making continues to be that much more subjective.

ETHICAL FOUNDATION

In the nonprofit sector, investment projects or public policies generally have ramifications in three directions: economic, social, and political. They cause reallocation of scarce resources from one use to another, distribute desirable and undesirable effects, and create conflict among partisan interests. The decision maker cannot afford to overlook any of these aspects; the alternative chosen must be economically efficient, socially acceptable, and politically feasible.

Cost-benefit analysis focuses on the social welfare effects of the alternatives under consideration. Its central concern is allocative efficiency: Will the reallocation of scarce resources expected from a proposal be an improvement (in the welfare sense) over their existing use? That is, will the social benefits that may stem from the expected rearrangement exceed the social costs? Here social benefit (cost) is defined as the *aggregate* of benefits (costs) to all individuals. Benefit refers to increase in individual welfare. It is usually measured as the net dollar amount an individual would be willing (and able) to pay in order to have the proposed rearrangement rather than do without it. Cost is simply the opposite of benefit; it refers to decrease in welfare, which is the same as sacrifice of benefits.

The framework described above incorporates some normative judgments which should be explicitly noted. For one, the framework is based on the position that the assessment of whether a proposed rearrangement is beneficial should be made by the affected individuals themselves. It is they who should provide a valuation of individual welfare, while social welfare should be simply the aggregate of individual valuations. Implicit in this framework is the ethical judgment that, in social choice, individual preference should count. Even in democratic countries, however, people may have serious reservations about a simple democracy such as is implied above. Individuals may not know what is "good" for them, for example, if they are mentally disturbed; individuals may be myopic and fail to see the good that lies in the distant future, for example, the long-run benefits of education; and individuals may not be sufficiently well informed to be in a position to assess the value to them of a proposed project or policy, for example, the benefits of forest preservation.

Second, the question of distributional equity and fairness—of who the beneficiaries are and who the losers—is outside the framework of traditional cost-benefit analysis. Such an ethical judgment is up to the decision maker to consider.

Third, in the calculus of aggregated individual benefits and costs, only the ends count, not the means. For example, the raids of Robin Hood or the robberies of an indigent bandit may fare no worse in the cost-benefit equation than the transfer payments arranged by the government. Whether ends justify means is an ethical question outside the framework of cost-benefit analysis. This ethical judgment is also up to the decision maker to consider.

Finally, the framework incorporates the value judgment that what should count are not the *desires* of individuals but their *demands*, reflected by their willingness to pay and backed by their ability to pay. Of course, ability to pay depends upon whether the individual is rich or poor. Thus, although cost-benefit analysis is not concerned with the distributional consequences of the alternatives under consideration, it evaluates the worthiness of the alternatives by using measures which depend upon the wealth and income distribution patterns already existing in the society. In summary, cost-benefit appraisal is not entirely value-free. It regards the individual as sovereign and defers to the individual's preferences. It looks at what individuals demand, not at what they need or desire, or what might be good for them. It accepts the current economic regime and tallies the demands of poor and rich without distinction—but also without heed to the fact that a poor man's willingness to pay $1 means much more than a rich man's willingness to pay $1. The rationale for such aggregation is discussed next.

Social Choice and the Compensation Principle

An incontroversial rule for making social choice is the Pareto *unanimity rule:* If everyone prefers a proposed change in the existing pattern of resource allocation, then the proposal is judged socially preferred as well.

The scope of the unanimity rule is extended somewhat in the Pareto *optimality rule:* If some individuals prefer a proposed change while all others are *indifferent* to it, then again the proposal is deemed to be socially preferred. Often, the optimality rule is expressed loosely as follows: If some individuals are made better off by a change while all others are not made any worse off, then the change is socially preferred. This latter version may not be acceptable on grounds of distributional equity in that a change by which the rich become richer but the poor remain as they are may not be socially preferred over the status quo.

Situations of unanimity or optimality are seldom found in practice. Usually, public policy and projects entail benefits to some and costs to others. The Pareto criterion then fails to provide any guidance.

The scope of the Pareto principle is widened to cover situations of nonunanimity in the Kaldor-Hicks *compensation principle:* A proposed change is socially preferred if those benefiting by the change could compensate the losers and still be left better off. This principle provides the rationale for the aggregation of benefits and costs in cost-benefit analysis.

There are some serious objections against the Kaldor-Hicks compensation principle as a criterion of social choice. First, a change judged socially preferred under the principle is not guaranteed to yield social improvement unless the compensation is actually paid, in which case the compensation principle reduces to the Pareto optimality criterion. Alternatively, an explicit moral judgment must be made that the proposed beneficiaries indeed deserve to be made better off at a cost to the losers.

The second objection is the *Scitovsky paradox.* Let the status quo be *S;* and consider a change to state *T* creating both beneficiaries and losers. Assume *T* is socially preferred to *S* under the compensation principle and a move is made to *T,* but no compensations are paid. Then it can be shown that in some situations, starting from *T* as the status quo, a move back to *S* will also be socially preferred under the compensation principle! What is society to do in such a case? There is no answer to this except that such pathological situations, while possible in theory, are reasonably unlikely in practice.

Third, if compensation payments were to be actually arranged, serious issues would arise relating to the compensation mechanism and its consequences. The mechanism would involve both information-gathering costs to determine who the beneficiaries and losers were and by how much, and administrative costs to actually arrange and oversee the transfer payments. It would raise questions of whether the compensation should be financed by a levy on the beneficiaries or a tax on some other group—for example, the rich. The compensation mechanism might have consequences in several directions such as work incentive or disincentive on those taxed and those awarded compensation, the economic and political impact on the agency in charge of the project, and the political and social repercussions on the desirability of the project itself.

Finally, it is important to remember that the relative weights of individual votes in the political process are not necessarily the same as in the aggregate economic measure of social welfare. Thus, a project, although economically efficient in the aggregate sense, may well be politically unacceptable, particularly in light of a proposed compensation mechanism.

The above is not to deprecate the cost-benefit approach; it is to alert the decision maker to the value judgments and limitations inherent in the approach.

ECONOMIC FOUNDATION

It will help the decision maker to have a good understanding of the basic concepts on which the practice of cost-benefit analysis is founded. The key conceptual issue is how to measure the change in individual welfare. There are several ways to assign a value to the change. But underlying all evaluations is the economic notion of compensation.

For illustration, take an individual with an expenditure budget of $200 (per week). Assume that the current price of gasoline is 69¢ per gallon and the individual's weekly basket includes 40 gallons of gasoline. Suppose it is proposed to reduce the price of gasoline to 59¢ per gallon. All else remaining the same, the proposal would mean a $4 saving in expenditure on the current basket. The individual could use this saving to satisfy more needs, thus increasing welfare. But this is not the only source of welfare gain to the individual. When the gasoline price is reduced, the individual could also rearrange the composition of the demanded basket, increasing the quantity of some items while reducing the quantity of others, so as to attain an even higher level of satisfaction. Say the individual would demand 55 gallons of gasoline if its price were 59¢ per gallon. The issue is how to measure the welfare gain (or benefit) that the price reduction would confer upon the individual.

Compensating Variation or Willingness to Pay

A commonly used measure of gain or loss of welfare to an individual owing to any proposed change is the maximum money amount (plus or minus) the individual would be willing to pay out of the available budget in order to have the proposed change rather than go without it. Such an amount is called *willingness to pay* (WTP) or *compensating variation* (CV). CV is the individual's maximum bid price (plus or minus) for the proposed change. Whether or not the individual would in fact be required to pay this price is another matter. In effect, the central question in CV approach is what net budget in conjunction with the proposed change the individual regards as welfare equivalent to the status quo.

It will be a mistake to presume that, in the foregoing illustration, the maximum price the individual would be willing to pay for the right to buy gasoline at 59¢ per gallon equals the resulting $4 (per week) saving in expenditure on the existing basket. It can be shown that the CV of price reduction of a good is always more than the saving on the existing basket owing to price reduction. In the present example, therefore, the CV is necessarily more than the $4 (per week) saving. Say the CV is $4.50 (per week). This means the individual is indifferent between a reduced budget of $195.50 with gasoline at 59¢ per gallon and the status quo, or a budget of $200 with gasoline at 69¢ per gallon. Stated another way, the individual would be willing to pay a maximum of $4.50 (per week) for the right to buy gasoline at 59¢ per gallon. This willingness to pay is a measure of how much the proposed price reduction is worth to our individual.

For another example, consider the symmetrically opposite change. The individual's weekly budget is $200, but the price of gasoline is 59¢ per gallon. It is proposed to hike the gasoline price to 69¢ per gallon. In this case, our individual must be paid a bounty (or compensation) so as to offset the welfare loss brought about by the price hike. The bounty depends upon the budget, which (with gasoline at 69¢ per gallon) the individual regards as welfare equivalent to the status quo of a $200 weekly budget with gasoline at 59¢ per gallon. Say the budget needed is $205 (per week). In other words, the CV of the proposed price hike is $5 (per week), which is a measure of the welfare loss the proposed price hike will bring to our individual.

Variation Surplus or Value of Net Benefit

Consider again the first illustration and recall that our individual would be willing to pay a maximum of $4.50 (per week) to see the gasoline price reduced from 69¢ to 59¢ per gallon. Assume now that the individual is issued a license to buy as much gasoline as needed for his own consumption at 59¢ per gallon, and the charge for license is $4.50 (per week). This arrangement neither brings any benefit to the individual nor causes a sacrifice. The gain in welfare owing to the price reduction is exactly offset by the loss in welfare owing to the payment of the license fee of $4.50 (per week). If, however, the individual were charged a license fee less than the CV of $4.50 (per week), then there would indeed be a *net* increase in the welfare of the individual as measured by the *variation surplus* equaling the CV minus the actual payment extracted. For instance, if the license fee charged were $1.50 (per week), the arrangement would confer a net benefit "worth" $3 (per week) to the individual.

In general, for any proposed rearrangement of the status quo, an individual's variation surplus, calculated as the amount (plus or minus) the individual would be willing to pay for the rearrangement less the amount that is actually paid, measures the value of the net benefit that accrues to the individual from the proposed rearrangement.

It is important to fully appreciate what the individual is assumed in theory to have already taken into account in arriving at the magnitude of the CV or variation surplus for any proposed change. To proceed by way of example, suppose a commuter who drives around a hill to go to work is willing to pay at most $10 per week for the use of a proposed tunnel. Then, in making this assessment, the commuter is assumed in theory to have given due consideration to all welfare effects that stem from using the tunnel: (1) change in personal qualitative factors considered relevant by the commuter, such as reduced driving aggravation, extra sleeping time in the morning, and more leisure time in the evening; and (2) change in the composition of the demanded basket of goods and services after including therein the use of tunnel service at a "price" of $10 per week. Thus, for instance, if the commuter would reallocate the remainder budget so as to demand one less bottle of wine per week, then the welfare loss due to this sacrifice is already included in the assessment of the $10 CV for the use of the tunnel. By definition of CV, the use of the tunnel, a reduction of $10 in the budget, *and the attendant rearrangement of the consumption basket* are what the commuter regards as welfare equivalent to the status quo.

In practice, the willingness-to-pay measure of welfare has to be estimated almost always by indirect methods. The onus then is on the cost-benefit analyst to take into account all that an individual is assumed in theory to have taken into account in assessing the CV. To be sure, in principle, one could use statistical survey techniques to estimate the aggregate measure by directly questioning a sample of the individuals involved; and, in some situations, this might be the best estimation method available. The problem is that there is no way to know whether the sampled individuals' responses are truthful. In other words, CV or willingness to pay is an unobservable magnitude for it involves a personal assessment which cannot be objectively verified.

What is observable is the individual's demand behavior. Given a budget and faced with a set of prices, the individual demands certain quantities of goods and services and so reveals his or her preference. The preference revealed through demand behavior can be used to infer the magnitude of the otherwise unobservable CV. To this task we turn our attention next.

Demand Schedule

Fix attention on goods and services which (1) can be denied, in principle, to one individual without denying them to others, and (2) can be demanded in variable amounts or levels of use. Condition 1 excludes from consideration items such as clean air, noise-free environment, and national defense, but admits items such as filtered water, parks, museums, and health care. Goods and services that can be denied to individuals selectively are, in principle, marketable.

Condition 2 merely establishes a viewpoint. All items, whether they are minutely divisible in quantity such as filtered water, or are "lumpy," such as a civic hall, can be made to satisfy condition two by agreeing to measure their quantities in terms of *rates of use*.

Suppose a good, say, the services of a city park, is offered to an individual at varying prices while keeping the prices of all other goods and services constant. Assume the individual has consistent preferences and is a price taker, that is, accepts prices as given in making demand decisions. It is then possible to conceive the following two schedules of prices versus corresponding quantities demanded by the individual (see Figure 8–1).

Marshallian or observable demand schedule. The Marshallian demand schedule refers to the demand of the individual when his or her total

FIGURE 8-1. *Demand schedules.*

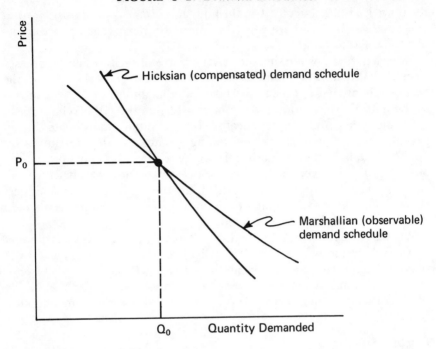

budget is held fixed as the price of the good is varied. The schedule is observable because its determination does not require knowing magnitudes that are subjective to the individual. Each price-quantity point of the demand schedule determines the expenditure (price × quantity) the individual allocates to the good at that price. This allocation may or may not change from one point of the demand schedule to another; but, if it changes, then the remaining amount allocated to all other goods and services in the demand basket changes correspondingly, resulting for sure in a change in the demand for these other items as well. Different points of the demand schedule represent different levels of welfare—the lower the price of the good, the greater the welfare of the individual, and vice versa. To see this, note that, following a price reduction, the individual can still buy what he or she was buying before but with some money to spare, which goes to increase welfare. Finally, for normal goods, a decrease in price necessarily leads to an increase in demand if satiation does not set in.

Hicksian or compensated demand schedule. The Hicksian schedule refers to the demand of the individual when his or her level of welfare is held constant as the asking price of the good is varied. To see what this involves, take a reference point (the point P_0, Q_0 in Figure 8–1) on the individual's Marshallian demand schedule. This point is a surrogate for the welfare level enjoyed by the individual in consuming the reference basket of goods and services. A decrease in price increases welfare. Hence, for each price less than the reference price P_0, a tax equal to the CV of the price change must be extracted from the individual so as to bring the welfare back to the reference level. The quantity of the good then demanded with the reduced budget is the *compensated demand* at the lesser asking price. Because the available budget now is smaller, the compensated demand is necessarily less than the corresponding Marshallian demand. For prices greater than P_0, the situation is symmetrically opposite. An increase in price diminishes welfare. Hence, for each price greater than P_0, a bounty equal to the CV of the price change must be granted to the individual to compensate for the welfare loss. Because the available budget in this case is larger, the compensated demand is necessarily greater than the corresponding Marshallian demand. The individual is, of course, free to allocate the available budget (reference budget plus or minus CV) so as to attain the highest level of welfare. This means that changing the asking price of the good in question may lead the individual to change the demand for the other items in the demand basket as well.

But CV is an unobservable magnitude; hence the Hicksian compensated demand schedule is an unobservable construct. Its usefulness is that it clarifies how CV may be estimated from the observable Marshallian demand schedule. This is discussed in the next section.

Consumer's Surplus

Without doubt, consumer's surplus is the most crucial concept in cost-benefit analysis. Although the idea originated in 1844, convergence in professional opinion has been slow in coming; in fact, a full consensus on its meaning or usefulness still does not exist. The development below is somewhat different from that usually found in the present-day textbooks; it is believed to be more revealing.

The basic problem at hand is to estimate the CV or willingness to pay from the individual's *observable* demand behavior. To proceed with an example, take the situation where the present price of gasoline $P_0 = 59¢$ per gallon, and the consumer having a (weekly) budget of \$200 includes $Q_0 = 55$ gallons of gasoline in the consumption basket. One can conceive a Marshallian (observable) demand schedule and a Hicksian (compensated) demand schedule passing through the point P_0, Q_0 (see Figure 8–2). The former schedule is with the budget kept constant at \$200, while the latter is with the welfare level kept constant and equal to that at P_0, Q_0. Holding the prices of all other goods and services fixed, it is proposed

FIGURE 8-2. *Compensating variation.*

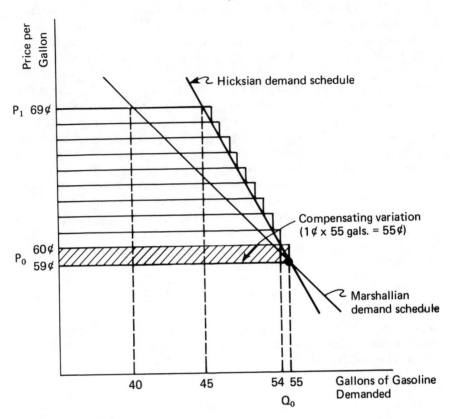

to increase the price of gasoline by 10¢ per gallon to $P_1 = 69$¢ per gallon, which would mean an increase of $5.50 in the expenditure on the *existing* consumption basket of the consumer. We wish to know how the consumer's assessment of CV relates to his or her demand behavior.

Recall from the discussion earlier that, for any finite increase (decrease) in the price of normal goods, the compensation to be given to (extracted from) the consumer does *not* equal the corresponding increase (saving) in expenditure on the existing consumption basket. However, it can be shown that, for an *infinitesimally* small change in the price of a good, the (infinitesimally small) CV is exactly equal to the change in expenditure on the existing consumption basket—and this despite the fact that, as the price changes, the consumer may be changing the composition of the basket in all manner of ways.

To illustrate, let the proposed price increase be made in steps of 1¢ per gallon. Then, no matter how the consumer changes the composition of the basket, the CV for the first step will be approximately 55¢ (1¢ × 55 gallons)—the smaller the steps of price change, the closer the approximation. Referring to Figure 8–2, this CV is given by the area of the shaded horizontal strip, whose length equals the initial demand (Q_0 = 55 gallons) and width equals 1¢.

What is the CV for the second 1¢ increase in the gasoline price? To calculate this, we need to know the consumer's demand for gasoline subsequent to the first 1¢ increase in price accompanied by a compensation of 55¢ to the consumer to keep his or her welfare constant. In other words, we need to know the consumer's (observable) demand for gasoline when the budget is $200.55 and the price of gasoline is 60¢ per gallon. Say the demand is 54 gallons. Then, as before, the CV for the second 1¢ price increase equals approximately 54¢ (1¢ × 54 gallons), and is given by the area of the second horizontal strip.

Proceeding step by step, the total CV for ten price increases of 1¢ each is approximately equal to the area of the pyramid of ten horizontal strips between the prices 59¢ and 69¢ in Figure 8–2. Of course, the CV for a price increase of 10¢ must be the same as that of ten price increases of 1¢ each. Making the steps smaller and smaller, we see that, in the limit, the total CV for any contemplated price increase equals the area of the strip sandwiched between the initial and final price horizontals and bounded by the consumer's compensated demand schedule passing through the initial point.

Now we can see how to estimate the magnitude of CV using only observable data. The CV is measured approximately by the area of the strip between the initial and final price horizontals extended up to the observable Marshallian demand schedule. Also, as long as the prices of all other goods and services remain constant, the CV so measured fully incorporates the welfare consideration of all related adjustments in the consumer's demand for other goods and services.

The approximation using the consumer's observable (Marshallian) demand schedule instead of the compensated demand schedule is close enough, considering other unavoidable estimation errors. But the approximation breaks down (1) if the variations under consideration are too large a part of the total economy of the person or society, or (2) if, for a small change in the consumer's income, the percentage change in demand is sizable compared to the percentage change in income.

In practice, it is convenient to associate with each price a magnitude called *consumer's surplus* and defined as the area bounded by the observable demand schedule and the price horizontal (see Figure 8–3). Then the CV for any particular price change simply equals the final value of the consumer's surplus *minus* the initial value of the consumer's surplus. In other words, the CV for any price change equals the change in the associated consumer's surplus.

Consumer's surplus is a special case of variation surplus because it can be interpreted as the amount a consumer is willing to pay for the actual quantity demanded at any given price *less* the amount actually paid for the quantity. This is the classical interpretation of consumer's surplus. It is instructive to go over the reasoning underlying this interpretation.

In Figure 8–4, a consumer demands 55 gallons of gasoline at 59¢ per gallon. The amount *actually* paid is the rectangular area 59¢ × 55 gallons. How much is the consumer *willing to pay* for 55 gallons? How much is he willing to pay for the *fifty-fifth* gallon?

To answer the second question, note that the consumer willingly pays 59¢ for each gallon until the last desired gallon is purchased. The fact that he does not purchase one more unit of gasoline beyond 55 gallons

FIGURE 8–3. *Consumer's surplus.*

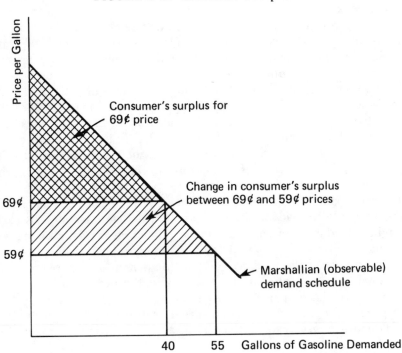

reveals that the satisfaction to be derived from the last (or 55th gallon) must be just equal to that attainable with the best alternative use of the 59¢ paid for the last gallon. In other words, 59¢ is (approximately) how much the 55th gallon is worth to the consumer.

To see how much, say, the 49th gallon is worth to the consumer, draw a vertical line from the 49-gallon mark to the observable demand schedule and read the corresponding price as 63¢. This says that, with gasoline at 63¢ per gallon, the consumer's observable demand is 49 gallons. Then, using the same reasoning as above, the 49th gallon is worth approximately 63¢ to our consumer. Now, to answer the first question, repeat the argument for each infinitesimal demand from 0 to 55 gallons and note that the consumer's *willingness to pay* is given by the area under the observable demand curve, bounded on the right by the 55-gallon quantity vertical.

Thus consumer's surplus is the difference between the area identified as measuring the willingness to pay and the rectangle representing the amount actually paid. This establishes that consumer's surplus is a special

FIGURE 8-4. *Willingness to pay.*

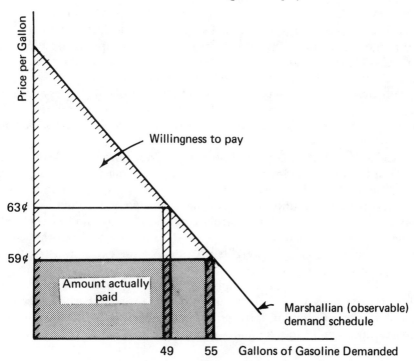

case of variation surplus, and measures the net welfare that accrues to the consumer in satisfying his demand at the given price.

Social Benefit and Consumers' Surplus

In cost-benefit analysis, the value of social benefit is taken as the aggregate of the values of individuals' benefits as measured by the change in their consumers' surplus. For the aggregate, it is convenient to define *consumers' surplus* using the market (or aggregate) observable demand schedule, exactly as consumer's surplus is defined for the individual using the individual demand schedule. The (classical) argument for consumers' surplus is the same as before. There are some consumers who would have paid a higher price for the product than its prevailing price. And the value of the social benefit due to a price change is given by the change in consumers' surplus.

Estimating the market demand schedule usually involves econometric and forecasting methods, which are outside the scope of this chapter. The estimates are necessarily imprecise—more so if they refer to future demand. The decision maker should be sure to carefully review the assumptions that go into making the estimates.

In practical cost-benefit analysis, the market demand schedule is frequently assumed to be a (downward sloping) straight line, at least within the range of the initial and final prices. This assumption considerably simplifies the calculations. For example, the change in consumers' surplus then equals the change in price times average demand.

Controversy still surrounds the conceptual meaning of (aggregate) consumers' surplus. The justification for the interpersonal comparison implicit in such aggregation is provided by the Kaldor-Hicks compensation principle discussed earlier.

Social welfare is the welfare of individual citizens, and no single measure of it can be constructed without (implicitly) assigning relative weights to the individual's welfare. Measuring social welfare by reference to consumers' surplus amounts to measuring and aggregating market votes expressed in a competitive marketplace or votes that would be expressed if there were a competitive marketplace. The relative weights implicit in this scheme are clearly the weights provided by the existing distribution of the market power (or income) among individuals. Such weighting is obviously different from the weighting underlying "political vote" even when the latter is modified by the lobbying process. For this reason, considerations of economic efficiency can conflict with political and social considerations in a fundamental way.

Social Cost of Resources Used

Resources used in any project are resources diverted from their existing use. The diversion would result in an improvement in economic efficiency (in the aggregate welfare sense) only if the value of social benefits gained from the project exceeded the value of social benefits forgone in the existing use of resources. Thus, from society's point of view, the cost of a project is the social opportunity cost of the resources used in the project. Money cost of the resources is irrelevant, because money payments simply serve to redistribute benefits and costs among the individuals of society.

For example, suppose a project hires an otherwise unemployed person for wages equal to $24, producing benefits valued at $50. No other resources are used. Then the money cost of the labor used is $24, while its social opportunity cost is $0. In the aggregate, society gains a net value of $50 by undertaking the project as opposed to not undertaking it. The payment of $24 as wages simply transfers $24 of the produced value to the worker, leaving $26 of the produced value to be enjoyed by other individuals. For another example, suppose, instead, that the person is employed elsewhere for $14, producing a value of $20. If this person is switched to a job on the project, then the social opportunity cost of labor is $20, and there is a saving of $14 in wages which were being paid to the worker. In these examples it is assumed that the person has no preference for one occupation or the other.

The social opportunity cost of a resource is the amount consumers are willing to pay for the product of the resource in its existing use; it equals what the consumers actually pay plus the consumers' surplus. In the case of labor, adjustments should also be made to reflect the gain or loss of welfare that might arise, for example, because an individual prefers to remain idle or prefers one occupation rather than another (see paragraph 3 below).

In practical cost-benefit analysis, it is usual to take the prevailing market price of resources as a close enough measure of their social opportunity cost unless special circumstances warrant otherwise. In this respect there is a clear asymmetry in the valuation of benefits and costs. The bias of this asymmetry is toward understating the costs, because the consumers' surplus component of the social opportunity cost is ignored. This is explained below.

In a competitive market equilibrium, the market price of each factor of production necessarily equals the value of its marginal product. In other words, the price of a very small quantity of a factor is equal to the value of the incremental product obtained from that much additional quantity of the factor with all else remaining the same. For if the price were less, profit seekers would continue buying the factor, converting it into the product and gaining by the differences, thus, driving up the price of the *factor;* and if the price were more, producers would stop converting the factor into that particular product until the price of the *product* is driven up sufficiently. It follows that, when a nonprofit organization bids away a resource for use in a project, the market price of the resource is a close enough measure of the value sacrificed in the existing use of the resource unless (1) the resource price rises because of such demand, that is, the quantity of the resource diverted is not small, or (2) the market for the resource or its product is not perfectly competitive. In such cases, the consumers' surplus component of the social cost is not neglible, and proper accounting of it becomes essential.

For example, consider the demand and supply schedules for a product using a resource that is needed for some project (see Figure 8–5). To keep things simple, assume the product uses no other resources. To begin with, the equilibrium is at point A. In order to release sufficient quantity of the resource for the project, the product demand must contract from quantity B to, say, quantity C. This is possible if the supply schedule moves from its present position S to the position S' by a rise in the resource price. Then the value of social benefits *lost* by redeploying the resource is given by the willingness-to-pay shaded area $ABCD$. On the other hand, the current market price of the diverted resource is represented by the rectangular area $ABCE$. Thus, if market price is used as the measure of social opportunity cost, it would have a downward bias equal to the lost consumers' surplus AED. The analysis for the case of imperfect competition is similar, and is omitted.

The following are some illustrative special circumstances in which the current market prices fail to approximate the social opportunity cost of resources used.

1. When the quantity of a resource used is large enough to affect its price, the social opportunity cost should be determined by reference to the area under the relevant portion of the demand schedule for the resource in its alternative uses. Assuming linear demand and perfect competition, the social cost equals the quantity demanded times the average price. This corresponds to the willingness-to-pay area $ABCD$ in Figure 8–5.

2. If the project's demand for a factor will extend over a long period, the social opportunity cost should be determined by reference to estimated demand schedule for each year (or each suitable segment of time) in the future. Due consideration should be given to the possibility that, in the long run, the supply of the factor might increase or decrease, for

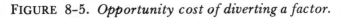

FIGURE 8-5. *Opportunity cost of diverting a factor.*

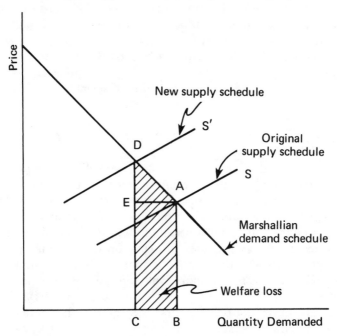

example, because of increased production or import, or depletion of natural resources such as oil and silver.

3. The social opportunity cost of labor should be taken as the value of its marginal product in the existing occupation—the value being zero if the individual is unemployed—plus the minimum compensation that will induce the individual to change the occupation. The compensation is a plus amount if the individual prefers the current occupation (for example, remaining idle if currently unemployed) and is a minus amount if the individual prefers the new occupation. In addition, any reduction in the unemployment benefit the individual might be currently receiving should be accounted for as a social saving. For example, suppose a person is unemployed and is receiving $59 per week unemployment benefits. The person considers $70 per week as the minimum wages for which it will be "worthwhile" to accept a job rather than remain idle and "collect unemployment." Then the social opportunity cost of employing the person net of social saving is $11 ($70 − $59) per week. In other words, if the marginal product of the individual in the new occupation is *less* than $11 per week, then, from the viewpoint of economic efficiency, society

is better off leaving the individual unemployed. On the other hand, if the marginal product of the individual is $11 or more, society is better off in paying the individual $70 per week to work even though the marginal product is less than $70 per week.

The above example also illustrates how cost-benefit analysis may call for construction of *accounting prices* or *shadow prices* different from market prices in order to correctly assess the value of social benefits net of social costs.

ACCOUNTING FOR COST AND BENEFIT FLOWS

Social returns and financial returns are two different perspectives on capital investments; both provide important insights into nonprofit undertakings. The accounting of social costs and benefits provides information on whether a nonprofit project is economically efficient in the aggregate welfare sense. In contrast, the accounting of revenues and operating expenditures provides information on the annual financing (budgetary) demands of the nonprofit agency administering the project and thus forms a basis for periodic evaluation of the performance of the agency itself (as opposed to the performance of the project). If the social justification behind a nonprofit project is forgotten, the agency in charge might get faulted for its inefficiency in not managing to break even. Such complaints (right or wrong) are often heard, for example, against the U.S. Postal Service and transit authorities of many metropolitan cities.

In making a cost-benefit calculation, it is important to specify at the outset all alternatives that will be covered by the evaluation. Also, (relevant) political constraints must be explicitly identified. Such constraints may affect the valuations of benefits or costs by restricting alternative opportunities or by specifying economic policy that must prevail. For example, a developing country might set priority on items whose import will be restricted in case of a foreign exchange shortage; such a constraint will affect the opportunity cost placed on an imported resource needed for a project. It does not matter whether the policies and constraints make economic sense; they define the political and economic framework within which social welfare is sought.

Accounting for capital undertakings is conveniently split into two parts: (1) expected capital costs and their timing, and (2) expected annual flows of benefits and costs. In cost-benefit analysis, all costs including expected capital costs are reckoned in terms of social opportunity costs as opposed to outlays of funds. The categories of social benefit and cost flows are shown below:

Benefits	*Costs*
Direct benefits (new or incremental)	Direct costs (new or incremental)
Indirect or spillover benefits	Indirect or spillover costs
Cost savings	Forgone benefits or opportunity costs due to redeployment of resources

Any partial netting out of benefits and costs makes no difference in the net benefit (cost) of the project; but it does make a difference in the gross amounts of benefits and costs and, hence, in various cost-benefit ratios (if any are computed).

A major problem in the accounting for cost and benefit flows is to decide what is to count and what is not to count in the evaluation of a project; it is easy to slip into the error of double counting. A second major problem is that some benefits and losses are not priced in the market; their values must be estimated by indirect means requiring assumptions which may be tenuous at best. The decision maker should critically evaluate every assumption before placing trust in the results of a study. The accounting of social cost and benefit flows is explained below, illustrated by simple situations that serve as building blocks for more complex situations.

Introduction of a New Good or Service

The most basic case is the social accounting for a new good or service. To make things concrete, consider the introduction of a rapid transit system where none existed before. Suppose the service is made available to the community at a unit price P, the quantity of transit service demanded is Q, and, for this quantity, the average operating cost per unit exclusive of cost of capital is C (see Figure 8–6). Let the community's aggregate (Marshallian) demand schedule for the rapid transit service be the straight line AB. This assumes as given (1) the prices of all other products, (2) population size, (3) distribution of income, (4) real per capita income, and (5) tastes of individuals.

1. The area $ADQO$ under the demand schedule represents what the community is willing to pay for the quantity Q actually demanded at price P. This measures the worth of the transit service to the community, *assuming there is no change in the prices of other products.*

2. The actual payment extracted from the consumers is the area $PDQO$, which is equal to price OP times quantity OQ. This amount is a (financial) cost to consumers but a revenue to Transit Authority. Thus, from the

FIGURE 8-6. *Consumers' surplus and operating surplus.*

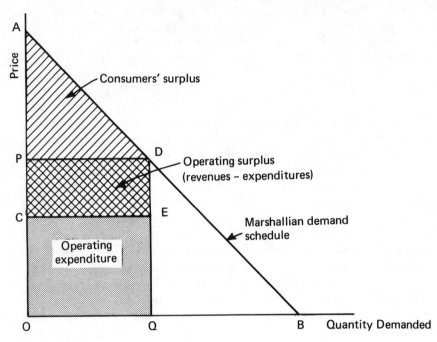

community's viewpoint, the consumers' cost is a mere transfer or redistribution of benefit. The remainder is the consumers' surplus area *ADP*, and counts as a social benefit accruing directly to the individuals in the community.

3. The operating expenditure of Transit Authority is the area *CEQO*, which is equal to average cost *OC* times quantity *OQ*. While a (financial) cost to Transit Authority, this amount is an income to the owners of the various factors demanded by Transit Authority. The difference, agency's revenue minus operating cost, is the area *PDEC*; this is the net financial operating surplus (loss) of Transit Authority and counts as a social benefit retained (forgone) by that agency on behalf of the community.

4. Continuing with the accounting of the income to factor owners, first assume the factor owners are all "foreigners" to the community. Then their factor income does nothing for the welfare of the community and so does not count as a social benefit. Hence, the accounting ends here. Next, assume the factor owners are all "domestic" to the community. Then the operating cost of Transit Authority is a mere transfer of benefits

to factor owners. Its further accounting may then take one of several directions:

• Income received by factors (except labor) which were otherwise idle goes to increase the welfare of factor owners, and so counts as a social benefit.

• Income received by unemployed labor counts as a social benefit against which must be charged a social cost (plus or minus) equal to the compensating variation (CV) needed for the workers to switch from their "idle occupation" to the job with Transit Authority.

• For factors which were fully employed, if the factor markets are competitive and the quantities demanded are relatively small, then the factor-income received from Transit Authority exactly offsets the benefits forgone in the existing use of the factors. Hence, such factor-income does not count as social benefit and the accounting ends. If, on the other hand, the factor markets are not competitive or factor demands are sizable, then the factor-income received from Transit Authority is *less* than the benefits forgone in the existing use of the factors. Hence, to complete the accounting, a charge must be made for the loss of social welfare over and above the money income to factor owners.

5. In subsequent years, the demand schedule *AB* might shift for one of several reasons. For instance, it would shift outwards if there is an increase in population, change of community's taste (increased desire to live in suburbia), development of attractions such as shopping centers in suburbia or music hall in the city center, and increase in real per capita income. The demand schedule would shift inwards, for instance, owing to the introduction of more desirable substitutes for the rapid transit. Whatever the reason for the shift, subsequent years' benefits should be calculated by reference to the anticipated changed position of the demand schedule. The analyst should attempt to forecast such changes as best as possible.

6. Whatever amount consumers spend on the transit service goes to reduce their budget for other goods and services. The demand schedule for such other items will, therefore, shift after the transit service is introduced. So long as there is no induced change in the price of all these other goods and services, the demand shift for such items does not affect the accounting for benefits and costs. Whatever trade-off the consumers make, it is already incorporated in their willingness-to-pay measure of the transit service.

7. The accounting for net annual benefits of a new product* (assuming

---

*"Product" here is defined broadly to include goods and services provided by a nonprofit organization.

prices of all factors and other products remain constant) is essentially a breakdown of the following accounting equation: Net benefit equals willingness to pay *minus* opportunity cost of factors of production. The accounting is as follows:

- Consumers' surplus due to the new product (excluding benefits that accrue to foreigners in their capacity as consumers).
  Less Loss of consumers' surplus (to domestic population) due to the diversion of previously employed factors.
- Nonprofit agency's operating surplus (loss), equaling operating revenues *less* expenditures.
- Income to previously unemployed factors owned by domestic population.
  Less Compensation to factor owners for agreeing to employ the factors rather than leave them unemployed.†
- Income to previously employed factors owned by domestic population.
  Less Income earned by such factors in their previous employment.
  Less Compensation to factor owners for agreeing to switch the factors from their existing use to the new use.†

This breakdown is important for two reasons. First, it shows the relationship between the social benefit and cost accounts and the nonprofit agency's operating accounts. Second, it provides a foundation for incremental analysis—analysis for changes in net benefit when a nonprofit project is designed to introduce a change (such as a cost reduction) as opposed to a new product.

Cost Reduction and Change of Price

Examples of cost reduction projects are the acquisition of an automatic blood analyzer for a hospital and an energy-efficient motive power for a rapid transit system. The accounting for social benefits and costs in such cases is simply accounting for changes in the various components listed in paragraph 7 above.

1. First, assume that the cost reduction comes from using a smaller quantity of factor inputs, that the prices of all goods and services remain unchanged, and that the nonprofit agency does not pass the cost reduction to the consumers. Then there is no change in consumers' surplus. The reduction in the agency's expenditures is a social benefit referred to as *cost saving*. If some of the released factors become unemployed, then the loss in (money) income to such factors is a social cost. As for the released

---

†This compensation arises only if the factor owners have a preference for where the factor is employed.

factors finding alternative use, the accounting takes one of two directions. If factor market is competitive and quantity released is relatively small, then no further accounting is needed because the released factors will earn the same amount elsewhere while producing (marginal) product of equal value. But if either of the two conditions does not hold, there will be additional social gain or loss on this count (for example, owing to a change in the factor price). Finally, there may be some gain or loss associated with labor having to switch occupations. It should be noted that "unemployment benefits" are neither a social gain nor a social loss; they are simply transfer of benefits from the employed to the unemployed.

2. Next consider the case when cost savings are passed on to the consumer (in part or full) in the form of a price reduction, but the prices of all other products remain unchanged. This situation is depicted in Figure 8–7 (which is similar to Figure 8–6). The subscripts 1 and 2 refer, respectively, to conditions before and after the project; P stands for the price of the product, Q for the quantity demanded, and C for the average cost per unit exclusive of the cost of capital.

FIGURE 8-7. *Change in consumers' surplus cum operating surplus.*

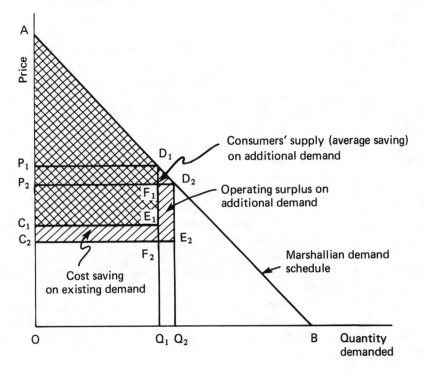

The increase in consumers' surplus is the area $P_1D_1D_2P_2$; the increase in the agency's operating surplus is the area $P_2D_2E_2C_2$ minus area $P_1D_1E_1C_1$. The increase in consumers' surplus cum operating surplus is the hatched border consisting of three parts: (1) area $C_1E_1F_2C_2$, representing the cost saving on the existing level of service (equaling unit cost saving C_2C_1 times the existing quantity C_1E_1); (2) area $F_1D_2E_2F_2$, representing the operating surplus on the additional demand Q_1Q_2 (at new unit price less new unit cost); and (3) area $D_1D_2F_1$, representing consumers' surplus associated with the additional demand.

In general, the following accounting equation always holds: Change in consumers' surplus cum operating surplus equals cost saving on the original demand *plus* operating surplus on the additional demand *plus* consumers' surplus on the additional demand. Furthermore, assuming the demand schedule is a straight line, consumers' surplus on additional demand is simply the *average saving* $[(D_1F_1 \times F_1D_2)/2]$ to the consumers on the additional demand. Of course, as before, account should also be taken of the change in social welfare associated with the release (additional demand) of various factors of production.

It should be borne in mind that the demand for all other products may alter in all manner of ways as a result of the price decline under consideration; but so long as the prices of the other products remain unchanged, no further account of the shift in demand should be taken.

3. Finally, consider the general case wherein the project-induced shift in demand for other goods and services results in a change of price of one or more such good or service. For example, suppose X and Y are substitute goods and a nonprofit project reduces the price of X to consumers. Then the aggregate demand for Y will decrease as consumers switch to more of X. As a result, there will be an inward shift of the aggregate demand schedule for Y. This, in turn, will lead to a fall in the price of Y if its supply schedule is upward sloping, but will lead to a rise in price if the supply schedule is downward sloping (see Figure 8–8). Alternatively, if X and Y are complementary goods, then an increased demand for X will give rise to an increased aggregate demand for Y; and the price of Y will rise or fall depending on whether the supply schedule for Y is upward sloping or downward sloping.

In such cases of concomitant price changes, the total compensating variation is the sum of the compensating variation for the price change of each good. Thus, for example, when the price of X falls, with all other prices remaining the same, there is an increase in consumers' surplus. Then, with the price of X held at this new level, the demand for Y shifts. As has been emphasized several times, shifts of demand schedule do not

FIGURE 8-8. *Changes in consumers' surplus resulting from price changes that accompany induced shifts in demand.*

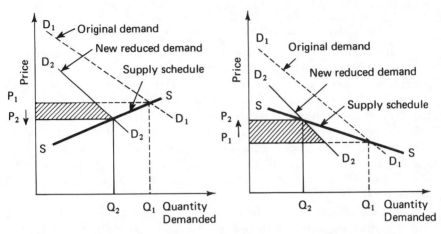

(a) Upward-sloping supply schedule   (b) Downward-sloping supply schedule

call for compensating variations; hence, changes in area accompanying such shifts do not count as changes in welfare. But as the price of *Y* falls (rises), there is a further increase (decrease) in consumers' surplus *measured by reference to the shifted demand schedule*—shown as the shaded area in Figure 8–8.

Implicit Versus Explicit Accounting

Consider the following situation. An indirect suburban route already exists from a city center to a far suburban township. A direct link is proposed, which will reduce both the cost of service and time of travel. One way to proceed with the cost-benefit analysis would be to estimate the aggregate demand schedule for this new service so as to use the accounting shown under paragraph 7 above. It is understood that the commuters have fully taken into consideration all benefits of the new service such as time saving, comfort, and reduced stress, and have given due thought to the trade-offs concerning other alternatives available at prevailing prices.

An alternative way to proceed would be to explicitly estimate the value of each such benefit separately, giving due consideration to the expected increase in the number of paid journeys when the present commuters switch from alternative modes of travel and present noncommuters switch to the status of a commuter. Whichever method of analysis is adopted, spillover benefits will have to be valued separately—benefits such as reduced congestion on roadways and other modes of commuting presently in use.

Miscellaneous Accounting Hints

1. Ordinarily, a rise in population with no change in real per capita income is regarded as no change in society's level of welfare. Population growth may, however, lead to an outward shift of the aggregate demand schedule for some goods and services. Of course, the shift in the demand schedule does not imply increased welfare; but it does imply increased willingness to pay in the aggregate. For this reason, a project not justified with the smaller population may become justified with the increased population. Welfare calculation for any year, as already explained, must be made by reference to the aggregate demand schedule expected to prevail at that time.

2. Income redistributions do not change aggregate social welfare. There can be secondary effects, however, owing to substantive changes in demand patterns if the redistributions are of sizable magnitude.

3. Change in real per capita income, which may stem, for instance, from technological change, may shift the aggregate demand curve and so increase the willingness-to-pay measure of social benefit as do changes in population.

4. Spontaneous changes in tastes show up as shifts in demand schedule. The remarks of paragraph 1 above are applicable here as well. Changes in tastes often lead to social waste of capital resources which are "sunk" costs. Hence, from the viewpoint of cost-benefit analysis, resources spent for inducing changes in society's tastes are misallocations.

5. Introduction of a duplicate service may take away demand from an existing facility. Such switching of demand does not constitute a loss in consumers' surplus with reference to the existing facility. As emphasized earlier, only a change in price entails a compensating variation or welfare effect. The duplicate project should not be faulted purely because a facility providing similar services already exists.

6. Taxes and bounties within the society are purely internal redistributions and must not be counted as costs or benefits. Thus, for example, if a crosstown highway in a metropolitan area is not justified on the basis of cost-benefit analysis without a bounty from the federal government, then it is also not justified in the presence of a bounty, no matter how large the bounty is.

7. Taxes by foreign countries are costs just as tariffs on foreign imports are benefits to the home nation. A foreign investment brings social ben-

efits only to the extent that it leads to an increase in the total proceeds to the home country net of foreign taxes.

8. If the project under consideration uses some imported factor, the valuation of the factor may require constructing a *shadow price*. The actual construction will depend upon political constraints. Consider the following values of an imported factor: (a) its current world price; (b) its price in the domestic market; (c) value in the domestic market of the imported good that will be cut out so as to import the factor required for the project; and (d) value in the domestic market of the good that will have to be exported to raise sufficient additional foreign exchange to pay for the import of the needed factor—taking into account the fact that more offering for export may depress the export price of the good. In the presence of foreign exchange shortage, (a) above is obviously not the proper value to use in cost-benefit analysis; (b), (c), or (d) should be used depending upon the political constraint.

9. If the output of the project in question is intended for export, the value of the social benefit from the project is not the money value of the foreign exchange so earned; rather, it is the domestic value of the goods that are intended to be imported by using the earned foreign exchange. If necessary, a domestic price index or national parameter for the value of foreign exchange may be constructed by reference to the basket of the usually imported goods. This index acts as the shadow price of the earned foreign exchange and is, obviously, different from the exchange rate prevailing in the money markets.

Accounting for Spillovers

Suppose a municipal project for cleaning the effluents going into a river has two further consequences: (1) the cost of a downriver vegetable producer is reduced; and (2) the demand and, therefore, rent for pleasure boats is increased, which entails a loss of welfare to the regular boaters. Both effects exemplify dependency of an individual's welfare on the activities and choices of others. But the gain to the vegetable producer is transmitted directly without the mediation of the price mechanism, whereas the loss to the boaters is transmitted via a price effect. When the choices made by an economic agent affect the welfare of another individual without the mediation of the price system and the agent does not pay (or extract) the corresponding compensating variation, then such an effect on welfare is called an externality or a spillover.

Spillovers may be benefits or costs. Some standard examples of spillovers are noise pollution, air pollution, adverse effects of deforestation, and congestion in a city center owing to an arterial inlet. Satisfactions or grievances not considered legitimate within the social ethic are not spillovers. For instance, a person's jealousy of a neighbor's buying a Rolls Royce does not qualify as a spillover cost.

Spillovers arise because some inputs used or outputs produced cannot be privatized or have not been privatized. In situations where definition and enforcement of property rights are feasible, a spillover can be eliminated by denying its perpetrator access to the property rights or by having a market for spillovers. Alternatively, the perpetrator of a spillover cost may choose to compensate the losers regardless of considerations of property rights. Then the spillover cost is said to have been internalized by the perpetrator.

Cost-benefit analysis is conducted within the framework of existing property rights, legal structure, and institutions. To see what difference the law makes, note that if, for example, the law is silent on environmental protection, then the value of clean air is the sum of the compensating variation that can be extracted from all affected individuals for incorporating pollution control in a project. On the other hand, if the law protects the rights of individuals to have clean air, then the value of clean air is the sum of the compensating variation that will need to be paid to all affected individuals for obtaining their permission to pollute the air.

The ecological spillovers of major projects such as the Tennessee Valley dam or the Alaskan pipeline are usually slow in unfolding and necessarily accrue to future generations. Since the preferences of posterity are not revealed through demand behavior as are the preferences of the present generation, the cost-benefit analyst is forced to assume that future generations will have the same want structure as the present generation. Unfortunately, ecological spillovers are usually irreversible and the future generations are denied the option of restoring the status quo should they so desire. For this reason, some have argued that, in case of irreversibilities, keeping the options open is a benefit and should be valued as such. The other side of the argument is that the consumption of all mineral resources is an irreversible process, and keeping the options open is an argument that will carry over to every future generation in turn. Are we, therefore, to leave all depleting mineral resources untouched forever?

Aside from the problems discussed above, the accounting for spillovers introduces no new conceptual problem. For instance, the spillover social benefit due to the reduction in the vegetable grower's production cost is accounted for exactly as any other cost reduction. The problems in accounting for spillovers are mostly the practical problems of valuation, particularly, when spillovers involve situations where property rights cannot be defined or enforced. For such spillovers, no market can exist even in theory; so they are inherently unpriced and share the valuation problems of all unpriced benefits and costs.

Valuation of Unpriced Benefits and Costs

Valuation of unpriced benefits and costs is the most vulnerable side of cost-benefit analysis. It often involves assumptions that are tenuous at best and estimates that are coarse and based on informed guesswork. The decision maker should be sure to review the assumptions and bases of valuation critically before accepting the results of a study as a guide to social policy.

One way of resolving the valuation problem is to construct a shadow price by reference to prices of similar goods or services elsewhere. For instance, the social valuation of a new proposed museum in city A may be arrived at on the basis of the demand of a similar museum in city B. This approach does not fully solve the estimation problem because even in city B the demand for the museum is not market based.

A second way of resolving the problem is by reference to some implied consequences. For instance, the spillover cost to society because of air pollution from a steel plant may be valued by reference to increased repairs and maintenance costs of buildings and structures and increased health-related costs attributable to air pollution. It bears emphasizing that the practical problem of valuation is no license for violating the theoretical concept of compensating variation on which cost-benefit analysis rests. For example, if the steel plant already exists, the value of spillover cost it perpetrates is the compensating variation by reference to the level of welfare prevailing under the existing pollution. On the other hand, if the steel plant does not presently exist, the value of the spillover cost it will perpetrate is the compensating variation by reference to the level of welfare prevailing under the present clean environment.

A third way to resolve the valuation problem is to impute bounds on the value of the benefit or cost after all other calculations have been made. For example, an unpriced benefit is assigned a minimum value equal to the total costs minus the total benefits already quantified in the study. The reasoning is that, if the value of the unpriced benefit is less than this minimum, then the net benefit of the project will be a negative quantity indicating that the project is socially inefficient. It is left to the decision maker to judge whether the imputed minimum (maximum) value of the unpriced benefit (cost) is reasonable.

A variation on the approach mentioned above is to impute the value of, say, a benefit by reference to some other already accepted nonprofit project involving similar unpriced benefit. Here the reasoning is that, since the reference project has already been accepted, a (minimum) value has implicitly been assigned to the unpriced benefit. There are several objections to this procedure. First, this approach introduces a valuation method which cannot be tied to the basic economic concept of compensating variation. Second, the final choice of the reference project may have been made on social and political considerations and not on economic considerations involving imputation of value to the unpriced benefit. And third, cost-benefit calculations made at the planning stage may not have materialized later, or the decision may not be a right one when seen with hindsight.

Another way to resolve the problem of valuation is to leave the unpriced benefits and costs outside the equation and draw attention to them explicitly. The decision maker may then use this information, for instance, as a "tie breaker," should two alternatives under consideration turn out to be too close to call otherwise.

Examples of Valuations of Unpriced Effects

The examples that follow are meant to illustrate the variety of approaches that have been used for coming to grips with a problem which is admittedly difficult, but which is also at the heart of cost-benefit analysis. These examples should not be viewed as guidelines or as suggested practice.

1. *Valuation of improved quality of water.* In situations where improved quality of water can be considered as a public good to be enjoyed by all and sundry in a community, the possibility of simply surveying people for their willingness to pay for the improvement could be a viable alternative. The problem is that one cannot be sure that people will reveal their true assessment. If people believed that their answer might somehow be used to in fact levy a financial cost on them, they would have an incentive to understate their willingness to pay. On the other hand, if they were assured that the project would be financed from general tax revenues, they would have an incentive to overstate their willingness to pay. Although there is no sure method to overcome this difficulty, if no other valuation method is feasible, a suitably designed referendum questionnaire would be better than no valuation.

2. *Demand for a specific recreation site.* A well-known valuation approach is the Clawson-Knetsch travel cost method for valuing an existing recreation site. The country surrounding the site is divided into concentric annular zones of specific money cost of travel. The visitors at the site are sampled to determine the zone they came from, and visitor-days per capita are estimated for each zone. This visitation rate is regressed on travel cost and socioeconomic variables, such as income and education

level. The observed total visitation at the present admission price, of course, is one price-demand point. To find other price-demand points, it is assumed that individuals will react to a $1 increase in admissions charge in the same way as to a $1 increase in travel cost. Then, using the regression equation, the visitation rate for each travel cost zone is calculated for different (hypothetical) increments in travel cost.

The travel cost method has also been extended to include both money cost and time cost of travel.

3. *The value of a person's time.* The common practice is to value a person's time (saved or used up) at a rate equaling the (social) value of the person's marginal product. Current wage rate may or may not reflect the social value of a person's time and may have to be adjusted to construct a suitable shadow price. Note that the structure of the time saved must be explicitly considered in making the valuation. Commuting time may be a cost; but vacation time is a benefit. Also, there is some minimum threshold below which any saving in time has no value. For example, a project that cuts the daily commuting time by one minute (out of thirty) can hardly be regarded as conferring a sensible benefit.

4. *The social cost of labor hired.* In general, a (nonprofit) project draws labor from both the employed and unemployed pools of workforce. The proportion of labor drawn from the two pools depends upon the demographic distribution of the labor hired, the type of occupation, and the prevailing rate of unemployment. The social cost of labor hired is the weighted average opportunity cost of labor drawn from each of the two pools. Of course, the social cost is less than the wage bill of the hired labor.

5. *The social cost of loss of life or limb.* This valuation is an emotionally sensitive issue on which there is still no consensus. The reasoning of the last two valuation approaches extends to valuing loss of life or limb by viewing it as loss of *economic activity.* There is disagreement among researchers as to whether the loss is (a) loss of earnings, (b) loss of expenditure on consumption goods, (c) loss of consumer's surplus, or (d) loss of net contribution to others in the society, that is, loss of marginal product less consumption expenditure of the individual. Note that, under viewpoint (d), extending the life of nonworking poor, disabled, and senior citizens would count as a social *cost.*

Another approach is to view loss of life or limb as loss of an *economic resource* or human capital whose replacement will cost the society a certain amount. This idea has not been extensively explored as yet.

A third approach is to invoke the *insurance principle* and estimate the value a person places on his or her own life. The value equals the life insurance premium a person is willing to pay divided by the probability of the person being killed. The objection to this method is that, at best, it is based on compensation to others in the event of a person's death.

The only method consistent with the concept of compensating variation is to value a person's life or limb by reference to what the person is willing to accept as compensation for an increased exposure to risk of such a loss. While no amount of compensation will suffice for an individual to agree to give up life or limb for sure at some near date, it is commonplace for individuals to accept more risk in exchange for money compensations. Of course, a voluntary assumption of risk such as by smokers or sky jumpers can hardly be viewed as a loss of welfare. But when a project imposes an involuntary increase of risk on some individuals or on the community as a whole, then it must count as a spillover cost. The problem with this method is that as risk increases, additional increments of risk become increasingly costly from the viewpoint of the individual.

Accounting for Uncertainty.

In accounting for future flows of benefits and costs, the analyst must come to grips with uncertainty. In practice, a distinction is sometimes drawn between *estimation* uncertainty and *forecast* uncertainty although, at the formal theoretical level, there is no difference between them for both refer to lack of knowledge. For instance, in evaluating a flood control project, one problem is to estimate the value of damage to crop and property that occurs when a flood of some specific magnitude exceeds the reservoir capacity under consideration. A second problem is to estimate the chances (probability) that a flood of such a magnitude will in fact occur. Several avenues are open to the cost-benefit analyst for handling uncertainty.

1. *Point estimate.* A point estimate is a single estimate of the value in question. When no formal consideration is given to the probabilities of alternative scenarios, the point estimate represents either the most likely value or a conservative assessment in the judgment of the analyst. Alternatively, a mental calculation is made to arrive at a weighted average value, or *expected value*, where the weights are the probabilities of alternative scenarios. For example, if a crop loss of $10,000 is expected with a probability of .4 and a crop loss of $15,000 is expected with a probability of .6, then the weighted average loss is $13,000 ($10,000 × .4 + 15,000 × .6).

Point estimates may be made using the formal methods of the theory of probability and statistics. There are two approaches here, the classical approach and the Bayesian approach. The latter may also take into consideration the *loss function*, that is, the possible ill effects of making incorrect estimates, where the ill effects depend upon the extent of error.

The formal methods of the theory of probability and statistics are outside the scope of this chapter.

2. *Three-point estimate or interval estimate.* Alternatively, the analyst may specify a range of values, usually communicated by specifying a conservative estimate, the most likely value, and an optimistic estimate. This way, the decision maker is afforded the opportunity to exercise additional judgment instead of having to depend entirely on a point estimate chosen by the analyst.

Again, formal methods of probability and statistics are available to assess a range which covers the true but unknown value with a specifiable degree of confidence.

3. *Explicit statement of plausible scenarios.* In the rare case when the analyst is unable to make any judgment whatsoever of the probabilities of alternative scenarios, there is no alternative but to report the costs and benefits for each plausible scenario. The decision maker can then exercise some judgment or use decision techniques suitable for such uncertain situations.

It bears emphasizing that a point estimate or range estimate is merely a construct to comprehend before the fact what the future might hold. After the fact, one and only one outcome will occur. If the actual outcome does not coincide with the estimate which formed the basis of the decision, it does not necessarily mean that the decision maker was at fault.

The Common Error of Double Counting

A cost or benefit may be viewed either as a flow accruing time after time or as an asset value—that is, the lump-sum value that people would be willing to pay to acquire the claim to such a flow. In the accounting of benefits and costs, care should be taken to count either the flows or the consequent asset values, but not both. For example, the construction of a rapid transit system provides a flow of benefits such as reducing commuting time, increasing job opportunities, and opening ready access to the amenities of the city center. The aggregate demand schedule, from which the consumers' surplus measure of the increase in welfare is calculated, implicitly takes all these benefits into consideration.

The opening of a rapid transit system will also lead to a rise in the land and real estate values. To include these increments also in the evaluation of benefits will be to engage in double counting. The reason the real estate values increase is that a flow of benefits becomes available to the residents. Indeed, when the valuation of flows is too crude, it might become necessary to use the increases in asset values as a better estimate of the social benefits of a project. For instance, the benefit of an irrigation canal may have to be estimated by reference to the increase in the farmland values instead of the incremental annual crop yield values.

A second common exposure to double counting arises in the case of projects directed toward cost saving. The annual benefits of such projects correctly include the cost savings on the existing demand *plus* operating gains and consumers' surplus on the additional demand induced by the reduction of market price (if any). To also include as benefits the profit of middlemen, the saving to consumers, and the like would be to engage in double counting.

A third exposure to double counting arises in the case of spillovers in the presence of full employment. Suppose a nonprofit project is undertaken to clean up a lake for recreational use and, as a spillover, a resort hotel is constructed on the lakefront by a private enterprise. The consumers' surplus associated with the demand for hotel is properly a benefit. But treating factor incomes generated by the hotel service also as benefits would be double counting if there is full employment in the economy. The benefit to factor owners is canceled by the sacrificed value of their marginal product in alternative use.

Summary of Costs and Benefits

For each alternative (and, if necessary, for each scenario) the estimates are summarized as a time schedule of costs and benefits which consist partly of outlays and receipts of funds and partly of decreases and increases of social welfare. Table 8–1 suggests one way of summarizing the information, keeping in view the fact that, while the objective is to evaluate the economic efficiency of projects in the social welfare sense, availability of funds and continued financing of the project can be important constraints.

INVESTMENT CRITERIA

The investment decision, by definition, involves incurring costs (or sacrifices) in the present so as to enjoy a greater stream of net benefits in the future. Having determined the yearly schedule of costs and benefits for all alternatives under consideration, the decision maker needs a rule:

- To decide whether or not a project represents an increase in economic efficiency in the aggregate social welfare sense.
- To rank alternative projects according to their economic efficiency.
- To allocate limited funds among the available projects so as to maximally enhance social welfare.

A straightforward summation of all future costs and benefits into a single net benefit number is unsatisfactory because this rule pays no attention to the fact that, all else being the same, a project which promises

TABLE 8–1. *Time schedule of costs and benefits.*

	Year 1	Year 2	...
Funds flows			
Capital outlays	(_ _ _ _ _)	(_ _ _ _ _)	
Operating revenues	_ _ _ _ _	_ _ _ _ _	
Operating expenditures	(_ _ _ _ _)	(_ _ _ _ _)	
Net funds inflows (outflows)	_ _ _ _ _	_ _ _ _ _	
Social welfare flows			
Adjustment for social cost of capital resources	(_ _ _ _ _)	(_ _ _ _ _)	
Social welfare benefits	_ _ _ _ _	_ _ _ _ _	
Social welfare costs	(_ _ _ _ _)	(_ _ _ _ _)	
Net adjustment for social welfare effects	_ _ _ _ _	_ _ _ _ _	
Net social benefit (cost)	_ _ _ _ _	_ _ _ _ _	

Note: Parentheses indicate subtraction.

benefits later is less preferred to the one promising the same benefits earlier. A suitable weighting scheme must be used to properly take into account the timing of costs and benefits. Consensus is lacking on what weighting scheme to use.

The discussion below explores how an individual comes to assign more weight to near-term benefits compared to distant benefits, and explains the resulting arithmetic of time adjustment calculus (commonly referred to as *discounting*). The discussion then moves on to social time adjustment calculus and its use in cost-benefit approach to capital expenditures.

Individual's Time Adjustment Calculus

There are several possible reasons why individuals generally assign greater weight to near-term benefits and costs compared to the distant ones: Individuals are impatient to consume; they know they are not getting any younger and wish to enjoy life now; they believe that their future income will be greater; and know that capital investments produce increased future benefits, providing opportunities for positive returns; they recognize the uncertainty of future benefits and hedge for possible losses by demanding more; and they abhor riskiness in general and therefore attach a cost to it. Each of these reasons is explored further before going into the arithmetic of time adjustment.

Impatience. Individuals are generally not willing to sacrifice today's consumption unless they are suitably compensated for having to wait. This impatience puts a cost on waiting. The cost per period is conveniently expressed as a percentage surcharge on the amount sacrificed at the beginning of the period, and is referred to as the individual's required rate of return.

Why would an individual prefer to consume now rather than a year from now? First, because there is a risk that a year from now the consumption goods may not materialize. Second, there is the risk that a year from now the person may not be there (or may have less "spark") to enjoy consumption. And third, the person may believe that the future holds promise of higher levels of consumption anyway, so that it is not worthwhile to defer today's consumption. The three components of impatience, then, are risk premium, risk of death, and time preference.

Time preference. Suppose today an individual has a well-defined preference structure not only on today's consumptions but also on the consumptions at future dates. Assume that, at every date, each incremental consumption brings decreasing amounts of additional satisfaction to the individual. If the individual believes that the future holds promise of higher levels of income, then a small (marginal) increase in consumption today will be seen by the individual as giving more satisfaction than that given by the same increment at future dates. In other words, $1 of future consumption must be reckoned "worth" less (in terms of satisfaction) than $1 of today's consumption, because the base income is expected to be greater in the future than it is today. As before, this relative weighting across time may be expressed as a percentage rate of return charged on the amount sacrificed at the beginning of the period.

Marginal productivity of capital. It is an empirical fact that a consumption forgone today and invested as capital can be made to produce a larger amount of output over a period of time. The capital markets always stand ready to borrow, or accept as equity, funds from individuals in lieu of a return in the form of periodic interest or dividends. This rate of return is the opportunity cost to the individual for consuming $1 today instead of leaving it in the private investment market.

The obverse side to the point above is that a producer should not invest funds into the productive process unless such investment is expected to generate a sufficient value of product to cover the *cost of capital,* which, in general, will be weighted average cost of debt and equity.

Cost of risk. Suppose an individual loans $100 for one year to each of 50 persons, knowing well that, statistically speaking, an average of 12 percent (six persons) will not repay the loan for whatever reason. Assume the individual wishes to have a 10 percent per year net return on invested funds. In other words, at the end of one year, the individual must receive back $5,500 ($5,000 initial investment plus $500 return), and this must come from 44 persons expected to repay the loan. The loan agreement, therefore, should require repayment of $125 ($5,500/44) per person. The nominal or *ex ante* interest rate here is 25 percent per year although the expected realized interest rate is only 10 percent per year. The difference arises because, as a hedge against loss, the individual spreads the cost of expected defaults on all borrowers. The nominal interest rate can be reduced if the borrowers as a class become less risky.

The argument remains unchanged if, instead of lending the money to 50 people, the individual chooses to invest money in 50 projects whose return is risky. Once again, the nominal rate of return from each project must be more than the required rate of return by an amount representing the cost of risk.

Risk aversion and risk premium. Suppose an individual abhors risk, so much so that, if owning a fair lottery giving a 50–50 chance at winning or losing $10, the individual would be happy to pay $1 to get rid of the lottery. The expected value of the lottery was zero, but the individual valued it at negative $1. The difference between its value to an individual and the expected value of a lottery is called *risk premium*. Of course, the risk premium for a lottery depends upon the size of the lottery as well as the size of the individual's assets. To a Rockefeller, a 50–50 chance at winning or losing $100 will have less risk abhorrence than to a professor at the University of Pittsburgh. In fact, some individuals may even love the gamble; however, even for such risk lovers, beyond some size, risk becomes unattractive.

Suppose a risk-averse individual requires 10 percent per year return on nonrisky investments. In other words, the individual doesn't mind investing $100 for a sure return of $110 after one year. For a risky future return, the individual will require additional compensation to assume the risk, thus raising the return requirement to, say, 15 percent per year. The additional 5 percent is the individual's risk premium for accepting the risk (as opposed to the premium for getting rid of one). Needless to say, the risk premium for accepting risk will vary directly with the "riskiness" of the promised return.

The risk premium notion should not be confused with the notion of cost of risk discussed in the previous section. The 5 percent risk premium in the above example is purely a function of the individual's risk-aversion characteristic. If, for instance, the individual were risk neutral, the risk premium would be zero.

Arithmetic of Time Adjustment
(or Counting and Discounting of Interest)

Assume an individual's required rate of return (also called discount rate) is 10 percent per year. This means that the individual is indifferent between $100 at any given date and $110 one year later. Repeating the argument one more time, the individual is indifferent between $110 one year later and $121 ($110 × 1.1) two years later. This calculation is like counting interest at a compounded rate.

In the above example, $110 is called the *future value* (FV) after one year of $100 now. Thus, $121 is the future value after one year of $110 now, or future value after two years of $100 now.

The calculation works backward as well. The individual is indifferent between $100 at any given date and $90.91 ($100/1.1) one year earlier. For $90.91 together with one year's return at 10 percent per year equals $100. Similarly, the individual is indifferent between $90.91 one year earlier and $82.64 two years earlier. For $82.64 together with one year's return equals $90.91. This calculation is called *discounting* (of interest at compounded rate).

In the above example, $90.91 is called the *present* (discounted) *value* of $100 one year from now. Thus, $82.64 is the present discounted value of $90.91 one year from now or present discounted value of $100 two years from now.

Tables of future value (FV) and present value (PV) of $1 at different discount rates per period and covering 1 to 50 (or more) periods help simplify the arithmetic.

Consider a project with net (costs) benefits equaling ($100), $40, $90, and ($14) at year 0 and at the end of three succeeding years respectively. The arithmetic of time adjustment is shown in Table 8–2. A positive net present (future) value indicates that the project more than compensates the individual for all costs as well as for the return required on the costs outstanding at the beginning of each period. Hence, economically, the project is better than the status quo.

Interpretation of Net Present (Future) Value

It is instructive to look at the meaning of net present (future) value from several different angles.

1. *Loan accounting and reinvestment assumption.* One way to view the project is to see it as consisting of loaning $100 to a producer on the condition

TABLE 8–2. *Arithmetic of time adjustment.*

Year End	Flow	PV at Time 0		FV at Year End 4	
0	$(100)	(100) × 1.0000	$(100.00)	(100) × 1.331	$(133.10)
1	40	40 × .9091	36.36	40 × 1.210	48.40
2	90	90 × .8264	74.38	90 × 1.100	99.00
3	(14)	(14) × .7513	(10.52)	(14) × 1.000	(14.00)
Net time-adjusted value			$ .22		$ .30

that the producer pay $40 and $90 at year ends 1 and 2 respectively, and receive $14 at year end 3. We will say that $100 is loaned to the project. The required rate of return is 10 percent per year. Then, at year end 1, the project "owes" $110 ($100 outstanding investment *plus* $10 return on outstanding investment). Of this amount, $40 is received, leaving an outstanding "loan" of $70. At year end 2, the project "owes" $77 ($70 outstanding investment *plus* $7 return on outstanding investment); however, $90 is received, which is $13 more than the net outstanding debt on date. Assume it is possible to reinvest $13 for any length of time at the required rate. Then, at year end 3, the reinvestment would provide a total of $14.30 ($13.00 + $1.30 return), of which $14 is paid back to the project, leaving a net balance of $.30. This is the net future value of the project— the balance remaining after reimbursing all costs and after paying the required return on costs outstanding at the beginning of each period, *assuming the return rate and reinvestment rate are equal.*

If the individual's reinvestment rate were only 5 percent per year, then at year end 3 the reinvestment would provide a total of only $13.65, which falls short of the $14 obligation at year end; hence, the project would be economically unacceptable.

There is no change in the above discussion if, instead of loaning $100 to a producer, the sum is invested, say, in a machine and the investment is looked upon as a "loan" to the machine.

2. *Loan accounting and equality of borrowing and lending rates.* Assume the initial $100 is borrowed from a bank at 10 percent per year, with the loan to be repaid from the receipts of the project. The accounting for the loan obligation is exactly the same as before, except now the focus is on what is owed to the bank. At year end 2, $13 is left over after full repayment of the loan and all related interest charges. Assume the *lending (or reinvestment) rate equals the borrowing rate.* Then, as before, the net future value at year end 3 is $.30, and the project is economically viable. But if the lending (or reinvestment) rate is only 5 percent per year, then economically the project is unacceptable.

Note that any (partial) repayment of a debt carrying a 10 percent per year interest rate is tantamount to investing funds at 10 percent. Thus, as long as there is any debt outstanding, it is always possible to reinvest funds at the debt rate. The question of equality of borrowing and lending rate emerges only after the debt is fully paid off.

3. *Willingness to pay for consumption claims.* Let us change the setting slightly. Assume costs and benefits refer, respectively, to units of consumption sacrificed and received by an individual. The project requires an initial sacrifice of 100 units of consumption at time 0. It promises 40 units of (additional) consumption at year end 1, 90 units of (additional) consumption at year end 2, and a sacrifice of 14 units of consumption at year end 3. Assume the individual's time preference is 10 percent per year.

At time 0, the individual is willing to sacrifice at most 36.36 units of consumption for a claim on 40 units of consumption at year end 1, and 74.38 units for a claim on 90 units of consumption at year end 2 (see the PV calculations in Table 8–2). In other words, an individual's present value of a future consumption claim is the compensating variation that can be extracted from him on grant of the claim so as to keep his welfare level unchanged.

What are we to make of the PV of 14 units of sacrifice required at year end 3? Assume that the individual is alone and is *as much willing to consume now and sacrifice later as to do the reverse—namely, to consume later and sacrifice now.* Then the compensating variation that he must be paid as a bounty at time 0 in lieu of the 14 units he will have to sacrifice at year end 3 equals 10.52 units of consumption. His net willingness to pay, therefore, is 100.22 units (36.36 + 74.38 − 10.52). Since the required sacrifice is only 100 units, the project represents a variation surplus of .22 units, representing a net increase in the individual's welfare.

Next, assume instead that the individual is not alone—there is one other beside him. Then, for the project to be acceptable, at least one of the two men should be willing to consume earlier and pay later. Whoever is willing will be granted 10.52 units of consumption at time 0 against a promise to sacrifice 14 units at year end 3. This brings capital markets back into the picture. The two men trade their consumption claims of different dates to reach a distribution which is more desirable for both of them.

SOCIAL TIME ADJUSTMENT CALCULUS

The evaluation criterion has the same structure for nonprofit capital expenditures as for individual or private sector expenditures. The project represents an improvement in economic efficiency in the aggregate social welfare sense if the present (future) value of social benefits exceeds the present (future) value of social costs. Two basic issues need consideration here: What social discount rate is meaningful to use and what, if any, conceptual problems are introduced by discounting the aggregates at the social level.

Social Discount Rate

The social discount rate is the relative weighting of future social costs and benefits against present costs and benefits. There are two schools of thought on the "right" approach for determining the social discount rate: (1) the opportunity rate on private investment (assuming it also represents the *social* yield of private investment), and (2) social rate of time preference. Controversy also surrounds the question of whether the social discount rate, however determined, should include a risk premium or should be riskless.

1. *Market opportunity rate.* According to proponents of the opportunity rate approach, the source of funds for any nonprofit (public) project is ultimately the private sector. Thus, the rate of return on private sector investments should serve as the opportunity cost for funds used in public projects.

In an ideal situation, each person's rate of time preference—that is, the interest rate that makes a person indifferent between consuming now and consuming in the next period—must become equal (at the margin) to the market interest rate. Let us see why. Suppose an individual's rate of time preference is 5 percent per year, while the market interest rate is 6 percent per year. Then the individual will increase his lendings—will give up today's consumption in exchange for tomorrow's—until his rate of time preference increases to equal the market interest rate. In the opposite case, the individual will increase his borrowings until the equality of rates obtains. Thus, ideally, every individual's rate of time preference equals the riskless market interest rate represented by the (long-term) government bond rate—which, therefore, may be taken as a surrogate for social rate of time preference.

In real life, considerations of corporate income tax and risk premiums lead private sector investments to have a *higher* rate of return than the government bond rate. In theory, nonprofit projects should be evaluated at the private sector's *before-tax* rate of return, because, for society as a whole, taxation is only a transfer of product from the private sector to the government sector.

This view assumes that the rate of return of private sector investments equals the *social* yield of private investment. Strictly speaking, the two could be different, because the private sector rate of return is calculated by reference to funds flow and ignores welfare effects such as consumers' surplus and externalities (see Table 8–2 above).

2. *Social rate of time preference.* Proponents of this approach argue that people suffer from myopia, which leads them to discount their future wants too heavily. To such myopia, people unavoidably bring in a component identifiable as the risk-of-death discount rate. Further, the argument goes that future generations are not even represented in the market determination of the government bond rate. Hence, the government bond rate is not representative of the "true" social rate of time preference; it is biased on the higher side.

Society today has an obligation to posterity. It is the custodian not only of the welfare of present generations but of the welfare of future generations as well. Thus it should be responsible to hold in check the irrationality of individuals and institutions, especially because the use of a large social discount rate is tantamount to assigning a small weight to distant costs and benefits. The seriousness of such shortsightedness gets multiplied, for instance, when costs are irreversible.

According to the proponents of this approach, some political process should determine the appropriate rate of social time preference. A suitable mechanism for making the social choice poses a design problem of no mean magnitude.

Some Unresolved Issues in Social Discounting

There are several unresolved issues related to discounting of costs and benefits of nonprofit projects. Consider the numerical example shown in Table 8–2. Suppose the flows of benefits and costs refer to generations instead of years. Then it is difficult to interpret discounting of a future generation's cost. The present generation speaks for itself in expressing a willingness to sacrifice consumption so that a future generation may benefit. However, it is incorrect to presume that the reverse is true—for instance, that the third generation will be equally willing to bear the sacrifice of $14 for the present generation's enjoyment of benefits.

A second problem is the so-called Strotz paradox of inconsistent planning. The argument is somewhat involved and, so, will not be repeated here. The essence of the paradox is this. Suppose a consumer chooses a plan today, allocating a fixed stock of goods for consumption over different dates so as to maximize present welfare. When tomorrow comes and the consumer reconsiders the plan, he will generally want to *revise* the plan even when there is no change of expectation in the interim. If the project involves irreversible changes, the revision will not be possible when the present or the next generation reevaluates the project.

A third problem concerns the fact that the future generations cannot negotiate with the present generation. In the foregoing numerical illustration, once the project is accepted, there is no assurance that the second generation will reinvest a sufficient amount from the $90 income to provide for the cost of $14 to the third generation. Were it possible for the two generations to negotiate, the intergenerational distribution of costs and benefits could well be different.

The above considerations suggest that when a project involves throw-over costs to future generations and, particularly, irreversibilities, the decision maker must bring to bear judgments that go beyond cost-benefit analysis.

Weighted Social Discount Rate

In practice, the social rate of time preference is estimated by reference to the government bond discount rate, say, 8 percent per year. Estimation of the rate of return on private sector investments poses econometric problems because market imperfection and riskiness of investments lead to the prevalence of a different social rate of return, say, 13 percent per year. A weighted social discount rate is used, depending upon the constraints placed on the source of funds and their use in nonprofit projects. Three cases are possible.

1. The funds are allocated to the nonprofit agency for investment only in the nonprofit sector, so as to provide a social value higher than the sacrificed current social consumption. In this case, the appropriate social discount rate is the social rate of time preference. Private sector rate of return is inappropriate because of the injunction concerning the allocation of funds.

2. The funds are allocated to the nonprofit agency for investment in any way that best furthers social welfare. In this case, the appropriate social discount rate is the private sector rate of return, because this investment opportunity is always open to the nonprofit agency.

3. The funds are allocated to the nonprofit agency for investment in only those nonprofit projects that are superior to the alternative of leaving the funds in the private sector. If the funds withdrawn reduce only current consumption, then, as in case 1 above, the appropriate social discount rate is the social rate of time preference. If the funds withdrawn reduce only private investment, then, as in case 2 above, the appropriate social discount rate is the private sector rate of return. Finally, if the funds withdrawn reduce both current consumption and private investment, a weighted average discount rate is used.

For example, suppose an increase of taxation generates $100 million needed for the construction of a dam, of which $10 million is estimated to come from a reduction in current savings and, therefore, from a reduction in current private investment (assuming a full-employment economy). Then $90 million must come from a reduction in the current disposable income, so that the weighted average social discount rate is 8.5 percent ([.10 × 13] + [.9 × 8]) per year.

Other, more complex weighting schemes have been suggested in the literature based on the assumption that the returns from private sector investments are usually partly consumed and partly reinvested. The assumption produces a somewhat lower weighted average discount rate than the one calculated above.

A Short Note on Capital Rationing

Often the funds available are limited and the decision maker must choose the best combination among available alternative projects. Constraints may be placed only on current funds or on future availability of funds as well. The solution of such complex problems requires mathematical procedures best handled on electronic computers.

If the budget constraint is only in the initial capital outlay, then the decision maker can often arrive at the optimal combination of projects in a fairly straightforward manner. The problem here is to achieve the best *utilization* of each capital dollar:

$$\text{Utilization index} = \frac{\text{net PV of the project}}{\text{initial investment}}$$

The projects are listed in the order of their utilization index. The capital budget is allocated to the project with the highest utilization index first, and so on down the list. If the alternatives available are large in number and vary widely in the size of the initial capital investment, it may become necessary to use mathematical methods to find the best combination.

For example, suppose the capital budget is $8 million. Three different services—X, Y, and Z—are under consideration. For service X, there are three proposed projects; for service Y there are four proposed projects; and for service Z, there are two proposed projects. At most one project is to be selected for each service. The utilization indexes of the alternatives proposed for each service are tabulated below, with capital investment needed, in millions of dollars, given in brackets.

X	.15 [2.8]	.28 [1.9]	.32 [4.0]	
Y	.10 [3.3]	.20 [4.4]	.35 [4.8]	.45 [3.6]
Z	.26 [5.0]	.30 [2.0]		

The rows have been arranged in ascending order of the utilization index.

In each row, the project with the highest utilization index is picked, and listed in decreasing order of the index value together with the corresponding magnitude of the investment needed: Y = .45 [3.6], X = .32 [4.0], and Z = .30 [2.0]. Then the choice is Y and X, calling for a $7.6 million (3.6 + 4.0) capital expenditure and yielding a net present value of benefits of $2.9 million ([.45 × 3.6] + [.32 × 4.0]).

The simple procedure outlined above becomes ineffective if a relatively large amount of the capital budget remains unallocated.

Other Decision Criteria

Other decision criteria have often been proposed for use in capital expenditure decisions. These include internal rate of return, cost-benefit ratio, payback period, and discounted payback period. It is now well understood that such criteria give the right comparison only in special circumstances. They are, therefore, not presented here in detail. The decision maker will do well to avoid them.

SUMMARY

Cost-benefit analysis has been used for many years. However, on many theoretical and practical issues, full consensus does not yet exist. Difficult problems are encountered in the valuation of unpriced welfare effects, which are at the heart of the problem of social choice. Controversy is still not quiet on the matter of the social discount rate and the validity of time-adjusting the benefits and costs which accrue to unborn generations. Nevertheless, cost-benefit analysis provides a well-structured framework for taking into account the social welfare effects of a proposed project. The quantities in the analysis are not exact, but they provide a handle on the order of magnitudes involved.

Because cost-benefit analysis brings structure to the problem of social choice, it can be a powerful aid to the decision maker. By the same token, used injudiciously, it can be a damaging tool. A poorly conducted cost-benefit analysis, in the garb of quantitative definiteness, can lead to social injustice. For this reason, a greater responsibility falls on the decision maker. All assumptions must be critically examined, deliberated upon, and accepted as reasonable before any reliance is placed on the quantitative results. This indeed is the main theme of the chapter. For this reason, emphasis has been placed on explanation of concepts and their significance to the decision maker who does not conduct the analysis but who is called upon to evaluate its results and to act upon them. Study of the chapter can help the decision maker carry the burden of social choice with care and caution.

CHAPTER 9

Strategic Planning in Nonprofit Organizations

William R. King

Editor's Note   *Strategic planning is the organized activity through which an organization prepares for its future. It involves basic and important choices such as an organization's mission, objectives, strategy, policies, programs, goals, and strategic resource allocation. Planning is an essential ingredient in organizational effectiveness. Every manager should be aware of the alternative approaches to planning and be able to recognize the problems associated with planning. This chapter helps the reader gain such an awareness by introducing the basics of planning: the decision elements, basic premises, and subsystems of a strategic planning system (SPS).*

The mission refers to the organization's business, which has to be periodically reviewed and analyzed. The objectives are the general broad-based things the organization wishes to accomplish. Strategy is the general direction in which objectives are to be pursued. Policies are the broad guidelines developed to guide lower-level tactical decision making. Programs are resource-consuming activities through which strategies are pursued to achieve objectives. Goals are narrow, specific statements of objectives. Strategic resource allocation is the allocation of resources to programs, usually through budgets.

The author presents useful basic premises which form the basis of an organizational climate that is conducive to effective and useful planning. The implementation of these basic premises requires the operation of an SPS in the organization which consists of a system of plans, planning process, planning decision subsystem, planning information subsystem, facilitative planning organization, and planning management system. The system of plans consists of the mission plan outlining the broad mission/objective/strategy of the organization, organization development plan, divestment plan, diversification plan, R&D plan, program and project plans, and operations plan. The planning process begins with four basic inputs—forecasts, assumptions, strengths and weaknesses, and competitive information—and proceeds through a sequential selection of various strategic decision elements to the development of implementation and control strategies and the taking of action based on the system of plans. The planning decision subsystem is the formalized process for strategic decision making. A good planning information subsystem should focus on these environmental and competitive elements of the organization that will most critically affect its future. A facilitative planning organization is innovative, and it facilitates rather than inhibits strategic planning. The planning management subsystem involves giving attention to the organization climate necessary for creative planning. The best way to create a proper climate is to permeate the organization with planning and to make use of it to demonstrate that it works. For planning to have any significant effect on the strategic choices it should become part of the organization culture.

Strategic planning is the activity through which an organization prepares for its future. Of course, many of the daily decisions and actions taken by managers and administrators have consequences which will be realized only in the future, so in some sense all such activities involve preparation for the future. *Strategic planning, however, involves the organization's most basic and important choices—the choice of its mission, objectives, strategy, policies, programs, goals and strategic resource allocations.* These basic strategic choices, taken together, will largely determine the organization's overall future, whereas individual managerial decisions, particularly if made within the guidelines of established organization strategy and policy, will merely influence some aspect of the future.

Thus, while the decisions made by a police administrator concerning how many patrol cars to assign to various areas or what stance to take in an upcoming contract negotiation are important, they are not strategic. Choices which refocus the basic role of the department in helping society to achieve its goals are strategic. For instance, a police department which chose to shift attention from crime deterrence to crime prevention or one that decided to leave the protection of business facilities to private security organizations would be making such a strategic choice.

Strategic choices—those which affect the basic values and modus operandi of the organization—are made by all organizations. Sometimes they are made implicitly and sometimes even unknowingly, but they are inevitably made through the actions or inactions of the organization's administrators. The United States made such a choice when it chose to seek new values through the adoption of a Social Security program, when it chose to take responsibility for the welfare of large new segments of the population, and when it chose to rely on a volunteer system to man the military. The Social Security and welfare decisions were strategic because they affected the basic role of government and the values that it was seeking. The volunteer military decision was strategic because it changed the entire way in which the Department of Defense conducted its huge personnel system.

Indeed, strategic decisions may even involve changes in the basic business of the organization. When the March of Dimes chose to redirect its attention from polio to birth defects, it got into a new business, with new clients, new competitors, new strategies, and the need for new, or updated, organizational skills and structure.

Strategic planning is the organized process through which such strategic decisions can be systematically and rationally analyzed and made. Without such an organized process, the far-reaching impact of strategic decisions will probably not be foreseen. For instance, the volunteer military was introduced in the United States without due consideration of many of the social and cultural impacts that it might produce. The result is a military that is disproportionately made up of black young men, that has an extremely high attrition rate, and which may be unable to attract the quantity and quality of volunteers that are required. The impact of the volunteer military on the credibility which the public and potential adversaries ascribe to the military, the level of patriotism in the country, and the effect on the youth of America were also not seriously considered in the making of this strategic national choice (see King, 1977).

A good strategic planning process ensures that such potential impacts are identified and given appropriate consideration. An urban police department which systematically identified and investigated those public values to which it could best contribute—better public transportation, greater personal security, an improved environment, and so forth—was able to develop a program structure and resource allocations to such activities as crime investigation, crime repression, and traffic control to reflect clearly defined objectives of increased arrests, reduced crime, and decreased accidents. This planning process produced a set of choices which had an underlying rationale for what the department wished its role to be, what it planned to accomplish, and how it would measure progress toward its goals.

The alternative to such strategic planning is often a series of ad hoc unrelated choices made in response to the exigencies of the moment. Such strategic choices are usually not synergistic (mutually reinforcing), and they may even be contradictory. The lack of overall strategic planning at the national level in the United States is such a case. The federal government simultaneously funds tobacco growing and cancer prevention, even though the two are known to be contradictory. This is because such choices have been made independently to achieve different objectives. A strategic planning process would ensure that they be considered together in terms of their net impact on a broad range of national objectives.

THE DECISION ELEMENTS OF PLANNING

Despite the wide acceptance of need for strategic planning, there is no single unified concept of planning which is generally accepted and applied. Various organizations do different kinds of planning: some focus primarily on financial planning; others do program planning; still others plan for the long-term future only in terms of specific areas such as facilities or programs.

Planning also has different levels of perceived importance in various organizations. Some rely on planning so much that people in the organization feel that nothing can get done that has not passed through the planning process. Other organizations use planning more as a once-a-year process which serves as an opportunity for the review of past accomplishments and the setting of new objectives, with decisions being made on a day-to-day basis in a manner which is not directly related to the formal planning process. Some espouse an "antiplanning" philosophy regarding highly formalized planning (see Wrapp, 1967), but most modern organizations formally plan at one level of intensity or another.

The specific strategic choices that an organization makes in its planning process affect the kind of planning that it does and how important its planning is perceived to be. To understand these differences in approaches to planning and differences in the importance of planning, one must understand the various strategic decision elements which may be incorporated into the strategic planning process.

The Mission

The choice of an organizational mission—the business that the organization is to be in—is its most basic and most important strategic choice. Many people believe that their organization's mission is preordained—for example, "We made widgets" or "We exist to help the poor." In fact, the mission is a *choice* that should be periodically reviewed and analyzed, even in those organizations whose mission is established by statute. This is so because missions become outdated, because organizations change in terms of those things which they are well equipped to do, and most important because the outside world is constantly changing.

Even so well-defined an organization as an urban police department has had to redefine its mission over the years. For instance, the maintenance of civil order became a primary police mission in the 1960s, whereas it had been only a secondary mission earlier.

Objectives

Objectives* are the *general things that an organization wishes* to accomplish. Generally, objectives are stated in broad and timeless terms—for example, "To decrease the number of households whose income is below the poverty level," or "To substantially increase the proportion of small businesses that use our service."

Two varieties of objectives must be considered—those involving prospective levels of attainment (such as those just illustrated), and those described in terms of states to be retained (for instance, "to continue to be recognized as the primary health research funding agency"). Retentive objectives often serve as constraints under which the organization must operate.

Objectives directly involve those values that the organization is trying to attain or retain for its clientele. A public agency exists to serve the public in a given sector. Inherent in this service are a variety of public values to be enhanced. For instance, the U.S. military has the primary duty of defense, yet many of the strategic choices which it must make affect the employment situation in various areas, the well-being of military personnel and families, the economic position of businesses, and so on. A good planning process will identify these various clientele groups, specify objectives which are related to each, and permit the making of informed choices rather than choices which inadvertently affect some clients in unanticipated ways.

Strategy

A strategy is a general direction in which objectives are to be pursued. Often, strategies are stated in product-market terms—that is, the products or services to be produced and the markets or constituencies to be served. For instance, one strategy might be to introduce new programs that will

---

*In some contexts, it is common to interchange the role of "objectives" and "goals" as the terms are used here.

affect the income levels of current clients. An alternative strategy might be to expand current programs to serve new clientele groups.

Policies

The organization's policies are those broad guidelines which are developed to guide lower-level tactical decision making. Policies may be thought of as being of the same nature as strategies, but generally policies are not product-market oriented as are strategies. Also, policies are often more enduring than are strategies. For instance, organization policies might direct managers to follow a prescribed set of hiring practices, to promote solely on a merit basis, or to recommend new programs only if they meet established criteria.

Policies are often directly related to retentive objectives in that policies may be the instruments through which constraints are imposed on lower-level decision making.

Goals

Goals, like objectives, are things to be sought. However, they are more narrow, specific, and timely statements than are objectives. Thus, an objective of increasing the number of clients who have incomes above the poverty level might translate into specific goals of numbers and dates—100,000 in 1979, 120,000 in 1980, and so on.

Programs

Programs are the resource-consuming collections of activities through which strategies are pursued to achieve objectives. Programs have clearly defined goals and they are associated with organizational resources which have been allocated for the achievement of those goals. Illustrative of a program is a community aquatics program to attain improved community health levels through water sports. Such a program would have specific numerical goals, a program manager, a staff, and a budget.

Strategic Resource Allocations

Resources are allocated, usually through the mechanism of budgets, to programs, and sometimes to specific objectives and strategies. The array of resources, as allocated to various program and other entities, represent a choice which translates all the other planning choices into dollar and cents terms. The resource allocations, along with individual program and project plans (which involve schedules and manpower and facility plans, and which are usually not thought of as an element of organizational *strategic* planning), reflect the array of resources which are allocated to the various programs of the organization.

These strategic decision elements—mission, objectives, strategy, policies, goals, programs, and strategic resource allocations—constitute the choices which may be made through strategic planning. All organizations do not formally deal with all these elements; for instance, some see their mission and objectives as being fixed by law or tradition. Others behave as though they have no clear strategy in that they expend resources in many directions, often without allocating adequate resources in any one area to produce significant results. Moreover, even among those organizations that do explicitly decide on all these strategic decision elements, some do so in an unintegrated fashion—for example, allocating resources to programs that are not directly related to organizational objectives. (Often, one sees this latter phenomenon with regard to research programs which, although meritorious, are not directly related to fulfillment of overall organizational objectives.)

A VIEWPOINT ON STRATEGIC PLANNING

In analzying these various strategic decision elements, one can readily see how different perspectives might result in quite different approaches to planning. For instance, the organization which sees its mission to be predetermined and unchanging will plan differently from the one that views the world as a bundle of opportunities to be evaluated and exploited. An organization that is hierarchical and bureaucratic will probably involve people in the planning process in different ways from the one in which decisions are routinely made more participatively, such as might be the case in a research environment.

Thus, one cannot expound an all-inclusive viewpoint of planning. The way in which planning is done (indeed, the best variety of planning which can be done) depends very much on the specific organization, its structure and history, and on the nature of the people who make up the organization.

Although the planning viewpoint which is put forth here is not necessarily valid in all cases, it does reflect much of what has been learned by business and nonprofit organizations over the past several decades, and it has been implemented and positively evaluated in a variety of organizations. However, it should not be taken to be, and is not intended to be, the only correct viewpoint on planning.

To make this viewpoint explicit, a variety of planning premises will be stated. These premises, which represent the foundations of the remainder of the chapter, are not established truths, but they have been developed and tested in real-life situations to a degree that makes them worthy of serious consideration by any organization with a need and desire to do better strategic planning. These basic premises are as follows:

• Professional planners can facilitate a planning process, but they cannot themselves do the organization's planning.

• Planning activities should be performed by the managers who will ultimately be responsible for the implementation of the plans.

• Creative strategic planning is inherently a group activity, since it must involve many different subunits of the organization and many different varieties of expertise.

• A planning organization must be created to deal with the conception and development of strategic plans. This organization provides the climate and mechanism through which individuals at various levels are provided a greater opportunity to participate in determining the organization's future.

• Managers must be motivated to spend time on strategic planning through a formalized system and organization approach which also permits their contribution to the planning process to be assessed.

• The planning process must provide for the development of relevant data bases—qualitative as well as quantitative—which facilitate the evaluation of strategic alternatives.

• An evaluation of future environmental trends, competitive threats, and internal organizational strengths and weaknesses is essential to the strategic planning process.

• Evolving ideas of organization participants must be captured and incorporated into strategic decision making.

• The chief executive's responsibility for planning revolves around the development of a strategy culture in the organization, the final evaluation and selection of strategic alternatives, and the design of a master plan for implementation of the plan.

A STRATEGIC PLANNING SYSTEM (SPS)

The implementation of these premises requires that a strategic planning system (SPS) operate in the organization. The SPS to be described here operationalizes the planning premises with emphasis on effectively and efficiently addressing the strategic decision elements of the organization.

The SPS has a number of elements, or subsystems, which will be described. Every organization need not have all these SPS subsystems to plan effectively; just as with the strategic choice elements, an organization may consciously or unconsciously decide not to recognize the need for, or value of, one or more planning system components. However, taken together these elements form a comprehensive modern system to facilitate strategic planning.

The elements of an organizational strategic planning system are:

A system of plans.
A planning process.
A planning decision subsystem.
A planning information subsystem.
A facilitative planning organization.
A planning management system.

A System of Plans

The outputs of the planning process consist of a set of decisions concerning mission, strategy, objectives, and so on. These decisions are reflected in "the plan," or the documentary output of planning. However, for a sophisticated organization, the plan cannot be a simple entity. Rather, it is a system of interrelated and interdependent subplans which reflect the various dimensions of the environments being faced, the opportunities which exist, the relevant organizational clientele groups, and the interrelationships among these elements.

Figure 9–1 shows a schematic diagram of a system of plans. Much of the terminology used in that figure and the ensuing discussion is in product-market terms, which have been traditionally associated with business firms but which are increasingly being applied to public organizations (see Kotler, 1975).

Mission plan. The mission plan of the organization is at the summit of all the plans; it outlines the broad mission of the organization and the objectives and strategies that the organization wants to pursue. It includes the answers to such questions as:

- What are the broad missions and roles of the organization?
- What clientele is to be served?
- What are the values expected by each client group?
- How can our objectives serve to enhance these values?
- What general strategy is required to move from today's position to the position desired in the future?
- What strategic attributes of the organization are to be the foundations for its future development?
- What image does the organization want to portray in the greater system (social, economic, political) of which it is a part?
- What are the major guidelines under which other lower-level plans are to be formulated and general constraints that they must recognize?

Often, a mission plan will explicitly identify major client groups and their objectives. This permits the identification of organizational objectives, general strategies and policies which can contribute to the fulfillment of client expectations, and strategic organizational attributes. Figure

FIGURE 9-1. *The system of plans.*

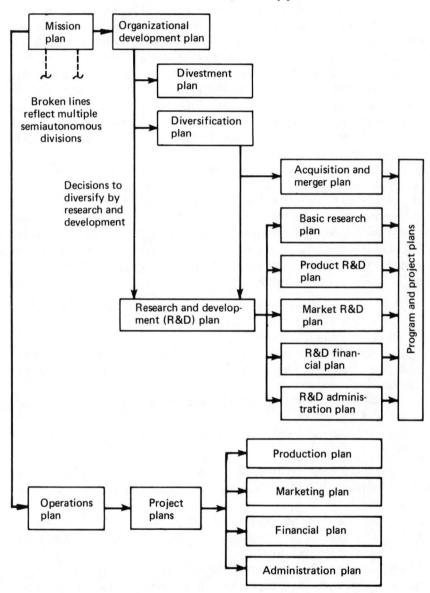

Source: Adapted from *A Framework for Business Planning,* Report No. 162 (Menlo Park, Cal.: Long-Range Planning Service, Stanford Research Institute, 1963).

9–2 shows how a business firm might delineate these relationships in its mission plan. At the top of the figure are various client groups which the firm has identified. The mission plan delineates organizational objectives, strategies, and strategic attributes which are to form the foundation for more detailed plans. Each of these illustrative elements is followed by a parenthetical code which identifies the client groups from which it primarily derives or the objective to which it relates. For instance, O_6, the elimination of vulnerability to the business cycle, is based principally on consideration of stockholder (S) and creditor (Cr) values and objectives. In turn, the diversification strategy is based on this objective as well as the one related to earnings (O_1).

The mission plan is important because it becomes a standard for deciding what direction the subsidiary plans in the organization should take.

Organizational development plan. The next echelon in the system of plans is the organizational development plan, which determines the activities necessary for a new generation of outputs. At the same time, the organizational development plan maps in greater detail the route toward the future position of the organization that has been specified by the mission plan. It deals with such questions as:

- What will the future environment consist of in terms of demand for our outputs and services? What will be expected of our organization in that future time period?
- What favorable conditions must be created within the organization in order that new outputs and new markets can be conceived and defined?
- What techniques will be used to screen out poor investments and high-risk ventures?
- What are the expected resources available for the new outputs or services?

The organizational development plan provides the guidance for the divestment plan, the diversification plan, and the research and development plan.

Divestment plan. This plan deals with the divestiture of major elements of the organization. These elements can consist of outputs, services, property, or organizational entities.

Diversification plan. This plan describes the development of new outputs, services, and markets to join or replace the current generation of outputs. It selects new opportunity areas and determines when entry should be made by acquisition of other organizations which possess required capabilities, by merger with another organization, or by conducting in-house research and development which builds in existing competence.

FIGURE 9–2. *The mission plan and its relationship to organizational clients.*

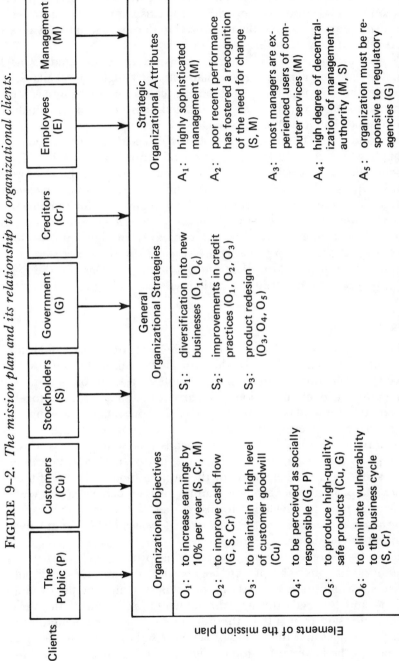

Research and development plan. This plan specifies actions oriented to the creation of new outputs or new clients for existing outputs and services. It is through this plan that the organization does research to advance or improve what it has to offer.

Program and project plans. Program plans are the basic building blocks of the system of plans. Program plans support higher-level plans; for example, the organizational development plan is supported by a complex of program plans which cover the detailed activities through which organizational change will be pursued.

Operations plan. The operations plan is directed toward the activities through which the current generation of outputs and services serves existing clients. Normally of one to two years' duration, the operations plan is supported by plans in each functional area. It is not an element of strategic planning, but is incorporated into Figure 9–1 for completeness.

Relationships among subplans in the system of plans. Figure 9–3 shows the system of plans in a slightly different context from Figure 9–1 in that it emphasizes the *relationships among the various different kinds of plans* in the overall system of plans, together with *typical time horizons* and the *specific foci of the various plans.* The organization reflected in Figure 9–3 is a school district.

A Planning Process

If a complex system of plans is to be effectively developed and utilized by an organization, it must be done in an organized fashion. A loose process for planning might well be feasible in a small organization, or even in one in which the various subplans can be simply stapled together to form the overall plan. However, one basic aspiration of planning is the achievement of synergy—that the whole plan be more than the sum of the component parts. This, in turn, means that some process must be developed for assessing the relationships, interactions, and interdependencies among the subelements of the organization and among the activities and programs of each. For planning to truly achieve synergy, some mechanism must be developed for using these assessments as a basis for *taking advantage of the interactions and interdependencies* which exist between organizational units and programs.

Figure 9–4 shows a substantive planning process such as is used in many organizations. The process begins with four varieties of inputs—forecasts, assumptions, strengths and weaknesses, and competitive information—and proceeds through the sequential selection of the various strategic decision elements to the development of implementation and control strategies and the taking of action based on the system of plans.

Although the boxes at the top of Figure 9–4 appear to describe infor-

FIGURE 9-3. *A system of plans for a school district.*

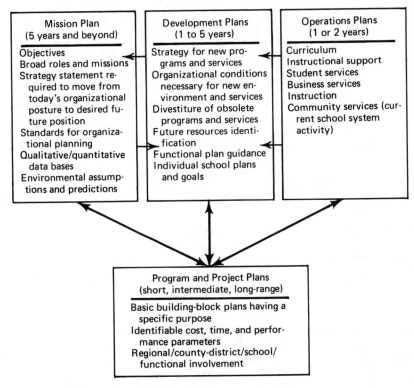

mational inputs rather than planning process elements, this is not the case. If a planning system is to be based on the underlying premises, these informational choices must themselves be an element of the overall planning process. Otherwise analysts, not managers, would be making important strategic choices.

These information elements are referred to as choices because any useful and manageable set of strategic information about such things as competition and organizational strengths and weaknesses must be chosen from the voluminous data which are potentially available on these topics. They must also be based on, but not limited to, the salient and strategic organizational attributes which have been identified in the mission plan. In a participative planning process, the evaluations of the vast quantities of data which form the raw input for the development of useful and manageable sets of input information may be performed by task forces, or teams of managers representing diverse interests within the organization. *In this way, the organization can be assured that the evaluation does not*

FIGURE 9-4. *The strategic planning process.*

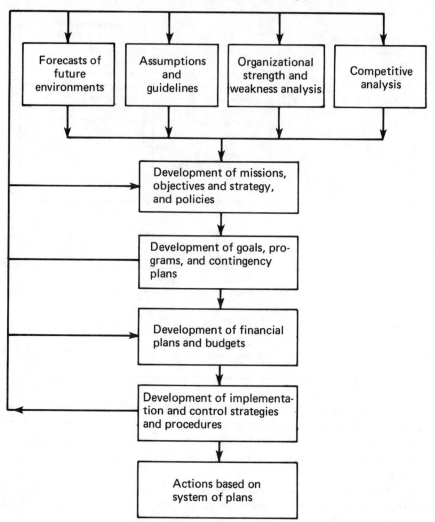

represent one narrow point of view, or only the parochial viewpoint of analysts.

These teams of managers, supported by staff, may be charged with arriving at conclusions concerning a specified number (usually from 10 to 15) of the most important factors affecting the future of the organization in a specified area. For instance, the development of conclusions on the 10 to 15 most important organizational strengths and weaknesses can be, as any experienced manager knows, a difficult task, when it involves managers representing various organizational interests and points of view. Developing a 20-page list of strengths and weaknesses could be accomplished relatively easily, but a list of the 10 to 15 most significant strengths and weaknesses involves analysis and negotiation. This is so both because of the judgments involved and the potential organizational impact which such a list can have through the strategic choice process.

It is useful to contrast this participative process for developing strategic inputs to the planning process with the one more commonly used to prepare the informational inputs to planning. This common approach relies on staff analysts, who gather data and prepare documents which are to serve as background information supporting planning activities and choices. Because the planners and analysts who perform these tasks often have neither the managerial expertise nor the authority to make the significant choices involved in any information evaluation process, the typical output of such an exercise is a document which seems to have been prepared on the basis of "not leaving anything out."

Such an emphasis on ensuring that nothing relevant is omitted rather than on attempting to distinguish the most relevant information from the mass of less relevant and the irrelevant serves only to perpetuate the existing state of affairs regarding the informational support provided to managers at all levels: the manager who is preparing plans is deluged with irrelevant information, while at the same time, he is unable to find elements of information which are crucial to his function. (For a full exposition, see Ackoff, 1967.)

Table 9–1 illustrates the kinds of strengths and weaknesses which a public agency might list from this stage of the planning process. The agency has preliminarily determined that its strengths revolve about its client contacts, data base, client service skills, technical skills in one area, and computer resources. Its weaknesses lie in areas of management systems and skills, two areas of technical expertise, and an inadequate compensation system. Since these strength-weakness assessments are the re-

TABLE 9–1. *Strengths and weaknesses of a public agency.*

Major Strengths	Major Weaknesses
Contacts with clients in special education sector.	Lack of personnel development system.
Computerized client data base.	Lack of technical skill in vocational education.
Administrative skills in client service.	Inadequate compensation to attract individuals with vocational education skills.
Technical skills in area of special education.	Inadequate R&D capability with respect to computer applications.
Computer hardware and systems.	Lack of planning skills and systems.

sult of data analysis and negotiation among the interested parties, they represent a foundation on which further strategic choices may be based. Most organizations should choose strategies which build on the strengths and avoid those whose success could be significantly affected by the weaknesses.

A major feature of Figure 9–4 is the series of feedback loops illustrating how tentative decisions are made at each step and fed into the choice process in the subsequent step. After each step in the process, the implications of the tentative choices to the prior steps are assessed. Thus a strategy may be tentatively chosen which requires that a particular organizational strength be reassessed to make it more specific, or an assumption may be called into question because of a strategy which appears to be promising but is inconsistent with a previously stated assumption. In this way, prior choices are continuously reviewed for validity and merit as the sequential planning process is executed.

A Planning Decision Subsystem

Planning intrinsically involves decision making, yet many organizations have attempted to institute formal planning without formally defining and specifying the decision mechanisms to be used. Some formal recognition must be given to the way in which decisions are made in the planning process. Those organizations which have failed to do this have established elaborate planning processes which degenerate into either unfocused discussion or exercises in filling out forms. In either case, the real decisions are made outside the process. In some cases this may mean that the agency executive or planners make the real choices. In others, these choices are made by default.

Some organizations, however, are required to use a formalized process for strategic decision making. Whether the process be PPB (planning, programming, and budgeting) (Macleod, 1971), zero-based budgeting (Stonich, 1977), or something else, the purpose of all such approaches is the same—making the decision processes involved in planning more objective and systematic and less arbitrary and subjective.

A Planning Information Subsystem

The incorporation of a decision subsystem into the planning system serves to emphasize the decision aspect of planning. It also requires that certain information be obtained and processed in a fashion which will contribute to better decisions.

Many planning failures have been caused by a lack of supportive information which is directly relevant to planning choices. Most of the information that has traditionally been processed by organizational information systems is internally oriented and related only to describing the past history of the organization. To be useful for strategic planning, such information must be prospective—it must be directed toward those environmental and competitive elements of the organization that will most critically affect its future.

Table 9–2 illustrates a variety of planning information subsystems, which are related to a basic four-step planning process—situation assessment, goal development, constraint identification, and strategy selection. Table 9–2 also shows a number of key sources of strategic information in the righthand column.

The middle column lists a number of information subsystems which may be developed to facilitate strategic planning. For example, the image subsystem, derived from data from clientele/groups, is based on the answers to the basic question, "What is our current situation?" This question implies more complexity than a statement of the organization's position or status in the usual terms. The usual objective data must be complemented with external data on how the organization is perceived among its clientele. Many organizations have been shown to have a biased and distorted understanding of how they are perceived by outsiders. Yet, such perceptions form the basis for the organization's future success, since it is its clientele who "pay the bills" either directly or indirectly. Surveys of

TABLE 9–2. *Information subsystems relating information sources to the planning process.*

Strategic Planning Process	Planning Information Subsystems	Strategic Information Sources
Situation assessment		
What is our current situation?	Image subsystem Customer subsystem	Clientele groups
Goal development		
What do we want our future situation to be?	Potential clientele subsystem Forecasting subsystem	Potential clientele groups External—technological, economic, and social
Constraint identification		
What constraints might inhibit us?	Competitive profile subsystem Regulatory subsystem	Competitive organizations Government
Selection of strategies		
What actions should we take to achieve our goals?	Cost-benefit subsystem	Other external sources

Source: Based on W. R. King and D. I. Cleland, "Environmental Information Systems for Strategic Marketing Planning," *Journal of Marketing,* October 1974, p. 31.

clientele image perceptions may be conducted on a routine basis and fed into the organization's information system. Such data permit the organization to establish image-related goals and to assess whether the goals are being achieved.

Other elements of Table 9–2 show other such subsystems which may be established to support planning. A customer subsystem deals with more traditional data on how well the organization is doing—that is, data for program evaluation. The potential clientele subsystem recognizes the need to have data on client groups which are not currently served, in order to provide opportunities for growth and expansion.

The forecasting subsystem uses data from external sources to make forecasts of the future environment. The competitive profile subsystem maintains data on competitive organizations, their strengths, weaknesses, and capabilities. The regulatory subsystem maintains records of government regulations and rulings which constrain future actions. The cost-benefit subsystem is the interface with the decision subsystem in that it maintains the cost-benefit data which may be used in planning decision models.

Just as with other SPS subsystems, the information subsystem actually required by a particular organization may not be as sophisticated or extensive as is implied in Table 9–2. However, this presentation serves to demonstrate the nature and potential utility of planning information support systems.

A Facilitative Planning Organization

There are a variety of well-known planning-related organizational concepts. Among these are:

- A strong central planning staff that develops long-range strategies.
- A central planning staff that facilitates long-range planning by providing supporting services to operating organizational elements which are engaged in planning.
- The decentralization of long-range planning responsibilities to "profit center" executives responsible for carrying out the long-range plans.

In order to operationalize basic premises, the planning organization must be innovative and must facilitate, rather than inhibit, strategic planning. The concept of a planning organization is itself not well understood in any context other than that of a professional planning staff. Many organizations operate as though strategic planning were simply another aspect of the manager's job, or alternately, as though only top management and professional planners should have anything of substance to do with strategic planning for the overall organization. These two concepts, either alone or in combination, presume that strategic planning should be done within the framework of the existing traditional bureaucratic organization.

Modern organizations are much too complex for either of these simplistic approaches. If the organization is to be opportunistic, to adapt to change, and to influence the future—all the things that planners constantly promise as the benefits of comprehensive organizational strategic planning—it must not be bound to either the practices or the organizational structures of the past.

Innovative ideas, the harbingers of the organization's future, may be lost in the bureaucratic milieu. If, for instance, new services and markets are to be developed that are not simply extensions of existing ones, effective ways of generating ideas, evaluating those ideas, and developing them to fruition must be found. To achieve these goals, the planning effort must be supported with the skills and knowledge that exist in the organization at all levels and in all subunits. In most organizations, good ideas are lost between the cracks of interfacing subunits. The goal of a strategic planning system should be to convert those ideas into organizational assets to be used in the creation of the organizations' future.

According to the concept of planning organization, the overall organization is made up two (or more) parallel organizations, represented by the charts in Figure 9–5. There, the two organizations are in parallel and the *same people play different roles in each*. Thus the cross in Figure 9–5 represents an individual filling one slot on the operating organizational chart and another slot on the planning organizational chart. He or she may, within one day, move back and forth several times between the two jobs in the two parallel suborganizations which make up the overall organization. In this way—through parallel organizations—the operating and planning goals and activities can be separated to some degree and each may be dealt with effectively and efficiently.

The Planning Management Subsystem

Strategic planning does not just happen; it must be motivated. An important aspect of motivation is the attitude that managers create and the climate that exists in the organization. Since it is people who perform the planning functions, the strategic planning process must itself be structured and managed.

Just as the planning process described earlier dictates that a strategy for the implementation *of plans* be developed, so too is a strategy for the implementation *of planning* required if strategic planning is to be newly introduced or radically changed in an organization. Thus planning must itself be planned for and managed.

FIGURE 9-5. *Parallel organizations within a single organization.*

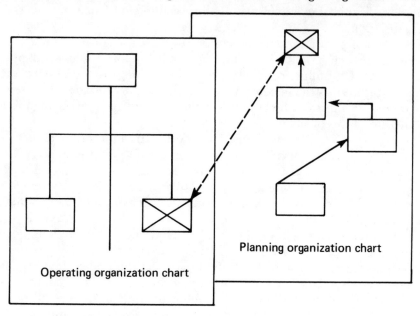

Operating organization chart

Planning organization chart

This seeming play on words is, in fact, most crucial to successful planning. Planning is a major time- and resource-consuming organizational
activity. As such, it will degenerate if it is not perceived as being important,
if people are not positively motivated toward it, and if it is not carefully
managed in the same way that other organizational activities are managed.

Part of this management of planning involves giving attention to the
organizational climate necessary for creative planning. An effective way
of enhancing the climate for such planning is to encourage widespread
participation at all levels. Individuals can be encouraged to submit their
own planning ideas in terms of program modifications, new programs,
new organizational arrangements, new strategy for the organization, and
so forth. Such ideas should have enough justification and documentation
to enable the planning staff to make an initial appraisal to see if each idea
is worthy of further investigation.

In creating a suitable climate for strategic planning, the role of top
management is critical:

Top managers must be change seekers. Their leadership role is to provide a climate for rapid improvement toward excellence. The success their business achieves in the future will be in geometric proportion to their understanding of, planning for, dedication to, personal involvement in, and self-motivation toward the implementation of purposeful change. For many companies this demands a reorientation in the thinking of senior executives. It means honest commitment to a new concept. Insincerity or lip service will soon destroy confidence. (Irwin and Langham, 1966).

Of course, the only truly effective way of creating a proper climate for strategic planning is to permeate the organization with planning, to demonstrate that it works, and to make use of it. When this pragmatic test of results has been passed, skeptics will be stilled and the organizational climate will be ripe for the institution of sophisticated strategic planning.

SUMMARY

Planning is an activity that may be rather easy to order into being in a not-for-profit organization; however, it is difficult to make effective. The establishment of a planning unit and the appurtenances of planning can be accomplished with the stroke of a pen and the allocation of funds. However, for planning to have significant impact on the strategic choices which are made, it must become a part of the organizational culture.

The planning premises enunciated in this chapter form the basis for such a process of culture development. When they are implemented through a strategic planning system (SPS), the processes and systems can become an established part of the organization. Taken together, this planning philosophy and system provide the framework around which planning may be instituted, perpetuated, and made to aid the organization in facing the uncertain future.

REFERENCES

Ackoff, R. L. "Management Misinformation Systems," *Management Science*, December 1967, pp. B147–B156.

Branch, M. C. *The Corporate Planning Process* (New York: American Management Association, 1962).

Brewer, Garry D. *Politicians, Bureaucrats, and the Consultant* (New York: Basic Books, 1973).

Briggs, B. B., et al. *The Politics of Planning* (San Francisco: Institute for Contemporary Studies, 1976).

Burton, R., D. Dellinger, and William R. King. "Alternative Strategies for Legislative Analysis of Public Policy," *Urban Systems*, Vol. 3 (1978), pp. 9–20.

Ghymn, K. I., and William R. King. "Design of a Strategic Planning Management Information System," *OMEGA*, October 1976, pp. 595–607.

Greensberger, M., M. A. Crenson, and B. L. Crissey. *Models in the Policy Process* (New York: Russell Sage Foundation, 1976).

Hoos, I. R. *Systems Analysis in Public Policy: A Critique* (Berkeley: University of California Press, 1972).

Irwin, P. M., and F. W. Langham, Jr. "The Change Seekers," *Harvard Business Review*, January–February 1966, p. 83.

King, William R., and D. I. Cleland. "Information for More Effective Strategic Planning," *Long-Range Planning*, February 1977, pp. 59–64.

King, William R., "Achieving America's Goals: National Service or the All-Volunteer Armed Force?" Washington, D.C.: U.S. Senate Committee on Armed Services, U.S. Government Printing Office, February 1977.

King, William R., and David I. Cleland. *Strategic Planning and Policy* (New York: Van Nostrand Reinhold, 1978).

Kotler, P. *Marketing for Nonprofit Organizations* (Englewood Cliffs, N.J.: Prentice-Hall, 1975).

Macleod, R. K. "Program Budgeting Works in Nonprofit Institutions," *Harvard Business Review*, September 1971, pp. 45–56.

Mitroff, I. I., and L. R. Pondy. "On the Organization of Inquiry: A Comparison of Some Radically Different Approaches to Policy Analysis," *Public Administration Review*, Vol. 34 (1974).

Niskanen, W. A., Jr. *Bureaucracy and Representative Government* (Chicago: Aldine-Atherton, 1971).

Rivlin, A. M. *Systematic Thinking for Social Action* (Washington, D.C.: Brookings Institution, 1971).

Rodriguez, J. I., and William R. King. "Competitive Information Systems," *Long-Range Planning*, Vol. 10 (1978), pp. 45–50.

Stonich, P. J. *Zero-Base Planning and Budgeting* (Homewood, Ill.: Dow Jones-Irwin, 1977).

Williams, W. *Social Policy Research and Analysis: The Experiences in the Federal Social Agencies* (New York: Elsevier, 1975).

Wrapp, H. E. "Good Managers Don't Make Policy Decisions," *Harvard Business Review*, September–October 1967, pp. 91–99.

CHAPTER 10

Marketing Management

Rohit Deshpande

Editor's Note   *Changing demand, increasingly scarce funding, and increased competition are some of the major problems that nonprofit organizations are facing today. For these and other reasons it is important to the survival of a nonprofit organization that it interact with its environment as effectively as possible. Hence, managers in the nonprofit sector must understand the fundamental principles of marketing which are especially appropriate for interacting with various groups in the environment. This chapter introduces several marketing management concepts and their relevance to the nonprofit organization. Marketing management is defined as the process of planning, organizing, staffing, and controlling programs concerning the exchange of valued products and services between individuals (or groups of individuals) and the organization to satisfy organizational goals.*

The author suggests that the very first marketing task is to learn the needs of the client or target audience. This may involve the segmentation or subdivision of the client audience into homogeneous subsets of customers, so that selected program offerings can be made to each subset. The more precise the segmentation, the more specific the program offerings can be, and the more satisfied clients will be.

Having selected a target audience, the manager has to design the marketing program by manipulating the marketing mix or the four P's—product, price, promotion, and placement. The product or service design can be carried out by allowing the target community to design the product/service to suit its need, by designing the product or service within the organization according to the perceived needs of the community, or by a combination of both methods.

A nonprofit service can be classified as a tangible, a core, or an augmented service. A tangible service is what is being offered, a core service is the essential utility being exchanged, and the augmented service is the entire bundle of costs and benefits the individual receives. Other important concepts for the manager to

363

know are the service life cycle and the process of diffusion of innovations. A manager may adopt any one of the following strategies for his or her product or service. A service addition strategy involves broadening the line of services offered to get increased patronage from existing publics or to attract new ones. A service modification strategy involves tangible changes in service quality features, styling, brand name, or packaging. A service elimination strategy involves a decision by program management to drop current services that do not contribute to organizational objectives.

The author describes nine types of pricing policies which may be used in making decisions for nonprofit organizations. They are cost recovery pricing, penetration pricing, no-fare pricing, demarketing pricing, profit maximization, price stabilization, cost-plus pricing, variable pricing, and discriminatory pricing. Price elasticity of demand is also an important concept for the manager to be aware of.

Promotion includes advertising, personal selling, sales promotion, and publicity. Advertising is any paid form of nonpersonal presentation and promotion of ideas or services by an identified sponsor. In the preparation of an advertising campaign, a manager has to set advertising objectives and budgets, determine creative strategy, choose media, and conduct effectiveness measurements. Personal selling is an oral presentation in a conversation with one or more prospective purchasers for the purpose of making sales. Sales promotion includes activities like displays, shows, exhibitions, and demonstrations that stimulate purchase behavior. Publicity which produces a nonpersonal demand stimulation for a service involves planting commercially significant news in communication media; such publicity is not paid for by the sponsor. Placement or distribution involves selection of distribution channels to effectively and efficiently distribute the product or service within given cost constraints.

This chapter also discusses the concept of a marketing audit, which is an independent examination of the entire marketing effort of an organization in order to evaluate what is being done and to plan for the future. The audit is designed to help the organization manage its environment rather than simply react to it.

The core of the marketing process is concerned with exchange. Any two individuals or groups of individuals who possess items of value to each other may or may not be interested in exchanging those items for something of equivalent or greater value. These individuals can then be said to have the necessary potential for exchange. The transaction itself (if it occurs) may involve products such as pharmaceutical drugs and family planning devices, or services such as home repair and health education. In return for these products and services, the exchange process may involve either money or a variety of products and services considered to be of equivalent or greater value.

Yet marketing has been traditionally misconceived to be the same as advertising or selling. In newspaper reports or television discussions, the professional marketer is seen as someone who knows a better way to get a consumer to purchase household appliances or automobiles. However, marketing involves much more than these functions of advertising and selling.

A professional marketer is not necessarily the advertiser or manufacturer of consumer products, but rather the person who is "very good at understanding, planning, and managing exchanges" (Kotler, 1975, p. 5). The process of marketing can therefore be defined as *the planning, organization, staffing, and control of programs to achieve the exchange between individuals or groups of individuals of valued products and services.*

Let us look at this definition a little more closely. Since it refers to products and services of value to individuals, it goes beyond the conventional marketing perspective of consumer products such as household commodities or even industrial goods such as telecommunication systems. This definition is equally concerned with the marketing of education, of nutrition, or of drug abuse programs. Moreover, since the definition includes program planning, organizing, staffing, and control over a plethora of activities, marketing is considerably more than a selling or advertising function.

A further requirement of our definition of marketing calls for a goal-oriented activity, and it is at this point that marketing management can be considered. When an organization plans a marketing program, it generally wishes to achieve certain prespecified objectives, such as increased literacy, greater energy conservation, or higher profitability. Marketing management, therefore, is the planning, organization, staffing, and control of programs concerning the exchange between individuals or groups of individuals of valued products and services so as to achieve organizational objectives.

THE MARKETING CONCEPT

Marketing is generally viewed as having to do with selling or promotion. There are good reasons for this. Historically, the exchange of goods and services occurred in economies having few producers and several buyers. Since the demand far exceeded the supply, in these situations marketing

professionals were more concerned with what is called a product or operational orientation. They believed that if a product was designed well,
it would, in effect, sell itself.

This picture changed dramatically with economic growth and increasing competition. Several very similar products were produced for the
same target markets of consumers. Clearly, a change in strategy was
required, and organizations moved from a product to a selling orientation,
which involved going out and attempting to find customers, who were
now in short supply (since they had a variety of equivalent products to
choose from). More salespeople were recruited by organizations, and
increasing amounts of money were spent on the use of mass media
advertising.

Recently, however, the selling orientation has given way to one that can
truly be called marketing. It embodies the marketing concept in that it
is concerned primarily with *the satisfaction of customer needs*. The customer
or client therefore becomes the focus of all program planning, and various
methods of determining what the client markets are, what their individual
needs are, and how best these needs can be serviced by the organization
constitute the tasks of today's marketing professionals.

Naturally, organizations differ in the extent to which they subscribe to
the marketing concept. Various consumer goods industries, for example,
have moved farther ahead than industrial product manufacturers in their
orientation to user need. However, the difference is most strongly marked
in the case of nonprofit organizations. The majority of organizations in
the health care, educational, and social action fields operate from a product or operational orientation. A few have realized the extent of available
competitive services and their demands for equal attention and funding
and have moved to selling orientations. Extremely few, unfortunately,
embody a real marketing concept.

THE NEED FOR MARKETING MANAGEMENT

Is there really a need for marketing management in the nonprofit
sector? And what can marketing do to help better achieve the objectives
of nonprofit organizations? To answer these questions, we need first of
all to consider some of the past objections to incorporating a marketing
orientation. These stem basically from an emphasis on the differences
rather than the similarities between for-profit and not-for-profit organizations (see Lovelock and Weinberg, 1978).

The first of these dissimilarities concerns the differentiation between
resource attraction and resource allocation in nonprofit institutions. Unlike for-profit firms whose customers pay money for products or services

received, the nonprofit organization has dealings with multiple publics, such as donors or funding agencies and target audiences or client communities. Frequently these are two quite different sets of people or organizations. Therefore, it has been claimed, what may be a reasonably easy job in developing marketing plans for consumers becomes much more complicated and even qualitatively different when attempting to market to diverse publics.

This difference, however, is an oversimplification. Besides being concerned with the needs of the consumers who buy their marketed products, for-profit firms are also involved in the social system with shareholders, with governmental regulatory agencies, with competitors, with state and federal government lawmakers, and with environmental protection groups, to name a few. All these groups have their own sets of needs that must be determined and satisfied. No corporate entity can survive in total disregard of other members of the social system. Figure 10–1 indicates the similarity rather than the difference between for-profit and not-for-profit organizations with regard to multiple publics.

Another cited difference between for-profit and nonprofit organizations is that the former are concerned primarily with the distribution of physical goods while the latter are more concerned with the distribution of services. It is indeed true that the marketing of tangible commodities such as grocery produce or automobiles has taken up a lot of professional attention over the past several years. Yet for-profit marketers are as concerned with the distribution of entertainment services (such as the movie industry), remedial services (for example, home and automobile repair), telecommunication services (data processing equipment maintenance), and leisure services (vacation flights or cruises). Clearly, once again, there are several similarities between the service industries in for-profit and nonprofit organizations that can provide for an effective interchange of bodies of knowledge that have been developed in one or the other of them.

A final distinction lies in the very terms "for-profit" and "nonprofit." It is claimed that since corporate firms are interested in marketing their products or services at reasonable returns on investment and since nonprofit organizations frequently operate on deficits, the financial objectives of the two sets of organizations are markedly different. This is certainly true in that a business firm that operates continually at a loss would soon go out of business altogether or at the very least be acquired by another corporate entity that hopes to turn the red ink into black on the income statement. Yet even acknowledging this difference, we can go back to the definitions of marketing and marketing management considered in the light of the marketing concept and see that there is an overarching sim-

FIGURE 10-1. *Multiple publics in for-profit and nonprofit organizations.*

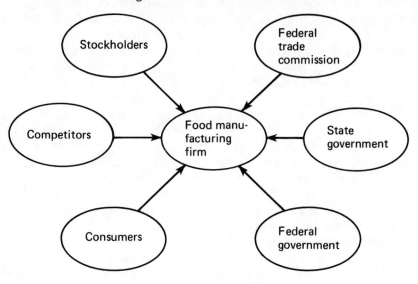

(a) For-profit organization

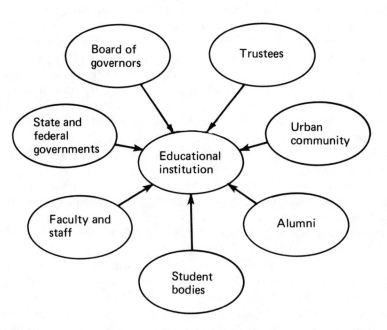

(b) Nonprofit organization

ilarity in the two types of institutions. As mentioned earlier, the marketing concept is concerned with increased customer satisfaction. If profitability were the sole consideration, business firms would get into new markets, charge as high prices as possible for their products, and produce those products at substandard quality. It is obvious that this can only be a short-term phenomenon. Both growing competition and consumer disapproval would combine to force such firms to either declare bankruptcy or else completely revamp their strategies. The important point here is that for-profit organizations like their nonprofit counterparts are interested in continued customer goodwill. This goodwill brings customers back with repeated demands for offered products and services and in the long term will perpetuate the organizations' programs.

It can be seen, therefore, that both for-profit and nonprofit organizations have similar interests in terms of multiple publics, service distribution orientations, and the maintenance of long-run client goodwill through effective need satisfaction. Individuals in both groups of organizations can capitalize on the available concepts, theories, and techniques that marketing has to offer.

We began this section with two questions. The obvious similarities in overall objectives, that is, those dealing with the satisfaction of customer or client needs, led us to conclude that nonprofit organizations can gain from a marketing concept orientation. But what are the gains that can accrue? And how best can they be achieved? A discussion of these issues takes us into the realm of the marketing management function.

THE FUNCTION OF MARKETING MANAGEMENT

Let us begin by restating the definition of marketing management as the planning, organization, staffing, and control of programs concerning the exchange between individuals or groups of individuals of valued products and services so as to achieve organizational objectives. The starting point for a manager of any profit or nonprofit organization is to *prepare a marketing plan*. This plan is a statement of the program objectives (clarified in as much detail as possible) together with an outline of how these objectives can be achieved with a given budget over a stipulated period of time. Generally, marketing plans are prepared annually with quarterly reviews for amendments and revisions.

To facilitate understanding of a nonprofit organization's marketing function, we will use a specific example, that of a health education resources center. Let us assume for the sake of illustration that the health education organization (HEO) wishes to institute an antismoking program. If the HEO is strongly oriented toward the marketing concept, it will first determine whether a felt need exists among the intended audience for information about the dangers of cigarette smoking. It is interesting to note here that if the HEO were product-oriented, it would automatically assume that such a need *did* exist and that all it had to do was promulgate information on the issue and the problems would be taken care of. There have been several cases in the public health education area of programs searching for people who need them; many such programs have been unsuccessful (Sutherland, 1972, p. 84). Rather than designing a complete program at the outset, it is necessary to *investigate what the needs of the target audience are*. Then a program can be designed. (It is assumed, for the moment, that program planners know-exactly who their target audience is. Obviously, in order to specify what program objectives are going to be for a forthcoming year, and given the fact that these objectives must have some specificity, a program manager should know for whom the program will be primarily designed.)

Who are the people that the HEO might be interested in educating about the dangers of cigarette smoking—adults, teenagers, nonsmokers, smokers, heavy/medium/light smokers, or some combination of these groups? Assume that our particular program manager is interested in teenagers (both smokers and nonsmokers) as the target audience. Having made this decision, it is still premature to attempt to specify program objectives, because any large group of people is invariably composed of smaller subsets who think, act, and behave differently. Any marketing program that approaches these subgroups with a uniform set of promotional or selling appeals is wasting a lot of money and energy. It is necessary to define how many subgroups exist and what their differentiated needs are, that is, *the program manager should segment the target audience into its component subgroups based on their individual characteristics and needs*.

MARKET SEGMENTATION

"Market segmentation" has been formally defined as "the subdivision of a market into homogeneous subsets of customers, where any subset may conceivably be selected as a market target to be reached" (Kotler, 1975, p. 166). In our HEO example, it is possible to consider segmentation in a variety of ways, as shown in Figure 10–2. The first segmentation variable—attitudes toward cigarette smoking (Figure 10–2a)—would indicate the number of teenagers in each subgroup. The HEO program manager would then be in a position to indicate (in a statement of program objectives) not only how large the groups to be educated were at the

FIGURE 10-2. *Segmentation of teenage market by attitude toward cigarette smoking, geographic location, and formal education.*

	Indifferent	Hardcore
Smokers		
Nonsmokers		

(*a*) Attitude toward cigarette smoking

	Urban	Rural
Smokers		
Nonsmokers		

(*b*) Geographic location

	No School	School Dropouts	High School
Smokers			
Nonsmokers			

(*c*) Formal education

outset, but also what proportion of these groups would be reached over a given time period with program literature and educational campaigns. He would be able to set targets and to allow for a greater degree of specificity in the marketing plan.

Figures 10–2*b* and 10–2*c* indicate other ways of segmenting target audiences on the basis of demographic characteristics. The marketing manager may have reason to believe that a rural/urban dichotomy or a formal education segmentation would prove useful. Again, program objectives could be specified more precisely in these terms. Segmentation could also be carried out using a variety of such variables in combination to describe the total target audience. In the health area, Henrik Blum has suggested a typology of "communities" that can be used for segmenting clients of health education program offerings. This typology is reproduced in Figure 10–3. With slight modifications it could be used in any nonprofit organization setting, and it amply illustrates our earlier discussion on multiple publics.

Another method of segmentation is offered in the idealized scheme suggested by Julian Simon for the birth control market (see Figure 10–4). This looks at both the target audiences that do and do not want to regulate their fertility, as well as at the types of methods that can be used for regulation.

It is clear that *the more precise the segmentation, the more specific program offerings can be.* Behavior patterns of particular subgroups may be so different that further program focus (in following marketing plan years) can be accordingly directed at them. A study of the nonuse of automobile safety belts, for example, found that the greatest nonusage was associated with females and among persons with less than high school education or low income (Helsing and Comstock, 1977). Obviously, the needs of such groups are different from those having other socioeconomic and demographic characteristics.

FIGURE 10-3. *Community segmentation in planning for health.*

Source: Adapted from Henrik L. Blum, *Planning for Health: Development and Application of Social Change Theory* (New York: Human Sciences Press, 1974), pp. 496–507.

A final point in regard to market segmentation is that the program manager should attempt to *forecast the emergence of client groups which do not presently exist.* This can be shown in our HEO example by the pre-teenager cohort which would perhaps become a potential target audience for the educational program if the program was maintained over several years. It becomes important to know which new client segments will become part of the target audience, and also, which old segments will leave the audience (Bauer, 1974, p. 25).

THE MARKETING MIX

Having considered the specific target audiences to which a program can be directed, the program manager decides on how best to design the program itself. This decision is made on the basis of the manipulation of different marketing variables. The set of these variables is commonly

FIGURE 10-4. *An idealized scheme of birth control market segmentation.*

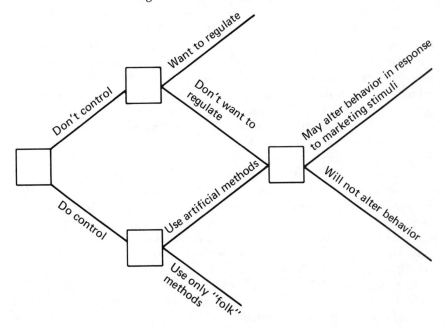

Source: Julian L. Simon, "Strategy and Segmentation of the Birth Control Market: This Side of Family Planning," in Michael McMillan, ed., *Using Commercial Resources in Family Planning Communication Programs* (Honolulu, Hawaii: East-West Communication Institute, East-West Center, May 1973), p. 35.

referred to as the "marketing mix" and is conventionally summarized in terms of four P's—product, price, promotion, and placement (McCarthy, 1964, pp. 38–49). In for-profit marketing organizations, each of these P's involves a multitude of managerial decisions that frequently require specialized professional attention. The appropriate combination of all the marketing mix variables forms the body of the marketing plan. We shall discuss each variable in the context of nonprofit organizations and then indicate how a policy orientation can be utilized to put them together. In this discussion, illustrations will be chosen from several nonprofit areas both to demonstrate the extensive applicability of marketing concepts and to provide guidelines for particular organizational contexts.

The Product or Service

Decisions regarding what the program offerings will be compose the "product" or "service" issues in the marketing plan. These decisions have their bases in the needs expressed by various segments of the target community. Three main approaches can be used in product or service design—to allow the target community to design their own products or services according to their needs; to design the product or service in the nonprofit organization according to the felt needs of the target community; and to design the product or service by a combination of the above two methods. Let us consider each of these approaches using illustrative organizational contexts.

The formation of day care centers provides an example of a service that was designed by a community in response to its own needs. Since working mothers who had infant children required some means of having them taken care of during the working week, the concept of a day care center came into existence, frequently with the assistance of church-support organizations. These support groups would recruit the assistance of mothers on welfare to provide some of the daytime help. In addition, women who worked on part-time jobs would contribute some of their nonwork hours to the day care center. In this manner, the needs of the community were satisfied by community members themselves.

Another approach to product or service design is for a nonprofit organization to provide the service according to the needs expressed by the target community. Examples are provided in several developing countries where funding is provided by multilateral lending institutions such as the International Bank for Reconstruction and Development. A country may require technical know-how and funds to construct an irrigation project, and these would be provided by the multilateral institution after the project had been appraised for its feasibility.

A third type of service design, which combines the above two approaches, is based largely on the fact that a target community frequently wishes to modify or adapt a service according to its own specific needs. In cases such as these, the service is primarily provided in a somewhat rough or unstructured form and then client community members are allowed to modify it as they wish (Agarwala-Rogers, 1976). An illustration of this approach is the satellite-based educational experiments being conducted in third world countries. Villages equipped with community television sets are beamed educational programs concerning agricultural innovations, health improvement methods, welfare reforms, and so on. Repeated survey research gathers information on exactly what the village populations want in program content. This information is then fed back to the programming centers to modify further programs according to target audience needs.

The major point behind each of these three approaches is that *the program manager should base product or service design on the needs of the target community rather than only on what the nonprofit organization wishes to provide.* This leads to a set of extremely important guidelines which are based on the fact that *no high degree of precision in determining client needs can result without a continued and intensive association with the client community.* As Hessler and Walters (1974, pp. 4–5) comment about the health area, "The effectiveness of services and the degree to which services are consonant with the expectations and needs of consumers depend in part on the relationship between consumers and providers. In order for this relationship to be meaningful, there must be continuity in the sense of a routinized process of provider-consumer exchange."

In making product or service design decisions, it is frequently useful to think in terms of the product concept components suggested by Kotler (1975, pp. 164–166). A nonprofit service can be conceptualized as the tangible service, the core service, and the augmented service. The *tangible service* is what is actually offered to the target market. A government income tax advisory service, for example, can be looked at in terms of its quality level (the degree of competence of the tax advisers), its features (being free to taxpayers but requiring more time to supply service than for-profit competitive tax advisory services), its styling (brevity, cursoriness, impersonality), its brand name (the "federal income tax advisory service"), and its packaging (branch offices located at various points in different cities).

Next, the *core service* is the essential utility that is being exchanged. In the case of the tax advisory service this could be the freedom from later aggravation or worry in paying taxes coupled with the security of knowing exactly what one's income tax position is as far as government assessment is concerned.

The *augmented service* is the entire bundle of costs and benefits that an individual receives when the service is obtained. This includes not only the above two components but also the time, energy, and money expended in traveling to and from the branch office of the tax advisor, the opportunity costs or benefits of not taking the tax problem to a private consultant, and so on.

Thinking about a product or service in this manner can be helpful in two ways to the marketing manager in a nonprofit organization. First, it provides a total perspective of what an offered product or service is composed of (and thus avoids the myopia associated with looking only at the tangible or core service), and second, it provides a way of thinking about how the *client* perceives the product or service. This last point is very important. Several marketing mistakes have been made because management would not empathize with how consumers saw their product offerings. To the manufacturer or product designer, a product is always "optimal." To the consumer, however, it may be totally inappropriate.

This brings us to the concept of product or service differentiation. *In an increasingly competitive marketplace, it is essential to differentiate a program or service from all other programs or services being offered to the target audience.* This involves building into the product or service a unique selling proposition. We shall come back to this concept in the section on the promotion variable, but it can be said here that however vital a nonprofit organization may think its programs to be, if consumers think that there are several equally worthy causes which offer either similar or superior programs, then they will be partly indifferent to the organization concerned. The nonprofit institution, therefore, needs to design its product or service to be as different as possible from the available competitive services. Once again, this is best done when the service design is based on an accurate reading of client audience needs—perhaps even with client involvement in the design process itself. This makes for ensured commitment to later program offerings.

In the context of product design amidst competition, it is relevant to note that every service has a certain history. The life of the service involves four different phases which are referred to as the introduction, growth, maturity, and decline stages of the service life cycle. The concept of the *service life cycle* is illustrated in Figure 10–5. A new service that has recently been introduced into the market will have a quick upsurge in growth as more and more people become aware of and subscribe to it. After a certain time period (which will vary according to the type of service, its distribution, location, the amount of competition, federal and state government interest and funding, and so on) the growth of the service will begin to stabilize, plateau, and finally decline. Program managers should

FIGURE 10-5. *Stages in the service life cycle.*

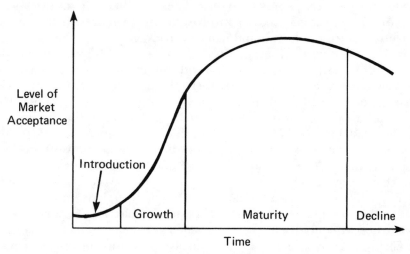

be aware of the fact that some services in their decline stage can be extended into further growth by modifications of the basic program. A case in point is the decision by health service programmers in California to cater not just to people who are sick or unhealthy, but also to those who are healthy and wish to maintain their level of health. This decision requires program amendments that will contribute to an extended growth in the service life cycle.

This takes us into the realm of the three chief product or service strategy decisions: addition, modification, and elimination.

A *service addition strategy* involves broadening the line of services offered so as to increase patronage from existing publics and to attract new ones. Examples are provided in the field of art by museums which are seeking to appeal to a wider audience (Ricklefs, 1975). For example, New York's Metropolitan Museum offers cookbooks with medieval recipes based on the fourteenth-century epicurean tastes of royalty. The museum even offers to supply by mail the necessary ingredients (herbs and spices) that may be unavailable at local supermarkets. California's Oakland Museum organizes annual festivals celebrating the ethnic heritage of Chinese, Mexicans, Africans, and Greeks, among others, and attracts at each festival 30,000 to 50,000 visitors—some of whom have never been in the museum before. The Art Institute of Chicago has doubled the size of its museum store in five years and stocks items such as antique English paper weights and decorative Philippine baskets. Both the National Gallery in Washington, D.C. and the Metropolitan in New York have developed special programs for preschoolers. They attract children as young as two and a half (who frequently have their parents build up an interest too).

A *service modification strategy* involves tangible changes in the service quality, features, styling, brand name, or packaging. This strategy is similar to that of suiting program offerings to client needs by modifying the product or service. In order to deal with community social problems on a preventive rather than a crisis basis, the Simi Valley, California city management opted for a community Safety Agency in 1972 rather than the traditional police force (Altman, 1977, pp. 190–193). Since 88 percent of the 62,500 residents were less than thirty-five years of age, the safety agency recruited supervisors, youth coordinators, and safety officers having a minimum of two years of college and an average of six years of police experience. The "young professional" image was also enhanced by having firearms concealed in pockets of specially designed green blazers rather than ostentatiously displayed in external holsters. The "new image" police department idea has been evaluated as being extremely successful.

Finally, a *service elimination strategy* involves a decision by program management to drop current products or services that do not contribute to organizational objectives. This was a decision made recently by New York University when it discontinued its School of Social Work after cost-cutting measures were necessitated by a $5 million annual deficit (Kotler, 1975, pp. 173–174).

All three of the above service strategy decisions relate to existent program offerings of products and services. The development of entirely new programs entails a different outlook. New product decisions in marketing are aided by a body of theory that has come to be called the diffusion of innovations. In this theory, an innovation is defined as any idea, practice, or object that is perceived as new by an individual or group of individuals (Rogers and Shoemaker, 1971, p. 19). Diffusion refers to the process by which an innovation spreads through a particular social system.

Diffusion of innovations theory studies how individuals or groups of individuals adopt new ideas and products, that is, the mental process through which individuals pass from first hearing about the innovation to the point of acquiring and using it (Rogers, 1962). The study of this mental process has revealed four distinct categories of adopters. They have been called the early adopters, the early majority, the late majority, and the laggards. Figure 10–6 illustrates adopter categories on the basis of their relative adoption times. Studies in rural sociology and later in marketing have shown that on this basis, innovators form about 2.5 percent of the social system, the early adopters around 13.5 percent, the

FIGURE 10-6. *Categories of adopters of innovations.*

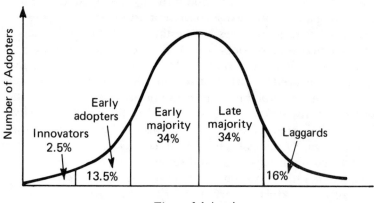

Time of Adoption

Source: Based on Everett M. Rogers, *Diffusion of Innovations* (New York: Free Press, 1962), p. 162.

early majority about 34 percent, the late majority approximately 34 percent, and the laggards about 16 percent.

Further research indicates certain characteristics associated with different adopter categories. *Innovators* are venturesome, like to try new ideas, and are cosmopolite in outlook. *Early adopters* exhibit a dominant characteristic of being respected by other social system members for their standing in the community. The *early majority* are deliberate and like trying new ideas although not before other people. The *late majority* and *laggards* are skeptical and traditional, respectively, and are generally suspicious of change and modernity. Although these are initial research findings, they show the interesting divisions in the social system based on reactions to new ideas and products. Further work has been done in several contexts to investigate how particular adopter groups behave in different marketplace and social situations (Rogers, 1973).

When a new product or service is being marketed, it becomes important to test its potential viability. Two main modes of testing this product or service viability are *concept testing* and the *test market.* The former will be discussed in detail in a later section. The test market refers to a kind of dry run of a program's offerings, testing them in a small-scale situation that is considered representative of the target audience. Family planners wishing to research the rate of adoption of a contraceptive device may wish, for example, to distribute it in a limited geographical area before going national. A survey of adopters and nonadopters over a time period may then reveal whether any modifications are needed in the device before starting a nationwide distribution program with the same product. The test market thus provides both estimates of the likely acceptability of new products and services and a low-cost means of trying various product modifications on a small scale. For example, the contraceptive device can be offered in different regions at different prices. Assuming that the regions are similar in socioeconomic profiles (or can be statistically controlled for any differences that may exist), the price sensitivity of the product can be tested. Needless to say, this can be done for a variety of other marketing variables such as product packaging, location of distribution, advertising media used, and so on.

A final element in the product or service design decision is the usage situation of the product or service. Work that is currently being done in this area (Srivastava, 1978) looks at the different perceptions of individuals of identical products depending on how and where those products are being used. To go back to our family planning example, for instance, the usage patterns of contraceptives can vary according to the degree of privacy-in-use that they embody. Intrauterine devices require women to go to a medical clinic for insertion. Oral contraceptives, on the other hand, can be taken at home. This issue of the usage situation can dramatically affect whether a particular program is successful or not. The concept of privacy can work the other way as well. When a product or service is acquired for group rather than individual consumption, the person making the purchase or acquisition decision may be more tempted to underrate the cost of the product or service. Marketing of the entertainment arts provides such an illustration. A person who would buy cheaper seats to the opera when alone or with family members may buy more expensive ones when accompanied by individuals whom he or she wishes to impress. *The program manager should therefore consider not only how an offered product or service is perceived but also how it is perceived in different usage situations by customers.*

The Price

The price of a product or service is an extremely important part of the marketing plan. Although nonprofit organizations are typically not interested in the rates of return on investment that stimulate corporate activity, the cost of staying in business is a very vital part of nonprofit organizational budgeting systems. The price element can occur in various ways ranging from education tuition, to utility rates, to highway commission tolls, to income and other levied taxes. The program manager has a series of inputs to make concerning price variable decisions.

In a consideration of pricing decisions, it is important to understand the concept itself. We began this chapter by describing marketing as a process of exchange of items of perceived value between two or more individuals or groups of individuals. This value is perceived in terms of the utility of the particular product or service that is to be exchanged. Monetary price, then, is the utility expressed in terms of dollars and cents. Psychological price, which we shall later discuss, imputes a nonmonetary or symbolic value to a product or service.

There are two sets of pricing strategies, the first set applying to organizations marketing new products or services, and the second set to products or services that have already been in the market for a time. Let us first consider how a marketing manager can go about pricing a new program offering.

Nine types of pricing policies can be used in making decisions for nonprofit organization programs. These are cost recovery, market penetration, no-fare pricing, demarketing pricing, profit maximization, price stabilization, cost-plus pricing, variable pricing, and discriminatory pricing. The type of policy selected will depend upon the marketing objectives of the organization.

Cost recovery pricing. A nonprofit institution that is interested in recovering a certain amount of the costs incurred in providing a program uses a price that is considered reasonable to effect this goal. Examples of cost recovery pricing policies are highway toll commissions, postal services, and some mass transit public transportation services. The extent of the costs that can be recovered through product or service pricing is a decision that is generally made by the administrators of particular organizations. Universities, for instance, traditionally attempt to recover only their operating costs and depend on state and private funding for the remainder.

Penetration pricing. A market penetration pricing policy is used by an organization that is interested in attracting as many customers as possible in the shortest period of time. Such an organization would charge a very low price for its services in the hope that the resultant demand for the service would generate in volume what the price itself would not if it had been higher (that is, increased revenues). Lovelock and Twichell cite the cases of low fare transit plans used by the Metropolitan Atlanta Rapid Transit Authority in 1972 when it charged a fifteen-cent fare with free transfers as opposed to its earlier forty-cent fare plus a five-cent transfer charge. This policy was also used in 1975 by the Southern California Rapid Transit District which adopted a flat twenty-five-cent fare with a ten-cent transfer for all services within the Los Angeles county area. The objectives of these pricing policies were to get automobile users to shift to mass transit thereby reducing pollution and traffic congestion, to help senior citizens and handicapped persons with limited disposable incomes, to encourage travel to downtown locations and thus stimulate economic activity there, and to eliminate the zonal fares for people who traveled long distances (Lovelock and Twichell, 1977, pp. 325–331).

No-fare pricing. A pricing policy that has similar marketing objectives to market penetration is that of no-fare pricing. This policy was used in 1973 by the city of Seattle when it introduced a program for mass transit use in the central city region for no charge. The policy, which had an enthusiastic response, was in answer to the problems caused by automobile traffic congestion and pollution. The concept of a no-fare transit can be applied also to specific groups, such as the elderly, to the entire city at all times, and to special times, such as rush-hour (Lovelock and Twichell, pp. 318–324).

Demarketing pricing. The objective of demarketing pricing is the reverse of the above two types of pricing policies. The aim here is to reduce the use of consumption of a particular product or service as much as possible. The policy uses an extremely high level of pricing in order to achieve this objective. Frequently, taxation systems are based on this kind of policy. Graduated income tax, for example, attempts to tax individuals in higher salary brackets more than it taxes lower income groups. Sales tax on items classified as luxuries is generally higher than the tax on convenience goods that are for the everyday use of a larger percentage of the population. Similarly, demarketing pricing could be used by a nonprofit organization when faced with a critical shortage of a particular product or raw material. Energy conservation is one recent area that has seen the use of this type of pricing policy.

Profit maximization pricing. Although it seems unlikely that a nonprofit organization would resort to a profit maximization type of pricing policy, there are certain situations in which the objectives dictate such a policy being used. For example, tickets to a ball held to raise money for a public charity are generally priced at an extremely high level in order to maximize profits.

Price stabilization. A price stabilization policy is often referred to as going-rate pricing. When an organization markets a product for which a fair amount of competition exists, it resorts to this kind of policy to circumvent the problems raised by the difficulty in estimating costs and by the need to avoid undue publicity by charging either much higher or lower than what the "industry" maintains. Obviously, this type of pricing policy is not advocated for an organization that markets a highly differentiated product or service. It is only when the client audience perceives several competitive program offerings to be similar that price stabilization can be used.

Cost-plus pricing. Cost-plus pricing is implemented by charging a price that is based on the unit cost of the product or service with the addition of a predetermined markup. Frequently, a particular division or section of a nonprofit organization will use this type of pricing policy. It is common, for example, in museum stores where gift items are priced above cost so as to generate profits that can later be used in covering cost overruns in other museum services. This type of pricing policy is more frequent in situations where the organization (or some part of it) offers a semimonopolistic service. Gift shops in museums, for instance, sell items such as antiques, curios, and prints of masterpieces which may be unavailable elsewhere in that city or even in the country.

Variable pricing. Variable pricing is the policy that advocates that prices be linked to the demand for a product or service. When the demand for a service is high, a high price is charged in order to shift some portion of the clientele into off-peak times, when the price charged is lower. This type of policy is not based on the costs of providing the service since these are identical at both peak and off-peak moments.

Discriminatory pricing. Finally, discriminatory pricing is a form of variable pricing which has either a customer, product-version, or place basis (Kotler, 1975, pp. 183–184). Customer-based discriminatory pricing is illustrated by a museum's charging lower prices to students than the general public. Product-version discriminatory pricing is shown in the case of the U.S. Postal Service's charging higher rates for registered rather than for unregistered mail. Place-based discriminatory pricing can be seen in the example of a symphony or ballet company that charges more for front-row rather than back-row seats. For these types of price discrimination to work, four conditions must be satisfied: it should be possible to segment the market on the basis of the different demand in different segments; there should be no possibility of a lower-charged segment selling its product or service to a higher-charged segment; it should not be possible for competition to charge lower prices and thereby undersell the organization; and the cost of segmenting the target market and instituting price discrimination should not be higher than the additional revenue generated by using this type of pricing policy.

We mentioned earlier that there were two sets of pricing strategies— those that were applicable to new program offerings and those that were applicable to existing products and services. Some of the above policies can indeed be used when pricing products that already exist. However, a few considerations need to be kept in mind by the program manager. These considerations revolve around the issues of price elasticity and the psychological components of pricing.

The concept of *price elasticity of demand* refers to the ratio of the percentage change in the quantity of a product or service sold in a period to the percentage change in the price of that product or service in the same period. This is expressed in symbols as:

$$E = \frac{Q_1 - Q_0}{Q_0} \Bigg/ \frac{P_1 - P_0}{P_0}$$

where E = price elasticity of demand,
  Q_0 = quantity of product or service sold before the price change
  Q_1 = quantity of product or service sold after the price change
  P_0 = old price
  P_1 = new price

If we make the assumption that the demand for a product or service will increase as the price of that item is decreased, then the price elasticity will always have a negative value (we will discuss a contravention of this assumption later). Therefore, if the price elasticity is -1, then the rise in sales is matched in percentage terms by the decrease in price. In this case there is no change in total revenue. This will be true also if the decrease in sales is matched by a proportionate increase in price.

A value of E of greater than -1 implies that the rise (or fall) in sales is greater than the percentage fall (or rise) in price. Here, total revenue will rise.

Finally, a price elasticity of less than -1 indicates that the rise (or fall) in sales is less than the percentage fall (or rise) in price and here the total revenue will fall.

In making pricing decisions, it is important for the program manager to get some sense of how price sensitive the offered product or service is. Is the product one that clients consider to be absolutely essential and hence are willing to pay a far higher price for (that is, the product is relatively price inelastic)? Or is the product considered to be one of marginal utility to the customer and hence one in which a slight increase in price would lead to a rapid decline in sales (that is, relatively price elastic)? The two scenarios for perfect price elasticity and inelasticity are shown in the familiar diagrams in Figure 10–7.

In the case of an organization marketing a health education service, assume that the price elasticity is -2. This means that the organization could increase its sales revenue by decreasing the price. On the other hand, if the elasticity for the same service was $-\frac{1}{4}$, then the organization would increase its revenue by increasing the price. This may seem relatively easy to do. However, the measurement of price elasticity poses several problems which stem from the fact that the relationship between changes in price and quantity is not a linear one. For a very small price change the elasticity may be small, but for a larger price change it may be substantial. Different price ranges may show different elasticities of

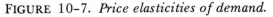

FIGURE 10-7. *Price elasticities of demand.*

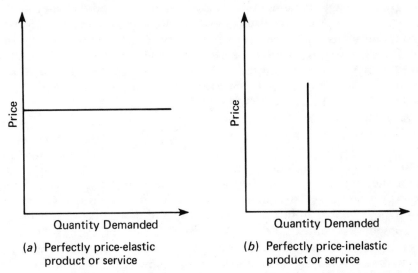

demand. Also there may be varying time lags before a price change is recorded in a demand change.

A final difficulty in measuring elasticity brings us to an assumption, mentioned earlier, that a decrease in price would always bring about an increase in demand. This may not necessarily be the case. There are several psychological imputations to the price variable. A decrease in price could well be interpreted as meaning that there was something wrong with the product or service. A "distress sale" for a consumer product such as a toilet preparation may not produce the same buying reaction as one for a health-related product or a family planning device. This has been found to be true in birth control programs in developing countries where products that were offered free were accepted and then discarded. Charging a certain minimal price had the effect of imputing a greater value to the product and also of getting more commitment toward eventual adoption and use.

This price-quality imputation is also related to products which are considered to have high prestige. Generally, these are products that are priced at high, or premium levels. A sharp cut in prices can undermine some of the prestige associated with that product.

Promotion

The term "promotion" summarizes a set of four marketing variables— advertising, personal selling, sales promotion, and publicity. We shall call the combination of these variables the *promotional mix*. The task of the program manager making promotion decisions is to find the best balance of each of the promotional mix variables so as to produce an effective communications campaign. In turn, this campaign will form part of the total marketing mix, discussed earlier, to achieve marketing plan objectives. In the discussion that follows we will describe each variable of the promotional mix and then demonstrate with illustrations how it has been and can be used by nonprofit organizations.

Advertising has been defined (Alexander, 1960) as "any paid form of nonpersonal presentation and promotion of ideas, goods, or services by an identified sponsor." The first task in planning an advertising campaign is to set the objectives. Similar to those of the overall marketing objectives, these should be as clear and specific as possible. In order to set advertising objectives it is necessary to know the function of advertising. Going beyond the formal definition of the term, it is helpful to think of advertising's purpose in the context of the AIDA principle (Strong, 1925, p. 9). This is an acronym for *a*wareness, *i*nterest, *d*esire, and *a*ction. If the nonprofit organization is marketing an entirely new product or service, it may first of all wish to make people aware that such a program is available. Once awareness has been created, the target audience needs to build up knowledge regarding how to acquire and use the product or service. Next, a desire to acquire the program offering must form. And finally, action needs to take place in making the actual acquisition.

All the above stages are based on the fact that the target market has been carefully segmented. In the use of advertising, perhaps only a part of the total market will be considered relevant. This further segmentation then needs to be made.

In the specification of advertising objectives it is also necessary to state what the reach of the advertising messages is to be (that is, the number of people in particular market segments that are to be reached by the advertisements), and also what the frequency of their exposure to the advertising is to be (that is, the number of times that an advertisement will appear in a specific time period, such as a year).

The next task is to decide on the size of the advertising budget. A rough estimate of these costs can be generated by using the following formula:

Total advertising cost = reach × frequency × average cost of
one exposure (in a particular medium—TV, radio, newspaper)

The magnitude of the budget is naturally predicated on the number of market segments to be considered, the geographical area to be covered by the advertising campaign, and on the time period over which the campaign will run.

The third task is to determine the creative strategy of the campaign. This involves deciding on what the major theme of the advertisements will be and producing both written copy and visuals that conform to this theme. The advertising theme is usually built around the "unique selling proposition" of the product or service—some physical or intangible attribute of the product or service that differentiates it from competitive program offerings. In the case of a college extension program for continuing adult education, the unique selling proposition could be class schedules that allow people who work full-time to take classes in the evenings or even on weekends. In the case of a blood bank for voluntary donors, it could be the blood-replenishment coverage offered to all members of the donor's family. In every instance, the nonprofit organization needs to indicate that its programs are discernibly different from all other programs. This is the focus of the creative strategy theme. The advertisements will then go through several developmental phases from rough layout to finished product to set the stage for the media strategy.

Decisions on media strategy involve determining primarily which of the major media types will be used (radio, television, newspapers, magazines, outdoor advertising). Then within each media type, particular media vehicles must be selected. For example, a decision on a medium such as magazines leads to a choice between *Time, Newsweek, Sports Illustrated, Fortune,* and so on. This choice depends on the suitability of the magazine's reader profile to the theme of the intended advertising campaign. Readership, circulation, and cost figures are generally available to match target segment profiles with those of the magazine's readers.

Finally, decisions must be made on how effective the advertising is. Measurement techniques for testing advertising abound, but there is some controversy on how effective each of them is relative to others. Basically, advertisements can be pre- or post-tested. *Pretesting* involves research to find out whether a particular advertising concept or theme will be successful. *Post-testing* research determines how successful an advertisement has been in terms of its achievement of stated objectives. Measurement techniques can be used (1) for advertising recognition (for example, the number of readers that remembered seeing an advertisement, that recalled seeing any part of an advertisement identifying a product or service, or that read at least half of the advertisement); (2) for advertising recall (for example, asking readers to indicate the advertisements they had seen recently, or aiding the recall by asking readers what advertisements for a particular product/service they had recently seen); (3) for product or service awareness (for example, asking respondents, "Considering continuing education programs, what schools or colleges can you think of?"); or (4) for product or service knowledge (where particular details about program offerings are asked about to determine the extent of understanding of program composition). Various mechanical instruments have also been developed to help in determining the effectiveness of advertisements in laboratory settings. These include measurements of pupil dilation, galvanic skin response, and reaction time (Lucas and Britt, 1963).

Each of the steps mentioned above is essential in the preparation of an advertising campaign. It is interesting also that advertising has been the most frequently used among the marketing mix variables by nonprofit organizations. Federal government advertising for the U.S. armed services alone exceeds the advertising budgets of such major advertisers as Lever Brothers, Coca-Cola, and Quaker Oats (Kotler, 1975, p. 203). A nonprofit organization, the Advertising Council, financed by American industry is estimated to place advertisements valued at well over $500 million to promote social causes. Some of these campaigns, such as Smokey the Bear, the American Red Cross, and the United Way, have extremely high recall and recognition ratings. Even smaller organizations enjoy a great deal of success in advertising efforts. The North Shore Animal League on Long Island, for example, got tremendous response to newspaper advertisements such as this one: "Ahab is a big beautiful gentle American short-haired gray-and-white cat with a head like a lion. But Ahab has only three paws. You wouldn't notice it unless we told you. He gets along just fine" (Mathewson, 1977, pp. 203–207).

Personal selling has been defined (Alexander, 1960) as "oral presentation in a conversation with one or more prospective purchasers for the purpose of making sales." This type of promotion has both advantages and disadvantages compared to advertising. The advantages result from the narrowed focus of the promotional effort. Personal selling involves direct interaction with members of the client community or their representatives. This allows for a clear understanding of community problems and needs and also provides for personalized service that is suited exactly to those needs and problems. Advertising, on the other hand, is a much more diffuse approach to promotion. However, it *is* cheaper than personal selling. The training of individual salespeople, the costs of traveling to and from client locations, and the costs of followup tend to be extremely high.

Yet nonprofit organizations have found that the advantages of personal contact exceed the cost disadvantages. In some cases, where volunteers are used—for example, social workers or political candidate canvassers— the incurred costs may even be minimal. Table 10–1 compares the relative merits of advertising and personal selling and is helpful in evaluating which mode of promotion is best suited to the marketing objectives of a particular nonprofit organization.

The planning of a personal selling program follows some of the initial

TABLE 10–1. *Comparative characteristics of advertising and personal selling.*

Advertising	Personal Selling
One-way form of communication	Two-way form of communication
Competes with other messages for client attention	Inherent flexibility in sales message (based on personal contact with clients)
Message designed for a large number of people and hence necessarily diffuse	Salesperson can ask for order and guarantee immediate sale
Reasonable cost (on a per reader, listener, or viewer basis)	High cost
Efficient	Effective

Source: Adapted from David T. Kollat, Roger D. Blackwell, and James F. Robeson, *Strategic Marketing* (New York: Holt, Rinehart & Winston, 1972), p. 367.

tasks of advertising programs. It begins with a determination of the client market segments that will be the targets of the personal selling effort. Next, the objectives of the effort are set out. In the case of a family planning agency, for instance, an objective might be to contact a certain number of fertile mothers with a specific product sample (such as an oral contraceptive) and a message (such as how to use the product safely and what it can do in terms of family welfare and long-run economic and health benefits) over a specific time period (a quarter of a year).

Following a statement of time-bound objectives, the next task is to recruit a sales force capable of carrying them out. These decisions are based on the size of the client markets to be covered, the geographical separation of market segments, the degree of difficulty involved in communicating the message, and the costs of salesperson expenses and travel time. Frequently this requires a systematic preliminary analysis to determine a working budget for the personal selling effort. This analysis is made by estimating the amount of time that each sales call will take and multiplying this figure by the total number of clients that will be contacted. Then a cost element based on the factors mentioned above is tacked on. The nature of the particular nonprofit organization and its purpose will determine certain additional costs. In the case of family planning agencies in developing countries, repeated personal contact may be necessary to reassure clients against fears about the harmful side effects of contraception. In the case of an educational outreach program to isolated rural communities, personal selling efforts may be geared to focus on relevant people who are held in high community esteem and who can themselves further the cause. In the case of an organization attempting to market a city symphony, efforts may be required to contact prominent business people who can attract their peers into providing necessary funding.

Personal selling efforts can therefore be designed for at least four different objectives. The first is to persuade a potential client to acquire a service, purchase a product, or provide monetary or material aid to the nonprofit organization. This is true of sales personnel for charities, alumni liaison groups, and health and welfare social workers. A second objective is to actually set up a further channel of communication. This is the case where influential people in communities are contacted so that they can contact their own sets of friends and associates. A third objective is to provide a service, for example a police officer or a museum official or guard. And the fourth objective is to act as a monitor to listen to the needs and the grievances of client groups and also to observe their possible interaction with competitive service organizations.

Once the sales force members are recruited they participate in training programs which would describe the philosophy of the nonprofit organization, its overall objectives, the goals of personal selling efforts, and typical client contact situations, and give a detailed account of what client segments to reach.

The level of compensation paid to salespeople will vary with the organization from absolutely nothing (for volunteers) to a basic wage plus a commission (similar to compensation plans used by for-profit firms). It is important that sales personnel understand the relevance and the importance of their jobs. Motivation is especially important for nonprofit organization promotion efforts since altruism rather than material gain is frequently the stimulus for accomplishing tasks satisfactorily.

As in the case of advertising, the personal selling efforts are evaluated at regular intervals to determine whether targets have been reached and objectives achieved. Any variance in task accomplishment would imply a need for changes and corrections, either in the promotional effort itself or in the statement of objectives.

Sales promotion is described (Alexander, 1960) as "those marketing activities, other than personal selling, advertising, and publicity, that stimulate consumer purchasing and dealer effectiveness, such as displays, shows and exhibitions, demonstrations, and various nonrecurrent selling efforts not in the ordinary routine." This description tends to be more applicable to for-profit marketing. In the case of nonprofit organizations, sales promotion largely takes the form of incentives. In referring to the family planning program in Asia, Rogers (1973) describes incentives as being the "direct or indirect payments in cash or in kind that are given to an individual, couple, or group, in order to encourage some overt behavioral change." Generally, behavioral change involves the purchase of a product such as a season ticket to ballet performances, or the adoption of a new practice such as an innovative agricultural technique (see also Pohlman, 1971).

The particular behavioral change desired depends on the objectives of the nonprofit organization. Once these objectives have been clarified, the program manager should decide to whom the incentive should go. In the case of family planning, for example, decisions need to be made on whether incentives should be targeted at the actual adopter of the birth control measure (the relevant male or female market segment), the decision maker about adoption (who might be either the husband or the wife), the promoter of the product or service (the individual who canvasses or recruits prospects), or doctors who initiate the diffusion process.

The incentive itself may be in the form of either cash or kind. In the United States, for instance, the Soil Conservation Service offered cash payments in the 1960s to farmers to encourage them to adopt conservation practices. In India, the Ministry of Health and Family Planning offered transistor radios to men undergoing sterilization after having two or three children.

Both positive and negative incentives can be used. The above examples are positive incentives. However, in 1975 and 1976, various state governments in India recommended a series of disincentives for individuals with large families. These ranged from mandatory sterilization for persons having three or more children to higher personal income tax rates for government officials whose family size was considered to be large. There is as yet inconclusive evidence as to the comparative merits of positive and negative incentives. Several cases exist, however, in which both types have been utilized.

Sales promotion efforts using incentives need a carefully controlled program of implementation. *The program manager should ensure that the incentives are indeed going to the particular market segments that they were designed for.* The larger the number of intermediaries involved in the promotion plan, the greater the chance that the effect of the incentive will not percolate to the lowest levels. Decisions regarding the size of offered incentives (neither too high nor too low for relevant target groups) and their administration must be regularly monitored. Incentives that are linked to quota fulfillment systems (for instance, where a recruiter of sterilization candidates is set certain achievement targets) run the danger that the wrong individuals will be selected (as in India recently, when men who were either past the reproductive age or young men who had no children were recruited so as to fulfill the mandated quotas).

Publicity is defined (Alexander, 1960) as "nonpersonal stimulation of demand for a product, service, or business unit by planting commercially significant news about it in a published medium or obtaining favorable presentation of it on radio, television, or stage that is not paid for by the sponsor." This is a promotional mix variable that is frequently used by nonprofit organizations. It is recommended strongly whenever there are severe financial constraints on the marketing budget. The costs involved in publicity revolve around the preparation of news releases by the organization and liaison with the major media personnel so that the news items are placed in prominent sections of newspapers, radio, or television.

An example of effective publicity is provided by the promotional effort of a summer school in Sewell, N.J. (Reinfeld, 1977, p. 209):

> A variety of news and feature stories was sent out, one or two a week. Highlighted were unusual courses offered, instructors teaching in the summer session, mechanics of registration. A bid to try college was made to seniors graduating from high school; mature citizens interested in further schooling were also sought.
>
> Each of the 14 releases, totaling more than 6,000 words, carried registration dates, times and places, and a phone number to call for further information. Stories about faculty were sent to the newspaper in their towns and to all newspapers in the college area. Releases went out in regular format from the college information center, whose director kept in touch with all facets of the campaign.
>
> Short- and long-range effects of the stories were felt. At least one area newspaper reader, unable to come during the summer, was stimulated enough by what she read to plan on fall attendance.

Needless to say, a publicity effort involves the same preliminary steps of specification of objectives and target segment definition as other promotional mix variables.

Placement

The fourth P of the marketing mix deals with the distribution channels used to get the product, service, or program from the nonprofit organization to the relevant market segment audiences. The most important decision that needs to be made in the context of distribution channels or the delivery system is one of perspective. If the marketing concept is used as the focus of decision making, decisions regarding how to distribute a nonprofit organization's products or services break down into decisions on how to optimize the efficiency of customer acquisition given the cost constraints.

Let us take an example to illustrate this point. Access to information regarding health and medical problems is frequently difficult, and particular problems have to be referred to qualified medical personnel. This generally necessitates trips to the nearest medical clinic or facility. In order to reduce the time spent in making these trips and the associated costs that may be incurred, the San Diego County Medical Society developed a medical tape library which comprises 225 three- to seven-minute tapes. When a caller requests medical information on a particular problem, the operator plays back the relevant tape which describes preventive health information and provides means of recognizing symptoms and methods of adjusting to serious illnesses. Additionally, a telephone referral number is given which can enable the caller to contact specific agencies such as the Lung Association of San Diego (Althafar, Butcher, and Fosburg, 1977, pp. 292–297).

The family planning area has seen a similar shift in focus from being medical facility centered to being customer oriented. Family planning agencies have recruited paramedical personnel to distribute products and information in rural areas and villages in countries where clinical facilities may be few and far between and where potential adopters of contraception may be reluctant to travel to urban or densely populated areas.

The innovative program in India provides an example of a different kind of delivery system use. Six major private sector marketing firms that had established distribution channels for such essential products as tea, cigarettes, matches, soap, and flashlight batteries were enlisted to distribute government-manufactured condoms. Their entrenched delivery systems provided a much more extensive coverage (at a minimum additional cost) than would have been the case for a specially developed public sector distribution network. The private sector corporations benefited in that their public relations efforts could illustrate their involvement in socially relevant programs.

We mentioned earlier that optimizing customer convenience can occur only at certain costs. Obviously, it would be impractical for a blood bank to solicit blood donations by going to the homes of all potential donors. This would be attempting to maximize rather than optimize consumer convenience. A balanced alternative would be to locate branch offices of the blood bank at certain strategic points of high population density in a city's downtown, work, and residential areas, providing a relative advantage over one centrally located facility.

This brings up the issue of logistics in planning delivery systems—the number and location of branches of an organization providing nonprofit products and services to a community. The problem is one that is continually facing for-profit manufacturers and distributors—how many facilities to provide, offering what quality of service, at what geographical locations so as to remain within the predetermined financial limits of the budget. Rather than advocate ad hoc solutions, it is more interesting and educative to see how particular nonprofit institutions handle the problem.

A national organization interested in distributing food to disadvantaged and elderly people is Meals on Wheels. Their delivery system involves having volunteers drive their own cars to deliver subsidized meals to people who, because of physical disability or age, are unable to get their own food. Meals on Wheels recruits its volunteers from local support groups such as church organizations.

The growth of university and college campuses around the country is greatly the function of the decentralization of large educational institutions. Regional campuses have been set up to serve students who were once forced to commute great distances for an education.

The concept of commuter education has been taken one step further by some universities on the East Coast. Realizing that a potential market existed in people who spent a certain portion of their day traveling to and from their workplace, these universities contracted to obtain railroad cars that are fully equipped as classrooms. Executives going to work each morning manage also to work their way in the rail-classrooms toward a degree that the universities award them on completion of course requirements.

Blood banks operate bloodmobiles that visit college campuses and business areas to increase accessibility to volunteer blood donors. Their blood drives are promoted so that students and office workers are aware of their arrival at particular locations in advance.

In addition to using private sector company distribution channels, the government of a developing country chose to place its federally manufactured male contraceptives at traditional retail outlets such as barbershops, small grocery merchants, tea stalls, and tobacconists. This placement increased both the acceptance and the availability of these products.

Closed-circuit television is a growing medium for centralized classroom instruction for schools at the primary and secondary level. The educational materials can be programmed in advance and played back whenever an individual instructor desires.

In 1969 the Bureau of Social Services in Chesapeake, Virginia devised a means of reducing costs and yet increasing the services offered. Its method involved setting up a mobile Social Service Office unit which operated on a regular weekly schedule (which was highly publicized), in nine city areas. The services offered included food stamps, Medicare, child welfare, work incentive programs for mothers receiving aid for dependent children, and services for the local juvenile and domestic relations court.

The four main components of the marketing mix should be considered in their cumulative effect on achieving an organization's marketing objectives. Figure 10–8 provides a comprehensive overview of the marketing plan.

The final section below describes a means of evaluating the efficiency of individual components of the marketing plan using a systematic auditing procedure. This provides a way for senior administrators in a nonprofit institution or agency to consider the worth of a marketing approach to their overall organization goals. The procedure described also demonstrates a method by which the contributions of marketing can be coordinated and controlled.

THE MARKETING AUDIT

The marketing audit has been described as "a systematic, critical, and unbiased review and appraisal of the basic objectives and policies of the marketing function and of the organization, methods, procedures, and

FIGURE 10-8. *Overview of the marketing plan.*

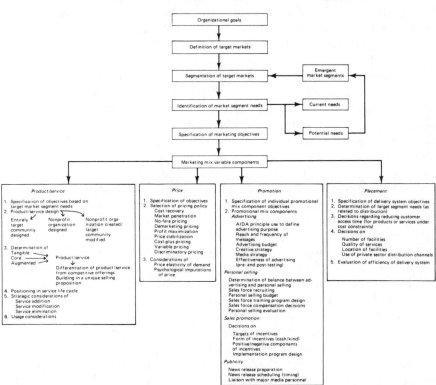

personnel employed to implement the policies and achieve the objectives"
(Oxenfeldt, 1959, pp. 25–36). There are four major tasks in conducting
a marketing audit:

1. To get a precise statement of the marketing objectives so as to evaluate them in terms of their adequacy and attainability.
2. To examine the marketing plan in terms of resource availability and
   the allocation of resources to specific market segments.
3. To look at the ways by which the plan has been put into action to
   achieve the organizational philosophy (as reflected in the marketing
   objectives).
4. To evaluate how well the personnel of the organization have been
   delegated tasks designed to attain particular goals (Wilson, 1973, p.
   104).

These four steps are shown in expanded form in Figure 10–9, which
provides a convenient method of evaluating the marketing performance
of a nonprofit agency using the five P's of policies, publics, problem,
personnel, and procedures. A systematic stepwise appraisal of the marketing function using this checklist will aid both in determining the effective contribution of each marketing plan component and in providing
a means of marketing control to ensure that the plan is being implemented
as designed.

A decision on how frequently the marketing audit can be used will
depend upon the time, manpower, and financial resources of the organization. At a minimum, a quarterly review is needed so midcourse corrections to the marketing plan can be made on the basis of any environmental or organizational fluctuations. For example, advocates of seat belts
are directly affected by energy conservation programs that might eventually produce fewer drivers on roads. State or federally funded education
programs are directly affected by policy changes on funding by government. Drought conditions in Midwestern or Western states directly affect
the purchasing power of rural communities, which in turn affects the
relative cost-benefit ratio of health education versus alternative commitments of limited money and time by community members. Any such
events that have not been planned for will necessitate marketing program
review and alterations. The more frequent the marketing audit, therefore,
the more likely that environmental and organizational changes can be
managed rather than simply reacted to. The important point is that the
marketing audit should be conducted regularly and under normal circumstances rather than infrequently, as and when crisis situations arise.

Finally, the issue of who should conduct the audit is handled differently
by different organizations. When the auditor or group of auditors is from
within the organization, a deep understanding of problems is gained, but

frequently at the cost of objectivity. Hiring an external consultant to conduct the audit is often expensive, but objectivity in evaluating marketing performance is generally enhanced. The decision is therefore largely dependent on the requirements of senior marketing personnel in the nonprofit agency or organization (Rosenberg, 1977, pp. 604–605).

FIGURE 10–9. *Marketing audit checklist for nonprofit organizations.*

I. POLICIES
   A. Organization
      1. What are the specific goals of the organization?
      2. Which target audiences are the organizational goals directed at?
      3. Are the organizational goals stated in a form that allows their achievement to be measured?
   B. Marketing
      1. What are the specific marketing objectives of the organization?
      2. How well do the marketing objectives conform to organizational goals?
      3. Are the marketing objectives stated in a form that allows them to be measured?

II. PUBLICS
   A. Customers
      1. What are the market segments to which the marketing plan is directed?
      2. What are the current needs of each market segment?
      3. What are the potential needs of each market segment?
      4. Which new market segments are likely to develop as a result of the marketing plan?
      5. Which new market segments are likely to develop regardless of the implementation of the marketing plan?
   B. Funders
      1. What are the principal sources of funding of the organization?
      2. How well do the major funders appreciate the needs of customer market segments?
      3. How much are the major funders in agreement with the marketing objectives of the organization?
      4. How is the current funding position likely to change in the next three to five years?
   C. Competitors
      1. Who are the major competitors of the organization in terms of serving the same customer markets?
      2. Who are the major competitors of the organization in terms of sources of funding?
      3. What is the competition's impact on the implementation of the organization's marketing plan?
   D. Regulators
      1. What are the regulatory agencies influencing the policies of the organization?
      2. What change in the current regulatory posture is foreseen in the next year? In the next three to five years?

III. THE PROBLEM
  A. As seen by the organization
      1. What is the specific nature of the problem (policy, organizational structure, people, product, or service)?
      2. How many individuals or groups of individuals are affected by the problem?
      3. Who are the individuals or groups of individuals affected by the problem?
      4. How long has the problem existed in its present form?
      5. What previous attempts have been made to deal with the problem?
      6. How dysfunctional is the problem?
      7. What is the location of the problem (geographically, socially, organizationally)?
      8. What are the nature and sources of resistance to dealing with the problem?
  B. As seen by the target audience(s)
      1. What is the specific nature of the problem (policy, organizational structure, people, product, or service)?
      2. How many individuals or groups of individuals are affected by the problem?
      3. Who are the individuals or groups of individuals affected by the problem?
      4. How long has the problem existed in its present form?
      5. What previous attempts have been made to deal with the problem?
      6. How dysfunctional is the problem?
      7. What is the location of the problem (geographically, socially, organizationally)?
      8. What are the nature and sources of resistance to dealing with the problem?

IV. PERSONNEL
    1. How many individuals in the organization have responsibilities that are tied solely to the achievement of marketing objectives?
    2. How well does the number of people reflect the importance of marketing to the organization?
    3. Does the controller of the marketing function report directly to the senior officials of the organization?
    4. What is the extent of training provided to the personnel concerned with implementing the marketing plan?
    5. How frequently is this training provided, and is it sufficient in quantity and quality to keep up with changes in the marketplace?
    6. How well are salespeople being compensated for their marketing efforts?
    7. Do all personnel in the organization (both marketing and nonmarketing) appreciate and practice the marketing concept?
    8. How frequently are the marketing activities of organizational personnel evaluated?

V. PROCEDURES
  A. The Product or Service
      1. How well are the needs of relevant market segments reflected in product or service offerings (as perceived by customers)?

2. Is there sufficient interaction between organizational representatives and target audience representatives in designing the product or service?
3. How adequate in conception are the tangible service, core service, and augmented service?
4. Where is the product or service currently in the life cycle? Where should it be?
5. How relevant are product strategies (addition, modification, elimination) to current market demand?
6. Is there a clear segmentation of customer markets by adopter categories?

B. Price
1. What was the past pricing history of the product or service being offered?
2. Does the current pricing strategy need to be changed to reflect changes in the customer market or in competition?
3. What are the psychological implications of the pricing strategy in terms of how customers perceive product or service quality? Is any change needed in the psychological connotations of price?

C. Promotion
1. How effectively do the promotional mix variables (advertising, personal selling, sales promotion, and publicity) conform to organizational and marketing objectives?
2. Are different market segments handled differently in terms of promotional appeals? How cost-effective is this differentiation?

D. Placement
1. Are there innovative ways of distributing the product or service that have not yet been considered?
2. How much effort (time, energy, money) does a customer expend in acquiring the product or service? Can this effort be reduced?

REFERENCES

Agarwala-Rogers, Rekha. "Re-Invention Limits on or Growth of Innovation," in Gerald Zaltman and Thomas V. Bonoma, eds., *Communication in Organizations* (New York: Free Press, 1976).

Alexander, Ralph S. *Marketing Definitions: A Glossary of Marketing Terms* (Chicago: American Marketing Association, 1960).

Althafer, Charles, Richard Butcher, and Capt. Richard G. Fosburg, "Now It's Health Information by Phone—Tel-Med," in Gaedeke, ed., *Marketing in Private and Public Nonprofit Organizations* (1977).

Altman, Bruce A. "A 'New Image' Police Department," in Gaedeke, ed., *Marketing in Private and Public Nonprofit Organizations* (1977).

Bauer, Katherine G. "Averting the Self-Inflicted Nemeses (Sins) from Dangerous Driving, Smoking, and Drinking," in Selma J. Mushkin, ed., *Consumer Incentives for Health Care* (Prodist, N.Y.: Milbank Memorial Fund, 1974).

Gaedeke, Ralph M., ed. *Marketing in Private and Public Nonprofit Organizations: Perspectives and Illustrations* (Santa Monica, Cal.: Goodyear, 1977).

Helsing, Knud J., and George W. Comstock. "What Kinds of People Do Not Use Seat Belts?" *American Journal of Public Health,* November 1977, pp. 1043–1050.

Hessler, Richard M., and Michael J. Walters. "Consumer Evaluation of Health Services: Implications for Methodology and Social Policy," paper presented at the annual meeting of the American Sociological Association, Montreal, Canada, August 1974.

Kollat, David T., Roger D. Blackwell, and James F. Robeson. *Strategic Marketing* (New York: Holt, Rinehart & Winston, 1972).

Kotler, Philip. *Marketing Management: Analysis, Planning, and Control* (Englewood Cliffs, N.J.: Prentice-Hall, 1967), Chap. 23.

Kotler, Philip. *Marketing for Nonprofit Organizations,* 2nd ed. (Englewood Cliffs, N.J.: Prentice-Hall, 1975).

Lovelock, Christopher H., and Jon Twichell. "Low-Fare Transit Plans Gain Nationwide Trials," in Gaedeke, ed., *Marketing in Private and Public Nonprofit Organizations* (1977).

Lovelock, Christopher, and Charles B. Weinberg. "Public and Nonprofit Marketing Comes of Age," in Gerald Zaltman and Thomas V. Bonoma, eds., *Review of Marketing 1978* (Chicago: American Marketing Association, 1978).

Lucas, Darrell B., and Stewart H. Britt. *Measuring Advertising Effectiveness* (New York: McGraw-Hill, 1963).

Mathewson, William. "With Right Tactics, It's Easy to Market a Three-Legged Cat," in Gaedeke, ed., *Marketing in Private and Public Nonprofit Organizations* (1977).

McCarthy, E. Jerome. *Basic Marketing: A Managerial Approach,* rev. ed. (Homewood, Ill.: Irwin, 1964).

Oxenfeldt, A. R. "The Marketing Audit as a Total Evaluation Program," in *Analyzing and Improving Marketing Performance,* Report No. 32 (New York: American Management Association, 1959).

Pohlman, Edward. *Incentives and Compensations in Birth Planning* (Chapel Hill, N.C.: University of North Carolina, Carolina Population Center, 1971).

Reinfeld, Patricia. "The Selling of the Summer School," in Gaedeke, ed., *Marketing in Private and Public Nonprofit Organizations* (1977).

Ricklefs, Roger. "Museums Merchandise More Shows and Wares to Broaden Patronage," *The Wall Street Journal,* August 14, 1975.

Rogers, Everett M. *Diffusion of Innovations* (New York: Free Press, 1962).

Rogers, Everett M. "Effects of Incentives on the Diffusion of Innovations: The Case of Family Planning in Asia," in Gerald Zaltman, ed., *Processes and Phenomena of Social Change* (New York: Wiley, 1973), pp. 133–152.

Rogers, Everett M., and F. Floyd Shoemaker. *Communication of Innovations: A Cross-Cultural Approach,* 2nd ed. (New York: Free Press, 1971).

Rosenberg, Larry J. *Marketing* (Englewood Cliffs, N.J.: Prentice-Hall, 1977).

Srivastava, Rajendra K. "Situational Influences on Competitive Market Structure: Implications for Marketing Planning," unpublished Ph.D. dissertation, University of Pittsburgh, 1978.

Strong, E. K. *The Psychology of Selling* (New York: McGraw-Hill, 1925).

Sutherland, Jean. "Why Methods Fail," in *Communication for Change with the Rural Disadvantaged* (Washington, D.C.: National Academy of Sciences, 1972).

Wilson, R. M. S. *Management Controls in Marketing* (London: Heinemann, 1973).

CHAPTER 11

Management Information Versus Misinformation Systems

Ian I. Mitroff
Ralph H. Kilmann
Vincent P. Barabba

Editor's Note *There is a need for the right information at the right time. Information is ever present for managers working in complicated and changing situations, and the need for a systematic procedure for acquiring and using information is also ever present. Without proper information at the appropriate time and available in a useful manner, the quality of most management decisions will suffer greatly. This chapter defines the fundamental ingredients of a management information system (MIS) and illustrates some of the basic problems involved in MIS design. The authors suggest that a poor design can convert a potentially valuable MIS into a potentially disastrous management misinformation system (MMIS). Many managers, perhaps even most, currently use an MMIS rather than an MIS. The authors also suggest a very broad problem-solving process applicable to strategic management problems.*

Most organizational difficulties, the authors contend, arise from a failure to identify the correct problems. Problem solving is generally easier than identifying the correct problem. Usually management information systems are to blame, because they are too narrow, limited, and sometimes misleading. Managers who spend adequate time designing an efficient and effective MIS are more likely to define problems correctly and thus avoid future waste of effort and resources.

Basic problems involved in MIS design are not technical in nature, but conceptual and human. Most MIS's are for purposes of problem solving, not for formulating or identifying the correct problem. Also, systems tend to be narrow and limited in scope as they fail to incorporate a broad range of potential users. MIS's are generally embodied in impersonal systems that ignore the human dimensions of information acquisition and use.

A traditional MIS model is introduced as a starting point for discussion. The authors argue that its value is substantially enhanced when additional banks or components are added. The incorporation of an assumption bank, a problem bank, an action bank, and a decision-maker bank satisfies various nonfinancial dimensions of value more effectively and efficiently.

Although there is no single process guaranteeing an optimal MIS design, there is a process to minimize MMIS errors. The process begins with identifying the participants in the design project. The participants are then divided into groups, one of which develops a list of critical research questions while the others develop an MIS to answer the research questions. These groups are split further into subgroups with different points of view. Constructive debates are encouraged among groups and subgroups. Each subgroup is allowed to develop in detail its own unique and individual perspective before moving into the most difficult and critical phase—synthesis. The groups uncover, inspect, and challenge each other's key assumptions before achieving synthesis. The authors contend that an MIS can be no better than the assumptions upon which it rests; therefore, the exposure of assumptions is critical to MIS design and to effective management in general.

DEFINITIONS AND ISSUES

The nature of information is such that, all other things being equal, it is presumably better to have more of it than less. Indeed, information is the stuff by which all of us supposedly run our lives. We generate it in the natural process of being curious; we use it in increasing quantities in making complex decisions. It is natural, therefore, that as institutions and problems have become more complex we should turn increasingly to systems which would aid us in making decisions. Essentially, this is the basic purpose of and rationale for management information systems.

As comforting as all this sounds, increasing doubts and criticisms are being raised as to whether the manager needs more information as the complexity of the decision he or she faces increases. Instead, the concern is with delivering "just the right amount and kind of information" the manager needs. The determination of the right amount and kind of information is the topic of this chapter.

The basic purposes of this chapter are (1) to define the fundamental ingredients of a management information system (or MIS for short), (2) to illustrate some of the basic problems connected with the design of MIS's, and (3) to suggest a very broad strategic problem-solving process that is applicable not only to the design of MIS's but to strategic management problems in general (public as well as private).

Some years ago in a now classic article, Ackoff (1967) described the properties of a class of systems he labeled (quite appropriately) management *mis*information systems. Although originally intended to serve as management informing systems, they had unwittingly become management *mis*informing systems. It is important to emphasize that these systems were not consciously designed by their creators to be misinforming. Indeed, their designers would have undoubtedly been both horrified and surprised to discover that their best intentions had gone awry. There is thus no reason to question the conscious intentions, motives, or goodwill of the designers. If the designers are to be faulted, it is with regard to their unconscious and unstated assumptions and intentions, not their stated aims. If anything, the designers were the unknowing victims of a set of widely held cultural norms regarding the role of technology in the solution of managerial problems.

Given the excellence of Ackoff's article, we would not even attempt to describe the full array of erroneous assumptions identified by him in the design of a management information system (MIS). The reader is strongly urged to consult Ackoff's paper as one of the best introductory treatises on avoiding the design of misinforming systems and on bringing about informing ones. Instead of attempting to summarize the assumptions Ackoff has identified, we shall list briefly in our terms the erroneous assumptions or factors that we have found in our own research and experience that leads to systems for managerial misinformation, not information.

In both our experience and research with using and designing systems, there are five areas or issues that are especially important to deal with in the design of any MIS. Failure to confront and to deal adequately with the assumptions underlying each of these areas can undermine the best intentions of any designer—that is, can convert a potential MIS into an MMIS.

The five issues are or involve: (1) the nature of the problem, (2) the kinds of clients/users and designers, (3) the evidence, (4) the system's boundaries, and (5) the design process. As we shall see, the assumptions involved with regard to each issue illustrate amply that the basic problems involved in MIS design are not primarily technical in nature as so many seem to assume. Rather, they are conceptual and human in nature—that is, interpersonal, organizational, and political.

It is important to note that these issues are neither random nor trivial. They follow from the basic definition of an MIS. The most generic definition (Mason and Mitroff, 1973, p. 475) is as follows: "An information system consists of at least one *person* of a certain *psychological type* who faces a *problem* with some *organizational context* for which he needs *evidence* to arrive at a solution (that is, to select some course of action) and the evidence is made available to him through some *mode of presentation*." In short, an information system is an organized process or procedure for uncovering, delivering, and presenting the appropriate evidence for the right problem to the right person in the correct part of an organization so that the person can take effective action in diagnosing and solving the problem. Put this way, the issues involved in discussing an MIS, let alone the effective design of an MIS, are exceedingly complex.

SOLVING THE RIGHT PROBLEM

The first issue in the design of any MIS is what we have called the nature of the problem. To discover the nature of the problem, the designer of an MIS has to face these critical questions: What are the classes of problems to which the system will restrict itself? Are the problems well known beforehand or are they unspecified—open-ended, dynamic, changing, vague, fuzzy, or even ill defined? Is the system to be designed under the presumption that the problems are already known and likely to stay the same and that therefore the purpose of the system is to help the user solve a given problem or a set of problems? Or is the system to be designed under the presumption that the problems are not completely known or fixed and that therefore the purpose of the system is to help the user formulate his or her own possibly unique problem, not to solve a given "canned" problem?

Very little recognition has been given to these important questions in the practice and the literature of design. Indeed, the vast majority if not nearly all the treatises on MIS design assume that the problem is given or known beforehand and therefore that the purpose of the system is to supply information or evidence with regard to an already known problem. With very few exceptions (see Joyner and Tunstall, 1970) there are literally no existent systems which help a user to formulate (or discover) his or her own problem. In short, most MIS's are problem-solving systems; they are not problem-forming ones.

As a result of this, most designers of MIS's commit what the authors call errors of the third kind of E_{III} (Kilmann, Lyles, and Mitroff, 1977; Mitroff, Barabba, and Kilmann, 1977; and Mitroff and Featheringham, 1974). It is customary in elementary courses in statistical decision theory to discuss extensively what are called errors of the first and second kinds, or E_I and E_{II} respectively. E_I and E_{II} essentially have to do with minimizing the conditions under which a true solution to a problem is wrongly rejected as false and a false solution is wrongly accepted as true.

It is shown in elementary courses that it is virtually impossible in all situations to minimize both of these errors simultaneously, so that a decision maker has to choose which one is of most importance to avoid. In any case, both errors presuppose that we have already formulated, know, or have had presented to us (given) the set of alternate solutions to a problem we wish to compare such that if we accept one as being true, we reject the other as being false. E_{III} steps back from this process and asks a more fundamental question: What is the problem to which the hypotheses are addressed?

E_I and E_{II} presuppose that we not only have already defined (identified) the problem but in addition we know that the definition we have formulated is the "correct" or the most fruitful one on which to work. Put slightly differently, E_{III} is more formally defined as "the probability of solving or working on the 'wrong' problem when one should have worked on (attempted to solve) the 'correct' problem" (Mitroff and Featheringham, 1974). In a word, E_I and E_{II} are associated with problem *solving*— that is, minimizing the rejection (or conversely, maximizing the acceptance) of the "correct" solution within a given formulation of the problem. E_{III}, on the other hand, is associated with problem *formulation* or problem *finding* (Kilmann, 1977; Mitroff, Barabba, and Kilmann, 1977). E_{III} challenges the decision maker (dm) to make sure that he or she is working on the right problem to begin with, before he or she attempts to secure a precise answer to a given problem. As the eminent statistician John Tukey once put it, "Far better an approximate solution to the right problem than an exact solution to the wrong problem."

To our knowledge, MIS designers have not utilized a process which would allow them to minimize E_{III}'s in the design of MIS's; moreover, we know of no system which attempts to allow a dm to systematically explore different formulations of his problem in order to assess explicitly E_{III}'s that he might be committing so that he might ultimately attempt to avoid them.

INVOLVING THE RIGHT PEOPLE IN DESIGN

The second issue in the design of an MIS is who should be involved in the design of the system. In our experience, it is vitally important to get as many potential users, clients, and stakeholders of the system deeply involved in as many phases of the MIS design as is possible. This means that there should not be a strict separation between the roles of users and designers. More than one designer has learned the painful consequences of not involving deeply and sincerely those who will use the system. Such consequences are underutilization and nonutilization of the system, passive and active opposition to it, indifference, termination of the system, and failure to initiate other such design efforts or projects in the future.

Without incorporating a broad range of potential users into the design phase, it has turned out far too often for comfort that the only users of the system are the technical designers; that is, the designers have ended up designing a system for themselves and only themselves. The designers become in effect the ultimate users of a system. The question therefore is how to broaden the potential class of designers in order to broaden the potential class of users and thereby to maximize use of the system.

We advocate broadening of the class of designers not just because many of the design issues are inherently political, and not merely technical, but because different parties have different conceptions of the aims of a system and the uses to which it will be put. The point is, again, that design is not just a technical process but a social and a political process involving negotiation, compromise, and bargaining. The process of design therefore means securing as many views of the proposed system as possible. We cannot overemphasize this last point for while many might agree on the need to involve many parties in the design process, there have been few attempts to outline a systematic process for incorporating, utilizing, and dealing with the views of differing parties and design perspectives.

DIFFERENT KINDS OF EVIDENCE

One of the most subtle issues involved in the design of an MIS is the role of evidence. Presumably, the basic justification for an MIS in the first place is that it provides evidence to answer some question. The issue is subtle because it involves the twin questions of "Evidence for whom?" (which kinds of users) and "Evidence for what?" (which kinds of problems). What is regarded as evidence by one type of user is not necessarily regarded as such by another kind of user. Recently a number of investigators have argued that there is an intimate connection between a person's cognitive style or personality and the type of information that he or she prefers and is even willing to label as "information" (McKenney and Keen, 1974; Mitroff, Barabba, and Kilmann, 1977).

On the following page are shown four very different notions of information as embodied in four different sources of information. The four notions were created by systematically applying Jungian personality theory to the concept of information. That is, each paragraph briefly describes what each of the four major Jungian personality types regards as information.

Since the application of the Jungian personality system to information systems has been extensively described elsewhere (Kilmann, 1977; Mitroff and Kilmann, 1978), we shall not pursue the details of the system here. (See also Chapter 6 in this volume for details of the system.) Suffice it to say that the four personality types result from the intersection of two dimensions: (1) a specificity (reductionistic)-generality (holistic) dimension, and (2) a personal-impersonal dimension. That is, each of the types represents one of the four possible combinations of the end points of the dimensions. Thus source A represents the generic archetype of a specific (analytic, reductionistic)-impersonal information system; source B, that of a specific-personalistic system; source C, that of a holistic-personal system; and source D, that of the holistic-impersonal system.

One of the most important aspects of the Jungian system is that in contrast to other systems it constantly stresses that no one personality type is superior in all respects or situations. Each type has major strengths as well as weaknesses. As a result, each needs the others to complement it, to make up for what it is weak on, for what it does not pay attention to or heed. Applied to the concept of information, this means that no one concept or type of information is superior or best for all situations. Consider the banking situation represented in the discussion of basic sources of information. Source A is the one which is typically embodied in most MIS's, especially accounting information systems. Indeed, implicit in the design of the vast majority of MIS's is the presumption that source A and only source A represents valid information. Source A is certainly the one that is most congruent with the design of computerized or mechanized MIS's.

There are strong senses, however, in which each of the other sources is valid. Consider, for example, source B. Given the complexity of many managerial problems, it is doubtful whether any standardized form would ever be sufficient to cover all contingencies. As a result, the manager or dm always needs to have recourse to information sources other than that represented in A. One of the most important of these other sources is B, another person that one knows and in whom one can place implicit trust to provide reliable personal information.

The question is what *is* the more rational course: (1) to place one's trust and confidence in vital matters in an impersonal information system where one may have had little involvement in the design and little control

Suppose that you were the chief loan officer of an important and highly respected banking institution. Suppose also that the decision to grant or not to grant a very large loan ($5,000,000) rested primarily on your shoulders. Suppose further that you had available the following *four* potential sources of information for either advising or helping you in reaching your decision:

A (Specific–Impersonal). Source A is an internally prepared, in-depth report and analysis by the bank's accounting division of the prospective loan applicant's financial status. The bank has a standardized, time-proven, and time-honored financial form that it requires of every loan applicant no matter what the size of the transaction. Based on the extensive, detailed factual data that this form calls for, the bank's accounting division performs a completely impartial and impersonal assessment of the applicant's "ability to pay back" the loan. It does this through a detailed and complicated analytical procedure which compares the applicant's past and current financial profile with the profiles of those applicants who have been granted a loan and have been successful in repaying it.

B (Specific–Personal). Source B is a fellow officer in the bank in charge of customer and public relations. B is also an old, trusted personal friend whom you can talk openly to about anything. B is extremely sociable and good at getting on with all kinds of people. He literally knows everyone who is anyone in the banking and business world. He also knows what everybody is currently thinking and doing. B bases his recommendations on whether to grant a loan entirely on facts. However, the kind of facts that B gathers are very different from those of source A. Since B knows a large number of people on a first-name basis, before he would make a recommendation to grant anybody a loan, he calls up a large number of his friends. Unless he can get a high proportion of his friends to personally vouch for (1) the financial status of the applicant and (2) the ability of the applicant to pay back the loan, he will not make a positive recommendation.

C (Holistic–Personal). Source C is a fellow officer in the bank in charge of special projects and assignments. He is the bank's general troubleshooter, problem solver, and all-around generalist. He is the only one in the bank who has a real grasp of the entire operation. C is also an old, trusted personal friend whom you can talk openly to about anything. While C is sociable and good at getting on with all kinds of people, he is best in dealing with people on a very personal one-to-one basis. C bases his recommendation to grant a loan on personal and social considerations, not on impersonal considerations. However, where B bases his recommendations on facts and on widespread social consensus, C relies entirely on his own judgment. C has an uncanny intuitive ability to "size up" any situation as well as any person. C also has the ability to visualize and open up new possibilities beyond merely granting or rejecting the specific loan at hand.

D (Holistic–Impersonal). Source D is an internally prepared, global report and analysis by the bank's management/behavioral science division of the prospective loan applicant's lifestyle. The management/behavioral science division conducts a series of probing, open-ended, far-ranging interviews designed to explore the prospective applicant's attitudes toward a wide variety of issues. Based on the large amount of subjective and personal data that this procedure uncovers, the bank's management/behavioral science division works up a series of multiple profiles on the loan applicant. Instead of merely recommending a single course of action, namely, the granting of a specific loan or not, the multiple profiles are designed to uncover a whole range of options for the bank.

over the validity of the input to the system (how the input data was collected, who collected it and checked it, under what circumstances it was collected, and so on); or (2) to place one's trust and confidence in a source that one can talk to face to face, challenge, and size up through a host of subtle verbal and nonverbal cues? By posing such a question we do not mean to imply that source B is more important than A, or A than B. Indeed, depending upon the circumstances, either one can be rational (or functional), both can be, or neither can be. By restricting themselves primarily to one of these sources for all situations, the majority of MIS's have assumed implicitly that one and only one type is best, rational, or superior.

THE SYSTEM'S BOUNDARIES

Closely related to differences in cognitive style—indeed, in a sense all the various assumptions we have been discussing follow from differences in cognitive style—is the issue of the boundaries, or limits, of a proposed MIS. Many MIS designers implicitly take the concept of an information system to be synonymous with that of a computerized system. As we shall see, such a limitation need not always be the case. A computerized system is only one out of a great variety of information systems. Sources B and C illustrate this point well.

The Organization as an Information System

Any formalized computerized MIS must be supported by both informal and formal organizational groups and processes. No system, mechanical or not, ever exists in a social vacuum. It is only there to begin with because it is expected to serve the goals of some groups within the organization or the organization as a whole. Indeed, it is important to take into account the degree to which the organization itself should be considered and designed to be the information system. It is clear that there is a variety of information system types, one of which is the people in an organization and the ways in which they are organized to facilitate or to inhibit the flow of information from person to person or from point to point. As Wilensky (1967) has shown, one of the most important MIS design questions is the organization's structure. Depending upon the kind of organization, one can very easily produce certain organizational information pathologies, such as the deliberate withholding and distortion of information. The reader is also referred to Kilmann (1977) for the relationship between information and organization design. To repeat: the organization itself is and must be considered as an information system. Not all the things an organization considers to be information can be stored in a computer or processed by it. At the very least, the organization is the supportive environment of the formal computerized system, and therefore the interface between the organization and computer must be carefully thought out and designed explicitly.

The Process of MIS Design

An important body of assumptions concerns the process that is used to design the MIS. We do not mean the technical process that is used to design the system hardware, because as the preceding paragraphs indicate it is not clear that any part of the MIS need be mechanized, let alone the whole of it. We are concerned with the behavioral and organizational processes that will be used to select, to bring together, and to motivate the participants to the design; we mean the social technology (Kilmann, 1977; Mitroff and Kilmann, 1978) that will be used to get people (designers) to consider all aspects of the system. Indeed, this very point will concern us most in the latter phases of this chapter.

THE DECISION-INFORMATION STRUCTURE OF AN MIS

Because of the extreme importance of avoiding the errors associated with each of the preceding sets of assumptions, we believe that we cannot overemphasize the foregoing points. Moreover, we believe it is important to show that these same concerns follow from an alternate approach. David Montgomery and Glen Urban (1969) have devised one of the best overall models available for thinking about the components of an MIS. A slightly modified version of the model is reproduced in Figure 11–1.

For Montgomery and Urban, an MIS consists of four principal "banks," components, or functions: (1) a statistical model bank, (2) a display system, (3) a model bank, and (4) a data bank. The purpose of the display system is to allow the user(s) to communicate with the system (via their input requests) and to allow the system to respond to the user(s) (via output of information). The purpose of the data bank is to accumulate and to store data (from surveys, studies, and the like) that are potentially useful in responding to a user's requests. The function of the statistical model and the model banks is to analyze the data. The statistical model bank analyzes or represents the data according to various statistical routines. The model bank—which can store large-scale corporate models of the whole organization and its long-term goals—is capable of analyzing the data for their impact on the organization's short-term and long-term future. The difference between the two is that the statistical model bank asks if there are statistically significant patterns or differences in the data—for example, whether the purchasing patterns for two different brands or products are the same. The model bank, on the other hand, asks what one is

FIGURE 11–1. *Structure of a decision-information system.*

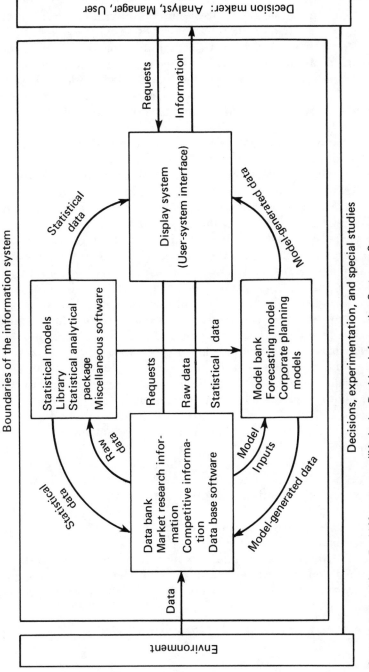

Source: Adapted from David Montgomery, "Marketing Decision Information Systems: Some Design Considerations," in Robert Ferber, ed., *Handbook of Marketing Research* (New York: McGraw Hill, 1974).

to make of a given set of statistically analyzed data, for example, what are the long-run implications for the organization for a given set of statistical analyses on market share, profit ratios, and so on.

The Montgomery and Urban decision-information system structure represents a substantial improvement over earlier conceptualizations of MIS's for conducting research.* It developed in greater detail these areas: (1) some of the important banks or components to consider in the design of an MIS, (2) some of the subcomponents of these banks, and (3) how the various banks are related to one another.

The value of the Montgomery and Urban model is enhanced when additional banks are added (see Figure 11–2). The importance of these additional banks has been stressed both implicitly and explicitly in the recent literature, primarily in the marketing literature. Failure to incorporate these additional banks explicitly into the design of an MIS means the difference between success and failure of a system.

The purpose of adding these additional banks is to make sure that explicit attention will be given to important design features of an MIS. For example, Cravens, Hills, and Woodruff (1976) accord a central role to problem analysis, particularly to the more subtle human aspects of problem recognition, in their model of the decision-making process. Not only do they recognize the need for a problem bank—that is, an MIS component that would keep track of and record the problems the organization has faced in the past and expects to face in the future—but they also imply strongly that an action bank is desirable. They suggest that the availability of such a bank will not only shorten the time of making decisions but also increase the likelihood of making correct ones.

Cravens, Hill, and Woodruff (1976) also argue implicitly for the existence of a decision-maker (dm) bank. In their judgment, the importance of a dm bank is to call explicit attention to the point that an MIS should be flexible enough to be compatible with and even act as an extension of a manager's analytical abilities, cognitive style, and general views. An MIS should attempt to identify the domain of potential dm's so that the MIS can be tailored explicitly to their style. This point is explicitly stressed by Little (1970) in his discussion of the factors affecting managerial usage of a model bank.

Kotler (1976) suggests that a dm bank is important to establish if only as a guide to knowing what data to collect. Different dm's will have different information needs even when they are all addressing the same

---

*The authors gratefully acknowledge the kind assistance of Gerald Zaltman in the preparation of this part of the chapter.

FIGURE 11-2. *Structure of an enhanced decision-information system.*

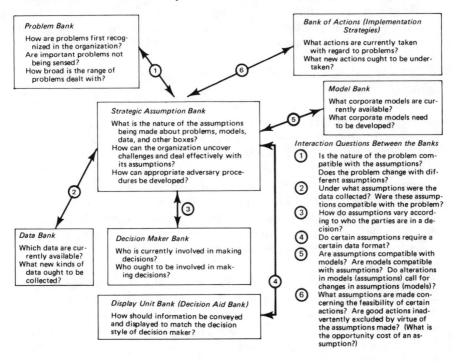

problem. These different needs may well stem from different assumptions; hence, it is also important to identify and to store these assumptions that are made over time by different dm's. This is the function of an assumption bank. For instance, Kotler distinguishes between "what is nice to know" and "what is necessary to know." Whether it is merely nice to have an answer to a question or absolutely necessary should be a function of the assumptions one makes about the nature of a problem.

Bell (1972) is one of the few in the field of marketing who has addressed in a serious manner the organizational implications of MIS's for conducting market research. As we have stressed previously, an MIS is an organizational entity. The structure of most organizations is based on the flow of authority rather than on information per se. Because information systems, when they are used at all, are typically incongruent with the structure of a firm, important dm's may not be served or served well by the MIS. For example, an MIS for marketing may fail if it is insensitive to the needs of nonmarketing personnel—such as the controller, or the vice-president for operations or manufacturing—who influence major marketing decisions such as launching a major product innovation. Thus, the dm bank requires the explicit identification of dm's on a firmwide basis and the types of marketing decisions in which they are likely to be involved.

Dickson and Simmons (1970) also addressed the problem of the organizational impact of information systems. They identify the various subgroups affected by an MIS and the dysfunctional behaviors these subgroups may display in response to an MIS. Dickson and Simmons do not directly address the issue of hidden and conflicting assumptions among these subgroups. However, it is clear from their discussion of the behavioral side of information systems that hidden assumptions and conflicting assumptions are at the root of many behavioral problems displayed by different subgroups. This points to the need for identifying and including an assumption bank in an information system for marketing decisions. Having an array of assumptions explicit in a system enables users to address them openly and without threat. The assumption bank makes the assumptions explicit.

Churchill (1976) has suggested that an assessment of each MIS user's decision-making style and capabilities is a fundamental criterion in the design of an MIS. One of the more important aspects of a dm's style is what we have repeatedly referred to as assumption making. For example, in making a decision does a brand manager typically make or entertain a large number of assumptions or a small number (say seven or less)? Do the assumptions made pertain more to problem definition or to remedial actions? Thus again, if decision style is an important MIS design consideration, then so is the existence of an assumption bank. Churchill also gives problem formulation a central role in the design of an information system and stresses the importance of tying problem formulations into the selection of actions. Although he doesn't call for an action bank, the existence of an information action bank is assumed. We feel that such a bank should be explicitly included. The formalization of an action bank has been suggested most recently in the general literature by Zaltman and Duncan (1977) and Zaltman, Florio, and Sikorski (1977).

Zaltman and Burger (1975) have also highlighted the importance of problem formulation and the generation of actions in response to market data. They discuss six facets of information which concern the nonfinancial value of information: (1) relevance, (2) reliability, (3) understandability, (4) significance, (5) sufficiency, and (6) practicality. These dimensions are briefly discussed below.

If a researcher can give managers information which will help determine policies, then the criterion of relevance is met. If the researcher and manager discuss with each other what information is needed, the information ultimately provided by the researcher will be more relevant.

Understandability indicates that a measure can be quantified (much marketing research data dealing with attitudes can be measured on suitable scales). It is understandable if it is simple, if it is consistent with how the marketing manager will find it useful, and if it can be compared with information to which it is similar and/or in contrast.

The types of decisions that utilize information will determine its significance. Data about consumer complaints take on a different meaning depending on whether they are used in a decision to retain or drop a product or in a decision to add packaging information on a label.

Sufficiency implies that just enough information was obtained to aid the marketing manager. It is not necessary, and it is certainly inefficient, to acquire extra information. A skilled researcher can fulfill management's needs without being superfluous and can feel assured that the information is adequate for making a decision. Information must be timely and have enough benefits in excess of costs to be practical.

There is obviously no simple way to measure all the dimensions of information. Some rating scale could be developed for each of these dimensions in addition to cost value, but different scales would have to be individualized for different types of decisions and their relative importance to the firm. Even if a researcher is not able to measure all the above criteria, however, their consideration in some judgmental way is necessary for data to be more meaningful.

Our position is that these nonfinancial dimensions of value are likely to be satisfied more effectively and more efficiently if an MIS incorporates an assumption bank, a problem bank, an action bank, and a decision-maker bank. The several marketing scholars cited here have been calling for the inclusion of these banks. These banks, together with those in the Montgomery design, should result in a more sensitive, more useful, and more sophisticated MIS.

SOME PRINCIPLES FOR AVOIDING AN MMIS

Following are 11 principles (design considerations) for avoiding the design of an MMIS. If these are adhered to in spirit, a well-functioning MIS should result. They are intended as much for discussion and stimulation as they are for implementation, and are offered as a critical guide to the design of information systems.

1. The system (MIS) ought to be attractive, even fun to use, and aes-

thetically pleasing in the sense that it is as easy and as pleasant for the user to use as possible. Experience indicates that MIS's that are merely factually correct, but boring, difficult, and dull to use, are not utilized to their full capability and may actually not justify their cost of installation. The Whirlpool Corporation (Sparks, 1976) has actually designed an operating MIS around the principle that the system should be fun to use, easily accessible, and integrated into the day-to-day activities of the managers. In order to encourage utilization of the system, it has been made as accessible as possible by locating it in a coffee room for managers. It is a normal part of the manager's everyday routine to start off with a visit to the coffee room and to interact with the system. The system displays such data as how the sales personnel under the managers supervision are performing and how the competitors are doing. The system is thus relevant to the manager's interests and needs.

2. The system ought to be designed with the capability of multiple methods of input, analysis, display, and output so that it can match a user's unique and normal style of inquiry; the system ought to be flexible enough to accommodate different kinds of users; the system ought to match the user instead of forcing the user to match the system.

3. The system ought to provide multiple and explicit alternative interpretations of whatever issue, question, or query is posed by a user; multiple conceptual and analytical models ought to be built into the system so that a user can witness alternate interpretations of his or her query. It is hoped in this way that dm's will minimize type three errors.

4. The system ought to guide and assist a user through all the phases of the problem-solving, inquiry process; it ought to help a user in formulating his or her problem, forming a conceptual model of it, building a formal analytical model, collecting data, forming action implications, and implementing the solution. This is generally the most important and yet most generally neglected aspect of problem-solving systems (MIS's). In other words, the system ought to help the user in formulating problems, and in exploring and reframing alternative assumptions and questions. In a similar fashion, it ought to actively assist the user in exploring different models of his or her problem.

5. In addition to providing factual explanations, data, and the like, the system ought to provide extrapolations and interpretations of the facts and data. It ought also to provide cautionary notes wherever such interpretations and extrapolations seem risky.

6. The system ought to include an explicit evaluation and implementation component; it ought to suggest strategies of taking action, of implementing the results of the inquiry/problem-solving process.

7. The system ought to keep track of past inquiries made by a user or

a group of users. A profile analysis ought to be conducted. The system ought to ask the user to consider asking other kinds of questions. It ought to assist him or her in asking other questions.

8. The system ought to serve as a warning device for alerting the user on what the competition is up to. It ought to raise disturbing issues that users may not want to raise for themselves.

9. The system should be evaluated in terms of its contribution to the effectiveness of the organization as a whole.

10. The system ought to encourage long-term strategic thinking about the corporation as a whole, its future products, services, needs, operating environments, customers, and competition; the system should not be designed to respond only to everyday, operational issues and problems.

11. The system ought to be designed to allow individuals to communicate potentially to anyone in the corporation in an anonymous mode so as to encourage the free and uninhibited exchange of ideas; persons ought to be encouraged to use the system to brainstorm, even to think of "harebrained" ideas; an inventory of such ideas ought to be kept and the more promising ones singled out for reward.

A DESIGN PROCESS FOR AN MIS

There is no single process whereby one can avoid the errors that prevent an MIS from being realized to its fullest and best advantage. However, we have found through our combined research, teaching, work experience, and consulting a process which works for us in the sense that it sheds insight on what is required to surface and it minimizes E_{III}'s. We have applied this process to various problems in ongoing organizations, as well as to the design of entirely new organizations themselves.* The process is schematically illustrated in Figure 11–3.

The process begins with the identification of participants to the design project. We have found that the outcome of the design effort will be most likely to be satisfactory to all participants and hence more likely to be implemented by the organization if the group of participants is as diverse as possible in order to insure that many viewpoints across all levels and perspectives from within the organization are included. This breadth of viewpoints not only helps to offset any potentially damaging charges of unrepresentativeness, which can often kill a planning or a design effort before it is even off the ground, but it also gets at a more fundamental

---

*In addition, this process emphasizes the importance of developing the strategic assumption bank as central to an effective MIS along with the other "banks" shown in Figures 11–1 and 11–2. Stated differently, assumption testing is a critical part of the MIS design process precisely because assumptions are implicit and usually ignored.

FIGURE 11-3. *A design process for MIS.*

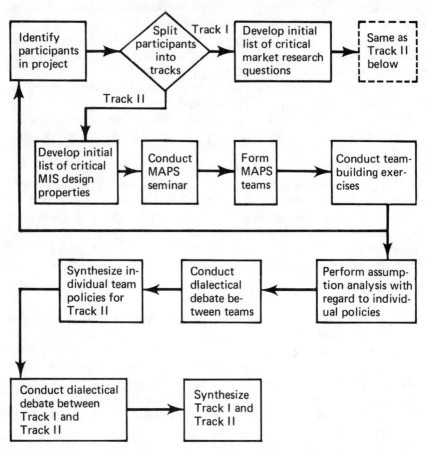

issue. Unlike other design or planning processes, the one we are presenting does not presuppose strong initial agreement between the parties
to the design—in fact, the case is quite the contrary. The process explicitly
presupposes the existence of strong differences in points of view in order
to insure that E_{III} will at least be controlled if not minimized. This is not
to say that there are not difficulties with the process at the beginning.
Indeed, right from the very start we face a basic dilemma: we are required
to have chosen via some means, or process, a group in order to start the
design process but we cannot be sure that we have made a proper choice
of participants until we have gotten far enough into the process. Since
the process is iterative and since every attempt is made to include diverse
viewpoints, this issue of circularity is not as damning as it might at first

appear. Because of its diversity in viewpoints and because of the self-reflectiveness the process encourages, every group we have worked with at some point raises for itself the question of whether new members ought to be included. Indeed, one of the most fruitful outcomes is for a group to become less exclusive, for example, for upper management to be willing to work with and seek the views of lower-level employees or for lower-level employees to become less afraid to state their views in front of their superiors.

The next step in the process is to divide the participants into two separate groups or tracks that will not be brought back together again until some time later. One track or group (I) is explicitly assigned to develop a list of critical market research questions that need answering whatever the MIS that is designed to potentially answer them. The other track (II) is explicitly assigned to develop an MIS for answering questions no matter what the set of questions that is put to the system. The basic reason for splitting the group in this manner is to assure (1) that the important questions that need addressing are not constrained by the system, and (2) that the design of the MIS is not constrained by a particular set of questions. In short, we do not want the questions to constrain or dictate the answering mechanism or the answering mechanism to dictate the kinds of questions that will be put to the system. If anything, we want to deliberately set the stage for an intense debate between two different views of the system in the attempt to make sure that an important aspect of the system is not being neglected.

Once the group of participants is split into two tracks, a further splitting occurs within each track. Since the process is basically the same within each track, we shall from here on merely illustrate it with reference to track II. Each track is divided into smaller subgroups in order to facilitate the participation and the discussion of each individual and to deliberately set up within each track explicit differences in points of view so that here as well a debate can take place later. That is, we are interested in having a debate take place both within each track and between tracks. The purpose of these debates is twofold: (1) to help insure that what one group takes for granted does not go unchallenged by another group of their peers, and (2) to help insure that important aspects of the system are not being neglected by the need for consensus that often develops in groups. If anything, we wish to deliberately induce conflict, but in such a manner that constructive use can be made of it. The use of controlled conflict is one of the cornerstones of a methodology for treating ill-structured problems (Mitroff, Barabba, and Kilmann, 1977; Mitroff and Kilmann, 1978).

It is beyond the scope of this chapter to describe the wide variety of methods that can be used to split groups into smaller working subunits

(Mitroff and Kilmann, 1978). (See Chapter 6 in this volume for a more extensive discussion of these methods.) The authors have worked most with two methods. One method divides groups along common personality lines similar to the A, B, C, and D personality types briefly described earlier. That is, all those individuals of the same personality type are put into a common subgroup. This not only facilitates their getting on with one another since they all have the same outlook but it also reduces the need for considering a large number of individual viewpoints. Instead of considering, say, twenty different views, we can consider and debate merely four. Most of all, this procedure does not leave to chance the generation of deliberately differing viewpoints of the system's design since the technique explicitly guarantees that each personality subgroup will tend to produce a very different version of the system: its detailed design properties, aims, objectives, assessments of feasibility, and the like. Once the individuals are assigned to one of four subgroups, each subgroup is instructed to develop in detail its own unique view of the system without reference to the others. Indeed, each group is deliberately instructed by us to make its view as different as possible from the others. This is insured by monitoring the output of each group. The technique would be extremely dangerous were we not assured that what one group ignores another pays explicit attention to because of the tendency of the personality system to produce completeness.

We have also worked with a formal method for organization and/or MIS design developed by Kilmann (1977) and known by the acronym MAPS (multivariate analysis, participation, and structure). The MAPS Design Technology essentially does three things. First, it breaks down a complicated set of tasks or issues into relatively homogeneous subsets of coherent or similar task clusters. Second, it breaks down a large and complicated group structure into relatively small and homogeneous subgroups, that is, manageable subgroups of eight to ten individuals that offer the promise of working effectively together. Third, it makes the best assignment of subgroups to task clusters; that is, it finds out which particular subgroup of individuals is best suited for working on which particular subset of issues. This is done for all subgroups and all task clusters so that each subgroup is assigned a unique task cluster of issues on which to work.

MAPS performs the preceding assignments by means of two question-naires. A tentative listing of the issues involved in a problem is developed by the individuals chosen for the MIS design. The individuals are then asked to indicate alongside each issue on a seven-point Likert scale (1) their degree of interest in working on the particular issue, and/or (2) their knowledge and expertise with regard to it. Similarly, a listing is made of all participating individuals who have responded to the first questionnaire. Individuals are now asked to indicate on a seven-point Likert scale, depending upon how much they know one another, either (1) the degree to which they like working with one another, (2) are interested in working with one another, and/or (3) feel they can work well together. Based on the responses to these two questionnaires, MAPS finds the best assignment of (1) issues to clusters of subissues, (2) individuals to subgroups, and (3) subgroups of people to clusters of subissues by means of multivariate statistical analyses.

Although this procedure seems to become circular, MAPS, in contrast to other techniques, not only recognizes this circularity explicitly but attempts to take positive advantage of it. The circularity arises as follows: the formal statistical aspects of the MAPS Design Technology are in many ways the smallest parts of the whole procedure. The resulting statistical assignments of individuals to subgroups, and so forth, are no better than the initial data inputs. Indeed, the validity of the output presupposes the validity of the input, which in turn presupposes that prior to their subgrouping the initial group of individuals have developed enough of an openness and a trusting relationship to give *behaviorally* valid information regarding how they feel about working with one another. This in turn presupposes that prior to the formal administration of the initial questionnaires, considerable group process work has been done in order to get the individuals to feel comfortable with one another and their feelings, so that the individuals will honestly fill out the questionnaires once they are organized, and will contribute honestly to the development of the questionnaires themselves. Since everything which follows presupposes the basic meaningfulness and validity of the input, one of the ways of securing this validity is to involve the individuals right from the very beginning in the development of the instruments to which they will be responding. But such involvement inevitably raises the question of the representativeness of the initial group, touched on earlier. See Kilmann and Ghymn (1976) for an illustration of applying the MAPS Design Technology to develop a strategic intelligence system (much like an MIS for strategic planning) for a multinational corporation.

After each subgroup has worked for some time to develop in detail its own individual and unique perspective on the design issue, the process moves into one of its most critical and difficult phases: the uncovering, inspection, and challenging of the key assumptions which underlie its design policy. One of the reasons why the design of an MIS is so difficult and why different groups often disagree about the nature of the design is, as we have repeatedly stressed throughout this chapter, that they posit fundamentally different assumptions about who the users of the system will be, their needs, objectives, and psychological style, and hence the kinds of problems they have and the data which are needed to respond to them. A key if not central feature of the process represented in Figure 11–3 is the systematic and explicit surfacing and examination of assumptions between the various groups.

We can perhaps best illustrate this part of the process by discussing an actual case in which the techniques were applied. The situation concerns a drug company faced with a major pricing policy decision on one of its most important products.* The decision was so significant that it would have vast impact on the economic structure of the entire company. As a result, the decision required analysis of the entire internal financial structure of the company, as well as various market considerations. When the problem surfaced, there were three already existing and significant groups of managers within the drug company, each of whom had a significantly different policy with respect to the pricing of the drug. These groups were, for easy identification, the high-price group, the low-price group, and the mid-price group. Each of the three groups, it turned out, was making assumptions very different from the other groups from a macro level regarding who were the important stakeholders, and each had very different detailed micro assumptions about the problem.

Mitroff and Emshoff (1979) used a technique known as *stakeholder analysis* to identify the assumptions of each group. In contrast to *stock*holder analysis, *stake*holder analysis asks a manager or dm to consider all the parties who will be affected by or who affect an important decision. It asks the manager to list as many parties or interest groups as he or she can who have a stake in the policy under consideration. This list of parties is typically much broader than the single category of stockholders which, while important, to be sure, is only one out of many contending groups which have an impact on and a stake in a corporation; it is neither the only group nor always the single most important group. In this particular case, the managers were with our help and prodding able to list the stakeholders in Figure 11–4. We would contend that for the most part the categories are generic, and hence, with little modification, they apply to most business situations. For example, in the present case, the retailers are pharmacists, although it turned out it was important to differentiate between large-scale, chain retailers and small-scale, singly owned pharmaceutical outlets.

It can easily be seen from Figure 11–4 that assumptions about each stakeholder category greatly affect the resultant policy. The whole point of getting managers to identify the important stakeholders in their situation is to help them confront the important question: "What is it that

---

*The same technique has also been applied to not-for-profit organizations.

FIGURE 11-4. *Functional stakeholder analysis for a pharmaceuticals company.*

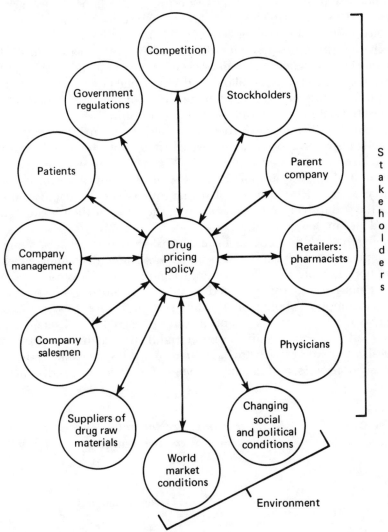

you have been assuming about the stakeholders or that you have had to assume about them so that *starting from* these assumptions you are able to *derive* your policy?" Stakeholder analysis thus asks and helps a manager to work backward. Instead of regarding the problem at the level of the resultant derived policy, it asks the manager to focus on the underlying assumptions and to regard the real problem as being at this level. What assumptions has he been making and why? What is the effect of making other assumptions? Can his policy stand up to other assumptions—can it tolerate them? Is it compatible with them? Is the current set of assumptions internally consistent with other assumptions? These are only a few of the uses to which stakeholder analysis can be put.

Once a subgroup feels it has adequately identified the assumptions which underlie its design policy, the process proceeds to a sorting of them via a technique called *belief assessment analysis* (Saaty and Rogers, 1976). Essentially, the technique allows a decision maker to derive a relative weighting of the importance of an entire set of objectives, goals, means, assumptions, and objects with regard to one another.

The significance of this procedure is illustrated in Figure 11–5. It is not only instructive, but vital to have a group apply the belief assessment procedure to two basic questions: (1) With respect to the set of assumptions underlying the support of a policy or plan, which assumptions are seen as *more important* to the plan than others? (2) Which assumptions does the group feel *most certain* about in the sense of their validity, their confidence in them, and the like?

Going through the belief assessment procedure twice, that is, rating the assumptions on both these questions, allows one to determine which assumptions fall into which quadrant of Figure 11–5. For obvious reasons, we are not particularly interested in, or at least much less interested in, those assumptions falling in the left side of Figure 11–5. Moreover, whereas the assumptions falling in the upper righthand quadrant are important, those falling in the lower righthand quadrant are the most critical. They are precisely the kind of assumptions one looks to the belief assessment process, and the methodology as a whole, to identify. Because

FIGURE 11-5. *Belief assessment of the importance versus the certainty of critical assumptions.*

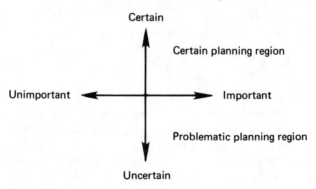

the assumptions in the lower righthand quadrant are important and yet because dm's are uncertain of their plausibility, truth, reasonableness, and the like, they deserve the most intensive discussion with regard to what if anything could be done to make their occurrence or their validation more certain. In fact, we take the identification and verification of these kinds of assumptions to be at the heart of strategic planning or strategic design.

There is an important reason for prioritizing assumptions in the way described above. We have found that individual design or strategic planning policies not only differ with regard to the detailed assumptions they make regarding stakeholders but that typically they assume very different macro stakeholder categories altogether. What one group or policy sees as an important or potentially important party another sees as relatively unimportant. The strongest way of putting this is to say that we have found that when one uses the belief assessment technique to assess the assumptions of the different policies pertaining to the different stakeholder categories, the categories typically fall into the diametrically opposite quadrants of Figure 11–5. What one group or policy takes as a relatively unimportant and certain assumption, another often takes as important and uncertain. The stage is thus typically set for an intense dialectical debate between the proponents of the different policies regarding their respective assumptions.

The purpose of the dialectical debate is not for each group to convince the other of the uncontested truth of its position, but rather to show how each group views the situation as it does and what its viewpoint entails, so that the various parties learn that there are different ways of viewing the situation and that what each takes as a natural set of "givens" (natural assumptions), the others take as an unnatural set of "takens" (unwarranted assumptions). The exercise is meant to demonstrate to both sides that there really are no "givens" in the first place, but that there are only "takens." Since this is the case, we want to make sure we have done everything in our power to locate, expose, and challenge these "takens." We know of no better way of doing this than through conducting a dialectical debate with regard to key assumptions.

The dialectical debate proceeds in much the same manner as described by Mason (1969) with some important additions. Through belief assessment analysis, we are able to identify for each design policy its key underlying assumptions—those assumptions falling in the "important" quadrants of Figure 11–5. Typically we have found that it is possible to reduce the number of these assumptions to one or two really critical or key assumptions. These generally fall into the "important" and "uncertain" quadrant. This sorting out shortens immensely the debate between policies. Instead of having to debate ten to fifteen assumptions, one can focus on the critical items and hence make the debate both more manageable and more productive.

Up to the point of the dialectic debate, we have found it advisable to work with each individual policy group separately. We have found that this helps each group to develop the best case for its position. Otherwise, groups spend too much time thinking about each other and tend to soften their position rather than building the strongest, most extreme case for their position. In our culture, at least, we are unconsciously trained for compromise. We therefore find it necessary to consciously train dm's to appreciate the value of adversarial policy making (Mason and Mitroff, 1973; Mitroff and Kilmann, 1978). The danger is not in reaching compromise, but in reaching it too soon and for the wrong reasons, for example, because of the inability to tolerate conflict as a sometimes necessary and valuable tool for policy making. Notice that we are not saying that in itself conflict is always desirable. We are saying that the outright rejection and unconsidered avoidance of conflict is undesirable.

The conduct of the debate proceeds by having the spokesperson of each individual policy list the one or two key assumptions associated with that policy. Each spokesperson then argues why his or her assumptions are critical to the policy, that is, why it is dependent upon them. Only after each group has made its presentation and every group has understood why the assumptions of each individual group are critical to that group's policy does the method enter the last, the most difficult, and the most critical phase—the negotiation of assumptions. Before this can proceed, however, it is vital that each group understand the assumptions of the other groups and why they are critical for those groups. We do not ask each group to necessarily accept alternate assumptions, merely to try to understand them. We have found as a rule that the more a group can begin to understand the assumptions of an opposing policy, the closer they will be to later appreciating the value of entertaining alternate assumptions and, hence, achieving compromise.

The most difficult part of the process is achieving compromise between assumptions. It is even more difficult to come up with an entirely new, synthesized set of assumptions that bridge the old policies and go beyond them as well.

In an attempt to achieve synthesis, and at the very least compromise, we have worked out an assumption negotiation procedure. After each group has listed its key assumptions on a blackboard for public inspection by all the other groups, we ask each group individually to identify the most perturbing assumptions from the other groups, that is, those assumptions (key or otherwise) which are the hardest for each group to live with. After each group has done this, we ask all the groups to engage, to the extent they can, in assumption modification. We ask each group to soften *its* assumptions to the point where they just barely support its policies, that is, where if the group relaxed its assumptions any further, it could no longer derive or support its own policy. In this way, we hope by successively working back and forth between the assumptions of the different groups to obtain a zone of compromise, if one is possible, and from this zone to extract a set of compromise assumptions. If such a compromise is not possible, and it frequently is not, then the participants will at least have achieved a better, a deeper understanding of the underlying reasons that have divided them in the past and will continue to divide them in the future. They will have at least achieved the important understanding that if they decide to act on or accept any one of the original policies, then they are in a better position to consider what might happen if the assumptions of the design policy they have chosen to implement no longer prove valid. They can at least defend their choice to their superiors by arguing that they have made their choice under the most critically challenging test conditions.

CONCLUSION

None of the preceding discussion is meant to imply, let alone guarantee, that the design of an MIS produced by the process will be *the* correct one. In the realm of ill-structured problems there may be no single best or right solution (Rittel, 1971), merely relatively better ones, where "better" means a design that is produced under conditions of awareness of one's assumptions. At least this much we can hope for and try to achieve. If ignorance of assumptions is not a desirable property for well-structured problems, it is even less of a desirable property for ill-structured problems where even more is at stake and dependent upon examining key assumptions.

The whole design process we have outlined in this chapter rests upon *our* key operating assumption: that an MIS can be no better than the assumptions upon which it rests; therefore, the exposure of assumptions is critical to MIS design. We hope that we have sufficiently exposed our own assumptions so that they as well can be challenged.

REFERENCES

Ackoff, Russell L. "Management Misinformation Systems," *Management Science*, December 1967, pp. B-147–B-156.
Bell, Martin L. *Marketing: Concepts and Strategy*, 2nd ed. (Boston: Houghton Mifflin, 1972).

Churchill, Gilbert A., Jr. *Marketing Research: Methodological Foundations* (Hinsdale, Ill.: Dryden Press, 1976).

Cravens, David W., Gerald E. Hills, and Robert B. Woodruff. *Marketing Decision Making: Concepts and Strategy* (Homewood, Ill.: Irwin, 1976).

Dickson, G. W., and John K. Simmons. "The Behavioral Side of MIS," *Business Horizons*, August 1970, pp. 59–71.

Edström, Anders. "User Influence and the Success of MIS Projects: A Contingency Approach," *Human Relations*, Vol. 30, No. 7 (1977), pp. 589–607.

Joyner, Robert, and Kenneth Tunstall. "Computer Augmented Organization Problem Solving," *Management Science*, December 1970, pp. B-212–B-225.

Jung, C. G. *Psychological Types* (London: Rutledge, 1923).

Kilmann, Ralph H. *Social Systems Design: Normative Theory and the MAPS Design Technology.* (New York: Elsevier, 1977).

Kilmann, Ralph H., Marjorie A. Lyles, and Ian I. Mitroff. "Designing an Effective Problem Solving Organization with the MAPS Design Technology," *Journal of Management*, Vol. 2 (1977), pp. 1–16.

Kotler, Philip. *Marketing Management: Analysis, Planning, and Control*, 3rd ed. (Englewood Cliffs, N.J.: Prentice-Hall, 1976).

Little, John D. C. "Models and Managers: The Concept of a Decision Calculus," *Management Science*, April 1970, pp. B-469–B-470.

Mason, Richard O. "A Dialectical Approach to Strategic Planning," *Management Science*, April 1969, pp. B-403–B-414.

Mason Richard O., and Ian I. Mitroff. "A Program for Research on Management Information Systems," *Management Science*, January 1973, pp. 475–487.

McKenney, James L., and Peter G. W. Keen. "How Managers' Minds Work," *Harvard Business Review*, May–June 1974.

Mitroff, Ian I., Vincent P. Barabba, and Ralph H. Kilmann. "The Application of Behavioral and Philosophical Technologies to Strategic Planning: A Case Study of a Large Federal Agency," *Management Science*, September 1977, pp. 44–58.

Mitroff, Ian I., and Ralph H. Kilmann. "On Integrating Behavioral and Philosophical Systems: Towards a Unified Theory of Problem Solving," *Annual Series in Sociology*, Vol. 1 (1978).

Mitroff, Ian I., and Tom R. Featheringham. "On Systematic Problem Solving and the Error of the Third Kind," *Behavioral Science*, November 1974, pp. 383–393.

Mitroff, Ian I., and James Emshoff. "On Strategic Assumption-Making," *Academy of Management Review*, in press (1979).

Montgomery, David B. "Marketing Decision Information Systems: Some Design Considerations," in Robert Ferber, ed., *Handbook of Marketing Research* (New York: McGraw-Hill, 1974).

Montgomery, David, and Glen L. Urban. *Management Science in Marketing* (Englewood Cliffs, N.J.: Prentice-Hall, 1969).

Myers-Briggs, I. *Manual for the Myers-Briggs Type Indicator* (Princeton, N.J.: Educational Testing Service, 1962).

Pounds, William F. "The Process of Problem Finding," *Industrial Management Review*, Fall 1969.

Rittel, H. "Some Principles for the Design of an Educational System for Design," *Journal of Architectural Education*, Vol. 26 (1971), pp. 16–27.

Saaty, T. L., and P. C. Rogers. "Higher Education in the United States (1985–2000): Scenario Construction Using a Hierarchical Framework with Eigenvector Weighting," *Socio-Economic Planning*, Vol. 10 (1976), pp. 251–263.

Sparks, Jack D. "Taming the 'Paper Elephant' in Marketing Information Systems," *Journal of Marketing*, Vol. 40 (1976), pp. 83–91.

Wilensky, Harold L. *Organizational Intelligence* (New York: Basic Books, 1967).

Zaltman, Gerald, and Robert Duncan. *Strategies for Planned Change* (New York: Wiley-Interscience, 1977).

Zaltman, Gerald, David Florio, and Linda Sikorski. *Dynamic Educational Change: Models, Strategies, Tactics, and Management* (New York: Free Press, 1977).

Zaltman, Gerald, and Philip Burger. *Marketing Research: Fundamentals and Dynamics* (Hinsdale, Ill.: Dryden Press, 1975).

PART III
Control

CHAPTER 12

Fund Accounting

James M. Patton

Editor's Note *Fund accounting measures the extent to which managers' resources meet their fiduciary responsibilities to constituents. Thus fund accounting is a vital procedure of concern to many people associated with nonprofit organizations. This chapter introduces the fund accounting system, its concepts, characteristics, and limitations. The basic theory and practice are dealt with in the context of municipal government units, and the results are evaluted to help the reader recognize its strengths and weaknesses.*

Fund accounting is a unit of information peculiar to nonprofit organizations. It was developed as a result of the characteristics of the organizations and of the users and uses of information. Nonprofit organizations are characterized by their focus on social benefits, their relative absence of profit-motivated behavior by resource contributors, and special government- and constituent-imposed constraints on activities. The users of fund accounting information are a diverse group, both internal and external to the organization.

Fund accounting is similar to private enterprise accounting in its activities, terminology, and qualitative objectives. But whereas private enterprises use a single-entity focus, fund accounting may involve many fragmented financial reports, focusing on separate individual funds and the flow of liquid assets instead of income. For example, municipal fund accounting divides a municipality into eight types of fund entities and two groups of accounts. The general fund is established to account for the unrestricted resources of the municipality and resources not accounted for in any other fund or group of accounts. The basic operating statements of the general fund are revenues, expenditures, and encumbrances and changes in fund balances. Debt service funds keep track of resources segregated for paying interest and principal on a municipal general obligation debt. Capital project funds are established to account for resources segregated for the purpose of acquiring major fixed assets. Financial reports for capital project funds seek to present sources, uses, and available resources for individual projects.

The general fixed-assets group is created to establish control of general fund assets of the municipality. The general long-term-debt group is designed to report the amount and status of debt obligation. Proprietary funds account for commercial activities and are of two types: enterprise funds, which account for self-supporting municipal operations that provide goods and services to the general public on a user-charge basis; and internal service funds, which cover the same activities in cases where consumers are other departments in the municipality. Fiduciary funds are established to account for resources held by the municipality as an agent or trustee for some other person, group, or government.

Municipal financial reports may be useful for financial planning and control but they have been criticized for their fragmented nature, use of a modified accrual system of accounting in general government fund activities, and treatment of depreciation. The author also examines the accounting practices and special characteristics of hospitals and colleges, sources of generally accepted accounting principles (GAAP) for these nonprofit entities, and the similarities and differences between GAAP and their financial reporting practices.

This chapter introduces a fundamental component of information systems in not-for-profit (NFP) organizations: the fund accounting system. In the sections that follow, the conceptual basis, characteristics, and limitations of fund accounting will be described. The basic theory and practice of fund accounting will be examined in the context of municipal government units. The information produced by fund accounting practices will be examined to help users recognize the strengths and limitations of financial reports. The chapter ends with a review of the special characteristics of fund accounting in nongovernment nonprofit organizations.

Accounting has been defined in different ways over time. Nearly all the definitions recognize accounting as a service activity, designed to provide information useful for making decisions. To fulfill this function, the accountant must decide which phenomena are relevant, how to measure and record their effects, and how to classify, summarize, and report the data for use by interested parties.

Such decisions are generally influenced by (1) the characteristics of the entity being reported upon and (2) the users/uses of the information. In NFP organizations, these two factors have led to the development of accounting practices commonly called "fund accounting."

CHARACTERISTICS OF NOT-FOR-PROFIT ORGANIZATIONS

Not-for-profit organizations can be distinguished from for-profit entities primarily on the basis of differing organizational objectives. This fundamental difference creates other important differences in organizational structures, constraints on activities, and the relationship of revenues to output. These factors, which affect the accounting system and financial reports of NFP organizations, are discussed below.

Although most organizations have multiple objectives, the primary goal of private enterprise businesses is frequently assumed to be maximization of long-run profit or shareholders' wealth. In contrast, NFP organizations generally focus on the satisfaction of some nonfinancial social objectives. Although for-profit and NFP organizations sometimes engage in similar activities, this difference in goals leads accountants to measure, record, and report different types of information for the two organizations. For example, since the profit motive is not an important factor in NFP organizations, this measure of performance (revenues less expenses) is not calculated for most NFP activities. Rather, NFP organizations report primarily on the control and use of current financial resources. The fund accounting system described in this chapter aids in control over the use of these assets. (Other chapters in this book describe managerial accounting information systems in NFP organizations.)

The differing objectives of NFP and for-profit organizations are also reflected in the organizational structures of NFP entities. Unlike for-profit businesses, NFP organizations do not have equity interests based on *ownership* of the entity. Thus the management of NFP organizations has a different set of constituencies to report to than does private enterprise management. In addition, the influence of constituents in NFP organizations is not usually directly proportional to the individual "contribution" of resources to the NFP organizations. Thus the structure and financial reports of NFP organizations are not usually centered upon shareholder-director-management stewardship relations. Rather, NFP organizations are more likely to be structured around the members, the public, or the consumers of the service provided.

Private enterprises and NFP organizations operate within the same general framework of society. However, private enterprise businesses are primarily guided by the market forces created by competition for profits. This profit motive, which influences much of private enterprise decision making, is absent from NFP organizations. Thus NFP organizations (especially governments) can continue to operate in spite of inefficient or nonprofitable activities. Because they lack an automatic constraint on activities, NFP organizations are frequently subjected to more extensive formal regulation and controls. These controls may be imposed by the government granting NFP status or by the constituents of the organization itself and are designed to limit the activities of the NFP organization to the achievement of basic social goals. The fund accounting system is designed to help enforce some of these limitations on NFP organizational activities.

Another distinguishing characteristic of NFP organizations, also tracable to the nonprofit objective, is the fact that the revenues of the entity are rarely related to the services or goods it provides. Private enterprises rely on supply and demand factors to determine what to charge the customers for goods and services sold. This has led private enterprise accounting to attempt to "match" revenues and expenses in order to measure the profit earned. In NFP organizations, in contrast, "customers" are not charged so the organization can achieve a profit. The NFP organization receives its resources from contributions, taxes, earnings from endowments, cost-based user charges, and other nonoutput-related sources. Thus, instead of attempting to match revenues and expenses, NFP organizations typically trace the flows of financial resources through the entity. Fund accounting practices have been developed to aid this function.

USERS OF NFP ACCOUNTING INFORMATION

The characteristics of NFP organizations discussed above have a direct impact on the number and types of NFP accounting information. For example, since there are no shares of stock in NFP organizations, equity investors are not potential users of accounting information. The potential users of NFP accounting information can be divided into two groups: internal and external. (Although the distinction between internal and external users is sometimes unclear, the basic difference lies in the extent to which the user is directly involved in the day-to-day operation of the NFP organization.) Few systematic studies have been made of actual users of NFP accounting reports. The list at the top of the next page describes the groups that are generally thought to be users, actual or potential.

Within this list, the groups concerned with accountability for the use of financial resources have been emphasized in the development of fund accounting for NFP organizations. For example, in a municipal context, some information users want to ensure that the resources appropriated have been spent legally and in accordance with the legislators' directions. Fund accounting seems to do a good job on this type of accountability

Internal	*External*
Managers	Public
Auditors	Regulators
Legislators	Investors
	Creditors
	Independent auditors
	Foundations
	Other NFP organizations
	Employees
	Accreditation groups
	Directors
	Constituencies (voters, members, consumers)
	Suppliers

and control. Other internal and external users are apparently not served as well. This limitation will be discussed below.

FUND ACCOUNTING

The sections above established the conceptual basis for differences between NFP and private enterprise accounting—namely, different characteristics of the economic entity and the emphasis on different users and uses of the information. In this section we examine the specific fund accounting practices that reflect these basic conceptual differences. These differences are illustrated in the context of accounting for municipal NFP organizations. Later, the special characteristics of fund accounting in other NFP organizations will be discussed.

Fund Accounting Versus Private Enterprise Accounting

There are some fundamental similarities between fund accounting and private enterprise accounting. There are also a significant number of differences that lead to distinctly different reporting practices by the two types of organizations.

Similarities. Both private enterprise and fund accounting systems are based on observing events and phenomena that can be measured and reported in monetary terms. (Although nonfinancial measures of output are important in NFP organizations, these measures are not part of the fund accounting system). The two systems are also similar in that (1) both use a double-entry bookkeeping system, with the same basic terminology; (2) certain activities (such as electric utility operations) are accounted for in roughly the same way; and (3) both are based on objectivity, consistency, disclosure, and other qualitative objectives of accounting.

Differences. Private enterprise organizations report on their financial position and operations using a single-entity focus. Thus, although a conglomerate may be involved in diversified activities, the company constructs one set of reports to describe its financial position and results of operations. In contrast, most NFP organizations prepare highly fragmented financial reports which focus on the individual *funds* as separate fiscal and accounting entities. Instead of reporting a single set of consolidated statements, NFP organizations prepare a series of reports on individual fund entities to reflect the operations and position of the organization. The nature of these individual subunits is described in detail below.

Another fundamental difference between private enterprise and fund accounting is the basis of accounting. In a municipality, the general government fund entities employ a *modified accrual* system. Unlike the private enterprise full accrual system, which focuses on income, such funds focus on the flow of liquid assets. As a result, the operating statements reflect revenues and *expenditures* (versus expenses) of the individual fund entities. Revenues are recorded when they are judged to be measurable and available for meeting obligations; expenditures are recorded when new obligations of the fund are incurred. The balance sheets of such funds also emphasize current financial resources. Thus normally only short-term monetary items will appear as assets in general government fund entities.

Private enterprise accounting and fund accounting also differ in the effect of budgeting on operations and reports. In NFP fund accounting, control over activities is often extended by imposing formal budgetary constraints on managers (especially in government units). Once the intent of the directors or elected officials is formalized, all subsequent expenditures must be traced to some budgetary authorization or appropriation. This control point ensures that the expenditures are legal and appropriate to the object (service) acquired and the amount expended. Budget information may also be included in the financial reports of the general fund and certain special revenue funds. Comparisons of actual versus budgeted revenues and expenditures monitor the adherence to authorized spending limits. Although budgets are an important planning and control tool in private enterprise, they are not recorded in the accounts or reported in the financial statements of business.

A final basic difference between NFP and private enterprise accounting is the source of generally accepted accounting principles (GAAP). In 1934 the Securities and Exchange Commission (SEC) was created to administer the Securities Acts. The SEC was given (and retains) the authority to establish GAAP for private enterprises. The SEC has delegated much of its authority to the accounting profession. Thus the Financial Accounting

Standards Board (FASB), an independent group of individuals familiar with accounting issues, is currently the basic source of private enterprise GAAP in the United States. However, until recently NFP organizations have not been the subject of much SEC or FASB attention. Rather, other private groups [such as the Municipal Finance Officers Association (MFOA), the National Association of College and University Business Officers (NACUBO), the American Hospital Association, and the American Institute of Certified Public Accountants (AICPA) audit guide committees] have established GAAP for NFP organizations.

Because of this dispersal of authority, the accounting principles for the different types of NFP organizations (municipalities, colleges, hospitals) are somewhat unique (although they do share some common characteristics, such as the fund entity concept). In addition, the actual accounting and financial reporting practices of such organizations have not always conformed to GAAP. Thus generally acccepted fund accounting principles are applied differently in different types of NFP organizations and are not always followed uniformly among NFP organizations of the same type.

An understanding of the basic fund accounting principles described above is only part of the preparation necessary for understanding and using NFP fund accounting financial statements. The section that follows describes the unique features of fund accounting in a municipal setting. A later section will examine the features of fund accounting in hospitals and colleges.

MUNICIPAL FUND ACCOUNTING

Municipal fund accounting divides a municipality into eight types of fund entities and two groups of accounts. The eight funds can be grouped according to the primary function they serve:

Funds
  General government
    General fund
    Special revenue funds
    Capital project funds
    Special assessment funds
    Debt service funds
  Proprietary (self-supporting)
    Enterprise funds
    Internal service funds
  Fiduciary
    Trust and agency funds

Groups of Accounts
    General fixed-assets group
    General long-term-debt group

In municipal accounting, a fund is defined as "an independent fiscal and accounting entity with a self-balancing set of accounts recording cash and/or other financial resources together with all related liabilities and residual entities . . . which are segregated for the purpose of carrying on specific activities or attaining certain objectives" (NCGA, 1977, pp. 2–10). As noted above, these fund entities are the focus of the financial accounting and reporting system. Because general government funds focus on the flow of current assets, general fixed-asset and long-term-debt *groups of accounts* are also needed to account for noncurrent general government items. These groups of accounts are not fund entities, since they are not comprised of resources and related obligations segregated for a specific purpose. Rather, they are records designed to aid in the control of non-current assets and liabilities of municipalities.

General Fund Accounting

In any accounting system, the accountant must first decide which events to measure and record. In a fund accounting system the next decision involves which fund entity(ies) to use to record the effect of the events. The general fund is established to account for unrestricted resources of the municipality and resources not accounted for in any other fund or group of accounts. The general fund is most often the major (sometimes the only) fund entity used by a municipality. It is a general government or expendable type of fund. As described above, general government funds reflect the flow of liquid resources. The sample financial reports (balance sheet; statement of revenues; statement of expenditures and encumbrances; and statement of changes in fund balance) reproduced in Figures 12–1 to 12–4 illustrate the type of information on the general fund provided by the fund accounting system. The economic events and phenomena that underlie such reports are discussed below.

The general fund balance sheet (Figure 12–1) reflects the current asset/ obligation focus of government funds as well as the separate fund-by-fund approach in municipal accounting. The basic relationship within the statement of financial position is as follows:

$$\text{Assets} = \text{liabilities} + \text{fund balance}$$

The assets recorded in the general fund are not classified into current and noncurrent, since they are all short term in nature. All these assets (except the inventory of supplies) represent cash, claims on other eco-

FIGURE 12–1. *General fund balance sheet.*

Municipal Government
General Fund
Comparative Balance Sheets (December 31)

	1978	1977
Assets		
Cash	$ XXX	$ XXX
Certificates of deposit	XXX	XXX
Property tax receivable	XXX	XXX
Less: Allowance for uncollectibles	(XXX)	(XXX)
Due from other funds	XXX	XXX
Inventory of supplies	XXX	XXX
Total	$XXXX	$XXXX
Liabilities, Reserves, Fund Balance		
Vouchers payable	$ XXX	$ XXX
Accounts payable	XXX	XXX
Due to other funds	XXX	XXX
Reserve for inventory	XXX	XXX
Reserve for encumbrances	XXX	XXX
Fund balance	XXX	XXX
Total	$XXXX	$XXXX

nomic entities for receipts of cash, or temporary investments of cash. Thus the general fund assets represent the current position of this fund entity—that is, the pool of liquid resources that can be appropriated for the activities accounted for by the general fund. The exception to this rule, the inventory of supplies, reflects the cost of the miscellaneous supplies held by the municipality. It is included to help complete the description of the current position of the general fund. However, since inventory does not represent an appropriable asset, the inventory amount is offset on the balance sheet by an equal amount in a fund balance reserve account (discussed below). The inventory of supplies and the investment securities are generally recorded at cost (with market value disclosed parenthetically for investments). However, the other assets of the general fund are reported at their net realizable value—that is, the amount that would be received if the claims were converted to cash.

The separate-entity focus of fund accounting is illustrated by the general fund asset account called "due from other funds." Although this account represents an asset of the general fund, it cannot be considered an asset of the municipality as a whole. It represents the right of the general fund to receive cash from some other fund entity within the municipality. A corresponding liability will appear on another fund's balance sheet.

In addition to describing the assets of the fund, the balance sheet reports the claims upon such assets. Debts of the municipality that are not directly related to the assets of the general fund are not reflected in the general fund balance sheet. The obligations reported are generally short term in nature and reflect the current obligation of the general fund to other economic entites (including other funds within the municipality).

The other major section of the balance sheet, the fund balance, reflects the excess of assets over the liabilities of the fund. The fund balance can be further divided into reserves and the free fund balance. The free fund balance reflects the net assets of the fund that are available for further budgetary appropriations. The "reserve" subcategory reflects varying degrees of claims or limitations on the assets. For example, the reserve for inventory is created to offset recognition of the nonappropriable asset inventory. Although it may be useful to disclose the existence of this current asset, including its value in the fund balance would misstate the available appropriable resources.

The reserve for encumbrances is another aspect of the modified accrual system used in municipal government. The amount of expenditures that can be made for specific objects or purposes is frequently restricted by a budgetary appropriation. Thus it is important to keep track of the consumption of such authorizations for spending. The reserve for encumbrances shows that the process of incurring obligations or disbursing resources has begun. Although a formal obligation has not yet been created, the appropriable resources are expected to be consumed as a result of current actions. For example, issuance of a purchase order for supplies begins the expenditure process. Although the general fund liability and expenditure are not created until the supplies are actually delivered, the balance sheet should reflect the fact that resources have been encumbered by the purchase order. Through this process, the actual fund balance account remains an accurate representation of the net resources free for further appropriation.

In summary, the balance sheet in Figure 12–1 reflects the assets, obligations, and residual equity of the general fund. The general fund resources are generally available for use in any authorized activity of the municipality.

The basic operating statements of the general fund are the statements of (1) revenues, (2) expenditures and encumbrances, and (3) changes in fund balance. These statements trace the flow of general fund assets and explain changes in general fund balance sheets over time. As noted above, these statements do not focus on income. Rather, they trace the flow of appropriate liquid assets through the fund entity.

In the modified accrual accounting system for municipal general funds, revenues of a fund entity consist of increases in assets which are not accompanied by increases in obligations or decreases in other assets. As illustrated in Figure 12–2, revenues are typically reported by various sources and compared with budgeted amounts. Interfund transfers are treated as a special type of source and reported separately. Revenues are generally recorded when received in cash. However, some revenues (such as property taxes) may be recorded on an *accrual* basis. Such revenues may be recorded when they become *measurable* and *available*.

Recording revenue is clearly inappropriate until an objective measure of the ultimate inflow of assets can be made. In this respect NFP accounting resembles private enterprise accounting. Municipal revenues are said to be available when appropriable assets flow in soon enough to finance the activities accounted for in the fund during the current year. If GAAP are followed, the figure reported as actual revenues of a period should reflect the gross increase in financial resources of the fund from various sources. Underestimating uncollectible accounts and recording revenues prematurely will distort the financial picture presented and misstate the resources available for pursuing the NFP organization's goals.

FIGURE 12–2. *General fund revenue statement.*

Municipal Government
General Fund
Statement of Revenue—Estimated and Actual
For the Year Ending December 31, 1978

Source	Estimated Revenue	Actual Revenue	Actual Over (Under) Estimate
Property tax	$ XXX	$ XXX	$ XXX
Licenses and permits	XXX	XXX	XXX
Intergovernmental funds	XXX	XXX	XXX
Charges for services	XXX	XXX	XXX
Fines and forfeits	XXX	XXX	XXX
Interest	XXX	XXX	XXX
Transfers from other funds	XXX	XXX	XXX
Total	$XXXX	$XXXX	$XXXX

The statement of general fund expenditures and encumbrances (Figure 12–3) traces the flow of appropriable assets out of the fund entity during a fiscal period. The statement illustrates how the modified accrual approach applies to outflows. As noted above, the modified accrual system focuses on expenditure accrual rather than expense accrual. In addition, the accruals are not matched with the revenue accruals in an attempt to measure income. This distinction is fundamental to understanding the information contained in the operating statement. Expenditures for buildings and other fixed assets are treated the same basic way as expenditures for items or services consumed in the same period as acquired. The only difference is that fixed assets acquired by the municipality through general fund expenditures are also recorded in the general fixed-asset group of accounts (discussed below). Thus, from the point of view of general fund operating and position statements, fixed-asset expenditures and current operating expenditures are equivalent.

General fund expenditures are recorded when an obligation is incurred or assets are distributed. These expenditures are typically classified and reported according to the function they serve within the municipality. They may also be classified and reported by (1) the organizational unit with the municipality making the expenditure (such as the police or sanitation department), (2) the character of the expenditure (current, capital, or debt service), and (3) the object of the expenditure (such as supplies

FIGURE 12–3. *General fund expenditures statement.*

	Municipal Government			
	General Fund			
	Statement of Expenditures and Encumbrances			
	For the Year Ending December 31			
	1978	1978	*Over (Under)*	1977
Function	*Budget*	*Actual*	*Budget*	*Actual*
General government	$ XXX	$ XXX	$ XXX	$ XXX
Public safety	XXX	XXX	XXX	XXX
Highways and streets	XXX	XXX	XXX	XXX
Sanitation	XXX	XXX	XXX	XXX
Health	XXX	XXX	XXX	XXX
Welfare	XXX	XXX	XXX	XXX
Culture and recreation	XXX	XXX	XXX	XXX
Education	XXX	XXX	XXX	XXX
Transfers to other funds	XXX	XXX	XXX	XXX
Total	$XXXX	$XXXX	$XXXX	$XXXX

or labor services). Each of these classification schemes may be useful to certain users.

Since budgetary control is important in fund accounting, encumbrances and budgetary figures may also be included in the operating statements. Comparative statements allow the reader to compare the amounts budgeted for some function with the actual amounts expended and encumbered. In addition, the current year's budgeted and actual expenditures and encumbrances can be compared with previous year's actual figures to give some idea of the trend of current expenditures. Such statements do not, however, reflect the utlization or consumption of all the resources applied to a certain function. (This distinction is discussed in the limitations section below.)

The final basic financial statement prepared for the general fund entity is the statement of changes in fund balance (Figure 12-2). As the title suggests, this report summarizes the events that affect the balance of the general fund, linking the general fund balance sheets over time. Since the fund balance in the general fund reflects the net appropriable resources of the fund, the items that affect the statement are the beginning fund balance, revenues, expenditures. and encumbrances.

The basic principles for municipal general fund accounting and reporting also apply to the special revenue fund (SRF). SRFs account for and report on resources that come from special revenue sources or that are restricted to more specific purposes than the general fund. They constitute a separate class of fund entities and are reported on separately, using the same basic principles as the general fund. Therefore, they are not discussed as a separate item in this chapter. The interpretation and

FIGURE 12–4. *General fund statement of changes in fund balance.*

Municipal Government		
General Fund		
Analysis of Changes in Fund Balance		
For the Year Ending December 31, 1978		
	1978	*1978*
	Estimated	*Actual*
Fund balance January 1, 1978	$ XXX	$ XXX
Add: Revenues	XXX	XXX
Less: Expenditures	(XXX)	(XXX)
Less: Increase in reserve for encumbrances	(XXX)	(XXX)
Fund balance December 31, 1978	$XXXX	$XXXX

limitations of the information produced by GAAP for these fund entities are discussed below.

Debt Service Funds

In some municipalities only the general fund is used. However, in larger municipalities which require specialized accounting for certain types of resources or activities, other (distinctly different) fund entities must be created. For example, when a municipality issues general obligation bonds, it may be required to establish one or more debt service funds (DSFs). Debt service funds are created to keep track of resources that are segregated for the purpose of paying interest and principal on a municipal general obligation debt. The financial accounting and reporting practices required for a DSF reflect the attempt to identify the sources and amounts of resources available for debt servicing.

The balance sheet in Figure 12–5 shows the type of assets, liabilities, and fund balance found in the DSF. One DSF has been created for each of several bond issues. These items reflect the familiar focus on current resources and obligations, since the modified accrual basis of accounting is also applied in the DSF. Thus the assets of the DSF consist of cash and

FIGURE 12–5. *Debt service funds balance sheet.*

Municipal Government
Debt Service Funds
Balance Sheet
December 31, 1978

	1985 (Parks)	1988 (Bridges)	1992 (Civic Center)	Total
Assets				
Cash	$ XXX	$ XXX	$ XXX	$ XXX
Cash with fiscal agent	XXX	XXX	XXX	XXX
Taxes receivable (net)	XXX	XXX	XXX	XXX
Investments	XXX	XXX	XXX	XXX
Interest receivable	XXX	XXX	XXX	XXX
Total	$XXXX	$XXXX	$XXXX	$XXXX
Liabilities and Fund Balance				
Matured bonds payable	$ XXX	$ XXX	$ XXX	$ XXX
Matured interest payable	XXX	XXX	XXX	XXX
Fund balance	XXX	XXX	XXX	XXX
Total	$XXXX	$XXXX	$XXXX	$XXXX

near-cash items (receivables and investment securities). Since there may be a significant interval between the time revenues are received by the DSF and the time that interest and principal expenditures are required, sound financial management practice requires that the liquid resources be invested in safe securities for that interval. The liabilities reflect unpaid amounts of interest due or bonds that have matured. General obligation bonds that have not matured are not a liability of any specific fund entity and therefore do not appear as a liability of the debt service fund. Rather, these bonds are accounted for in the long-term-debt group of accounts (discussed below). The fund balance represents the net balance of assets available for future debt service activity.

The operating statements of the DSF trace the flow of liquid assets in and out of the fund entity (Figure 12–6). Revenues for debt service are usually based on general property taxes. However, other sources may be

FIGURE 12–6. *Debt service funds operating statement.*

	1985 (Parks)	1988 (Bridges)	1992 (Civic Center)	Total
Revenues				
Property tax	$ XXX	$ XXX	$ XXX	$ XXXX
Interest on investments	XXX	XXX	XXX	XXXX
Intergovernmental funds	XXX	XXX	XXX	XXXX
Contributions of other funds	XXX	XXX	XXX	XXXX
Total	$XXXX	$XXXX	$XXXX	$XXXXX
Expenditures				
Matured bonds	$ XXX	$ XXX	$ XXX	$ XXXX
Interest paid	XXX	XXX	XXX	XXXX
Fiscal agent fees	XXX	XXX	XXX	XXXX
Total	$XXXX	$XXXX	$XXXX	$XXXXX
Fund balance January 1, 1978	$ XXX	$ XXX	$ XXX	$ XXXX
Excess of revenues over expenditures	XXX	XXX	XXX	XXXX
Fund balance December 31, 1978	$XXXX	$XXXX	$XXXX	$XXXXX

Municipal Government
Debt Service Funds
Statement of Revenues, Expenditures, and Changes in Fund Balance
For the Year Ending December 31, 1978

available, such as transfers from other funds and investment income. As in the general fund, revenue should be accrued when it is measurable and available.

The financial statement tracing the outflows of resources from the DSF focuses on the expenditures made during the period. Since payments for interest and principal are usually prescribed by the bond indenture, the operations of the DSF are generally not compared with budgeted figures in the financial reports. In the DSF, the modified accrual system of accounting requires the recording of expenditures when legal obligations are created. In fund accounting, when bonds mature they cease to be general obligations of the municipality as a whole and become obligations of the debt service fund. At this point an expenditure and liability are recognized in the DSF. In addition, when interest becomes payable, the DSF records an expenditure. Thus encumbrances and interest *expense* accruals are not made within the DSF. That is, no accrual is made for interest charged (but not paid) on bonds for the period between the last payment of interest and the end of the fiscal period. For example, if a fiscal period ends on December 31 and an interest payment is due on January 1, neither the expenditure nor the obligation will be recorded on the DSF financial reports (unless it is prepaid).

Capital Project Funds

The final type of general government fund entity is the capital project fund. (Special assessment funds are not discussed here since they simply combine the accounting and reporting practices of special revenue, capital project, and debt service funds.) Capital project funds (CPFs) are established to account for resources segregated for the purpose of acquiring major fixed assets. A separate capital project fund is normally established for each project.

Financial reports of the CPF present the sources, uses, and available pool of resources for individual projects. Like the other general government fund entities, the CPF focuses on current resources and obligations. Thus the balance sheet (Figure 12–7) shows the typical set of highly liquid assets and current obligations. "Retained percentage," a special type of liability, is also included. This account reflects the fact that the municipality will not pay a portion of the contract price until the project is completed and accepted. Thus the municipality has an obligation resulting from services that it has already received.

Capital projects are subject to capital budgeting plans. Thus the reserve for encumbrance account may also appear in the CPF balance sheets. The fund balance in the CPF reflects the net resources currently available for completing the project. Note that no fixed assets appear on the CPF

FIGURE 12–7. *Capital project funds balance sheet.*

Municipal Government
Capital Project Funds
Balance Sheet December 31, 1978

Assets	Civic Center	Bridges	Total
Cash	$ XXX	$ XXX	$ XXX
Due from other funds	XXX	XXX	XXX
Due from other governments	XXX	XXX	XXX
Investments	XXX	XXX	XXX
Total	$XXXX	$XXXX	$XXXX
Liabilities, Reserves, Fund Balance			
Vouchers payable	$ XXX	$ XXX	$ XXX
Contracts payable	XXX	XXX	XXX
Retained percentage	XXX	XXX	XXX
Due to other funds	XXX	XXX	XXX
Reserve for encumbrances	XXX	XXX	XXX
Fund balance	XXX	XXX	XXX
Total	$XXXX	$XXXX	$XXXX

balance sheet. The fixed assets (in progress or completed) become assets of the municipality as a whole rather than of the CPF. Therefore, they are recorded in the general fixed-asset group of accounts.

The two operating statements recommended for the CPF are the statement of revenue and the statement of changes in fund balance (Figures 12–8 and 12–9). A revenue was defined earlier as an increase in fund assets without a concurrent increase in obligations or decrease in assets of the fund. Frequently, capital projects will be financed by issuing municipal bonds. The proceeds from the sale of the bonds become an asset of the CPF. The liability is recorded separately in the general long-term-debt group of accounts. Thus, technically, the issuing of debt provides revenue for the CPF. However, from the point of view of the municipality as a whole, the debt issue clearly does not provide an increase in net assets. Because of the special nature of this source of funds for the CPF, it should be reported separately on the statement of revenue. Other sources of revenue for the CPF include contributions from other fund entities and intergovernmental grants.

No separate statement of expenditures and encumbrances is recommended for the CPF. Rather, a condensed statement of changes in fund

FIGURE 12–8. *Capital project funds statement of revenue.*

Municipal Government *Capital Project Funds* *Statement of Revenue, Estimated and Actual* *For the Year Ending December 31, 1978*		
Fund and Source of Revenue	*Estimated*	*Actual*
Civic Center		
Sale of bonds	$ XXX	$ XXX
Transfers from other funds	XXX	XXX
Intergovernmental funds	XXX	XXX
Bridges		
Transfers from other funds	$ XXX	$ XXX
Intergovernmental funds	XXX	XXX
Interest	XXX	XXX
Total	$XXXX	$XXXX

balance is presented. This report summarizes all the events of the period that affected the fund balance of the CPF. All the expenditures in the CPF should be related to capital asset acquisition. To the extent that current operating expenditures are included among the capital expenditures, the current position and operation of the CPF and general fund or special revenue fund may be misstated.

FIGURE 12–9. *Capital project funds statement of changes in fund balance.*

Municipal Government *Capital Project Funds* *Analysis of Changes in Fund Balance* *For the Year Ending December 31, 1978*			
	Civic Center	*Bridges*	*Total*
Initial project authorization	$ XXX	$ XXX	$ XXX
Fund balance January 1, 1978	XXX	XXX	XXX
Add: Revenues	XXX	XXX	XXX
Less: Expenditures	(XXX)	(XXX)	(XXX)
Less: Reserve for encumbrances	(XXX)	(XXX)	(XXX)
Fund balance December 31, 1978	$ XXXX	$XXXX	$XXXX

Groups of Accounts

The descriptions of the general government fund entities in municipalities have made it clear that such funds are created to account for and control the flow of liquid resources. Long-term assets and obligations are not included in the balance sheet reports of these fund entities. However, it would be impossible to control such assets and liabilities if their existence was not somehow recorded and disclosed. Two separate groups of accounts serve this function: the general fixed-assets group and the general long-term-debt group.

General fixed-assets group. A capital expenditure accounted for in a general government fund will affect two municipal subentities: (1) an expenditure in the general government fund and (2) an increase in the stock of the general fixed-assets (GFA) group. In each case the transactions will be recorded at acquisition cost. An expenditure is recorded in the general government fund because the capital asset acquired is not recorded as an asset of the fund. The general government capital assets are reported in the GFA group, based on the type of asset and the source (fund) financing the acquisition (Figure 12–10). In addition to this balance sheet, supplemental statements describing changes (additions, disposals)

FIGURE 12–10. *General fixed assets balance sheet.*

Municipal Government	
Statement of General Fixed Assets	
December 31, 1978	
General Fixed Assets	
Land	$ XXX
Buildings	XXX
Improvements other than buildings	XXX
Equipment	XXX
Construction in process	XXX
Total	$XXXX
Sources of General Fixed Assets	
General fund revenues	$ XXX
Special assessments	XXX
Capital project funds	XXX
General obligation bonds	XXX
Intergovernmental funds	XXX
Total	$XXXX

in the GFA may be presented. The GFA may also be classified by the function served within the municipality or by the fund source (as shown in Figure 12–10). No depreciation is recorded on these assets in the government funds. However, depreciation may be calculated separately for special cost-finding purposes. The GFA is created to establish control over the general fixed assets of the municipality.

General long-term-debt group. Debt obligations that are not direct liabilities of specific fund entities are accounted for and reported on in the general long-term-debt (GLTD) group. These obligations are typically general obligation municipal debt issues, but may also include noncurrent lease and pension obligations. The financial reporting of the GLTD group reflects the amounts and status of the debt obligations. A balance sheet (Figure 12–11) summarizes the amount of the various types of debt that are outstanding. In addition, a record is made of the amount of liquid resources available in the debt service fund that have been segregated for the purpose of paying principal amounts. The annual financial report should also include a detailed schedule describing the specific terms of the individual debt issues.

Proprietary (Self-Supporting) Funds

Although the primary objective of most NFP organizations is to provide social services, municipalities are frequently involved in more commercial types of activities. Separate proprietary fund entities should be established within the accounting structure in order to account for these commercial activities. The two basic types of proprietary funds are enterprise funds and internal service funds. Enterprise funds are established to account

FIGURE 12–11. *General long-term debt balance sheet.*

Municipal Government	
Statement of General Long-Term Debt	
December 31, 1978	
Amounts Available and to Be Provided	
Amounts available in debt service fund	$ XXX
Amounts to be provided	XXX
Total	$XXXX
General Long-Term Debt	
Bonds payable	$ XXX
Total	$XXXX

for self-supporting municipal operations that provide goods and services to the general public on a user-charge basis. Internal service funds are established to reflect the same activities in cases where consumers of the goods and services are other departments within the municipality. The accounting principles for both types of entities are basically the same. Therefore, only enterprise fund accounting and reporting will be discussed in this chapter.

The general government fund entities discussed above are not expected to be self-supporting. The fund entities receive resources from external sources with the expectation that these assets will be depleted through expenditures during a period. Thus general government funds are sometimes referred to as "expendable" funds. In contrast, enterprise funds (and internal service funds) are intended to be self-supporting in their operations. Because of this difference in operating objectives, general government and enterprise municipal fund entities have distinctly different accounting reports. Since enterprise funds basically follow the private enterprise accrual accounting system, statements of income, position, and funds or cash flow should be prepared for these activities. These standard business-type financial statements are not illustrated in this chapter but are discussed below.

The operating objectives of the enterprise fund require that all the assets and obligations associated with its activities be reflected in the fund accounts. Thus the position statement should show current and noncurrent assets as well as short-term and long-term liabilities. This practice affects the interpretation of the assets-less-liabilities difference in enterprise funds. In general government fund entities, the residual is the fund balance, which is interpreted as the net appropriable assets available for continuing activities of the fund. In the enterprise fund, the residual of assets minus liabilities is not so easily interpreted. The residual represents the initial contributions (discussed below) to the fund and the *retained earnings* to date. Retained earnings should not be equated with the fund balance. The accounting processes followed to achieve the two figures are completely different.

One important difference between a private enterprise balance sheet and the enterprise fund position statement is that instead of reporting owner's contributed equity capital, the enterprise fund reports "contributions." These generally reflect the municipal resources allocated to begin the enterprise.

Since enterprise funds are supposed to be self-supporting, net income is calculated. The standard private enterprise revenue recognition and expense accrual principles are followed in preparing the statement of income. Since enterprise funds are separate subentities within municipalities, they may be involved in interfund activities. Thus revenue may be generated by providing service to other departments within the municipality. In addition, payments in lieu of taxes made to the municipality may be reflected as an expense or liability in the enterprise fund financial statements. Finally, if a portion of net income for the period is converted into liquid assets and distributed to another fund entity within the municipality, such a distribution should be treated like a dividend and deducted from the retained earnings of the fund.

In summary, proprietary fund entities are basically accounted for as separate private enterprise operations within a municipality.

Fiduciary Funds

The final type of municipal fund entity to be discussed in this chapter is the fiduciary fund. Trust and agency funds, the two principal types of fiduciary funds, are established to account for resources held by the municipality as an agent or trustee for some other person, group, or government. The agency fund normally serves as a clearinghouse for collections made by the municipality for some other organization. Thus it is an expendable fund that collects and transmits monies. Two basic financial reports are constructed to reflect this function: a balance sheet and a cash flow statement. Since these statements are very similar to previous illustrations, they will not be illustrated here.

Accounting and reporting for trust funds can be significantly more complicated than that for agency funds. Trust funds are separate fiscal entities created to receive, invest, and spend certain assets in accordance with the specific constraints placed on the use of the assets. Trust funds can be expendable or nonexpendable depending on the trust agreement. For example, some trusts may restrict the consumption of resources to the income earned by the body of the trust (nonexpendable). Other trusts may permit the spending of the principal as well (expendable). The accounting system and financial reports must reflect the nature of the trust agreement and the extent to which it has been followed.

Public retirement funds are one of the most important activities accounted for in a municipal trust fund. Full coverage of the accounting and reporting for such entities is beyond the scope of this section. However, it should be noted that the financial reports should reflect the specific nature of the trust agreement. All such funds should produce a balance sheet, statement of cash flows, and change in fund balance. In addition, retirement trust funds should report on the retirement reserves. The problem of unfunded (and sometimes undisclosed) actuarial retirement fund obligations is currently being addressed by municipal finance officers and the accounting profession. Such obligations may be important considerations for some users' tasks and decisions.

Financial Reporting in Municipal Fund Accounting

The sections above have discussed the accounting and financial reporting practices prescribed for the individual types of fund entities. These individual fund reports form the core of the municipal annual report. However, additional financial reports may also be made as a summary of the individual fund reports. Specifically, the following types of combined reports are recommended:

1. Combined balance sheet for all funds and groups of accounts.
2. Combined statement of revenues, expenditures, and changes in fund balances for all general government funds.
3. Combined statement of revenues, expenses, and changes in retained earnings for all proprietary (self-supporting) funds.
4. Other combined schedules.

It is important to note that these combined reports are not consolidated. They should still reflect interfund activity. The type of statement to be provided is illustrated by the combined balance sheet in Figure 12–12. If there is more than one special revenue, debt service fund, and so on, the individual funds should be aggregated first, with the summary statement of each type of fund provided in one column in the combined balance sheet. Since the summation of assets from various types of funds may be difficult to interpret, GAAP require that any "total" column be labeled "Memorandum Only" so that the users will not be misled.

Other types of special schedules and statistics may also be presented to supplement (rather than replace) the fund entity approach to municipal financial reporting.

Usefulness of Municipal Fund Accounting Practices

Measuring the usefulness of accounting reports is a difficult task. In most cases the role that accounting information actually plays in decision making is not known. The situation is complicated by the timeliness of the information and the information available from other sources. Therefore, it is difficult to determine which accounting and reporting technique is the best for a given user. In addition, if financial reports are to be general in purpose, the choice of a preferred accounting and reporting technique must involve trade-offs among potential user groups. Therefore, there is currently no single best method for resolving debates over accounting alternatives.

One source of evidence on the usefulness of accounting reports is the opinions of individuals familiar with the problem. This section will review some positive and negative comments by users about municipal fund accounting reports. This review should expose some of the strengths and

FIGURE 12–12. Combined balance sheet.

Municipal Government
Combined Statement of Position
December 31, 1978

Assets/Debits	General Fund	Special Revenue Funds	Capital Project Funds	Debt Service Fund	Trust and Agency Funds	Enterprise Funds	General Long-Term-Debt Group	General Fixed-Assets Group
Cash	$ XXX	$ XXX	$ XXX	$ XXX	$ XXX	$ XXX		
Investments	XXX	XXX	XXX	XXX	XXX	XXX		
Interest receivable	XXX	XXX		XXX	XXX	XXX		
Accounts receivable		XXX			XXX	XXX		
Tax receivable	XXX	XXX		XXX				
Less: Estimated uncollectible tax	(XXX)	(XXX)		(XXX)				
Tax receivable for other governments					XXX			
Advances to other funds	XXX							
Due from other funds	XXX	XXX			XXX	XXX		
Prepaid expense			XXX					
Due from other governments		XXX						
Inventory	XXX	XXX						
Land						XXX		$ XXX
Buildings and improvements						XXX		XXX
Less: Accumulated depreciation						(XXX)		
Machinery						XXX		XXX
Less: Accumulated depreciation						(XXX)		

Construction							$ XXX
Amount available for bond retirement						XXX	
Amount to be provided for bond retirement						XXX	
Total	$XXXXX	$XXXXX	$XXXXX	$XXXXX	$XXXXX	$XXXXX	$XXXXX
Claims on Resources/ Reserves/Fund Balances							
Vouchers payable	$ XXX	$ XXX	$ XXX	$ XXX	$XXX		
Accounts payable	XXX	XXX	XXX	XXX			
Contracts payable	XXX	XXX	XXX	XXX			
Due to other funds	XXX	XXX	$ XXX	$ XXX	XXX		
Due to other governments	XXX			XXX			
Benefits payable							
Advance from general fund			XXX	XXX			
Mature interest payable			XXX				
Bonds payable							
Mature bonds payable			XXX		XXX	$ XXX	
Reserve for encumbrances	XXX	XXX	XXX				
Reserve for inventory	XXX	XXX					
Reserve for bond requirements				XXX			
Reserve for advances	XXX				XXX		
Reserve for retirement system				XXX	XXX		
Contributed capital					XXX		
Investment in general fixed assets						XXX	
Fund balance	(XXX)	(XXX)	XXX	(XXX)	XXX	(XXX)	$ XXX
Total	$XXXXX	$XXXXX	$XXXXX	$XXXXX	$XXXXX	$XXXXX	$XXXXX

weaknesses of fund accounting and help the reader understand current and future developments in municipal GAAP.

A recent survey (Patton, 1976) revealed that users consider municipal financial reports useful for control and financial planning. This finding is consistent with the focus on dollar accountability and control in general government fund entities. As described above, the financial reports for such funds trace the flows of appropriable resources through the municipality. Thus those users who are interested in reports on current resources seem to be well served by current fund accounting practices.

The survey cited above also revealed that a significant number of users were unsatisfied with municipal reports. The most common criticisms can be understood by reviewing recommendations for change that have recently appeared in the municipal accounting literature. Although these recommendations have not been rigorously examined to determine if they would actually improve users' decisions, they may indicate the nature of future municipal financial reports.

Two fundamental criticisms of current municipal GAAP focus on (1) the fragmented nature of the fund-by-fund financial reports and (2) the use of the modified accrual system of accounting in general government funds—specifically, whether depreciation (asset consumption) rather than expenditures (asset acquisition) should be recognized in the reports.

The most frequent suggestion for eliminating the fragmented fund-by-fund approach is the consolidated report. As discussed above, current GAAP do not encourage the presentation of such a report. Those who advocate consolidated financial reports feel that the fund-by-fund report is too detailed a document to be understood by most potential users. In addition to the potential information overload (New York City's annual report for 1975 was over 550 pages), critics claim that the position and operation of the municipality from the fund-by-fund financial report as a whole are of interest to many users. These user groups may not understand the overall financial position and operation of the municipality from the fund-by-fund financial report. The advocates of consolidated municipal financial reports do not all agree on the form the consolidation should take. One potential consolidation solution is illustrated in Figure 12–13. Although such a report can clearly reduce the bulk of municipal financial reports, questions still remain about the effects of the change on users' decisions. This issue is currently unresolved.

The debate over recognition of depreciation expense has been carried on for many years in both private enterprise and municipal accounting. Currently private enterprise financial reports include depreciation, while general government municipal fund entities do not. One criticism of municipal accounting practices comes from the American Accounting Association (AAA) committee report:

FIGURE 12–13. *Consolidated statement of position.*

Municipal Government
Consolidated Statement of Position
December 31, 1978

	Operating* Funds	Restricted** Funds	Enterprise*** Funds
Assets/Debits			
Cash	$ XXX	$ XXX	$ XXX
Investments	XXX	XXX	XXX
Interest receivable	XXX	XXX	XXX
Accounts receivable	XXX		XXX
Tax receivable	XXX	XXX	
Less: Estimated uncollectible tax	(XXX)	(XXX)	
Tax receivable for other governments		XXX	
Prepaid expense			XXX
Due from other governments	XXX	XXX	
Inventory	XXX	XXX	XXX
Land	XXX		
Buildings and improvements	XXX		XXX
Less: Accumulated depreciation			(XXX)
Construction	XXX		XXX
Total	$XXXX	$XXXX	$XXXX
Claims on Resources/			
Reserves/Fund Balances			
Vouchers payable	$ XXX	$ XXX	
Accounts payable	XXX		$ XXX
Contracts payable	XXX	XXX	XXX
Due to other governments	XXX	XXX	
Mature interest payable		XXX	
Bonds payable	XXX		XXX
Mature bonds payable		XXX	
Reserve for encumbrances	XXX	XXX	
Reserve for inventory	XXX		
Reserve for bond requirements			XXX
Reserve for retirement system		XXX	
Reserve for advances	XXX		
Contributed capital			XXX
Fund balance	(XXX)	XXX	XXX
Excess cost of general fixed assets over general long term debt	XXX		
Total	$XXXX	$XXXX	$XXXX

*General and special revenue funds; general fixed-asset group and general long-term-debt group.
**Capital projects, debt service, trust, and agency funds.
***Municipality-owned utility and recreation facilities.

The accounting records and related reports of a not-for-profit organization should disclose the cost of use or consumption of assets allocated to services and/or time periods as appropriate. . . . An informed estimate of the periodic expiration of fixed-asset costs is much more objective and useful information about resource use than the information developed by [expenditure-based methods] (AAA, 1971, pp. 115–116, 119).

The 1975 AAA committee report added:

Funds-flow [expenditure] accounting also frequently fails to reflect that outputs result from a complex chain of resource transformations. . . . Expenditures only coincidentally represent resource-use cost [expenses] of outputs. . . . The expense concept of "cost" is generally considered to be more useful than the expenditure concept of cost (AAA, 1975, p. 18).

The AAA committee felt that better decisions (especially those concerned with efficiency of operation) would be made with expense accrual data than with the current liquid resource flow information. In addition, the committee suggested that (1) stewardship of total resources is better reflected by reports including depreciation (AAA, 1971, pp. 113–114) and (2) the going-concern concept is violated by the focus on current asset flows (AAA, 1971, p. 119).

The resolution of these controversial issues in municipal fund accounting is still in progress. More research into the consequences of these and other solutions may provide some help in gaining consensus on the appropriate choice. Currently, however, GAAP do not prescribe the use of consolidated statements or depreciation accounting in municipalities.

FUND ACCOUNTING IN OTHER NFP ORGANIZATIONS

This section examines the accounting practices of hospitals and colleges. Some special characteristics of these NFP organizations will be noted, along with a description of the sources of generally accepted accounting principles for these NFP entities. Finally, some of the major similarities and differences in GAAP and financial reporting practices for the different entities will be discussed and illustrated.

Special Characteristics

As noted earlier, the characteristics common to all NFP entities include (1) the objective of social benefits, (2) the related absence of profit-motivated behavior on the part of the contributors of resources, and (3) the special government-constituent-imposed constraints on the activities to be conducted in the name of the NFP organization. These special characteristics are responsible, in part, for the development of fund accounting to monitor whether managers of an NFP organization's resources meet their fiduciary responsibilities to constituents.

Most of this chapter has focused on fund accounting in the context of municipal financial reporting. Government entities are unique in that they are able to obtain resources through taxation of the public within their jurisdiction. This and other special characteristics raise financial reporting problems peculiar to governmental accounting. Other NFP organizations also have peculiar characteristics which pose financial reporting problems. For example, hospitals receive payments for services rendered to patients from third-party payors (Medicare, Medicaid, Blue Cross, and/or private insurance carriers). Third-party payors also are a factor for colleges and universities.

Hospitals, colleges, and universities charge their "customers" for services rendered. However, the charges often are not sufficient to cover all costs for all services provided. Thus these NFP organizations seek support from other sources—such as governments, philanthropists, philanthropic foundations, and the general public. Because of this reliance on outside sources, the organization must report on operations in a manner that satisfies conditions set forth by contributors. For example, when the NFP organization relies on substantial government support, its accounting system may resemble that of the government more closely than that of similar NFP organizations with only minor reliance on government funding.

Sources of GAAP for Nongovernment NFP Organizations

Although all types of NFP organizations generally follow fund accounting principles, the GAAP are not homogeneous. Variations in not-for-profit GAAP can be explained, in part, by the fact that different authoritative publications govern the different categories of not-for-profit organizations. Accounting practices for hospitals, colleges, universities, and voluntary health and welfare organizations are based primarily on authoritative publications from two types of professional groups: accountants (primarily through the AICPA) and nonprofit professional organizations.

The AICPA has published two audit guides that serve (in part) as listings of GAAP for nonprofit organizations other than governments. These are the *Hospital Audit Guide* (1972) and *Audits of Colleges and Universities* (1973). Each was prepared by a separate committee of the AICPA. The differing views of the committees, coupled with the differing industry practices that had already evolved (sometimes in response to funding agency reporting requirements), are responsible for certain differences between these audit guides and the audit guide for state and local governments. The existence of differences (apparent inconsistencies) between the audit guides is not necessarily undesirable. Different categories of NFP organizations may have certain characteristics or user groups that warrant special accounting and financial reporting principles. Whether such differences can be justified is still subject to debate and research. An expanded discussion of these issues is beyond the scope of this chapter.

Various professional societies have also published authoritative statements on what constitutes generally accepted accounting practices. The American Hospital Association's *Chart of Accounts for Hospitals* (1976), which recommends the types of funds to be used by hospitals, provides a coding scheme for the chart of accounts and discusses the recording and reporting procedures that should be followed. In addition, a committee from NACUBO (National Association of College and University Business Officers) prepared *College and University Business Administration* (1974), which sets guidelines for accounting practices in colleges and universities. In general, the audit guides of the AICPA and the above publications agree on the acceptable accounting practices for the respective nonprofit organizations. However, when discrepancies exist, the independent (CPA) auditor is expected to follow the AICPA audit guides.

Influences on GAAP are not limited to the above institutions. The audit guides specifically state that relevant pronouncements of the organizations setting accounting standards (FASB Statements, APB Opinions, and Accounting Research Bulletins) should be applied. Other influences on accounting practices for NFP organizations include literature published by societies such as the Hospital Financial Management Association.

Financial Reporting for Colleges and Universities

This section examines the generally accepted fund accounting practices of colleges and universities and compares them with the practices and principles of other NFP organizations.

The balance sheet illustrated in Figure 12–14 reflects the concept that each college and university fund is a separate accounting entity. The balance sheet is composed of several balance sheets, one for each fund group. These include (1) current funds (restricted and unrestricted), (2) loan funds, (3) endowment funds, and (4) plant funds (unexpended, renewal, retirement of debt, and investment in plant). The functions accounted for in each of these subentities are described below.

As indicated above, the current funds group is divided into unrestricted and restricted current funds. The unrestricted current fund is similar to the current fund of hospital accounting and the general fund of municipal accounting in that it accounts for resources that have not been externally restricted. The accounting practices for the unrestricted current fund parallel those of the municipal general fund. Externally restricted resources that are expendable for operating purposes are accounted for in the restricted current fund subgroup. This subgroup is analogous to a

FIGURE 12–14. Balance sheet for a college.

College
Balance Sheet
June 30, 1977
With Comparative Figures for 1976

CURRENT FUNDS

Assets	1977	1976	Liabilities and Fund Balances	1977	1976
Unrestricted			*Unrestricted*		
Cash	$ XXX	$ XXX	Accrued liabilities	$ XXX	$ XXX
Investments	XXX	XXX	Students' deposits	XXX	XXX
Accounts receivable (net)	XXX	XXX	Due to other funds	XXX	XXX
Inventories	XXX	XXX	Fund balances	XXX	XXX
Total unrestricted	$XXXX	$XXXX	Total unrestricted	$XXXX	$XXXX
Restricted			*Restricted*		
Cash	$ XXX	$ XXX	Accounts payable	$ XXX	$ XXX
Investments	XXX	XXX	Fund balances	XXX	XXX
Accounts receivable (net)	XXX	XXX			
Total restricted	$ XXX	$ XXX	Total restricted	$ XXX	$ XXX
Total current funds	$XXXX	$XXXX	Total current funds	$XXXX	$XXXX

LOAN FUNDS

Assets	1977	1976	Liabilities and Fund Balances	1977	1976
Cash	$ XXX	$ XXX	Fund balances	$ XXX	$ XXX
Investments	XXX	XXX			
Loans to students, faculty, and staff (net)	XXX	XXX			
Total loan funds	$XXXX	$XXXX	Total loan funds	$XXXX	$XXXX

FIGURE 12–14. (cont.)

College
Balance Sheet
June 30, 1977
With Comparative Figures for 1976

ENDOWMENT AND SIMILAR FUNDS

Assets	1977	1976	Liabilities and Fund Balances	1977	1976
Cash	$ XXX	$ XXX	Annuities payable	$ XXX	$ XXX
Investments	XXX	XXX	Income payable	XXX	XXX
			Fund balances		
			Endowment	XXX	XXX
			Annuity	XXX	XXX
			Life income	XXX	XXX
Total endowment and similar funds	$XXXXX	$XXXXX	Total endowment and similar funds	$XXXXX	$XXXXX

PLANT FUNDS

Assets	1977	1976	Liabilities and Fund Balances	1977	1976
Unexpended			*Unexpended*		
Cash	$ XXX	$ XXX	Accounts payable	$ XXX	$ XXX
Investments	XXX	XXX	Bonds payable	XXX	XXX
Due from unrestricted current funds	XXX	XXX	Fund balances:		
			Restricted	XXX	XXX
			Unrestricted	XXX	XXX
Total unexpended	$XXXXX	$XXXXX	Total unexpended	$XXXXX	$XXXXX

Renewal and Replacement			Renewal and Replacement		
Cash	$ XXX	$ XXX	Fund balances:		
Investments	XXX	XXX	Restricted	$ XXX	$ XXX
Deposits with trustees	XXX		Unrestricted	XXX	XXX
Total renewal and replacement	XXX	$ XXX	Total Renewal and Replacement	$ XXX	$ XXX
Retirement of Indebtedness			**Retirement of Indebtedness**		
Cash	$ XXX	$ XXX	Fund balances:		
Deposits with trustees	XXX	XXX	Restricted	$ XXX	$ XXX
			Unrestricted	XXX	XXX
Total retirement of indebtedness	$ XXX	$ XXX	Total retirement of indebtedness	$ XXX	$ XXX
Investment in Plant			**Investment in Plant**		
Land and improvements	$ XXX	$ XXX	Bonds payable	$ XXX	$ XXX
Buildings	XXX	XXX	Mortgages payable	XXX	XXX
Equipment	XXX	XXX	Net investment in plant	XXX	XXX
Total investment in plant	$ XXX	$ XXX	Total investment in plant	$ XXX	$ XXX
Total plant funds	$ XXX	$ XXX	Total plant funds	$ XXX	$ XXX

Source: Adapted from AICPA *Audits of Colleges and Universities* (1973).

municipal government's special revenue fund. However, certain revenue recognition practices (discussed below) are distinctly different.

Loan funds have no real counterpart in hospital or government fund accounting. They account for those resources which the college or university may loan to students, faculty, and staff. When only the income produced by a particular resource may be loaned, the income is accounted for through the loan fund group and the principal is accounted for in an endowment fund. Endowment funds are used to account for resources held (invested) to provide payments for purposes designated by the donors. These payments may be annuities or they may consist solely of the income earned by the donated resources. The fund accounting system must be designed to ensure that the restrictions (amounts, purposes) have not been violated. Thus the accounting for endowments is similar to the municipal trust for accounting.

In college and university fund accounting, the plant fund group accounts for (1) unexpended resources earmarked for plant asset acquisitions; (2) resources used for renewal and replacement of fixed assets; (3) resources used to retire debts relating to the acquisition, renewal, and replacement of fixed assets; and (4) the actual investment in plant assets used in the operations of the college or university. The plant fund group is also used to account for indebtedness relating to fixed assets. Thus the plant fund serves functions similar to the general long-term-debt group, general fixed-assets group, and special revenue funds in municipalities.

In addition to a balance sheet, the AICPA recommends a statement of current funds revenues, expenditures, and other changes (Figure 12–15), as well as a statement of changes in fund balance. In examining Figure 12–15, note that college or university current fund accounting is concerned primarily with expenditures as opposed to expenses. This is similar to general government municipal accounting and contrasts with hospital accounting. Consistent with the expenditure orientation, recording depreciation is not a required accounting procedure (except in certain endowment funds). College and university reports also use a fund-by-fund approach similar to municipal accounting. Transfers among various fund groups are reported in the individual college resource flow statements. Most of the titles under revenues and expenditures are self-explanatory. Auxiliary enterprise items reflect the operation of activities such as dormitories and bookstores.

One important feature of accounting for resource flows in current restricted funds should be noted. *Nonrestricted* current funds use the standard modified accrual method of recognizing revenue when it becomes measurable and available. However, *restricted* current funds recognize "revenues" only when expenditures are made for the restricted purpose. That is, the resources are not considered to be "earned" until they have been used for the designated purpose. Other additions to the resources of the restricted fund are reflected in the change in fund balance. Thus, although reported revenues may equal expenditures in a restricted fund, the actual fund balance need not remain constant.

The accounting practices of colleges and universities have been criticized in much the same way as municipal accounting, reported above. Critics argue that the fund-by-fund approach combined with an expenditure-based system yields information that is hard to interpret by those accustomed to private enterprise reports. Thus some observers (Price Waterhouse, 1975; Skousen et al., 1975) recommend consolidation (aggregation) of statements and recognition of depreciation expense in the reports. Some critics also maintain that the interpretation of the term "revenue" can be complicated by the context in which it is used (for example, restricted versus nonrestricted funds). As a result, they suggest that this term be dropped or used only in circumstances where its meaning is consistent with the modified accrual method of accounting. Finally, the reader should be wary of simplistic interschool comparisons. The dollar amounts of various revenue sources and expenditures may reflect alternative classification schemes rather than significantly different operations.

As with the criticisms of municipal accounting, the impact of these recommended changes has not been systematically investigated. However, the suggestions may indicate the direction of any future changes in college and university financial reporting.

Financial Accounting and Reporting for Hospitals

This section describes the special fund accounting principles applicable to hospitals. The discussion is based primarily on the AICPA's *Hospital Audit Guide*. The form of the hospital financial reports recommended by the AICPA is similar to that of college and university statements. University and hospital accounting also share the same revenue recognition practices in certain types of restricted fund entities. However, there are significant differences between accounting practices for hospitals and other NFP organizations. For example, hospitals employ a *full accrual* system of accounting in their unrestricted funds. That is, revenues are recognized when services are provided (not when cash is paid) and expenses are recorded when goods are consumed (not purchased). There are therefore significant differences in the statements of financial position and operations in hospitals versus other NFP organizations. These differences are noted in the discussions that follow.

Hospitals typically present a balance sheet, a statement of revenues and expenses, and a statement of changes in fund balances. The AICPA-recommended balance sheet (Figure 12–16) reflects the concept of hospital funds as separate accounting entities. Each major fund has a

FIGURE 12–15. Statement of current funds, revenues, and expenditures for a college.

College
Statement of Current Funds, Revenues,
Expenditures, and Other Changes
Year Ended June 20, 1977
With Comparative Figures for 1976

| | 1977 | | | 1976 |
	Unrestricted	Restricted	Total	Total
Revenues				
Educational and general:				
Student tuition and fees	$ XXX		$ XXX	$ XXX
Governmental appropriations	XXX		XXX	XXX
Gifts and private grants	XXX	$ XXX	XXX	XXX
Endowment income	XXX	XXX	XXX	XXX
Sales and services of educational departments	XXX		XXX	XXX
Total educational and general	$XXXX	$XXXX	$XXXX	$XXXX
Auxiliary enterprises	XXX	XXX	XXX	XXX
Total revenues	$XXXX	$XXXX	$XXXX	$XXXX

Expenditures and Mandatory Transfers

Educational and general:

Instruction and departmental research	$ XXX	$ XXXX	$ XXX
Sponsored research		XXX	XXX
Extension and public service	XXX		XXX
Libraries	XXX		XXX
Student services	XXX		XXX
Operation and maintenance of plant	XXX		XXX
General administration	XXX		XXX
Student aid	XXX	XXX	XXX
Total educational and general	$XXXXX	$XXXXX	$XXXXX
Mandatory transfers for:			
Principal and interest	$ XXX	$ XXX	$ XXX
Renewals and replacements	XXX		XXX
Total educational and general	$XXXXX	$XXXXX	$XXXXX
Auxiliary enterprises	$ XXX		
Other transfers and additions (deductions):			
Excess of restricted receipts over transfers to revenues	$ XXX	$ XXX	$ XXX
Net increase in fund balances	$XXXXX	$XXXXX	$XXXXX

Source: Adapted from AICPA *Audits of Colleges and Universities* (1973).

FIGURE 12–16. Balance sheet for a hospital.

Hospital
Balance Sheet
December 31, 1977
With Comparative Figures for 1976

UNRESTRICTED FUNDS

Assets	1977	1976	Liabilities and Fund Balances	1977	1976
Current			*Current*		
Cash	$ XXX	$ XXX	Accounts payable	$ XXX	$ XXX
Due from restricted funds	XXX	XXX	Accrued expenses	XXX	XXX
Inventories	XXX	XXX	Advances from third-party payors	XXX	XXX
Total current assets	$XXXX	$XXXX	Total current liabilities	$XXXX	$XXXX
Other			*Long-term debt*		
Investments	$ XXX	$ XXX	Mortgage notes	$ XXX	$ XXX
Property, plant, and equipment (net of accumulated depreciation)	XXX	XXX	Fund balance	XXX	XXX
Total other	$XXXX	$XXXX	Total other	$XXXX	$XXXX

RESTRICTED FUNDS

Specific Purpose Funds

Cash	$ XXX	$ XXX
Investments		XXX
Grants receivable		XXX
Total specific purpose funds		$XXXX

Plant Replacement and Expansion Funds

Cash	$ XXX	$ XXX
Investments		XXX
Pledges receivable (net)		XXX
Total plant replacement and ex-pansion funds		$XXXX

Endowment Funds

Cash	$ XXX	$ XXX
Investments		XXX
Total endowment funds		$XXXX

Specific-Purpose Funds

Due to unrestricted funds	$ XXX	$ XXX
Fund balance		XXX
Total specific purpose funds		$XXXX

Plant Replacement and Expansion Funds

Fund balances	$ XXX	$ XXX
Total plant replacement and expansion funds		$XXXX

Endowment funds

Fund balance	$ XXX	$ XXX
Total endowment funds		$XXXX

Source: Adapted from AICPA *Hospital Audit Guide* (1972).

set of self-balancing accounts (assets = liabilities + fund balance). The primary types of funds are the unrestricted (operating) fund and three restricted funds: specific purpose, endowment, and plant. The restricted funds reflect limitations that have been imposed by individuals or groups external to the hospital.

The unrestricted funds balance sheet reflects both liquid and noncurrent assets that have not been externally restricted. Related current and noncurrent liabilities are also reported. The restricted fund balance sheet reflects the liquid resources (and related liabilities) that have been externally restricted for specific purposes. The specific purpose funds are similar to municipal special revenue funds and college and university restricted current funds. The hospital endowment fund is similar to college and university endowment funds and municipal nonexpendable trust funds. The plant fund balance sheet (under the AICPA audit guide approach) reports the resources that have been restricted for acquisition and replacement of plant and equipment.

The statement of changes in fund balances (Figure 12–17) provides a financial explanation of the change in each of the balance sheet fund balance accounts (assets minus liabilities). This combined financial statement also reflects the financial interactions among the hospital fund entities. The unrestricted changes in fund balance can be traced to the revenues and *expenses* of operations (see Figure 12–18) as well as to other transfers of assets. For example, the unrestricted fund may provide resources to the plant fund for future acquisitions of plant and equipment. In addition, the unrestricted fund may receive assets for fixed-assets expenditures from the plant fund. When additions are made to plant assets, the cost is recorded in the property and plant and equipment accounts of the unrestricted fund.

Similar relationships may exist between the unrestricted fund and other restricted funds (specific purpose and endowment). For example, in Figure 12–17 the specific purpose fund balance is increased by various inflows of resources from external sources and is reduced by transfers of resources to the unrestricted fund. This transfer reflects the unusual revenue recognition practices of specific purpose funds—that is, revenues are not recognized until resources have been expended for the specified purpose of the fund. Other increases in resources are reflected by increases in the fund balance. This practice is also followed by restricted current funds in colleges and universities.

Figure 12–18 illustrates the AICPA-recommended statement of revenues and expenses. Two features should be noted: (1) expenses rather than expenditures are reported and (2) revenues and expenses may reflect activities in various fund entities within the hospital.

FIGURE 12–17. *Statement of changes in fund balances for a hospital.*

Hospital		
Statement of Changes in Fund Balances		
Year Ended December 31, 1977		
With Comparative Figures for 1976		
Unrestricted Funds	*1977*	*1976*
Balance at beginning of year	$ XXX	$ XXX
Excess of revenues over expense	XXX	XXX
Transferred from plant replacement and		
expansion funds	XXX	XXX
Transferred to plant replacement and		
expansion funds	(XXX)	(XXX)
Balance at end of year	$XXXX	$XXXX
Restricted Funds		
Specific Purpose Funds		
Balance at beginning of year	$ XXX	$ XXX
Restricted gifts and bequests	XXX	XXX
Research grants	XXX	XXX
Income from investments	XXX	XXX
Transferred to other operating revenue	(XXX)	(XXX)
Balance at end of year	$XXXX	$XXXX
Plant Replacement and Expansion Funds		
Balance at beginning of year	$ XXX	$ XXX
Restricted gifts and bequests	XXX	XXX
Income from investments	XXX	XXX
Transferred to unrestricted funds	(XXX)	(XXX)
Transferred from unrestricted funds	XXX	XXX
Balance at end of year	$XXXX	$XXXX
Endowment Funds		
Balance at beginning of year	$ XXX	$ XXX
Restricted gifts and bequests	XXX	XXX
Balance at end of year	$XXXX	$XXXX

Source: Adapted from AICPA *Hospital Audit Guide* (1972).

Whereas other NFP organizations focus almost exclusively on the flow of liquid resources through the fund, hospitals report *income* on a full accrual basis. Thus expenses (including depreciation on fixed assets employed) are reported. Because of this private enterprise style of reporting,

FIGURE 12–18. *Statement of revenues and expenses for a hospital.*

Hospital
Statement of Revenues and Expenses
Year Ended December 31, 1977
With Comparative Figures for 1976

	1977	1976
Patient service revenue	$ XXX	$ XXX
Less: Allowances and uncollectible accounts	(XXX)	(XXX)
Net patient service revenue	$ XXX	$ XXX
Other operating revenue (including $XX transferred from specific purpose funds)	XXX	XXX
Total operating revenue	$XXXX	$XXXX
Operating expenses		
Nursing services	$ XXX	$ XXX
General services	XXX	XXX
Fiscal services	XXX	XXX
Administrative services	XXX	XXX
Provision for depreciation	XXX	XXX
Total operating expenses	$ XXX	$ XXX
Gain (loss) from operations	$XXXX	$(XXXX)
Nonoperating revenue		
Unrestricted gifts and bequests	$ XXX	$ XXX
Unrestricted income from endowment funds	XXX	XXX
Total nonoperating revenue	$ XXX	$ XXX
Excess of revenues over expenses	$XXXX	$XXXX

Source: Adapted from AICPA *Hospital Audit Guide* (1972).

the AICPA recommends the presentation of a statement of changes in financial position (funds flow) for the unrestricted fund activities.

Revenues are recognized in hospitals when resources become available for unrestricted use or when restricted resources are expended for the intended purpose. Therefore, the statement of revenues reports on billings for services, unrestricted gifts, unrestricted earnings on endowments, and transfers from specific purpose funds. The billings for services should be accrued as revenue in an amount equal to the full established rates, whether or not the hospital expects to collect this full amount. Allowances for contractual adjustments by third-party payors (Medicare, Blue Cross, and so on) should be recorded as a deduction allowance on the statement of revenues and expenses (Figure 12–18). Transfers from specific funds reflect revenue recognized in an amount equal to the costs incurred during the period. The assumption is that such revenue is not earned until the resources have been expended in accordance with external restrictions.

The financial reports prepared by hospitals reflect a combination of fund and private enterprise accounting practices. The fund-by-fund approach is reflected in the balance sheet and statement of changes in fund balances but is suppressed in the statement of hospital revenues and expenses. The user of such reports must be aware of the special definitions and accounting practices used by hospitals.

CONCLUSION

This chapter has described, illustrated, and discussed fund accounting in several contexts. Various specific fund accounting practices have been adopted to serve different groups of users and to reflect different types of economic events and phenomena. Thus users must be aware of the types of NFP organizations and the specific context involved in order to understand and interpret the fund accounting reports.

References

American Accounting Association (AAA). "Report of the Committee on Accounting Practices of Not-for-Profit Organizations," *The Accounting Review* (Supplement, 1971).

AAA. "Report of the Committee on Not-for-Profit Organizations," *The Accounting Review* (Supplement, 1974).

AAA. "Report of the Committee on Nonprofit Organizations," *The Accounting Review* (Supplement, 1975).

American Hospital Association. *Chart of Accounts for Hospitals* (1976).

American Institute of Certified Public Accountants (AICPA). *Hospital Audit Guide* (1972).

AICPA. *Audits of Colleges and Universities* (1973).

AICPA. *Audits of State and Local Governmental Units* (1974).

Davidson, Sidney, et al. *Financial Reporting by State and Local Government Units* (Chicago: University of Chicago Press, 1977).

Freeman, Robert J. "New Thoughts in Governmental Accounting," *Governmental Finance*, November 1972.

Hay, Leon E., and R. M. Mikesell. *Governmental Accounting*, 5th ed. (Homewood, Ill.: Irwin, 1974).

Henke, Emerson O. *Accounting for Nonprofit Organizations*, 2nd ed. (Belmont, Cal.: Wadsworth, 1977).

Lynn, Edward S., and Robert J. Freeman. *Fund Accounting: Theory and Practice* (Englewood Cliffs, N.J.: Prentice-Hall, 1974).

National Association of College and University Business Officers (NACUBO). *College and University Business Administration* (1974).

National Committee on Governmental Accounting (NCGA). *Governmental Accounting, Auditing, and Financial Reporting* (Municipal Finance Officers Association, 1968).

NCGA. *GAAFR Restatement: Introduction and Principles* (working draft, 1977).

Patton, James M. "Standardization and Utility of Municipal Accounting and Reporting Practices: A Survey," *Governmental Finance*, May 1976.

Price Waterhouse and Co. *Position Paper on College and University Reporting* (1975).

Skousen, K. Fred, Jay M. Smith, and Leon W. Woodfield. *User Needs: An Empirical Study of College and University Financial Reporting* (Washington, D.C.: NACUBO, 1975).

CHAPTER 13

Accounting Information for Operating Decisions

Jacob Birnberg

Editor's Note *Managers involved in planning and controlling need information on prior activities, problem areas, and possible solutions to problems. Accounting data provide this information. Thus an understanding of accounting terminology and methods is essential for managers. This chapter focuses on accounting data useful to managers in planning and control. Specifically, it deals with reporting, evaluation, and short-term decisions. Examples and cases are used to illustrate the principles.*

The author introduces the reader to the basic terminology of accounting. Cost-funding-volume and incremental cash flow analyses are concerned with plans or decisions. They deal with the rational allocation of scarce resources at the beginning of the period. Cost-funding-volume analysis helps to sort out alternatives and examine the effects of constraints on the organization. It is a general tool which helps the manager see issues more clearly and choose between alternatives more effectively.

Budgets are detailed analyses of funding to implement plans. They indicate the resources needed, their costs, and coordinate resource utilization by units of the organization. They may be either fixed or flexible. One of the more important budgets is the cash budget, which examines the flow of funds over time and the volume of cash flows in and out of the organization.

Responsibility accounting is concerned with the efficient utilization of budgeted resources. It is the structuring of accounts to highlight costs that can be controlled by department or unit heads. Responsibility accounting varies from agency to agency, and its design must reflect the lines of authority in a given agency. Key steps in developing the system are described in the chapter. Though responsibility accounts appear to be trivial, they usually represent an important step in reorienting the accounting system to assist management.

In the evaluation of performance, standards are used to assess costs incurred. Together, budgets, responsibility accounts, and standards transform accounting data from merely serving as a scorecard to directing attention to problem areas.

The role of economic considerations in decision making varies. In some cases, the organization will be interested in the least costly course of action; in others, it will incur extensive costs to achieve a highly designed goal. Accounting information will try to answer the questions of cash inflows and outflows, increases or decreases, and the sum total of these flows.

Appended to this chapter is a section describing the basic framework and tools of cost estimation.

The role of the accounting system in any organization is to assist management in performing its duties and achieving the organization's goals. In this capacity accounting systems and accounting reports are not ends in themselves. Rather, they are tools to assist managers in performing their function. This chapter deals with two questions: What information can managers expect to find in their organization's accounting system? What techniques are available to provide managers with useful data from the accounting system?

FUNCTIONS OF ACCOUNTING SYSTEMS

The functions of accounting are usually the same for all organizations. It makes no difference whether the organization is profit oriented or not for profit; whether it provides a service or a product; or even whether it is a large, multinational corporation such as General Motors, an agency of the United Nations, or an entity as geographically restricted in scope as the local boy's club. In all cases the accounting system should be designed to serve three purposes:

1. Provide reports to various external groups to whom the organization has an obligation to report.

2. Assist management in planning and controlling the organization's ongoing activities.

3. Assist management in undertaking long-range planning of the organization's activities.

It would be foolish to argue that any one of the functions is more important than the other two. Rather, their relative importance depends upon the individual's position in the organization and the problems currently facing it. To the treasurer wrestling with tax forms (or tax-exemption forms), it is clear that formal reports are most important. To a group charged with producing a five-year plan to support a proposal for funding, the long-range planning function is most important.

In this chapter we will concentrate on the second point—the use of accounting data to assist management in planning and controlling. This function has a much more significant effect than the other two on the financial health of the organization. The filing of various reports is required by law or by convention. However, such reports, once filed, offer the organization only the right to continue to exist. They do not tell management how well it is doing in meeting intended objectives. (The reporting function of accounting is covered in Chapter 12.) Similarly, long-range planning may provide future managements with a viable economic unit. However, the existence of resources cannot guarantee that those managements will properly exploit their advantage. (Many of the accounting tools for long-range planning are described in Chapters 8 and 9.) Thus it is in the ongoing operations of the organization that accounting is best able to assist management.

To facilitate the planning and controlling function, three kinds of information are needed. These are frequently called scorekeeping, attention-directing, and problem-solving information. Scorekeeping data report on prior activities of the organization. As such, they are intended to be statements of fact rather than evaluations of performance. The reports discussed in Chapter 12 are examples. Such reports typically are prepared and distributed at regular intervals. Figure 13–1 shows another report of this type.

Attention-directing reports highlight any problem areas or areas of better-than-expected performance. They therefore differ in intent and format from scorekeeping reports. In Figure 13–2 the scorecard data from Figure 13–1 have been combined with the budget for the X-ray department for that period. The result is a report intended to direct the user's attention toward problem areas. This report is part of a system called responsibility accounting, which is intended to match the accounting measures of effort and performance with the individuals or units

FIGURE 13–1.
Performance report.

Kennington Hospital X-Ray Department January 1979	
Account	Amount
Personnel	$2,500
Supplies	300
Utilities	200
	$3,000

FIGURE 13–2. *Performance report with budget variances.*

Kennington Hospital X-Ray Department January 1979			
Account	Actual Costs	Budget	Variance
Personnel	$2,500	$2,500	0
Supplies	300	290	$10 U*
Utilities	200	180	20 U
	$3,000	$2,970	$30 U

*Indicates an unfavorable variance. Outlay exceeded the budget allowed.

responsible for them. (The details of responsibility accounting will be discussed later in this chapter.)

Problem-solving information can take a variety of forms, for an organization's problems take many different forms. Problems can be classified according to their time horizon or according to the specific activity being contemplated and its urgency. In this book accounting data and techniques have been separated according to time horizon. Those of relatively short duration are discussed in this chapter. Those with a longer time horizon (arbitrarily set as one year) are discussed in Chapters 8 and 9.

Problem-solving reports usually utilize different accounting concepts than do scorekeeping and attention-directing reports. For example, they might measure the *economic* costs of employing an additional bookkeeper as opposed to the cost of hiring a service to do the same work.

In summary, while accounting data are useful to managers in many ways, this chapter will focus on the usefulness of the data to managers in planning and controlling the ongoing operations of an organization. Illustrations of the data and techniques required for these purposes will draw most heavily on attention-directing and problem-solving reports. In the remaining sections of this chapter, relevant terms will be defined and appropriate techniques explained and illustrated. It is difficult to offer examples appropriate to every reader. However, it is hoped that through the liberal use of examples and terminology, along with the list of references at the end of the chapter, the reader will gain an idea of the appropriate literature in his or her area as well as the expanding literature on managing the not-for-profit organization.

Since most planning and control activities are concerned with resource utilization, much of the analysis utilizes cost data of one type or another. Thus accountants and managers have developed a variety of classification schemes for costs and labels for these categories. The categories discussed below reflect the relationships between costs incurred and the volume of activity, type of activity, and responsibility.

COST-VOLUME RELATIONSHIPS

The simplest dichotomy in costs involves changes in the level of an organization's activities. Costs are divided into fixed and variable. A *fixed* cost is one that does not change with a change in volume. Examples are rent for facilities used by the organization and salaries of administrative personnel. Over fairly broad ranges of activities these costs are likely to remain the same. Figure 13–3a shows how a fixed cost (rent) responds to changes in the number of cases processed.

Variable costs are those that change with the volume of activity. Many types of supplies, utilities, and wages fit into this broad category. Figure 13–3b shows several examples of variable costs. All increase with volume, though they reflect very different patterns of cost incurrence in response to changes in volume. Cost function OY fits the definition usually offered

FIGURE 13-3. *Cost-volume behavior.*

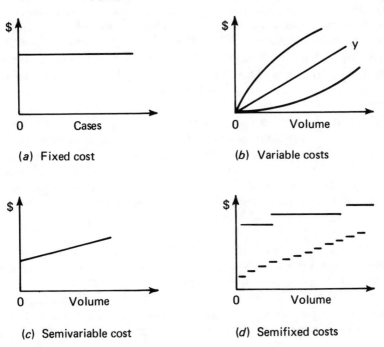

(a) Fixed cost

(b) Variable costs

(c) Semivariable cost

(d) Semifixed costs

to describe variable costs: a cost which is zero when volume is zero and increases by a constant amount per unit of activity as volume increases. In practice, the definition is viewed as an approximate one; it should be looked upon as a guide rather than a rigid rule.

There are, of course, costs which are neither fixed nor variable. Figures 13–3c and 13–3d are examples. In each case the relationship between cost and the level of activity resembles one of the definitions but does not completely fit it. Figure 13–3c could represent the cost of utilities. Regardless of volume, certain amounts must be consumed once the organization commits itself to operating in a given period. Additional costs are incurred roughly in proportion to activity. Costs of this type, which are a mix of both fixed and variable costs, are called *semivariable* costs. They increase by a constant amount as activity increases but are not zero when volume is zero.

Semivariable costs are typical of a wide range of cost categories when they are viewed over some relevant range of planned activities, say, 1,000 to 1,500 cases per month. The cost of each additional case raises the total cost of handling casework. In that sense it is variable. However, should no cases be processed during the period, there would still be a significant element of cost which remains fixed.

Figure 13–3d shows two patterns that costs might follow over the range of activities the organization is likely to experience. One consists of a series of short "steps" where costs are unchanged over small changes in volume. If the vertical axis is labeled "dollars of instructional costs" and the horizontal axis "students," each step might be about 25 to 30 students in length. In a large school district these steps would be very small relative to the total number of students, probably small enough to be ignored and to permit the cost to be considered variable or semivariable.

In contrast, the second cost pattern in Figure 13–3d consists of very broad steps. Such steps might relate to the cost of hospital maintenance. A given level of maintenance probably will cost about the same amount over very broad ranges of occupancy. The cost might be less if occupancy fell to significantly lower levels. However, over the range of occupancy rates that the hospital expects to incur, the level of costs is essentially fixed. Costs exhibiting the latter pattern of cost-volume behavior are called *semifixed*.

Some costs are not only independent of volume but are influenced very strongly by managerial decisions. They can be altered (if not totally deferred) without affecting current operations. These costs, called *administered* costs, are set at a given level by managerial policies and are independent of volume. Sometimes they are referred to as *discretionary* costs to emphasize management's control over their level. Figure 13–4 shows

FIGURE 13-4. *Administered costs.*

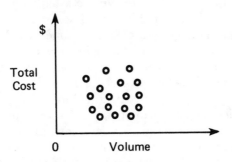

that administered costs bear no relation to volume. Discretionary costs exist even in not-for-profit organizations. Often, however, the discretion is not absolute but rather one of degree. Examples include funds allocated for sabbatical leaves in a university and funds allocated for conferences, travel, and educational activities in a hospital or social service agency.

With the restriction of managerial prerogatives by new legislation and labor agreements, the role of administered costs has declined or taken different forms.

Administered costs can play an important role in managing an organization. Fixed costs usually give rise to commitments to make outlays during an operating period. Variable costs are the inevitable result of operation. Thus typically neither can be reduced significantly or avoided *if the organization is already operating effectively.* Administered costs may be reduced if necessary. While some harm may occur as the result of such a reduction—for example, lowered morale among those denied support to travel to a conference or training program—it may be the only course of action open. Similarly, the organization may suffer in future periods because of the decision to defer an expenditure such as training or preventive maintenance.

Books dealing with the management of for-profit organizations make no mention of the behavior of revenues (resource inflows) in response to changes in volume. The presumption is that revenue is a variable item. That is, the greater the quantity of goods or services provided, the greater the revenue. Indeed, if the price at which goods or services are to be provided is fixed in advance, the revenues are a linear function of volume and fit the definition of a variable cost. For practical purposes, this is the case.

In the not-for-profit sector revenues or budgets are more complex. For example, a social welfare agency may have a fixed budget within which it must operate for the year. The revenue for such an organization essentially is fixed for the period. Other agencies may receive a mixed budget. The funding source may allocate a flat sum to cover the fixed costs of the agency plus an increment of some predetermined amount per case or client. This gives the agency some flexibility in relating its resources to its level of activity. In such a case the agency's revenues would resemble a semivariable cost in its functional relationship to activity. A college or university also exhibits such a pattern.

Many other functions could be described to fit the unique situations of particular agencies and classes of agencies. For example, the fund-raising appeal represents a revenue category very similar to an administered cost. That is, its level is related to the agency's efforts and skills rather than to its operating activity. The processing of an additional case, the educating of an additional student, or the presence of one more patient does not automatically give rise to revenues. Nor do contributions usually come in just because the unit opened its door. (How many loyal alumni or contributors would continue to mail in their checks if the annual fund drive or dinner was dropped?)

We will discuss the nature of both cost and revenue functions in greater detail in the section on cost-funding-volume relationships.

COST-RESPONSIBILITY RELATIONSHIPS

Another breakdown of costs relates to those individuals responsible for determining the amount expended to procure a given resource or service. This is referred to as controllability. The underlying rationale is that a significant portion of any organization's costs are affected by someone's behavior. Even variable costs can be affected by someone's decisions about how efficiently a given quality and quantity of service will be provided. The notion of competitive bids reflects the idea that identical services can be secured at markedly different prices. Controllability is independent of the cost-volume relations described in the previous section. Thus examples can be found of both controllable and uncontrollable costs for all the cost-volume relationships.

A cost is said to be controllable to a given individual when that party can alter the level of expenditure. A cost is uncontrollable when the individual cannot affect its level. It should be readily apparent that aside from taxes most costs are at *some time* the responsibility of *someone, somewhere* in the organization.

For example, once a contract is signed with a craftsmen's union, the rate of pay per hour is uncontrollable to the foreman assigning various tasks. However, the cost per job may still be determined by how well the foreman performs his job, since he is responsible for supervising the craftsmen's work. Thus what is controllable to the foreman is the efficiency with which the craftsmen work. Such a situation is typical of what is likely to exist in any organization. The individual responsible for controlling costs does not have total control. Rather, he controls by affecting a small subset of relevant factors. Still, this can result in significant savings (or nonsquandering) of an organization's limited resources. These concepts will now be used to illustrate how accounting data can assist managers.

ACCOUNTING AND PLANNING: COST-FUNDING-VOLUME ANALYSIS

The first step in any operating cycle is the plan. "How would we like things to be during the coming year?" Then, realistically, "What can we expect our inflows and outflows to be during that period?" Finally, "Are the two compatible?" Like a family trying to live within its means, the organization must take certain steps to see if the available economic resources are adequate for the mission it desires to undertake.

To solve this problem, the organization must conduct a cost-funding-volume analysis. Three questions must be answered:

1. What is the range and scope of activities planned for the period?
2. What costs are associated with these activities?
3. What are the various resources the organization expects to have available during that period?

The first question sets the frame of reference for the analysis. It specifies the activities which the organization desires to undertake. These, in turn, are needed so that the costs can be estimated; and if the organization receives fees for its services from either the client or a funding source (or both), the resources available can be calculated.

The second question asks for a general statement about the nature of the costs incurred in performing these activities. Initially, in the planning phase, the organization is not interested in the details of such costs. Rather, it is interested in the general form of the total cost function. In the language of the earlier section, these are the fixed and variable costs. Thus, in cost-funding-volume analysis, we are concerned with the general shape of the agency's cost function. As we will see below, the various cost categories will be aggregated to form a single cost function. Usually it is of this form:

$$\text{Fixed costs} + (\text{variable cost per unit} \times \text{level of activity}) = \text{total cost}$$

Thus the total cost at any given level is a function of some unavoidable fixed costs and the added resources expended to achieve that volume of activity.

The third question raises essentially the same issues about the agency's funding. To answer it, we may need to look beyond the confines of the agency. Still, a good manager may have a better idea of the next period's budget, contributions, fees, and grants than he does of the agency's costs. Traditionally, the funding side has been of great concern for not-for-profit agencies. This is because funding is often a competitive and political process. In addition, providing increased services can incur more costs, but (unlike the for-profit counterpart) it does not necessarily result in added inflows of resources. Thus administrators have developed great skill in anticipating their budgets.

Because not-for-profit agencies are such diverse organizations, a single example of cost-funding-volume analysis is unlikely to satisfy everyone. Thus a series of examples is given below. In general, Case 1 should be read by everyone, since it includes the most thorough discussion of the costs involved. The other examples vary the assumptions about the nature of the agency's costs and/or funding sources.

Case 1: Funding Fixed and Provided by a Single Source

Assume that we are part of a social service agency that is planning for the coming year. The agency's sole source of funding is a fixed government grant. There are no outside sources of funds such as foundations, charitable drives, or deficiency appropriations later in the year if we overspend our budget. Thus the revenues appear as a horizontal line (Figure 13-5); they are fixed independent of the agency's activity (though their initial level may purport to be related to activity).

In contrast, the total cost function of the agency resembles a semivariable cost. The range of activities the agency expects to undertake (the "relevant range") can be approximated by a linear cost function with a nonzero intercept. That is, at the start of the period the agency incurs or commits itself to certain costs—wages, rent, and so on. These costs are initially set at a level consistent with the agency's expected activities. This constitutes the fixed element. Other costs will be incurred in proportion

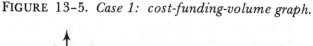

FIGURE 13-5. *Case 1: cost-funding-volume graph.*

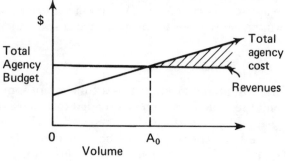

to the exact volume of work performed. These costs are the variable portion.

One agency that fits these assumptions is a social welfare agency. The budget of the agency is a fixed amount. With this budget the directors hope to achieve the greatest possible scope of coverage. Their costs, in turn, consist of both personnel and other base costs. These are the costs of being ready to serve clients when the need presents itself. In addition, the servicing of each client will result in added costs. The form these costs take will depend upon the specific function of the agency. In a counseling agency these may be tests, phone calls, or travel costs of the social worker. If the agency provides welfare benefits, they would be the *extra* costs of providing these benefits plus the benefits themselves.

Thus in Figure 13–5 we would say that the agency exactly balances its budgeted inflows and outflows at activity level A_0. This is often called a *breakeven point*, for it is the activity level at which the two flows are equal in size. An agency of the sort described here would probably try to plan its activities so as to achieve this level of activity. It cannot reasonably expect to reach any level beyond A_0 under present circumstances. It does not have the resources to do so. The shaded area to the right of A_0 in Figure 13–5 represents the resources it would need to serve additional clients. Similarly, it is unlikely that the agency would be happy serving fewer than A_0 clients. In a period of diminishing resources there are usually more potential clients than available facilities.

Still, the administrator of the agency may feel that A_0 is too low. His goal for the present year may be some number in excess of A_0, say, A_G. The cost-revenue-volume analysis is valuable in telling the administrator approximately how many clients the agency can serve under present operating plans (outlays for various services); it also suggests ways in which the desired goal can be achieved. One obvious way is to try to reduce fixed costs. Perhaps fewer staff can be employed. If this is done, a larger portion of the projected funding could be devoted to meeting the variable costs of serving additional clients. Figure 13–6a shows the old plan as a broken line and the new one (utilizing fewer staff) as a solid line. In this case the administrator feels that by cutting back staff he will be able to reach the desired level. Obviously there are limits to such a trade-off. Administrators have only limited amounts of slack which can be reduced to achieve different goals. If staff is reduced to too low a level, no one will be available to service the added clients. Thus, while the trade-off may be present, it is likely to be severely limited.

Figure 13–6b shows another possible trade-off. However, this one is not necessarily available or desirable. In this instance, the agency's administrators have attempted to service more clients by raising the efficiency with which each is served. Remember, in this case, efficiency does

FIGURE 13-6. *Case 1: modified cost-funding-volume graphs.*

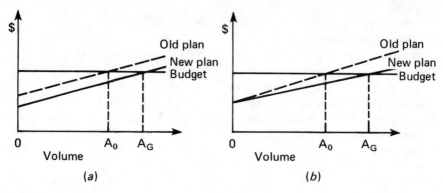

(a)   (b)

not mean faster; it means *incurring a smaller cash outflow per client.* Thus the administrators may attempt to reorganize caseloads in order to reduce the travel allowances of caseworkers or cut back the number of visits made by the caseworker to each client. The cash outlay per case falls and the budget can be spread over a larger number of cases. This is represented by the solid line in Figure 13–6b.

A numerical example of this case is given below. Similar examples in for-profit organizations can be found in the standard managerial accounting texts under "cost-volume-profit analysis" or "breakeven analysis."

Example: Burford Social Services Center was set up to administer training grants to unemployed minority high school graduates. Each client is interviewed by one of the center's caseworkers, given a battery of tests by the center's psychologist, and given a physical examination by one of Burford's doctors. The results of the interviews and the tests are used to ascertain the training program or vocational school most appropriate to the candidate. The intake process ends when the client is accepted into the designated program. During the client's stay in the program, he or she is visited twice a month by the caseworker. At the end of the period of study, the technical programs are responsible for placement. Burford's budget from the U.S. Department of Health, Education, and Welfare is $148,500. Its costs, divided into fixed and variable, are shown below:

	Variable (per client)	*Fixed*
Personnel		
Office costs and miscellaneous	$ 15	$80,000
Medical exams	50	10,000
Tuition	500	
Travel	20	
	$585	$90,000

In the above data the tuition costs are included as the average per client. There is no significant difference in cost among the courses. Travel includes only the mileage costs incurred by the caseworkers in the semi-monthly home visits while clients are enrolled in the program. The variable costs are the costs of sending one client through an entire program. For the sake of simplicity it is assumed that all the prospective clients have found a course consistent with their needs, interests, and abilities and that all clients finish a course once they start it.

Given the budget allowed the center by HEW, the first question raised by the director is "How many youths can we place?" To find out, we must see how much of the budget remains after the fixed costs of operating the center are deducted. The funds remaining are divided by the variable cost per client. The answer—100 youths—is shown computationally below and graphically in Figure 13–7.

Budget of Burford Social Services Center	$148,500
Less: Fixed operating costs	(90,000)
Amount available for tuition and other variable costs	$ 58,500

$$\frac{\text{Funds}}{\text{Cost per student}} = \frac{\$58,500}{\$585} = 100 \text{ students}$$

There are, of course, other questions the center's director might ask. For example, "What budget do we need to train 110 students?" From Figure 13–7 we can read off the cost line at 110 students the budget of $154,350. Alternatively, we could have calculated the answer using the cost-funding-volume equation:

Fixed costs	$ 90,000
Variable costs for 110 students ($585 × 110)	64,350
Budget required	$154,350

It might be interesting to see what the center's director would do if, in fact, the center's staff had estimated that a minimum of 130 students would need training. Costs such as tuition, rent of office space, and utilities cannot be reduced or altered materially. However, the personnel budget includes the salary for an additional part-time caseworker to make it possible for each worker to spend more time on case records and to move the maximum number of potential trainees up toward 150 students. This is about 25 more than the staff can handle at present. However, the plan could be dropped and, instead, the director could see clients when the caseworkers were overloaded. This would save $6,000, reducing fixed costs to $84,000. In addition, two procedural changes could be instituted. After the first month the caseworkers could visit the schools rather than

FIGURE 13-7. *Case 1: cost-funding-volume graph for Burford Social Service Center.*

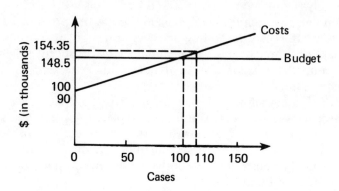

seeing the students at home. This would save not only travel costs but valuable caseworker time. The staff had considered this change in policy earlier but had deferred action on it. A second change which had been considered earlier but rejected involved sending clients for physicals only when the vocational training required it or when the caseworker believed it was needed to properly match the client to the training program. In this case, only about half of the students considered potentially trainable would probably be examined. Those found medically unfit would be placed in a different program, one for which they were qualified. These two changes (travel and medical exam) would reduce the variable cost per student by $30. To see if these changes are enough, we make the following calculations:

Fixed costs	$ 84,000
Variable costs (130 students at $555 per student)	72,150
Budget required	156,150
Budget available from HEW	154,350
Deficit	$ 1,800

You may wish to draw a graph similar to Figure 13–7 (using fixed costs of $84,000 and variable costs of $555 per student) in order to verify this calculation.

Case 2: More Than One Source of Funding

Given the deficiency present in Burford's budget, there is little hope for achieving the goal of at least 130 students unless some other source of funding can be found. One source that might be considered is a local foundation (a source of assistance we had ruled out in Case 1). The terms of the grant might be written in a variety of ways. The foundation might make a grant of some fixed amount which may be commingled with all other funds. Alternatively, it might agree to pay a subsidy of a fixed amount per trainee. The effect of adding these funds to the agency's HEW budget is shown in Figure 13–8.

Figure 13–8a shows the grant allowing the agency a fixed amount for the period. Figure 13–8b reflects the foundation's agreement to pay a fixed amount per trainee. Note that the graphs differ because the nature of the foundation's funding commitment differs. In Figure 13–8a the total funding of the agency is a fixed amount, but the sum consists of two sources. These appear as "layers" in the figure.

In Figure 13–8b the agency's funding is now dependent on how many trainees it places during the year. This is consonant with the foundation's and HEW's agreements with the agency. The agency might, of course, run a small surplus by actually cutting trainees back below 135 (if our estimates of costs are accurate), but we will ignore this possibility. The agency is operating to serve clients, not to show a budgetary surplus at year end. While the director wishes to use those resources wisely, he is committed to their use.

The general form of the calculations is the same as that shown earlier. The fixed grant from the foundation is exactly the same as in Case 1. Only the source of the funds is different. This does not affect the calculation of how many trainees can now be served or the adequacy of the budget to support a given level of activity.

The second case is slightly more complex in form, though its intent is the same. One possible solution is calculated below. For simplicity the foundation grant is treated as if it were a subsidy reducing the variable cost per trainee. This is the simplest approach for our purposes. However, in most cases the graphic form of presenting the data is the most useful. Note that in this situation the numbers do not come out even. The agency can train 135 students. The extra .3 is ignored.

Budget from HEW	$154,350
Less: Fixed operating costs	84,000
Budget remaining for variable costs	$ 70,350

$$\frac{\text{Budget remaining}}{\text{Adjusted rate*}} = \frac{\$70,350}{\$520} = 135.3$$

---

*The adjusted rate equals variable costs less foundation grant ($555 − $35 = $520).

FIGURE 13-8. *Case 2: modified cost-funding-volume graphs for Burford Social Service Center.*

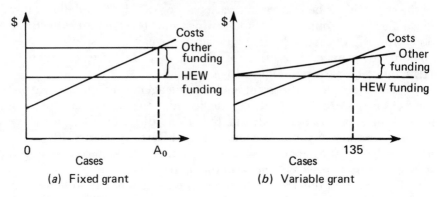

(a) Fixed grant   (b) Variable grant

Obviously, such agreements for extra funds could take many forms. For example, the foundation might limit its support to a maximum of 135 trainees. This means that the total-funding line in Figure 13–8b would stop rising after 135 trainees and flatten out. The agency's resources become fixed after 135 trainees, for no more funding is forthcoming from the foundation.

You may wish to see how the funds your agency receives would look in a cost-funding-volume graph. Obviously, some agencies' budgets will be more complex and some will have numerous funding sources.

Case 3: Quasi For-Profit Funding

In some instances, the not-for-profit unit may have as its primary source of funds revenues from a business or quasi-business operation. Hospitals and transport lines are extreme examples of how fund inflows in the form of fees for services rendered are paid by those to whom the service is rendered (or their agents through insurance). In such cases the fees constitute a significant portion of the unit's funding. Indeed, other sources of funding may base their support ("subsidy") on the deficit projected or incurred by the agency.

Consider a regional transport system planning for the coming year. Figure 13–9 shows the cost-volume relationships it faces. (This figure would be readily recognizable by any industrial manager.) The costs and receipts from patrons have been drawn so that it is feasible for the system to actually achieve a surplus of inflows over outflows *if volume is sufficiently large.* The expected level for the coming year, T_E, is below this point, and the difference between costs and revenues is the deficit which must be made up from some source other than fares. (*Note:* We are now talking

FIGURE 13-9. *Case 3: cost-volume relationship for a quasi for-profit agency (cash costs only).*

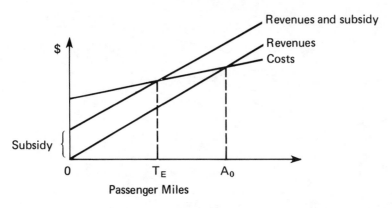

solely of cash costs. Thus depreciation on vehicles is not included among the costs.) Typically, it is an analysis of this form which supports an application for a subsidy or some other type of government support.

The price set for the transport service may be so low that the point where revenues cover costs is beyond the range of activities the coach line might achieve. While a for-profit firm would abandon this activity, some quasi-businesses may be deliberately planned in this manner. In the case of public transport, the government subsidy may be intended to encourage public transport over private vehicles.

Note again that Figure 13–9 reflects only the cash costs incurred by the transport company. Thus the deficiency of operating revenues relative to costs measures the amount of added cash the agency must find to pay its costs. As we move from agencies of the sort described in Cases 1 and 2 to quasi-businesses, we would expect to find significant amounts of capital investment. Any attempt to include a pro ration (such as depreciation) in the costs would raise the "deficit." (See Figure 13–10.) Undoubtedly, the transport company will need funds to replace vehicles as they wear out. Thus managers in a quasi-business may speak of two kinds of projections. One shows the amount needed to pay current bills (Figure 13–9). The second allows for recapturing the service potentials of the capital assets before equating inflows with costs (Figure 13–10). The latter breakeven point is analogous to the breakeven point in the for-profit sector.

Community mental health centers and similar agencies charge small fees according to the client's ability to pay. The total amount of such fees is not usually significant relative to the agency's budget. *In form* the funds

FIGURE 13-10. *Case 3: cost-volume relationship for a quasi for-profit agency (including depreciation costs).*

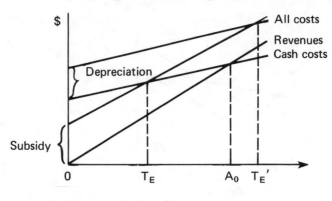

Passenger Miles

flow generated by these fees is similar to those in Figure 13–9. However, since they are so insignificant in amount, it is better to reflect them as the added increment to the budget. (See Figure 13–11.) Use of the form in Figure 13–9 might suggest that a massive subsidy is needed to recoup a large deficit. This is not the case. Rather, the small amount of fees collected supplements the budget.

In summary, the cost-funding-volume chart is a means of representing the resource flows of the agency. It provides a quick and heavily aggregated picture of the adequacy of the agency's resources for different levels of activity. Its purpose is to assist in making crude estimates of the agency's well-being under different conditions. In any given graph the cost function and revenue function can be held constant, with activity varied to estimate potential budget deficits and surpluses. It is also possible to devise different cost functions ("What happens if we attempt to undertake cost reductions?") or revenue functions ("What if we lose foundation support?") and compare the effects across two different cost-funding-volume graphs.

The strength of the approach is its simplicity, visual clarity, and the ease with which it can be used. However, because of its simplicity it must be supplemented by more detailed budgets once a choice among plans has been made.

BUDGETS

Cost-funding-volume graphs are snapshots of an agency's activities. Once a general course of action is decided upon, management requires

FIGURE 13-11. *Cost-volume relationship for trivial fees.*

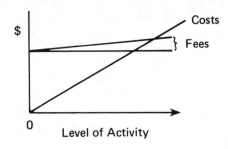

more detailed analyses of costs (and sometimes of funding) to implement the plan. These analyses are called *budgets* and are detailed forecasts of costs and funding for the next operating period. They are intended to serve two purposes. First, they indicate the nature and costs of resources needed and coordinate the utilization of these resources by different subunits of the agency. Second, they provide a yardstick against which performance can later be assessed. In this section we will consider the first purpose, the planning function. Later we will consider the use of budgets in controlling an agency's activities.

Accountants refer to two broad categories of budgets: static and flexible. A *static* budget is essentially what its name suggests. It remains fixed at a given level regardless of the activities of the agency. With a static budget, as with a fixed cost, we need to formulate only one plan of resource utilization regardless of anticipated activities. Quantities and total costs remain unchanged. Costs that are controlled by a static budget usually are truly fixed costs—for example, rental costs, and costs whose variability reflects administrative decisions rather than the agency's level of activities (such as reimbursed travel to conventions and meetings).

In a *flexible* budget, the costs involved are responsive to changes in the level of activity. Thus the total amount of the budget is "flexible." A flexible budget is really a series of budgets, one for each of several levels of activity. It gives the user relevant details concerning resources and costs of each level of activity. Consider a simple example—a local organization that must pay national headquarters $10 dues for each individual on its membership list during the year. In the cost-funding-volume graph, the national dues would be considered a variable cost and included in the total cost line. The flexible budget must also recognize this and requires that we plan accordingly. The budget for national membership dues if the organization has 40 members will be 40 × $10 = $400. For 50 members it will be 50 × $10 = $500. For any level of members, m, the budget will be $10m$.

This example shows how accountants avoid the need to calculate several different budgets for any one category of cost. The pattern of cost behavior discussed earlier is used to provide the "flex" in the flexible budgets. Only two budgets need to be formed: one during the planning cycle for the anticipated level of activity and another during the evaluation phase for the level of activity actually experienced.

Figure 13–12 depicts a series of budgets for the membership costs of an organization. Notice that the costs are both fixed (promotion and chapter fee to national headquarters) and variable (national per capita dues and costs of pins, cards, and so forth). The total cost for this budget can be found by the formula:

$$\text{Membership costs} = \$1{,}500 + \$25m$$

where m = number of members.

From this equation (and equations for the other individual categories of cost), a budget can be estimated for any level of expected membership. We could estimate the cost of any item in the budget (such as national dues) in the same manner. (The Appendix to this chapter discusses how these cost equations are developed.)

The administrator or the accountant develops a series of budgets to provide management with a detailed analysis of costs to be incurred at the volume of activity projected for the period in the agency's cost-funding-volume analysis. These budgets can be aggregated into a single master budget which summarizes all the inflows and outflows of the organization.

An extended example of how budgets are developed is beyond the scope of this chapter. The interested reader is referred to the appropriate works cited in the references. While these works do not discuss the plan-

FIGURE 13–12. *Membership budgets.*

	100 members	150 Members	200 Members
Variable costs			
Dues to national	$1,000	$1,500	$2,000
Pins	1,250	1,875	2,500
Supplies	250	375	500
Total variable costs	$2,500	$3,750	$5,000
Fixed costs			
Chapter fee	$ 500	$ 500	$ 500
Promotional expense	1,000	1,000	1,000
Total costs	$4,000	$5,250	$6,500

ning process for not-for-profit enterprises, the material is easily understood and can be readily adapted to the not-for-profit sector. The cash budget is discussed in detail below, since it is invaluable to managers of all organizations.

Cash Budgets

The cash budget examines the timing of cash flows into and out of the organization. While most budgets and statements aggregate the year's activities as if they occur at a single point in time, the cash budget disaggregates the cash flow into smaller time periods (monthly or even weekly). The resulting statement assists the agency's administrator in assessing the adequacy of the agency's cash on hand to meet obligations as they become due. It is not enough to expect future cash receipts when bills become payable; the cash must be on hand. An agency whose cash inflows will equal or exceed its outflows during the year may still need temporary bank financing to tide it over a period when cash inflows are expected to be low. Figure 13–13 shows a hypothetical cash budget for Studley Township. It covers the period from January through April 1979. This is a particularly difficult period for the township, since its fiscal-year

FIGURE 13–13. *Cash budget.*

Studley Township
Cash Budget
January–April 1979

	January	February	March	April
Balance on 1st of month	$ 2,500	$12,800	$ 1,800	$152,800
Receipts				
Wage tax payments	9,500			9,500
Property taxes paid	1,800	2,000	175,000	
Grants from county	20,000			
Total receipts	$31,300	$ 2,000	$175,000	$ 9,500
Disbursements				
Salaries				
Regular	$10,000	$10,000	$ 10,000	$ 10,000
Overtime	3,000	2,000	2,000	1,000
Supplies	8,000	6,000	7,000	10,000
Total disbursements	$21,000	$18,000	$ 19,000	$ 21,000
Net increase (decrease)	10,300	(16,000)	156,000	(11,500)
Loan		5,000	(5,000)	
Ending balance	$12,800	$ 1,800	$152,800	$141,300

responsibilities run from January to December but its primary sources of revenue, a wage tax and a property tax, are paid quarterly and annually respectively. In this simplified example the following data are assumed:

Cash Inflows

  Wage tax   Payments are due on the 15th of the month following the end of the quarter—in this case, January 15 and April 15.

  Property taxes   Payments are due by March 31. Normally 88 percent of all property taxes are paid in March. Of the remaining 12 percent unpaid, 1 percent of the total taxes are paid each month of the next 11 months along with the penalty. The remaining 1 percent is uncollectible.

  County grants   Grants are made by the county for services provided. Paid annually in January.

Cash Outflows

  Salaries   All wages and salaries are paid on the 15th and on the final day of the month in which they are earned. Overtime payments are made one month after the pay period in which they are earned. Thus the overtime earned in the first half of January is reported on January 15 and paid in the first pay period in February.

  Supplies   The township usually pays for its purchases approximately 60 days after purchase. Goods purchased by the township in January will be billed to it in the early part of February and paid in March. In some instances the township will make cash purchases of small items.

The statement in Figure 13–13 is the result of analyzing Studley Township's expected activities during the period and then extrapolating their cash flow effects. Thus it is the product of two sets of assumptions. One set concerns the details of the township's operations (hour worked, overtime, and so on). For the sake of simplicity they have not been listed, although many were required to prepare Figure 13–13. Fortunately, they usually are required in constructing the operating budgets. The other set consists of the data articulated above concerning the timing of the cash flows that result from these activities. Thus a cash budget, though valuable, can be tedious to construct.

Details of these calculations have been omitted from the example. Instead, they will be illustrated by explaining the source of the figures shown in the "January" column. The inflow consists of the payment of quarterly wage taxes for the period October to December 1978. (There are no collections in February and March because wage taxes are paid quarterly and we assume no late payments.) The property taxes paid and late fees represent late payments of those taxes due on March 15, 1978. The county's annual payment for service provided to the county by the township occurs in January.

Among the outflows, the wages consist of the "wages and salaries" earned in January and the "overtime" earned during the previous December. Supplies (other than those purchased for cash in January) were originally purchased in November 1978 and billed to Studley in December 1978.

At the end of January the township still expects to have a positive cash balance. However, as the figures for February and March show, some borrowing will be needed in those months to tide the township over until the property tax payments for 1979 begin in March. The township hopes to begin repaying the loans in March.

Banks would probably require an analysis such as the one above before making a temporary loan to Studley.

RESPONSIBILITY ACCOUNTING

The use of budgets to translate a cost-funding-volume graph into an operating plan is part of what accountants call responsibility accounting. Responsibility accounting is the structuring of the agency's accounts so that the costs (and, when appropriate, funds) can be associated with the subunit of the agency controlling them. The assumption underlying responsibility accounting is that if people and accounting data can be properly matched along lines of controllability (the authority to affect costs and revenues), the initial step has been taken toward improved performance. An accounting and reporting system structured according to whether the cost is controllable or uncontrollable gives managers data about those areas in which they can affect the level of costs and funding. Managers are not distracted by factors beyond their control. Responsibility accounting is what people usually have in mind when they speak of accountability.

One point must not be lost. Budgets and reports designed to reflect the controllability of costs and funding need not parallel the account structure legally imposed upon the agency for external disclosure. That is, good management accounting is not the same as strict compliance with legal requirements for disclosure. Some conflicts exist in the way costs are classified by the two methods. Thus the agency may keep "two sets of books," one to ensure compliance with statutory requirements and the other for management's use in planning and decision making. This is not unusual. In industry the conflict between the differing needs of the two sets of users has long been noted. As a result, special reports to assist management are the rule rather than the exception. This does not mean that the administrator is violating the law. Rather, it means that the same data can be arranged in different ways for different purposes.

It should be apparent that the form of a responsibility accounting system will vary from agency to agency, since its design must reflect each agency's lines of authority. Two agencies providing similar services need not be organized in the same manner. The examples in this section are intended as guides on how to ask the right questions, rather than as rigid examples of the only system of accounts. Occasionally, establishing responsibility units will reveal some conflicts between the preferred organizational structure for control purposes and the structure that has evolved. In these situations administrators will be required to make trade-offs between desired goals and a stronger control system. It must be remembered here that the control system is only a means to aid the agency in achieving its goals, not a goal in itself. However, few organizations can afford to deviate far from good practice without experiencing difficulties. This is particularly true when the organization's structure separates the authority for an activity and responsibility for it.

Developing the System

Five rules are involved in developing a responsibility accounting system:

1. The activities of the organization must be defined.
2. The main activities of the agency may be subdivided when this is consonant with the delegation of responsibility and authority within the agency or when the separation clarifies the association of the cost flows and the responsibilities of a particular individual.
3. Costs (and funds) must be associated with those administrators who control them.
4. If the scheme is to provide controls as well as activity reports, some yardstick must be developed against which performance can be assessed.
5. The system need not follow the same form as the reports filed with various external groups. However, it should not lead to any actions that would contravene any statutory rules.

The first four rules are the "dos" of any responsibility accounting system. They suggest the steps which must be taken to establish accountability. The fifth is the "don't" that must be borne in mind—a constraint that cannot be violated while designing the system.

The first two rules are concerned with determining the subunits which will serve as the responsibility units for the system. These responsibility units are called cost centers (if all they do is incur costs) or profit centers (if they generate revenues from their activities). The centers are hierarchical, so that the data can be aggregated upward in the organization. The nature of a superior's task makes him directly responsible for his own actions as well as indirectly responsible for those of his subordinates. Thus the head of a community mental health unit is ultimately responsible for all the unit's costs, while his subordinates will be accountable only for their own areas of authority. This is illustrated in greater detail later in the chapter.

The framework for accountability is developed with rules 1 and 2. Rule 3 is critical to the development of an effective system of organizational control. The association of costs (and funding) with those administrators who are able to affect their level (those who are "accountable") gives the administrators who should take corrective action the data they need to make their decision. This process is what we earlier labeled controllability. Remember that controllability does not mean that the administrator can reduce a cost to zero. It means only the *level of the cost* can be altered. Thus many fixed costs can be considered controllable, for we can control the *price* paid for a given service even though we cannot control the *quantity*. Similarly, a variable cost is controllable if we can affect either the price paid (per unit) or the quantity used to achieve a given level of activity (or both). Thus a union contract specifying the exact salary to be paid a professional and the workload of that professional in units of output (for example, so many clients seen or on the case list) would create a situation where the supervisor may have no control over an essentially variable cost. Similarly, the cost of teacher salaries probably is uncontrollable to everyone but the school district's board. Examples of this type are difficult to find but they do illustrate the notion that variable costs and controllable costs need not be synonymous.

The fourth rule is intended to assist the decision maker (whether it is the subordinate in charge of the activity or the head of the agency) in ascertaining not only the cost of a function but also the efficiency of its operation relative to some predetermined criteria. The budgets discussed earlier are examples of plans which, once formulated, provide both guidance to the manager and a measure of achievement at the end of a period. In general, criteria of this type are called standards.

Example of a Responsibility Accounting System

For illustrative purposes, a rather simple hypothetical organization has been selected—the Wolvercote Community Mental Health Center, which is assumed to provide only outpatient services. This example illustrates the principles of implementing responsibility accounting without using an elaborate set of facts, figures, and other data. Administrators directing hospitals and other quasi-businesses that have revenue inflows will find the concept of a contribution center more useful. (These concepts are discussed more extensively under the heading of "profit centers" in the traditional texts cited in the references.)

The Wolvercote Community Mental Health Center is administered by a director who is in charge of all administrative and support services. The chief clinical psychologist supervises testing and therapy, and the chief caseworker is responsible for directing the caseworkers' activities. Assuming that authority and responsibility are located in the same individual, the chief clinical psychologist, acting as a supervisor, receives reports concerning both testing and therapy. The chief caseworker receives reports on the scope of his authority and responsibility—the casework activities. The director of the center receives the same data they receive, as well as other data relevant to his job. This is the case because the director has ultimate responsibility for all the activities undertaken by the center, while the psychologist and the caseworker have responsibility only for their respective functions.

Figure 13–14 shows one possible format for the report the center's director might receive, summarizing the center's activities and highlighting the areas of responsibility. The three activities that the hypothetical agency performs which directly benefit the client—case workups, testing, and therapy—are indicated across the top of the report. Administration only indirectly benefits clients but is needed to maintain the center. Thus it too is included among the center's functions. The cost categories are shown down the left-hand side.

The head of each of the center's services would receive regular reports. However, the reports include only those costs relevant to that head's activities. In the case of Wolvercote, the report received by the chief caseworker would include only casework-related data. Such a report would be similar to the casework column in the administrator's report. As the person is responsible only for the efficient operation of the casework function, there is no need for detailed reports on the other activities of the center.

From a report such as that shown in Figure 13–14 the various administrators should be able to ascertain the level of costs for particular subcategories. When combined with data about the level of activities and the budget for these levels, reports such as this offer guidance concerning where time and effort should be expended to improve performance and what activities are being performed efficiently.

One difficulty in developing any responsibility accounting system is that some costs may be shared between centers and influenced by the activities of more than one department head or subordinate. Thus in preparing the data included in the report shown in Figure 13–14, it was assumed that the costs were associated solely with the function benefiting from

FIGURE 13–14. *Format for a responsibility accounting report.*

Cost Categories	Funtions			
	Casework	Testing	Therapy	Adminis-trative and Support Services
Direct costs				
Consultants		$ XXX*	$ XXX	
Testing supplies		XXX		
Direct travel costs	$ XXX			
Total direct costs	$XXXX	$XXXX	$XXXX	
Planned costs				
Salaries	XXX	XXX	XXX	XXX
Utilities and supplies	XXX	XXX	XXX	XXX
Total planned costs	$XXXX	$XXXX	$XXXX	$XXXX
Period costs				
Depreciation and rentals	XXX			XXX
Heat, light				XXX
Total period costs	$XXXX			$XXXX
Developmental costs				
Professional	XXX	XXX	XXX	XXX
Publicity	XXX	XXX	XXX	XXX
Total developmental costs	$XXXX	$XXXX	$XXXX	$XXXX

*XXXs are used in lieu of numbers. Costs are most likely to occur at those points where XXXs have been placed.

them. Many of the center's costs are clearly attributable to one and only one of the center's many functions. The cost of caseworkers' salaries is reflected only in the costs of that function, for their time is spent entirely on this activity.

However, this is not always the case. A caseworker may be qualified to do testing and will from time to time perform psychological tests when other personnel are unavailable. In such a situation, an allocation of the caseworker's salary between testing and casework is required. However, any allocation of the cost between them is essentially arbitrary and could result in conflict between the heads of two departments over how much of the caseworker's salary should have been included in each of their reports.

The presence of a large number of such items can disrupt the responsibility accounting system. They become a source of friction between the administrators and the system. The result usually is a reduction in the system's effectiveness. Typically, the conflict can be resolved by clarifying the lines of authority and responsibility.

The handling of administrative services in Figure 13–14 is an excellent example of a solution to the problem which still provides adequate cost control. Traditionally, these costs are considered common costs—that is, they are utilized by and benefit more than a single cost center. Thus the level of the cost is presumed to be affected by all centers, not by a single center. However, in the case of the administrative costs of smaller units, a significant degree of control may be vested in a single individual—the director—and a higher degree of control over these costs may be possible.

In contrast to administrative costs, other support costs may truly be common costs. Costs such as secretarial assistance, which provide pools of services utilized by all the centers within the agency, are affected by the activities of the various centers. However, they are under the complete control of no one. In such cases the responsibility for providing the pooled services efficiently probably rests with the central administration. This is the reason for including support costs with administrative costs, even though responsibility may be shared with others.

Many organizations do attempt to formulate their reports by functions, as shown in Figure 13–14. However, some administrators do so by allocating all the organization's costs in some predetermined ratio rather than by tracing the actual costs to the centers. Thus a director who feels that the agency's activities are divided 30 percent, 20 percent, and 50 percent among casework, testing, and therapy may allocate the agency's costs in that proportion. This is not responsibility accounting, for the costs allotted to the departments are not the costs they incurred. The costs so estimated need bear no relationship to the center's actual costs. For example, the personnel performing the tests may be so much better paid than the caseworkers that their total salary exceeds that of the caseworkers, even though there are fewer of them. An arbitrary rule of 30 percent, 20 percent, and 50 percent for allocating salaries would misclassify the costs. It allocates too much salary to the casework function and too little to the testing function compared with the costs actually incurred. A true responsibility accounting system must associate the costs actually incurred with the purpose for which they are incurred. An allocation scheme usually does not.

USE OF COST DATA FOR EVALUATION

The evaluation of performance is the next logical step once the measurement process has associated the costs with the center responsible for them. Doing this requires some criterion against which the costs can be assessed. This is usually called a *standard* in cost accounting and is common practice in manufacturing and many service industries. It undoubtedly will become much more common in not-for-profit agencies and quasi-businesses.

One such standard is the set of plans formulated prior to the beginning of a period. Budgets become a standard against which spending can be evaluated. Calculating the flexible budget for the period gives the administrator a standard against which to compare the costs incurred during the period. Figure 13–15 shows how a report might look for the case-worker function at Wolvercote. It includes not only the actual costs but also the budget for 600 client-contact hours and the difference (called a "variance" in accounting) between the actual and budgeted costs. Some reports would include one more column to measure the "variance" as a percentage of the budget. This, it is argued, aids the administrator in identifying areas of especially good or especially bad performance.

Budgets are used primarily to measure the costs of goods and services acquired from external sources. However, labor—particularly, the cost of skilled professionals—is likely to be a significant cost in any not-for-profit agency. If an agency is to make efficient use of its limited resources, it must do so not only by carefully marshaling the portion spent on items such as rent and supplies but also by utilizing its personnel wisely. This requires some standard against which the performance of these professionals can be compared.

An attempt to discuss standards in service industries is often greeted with statements that each case or client is different. While this is probably true from the staff professional's point of view, it does not necessarily mean that the clients must be considered so heterogeneous that a vast

FIGURE 13–15. *Responsibility accounting report for casework function.*

Wolvercote Community Mental Health Center			
Budget Report			
January 1979			
	Actual	Budget	Variance
Salaries	$6,000	$5,850	$150 U*
Direct travel costs	500	425	75 U
Utilities	100	125	25 F†
Supplies	45	50	5 F
Totals	$6,645	$6,450	$195 U

*U indicates an unfavorable variance (actual exceeded budget).
†F indicates a favorable variance (actual was less than budget).

array of standards for the efficient performance of a task must be set. The next section discusses how, when services are provided to a large volume of clients, a limited number of standards may be feasible.

Measuring Standard Performance

Implicit in any attempt to set standards is one of two assumptions. The first is that all the tasks performed by the agency are identical or, more realistically, that they are identical on certain key dimensions of the task that affect efficiency. This means that there are relatively few distinct classes of client problems. Thus, in our mental health example, whatever the client's problem, a caseworker can complete the partial screening process in a fixed period of time. This means that some clients may require a few time-consuming services and others may require many rather trivial services. In total they are expected to require about the same amount of caseworker time. When this happy coincidence exists, we can use a readily available index of activity as our measure of activity for purposes of control. In the caseworker example, an index of activity might be client-contact hours.

The second assumption is that, more typically, the services performed are not homogeneous in terms of the demands they make on the time of the professionals. Rather, some services to clients require a great deal of time, while others require only minimal time. This condition obviously raises some problems in setting standards, for we can no longer rely on simple, readily available measures of activity such as contact hours. Rather, we must somehow ascertain an *equivalent unit* that will serve as our standard unit of measure to assess the amount of work performed by each professional. Fortunately, this problem is not unique to the not-for-profit sector. Manufacturing and service firms also produce a variety of nonhomogeneous outputs. Methods applied to these problems would appear to be relevant to not-for-profit agencies.

Consider the following situation. The tasks performed by a caseworker may be diverse, but they are well known to the parties involved. Although a caseworker may handle many classes of clients with different problems, he or she will be able, as an experienced professional, to assess the relative time involved in each. For example, assume three kinds of cases—A, B, and C—are handled by a caseworker. B takes twice as much time as A, and C takes one and a half as much time as A. We can use these data to assess a caseworker's performance. A worker handling 10 A cases, 15 B cases, and 12 C cases would do the equivalent of 58 A cases: $(10 \times 1) + (15 \times 2) + (12 \times 1.5) = 58$. We ascertain the workload performed by a professional staff member by summing the quantity of each type of service performed and multiplying each class by the appropriate weight.

Thus when the clients of the agency reflect a relatively small number of identifiable and treatable problems and when each appears in significant numbers, standards can be established by assessing the relative time involved for each client class and measuring the workload of the professional as the sum of each caseload multiplied by its weight. Expressed mathematically:

$$L_t = W_i C_{it}$$

where L_t = the workload performed by the staff professional in period t

W_i = the relative weight of the ith client class

C_{it} = the number of clients in the ith client class seen during period t

Alternatively, the kinds of cases may be quite diverse and little homogeneity may exist. However, the services or treatments offered may consist of a few well-known standard procedures, and their relative times may be easily ascertained. In such a case, we may be able to assess the total work performed by evaluating each case in terms of the procedures utilized in servicing it. For example, assume that a given case required four procedures—W, X, Y, and Z—with known times of .1 hour, 3 hours, 1.5 hours, and 1.1 hours respectively. Then the total work performed on this case in standard hours is .1 + 3 + 1.5 + 1.1 = 5.7. In this manner we can estimate the *standard workload* involved in each case by relating it to its standard elements. The workload performed by the professional is the sum of the work performed for the individual clients.

Figure 13–16 shows a report based upon the idea of equivalent units. The relative weights used are assessed in terms of the standard office visit. The intake interview is rated as twice as time-consuming as a standard office visit. The home or school visit is one and a half times as time-consuming. In this particular report other activities such as staff training, professional development, and administration are assumed not to exist. These factors or some seasonal variation might explain why some caseworkers fell below standards. It could also be that the workers in question did not perform up to standard during that period.

Taken together, responsibility accounting, budgets, and standards transform accounting information from scorekeeping data to various attention-directing reports. This enriches the data available to managers and broadens the functions they can serve. In the next section we will examine how accounting data assist managers in the decision-making function. This is the third kind of data that accountants can supply managers. It is, as we shall see, the least structured of the three.

FIGURE 13–16. *Workload comparison.*

Comparison of Actual and Standard Workloads				
Wolvercote Community Mental Health Center				
January 1979				
Type of Activity	*Quantity*	× *Conversion*	=	*Standard Score*
Intake interviews	25	2		50.0
Standard office visit	110	1		110.0
School visit	65	.5		32.5
				192.5
Budgeted standard score	200.0			
Actual standard score	192.5			
Deficiency in standard score	7.5			

ACCOUNTING DATA FOR DECISION MAKING

Thus far we have been concerned with the more routine aspects of management, the day-to-day decisions for which management is responsible. These activities are at the core of the management function—the planning of operations, the efficient implementation of plans, and the efficient utilization of resources. From time to time the organization must consider changing the assumptions that underlie its plans and make a significant alteration in the nature of the organization and/or its activities. It is questions of this sort that concern us in this section.

Any decision involves a multiplicity of considerations. Many of these can be reduced to economic (monetary) terms. However, even in the for-profit sector, many cannot. The multi-objective set of goals affects all organizations to varying degrees. The role of the accountant is to measure the effect of any contemplated change on the organization's cash flows.

The role that economic considerations play in any decision will vary. In certain cases an organization will incur extensive costs in order to achieve a highly desired goal because the expenditure is considered worthwhile. Thus mental health centers use individual therapy sessions rather than group therapy sessions for a large number of patients because the benefits to the client are significantly greater. Yet group therapy is performed not only because it is often the more desirable form of treatment but also because the benefits of private therapy cannot justify the added cost. (This cost, of course, need not be entirely monetary. In expending greater resources on one patient, the center may be denying another patient services.)

But even with the wide range of goals and goal measures, scarce resources imply not that we avoid outlays but that we know the relative cost of the alternatives. Therefore in this section we will describe how managers should assess the cost of alternative courses of action—specifically, of those decisions that do not involve any capital investment. Multiperiod decisions involving capital investment require some discounting of costs and benefits and are discussed in Chapter 8.

Incremental Analysis

Any economic analysis for decision making involves isolating the change in costs (in whatever units of measure are to be used) and the change in benefits (measured in the same units). A potentially desirable alternative is one which results in a net increase in our welfare over the status quo. This is called *incremental analysis,* for it focuses on the changes that occur as we pass from the status quo to another state.

The format outlined below can be used in a variety of decisions. Typical of these are decisions concerning the operation of facilities (should we do our own cleanup or hire a service?) or the provision of support services (do we need an extra secretary?). These decisions are typical of a broad class of decisions an administrator faces as he tries to minimize the cost of undertaking necessary activities. All of them involve finding the least costly course of action. In some instances even a not-for-profit institution may be presented with the opportunity to provide services for a fee. (For example, it may run a special educational program or expand its services to include another political subdivision.) In these cases a critical element in the decision has to be the adequacy of the additional funding relative to the added cash outflows that will result.

Assessing the *financial* effects of any decision involves answering the following questions. (Similar questions must be answered for the nonfinancial costs and benefits as well.)

1. What increase (decrease), if any, will occur in the agency's cash inflows if the activity is undertaken?
2. What increase (decrease) will occur in the agency's cash outflows if the activity is undertaken?
3. Does the sum of any cash inflow increases and cash outflow decreases exceed the sum of the cash inflows lost and the increase in cash outflows?

The examples below will illustrate these points in detail. However, the reader should note that the items involved are all cash flows. What we will be concerned with is the effect of plans on *existing* and *potential* cash flows.

Case 1

Harlow School District needs a bus periodically to take children on field trips. It has already rejected the notion of buying a van or minibus. At present only one source of this service is being considered—Pluman Transport, which provides the bus service taking the district's children to and from school. A conference with Mr. Pluman has indicated the following costs:

- Trip between 9:00 A.M. and 3:00 P.M.: $10 per hour and $.25 per mile.
- Trip starting earlier or ending later than the above times: $25 per hour and $.25 per mile.

Using these figures, several teachers considered the cost of trips to the local museum. Since the trips could be fitted into the 9:00 A.M. to 3:00 P.M. period, the lower rate applied. One teacher estimated the cost at $27.50 for her trip to the museum. This consisted of 15 minutes for traveling in each direction, one and a half hours at the museum, a half hour total of waiting time at school to load and unload, and 10 miles of travel (2.5 hours at $10, and 10 miles at $.25).

A second teacher, planning a trip out of the district which would leave at 10:00 A.M. and not return until 5:00 P.M., estimated her costs to be $200 (7 hours at $25 and 100 miles at $.25).

At this point it is up to the teacher and others involved to decide if the trip is worth the expenditure. For example, $200 might take the same teacher's students to a special showing of the local ballet company, including the cost of tickets and transport.

Case 2

At this juncture the teacher became aware of a second alternative. Since she had a license to drive a bus or minibus, she decided to investigate the costs of renting the bus and driving it herself. These costs were:

One-day bus rental	$ 50
Mileage charge ($.15 per mile)	15
Gasoline	20
Insurance	15
	$100

Note that these costs make no allowance for the teacher's salary. What does this mean? First, that no additional cash outflow results from the teacher's driving. Apparently, she was to attend the field trip anyway. While driving may entail added "wear and tear" on her, this is not a relevant cost. Note, however, that gasoline and insurance are among the outflows. These must now be paid directly instead of implicitly in the rental fee.

What if, instead of going, the teacher had intended to stay at school? This would affect the cash flows. If a substitute must now be secured by the school, that cost too is part of the trip's costs, because it results in additional cash outflow. However, if two teachers swap duties, no added cost must be shown. Finally, should the union's contract with the school district require a payment of, say, $10 for a teacher who drives, that cost too must be included.

Both these cases are rather easy to analyze. In part this is due to the absence of any inflows or changes in the volume of services the agency supplies. In Case 3 some of these items will change.

Case 3

Kennington Hospital has been offered the chance to rent one wing (about 20 percent of its beds) to the local mental health unit for temporarily housing patients under observation. Patients would stay at this wing of Kennington for anywhere from a week to a month pending a decision on their mental state.

The mental health unit has agreed to make any alterations required in the hospital's facilities. These are relatively few and are of the sort that can be easily put in or removed. Kennington would receive a monthly rental and a fee per patient day for supplying food, nursing, and other care. Although the average occupancy rate at Kennington is only 75 percent, closing the wing will mean that some patients will be forced to go elsewhere during certain peak periods. Thus certain revenues will be lost.

Figure 13–17 shows an analysis of the cash inflows and outflows. The cash inflows include the fee from the mental health unit plus the estimated amount of the charge per patient day. Among the outflows is the cost of food, which includes only the added cash outflow of producing the meals. The manager of Kennington Hospital has ascertained that no extra personnel will be required in the kitchen. Thus the food charge reflects the amount expected to be paid for the edibles and an estimate of the added cash costs of cleanup, including the wages of any hourly personnel (but not personnel on salaries, for a full 40 hours will be worked under either

FIGURE 13–17. *Cash flows statement.*

Kennington Hospital
Analysis of Cash Flows
January 1979

Cash inflows

Monthly rental fee for wing		$ 5,000
Fee for patient care (500 patient-days at $40 per day)		20,000
Total cash inflows per month		$25,000

Cash outflows

Food (500 patient-days at $6 per day)	$3,000	
Linen (500 patient-days at $1 per day)	500	
Nursing (including fringes)	2,500	
Revenue forgone (60 patient-days at $150 per day)	9,000	
Total cash outflows per month		$15,000
Net cash inflow per month		$10,000

condition). Similar analysis was performed for linens. The nursing cost reflects the cost of hiring one added nurse so that the psychiatric wing will be adequately staffed even during peak periods of use of the hospital's other beds.

The revenue forgone by rental represents an "opportunity cost." This is a cash inflow which the hospital must forgo because it has reduced its capacity. Some patients will be forced to go elsewhere. These lost cash inflows are as real a consideration in decisions as the cash outflows incurred. In both cases the hospital has less cash resources as a result.

On the other hand, no depreciation is shown on the building wing. This is because the wear and tear will be present regardless of the use to which it is put. Rather, any unusual maintenance required because of its special use or because of its higher rate of use would be shown to the extent that *cash outflows are required.*

One obvious point is that the board of Kennington Hospital may still reject the plan because of its implications for the hospital in future years or its ability to serve its own patients. However, if it does so, the calculations in Figure 13–17 provide some insight into the economics of the situation.

SUMMARY

In this chapter we have examined a variety of tools that the accounting group can offer an administrator in the operation of the organization. For the most part we have discussed the current operations of the enterprise as distinct from any program evaluation or long-range planning. Thus the issue being addressed was "How can the administrator best utilize his resources?" To this end we have focused on three issues: reporting, evaluating, and short-term decisions. All three are concerned with resource utilization but in very different ways.

Cost-funding-volume and incremental cash flows analyses are concerned with plans and decisions. They deal with the rational allocation of scarce resources at the outset of the period. Cost-funding-volume analysis helps to sort out alternatives and examine the effects of the constraints affecting an organization. As such, it is a general tool which gives general answers. Since many estimates must be made before the graph can be drawn, there are many chances to err. Still, errors often offset one another, and a map that is roughly correct is preferable to no map at all.

In contrast, incremental analysis of cash flows is quite specific. The administrator faces certain alternatives, and choices must be made. The administrator may see the issues more clearly as a result. The role of accounting data in such a setting is to ensure that fiscal issues are not ignored.

The evaluation of performance requires that the data be structured so that people and programs are assessed according to their performance. To this end, the system of accounts for *internal* purposes has to be structured to highlight those costs which are controllable by a department head. This system, called responsibility accounting, should be implemented if an agency is concerned about the efficient utilization of its budgeted resources.

While responsibility accounting seems obvious, it may be a significant step in reorienting an organization's accounting system so that it assists the administrator in managing the organization, rather than being solely a necessary legal appendage. Moreover, responsibility accounting reinforces the role of the department and agency heads as administrators. Since they often serve also as professionals, it is important that one facet of their job is not lost to another, perhaps more interesting one.

Budgets and standards are the final link between a reporting system and one that facilitates evaluation. Much has been written on the behavioral problems of implementing such systems, in both the accounting and the behavioral science literature. Any organization trying to transform its accounting system from one focused primarily on legal concerns to one geared to serve managerial control as well must recognize that two changes are taking place. One is technical: the altering of an information system. The second is organizational: the revision of control relations and the establishing of new procedures. Unless the organization is properly prepared for the second, the first fails. If either sits in limbo, unused by those expected to benefit from it, or is openly rejected, the expenditure of time and effort is useless. In essence, since the budgets and standards are intended not only to alter the data available to administrators and others in the organization but also, through that information, to affect the attitudes and behavior of the members of the organization, both elements must be considered for successful implementation.

APPENDIX:
Cost Estimation

Much of the discussion in the chapter referred to costs by broad category (fixed or variable). However, to use the data for planning or controlling operations, the administrator needs more than the form of the cost function. He needs estimates of the values of the costs. While such costs may sometimes be found by reading labor contracts or invoices, in many instances past total costs must be compared with prior period levels of activities and the underlying relationship estimated. This relationship is called a cost function and is usually assumed to be linear in form. In this appendix we will examine the basic framework for cost estimation and the techniques available.

STEPS IN ANALYSIS

While it is tempting to focus on methodology, it is often true that the steps taken in selecting the data and deciding upon the appropriate methodology will be an important part of the analysis. Five steps are critical to this preanalysis stage and common to any of the techniques discussed later:

1. Examining the data to see if they have been affected by the accounting policy.
2. Selecting a measure of activity.
3. Considering if any events other than changes in the level of activities have occurred during the period to make the costs for the same activity differ in amount.
4. Plotting the data.
5. Deciding on how accurate an estimate of cost is necessary.

The first step ensures that accounting rules are not discovered instead of underlying cost functions. For example, accountants may allocate the fixed costs of a service department to other departments on the basis of some activity. The allocation of the costs of maintaining a hospital's personnel records to the other departments would probably be on a per capita basis. When costs of the departments are examined, the various levels of personnel will reflect different costs as if that portion of cost is variable. However, it need not be. All that has happened is that the accountant's allocation rule has been rediscovered.

Another accounting rule that can cause difficulties is the matching rule. In some instances accountants regard costs as expenses when paid for, not when used. Thus supplies may be shown as expenses in a period before use, while labor may be expensed in the month following the work. In the first instance the accountant has mismatched the costs too soon. In the other the mismatch is too late.

Problems of this sort, if serious, can be remedied by reexamining the raw data. Often, as in the case of labor costs mentioned above, all that needs to be done is to note that the activity shown for a given period is related to a cost that lags behind by one month. In such a case, the effort required to make such an adjustment is trivial.

The second step, selection of a basis to explain the change in cost, is often a matter of experience. Managers familiar with their organization's activities usually have at least a rough idea of how costs behave. Thus, in the first instance, judgment serves as the basis. Later, if the graph of the data shows no apparent relationship between cost and the measure of the activity selected, alternative bases can be considered. However, one caveat: the measure of activity selected should bear some a priori relationship to the cost in question. If it does not, any estimates resulting from a prior period's cost data could be spurious and useless for estimating a future period's costs.

The third step is often labeled "homogeneity" or "stationarity." That is, was the process unchanged throughout the period? For example, did inflation radically affect costs so that data that are two years old are not comparable to those for the most recent period? Or did a change in policy result in different shift sizes or different categories of professionals performing the task?

Depending upon the source of the difficulty, a solution to the stationarity problem may or may not be feasible. The effects of inflation on costs may be adjusted for, at least crudely, via price indices. However, changing the manner in which a task is performed probably leaves no alternative but to drop the earlier observations and utilize only those data that are homogeneous.

The fourth step, graphing the data, serves two purposes. First, any obvious relationships as well as the apparent absence of such relationships can be detected visually. This is helpful in either case, for it points out the direction for further work. If the relationship is obvious, a less sophisticated technique may well suffice. If none exists, a new measure of activity can be found *before* time and effort have been wasted on further analysis.

Second, any unusual characteristics of the data may appear at this time. Costs which appear to be unusually high or low relative to the other periods can be noted. Such outliers, as they are often called, may have to be eliminated because they are unrepresentative. However, only investigation can ascertain how unusual they really are. Graphing may also reveal seasonal patterns in the data. Because of differences in the amount of daylight, outside temperature, and sometimes the mix of activities undertaken at different times of the year, utility costs differ markedly between January and June. Thus, while it may be possible to analyze each season by itself to ascertain the cost function, analyzing two different seasons as one may produce a meaningless answer.

There is little point in paying more for cost estimation than is necessary. Each of the methods described below has different advantages and disadvantages. Some are essentially "quick and dirty"; others require more data points and are more time-consuming, more expensive, and usually more precise. The fifth and final step is for the administrator to select the method appropriate to the situation at hand. An elaborate technique should not be used if only a rough estimate is needed. Conversely, when great precision is necessary, a quick-and-dirty approach may be false economy.

TECHNIQUES

In this section we will describe four methods. Three of them are of the quick-and-dirty variety. As such, they can be quite useful when time and data are very limited. The fourth, statistical curve fitting, is both more rigorous and traditionally viewed as more time-consuming. Today, however, standard computer software packages are available for this purpose. In addition many of the pocket calculators now available fit a least-squares trend line to a fairly large data set. Thus, as a rule, the quick-and-dirty approaches should be used only when the number of observations is very small or any decisions will be relatively insensitive to variation in the estimates.

Analysis by Accounts

One of the simplest approaches to the cost estimation problem is the dichotomizing of each account into either fixed or variable. The broad category of costs involved is subdivided into the accounts which comprise it and these accounts are then examined. The argument supporting such a procedure is that while a broad category of costs need not be fixed or variable, the individual accounts are more likely to be. Figure A–1 shows an analysis by accounts for the support services of a social service agency. Activities in this example are measured by the number of cases handled. Note that the cost function finally developed is a semivariable cost. The variable portion was obtained by dividing the variable costs for January 1979 by that month's caseload.

The analysis by accounts requires minimal time and few observations (only one period's data), and will yield a function of some sort. However, it is also quite subjective, arbitrary, and subject to the vagaries of the period chosen. Thus two different estimators using the same raw data could disagree on the fixed-variable split. Similarly, the same estimator might analyze the February accounts into the same categories but arrive at a very different cost function if there is a high degree

FIGURE A–1. *Analysis by accounts.*

Account	Amount	Fixed	Variable
Utilities	$ 200	$ 200	
Salaries	3,800	3,800	
Supplies	100		$100
Rent on space used	100	100	
Xerox	300		300
Paper	150		150
Totals	$4,650	$4,100	$550

Cases handled in January: 110

Variable costs: $\dfrac{\$550}{110}$ = $5 per case

Cost function: $4,100 + $5 per case

of interperiod variability that is independent of the level of activity. Finally, the splitting of costs into only fixed or variable may be inappropriate. Thus, while utilities are essentially fixed, they do vary to a small degree in response to volume. This can be compensated for by splitting the semivariable cost between the two categories. In this example (Figure A–1) the utility cost could be allocated 80 percent to the fixed and 20 percent to the variable. Figure A–2 shows the revised calculation.

Visual Curve Fitting

The ranking of shortcut methods is difficult. Visual curve fitting is not better or worse than the analysis by accounts described above or the high-low method discussed below. Rather, it makes different compromises relative to the least-squares method, discussed in the final section of this appendix.

Figure A–3 shows a line fitted visually to two sets of data. In set *a* the data are grouped fairly close to a line. An examination of the cluster of observations in set *b* reveals no obvious line. The relative advantage of fitting the curve visually depends upon the obviousness of the function in the graphed data. In set *a*, many different observers would fit essentially the same line to the data. Thus, although quick and dirty, the method is quite useful under the circumstances. In set *b*, the same estimator might fit several different lines to the data. Under the method at hand we have no way of determining the "best" fit.

The most obvious difference between the analysis-by-accounts approach and visual curve fitting is the number of periods of data utilized. The analysis-by-accounts method requires that only one period's data be available; indeed, it could not utilize additional data if they were available. By contrast, in visual curve fitting several data points *must* be available before a line can be fitted with any hope of accuracy. Only then is the estimator able to ascertain the extent of the regularities present in the data.

The actual calculation of the cost function once a line has been visually fitted to the data can be done by extending the line to the vertical axis and reading

FIGURE A–2. *Analysis by accounts—revised method.*

Account	Amount	Fixed	Variable
Utilities	$ 200	$ 180	$ 20
Salaries	3,800	3,800	
Supplies	100		100
Rent on space used	100	100	
Xerox	300		300
Paper	150		150
Totals	$4,650	$4,080	$570

Cases handled in January: 110

Variable costs: $\dfrac{\$570}{110}$ = $5.18 per case

Cost function: $4,080 + $5.18 per case

values off of the chart. The calculations utilize the same computational procedures as the high-low method. Therefore, the discussion of how the cost function is derived will be covered in the next section.

High-Low Method

The high-low method utilizes the two extreme levels of activity to determine the cost function. The presumption is made that the two extreme values reflect the greatest variability among the data points. By comparing them we can isolate the change in total cost between the two levels. That change is attributed to the change in activity. As Figure A–4 shows, the variable cost per unit of activity (100 pages duplicated in this case) is found by dividing the change in cost by the change in activity. The fixed cost is that portion of the total cost at the high or low volume which is *not* accounted for by the variable costs. Similar calculations would be performed under visual curve fitting once the line has been drawn.

FIGURE A–3. *Cost data for visually fitting a cost function.*

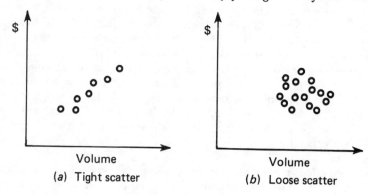

(a) Tight scatter   (b) Loose scatter

FIGURE A–4. *High-low method.*

Month	Duplicating Cost	Volume (batches of 100 copies)
January	$1,800	1,820
February	1,200	1,250
March	1,600	1,670
April	2,050	1,870
May	1,280	1,080
June	1,040	860

$$\text{Variable cost} = \frac{\text{cost}_{high} - \text{cost}_{low}}{\text{activity}_{high} - \text{activity}_{low}}$$

$$= \frac{\$2,050 - 1,040}{\$1,870 - 860} = \frac{\$1,010}{\$1,010} = \$1/\text{batch}$$

$$\begin{aligned}
\text{Fixed cost} &= \text{total cost} - \text{total variable cost} \\
&= \text{total cost} - (\text{variable cost per unit} \times \text{activity}) \\
&= \$2,050 - (\$1 \times 1,870) \\
&= \$2,050 - \$1,870 \\
&= \$180
\end{aligned}$$

The high-low approach is in many ways a variant of the visually fitted curve, without the subjectivity in setting the line. However, once the high and low values are used, a graph such as Figure A–3a can be used to determine how well the line fits the data. Under the high-low approach we still do not have a way to test the "best" fit, and unlike visual curve fitting much of the data in the intermediate values is ignored. Thus, if accurate estimates are needed, we must turn to the statistical techniques discussed briefly below.

Statistical Curve Fitting

The discussion of the quick-and-dirty methods revealed three weaknesses in these approaches. First, the high-low method and analysis by accounts did not use all the data available. Second, the visually fitted curve and the analysis by accounts are subjective. The same data could result in different estimates of the cost function by different people. Third, none of the methods offers an indication of how well the estimated cost function fits the data. The least-squares method resolves these problems.

At one time or another most readers have probably either calculated a least-squares trend line or used one that another person has produced. The least-squares method fits a trend line to the data which minimizes the sum of the squares of the differences between the data points and the trend line. Previously, the calculations were laborious and the quick-and-dirty methods saved a great deal of time. However, with the availability of pocket calculators the work has been cut significantly. In addition, many calculators contain a preprogrammed function that enables the user to calculate a least-squares trend line after putting the data points into the machine. Those organizations with their own computers can use preprogrammed software packages to calculate the desired results. The latter often provide a much more sophisticated analysis than we will discuss here.

Figure A–5 shows how the least-squares cost function is calculated. For simplicity, small numbers have been used. These do not affect the actual calculation, merely the number of digits to be manipulated. The columns of numbers i, x, y, x^2, xy, and y^2 are used in the "normal equations" which calculate a, the constant term, and b, the variable cost per unit. The r value reflects how the line fits the data. It can vary from $+1$ to -1. The larger the absolute value, the better the fit of the line to the data. The plus or minus sign refers to the slope of the line. A cost function should be increasing as it moves from left to right. This is a positive slope. It is difficult to imagine a cost whose general shape implies that the *total* cost will decrease as more of it is used. This is what a negative value implies. Sometimes an r^2 value is calculated. This number, found simply by squaring r, shows the percentage of the variability in the data that is explained by the cost function. In our example this value is quite high, for the value of r was high.

It should be apparent that for the extra effort involved the least-squares approach resolves many of the problems of the quick-and-dirty methods. Figure A–5 shows that all six data points were used to calculate the trend line. The normal equations mean that anyone given the data on production and costs should

FIGURE A–5. *Calculating a least-squares trend line.*

(i) Period	(x_i) Units Produced (in thousands)	(y_i) Total Cost (in thousands)	x^2	xy	y^2
1	1.0	$ 32	1.00	32.0	1,024
2	1.5	35	2.25	52.5	1,225
3	1.7	36	2.89	61.2	1,296
4	1.3	34	1.69	44.2	1,156
5	2.0	41	4.00	82.0	1,681
6	1.1	31	1.21	34.1	961
	8.6	$209	13.04	306.0	7,343

$$\Sigma y = na + b\Sigma x \quad \text{or} \quad 209 = 6a + 8.6b$$
$$\Sigma xy = a\Sigma x + b\Sigma x^2 \quad \text{or} \quad 306 = 8.6a + 13.04b$$
$$r = \frac{n\Sigma xy - (\Sigma x)(\Sigma y)}{\sqrt{n\Sigma x^2 - (\Sigma x)^2} \quad \sqrt{n\Sigma y^2 - (\Sigma y)^2}}$$
$$= \frac{6(306) - (8.6)(209)}{\sqrt{6(13.04) - (8.6)^2} \quad \sqrt{6(7,343) - (209)^2}}$$
$$= \frac{38.6}{40.2} = .96$$

calculate the same function. Finally, the r and r^2 values tell us the goodness of the fit.

The administrator in need of elaborate cost estimates will find the least-squares method worth pursuing further. Like any technique, it has its limitations. First, it can be no better than the data. If a good fit does not exist, least squares will still produce a cost function. The user must rely on the r value to recognize how poor the fit is. Second, the technique makes certain assumptions that we have not discussed here. The administrator considering extensive use of this technique should consult one of the more specialized texts to avoid difficulties. Such an administrator probably will be using one of the computer software packages, which contain the needed tests to guard against misuse. Finally, the least-squares method requires a reasonable number of observations over a fair range of activities. Some agencies may not be able to generate these data.

LIMITATIONS TO THE METHODS

It is worth reminding the potential user of the limitations to all the methods discussed. These limitations should be viewed as caveats for avoiding unnecessary problems.

Limited Range of Applicability

It seems obvious that no technique can be used authoritatively beyond the scope of the data from which it is derived. In other words, we cannot extend our cost estimates beyond the range of observations without risking great error. None of the methods purports to describe the form of cost behavior for levels of activity outside those examined in developing the cost function. Indeed, as we apply the estimates toward the ends of that range, we are less and less confident of their accuracy. Thus some discretion must be used in utilizing the estimates once they are developed.

Linear Form of the Cost Function

All the techniques above except for visual curve fitting are oriented toward the development of a linear cost function. Even the visual techniques were described as if only linear cost functions were to be developed. There are two reasons for this. First, over the range of observations, linear functions usually provide almost as good a fit to curvilinear data as a curvilinear function. Any improvement by using a curvilinear function is usually small. Second, the linear function is usually more familiar to the user and easier to analyze. For example, the linear function $TC = a + bx$ provides a convenient estimate of the variable costs via the value of b.

The statistical techniques used in curve fitting provide a fair range of alternative forms to the user. Thus nonlinear forms are available as part of the standard computer software package. This means that in those cases the choice between linear and nonlinear is a matter of preference and is not forced upon the user. Even in these cases, however, the user will typically find a linear cost function satisfactory.

FIGURE A-6. *Nonlinear total costs.*

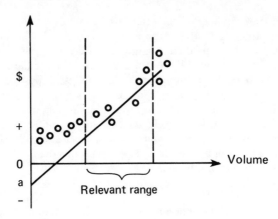

Fixed Costs Not Estimated

In the linear cost function described above, the *b* term was used as a measure of variable cost. However, the same cannot be said for *a* and fixed costs. In any of the estimation techniques the *a* term sets the relative height of the curve so that the proper level of total cost can be read off the *y* axis. This is not the same as fixed costs.

This may appear to go against intuition. However, consider the simple example where total costs are nonlinear over the entire range of activity (Figure A–6). Over the portion under examination, costs are rising quite rapidly. Any linear function fitted to the data shown could provide a good fit over the relevant range and still show a negative value for *a*. This would imply *negative* fixed costs if *a* is taken to measure fixed costs. That, obviously, is a logical contradiction and therefore cannot be the case. Other examples can be devised to show how *a* serves merely to calibrate the total cost curve. The one in Figure A–6 should suffice for our purposes.

REFERENCES

Birnberg, J. "Improving the Efficiency of a Community Mental Health Agency: An Accountant's View," *American Journal of Community Psychology,* Vol. 4 (1976), pp. 379–391.

Birnberg, J., and S. Birnberg. "The Zero-Based Budgeting Opportunity," *Professional Psychology,* November 1977, pp. 442–450.

Dopuch, N., J. Birnberg, and J. Demski. *Cost Accounting: Management Uses of Accounting Data,* 2nd ed (New York: Harcourt Brace Jovanovich, 1974).

Horngren, C. T. *Cost Accounting: A Managerial Emphasis,* 4th ed. (Englewood Cliffs, N.J.: Prentice-Hall, 1977).

Vatter, W. *Operating Budgets* (Belmont, Cal.: Wadsworth, 1969).

CHAPTER 14

Zero-Based Budgeting: Implications for Social Services

Gerard L. Otten

Editor's Note   *With the commitment to zero-based budgeting (ZBB) at the federal level, social science agencies may be faced with unique challenges. ZBB addresses many of the shortcomings of traditional budgeting. It can help managers of non-profit organizations serve their clients more efficiently and comprehensively. For example, ZBB can help eliminate and reduce low-priority programs for increased effectiveness. This chapter discusses the growing use of ZBB in government agencies and elsewhere and the implications for nonprofit organizations.*

The initial part of the chapter provides an overview of the three stages of budgetary reform: expenditure control, management control, and planning control. Expenditure control involves appropriation by line item and by object of expenditures. Management control emphasizes the efficiency with which activities are conducted. The planning, programming, and budgeting system (PPBS) has had significant impact on the theory of budgeting because it attempts to tie planning and budgeting in one analytical framework that focuses on programs.

The impetus for budgetary reform has led to ZBB. The format of traditional budgets is not conducive to end-product analysis, the absence of measurable objectives, and the incremental approach. ZBB tries to answer the questions of whether current activities are efficient and effective and whether they should be eliminated

---

From *Administration in Social Work*, Winter 1977, © 1978 by The Haworth Press. All rights reserved. Reprinted by permission.

or reduced to fund higher-priority programs or reduce spending. ZBB isolates decision units for analysis, evaluating and ranking them to facilitate approval or disapproval. The analysis is suggested by an example of a social service agency which highlights some significant shortcomings of ZBB.

Because ZBB has had limited application, valid conclusions about it cannot be drawn. ZBB faces significant barriers ahead. First, it needs widespread support in the political arena. ZBB requires additional staff involvement and paperwork, and, like PPBS, requires a statement of objectives—an alien activity for most public servants. The ability to collect the appropriate data and quantify it is another major hurdle. Social services must set clearer goals and objectives and use quantitative and cost data in developing budgets in the course of operationalizing ZBB.

With the election of Jimmy Carter to the presidency of the United States, a substantial portion of the population, especially social service professionals, probably saw renewed opportunities for the expansion and support of social service programs from the federal level. Those associated with the broadly defined field of social services probably felt a rejuvenated vitality and sense of direction for human services programs that had not existed during the preceding Republican administration. Whether reality will meet these expectations remains to be seen. The president's campaign rhetoric, laden with hopes and promises, must now be tested in a demanding political arena of divergent and conflicting interests; the author of *Why Not the Best?* will be hard pressed to make good on all his campaign assurances to the American people.

It is uncertain whether or not the president can achieve all of his stated goals. However, one of these, a commitment to the initiation of zero-based budgeting (ZBB) in all executive departments and agencies, remains firm. President Carter has already directed these organizations to prepare their budget estimates for fiscal year 1979 using a ZBB format (*Federal Register*, 1977).

As part of the president's commitment to efficiency through reorganization and renewed public trust in government, ZBB has rather significant implications for the operation and administration of our government. There appear to be particularly unique implications for the operation of social service programs and the associated stresses that will be placed upon them with the adoption of ZBB.

BUDGETARY REFORM

Author Allen Schick identifies three stages of budgetary reform: expenditure control, management control, and planning control (cited in Lee and Johnson, 1973, p. 101). Although these stages are not rigidly fixed to specific time periods, they do facilitate an understanding of how present budgetary philosophy has evolved. Expenditure control has been identified by a legislative concern for tight control over executive expenditures. The most prevalent means of exerting this type of expenditure control has been to appropriate by line item and by object of expenditures; financial audits are then used to ensure that money has in fact been spent for the items authorized for purchase. This focuses information for budgetary decision making upon the things government buys, such as personnel, travel, and supplies, rather than upon functions performed and the accomplishments of governmental activities. In other words, responsibility is achieved by controlling inputs; outputs are generally ignored.

The second stage is that of management control, which emphasizes the efficiency with which ongoing activities were conducted. Historically, this orientation has been associated with the New Deal through the first Hoover Commission (1949). Emphasis was placed upon holding administrators accountable for the efficiency of their activities through such methods as work performance measurement.

The third and, to the present, final stage of budgetary reform has been for the planning function to be served by budgets. President Lyndon B. Johnson's budget message of 1968 clearly emphasized programs and the relationship between revenues and expenditures in order to accomplish objectives (Lee and Johnson, 1973, p. 10). It was President Johnson who promulgated to federal agencies the adoption of the then heralded planning, programming, and budgeting system (PPBS) that had first been installed in the Defense Department by Robert McNamara.

PPBS had a brief yet significant impact upon the theory of budgeting because of its commitment to the concept of tying planning and budgeting in an analytical framework that focused on programs. However, because of a number of problems associated with PPBS, some political and some practical, the concept met a quiet and unspectacular death; its postmortem has been conducted in a number of professional and scholarly journals (see Mosher, 1969; Schick, 1972; Dougherty, 1971).

Although PPBS is now considered passé, the impetus for budgetary reform remains. There is, and has been, widespread dissatisfaction with traditional budgeting practices. The stakes are high in any budgeting procedure because "budgeting determines who gets what." Therefore, the crucial aspect of budgeting is whose preferences are to prevail in disputes about which activities are to be carried on and to what degree, in the light of limited resources (Wildavsky, 1974, p. 129). Given those realities, there is little wonder why elected officials, special interest groups, the general public, and agency officials have differing reactions to the cries for a budgetary reform that may produce a more efficient, more effective, and more accountable system.

Critics of the traditional budgetary approach cite a number of significant shortcomings that they feel encourage waste and inefficiency. First, they argue that line item formats prevent the analysis of end products. Thus, ends cannot be easily related to means (Wildavsky, 1974, p. 137). Second, traditional budgeting requires no statement of measurable objectives. For example, a budget request of X dollars will result in the placement of Y number of children in adoptive homes. Last, the traditional approach is incremental—only the increments over the preceding year's budget are analyzed. Consequently, the preceding year's budget, the base, is seldom analyzed. This incremental approach results in budgetary decisions that rarely question the merit of a program or an agency. It also limits the scope of legislative agreement because decisions are based on compromises that have been reached over the few extra dollars requested that are in excess over the previous year's budget. The base is taken as a given—the product of compromises reached in previous years. The budgetary decisions rarely involve basic differences in policy (Wildavsky, 1974, p. 136; for a discussion of the concept of analyzing small changes, or increments as they are called, see Lindblom, 1959).

Given the criticism of the traditional budgeting approach, there has been considerable interest in reform proposals that would address its deficiencies and achieve the goals of efficiency and effectiveness within a rational priority scheme. In the wake of the PPBS failure has risen the most recent hope for reform: zero-based budgeting.

ZBB OVERVIEW

ZBB focuses its activities on answering two basic questions (Pyhrr, 1977, p. 1): (a) Are the current activities efficient and effective? and (b) Should current activities be eliminated or reduced to fund higher-priority new programs or to reduce the current budget?

In order to address the issues associated with these two questions, the zero-based approach requires each agency systematically to evaluate and review all programs and activities (current as well as new). To do so, the agency must address four basic steps (Pyhrr, 1977, pp. 2–7):

1. *Identification of "decision units."* Zero-based budgeting attempts to fo-

cus an administrator's attention on evaluating activities and making decisions. Decision units are "meaningful elements" that can be isolated for analysis and decision making. In most agencies these may correspond to those budget units defined by traditional budget procedures (i.e., cost center).

2. *Analysis of decision units.* Each decision unit is analyzed in "typically" three decision packages, and more if possible. This enables each decision package to construct a "framework" of performance and funding. The decision package is the building block of the zero-based concept. It is a document that identifies and describes each decision unit in such a manner that management can (a) evaluate it and rank it against other decision units competing for funding and (b) decide whether to approve it or disapprove it.

The information contained in the decision package might include: purpose/objective; description of actions ("What are we going to do, and how are we going to do it?"); costs and benefits; work load and performance measures; alternative means of accomplishing objectives; and various levels of effort ("What benefits do we get for various levels of funding?").

3. *The ranking process.* This enables management to allocate its limited resources by making management concentrate on these questions: "How much should we spend?" and "Where should we spend it?"

4. *Preparation of a detailed operating budget.* The budget or appropriation requests prepared by each agency are usually subject to some form of legislative review or modification. Under the zero-based approach the decision packages and ranking determine specifically the actions required to achieve any budget reductions. If the legislature defines reductions in specific program areas, we can readily identify the corresponding decision packages and reduce the appropriate program and organizational budgets.

The following example briefly illustrates the type of analysis that would be conducted by an administrator to prepare a decision package. The decision unit in this case is a hypothetical adoptions division in a large state social service agency. The division's responsibility is to find suitable adoptive homes for children. The administrative head of this unit would (a) identify different ways of performing the function and (b) identify different levels of effort for the recommended decision package.

1. Different ways of performing the same function.
    a. Recommended decision package: Use the agency's county-based staff to complete all adoptions. This expenditure would permit the adoption of 500 children at a total cost of $250,000.

b. Alternatives not recommended (for same number of adoptions):
  (1) Contract with private agency XYZ. Cost: $310,000. The cost per adoption exceeds the projected cost for completing the adoptions using the county-based staff. Also, the administrative cost of administering the contract with agency XYZ is a factor.
  (2) Contract with public agency ABC which would operate from a central location. Cost: $290,000. Rejection is based on the same rationale as in the preceding alternative.
  (3) Use the agency's county-based staff to complete all adoptions. This expenditure would permit the adoption of 500 children at a total cost of $225,000. Although this alternative is clearly more economical than the recommended decision package, it incorporates the idea of reducing the depth and detail of the home study required to complete each adoption. A commensurate reduction in the staff resources necessary to perform home studies is responsible for a cost projection that is $25,000 less than the recommended decision package. The administrator has not recommended this alternative because of concern that the quality of adoption services would be reduced to a professionally unacceptable level.

In this example the recommended way of performing the adoption function would be chosen because the alternatives are either more expensive or offer no compensating advantages.

2. Different levels of effort for operation.
  a. Adoptions division (1 of 3), cost = $150,000. Minimum package: Complete adoptions on 300 children, and leave an approximate 1-year backlog of cases.
  b. Adoptions division (2 of 3), cost = $50,000 (levels 1 + 2 = $200,000). Complete adoptions on an additional 100 children, and reduce the case backlog to 6 months.
  c. Adoptions division (3 of 3), cost = $50,000 (levels 1 + 2 + 3 = $250,000). Complete adoptions on an additional 100 children, all of whom are so-called hard-to-place (older, handicapped, ethnic minority) children.

The chief administrator has thus prepared three decision packages (levels 1 of 3, 2 of 3, and 3 of 3). These three packages are then submitted to higher-level agency administrators who must incorporate them into the overall ranking scheme for the agency.

The ranking process establishes priorities among the incremental levels of each decision unit (i.e., decision package). The rankings therefore

TABLE 14–1. *Agency's ranking of decision packages.*

Rank	Decision Package	Incremental Cost	Cumulative Cost
1	Child day care (1 of 2)	$1,000,000	$1,000,000
2	Protective services (1 of 2)	2,000,000	3,000,000
3	Adoptions (1 of 3)	150,000	3,150,000
4	Child day care (2 of 2)	500,000	3,650,000
5	Adoptions (2 of 3)	50,000	3,700,000

display a marginal analysis (Pyhrr, 1973, pp. 130–135). An example of how the agency would rank its decision packages is shown in Table 14–1. This type of ranking would be completed for the entire agency. Once the agency's budget is approved, the total amount of funds would be matched with the corresponding cumulative cost, thereby identifying the decision packages that can be operationalized. For instance, if the agency were appropriated $3,200,000, only packages 1 through 3 could be afforded.

The above example can be used to highlight a significant shortcoming of the applicability of ZBB to the social services. Whereas an adoption service is a relatively easy service to understand and conceptualize in terms of goals and objectives (it is also politically "acceptable" and serves a deserving clientele), other social services are not. In contrast, for example, what constitutes the effectiveness of a substance abuse counseling service? Can the goals and objectives of such a service be stated in ways that lend themselves to statements about accomplishments or effectiveness? Can the social work administrator successfully argue that factors other than cost must be considered?

EXPERIENCES WITH ZBB

In looking at governmental experiences with zero-based budgeting, one would logically place a primary focus on the Georgia experience. Georgia was the first state to fully implement the concept; since this innovation occurred under the direction of Governor Carter's administration, inferences may be drawn about what might be expected when the federal government adopts zero-based budgeting. Additionally, there is a reasonable probability that states will rush (as many did with PPBS) to implement zero-based budgeting at the state level.

Were there to be a general transfer and application of the ZBB concept, as employed in Georgia with its associated strengths and difficulties, there might be a number of similar observations. Among the more noteworthy

were those offered by Peter Pyhrr, ZBB innovator and consultant to
Carter's budget director, after Georgia's first year of zero-based experience (Pyhrr, 1977, p. 8):

1. Zero-based budgeting can be effective and should be continued.
2. The quality of decision packages was poor but may improve with
   experience.
3. There is little incentive in government to be cost-effective.
4. Cost information was poor due to (a) the large number of discrete
   activities encompassed in budget units and (b) the fact that many
   managers/administrators who prepared packages generally never
   saw budgets or actual costs.
5. Agencies with large numbers of packages (exceeding 250–300) had
   difficulties in producing a single agency ranking.

Pyhrr (1973) presents a much more detailed critique in his book
Zero-Based Budgeting: A Practical Management Tool for Evaluating Expenses.
In a recent article Pyhrr (1977) suggests some significant strengths, which
he argues are four overriding reasons that make the zero-based approach
worthwhile: (a) low-priority programs can be eliminated or reduced; (b)
program effectiveness can be dramatically improved; (c) high-impact programs can obtain increased funding by shifting resources within an
agency, whereas the increased funding might not have been made available had the agency merely requested an increase in total funding; and
(d) tax increases can be retarded.

Pyhrr observes that there may be bureaucratic resistance to an approach
that involves an evaluation of program effectiveness. He also speculates
that it would be politically naive and unrealistic to assume that any one
major agency will be significantly defunded for the benefit of another.
Nevertheless, Pyhrr believes that ZBB should be considered a management and budgetary improvement effort that may require several years
to reach full utilization and effectiveness. He encourages patience and
perseverance.

It is quite interesting to contrast Pyhrr's comments about the Georgia
zero-based experience after its first year with the more recent comments
of Minmier and Herman. These two authors recently researched Georgia's budgeting systems and surmised that few financial resources were
reallocated directly due to the use of ZBB. They concluded that any
substantial reallocation of financial resources within state government
during Mr. Carter's administration was due primarily to Georgia's Executive Reorganization Act of 1972—not to zero-based budgeting. Mr.
Carter has argued that the Executive Reorganization was the primary
force behind allocation of financial resources, but added that success

would have been impossible without zero-based budgeting (Minmier, 1975, p. 11). Minmier and Herman conclude that ZBB appears to have served the best interests of the state of Georgia. They see great advantages accruing from the involvement of personnel at "activity" levels within the increased time and effort required for budget preparation (Minmier, 1975, p. 11).

Other state level experiences with ZBB have been somewhat limited—Texas and New Jersey have installed ZBB-type systems only recently, and evaluative reports are rather sketchy. However, it is interesting to note that New Mexico, because of dissatisfaction with the traditional budgeting process, conducted a limited experiment with ZBB in 1971. The conclusion of the author describing the zero-based program in New Mexico was that pure zero-based budgeting was probably a normative concept that needed modifications given the institutional nature of the traditional incremental approach. It was also felt that true reform cannot be realistically accomplished without the full cooperation and support of the legislature—it must be willing to learn and embrace fully the approach embodied in ZBB (LaFaver, 1974, p. 109).

PPBS RENAISSANCE?

Regardless of the depth of the analysis, it appears that the application of ZBB has been too limited to draw any definitive conclusions about its efficacy. Certainly, there appears to be no specific reference to the possible effects of such a reform on the "softest" of the generally soft governmental services—social services. Therefore, this author suggests that there are certain political, practical, and technical similarities between the now disfavored PPBS and ZBB that permit comparisons between the two and inferences about ZBB's potential for success. Consequently, it is suggested that ZBB must overcome significant barriers in order to preempt the publication of its obituary in scholarly and professional journals at some point in the future.

The first barrier that ZBB must surmount lies in the political arena. It is not sufficient for a governor or agency executive, or any one individual or group, to support and espouse the virtues of the concept. These endorsements must be accompanied by well-planned, coordinated efforts that are designed to garner broad support for change. Although there was a measure of support for PPBS, such support was not upheld by coordinated planning efforts. Consequently, with a few notable exceptions, it was never incorporated into the central budget and decision-making processes of state government (Schick, 1972, p. 13).

An associated issue in dealing with the problem of obtaining more than just nominal support is related to encouraging elected officials to move away from their bargaining-incremental tendencies of decision making. The difficulties of this task cannot be understated; considerable ramifications for our political system are inherent in this task. It is therefore unclear whether or not such a goal can be realistically achieved. The fundamental issue related to this political difficulty lies with the concept of politics as the "art of compromise." Virtually all legislative decisions, especially those involving the appropriation of tax dollars, are the products of give and take (i.e., bargaining). Consequently, our country's current political institutions are built on historically based compromises. A transition to ZBB would require the rejection of a familiar, traditional *modus operandi* and the adoption of what is considered by public administrators to be a more rational decision-making process.

If the political problems can be dispatched, there remain both practical and technical difficulties. In the practical vein, ZBB, like its percursor PPBS, requires additional staff involvement and the completion of a considerable amount of paperwork. It appears that (a) personnel resistance could subvert any transition to ZBB and (b) additional paperwork might be unduly burdensome. Furthermore, ZBB, like PPBS, requires a statement of objectives—an alien activity for most public servants. Surely technical problems are associated with such a requirement; there are certainly dilemmas when decision packages may have several possible objectives. Which one is chosen? For example, what is the objective of a penal institution? Punishment? Societal protection? Crime deterrence? Correction? Who decides? If the function of a penal institution is to attain all four of these objectives, what criteria are used to allocate the cost among them (Mosher, 1969, p. 163)?

It appears that all suggested budgetary reforms have strongly advocated the collection and application of more and better data. The empirical logic supporting such a feature is an obvious and quite justifiable effort to rationalize the entire budgetary process. In principle, there are probably few who would argue with such proposals. Unfortunately, the technical demands for such data are in many cases beyond the system's (or individual's) ability to deliver. In the first place, it appears that many governmental agencies collect voluminous data in formats that render them useless for budgetary processes like ZBB. Data are often collected so that certain local, state, or federal reporting requirements can be met; these are rarely uniform (this poses certain unique intergovernmental problems associated with federalism). Second, it is difficult to quantify many of the activities of governmental agencies. Certainly, this is true for social services as it is generally true for governmental operations. Given the inability to state objectives in any meaningful and quantifiable manner, it is obvious that these objectives cannot be evaluated and ranked in a way that facilitates budgetary decision making. Consequently, the adoption of ZBB would, in a sense, depend on: (a) the development of and adherence to a set of objectives for use in decision making; (b) the ability to develop meaningful objective criteria to incorporate in decision packages; (c) the collection of appropriate data; and (d) the ability to train administrators to think in nontraditional ways so they will use the data to develop these packages.

IMPLICATIONS FOR SOCIAL SERVICES

Certainly, any accelerated move for broad implementation of ZBB in governmental agencies will have significant and far-reaching implications for those agencies and the political environment in which they must function. This will be especially true for social service agencies and the programs they administer. It will undoubtedly create conflicts which will be most severe for lower-echelon supervisors (many of whom identify with the social work profession) who will be forced to apply quantitative and cost data in the development of budgets. Such activities are often foreign to such persons who have had little training in budgetary processes and who are often philosophically opposed to using cost concepts in the social services.

Prior to any attempts at operationalizing ZBB, it will become necessary to develop greater conceptual clarity about what social services are intended to accomplish; the adoption of the new language of goals, objectives, and measurement of outcomes may appear too mechanical and resemble the nonhumanistic efficiency identified with the previous administration and its budget cuts. However, the social work profession should, and must, move in this direction if it does not want its managerial role usurped by "pure" management types. Management technology, systems concepts, and information science can be important means for improving services even if they are not viewed as ends in themselves. The core values of social work and its concern for people must still be the base from which to use these concepts (Rosenberg and Brody, 1974, p. 346). Zero-based budgeting may have the potential to help us serve our clients more efficiently, effectively, and comprehensively than heretofore.

CONCLUSION

The preceding discussion does not present an exhaustive analysis of ZBB and the possible implementation difficulties it may present and encounter if adopted on a large-scale basis. The discussion has attempted to suggest to the reader what may be some of the more salient issues. Specific effects upon the social services have been, in most cases, left for the reader's inference.

One must not be too harsh in rendering premature judgment on ZBB. The concept squarely addresses many of the shortcomings of the traditional budgeting approach. That alone should provide an impetus for its consideration. Certainly, it presents a unique challenge for those who advocate accountability, and it offers an even greater challenge to those committed to delivering more effective services to the impoverished and disadvantaged of our nation.

REFERENCES

Dougherty, L. A. *Planning-Programming-Budgeting in State Government—Some Lessons Learned* (R-784-RC). Rand Corporation, August 1971.

Federal Register, May 2, 1977, *42* (84), 22341–22353.

LaFaver, J. "Zero-Based Budgeting in New Mexico (by the Legislative Finance Committee)," *State Government,* Spring 1974.

Lee, R. D., Jr., and R. W. Johnson. *Public Budgeting Systems* (Baltimore: University Park Press, 1973).

Lindblom, C. E. "The Science of Muddling Through," *Public Administration Review,* Spring 1959.

Minmier, G. S. *An Evaluation of Zero-Based Budgeting Systems in Government Institutions* (Atlanta: Georgia State University School of Business Administration, Publishing Services Division, 1975).

Mosher, F. C. "Limitations and Problems of PPBS in the States," *Public Administration Review,* March–April 1969.

Pyhrr, P. A. *Zero-Based Budgeting: A Practical Management Tool for Evaluating Expenses* (New York: Wiley, 1973).

Pyhrr, P. A. "The Zero-Base Approach to Government Budgeting." *Public Administration Review,* January–February 1977.

Rosenberg, M. L., and R. Brody. "The Threat or Challenge of Accountability," *Social Work,* May 1974.

Schick, A. "PPBS—A View from the States," *State Government,* Winter 1972.

Wildavsky, A. *The Politics of the Budgetary Process,* 2nd ed. (Canada: Little, Brown, 1974).

CHAPTER 15

Evaluation of Organizational Activities

Rekha Agarwala-Rogers
Janet K. Alexander

Editor's Note   *Every manager needs a way of perceiving issues clearly and judging activities after making a decision. Common sense and experience are two important perspectives; evaluation is a very useful third. This chapter deals with the need for evaluation, its importance, the various methods used, and a proposed management approach to evaluation design. The chapter also discusses the organizational environments characteristic of a nonprofit organization which uniquely affect evaluation activities.*

Evaluation is a type of research activity conducted to determine the effects on direct participants of an organization's plans, existing or potential programs, projects, or activities. Every manager needs a specific channel of communication, a solid source of feedback, and an objective way of arriving at a decision.

Managers may use formative evaluation, summative evaluation, or both. Formative evaluation, usually generated at the operating level, focuses on tentative and in-process measures of an ongoing program or activity and is a diagnostic tool for immediate decisions. Summative evaluation focuses on the effects or end results of a program and is usually generated at upper management levels. Evaluation methods may be very simple or very complex. The information used may be hard data, soft data, or both; it may be qualitative, quantitative, or both. The authors discuss two cases—a functional literacy and family life program in Thailand and a community health education program in California—where evaluation was beneficial.

Managers involved in evaluative design should be aware of the advantages and disadvantages of using explicit and implicit criteria for assessing products, services, or processes. Managers should consider such issues as ease of use, acceptability of results by colleagues, cost, measures, and how to improve a program through feedback.

The fact that nonprofit organizations are often centralized, less competitive than for-profit organizations, externally accountable, and concerned with social values and ethics has serious implications for evaluation. The authors conclude that for evaluation to be useful, managers must be educated to what evaluation can and cannot do. Managers should also be involved in evaluation from the initial stages.

Evaluation is an elastic word that stretches to cover judgments of many kinds.
Carol Weiss

It may be possible to undertake evaluation . . . which does not assume that . . . a bit of patchwork [is] required here and there to help the sick and the naughty to adjust properly.
Irwin Deutscher

WHAT IS EVALUATION?

Evaluation is a versatile, widely used term that has many different meanings and that changes meaning in the context of its use. Assessment, performance measurement, judgment, and appraisal are some of the commonly used synonyms for evaluation.

Evaluation is a type of research activity conducted to determine the effects of an organization's plans, existing or potential programs, projects, or activities on direct participants. Thus evaluation is carried out by measuring the outcomes of programs, projects, or activities under operating conditions and within the organizational context. Hence an evaluation is crucial to decision makers in rendering judgments about programs, projects, or activities. An evaluation is successful only insofar as it is useful in maintaining and improving quality. *Utility* is the key to successful evaluation.

Evaluation in the context of organizations is best described by the Yiddish word *sachel,* a well-informed sagacious judgment.* A manager needs evaluation for day-to-day operations as well as for making decisions about the future. Thus managers need some way to perceive keenly and judge their activities whenever decisions are made. An understanding of evaluation as a source of information provides them with needed sagacity.

A term which is becoming very popular among managers today is *evaluation research.*† Evaluation research is conducted to determine the effects of a program or activity under operating conditions in order to provide a scientific basis for decisions by program officials (Agarwala-Rogers, 1977).

The case of a national health-related voluntary organization illustrates how evaluation can provide information to solve problems. A program group wanted to prepare an informational print packet for teenagers. Some members felt that teenagers could be reached on the issue only through their parents and teachers, or radio. Others felt that teenagers would not be influenced by information coming from the association and thought the program would be a waste of time. Meetings were heavy with disagreement and deeply entrenched positions. The manager resolved the situation by persuading the group to conduct a short evaluation with a sample of teenagers to find out which of the assumptions was true. The group agreed and the manager contracted with an outside consultant to design the evaluation tasks in several stages. Stage one had to be completed successfully before going to stage two. Staff carried out the evaluation under a consultant's direction.

Informational items were designed and pretested by interviews with several small groups of teenagers. The results were convincing: teens were interested in the subject matter, strongly preferred the materials designed with teenage motifs (rock-poster style), and intensely disliked any attempt to write materials in a "pseudo-teen-talk dialect." The subject matter had a far higher interest to teens than had been supposed, and print was rated highly as a channel for such information, with radio being quite low. This and other information combined to persuade the group of the wisdom of one particular course of action. Funds were approved for the project, and additional funds were earmarked for further evaluation as the "pilot" test moved into the demonstration stage. This example suggests the practical nature of evaluation and its utility in addressing immediate and real organizational problems.

---

*The term *sachel* was brought to our attention by a friend and fellow evaluator, Marcia Guttentag.

†Some evaluation scholars note that evaluation research is unique, totally different both in its design and purpose from classical research. Classical research does not provide information for the decisions that must be made in the course of a program of change.

Evaluation research is quite different from classical research in its design and purpose. Decision makers require data obtained through the rigorous methods of classical research when making decisions about the ultimate worth of a program of activity, particularly if a large investment of resources is involved. For example, a decision about whether to disseminate a pilot program that appears to be working well, with good results, to a far larger number of sites requires dependable knowledge about the true worth of the program. Managers must be able to demonstrate to decision makers, in a precise and definite way, that the changes which occurred were a function of the particular program, intervention, or treatment applied and cannot be reasonably accounted for by other explanations. They must be able to answer the questions: "Did the program make a difference?" "If so, exactly how much and for whom?" Decision makers at this level require answers which may be derived from data gathered by the classical methods of the experiment or the quasi-experiment and subjected to statistical procedures. The data must be gathered and analyzed in ways that allow alternative explanations for the observed changes.

The rigorous methods appropriate to classical research and definitive evaluation of programs are not of central interest to managers of nonprofit organizations. They have little occasion to use such methods, and in cases where they need such evaluation, they most likely will call in expert consultants or contract with an established research firm. Thus this chapter will define and discuss evaluation issues which are likely to be most useful to nonprofit managers and which can be integrated into their work on a routine basis. The chapter focuses on the type of evaluation research that can provide useful data on an intermittent basis, for making decisions during the course of a program or action and for assessing the progress to date of ongoing organizational activities.

WHY DO MANAGERS EVALUATE?

Managers need to understand and appreciate evaluation as a technique for judging "merit." Scientific rigor and methodological sophistication are not required to evaluate programs. We believe strongly that evaluation should be used as a specialized channel of communication, a solid source of feedback, and an objective way of arriving at decisions.

Evaluation, in a general sense, is hardly a new topic for the organizational manager. Within any organizational structure, there are informational flows directed toward a variety of decision areas. For example, in one evaluation process, the budget review, monthly or quarterly reports compare actual expenses with projected expenses. The initial allocation of funds to projects is predicated upon some kind of evaluative or review process whereby competing forces for funds are put in priority and balanced within the overall budget. Personnel management is another area that relies on evaluative data. At the simplest level, the manager evaluates the résumés and recommendations of potential employees. Appraisals by supervisors and observation of the flow of work relative to the job description add more data. Performance in training programs and on-the-job actions are all pooled in some manner into an employee evaluation and review process that leads to raises and job promotions.

The importance of evaluation as a decision-making tool rests on a manager's appreciation of its value in judging merit. The ability to carry it out will depend on the manager's success in commanding resources to support it and his or her ability to stimulate staff enthusiasm for the activity. This, in turn, will depend on the manager's commitment to rational decision making—the desire to bring objective evidence to bear on organizational decisions whenever possible rather than to rely only on prior experience, subjective judgments, and ad hoc data. Common sense and experience are important to a manager; evaluation can add another string to his bow.

For evaluation to be useful, managers must want to reduce decisional uncertainty, improve their aim, and enhance their ability to make wise decisions. A curious mind is of value; the scientific rigor and methodological sophistication required for experimental research is superfluous for the majority of evaluation research activities useful to operational managers. Their main aim is to obtain information of immediate utility and to integrate it rapidly into their normal work routine with as little staff training as possible and with minimum requirements for "manager retreading."

The most important contribution the manager will make is a commitment to evaluation, a headset that demands systematic information and that builds in procedures to generate the required information flow on a continuing basis. The manager must provide the impetus for evaluation to begin and the atmosphere for it to flourish. The manager must also contribute to the growth of evaluation within an organization by carefully choosing the organizational problems and activities that can benefit from evaluative activities.

Some managers fear that evaluation is a gimmick that will replace their valued and hard-won experience. Nothing is further from the truth. Like any tool, evaluation may be put to good or bad purpose. But it can introduce a maximum of objective information into important decisions made by the organizational team. Evaluation is not a replacement for managerial functions; it is a tool to assist the manager. A case in point is the staff member who has strongly held but not necessarily well-informed opinions. This sticky situation can, in some measure, be resolved by the managerial attitude, "Well, let's look into that (if we have time and resources), and see if Bob's right." Similarly, a modest survey of "total participants" or a representative cross-section of users can put personal impressions of the response to services in proper perspective. For example, if Jane feels that "everyone wants to expand the information center at the clinic" but Fred thinks that "most people are interested in seeing the doctors and nurses more quickly," evaluation can help. A simple survey of participants, done systematically by clinic personnel, could shed light on who is right as well as help design programs and services that are responsive to real and perceived needs.

To facilitate evaluation, the manager must have an intimate knowledge of the objectives of the program and the nature of the target audience, an adequate evaluation strategy, command of resources to be deployed to this task area, and some skill in the design, analysis, and interpretation of evaluative data.

WHAT APPROACH TO USE

Managers need evaluation information that gives them a moving picture as well as a running commentary as they take actions and make decisions. The two types of evaluation that perform these functions are (1) formative evaluation and (2) summative evaluation (Scriven, 1967). These two types differ in the functions they perform, the methods they employ, and the way organizational structures carry them out. Each plays a distinct role in improving organizational and project effectiveness and in meeting both the manager's internal informational needs for decision making at the operational level and his need to provide external sources with a periodic accounting of organizational or project effectiveness.

Formative evaluation focuses on tentative and in-process measures of a program or activity. It is a diagnostic tool to be used for immediate decisions. It gives provisional information to program managers and, as such, builds an empirical basis for rational decision making about program directions. Formative evaluation is mainly concerned with assessing needs and plans and monitoring ongoing activities to detect early misfits between objectives and planned innovative programs before large investments are made.

For example, the producers of *Sesame Street* gave formative evaluation a big boost in 1967–1968 (Children's Television Workshop, 1972). This daily television program now reaches 40 percent of all U.S. children aged two to five. The team of television producers and evaluators pretests each program by showing a three-minute segment to a small audience of children and measuring the degree of attention, interest, and comprehension.

After the preview the producers modify, refilm, or reword the three-minute segment. Consequently, the success of *Sesame Street* is, in part, a product of formative evaluation.

Summative evaluation studies the demonstrated effects of a program, which become input in the decision-making process. The officials concerned with a program's continuation, discontinuation, modification, expansion, or curtailment use the information generated by summative evaluation to make such decisions. Traditionally, the majority of evaluations are of the summative type.

Distinctions Between Formative and Summative Evaluation

Often it is not possible to make clear-cut distinctions between summative and formative evaluations; in practice, they overlap. For example, certain kinds of summative evaluation may well be considered input for formative evaluation, leading to some set of plans which are in turn designed, implemented, and submitted to summative evaluation. The importance of distinguishing between the two functions is to avoid misunderstandings. Managers and their sponsors and evaluation personnel must have a common view of the purpose of evaluation before its design. The idea "Let's conduct an evaluation on this project or activity" may not be sufficient. The statement could mean different things to those participating in the project. For instance, if program operators want feedback information to improve performance, that must be specified. If managers want an overall statement on how a set of procedures works out after a definite period of time, that must be made clear. In the latter case, a very different set of data will be generated and the program operators will not be the central users of the information obtained.

Timing distinguishes formative from summative evaluation. Formative evaluation may be an ongoing but intermittent activity. Often it begins before a project is implemented—in the form of needs assessment or planning analysis. During the operational stages, it takes the form of monitoring or observational actions. Summative evaluation tends to be an event or set of events rather than a process and is conducted at specified time intervals before and/or after the program (intervals depend on the research design employed).

Several other useful distinctions can be made between formative and summative evaluation. For example, formative evaluation is usually carried on in-house by internal staff or those hired and supervised directly by them. Summative evaluation is usually undertaken by an external agency, often engaged by the director, the sponsor, or some other monitoring agency. Thus the main users of the results of formative evaluation are the program operators and managers at the actual site level, their colleagues, and immediate superiors. The information generated for summative evaluation is used primarily by those who are responsible for judging the program's performance as well as its future: upper-level decision makers, program sponsors, and policy makers. Consequently, the scope of the two types of evaluation varies in terms of the time involved of those who conduct the research and those who make use of it in future decision making.

Since formative evaluation tends to be generated at operating levels, its communication flow is horizontal and bottom-up. Information exchange goes on among peers and may cut across various functional units horizontally. As a result, the data obtained in formative evaluation are used in an immediate way in the local setting. In summative evaluation, by contrast, most of the information obtained is designed to assess ultimate outcomes of the project over time. The data are analyzed and organized into reports deemed appropriate for sponsors and other decision makers or the evaluator's professional colleagues. The information in such reports is utilized primarily by those at considerable functional and/or geographical distance from program managers and operators. Often, unfortunately, there is no direct communication link between the external summative evaluator and local managers of the activities being evaluated. Because of this, the data obtained in summative evaluation may not be used at operating levels.

Types of Evaluation and Stages of Organizational Activities

Managers tend to view the different stages of development of their organization's activities as a set of sequential decision points where information on progress to date feeds into the decisions affecting the next stage. Different stages of the development of organizational activities will have different decision points. As the nature of the decisions varies, so will the types of information required to make them. And as the type of information for decision making varies, so will the strategies for data collection and analysis. Table 15–1 relates the types of evaluation to the stages of project development and the evaluative functions at each stage. A review of the table will suggest the potential evaluation points to nonprofit managers.

Since managers need to decide at every step in the implementation of programs, a manager should attempt to evaluate whenever evaluation techniques can provide some of the information required to make decisions. Most individuals think evaluation is needed only after a decision is implemented. We suggest that managers need to evaluate at the planning and process stages of program development as well.

TABLE 15–1. *Evaluation and project development.*

Type of Evaluation	Stages of Project or Program (Activities and Type of Decision Making)
Formative Design evaluation	*Needs and plans assessments* Obtain data for input into preliminary program decisions; conduct needs assessment; devise preliminary plan of action for pilot or full-scale implementation; subject early plans to outside inspection; review available resources against plans and designs.
Process evaluation	*Operations and implementation assessments* Monitor operations in the field setting; obtain data during the ongoing program through systematic observation and monitoring by an evaluation team within the organization; use evaluation techniques appropriate to observing plan in action to detect problems, pitfalls, unintended results, lack of results, need for resource allocation, personnel problems, or other management concerns about program/project operations; assess rate and nature of progress toward long-term project goals on the part of client/participant groups through informal feedback and soft or semiquantitative techniques; obtain harder data to estimate the progress or movement to date toward goal achievement through observations at intermittent points.
Summative Impact evaluation	*Outcomes or results* Make systematic controlled observations to measure the state reached at the conclusion of a specific time segment for a pilot or demonstration project; obtain data that estimates the type and nature of changes, by population segment, that can be attributed to intervention, ruling out most alternative explanations for their occurrence (depends on study design); use evaluation team external to organization; provide a measure of cumulative program outcomes at program end. Analysis of the "before" and "after" data leads to reports to program/project sponsors and to academic peers on nature and outcomes of project and long-term recommendations; little focus on process or planning issues.

To carry this out, managers need to build evaluation into program operations and organize it so that evaluation is continuous. Evaluation then becomes a natural state of mind of the manager and a component of the total program operation.

WHAT METHODS TO USE

Methods of evaluation vary from simple quantitative approaches to very complex quantitative ones. The manager selects an evaluation method on the basis of whether the information it provides is usable in upcoming decisions. Time and money should not be wasted on obtaining more precise and sophisticated data than is required by the demands of the situation.

Types of Information

Since evaluation methods are determined in part by the characteristics of the information suitable for input into the decision-making process, we will note briefly the types of information that can be obtained through a variety of methods. Managers need (1) hard data and soft data and (2) qualitative and quantitative information.

Hard and soft data. Managers commonly need information which is labeled "hard data" and "soft data." The two terms actually refer to the qualitative as well as quantitative nature of information. Most *soft data* are used in qualitative decisions. For example, a program manager responsible for producing SITE* educational programs for Indian villages would worry about the content of programs, their informational value, entertainment value, and potential impact in bridging the knowledge gap among villagers in India. Hard data are used in quantitative decisions. They are precise and often based on the criterion of cost-effectiveness. For example, scientists at the Indian Space Research Organization needed to determine the cost of producing TV sets to be installed on experimental sites in order for financial officers to allocate resources adequately (Mody, 1976).

Media producers at Stanford University found that radio was most cost-effective for disseminating health innovations among Spanish-speaking people in California. This led to a reduction in the risk of heart disease as measured by the number of dollars spent in producing messages. Further, figures are now available on how much money is required to produce radio messages for a given size of audience.

The main distinction between soft and hard data is that soft data are

---

*SITE (Satellite Instructional Television Experiment) was a large-scale social experiment in India in 1975–1977 that used TV as an educational medium for national integration, literacy, and general development.

less precise, less extensive, less expensive, and easier to gather. They are good for providing the "flavor" and "color" of an activity. Hard data require money, personnel, professional skills, and decisions which are clearly *definitive* in nature.

Qualitative and quantitative information. Managers commonly need qualitative and quantitative information. *Qualitative* information is descriptive. Managers are likely to use it to determine the strengths and weaknesses of a decision and the consequences. It is anecdotal in nature; observation, experience, and keen perception are the tools. For example, one successful implementation of qualitative information stemmed from the keen observation, familiarity, experience, and common sense of an old Asia hand. He suggested to certain officials that field workers in Indonesian villages needed flashlights (to see snakes with and to drive away bad spirits), horses (to reach clients in the mountain areas), bicycles (to ride the plains), and shoes that don't stick in the mud (certain parts of Indonesia have lots of rain).

Quantitative information is numerical in nature. It provides an accounting—often of required efforts, spent resources, and desired results—in dollar terms. Financial reports and budgets are the ultimate form of quantitative information. A manager needs numbers to make decisions. For example, how many TV messages are required to introduce a new product? What should be the ratio of field workers to clients during a given time period so that information about a nutrition program will be properly understood?

Data-Gathering Techniques

How does a manager obtain data that will provide the information required on a subject? A variety of data-gathering techniques are commonly used. In the choice of an appropriate method, the "fit" between the characteristics of the information usable for decision making, the nature of the area under investigation, and the resources available to obtain data must all be considered (Rogers and Agarwala-Rogers, 1976a). Some commonly used techniques of information evaluation are:

Participant observation
Diary keeping
Panel of experts
Pilot programs
Pretesting
Individual questionnaires
Group interviews
Postevent recall

The following research design methods are often used for conducting summative evaluations that are useful to managers:

True field experiments
Quasi-experiments
Case studies
Panel of experts
Cost-effectiveness analysis
Records and documents analysis
Surveys
Zero-based budgeting
Goal attainment

Utility as the Key

The key to selecting appropriate methods of evaluation research is utility to the primary users. This suggests that classical research methods such as the experiment or quasi-experiment are not likely to be practical. However, the lessons learned from more rigorous research methods can provide a guide for selecting the most systematic method of data gathering within the time constraints facing managers.

Methods most useful to a manager have the following characteristics:

Systematic. The method is followed systematically so it is budgetable in time and dollars.
Purposeful. The method is narrow in scope and directed at the precise information needs of the manager, with no extraneous information.
Immediate. The information can be obtained in the time it is needed.
Affordable. The information can be obtained at a cost that is reasonable.
Pragmatic. The information obtained is concrete and useful in the decision process and does not address large, abstract issues tangential to decision-making needs. If information does not bear directly on the decision, but instead requires interpretation, it may not be useful to collect it.

EVALUATION IN ACTION

One of the themes of this chapter is that the manager's need to obtain and evaluate information for decision-making purposes can often be met through careful evaluation. This requires some dedication on the part of managers to building in mechanisms to obtain evaluative data on a regular basis. When managers take this special viewpoint and allocate resources in this direction, evaluative activities can take place routinely to assist decision makers in the design, planning, implementation, and operational stages of organizational endeavors.

In this section we present two case studies as examples of evaluation research in action. These examples point out the variety of evaluative activities undertaken by managers as they face decisions requiring several different types of information.

The first case study, a development project in Thailand, demonstrates how evaluation can be used in a national-level program. It illustrates some of the evaluation concepts discussed in the context of developing a long-range program of action. The second project, a health education research project in California, is an example of how managers can use evaluation research to solve a variety of problems and to assist in the ongoing management of a project. The evaluation conducted by the managers of the educational project in Thailand was much wider in scope than that conducted by the community health education research project in California. Each of the illustrations, however, points out how built-in evaluative activities can enhance a program's effectiveness.

Khit-Pen* and Evaluation in Rural Thailand

Evaluation has been used to assess the results of functional literacy and family life planning programs in Thailand. The objectives of the UNESCO-sponsored program were to help people cope with their environment by learning to read and write and to give them some basic, practical information to use in their daily lives. The evaluation of the functional literacy program followed these steps:

1. *Evaluation of the pilot phase* indicated that the project has been able to maintain the interest of its participants. The dropout rate over the six-month period was only 12.6 percent, compared with an average of 25 percent among Thailand's regular literacy classes.

2. *Preintervention and postintervention tests* were employed. The three areas of learning evaluated were reading, mathematics, and attitude change toward the concepts taught in the curriculum.

3. *The expansion phase* was evaluated to measure the attainment of abilities among participants. For these purposes an outside evaluator was hired.

4. *An evaluation strategy* was adopted as a framework for action. Evaluation was to comprise the context (Thai), the process, and the outcomes of the project.

5. *A conference* of 20 evaluators from around the world was held to critically review the evaluation strategy, preliminarily prepared by the Thai staff and external consultants.

---

*Khit-pen is an ability to think, to know that problems can be solved. The term is central to Thai culture and is Buddhist in origin.

6. *Postconference decisions* to design evaluation measures centered around three main issues:

- That learners' gains be measured in terms of literacy and numeric competence, knowledge of curriculum subjects, and attitude change. Methods to be used included literacy, numeric, and knowledge tests; attitude scores; simulated problem solving; and case studies, interviews, and observation.
- That the accuracy and relevance of the curriculum materials be measured. The focus would be on the text, classroom discussions, and methods for group participation. Evaluation methods included village surveys, questionnaires, and interviews with participants, teachers, and supervisors.
- That the teachers' performance be evaluated.

With the completion of the above evaluation, the project is being considered as a regular government-supported undertaking. The adult education division of the Thai Ministry of Education is planning to decentralize the teacher training, program materials, evaluation, and follow-up activities by creating adult education centers throughout Thailand. Two new pilot programs—radio correspondence schools and continuing education centers—are being planned to help the functional literacy program.

A new effort to bring classrooms out of the traditional setting into the workfields, temple grounds, and homes of villagers is under way. Thai walking teachers—influenced by the People's Republic of China's tradition of barefoot doctors—work in surroundings similar to their own and their clients' backgrounds. They are trained in school centers which emphasize informal educational techniques.

Community Health Education in California

The design and implementation plan for the California university-based research project called for the use of a variety of educational methods to address various project needs over time.

The three-community project. In the three-community project of the Stanford Heart Disease Prevention Program (SHDPP), the objectives were to influence the adult populations of two California towns to change their living habits so as to reduce the risk of premature heart attack and stroke. The intervention program (a mass-media campaign plus interpersonal group counseling in one town), held among adults ages 35 to 39, was designed to promote an increased awareness of the epidemic of coronary heart disease in the United States, an understanding of its probable causes, a knowledge of how living habits contribute to or reduce cardiovascular risk, and an awareness of the behavioral changes needed to make recommended adjustments in lifestyle.

To measure change in all these variables, a quasi-experimental before-and-after survey was conducted to provide evidence that changes in knowledge, attitudes, behaviors, and physiological indicators related to heart disease were, in fact, occurring as a result of the intervention program. Outcomes were assessed through surveys of a random sample of about 500 people in each town. Over a three-year period, a multimedia campaign was directed to two towns (a third town served as a control). In one of the two mass-media towns, the campaign was supplemented for a short while by group instruction offered to those with a particularly high risk of heart disease.

Summative evaluation. The three-community study required an assessment of the long-term impact of the intervention program on the target audience in the communities. This was accomplished through surveys of a probability sample of the target population and surveys of a comparable but untreated sample in a third town. The first or baseline survey occurred before the mass-media campaign was introduced. Follow-up surveys to track progress toward overall goals (a significant level of risk reduction for the entire population) occurred at the end of the first and second campaign years. From the scientists' and sponsors' point of view, the only data of interest were the "summative" data on program impact and the final outcomes of the study. This required another follow-up study after the third year. At this time, the function of the campaign was to reinforce prior change. (The campaign had shifted to a low level, providing occasional reminders of the messages sent out over the past two years.) After this third "holding" year, the fourth and final survey was undertaken to give project managers an idea of the stability of the changes induced through the mass media alone and through the mass media supplemented by group instruction.

Thus the follow-up survey at the end of the first campaign year served as an instrument of summative evaluation, a gauge of progress toward long-term outcomes, and a barometer of the "health" of the overall project. From the intervention managers' point of view, the second-year data had a formative function, since they were also used to trace the progress of various population segments from their starting place toward objectives. But the analysis of progress by the end of the first year was used to restructure the intervention strategy, refocus plans, and in general provide a new basis for judging the value of contemplated campaign items. The blur between summative and formative evaluation occurs only because two different sets of actors within the same organizational framework usually have different information needs and responsibilities, and because different decision points are required to carry out their jobs.

Formative evaluation. A distinctive feature of the media campaign was the ongoing use of many sources of data to guide the decision-making process during the design or planning stages and implementation (production, distribution, monitoring). Several types of information sources were used, and the data were pooled to build the "first wave" campaign plan. These sources were:

1. A pretest of the survey questionnaire on a similar population in Modeste. This provided baseline information such as what the target populations already knew about heart disease, what they believed either correctly or incorrectly, and what they were currently doing to reduce risk.
2. A precampaign survey in one of the three communities.
3. Interviews and discussions with key academic, professional, and political leaders with expertise on the subject matter, towns, and audience.
4. Marketing data on media usage patterns.
5. Personal interviews with key media gatekeepers.
6. Budget information, resource allocation, and time constraints.

Once the campaign was under way, it became necessary to supplement the formal data sources available (survey data) with occasional evaluations. The "minisurveys" were informal information-gathering actions to find the answers to questions that needed to be dealt with right away or not at all. The managers of the campaign supplemented their professional judgment, common sense, and experience with objective information decisions about production and distribution, monitoring the output system, monitoring acceptance of the intervention, projecting the utility of future productions, and monitoring the campaign "system."

MANAGEMENT APPROACH TO EVALUATION DESIGN

Managers should be aware of the pros and cons of using implicit and explicit criteria for assessing services, products, or processes. They should be concerned with such issues as ease of use, acceptability of the method to peers, cost and resources allocation required for developing and maintaining evaluative methods, coordination of the activities with other evaluation attempts, and (eventually) improvement of organizational activities through feedback.

It is possible to develop a measure of performance for nonprofit as well as for-profit organizations. For example, community mental-health center officials in Orange County, New York, decided to assess the use of services by the community. They used 130 needs indicators on the 1970 census, as developed by the National Institute of Mental Health. The use of needs indicators for social area analysis was simple and economical. Managers used the evaluation in decisions about the need for new services and planning activities.

What Criteria Should Be Used?

Managers of nonprofit organizations face a unique situation in critically looking at the services or products provided by their organizations. What are the bases for quality-related judgments? Are there implicit and/or explicit criteria?

The explicitness or implicitness of criteria for quality assessment are little known. Whatever is used is primarily in the manager's head. The problem becomes crucial when the quality judgments eventually become the criteria for funding or for the continuation of funding sources.

For example, in mental health therapy the manager is faced with variations not in the nature of diagnosis but in the therapies prescribed, which vary by more than the number of therapists assigning treatment. How is the overall effectiveness of the quality of care provided to clients to be measured? The Peninsula Hospital in Burlingame, California, uses a clinical case conference method for assessing the quality of care, based on the clinical and management problems related to the case and the type of decisions taken by the therapist. The case-by-case method depends on the implicit judgment of a group of clinical peers rather than on a comparison of client therapy to explicit, published criteria. The merits of such a method are that the clinical peers do take into account the complete view of the situation and have to be very thorough. Also, such an exercise forces the personnel to share knowledge and know-how with colleagues. Details of the costs as well as the choice of therapy are brought much more in the open. The system is not foolproof. However, it is an attempt to measure the quality of a nonprofit organization and the service or care provided by its staff.

Whose Criteria?

Decision makers and managers responsible for the delivery of services must agree on the criteria of measurement. The fact that the two groups share a common view is *sine qua non* for any evaluative efforts—both for evaluation to take place and for changes to be initiated as a result of feedback. For example, universities face an acute dilemma—how to measure effectiveness. Administrators and faculty may have very different perceptions about what constitutes effectiveness. For example, one may ask the administrators as well as the teaching faculty of a university the following question:

> Faculty members engage in various professional activities which are rewarding to them. However, organizations tend to motivate the kind of behavior they reward. How important are the following in decisions on the awarding of tenure, promotion, or salary increases in your institution?

> 1. Being a dedicated teacher.
> 2. Publishing professional work.
> 3. Being an innovative teacher.
> 4. Participating in departmental and universitywide government.
> 5. Being an empathetic adviser.
> 6. Bringing research resources into the institution.

The responses as to what constitute rewards and in turn measures of effectiveness would be very interesting. Administrators and teaching faculty would not have the same criteria for measuring effectiveness (Agarwala-Rogers, Rogers, and Wills, 1977; Lewis, 1975). To arrive at a mutually satisfactory measurement system is difficult in organizations, particularly academic institutions.

The issue that managers are constantly wrestling with is how to improve measurement of the quality of services, products, or processes. Measurement is particularly difficult when the output of an organization is a service. For example, it is easy to measure the quality of a chair. If the chair is comfortable, it has high quality. However, to measure the quality of a classroom practice as it affects student achievement is quite difficult and involves such sensitive issues as the following: Is achievement related to socioeconomic status? If so, to what extent? Do classroom innovations stimulate achievement over time?

Thus, for the managers of educational organizations, measurement of quality is particularly difficult and complex. Furthermore, it is often debatable as to what should be evaluated—teaching, publications, or student satisfaction. As one observer notes, the measurement of teaching effectiveness "is such a tangled skein that the more it is held up to examination, the more it seems that those who would have us ignore what goes on between the faculty and students possess a sort of primeval wisdom" (Lewis, 1975, p. 18).

How to Measure Quality

How should managers use quality measures as indicators of organizational effectiveness? How does a manager know that a product, process, or service is high in quality? For example, the quality of clinical services could be measured in terms of organizational facilities, process of care assessment, and results of services provided. Let us examine these three quality measures in the clinical services organizational setting.

Organizational facilities essentially refer to the type of personnel an organization has, their training and experiences, the availability of facilities and sufficient staff support, and sound fiscal and administrative procedures.

Process of care refers to the types of services, treatment, and care for a given type of client. Factors such as age, sex, and medical history are the basis for planning treatment. This measure, however, lies essentially in the hands of physicians. So here quality is measured in terms of classification of clients and the maximization of care to meet their needs.

Results of services provided are aggregate indicators of the level of improvement among certain groups of clients. Managers can use these measures as indicators of group rather than individual improvement.

How to Ask the Right Questions

It is difficult to set guidelines for asking the right evaluation questions and for developing and implementing an evaluation system. For example, in 1973 the Peace Corps, a voluntary organization, recognized that improvement of program evaluation was essential. Peace Corps officials were under pressure from Congress and the Office of Budget and Management to reestablish goals and assess performance against them. The stormy history of evaluation procedures and the negative connotations associated with evaluation made it difficult to set guidelines for asking the right questions. In an effort to reinstate evaluation as an integral part of the Peace Corps, managers established the following guidelines:

1. Internal and external needs for evaluation information are not mutually exclusive.
2. Evaluation information must be useful to the field staff.
3. Evaluation information must be integrated with other programming activities.
4. The evaluation system must be simple, and the basic tools must satisfy information needs at various levels.
5. Host country involvement in evaluation activities must be an integral part of the programming.

Asking the right questions to obtain needed information is crucial for making good decisions. The purpose of the evaluation influences the guidelines for asking questions. For example, evaluation in a nonformal education program in Ethiopia is being used as a diagnostic tool. The internal evaluation or "feedback" procedures are used to help answer questions on the soundness of the program. Managers ask such questions as: Is the curriculum relevant to audience needs? Are the materials used effective? Do visuals convey meaning? Are personnel available to help users?

ORGANIZATIONAL ENVIRONMENTS

Managers work in organizations, and organizations operate within environments. Nonprofit organizations are distinct in the way they relate to their environments. In this section we look at the implications of centralization and competitive markets for evaluation. The case of the U.S. Forest Service is cited to illustrate one organization's answer to external pressures. Later discussions focus on the roles played by various actors and the ethical issues that a manager faces as an evaluator.

Are Nonprofit Organizations More Centralized?

Centralization is one of the dominant characteristics of nonprofit organizations. It is not accidental that most for-profit organizations are decentralized. Why? In a for-profit organization performance can be measured by profits. Also the organization can attract professionals to responsible positions and can offer attractive salaries and professional freedom. In nonprofit organizations, which lack performance criteria for various parts of the organization, centralized design has generally dominated. The implications of centralization for evaluation are quite serious. For example, in hospitals authority and decision making are highly centralized. Participation by different levels in decision making is relatively limited. Consequently, it is difficult for managers to identify performance gaps—that is, discrepancies between the organization's expectations and actual performance (Rogers and Agarwala-Rogers, 1976a, p. 157). Less emphasis on centralized authority and greater participation in decision making increase the usefulness of evaluative information in closing performance gaps. However, because of centralization, managers can resolve conflicts easier and eliminate ambiguity about a decision.

Are Nonprofit Organizations Less Competitive?

Most nonprofit organizations operate under competitive market conditions. There is a lack of pressure to change. Most government organizations fall into this category. However, a newer form of organization (mostly nonprofit) has emerged in recent years: research or consulting companies associated with universities. These companies are relatively small and are staffed by competent researchers with a great deal of expertise. Their market represents a series of grants or contracts that they bid for competitively. The organization's ability to compete depends on attracting and keeping competent researchers and on maintaining the market image of being highly specialized. Interestingly, the market for the services of these organizations is highly stable. Thus market is not very relevant as an evaluation mechanism, since the quality of service, product, or process does not change drastically. The reputation for being avant garde remains shielded from the fluctuations of the market. Often the personal contacts and prestige of researchers are the most important assets of the organization. Managers measure effectiveness mainly in the form of internal feedback.

Are Nonprofit Organizations Externally Accountable?

All organizations resist change. However, managers sometimes encounter an external impetus to evaluate effectiveness in order to generate change. Nonprofit organizations are *externally accountable*—that is, they depend on outside sources for funds, personnel, and clients (Rogers and Agarwala-Rogers, 1976a, p. 160). For example, managers in the U.S. Forest Service need to work with the Bureau of Land Management in making decisions about building a road in national forest areas that are within the jurisdiction of the bureau. Thus the Forest Service (and other organizations) depends on interagency communication to coordinate its work.

External pressures can demand that managers provide evidence of organizational effectiveness in meeting certain goals. For example, there has been growing recognition in recent years of the problem of inadequate research utilization in the U.S. Forest Services. In 1972 (the latest year for which we obtained data), $54.3 million was spent on forestry research. Unfortunately, only a small share of this research has been rendered useful by practitioners in the forestry field (Agarwala-Rogers and Rogers, 1978).

The seriousness of the problem of research underutilization was accentuated in 1972 by a U.S. General Accounting Office report to Congress entitled *The Forest Service Needs to Ensure That the Best Possible Use Is Made of Its Research Program Findings.* After interviewing officials in the three main units of the U.S. Forest Service (research; the national forest system, which administers national forests; and the state and private forestry systems) and reviewing various documents and reports, the GAO report found: "Existing Forest Service procedures do not provide adequate means for (1) ensuring that the best possible use is made of research program results, and (2) furnishing research officials with feedback of information which could be useful in planning and directing future work under the program."

In responding to the GAO report, the acting chief of the U.S. Forest Service admitted there were problems: "The Forest Service recognizes that present procedures are not fully successful or satisfactory. We need to do better and we are making plans to do so."

Since the 1972 report, the Forest Service has made an effort to better utilize forestry research results, especially by the national forest system (the main audience for research results). Activities include creation of a research implementation working group in the Washington, D.C. offices of the U.S. Forest Service; creation of the position of Assistant Director for Planning and Application at each experiment station; establishment of a user-oriented information retrieval system; and commissioning research, development, and application (RD&A) programs, each under the leadership of a program manager.

Who Will Be Involved?

Managers must get all interested parties involved in evaluation. Of course, there will always be exceptions. However, information gathered must be used directly and must immediately benefit the people who helped gather it. The role played by various actors or interested parties is as crucial as the art of asking the right questions. For example, one federal agency uses different actors to evaluate products during the planning, implementation, and assessment stages. The seven actors are:

Policymakers
Agency's own staff
Advisory panel
Scholars and scientists
Change agents and linkers
Dissemination and training center
User of an innovation

The differing perceptions of evaluation among personnel at different echelons make evaluation as well as utilization of information difficult. Managers must make sure that policymakers share similar priorities, interpretations, and most of all uses of information gathered by evaluation.

Is Evaluation Ethical?

What can or should be evaluated? Managers, like social scientists, often find the reasons or "philosophy" for evaluating called into question. The early five-year program of the Soviet Union, the kibbutz movement in Israel, the modernization of a Peruvian village, the alteration of the agricultural customs of Punjabi farmers, and similar programs all represent attempts to bring about massive social changes by pragmatic means. Transfer of technology has been the main avenue for such change.

Can these programs be evaluated? Should they be evaluated? Is evaluation meaningful in this context? None of the above programs is an experimental or trial effort; hence evaluation does not apply. Furthermore, their failure to achieve intended goals is not due to the nature of the programs themselves. Rather, it has been attributed to administrative incompetency, organizational resistance to change, and sabotage by opposing parties. Quantification of such issues is often beyond numbers, but within the realm of ethics.

For example, the nature of activities of an organization like the Peace Corps raises some interesting ethical issues. The Peace Corps as a voluntary movement involves both the *intangible* issue of crosscultural exchange and the *measurable* issue of providing manpower assistance. The ethical dilemma faced by the volunteers is how to properly represent all dimensions.

HOW CAN EVALUATION BE UTILIZED?

Can a manager use evaluation to achieve desired goals? Yes. We have discussed the why, how, and when of evaluation for managers in earlier sections. How can managers get decision makers and policymakers to use the results of evaluation? The following are some guidelines for utilization.*

1. *Decision makers must be educated about what evaluation can and cannot do.* Frustrations often mount up when initial expectations about evaluation are unreasonable. Decision makers fear that their personal experience will be contradicted by the research and that the conclusions reached will not be relevant to problems.

2. *Decisions makers must be involved from the initial stages of evaluation.* Wooing decision makers, gaining their "blessings," and promoting their cooperation increases the probability that evaluation will be credible and useful.

3. *Decision makers are interested in useful information that will augment their judgments. Methodologies are less important.* It makes no difference whether the classical experiment, the quasi-experiment, or a combination of the two is used. Evaluation instruments are no substitute for good judgment.

4. *Decision makers must be provided with information on call.* Whether the program activity works or doesn't work, the manager must be able to provide information relevant for decisions. Evaluation data on programs must be collected, collated, and continually updated through the in-house information system.

5. *Decision makers need information for heuristic as well as comparative purposes.* Managers must know whether the information required indicates the success or failure of a program, or whether it enumerates conditions under which the program succeeded or failed. The difference between the two purposes is critical. Heuristic information triggers off the process of evaluation; comparative information may bring it to an end.

6. *Decision makers need information about the impact of the program on the organization, as well as on members.* The information is an indicator of

---

Utilization is the communication to practitioners of information produced to answer needs. (Agarwala-Rogers, 1977).

changes that have occurred organizationally. Most evaluation studies of correctional institutions, for example, indicate that the programs implemented over the past 20 years have changed but have failed to change offenders.

7. *Decision makers' needs for certain types of information must be courted and satisfied.* To be effective in creating change is to have a listening ear and a curious mind. The types of information needed for decisions regarding inequities, imbalances, or ineffectiveness should be researched by courting decision makers.

8. *Decision makers are concerned with measuring system improvement, changes in organizations, and the quality of services, products, and processes.*

9. *Decision makers are fallible.* Periodically decision makers may adopt a casual attitude about evaluation, but that does not mean they do not need evaluative information.

SUMMARY

This section provides some principles about evaluation that managers must be aware of in their efforts.

1. Managers need to evaluate as they face trade-offs and balances.
2. Evaluation is a specialized channel of communication for feedback.
3. Evaluation provides managers with information on which to base their judgments.
4. Utility is the keystone to successful evaluation.
5. Evaluation is a versatile term and changes meaning in the context of its use.
6. Evaluation is needed at the planning and implementation stages, as well as at the impact stage of decision making.
7. Evaluation provides both qualitative and quantitative information.
8. Information generated by evaluation varies in precision, cost, and ease of use.
9. Both formative and summative evaluations are relevant to managers.
10. Managers must be aware of the roles played by various actors in evaluation activities.
11. Centralization of an organization affects the nature of evaluation.
12. Market conditions and competition influence the nature of evaluation.
13. Managers must set guidelines for asking the right evaluation questions.
14. The perceptions of superiors as to what constitutes evaluation must be clearly understood by managers.
15. Managers must make sure that the goals and purposes of evaluation are understood by all levels in the organization.

16. The desired quality and quantity of evaluation depends on the nature of the organization.

17. Managers may find information for evaluation in management information systems.

18. Managers must clearly understand and use implicit and explicit criteria in evaluation.

19. Whether a method is "good" or "bad" depends on whether it provides adequate information for decisions.

20. Managers must get decision makers to understand the nature of evaluation information if changes are to be made within the organization.

21. Managers must get decision makers involved in evaluation early by wooing their cooperation and attending to the problems considered important by policymakers.

22. Decision makers will be genuinely interested in using evaluation information if it is in a form they can understand.

23. Managers must consider the ethical issues involved in evaluation.

REFERENCES

Agarwala-Rogers, Rekha. "Why Is Evaluation Research Not Utilized?" in Marcia Guttentag and Shalom Saar, eds., *Evaluation Studies Review Annual*, Vol. II (Beverly Hills, Cal.: SAGE Publications, 1977).

Agarwala-Rogers, Rekha. *Information Linkers*, in press (1979).

Agarwala-Rogers, Rekha, and Everett M. Rogers. *Linkers for Technology Transfer*, U.S. Forest Service, SEAM Program (Stanford, Cal.: Institute for Communication Research, 1978).

Agarwala-Rogers, Rekha, Everett M. Rogers, and Russel M. Wills. *Diffusion of IMPACT Innovations 1973–1976: Interpersonal Communication Networks Among University Professors* (Stanford, Cal.: Applied Communication Research, 1977).

Children's Television Workshop. "Production: The Making of *Sesame Street* and *The Electric Company*," in *A Special Report from the Children's Television Workshop* (New York: Office of Public Affairs, Children's Television Workshop, 1972).

Cyert, Richard M. *The Management of Nonprofit Organizations* (Concord, Mass.: Lexington Books, 1975).

Deutscher, Irwin. "Social Theory and Program Evaluation: A Methodological Note," paper presented at the American Sociological Association, San Francisco, 1975.

Lewis, Lionel S. *Scaling the Ivory Tower: Merit and Its Limits in Academic Careers* (Baltimore: Johns Hopkins University Press, 1975).

Mody, Bella. "Toward Formative Research in Television for Development," *Educational Broadcasting International*, Vol. 9 (1976).

Rogers, Everett M., and Rekha Agarwala-Rogers, eds. *Evaluation Research on Family Planning Communication*, UNESCO, Population Communication Technical Report No. 4 (1976a).

Rogers, Everett M., and Rekha Agarwala-Rogers. *Communication in Organizations* (New York: Free Press, 1976b).

Scriven, Michael. "The Methodology of Evaluation," in Ralph W. Tyler, *Perspectives in Curriculum Evaluation*, AERA Monograph Series on Curriculum Evaluation 1 (Chicago: Rand McNally, 1967).

Weiss, Carol H. *Evaluation Research* (Englewood Cliffs, N.J.: Prentice-Hall, 1972).

Biographical Notes

About the Editor

Gerald Zaltman is the Albert Wesley Frey Distinguished Professor of Marketing and professor of health services administration at the University of Pittsburgh, where he is also a member of the Center for Latin American Studies and the Western Pennsylvania Gerontology Center. He was formerly on the faculty of the Graduate School of Management and Graduate School of Education at Northwestern University. He holds a Ph.D. in sociology from Johns Hopkins University and an MBA from the University of Chicago. Dr. Zaltman is recognized internationally as a leader in the management field and is a management consultant to numerous organizations in the United States, Europe, Latin America, and Asia. He is the recipient of numerous grants and awards and is a frequent contributor to scholarly journals. Dr. Zaltman is the author or editor of 26 books, including, most recently, *Psychology for Managers, Strategies for Planned Change, Dynamic Educational Change, Innovations and Organizations,* and *Consumer Behavior: Basic Findings and Management Implications.* His special interests are in the management of social change, the adoption of new ideas, services, and products, and the utilization of research.

About the Contributors

Rekha Agarwala-Rogers is currently a private consultant in Palo Alto, California, and directs two projects on research utilization sponsored by the U.S. Forest Service. She has been a consultant with SRI International, American Institute for Research, National Institute of Education, and ABT Associates, and is an active author.

Janet K. Alexander is currently the director of media of the Stanford Heart Disease Prevention Program, Institute of Communication Re-

560

search, Stanford University. Over the past several years she has served as a consultant to several private and government agencies on health communication and mass media.

Vincent P. Barabba is manager of the Corporate Office of Market Research, Xerox Corporation. He received his BS at the California State University at Northridge and his MBA at the University of California, Los Angeles. His previous work experience was as a director for the U.S. Bureau of the Census. He is currently a vice president of the American Marketing Association and a fellow of the American Statistical Association.

Jacob Birnberg is professor of business administration at the Graduate School of Business, University of Pittsburgh, specializing in management accounting. In addition to publishing numerous articles in various journals, he has worked on the development of management accounting techniques for nonprofit organizations related to the evaluation of mental health delivery systems and the role of the accountant in them.

Thomas V. Bonoma is associate professor of business administration and psychology, a research associate at the University Center for International Studies, and a fellow of the Arms Control and International Security Studies Center—all at the University of Pittsburgh. He received his Ph.D. in 1972 in social psychology from SUNY–Albany and is a specialist in social influence, social conflict, decision behavior, and bargaining. He serves as an editorial consultant or referee for a number of journals in psychology, sociology, and marketing, and has published more than 50 books, monographs, and articles in these areas as well as in international studies. His most recent book is *Executive Survival Manual* (with D. P. Slevin).

Robert A. Cooke is associate research scientist in the Survey Research Center of the Institute for Social Research, University of Michigan. He is also affiliated with the Organizational Psychology Program of the Department of Psychology at Michigan. His research and teaching interests center around the social psychology of organizations, change and innovation in social systems, and organizational development. He has conducted studies on decision making and change in public schools, hospitals, research institutions, colleges and universities, voluntary associations, and government agencies.

James A. Craft is professor of business administration at the Graduate School of Business, University of Pittsburgh. He received his Ph.D. from the University of California, Berkeley. His teaching and research interests are in human resources management, industrial relations, and organizational behavior.

Rohit Deshpande is assistant professor of marketing at the Graduate School of Business, University of Texas at Austin. He received his MBA

from Northwestern University and his Ph.D. from the University of Pittsburgh. His research interests include marketing management, public policy, and the marketing of social change programs.

Wesley J. Johnston is assistant professor of marketing at the Ohio State
University. He was a summer fellow at the Center for Creative Leadership
in 1977. His research interests include the behavioral and industrial aspects of marketing management and leadership, and performance appraisal in sales-force management. Professor Johnston's publications include recent articles in *American Behavioral Scientist, Decision Sciences,* and
Industrial Marketing Management, plus a Marketing Science Institute monograph on industrial buying behavior.

Ralph H. Kilmann is professor of business administration at the Grad-
uate School of Business, University of Pittsburgh. He received his BS and
MS in management science from Carnegie-Mellon University and his
Ph.D. in management from the University of California, Los Angeles.
Dr. Kilmann is president of Organizational Design Consultants, Inc., and
is the author of numerous books and articles.

William R. King is professor of business administration at the Graduate
School of Business, University of Pittsburgh. He received a Ph.D. and MS
from Case Institute of Technology and a BS from the Pennsylvania State
University. He is the author of 8 books and more than 70 journal articles
in the fields of management science, strategic planning, and information
systems. He serves as a consultant in these areas to a variety of business
firms and public agencies.

Ian I. Mitroff is professor of business administration, information science, and sociology at the University of Pittsburgh and is the author of
over 100 articles and books. He is concerned with developing methods
for treating real-world problems and a theory of real-world problem
solving as it relates to strategic and operational planning.

Gerald L. Otten is director of the planning division of the United Way
of the Midlands in Columbia, South Carolina.

James M. Patton is assistant professor of business administration at the
Graduate School of Business, University of Pittsburgh. His major research
activities have focused on accounting for nonprofit organizations. Some
of his research has been published in *Governmental Finance* and *The Accounting Review.* He is a member of the Municipal Finance Officers Association, the Association of Government Accountants, and the American
Accounting Association.

Prem Prakash is professor of business administration at the Graduate
School of Business, University of Pittsburgh. He received his Ph.D. in
management science from the Massachusetts Institute of Technology. He
also holds graduate degrees in operations research and mechanical en-

gineering. His work experience includes five years in management positions and four years in the diplomatic corps for the government of India. His primary research interests are in economics and accounting, topics on which he has written frequently.

Dennis P. Slevin is associate professor of business administration and director of executive development at the Graduate School of Business, University of Pittsburgh. He received degrees from St. Vincent College, the Massachusetts Institute of Technology, and Carnegie-Mellon University before getting a Ph.D. from Stanford's Graduate School of Business. He is widely published and is a consultant on organizational behavior.

Melanie Wallendorf is assistant professor of marketing at the University of Michigan. Her research interests include the diffusion of innovations and the social aspects of consumer behavior. She has also studied the structure of exchange transactions and the effects of theoretical orientation on research results. Dr. Wallendorf is the co-author with Gerald Zaltman of *Consumer Behavior: Basic Findings and Management Implications*.

James A. Wilson is associate professor of business administration and assistant to the dean at the Graduate School of Business, University of Pittsburgh. As teacher, researcher, consultant, and psychotherapist, Dr. Wilson focuses on the relationship of the person to the group or organization, with special emphasis on mental health in industry.

Index